THE PLATINUM AGE OF TELEVISION

THE

PLATINUM AGE

OF

TELEVISION

FROM *I LOVE LUCY* TO *THE WALKING DEAD*,
HOW TV BECAME TERRIFIC

DAVID BIANCULLI

DOUBLEDAY

NEW YORK LONDON TORONTO

SYDNEY AUCKLAND

www.doubleday.com

DOUBLEDAY and the portrayal of an anchor with a dolphin are
registered trademarks of Penguin Random House LLC.

Book design by Pei Loi Koay
Jacket design by Michael J. Windsor
Jacket images: digital glitch © Igorstevanovic / Shutterstock;
error bars © Admirolas / Shutterstock; T.V. snow
© Shutterstock; test pattern © Donald Sawvel / Shutterstock

All photos are from the author's personal collection.

LIBRARY OF CONGRESS CATALOGING-IN-PUBLICATION DATA
Names: Bianculli, David, author.
Title: The platinum age of television : from I love Lucy to
The walking dead,
how TV became terrific / David Bianculli.
Description: First edition. | New York : Doubleday, 2016.
Identifiers: LCCN 2016027803 | ISBN 9780385540278 (hardcover)
| ISBN 9780385540285 (ebook)
Subjects: LCSH: Television programs—United States—
History. | Television producers and directors—United
States—Interviews. | BISAC: PERFORMING ARTS / Television /
History & Criticism. | PERFORMING ARTS /
Television / General.
Classification: LCC PN1992.3.U5 B57 2016 | DDC 791.450973—
dc23 LC record available at https://lccn.loc.gov/2016027803

MANUFACTURED IN THE UNITED STATES OF AMERICA

10 9 8 7 6 5 4 3 2 1

First Edition

To my children, Kristin and Mark Bianculli,

Their respective spouses, Roland Ochoa and Jessica Kozzi,

And the grandchildren they've given me—

My favorite examples of quality evolution . . .

CONTENTS

INTRODUCTION   1

1 CHILDREN'S PROGRAMS   15
The Mickey Mouse Club   21
Captain Kangaroo   24
Mister Rogers' Neighborhood   26
Sesame Street   29
Pee-Wee's Playhouse   32

2 ANIMATION   36
Rocky and His Friends/The Bullwinkle Show   43
The Flintstones   46
A Charlie Brown Christmas   49
The Simpsons   52
South Park   56

PROFILE MATT GROENING   60

3 VARIETY/SKETCH   67
Toast of the Town/The Ed Sullivan Show   70
Your Show of Shows   74
The Smothers Brothers Comedy Hour   80
The Carol Burnett Show   83
Saturday Night Live   88

PROFILE **MEL BROOKS**   98

PROFILE **CAROL BURNETT**   110

PROFILE **TOM SMOTHERS**   119

PROFILE **AMY SCHUMER**   125

4 SOAP OPERAS   129
   Peyton Place   131
   Mary Hartman, Mary Hartman   134
   Dallas   137
   Desperate Housewives   142
   Empire   145

5 CRIME   148
   Hill Street Blues   156
   NYPD Blue   162
   The Sopranos   166
   The Shield   170
   Breaking Bad   173

PROFILE **STEVEN BOCHCO**   178

PROFILE **DAVID CHASE**   186

PROFILE **KEVIN SPACEY**   191

PROFILE **VINCE GILLIGAN**   199

6 LEGAL   208
   Perry Mason   210
   L.A. Law   215

Boston Legal   219
Damages   221
The Good Wife   222

PROFILE **DAVID E. KELLEY**   226

PROFILE **ROBERT AND MICHELLE KING**   235

7 MEDICAL   241
Dr. Kildare   243
St. Elsewhere   245
ER   251
House, M.D.   255
Grey's Anatomy   257

8 FAMILY SITCOMS   260
I Love Lucy   264
All in the Family   271
The Cosby Show   276
Roseanne   280
Modern Family   283

PROFILE **NORMAN LEAR**   287

9 WORKPLACE SITCOMS   291
Fawlty Towers   292
Taxi   295
Cheers   297
The Larry Sanders Show   301
The Office   304

PROFILE **JAMES L. BROOKS**   310

PROFILE **GARRY SHANDLING**   318

10 SPLITCOMS   323
   The Andy Griffith Show   324
   The Dick Van Dyke Show   327
   The Bob Newhart Show   329
   Seinfeld   332
   Louie   334

PROFILE **CARL REINER**   338

PROFILE **BOB NEWHART**   344

PROFILE **LARRY DAVID**   351

PROFILE **LOUIS C.K.**   359

11 SINGLE WORKING WOMEN SITCOMS   371
   The Mary Tyler Moore Show   373
   The Days and Nights of Molly Dodd   375
   Murphy Brown   377
   Sex and the City   380
   Girls   382

PROFILE **JUDD APATOW**   385

12 SCI-FI/FANTASY/HORROR   395
   The Twilight Zone   396
   Star Trek   399
   The X-Files   403

Buffy the Vampire Slayer   405
The Walking Dead   409

13 WESTERNS   412
Gunsmoke   413
Maverick   416
Rawhide   417
Lonesome Dove   420
Deadwood   422

PROFILE DAVID MILCH   425

14 SPIES   431
The Avengers   435
Mission: Impossible   436
Alias   440
Homeland   441
The Americans   443

15 GENERAL DRAMA   446
Twin Peaks   447
The West Wing   450
Six Feet Under   453
The Wire   455
Mad Men   457

PROFILE DAVID SIMON   459

PROFILE AARON SORKIN   465

PROFILE MATTHEW WEINER   469

16 **WAR**   478
   Combat!   481
   M*A*S*H   482
   China Beach   488
   Band of Brothers   489
   Generation Kill   492

17 **MINISERIES**   495
   Roots   501
   The Singing Detective   505
   Lonesome Dove   509
   The Civil War   511
   Downton Abbey   513

PROFILE **KEN BURNS**   515

18 **TOPICAL COMEDY**   521
   That Was the Week That Was   522
   The Daily Show with Jon Stewart   525
   The Colbert Report   528
   Last Week Tonight with John Oliver   530
   The Nightly Show with Larry Wilmore   532

PROFILE **LARRY WILMORE**   535

CONCLUSION   544

ACKNOWLEDGMENTS   549

BIBLIOGRAPHY   553

INDEX   557

THE PLATINUM AGE OF TELEVISION

INTRODUCTION

If you're going to look at the history and evolution of television—quality TV in particular—there may be no better place to start than Mel Brooks. He was writing for Sid Caesar in TV's early days in the 1940s and 1950s and teamed with his fellow *Your Show of Shows* veteran Carl Reiner in the 1960s to record the first of several classic comedy albums featuring his "2000 Year Old Man." Brooks, in character as the oldest man alive, had seen everything and had his own funny spin on it all. And because Brooks, in real life, has been witness to the entire history of television, I asked him to put it all in perspective—his perspective.

"Hmmm," he says, warming to the challenge. "Let's begin. First of all, in the beginning, there's a, like, four-inch picture tube that you have to look at with a magnifying glass, to begin with. And now, in Carl Reiner's living room, there's a hundred-inch screen which will blind you, you know? That has changed dramatically.

"At the beginning . . . there were only a few shows, and very quickly there'd be a thing called a test pattern, with a kind of whistle, a whine at the end of it. That meant for you to wake up and turn off the TV, you know, so they had that sound. And everything, of course, was in black and white. And fuzzy. It was all fuzzy, and then it was clear. I don't remember when we went to color. We were in black and white for a long time . . .

"But today, all television has changed. I mean all television now—you can see really good writing. I mean really good writing . . . I love *Breaking Bad*. I love *The Good Wife*. I love *Downton Abbey*. I love *Justified*. I think these are wonderful. There are others, too, but these come to mind, and pop up, right away. They are ones that are wonderfully written and wonderfully acted, you know? I love that there are that many, and I'm glad that they're around."

As am I. As a TV critic for more than forty years, I find it's always the good television, not the bad stuff, that keeps me going. But how did television characters evolve from the meek high school science teacher Wally Cox played in 1952's *Mr. Peepers* NBC sitcom to the villainous one Bryan Cranston played in 2008's *Breaking Bad* AMC drama? What inspired the writers, directors, producers, and performers of some of TV's best shows to make their shows? And if the 1950s, because of the artistic achievements of such live anthology dramas as Paddy Chayefsky's *Marty* (later remade as an Oscar-winning movie) and Rod Serling's *Patterns,* are revered as "Television's Golden Age," what age are we in now? And when did that begin?

These questions turned out to be more difficult, more challenging, and ultimately more entertaining to answer than I originally thought. In evolutionary terms, you have to think both technologically (how advances in the medium, from videotape and color to satellite, cable, and streaming, impacted the product) and creatively (how, genre by genre and subject by subject, TV tended to become more sophisticated and complex). Then you have to define, and pinpoint the start of, your "new age" of television.

To test and advance my theories of TV evolution, I interviewed dozens of people whose work in television, over the decades, I have most admired, not only to learn what previous entertainers and programs had inspired and influenced their own, but also to ask about their early, formative relationships with popular culture. What did TV—and, for the more senior people, radio—mean to them when they were young? What, in particular, inspired them to do what they went on to do in the medium of television? And as I examined all these questions, I stumbled upon one more, which ended up informing and flavoring this book as well: What did television mean to me? Why had I become, and remained, a television critic, and what had that life given me in return?

The Platinum Age of Television addresses all those points. Starting right now.

The Platinum Age of Television

First, let's establish the meaning of the phrase "the Platinum Age of Television" and why I'm comfortable both employing and defining it. One of the earliest printed uses of the term comes in my own 1992 book, *Teleliteracy: Taking Television Seriously.* "If the Fifties were the Golden Age of television," I wrote then, "the quantity and quality of today's TV offerings make the modern era worthy of the appellation 'The Platinum Age of Television.'" And when we consider what was to come in the decades since, that "Platinum Age" term, which plays off the recording-industry standards awarding platinum records to indicate sales even higher than those of gold record sales winners, might have been prescient, but it was also a bit premature.

So when did "the Platinum Age of Television" begin? Eventually, I narrowed it down to three possible starting points. The earliest is 1970, when Grant Tinker created MTM Productions and launched *The Mary Tyler Moore Show* sitcom on CBS, starting a quality revolution in both comedy and drama. The next is 1981, with the debut of MTM Productions' *Hill Street Blues* on NBC, which changed the look, pace, and content of weekly TV drama series. And finally, there's 1999, the eve of the new century, when television gave us one of the last great dramas on broadcast TV, NBC's *West Wing,* as well as one of the first great cable dramas, HBO's hugely influential *Sopranos.* All three dates, and arguments, have merit, but I decided on the most recent as the most compelling. And I find that date persuasive because I've been an avid TV viewer through all those decades. Rather than reflexively arguing that the good old days were the best, I'm an old dog pointing out that the new tricks are even better. The Platinum Age of Television as I define it, therefore, is the period from 1999 to 2016 and beyond.

The Theory of Quality Television Evolution

Charles Darwin had his theory of evolution, and I have mine. Mine has to do with the concept of quality television: what it is, and, more crucially, how it got that way. Just as Darwin used fossil records to try to understand how today's life-forms developed from yesterday's ancestors, I'll use examples from the fossil records of television history—from past TV shows themselves—to draw links to the present and even to identify some of the "missing links" along the way.

Take, for example, the topic of single working women on television. In the 1950s, the prototypical single working woman was embodied in the CBS sitcom *Our Miss Brooks* by Eve Arden, portraying a man-hungry, marriage-seeking schoolteacher. In the 1960s, the ideal was Ann Marie, the character played by Marlo Thomas in ABC's *That Girl*: an aspiring actress in New York City, living alone but with a devoted boyfriend for the entire run of the series. By 1970, though, and *The Mary Tyler Moore Show*, things start getting more commendably complicated. Moore's single working woman, Mary Richards, dumps her boyfriend and moves to Minneapolis in the series premiere, setting up herself, and her series, as an example of independent feminism: focusing on her career, dating a series of men, and taking the Pill. At the end of the 1980s comes another single working woman in television, this time as the on-camera star: Candice Bergen as the newscaster Murphy Brown on CBS, a character who famously inflamed a national debate when she chose to have a baby out of wedlock, enraging the then vice president, Dan Quayle, by her "lifestyle choice." And in between Mary Richards and Murphy Brown, you have a key "missing link": Blair Brown in NBC's *Days and Nights of Molly Dodd*, playing a woman who has several serious relationships with men while trying to support herself in the publishing field in New York and define herself creatively and emotionally. Her status as a divorceé aside, Molly Dodd was a specific character type that would be explored again in the following decade in HBO's *Sex and the City*, starring Sarah Jessica Parker as the sex columnist Carrie Bradshaw, and the decade after that in HBO's *Girls*, starring Lena Dunham—who also created the show—as Hannah Horvath, an aspiring writer who, like Carrie in *Sex and the City*, surrounds herself with a cadre of friends to help her make her way through the trials and romances of life in the big city. From Mary Richards to Hannah Horvath is quite an evolution, but the steps along the way are clear and intriguing. And no matter the genre, this evolutionary pattern replicates itself as both the programs and the characters become significantly more complicated.

The Interviews

In seeking out people to interview to discuss the evolution of quality television, I restricted myself, first of all, to those who, in my observation as a lifelong TV critic, had contributed to that evolution. Start with those TV creators associated with the programs from the three possible starting points for the Platinum Age. From *The Mary Tyler Moore Show*, there's the co-creator James L. Brooks; from *Hill Street Blues*, the co-creator Steven

Bochco; and from 1999, the "winner" of the beginning of the Platinum Age of Television, we have the creator of *The West Wing*, Aaron Sorkin, and the creator of *The Sopranos*, David Chase. Or start chronologically, with Carl Reiner, the co-star and co-writer of NBC's landmark *Your Show of Shows* sketch variety series and the creator of CBS's *Dick Van Dyke Show*, and Norman Lear, the creator of *All in the Family* and so many other popular and formative sitcoms, and the aforementioned Mel Brooks. Or start in reverse chronological order, and begin with Amy Schumer of Comedy Central's *Inside Amy Schumer* and Judd Apatow of NBC's *Freaks and Geeks* and HBO's *Girls*.

Along the way are dozens of other creators whose contributions to TV have been entertaining and important, from Carol Burnett, Tom Smothers, Bob Newhart, and Garry Shandling to Larry David, Louis C.K., Kevin Spacey, and Larry Wilmore. Series creators are well represented, including David Simon of HBO's *Wire*, Matt Weiner of AMC's *Mad Men*, Vince Gilligan of AMC's *Breaking Bad*, David Milch of ABC's *NYPD Blue* and HBO's *Deadwood*, Tom Fontana of NBC's *St. Elsewhere* and HBO's *Oz*, David E. Kelley of Fox's *Ally McBeal* and ABC's *Boston Legal*, Ken Burns of PBS's *Civil War* and *Baseball*, and many more. And as they speak, you hear, quickly and consistently, of the threads connecting quality television past and present.

Bob Newhart and Carol Burnett listened to the radio programs of Jack Benny. Both Newhart and Tom Smothers were inspired by the low-key natural comedy of George Gobel. Burnett adored the sketch comedy of Sid Caesar, as performed by Carl Reiner and written by Mel Brooks. James L. Brooks, when creating *The Mary Tyler Moore Show*, adopted as his quality template Reiner's stellar script writing on *The Dick Van Dyke Show*. And so it goes, all through television history: David E. Kelley learned at the hand of Steven Bochco on *L.A. Law*, and Jason Katims of *Parenthood* and *Friday Night Lights* learned at the hand of Kelley on *Boston Public*. David Simon learned on the job from Tom Fontana, back on *Homicide: Life on the Street*. Matt Weiner watched the first episodes of David Chase's *Sopranos* on TV, thinking there was finally a place and time for his unproduced script to be appreciated and sending it to Chase, who hired him. Eventually, Weiner earned enough clout on *The Sopranos* to get that script produced as a series. Its title: *Mad Men*. And many connections were purely inspirational, with TV writer-producers seeing *The Larry Sanders Show* or *The Sopranos* or *The Shield* and saying, "Hey, things are different now, we can do it our way!"

And even earlier, back in that Golden Age, old TV shows inspired the creators of new ones and sometimes even caused young viewers to dream of entering show business themselves. When Matt Groening was imagining the family and townspeople of what came to be known as *The Simpsons,* he thought of Homer Simpson as a grown-up Eddie Haskell from *Leave It to Beaver* and the town where the Simpsons lived as a sort of Mayberry from *The Andy Griffith Show,* where supporting characters could recur occasionally but still be familiar, like Floyd the barber. Or, in the case of *The Simpsons,* Moe the bartender. When Kevin Spacey was young and watching *The Wild Wild West,* the character of Artemus Gordon, the chameleonic master of disguise, made him want to become an actor. Aaron Sorkin says, "The first writers I wanted to be were Jim Brooks and Larry Gelbart," and credits Gelbart's *M*A*S*H* as "the show, I think, that has informed everything that I've ever written." And throughout the decades, if one TV series inspired more of the people interviewed in this book than any other—inspired them to become writers and to make the sorts of TV shows they eventually did, or simply entertained them memorably when they were younger—it was *The Twilight Zone.* Mel Brooks cites it as a particular favorite, as do many of the writers and producers who followed him into television.

Each formative evolutionary step led to another, and by interviewing a galaxy of television's most creative people, I can trace many of those early, formative steps.

Creative Evolution Explained

In nature, the cleverest creatures adapt to survive, and thrive, even in hostile environments. Throughout television history, truly creative writers, producers, and performers have done the same, dealing with the restrictions and dangers around them while finding ways to pursue their individual visions. In every phase of television, creativity has found a way to break through.

In the earliest days of television, the way to survive, regardless of audience levels, was to find a sponsor that would finance and back your shows. That's how the TV pioneer Ernie Kovacs, despite bouncing from network to network over his career in the Golden Age, managed to keep going and to do all those crazy and wonderful things no one else on TV was even trying. His sponsor, Dutch Masters cigars, loved him, and that was enough. Once broadcast advertising in the United States went from single sponsorship to a spot-based model in the late 1950s, ratings counted for even more, but awards and acclaim still mattered. That's how *The Twilight Zone* and *The Dick Van Dyke Show,* to name two acclaimed and influential CBS shows, managed to persist and generate high-quality work despite modest ratings. Once ratings became dominant, demographics were introduced, which allowed some TV shows to pursue the coveted young audience (paving the way, for example, for *The Smothers Brothers Comedy Hour*). A new focus on demographics also made the lowest-ranked networks desperate enough to offer producers more freedom to generate the shows they really wanted to make, which was how NBC ended up with *Hill Street Blues.*

The launch of geosynchronous broadcast satellites in the 1970s sparked the creation and spread of cable networks. Eventually, some significant TV creators moved from broadcast to cable TV, like the first amphibians moving from water to land, and explored the freedom of their new environment. Tom Fontana, shifting from NBC's *St. Elsewhere* and *Homicide: Life on the Street* to HBO's *Oz,* was one of the very first (and, much later, was also one of the first to produce a series expressly for Netflix). Garry Shandling, Larry David, David Milch, Judd Apatow, Aaron Sorkin, Vince Gilligan—all of them evolved by shifting to cable and thriving in the freedoms found there. And with the advent of streaming services in the past decade, Kevin Spacey of *House of Cards* and Frank Spotnitz of *The Man in the High Castle* are among those staking early and impressive claims in a new environment. Broadcast television is not dead—Robert and Michelle King of *The Good Wife* on CBS proved that great work could still be done there—but these days there are many other places to seek, and find, quality TV. That's part of the evolution, too. Yet according to some, it's also fast becoming part of the problem, with a rising tide of available scripted television shows threatening to flood the landscape like the TV equivalent of climate change.

Does the Platinum Age Have "Too Much Television"?

Midway through 2015, John Landgraf, the CEO of FX, made national headlines at the semiannual Television Critics Association press tour trotting out facts and figures in support of his contention that the proliferation of new program providers, from Netflix and Hulu to basic cable networks such as

AMC and his own FX, has resulted in a growth of scripted TV series too large to be sustained. He predicted that 2015 would finish with more than 400 original scripted series for the year, compared with 280 in 2010, just five years earlier. "There is simply too much television," Landgraf told the assembled TV critics, in perhaps the ultimate example of preaching to the converted. And while the median scripted show may be better than before, the sheer glut of them may be making it harder for the best new shows to be found and sampled, much less supported and embraced. And Landgraf was right: in January 2016, his network researchers estimated the total number of prime-time scripted series on broadcast, cable, and streaming services in 2015 to be 409—the most in television history.

It was enough of a shot across the bow, and a thoughtful historical perspective, for me to contact Landgraf to discuss my Platinum Age of Television theory, and my start date of 1999, with him directly. After all, he was at NBC then as a programming development executive, when Aaron Sorkin created *The West Wing* there, as was David Nevins, the current president of the Showtime networks.

"We were both advocates," Landgraf says. "And we were facing a stiff wind, to tell you the truth, because the perception for most, at that time, was that politics was not suitable subject matter for an entertainment program on a broadcast network . . .

"But I think that's the date. I think you've picked the right date," he continues. "As much as I am a fan, and I hope a connoisseur, of many great television programs that preceded *The Sopranos*—all the way back to *Playhouse 90* and *Lucy* and *Mary Tyler Moore* and *M*A*S*H*, and certainly the important dramas like *St. Elsewhere* and *Hill Street Blues*—I really do think *The Sopranos* was the sort of tectonic shift in the industry." It was the first time, Landgraf confesses from the perspective of a former insider, that the broadcast networks looked at the audience levels for a cable drama, on the all-important, ultracompetitive Sunday night of television, and became worried that a show on an alternative programming source "could make a dent."

Competitively, HBO's *Sopranos*, and programs like it, had some distinct advantages, as Landgraf saw it. "They had certain arrows in their quiver that we at NBC didn't have. That is to say, they could portray language and nudity and sexuality and violence at a level that exceeded what was acceptable on broadcast television." They could also work at a less grueling pace: rather than being required to churn out twenty-two episodes per season (which, itself, was a reduction from the Golden Age's more common, almost unthinkable thirty-nine), HBO presented *The Sopranos* in chunks of thirteen episodes or fewer, often taking lengthy breaks between seasons, at the insistence of the show's creator. "What David Chase was able to do," Landgraf says admiringly, "was fit the number of episodes to the story, rather than fitting the story to the number of episodes. And that made all the difference in the world." Chase, for his part, admits his embrace of the British model of making television was as much a practical decision as a creative one ("The short season was welcomed by me," he says, "because I'd had enough of television completely"). But it began to catch on and eventually make possible such new TV innovations as the single-season anthology shows, such as FX's own *American Horror Story* and *Fargo* or HBO's *True Detective*, that would tell new self-contained stories every season.

Aaron Sorkin, who created *Sports Night* and *The West Wing* for broadcast TV before finally moving to HBO for the smaller-season orders of *The Newsroom*, had a running joke with the director Thomas Schlamme, his collaborator on both *Sports Night* and *The West Wing*. "When I was working on episode 14 of twenty-two of those shows," Sorkin says, "I would always say to Tommy, 'If we lived in the U.K. and this was on the BBC, we'd be done already.' And he'd say, 'Yeah, but we'd all be living in smaller houses.'" Sorkin laughs heartily and adds, "I'll take a smaller house. My last season of *The Newsroom* was six episodes, and it seemed worth it to me."

John Landgraf cares more about quality than quantity, too, and that's why his number crunching got so much attention in 2015. And in our conversation for this book, he crunched even more numbers and made another very valid point about the speed at which scripted television was multiplying, along with its imitators.

"In my head," he says, "there's a pantheon of greats that does, in fact, go all the way back to Ernie Kovacs and leads through Lucille Ball and Desi Arnaz, and through Norman Lear and through Steven Bochco . . . Essentially, it's about the people who took this medium and did something new and innovative, so that when we, the audience, were watching it, we were not only able to experience something great; we were able to experience something new, something breathtaking. Archie Bunker, saying what he was saying out loud, right? Lucille Ball, in that candy factory—it was an experience that was, in that moment, like nothing we had ever had before that television was giving to us."

Then came the numbers. "The modern era—the era in which television became an important thing in a room—roughly coincides with a few years after the end of World War II," Landgraf says. "So just for round numbers for a second, let's start it in the year 1949. And then let's say that *The Sopranos* came along in 1999 so we get a nice, round number, which is fifty years. And let's say that in fifty years, on average, there were about one hundred scripted television shows made a year—probably a lot less, in the early going.

"You and I are sitting here, having this conversation, in 2015. So it's been sixteen years since *The Sopranos* came out in 1999. Not fifty years. Sixteen—about a third of that amount. And we have now made as many [scripted] television shows in sixteen years as we made in [the previous] fifty." That exponential growth allowed for "an explosion of newness," as Landgraf calls it, but also, by this point, has encouraged a lot of new TV that "feels at least tangentially derivative of everything else." He acknowledges that wonderfully original programs continue to emerge on occasion, mentioning Amazon's *Transparent* in particular, but worries that with so many scripted TV slots to fill across the broadcast and cable and streaming playing field, "we now have people . . . making the clone of the clone of the clone." David Simon, who's spent his career making daringly original scripted dramas, agrees but, like Landgraf, is quick to point out some high-quality exceptions.

"I still think there's still an enormous amount of shit," Simon says bluntly. "But there's also an enormous number of channels: it's inevitable that there would be a lot of shit. But I'm, I think, a much harsher critic of a lot of television. I see a lot of shows that are put together as if they are thoughtful, premium narrative, and they have all the elements, but it's real ugly sewing, and I can see the seams. They're almost chopped together, as if they're thinking, 'If we put this much DNA of *The Sopranos* and this much of *Breaking Bad* and a little bit of *The Wire* . . . ,'" he says, and sighs. "But they're not starting with somebody's burning desire to tell this story and to have this take. And I think the best storytelling, not just TV, but in anything, begins with that." And he sees flashes of brilliance amid the clutter, from the first season of Netflix's *Orange Is the New Black* all the way back to the Canadian import *Slings & Arrows,* about a small Canadian troupe putting on Shakespeare. "That was magical," he says approvingly.

While I understand and accept the complaints of both Landgraf and Simon about TV's imitative and multiplying nature, I find myself thrilled by all the new programming venues and efforts—no matter how absurdly difficult it makes my job as a television critic. The expansion of available networks and the explosion of scripted programs have resulted in an ideal environment for creative growth—the TV equivalent of a biodiverse ecosystem, with the more species the better. I started my job in 1975, back when there were three broadcast networks and PBS and a brand-new cable "superstation" called TBS, the first of its kind. Now TV is everywhere, on every one of the screens in our lives, but so are excellent television programs unlikely to have ever surfaced on old-fashioned broadcast television, up to and including Amazon's new Frank Spotnitz series, *The Man in the High Castle,* based on the novel by Philip K. Dick, and *Fargo,* the Noah Hawley expansion of the Coen brothers' all-midwestern movie weirdness, televised by Landgraf's own FX. So long as scripted TV this excellent fights its way to the surface, regardless of the delivery system, there will never, in my mind, be too much television.

My Evolution with Television

Because what you're about to read are my theories and demonstrations of quality TV evolution, I feel you should understand my relationship with television, and I only began to understand that myself, to be honest, a year or so ago. That's when Steven Rand, executive director of the apexart gallery in New York's Tribeca district, invited me to be guest curator of an art show about TV—with, at first, no more guidance than that. My original idea was to mount five TV screens, each showing a chronologically displayed and synchronously timed video from television history, so you could watch the evolution of various television genres and subjects at once. And I did that, thanks to some invaluable assistance on both the video-editing and technical end. But the exhibit kept growing beyond that original "TV wall" as Rand kept pushing me to get more personal. By the time it opened, in November 2014, *Bianculli's Personal Theory of TV Evolution* was very personal indeed. I had reached out and borrowed such exciting artifacts as Rod Serling's typewriter, Ernie Kovacs's scripts, Fred Rogers's sweater and sneakers, and Vince Gilligan's scene-by-scene finale breakdown on the writers' room corkboard of *Breaking Bad.* But I'd also acknowledged, and displayed, my own lifelong relationship with television, including how and why I became a TV critic and how I was lucky enough to meet, and even interview and work with, some of the people whose television work impressed me the most. This book is a further outgrowth of that and—with the artists I was able to reach and the fact that I could publish the book at all—my culminating achievement as a television aficionado, critic, and historian.

One of the "artifacts" in that New York art exhibition was my diary, at age seven, containing such December 1960 entries as "Was PETER PAN good today!" and "Today at 6:00 I saw THE WIZARD OF OZ." Another was a reprint of my first professional TV review, from Florida's *Gainesville Sun*, in which I reviewed the first few episodes of a then-new NBC late-night series that had premiered in 1975: *Saturday Night Live.* "If you accept Malcolm Gladwell's concept of the '10,000-Hour Rule,' that it takes 10,000 hours working in a specific field before a person can be considered an expert," I wrote in the brochure to that apexart exhibit, "then, by that yardstick, I'm about four experts. I've been a professional TV critic for almost 40 years—and a TV viewer for 60."

Over those decades, the television I've enjoyed the most has rewarded me in other ways as well. I watched *The Smothers Brothers Comedy Hour* with my father each Sunday night and then, thirty years later, wrote a book about them and their show, spending hours and hours interviewing them in the process. I got to know Fred Rogers, Ken Burns, and Mel Brooks and interview Dennis Potter, Kurt Vonnegut, Jack Paar, Paul McCartney, and most of the people who shaped my tastes, interests, and politics. Thirty years ago, I fell into a job doing TV criticism for NPR's *Fresh Air with Terry Gross* and proudly remain associated with the show, and everyone working on it, today.

"I enjoy being a TV critic," I wrote elsewhere in that 2014 brochure. "It's a job that always changes, that demands you flex different muscles on different days, and that occasionally rewards you with brilliant, wonderful programs, some of which can enrich, and even change, your life. I've said for decades that sooner or later, everything I care about shows up on television, giving me the opportunity to write about music, theatre, politics, literature, comedy—anything telecast by anyone is fair game."

Streaming sites and the Internet have made that game more complicated than ever, but television critics, like TV itself, must adapt or die. In the 1970s, I used to have to drive an hour to sit in a Miami TV station's conference room to have videotapes of shows screened for me in advance. In time, I intercepted satellite transmissions, then received VHS tapes, then DVDs, and currently get e-mails with links for password-protected press website "screening rooms." Methods of writing and transmitting stories have changed just as dramatically, from electronically scanned typed pages to reviews typed on mini-monitors, on bulky "portable" machines called Telerams, and sent via a modem connection. And then came the laptops and relative freedom, but nothing was as freeing as the technical advancements on the home-viewing side of things. When I bought my first VCR the year I became a full-time TV critic, that Sony Betamax cost 10 percent of my gross annual salary but was worth it, because I could leave the house and still see a show I taped once I returned. Fast-forward a generation, and the DVR has loosened things up so much it's changed what, when, and how people watch television. I'd like to say I saw it coming, and I did.

In my 1992 book, *Teleliteracy: Taking Television Seriously,* in addition to using the term "the Platinum Age of Television," I laid out my prediction for the future of television:

> I suspect "real time" television will not vanish entirely. The instant availability of all types of music—on record albums, singles, cassettes, and CDs—hasn't killed radio . . . There's a lot to be said for the shared communal experience of a simultaneous national broadcast. Radio used to provide it; now television does. Even if tomorrow's version comes via satellite, or fiber-optic transmission, or a massive home-entertainment database, there will always be room for "real time" transmission and enjoyment of entertainment—not just news, sports, and weather. The likelihood is that viewers at home eventually will be able to call up any program they like—at any time—from a massive national network of databases, and store it on disc or tape (at a set fee, naturally) for retrieval and reviewing at their own leisure.

This was years before TiVo and Netflix were founded, but when I dug out and read that prescient passage to my son, Mark, recently, all he said was, "If you're so smart, why didn't you invest?" Damn good question.

Meanwhile, the four networks that were around when I wrote my first TV reviews in the mid-1970s have increased to hundreds, literally, making it more of a challenge, but more important than ever, to seek out and support the best that TV has to offer. The website I edit, TV Worth Watching, aims to do precisely that, with help from many other veteran TV critics, but John Landgraf is right. It's getting tougher to watch all the good television, much less cover it.

One final quotation from my art show brochure about television: "By 1988, when PBS presented Bill Moyers' six-part interview with mythologist Joseph Campbell under the title *Joseph Campbell and the Power of Myth*, and Campbell distilled his lifetime of research and teaching into three inspirational words of advice ('Follow your bliss'), I realized I already was following mine. I not only got to watch that fantastic TV series in advance and write about it for a New York newspaper in hopes of encouraging others to watch it, but got to interview Moyers about it in the process."

If my lifetime of research and teaching were distilled into a single phrase, it would be five words, not three—the same five words uttered by Chance the gardener, played by Peter Sellers, in the 1979 movie adaptation of the Jerzy Kosinski fable *Being There*. "I like to watch TV," Chance said simply.

When TV is good, I feel exactly the same way. Always have. And on the pages that follow are many of the programs, and the artists, who made me blissful.

The show of iconic television artifacts I curated for the Apex Art Gallery in lower Manhattan in 2014.

CHILDREN'S PROGRAMS

KEY EVOLUTIONARY STAGES

The Mickey Mouse Club	1955–59, ABC
Captain Kangaroo	1955–84, CBS
Mister Rogers' Neighborhood	1968–2001, NET/PBS
Sesame Street	1969–, PBS; 2016–, HBO
Pee-Wee's Playhouse	1986–91, CBS

No matter where you grew up, and for the most part no matter when, your TV was most likely populated by local shows made especially for children. The earliest ones were hosted by earnest, often costumed adults, presenting old theatrical cartoons and/or interacting with puppets or marionettes. Some of these early homegrown pioneers "matured" into national shows presented by one of the major broadcast networks, such as NBC's *Kukla, Fran, and Ollie,* which had begun on local TV in Chicago in 1947. But others, from 1948's *Junior Frolics* (a cartoon showcase from Newark, New Jersey, hosted by "Uncle Fred" Sayles) to 1950's *Popeye Theater* (a weekday afternoon Philadelphia children's show hosted for more than twenty years by the "cowgirl" Sally Starr), remained proudly local for their entire runs. Wherever you lived, if television was a part of your early life, so was children's TV. I was born in Pittsburgh in 1953, and one of my first TV memories is of watching a local public television show called *The Children's Corner,* hosted by Josie Carey starting in 1954, and featuring her interacting with such puppets as Daniel Striped Tiger and King Friday XIII—puppets created and voiced by the show's producer and music composer, Fred Rogers, years before he would launch his own successful children's series, *Mister Rogers' Neighborhood.*

Technically, the earliest TV children's show host might have been Burr Tillstrom, the puppeteer creator and voice of the clown-like Kukla, the friendly dragon Ollie, and other whimsical hand-puppet characters. He and his puppets appeared on TV before there was broadcast TV, as featured players during RCA's television exhibition at the 1939–40 New York World's Fair. After World War II, when television production began in earnest, Tillstrom teamed with the Chicago radio personality Fran Allison in 1947 on a local children's show, giving her equal billing with two of his puppet creations. Within a year, *Kukla, Fran, and Ollie* was a popular national offering on the NBC network, where it lasted for an entire decade.

That show's NBC lead-in, running at five o'clock weekdays on the East Coast, was even more popular and ranks as TV's first runaway children's TV hit. It began as *Puppet Playhouse* in 1947, back when NBC's "network" of stations was limited to a few cities along the northeast corridor, and premiered at a time when the concept of using television as a babysitter, previously unheard of, was instantly embraced. In a rave review of the debut of *Puppet Playhouse* that today would incense child advocates and women alike, *Variety* wrote, "In the middle-class home, there is perhaps nothing as welcome to the mother as something that will keep the small fry intently absorbed and out of possible mischief. This program can almost be guaranteed to pin down the squirmiest of the brood." *Puppet Playhouse* was created and hosted by "Buffalo" Bob Smith, but the show was quickly renamed *Howdy Doody,* after his marionette co-star. Like many children's shows that followed it, *Howdy Doody* featured a studio audience of overstimulated, sugar-engorged kids (called, in this case, the Peanut Gallery). It also featured a silent, horn-honking clown named Clarabell (played, over the course of the series, by three different actors, including the future *Captain Kangaroo* host, Bob Keeshan); the beautiful princess Summerfall Winterspring (played by Judy Tyler, who would go on to star in *Jailhouse Rock* opposite Elvis Presley); and a spineless character named Gumby, who was soon spun off into his own series. Give *Howdy Doody* credit, too, for the most unsettling finale in TV history: On the final show, Smith kept promising that Clarabell, then played by Lew Anderson, would have a special surprise. After thirteen years of silence, Clarabell ended the show, and the series, by staring into the camera and, in a choked whisper, saying, "Good-bye, kids."

Other early TV children's hits included ABC's *Super Circus* (like *Kukla, Fran, and Ollie,* going national in 1949 after starting in Chicago), hosted by Claude Kirchner and, later, Jerry Colonna and featuring the baton-catching, and eye-catching, baton twirler Mary Hartline. A singular children's star from the 1950s was Milton Hines, a.k.a. Soupy Sales, who had a unique career path by not only succeeding on network TV and in syndication but moving from one local market to another and conquering them individually. He started in Cincinnati, on a local 1950 show called *Soupy's Soda Shop,* then moved in 1953 to Detroit, where he simultaneously hosted a daytime kids' show (*Lunch with Soupy Sales*) and a slightly more mature late-night effort (*Soupy's On,* the surviving kinescopes of which include rare performance footage of the great jazz trumpeter Clifford Brown from 1956). The daytime show, with its pie-in-the-face comedy style (and I mean that literally), was so popular with kids ABC picked it up, renaming it *The Soupy Sales Show.* And when the host moved his base of operations again, this time to Los Angeles, the split-personality approach he had tapped in late-night Detroit TV sprouted in full bloom on his L.A. series. Even though he had the same furry, kid-friendly puppet sidekicks as always—including Pookie the little lion and the giant "dogs" White Fang and Black Tooth, who, except for their huge paws and arms, were heard but not seen—Soupy Sales attracted amazingly A-list adult guests, all of whom lined up eagerly to get cream pies in the face. Bob Hope, Sammy Davis Jr., Dean Martin, even Frank Sinatra, all came by to support the show's antic level of anarchy, as well as to get pies in the face.

Other approaches to children's TV evolved as well, not just from local to national, but in substance as well as style. There were the anything-goes "clubhouse" shows for children, typified by 1950's *Smilin' Ed McConnell and His Buster Brown Gang,* which bounced around several networks and time slots, with as many titles, throughout the decade. When the host died, his Western sidekick Andy Devine was cast as his replacement, and the series was renamed *Andy's Gang.* The content remained the same, though, with affable Andy entertaining little kids by reading stories, showing old cartoons and film shorts, and interacting with puppets, including Froggy the Gremlin, who would bedevil poor Andy after being summoned by the same rude-sounding catchphrase uttered by the previous host: "Pluck your magic twanger, Froggy!" Elsewhere, the vaudeville spirit thrived when channeled, literally, to a children's TV audience, thanks to the wild shenanigans of Pinky

Lee, a veteran comic whose *Pinky Lee Show,* an NBC offering from 1954 to 1956, had him entertaining kids while sporting a bow tie, a checkered suit, and a very childish attitude. Yet another popular children's TV franchise literally became a franchise, with a 1949 Los Angeles show, *Bozo's Circus,* evolving into Larry Harmon's Bozo the Clown broadcast business model in the mid-1950s, with each local station buying the rights to cast, produce, and present its own Bozo the Clown program.

Children's TV was full of such shows, emulating the basic formula and energy of *Howdy Doody* locally and nationally, but there were specialty shows, too. Live-action Westerns and sci-fi shows were big, from 1949's *Lone Ranger* on ABC to the same year's *Captain Video and His Video Rangers* on DuMont, a laughably cheap yet impressively durable weekday series that ran until the DuMont network itself collapsed in 1955. *Captain Video* encouraged its young viewers to sign up and receive special mailings—a practice copied by *Captain Midnight* on CBS, where a quarter and the seal from a jar of Ovaltine would get viewers a special decoder ring, which could be used to decipher special on-air messages.

From the beginning of network television, in addition to Westerns and science fiction and puppet shows, there was a subcategory of children's shows that could loosely be grouped under the term "educational." The earliest of these TV shows for children were offshoots from existing radio programs: NBC's *Juvenile Jury,* starting on television in 1947, featuring a panel of problem-solving youngsters, and the same network's *Quiz Kids,* which came to TV via Chicago in 1949 and featured kids answering the same sorts of increasingly tough queries in their chosen categories as adult contestants on *The $64,000 Question.* Those were shows that tested and rewarded knowledge; other shows set out to impart it.

These were sincere, gentle shows, in which the hosts talked slowly and sweetly, either directly to the viewers at home or to an in-studio surrogate. The former public school science teacher Don Herbert explored and explained the wonders of science on television for decades, starting with Chicago's *Mr. Wizard* in 1950, which moved to NBC a year later. Yet another show originating from Chicago, aimed at an even younger audience, was *Ding Dong School,* hosted by a soft-spoken, matronly hostess identified as Miss Frances. At the time, she was chair of what is now Roosevelt University and felt strongly that the new medium of television had a special responsibility to preschool viewers. She stared straight into the camera and addressed viewers directly, pausing to give them time to answer. "Do you remember the three ingredients to the sandwich we made today, besides bread?" she asks, waiting patiently for the unheard interactive reply. "That's right. Peanut butter. Lettuce. And . . . banana!" (Was Elvis watching?) NBC began broadcasting *Ding Dong School* nationally in 1952, only a few months after it premiered in Chicago.

Another preschool TV show that broke the fourth wall was *Romper Room*, which began as a local show in Baltimore in 1953. The producer Bert Claster had the simple but ingenious idea of letting his wife, Nancy, a nursery school teacher, bring her young students into the TV studio to play and work, with youngsters at home invited to watch as part of the action. "Miss Nancy" would do arts and crafts, sing songs, tell stories, and even advise on proper and improper social behavior, which would earn the classification of a "Do-Bee" or a "Don't-Be." And when, at the end of each show, "Miss Nancy" held up her magic mirror and looked through it, she would call out names of some of the children she "saw" watching *Romper Room* on her TV set. "I see Bobby, I see Cindy . . ." For the next several decades, *Romper Room* would be franchised, like Bozo the Clown, with each local TV market presenting its own Miss Somebody. The show's "magic mirror" gimmick made it seem interactive to young viewers at home, even if your name was never called.

For interactive TV gimmickry, though, nothing came close to *Winky Dink and You*, which ran on CBS from 1953 to 1957. It's described in detail in the chapter "Animation," but it armed young viewers with a "Winky Dink" kit—a cloth, a box of crayons, and a see-through plastic sheet—and encouraged them to draw missing details from the show's animation onto the sheet, which covered the TV screen.

Of all the programs and people associated with children's and family TV programming in the 1950s, one name rises above all others—a man whose name was already established, and beloved, in the world of theatrical cartoons and full-length animated movies and who would very quickly achieve amazing success as host of a prime-time anthology series, co-creator of a daytime children's series, and the visionary behind a wildly popular family theme park. In time, the empire he built would launch its own cable channel for children, purchase and run the ABC network, and establish a powerful cinematic studio operation that, in time, would absorb and present the latest offerings from Pixar, the Muppets, and *Star Wars*. That man, of course,

was Walt Disney, who had made his name with his first Mickey Mouse theatrical cartoon, *Steamboat Willie,* in 1928. In 1950, the year he first came to
television, Disney's big-screen releases included not only a dozen cartoon
shorts but the full-length movie *Cinderella* and the live-action feature *Treasure Island.* To cap off that very fruitful year, Disney co-hosted, with the
ventriloquist Edgar Bergen and the dummy sidekick Charlie McCarthy, his
first foray into TV: an NBC Christmas Day special called *One Hour in Wonderland.* The next year, he presented another Christmas Day TV special, this
time for CBS, and this time with himself as the sole host: *The Walt Disney
Christmas Show.*

Disney was eager to get into television because he recognized the value
of cross promotion and being able to show clips from, and stoke audience
interest for, his upcoming movies. He also had another pet project in mind,
a massive theme park, and television could be a major source of both rev-
enue and free publicity. NBC and CBS had already broadcast his Christmas
specials, and when he proposed a weekly prime-time series, all the networks,
even fledgling, low-rated ABC, were interested. Until that time, the major
studios were boycotting television, and to get a regular TV series produced
by the Walt Disney Studios would be a breakthrough. What resulted from
Disney's interest in TV turned out to be revolutionary for children's programming as well.

Disney's first regular series on television, produced for ABC, was a 1954
prime-time anthology series called *Disneyland,* named after a California
theme park of his that wouldn't open for another year. The opening installment of *Disneyland* was little more than a one-hour infomercial, but like
almost everything else Disney presented in the 1950s, it caught on quickly
and massively. One of the anthology show's first-season offerings was
Davy Crockett, a Fess Parker miniseries that sold millions of coonskin caps
to impressionable young kids and helped ABC land its first Top 10 series
of that decade. By the end of the 1954–55 TV season, *Disneyland* was the
No. 6 series on the air, proudly nestled between two long-established CBS
hits, Ed Sullivan's *Toast of the Town* and *The Jack Benny Program.* And in
the last half of 1955, Walt Disney enjoyed two other instant successes: his
Disneyland theme park, which opened in July, and a new daytime children's
show, which premiered in October and revolutionized children's television
significantly.

THE MICKEY MOUSE CLUB

1955–59, ABC. Creators: Walt Disney, Bill Walsh, Hal Adelquist. Host: Jimmie Dodd, aided by Roy Williams. Stars: Annette Funicello, Bobby Burgess, Darlene Gillespie, Cubby O'Brien, Karen Pendleton, Doreen Tracey, others.

To help create *The Mickey Mouse Club,* Walt Disney turned to Bill Walsh, who had written and produced Disney's two TV holiday specials. For inspiration, he reached back much further into his company's past—to 1930, when the success of Mickey Mouse as a theatrical cartoon character had sparked a series of local Mickey Mouse Clubs all over the country. More than two million kids signed up during the Depression before Disney stopped the enterprise, but clearly he never forgot it. In the mid-1950s, ABC,

The Mickey Mouse Club, starring Jimmie Dodd (top center), Annette Funicello (bottom left), and a gaggle of other all-white Mouseketeers.

already giddy over the success of Disney's prime-time series *Disneyland,* asked Walt Disney to produce a weekday children's show for late afternoons. He planned on a fifteen-minute feature, but ABC wanted an hour show, Monday through Friday, and got it.

The genius of *The Mickey Mouse Club* was present in almost every element. The opening, including the theme song and lots of lively animation, was packed with most of the Disney studio's most popular cartoon characters, from Mickey and Minnie Mouse to Donald Duck and Dumbo. It was more expensive and complex than any animation yet seen on TV and was longer, too, eating up close to two minutes of screen time, but those costs were amortized every single day, making it a wise investment indeed. Another wise investment was to shoot the series on 35-millimeter film, making it look crisp and fresh in 1955 (and, on DVD, in 2015 as well).

Other advancements were made in the casting and presentation. *The Mickey Mouse Club,* like so many children's shows before it, had adult hosts presiding over the fun—in this case, Jimmie Dodd (who wrote much of the show's music, including the opening and closing theme songs) and the Disney staff animator and illustrator Roy Williams. But the kids, instead of being relegated to a peanut gallery, were very actively involved: presenting cartoons, starring in live-action serials, and singing and dancing as part of their regular duties as Mouseketeers. There was a roll call at the start of each show, where the Mouseketeers, wearing big mouse-ear caps and with their first names emblazoned on their costumes, would walk right up to the camera and loudly and proudly identify themselves: "Annette!" "Bobby!" "Cubby!" "Darlene!" (That would be, in order, Annette Funicello, Bobby Burgess, Cubby O'Brien, and Darlene Gillespie, four of the original cast members.) They, and the other Mouseketeers, would be put through their paces on the show, because each day had a different theme: "Fun with Music Day" on Monday, "Guest Star Day" on Tuesday, "Anything Can Happen Day" on Wednesday, "Circus Day" on Thursday, and "Talent Round-Up Day" on Friday. Also included in the regular mix were newly made serials, echoing the Saturday morning movie matinee adventures or the *Davy Crockett* adventures from *Disneyland,* but starring young actors, as in *The Adventures of Spin and Marty* and *The Hardy Boys.* And, of course, there were loads of cartoons from the Disney vault, promotions for upcoming Disney movies, and other features as well. By the end of each one-hour episode, it was no wonder an overworked Jimmie Dodd slowed things down to lead the Mouseketeers in a tender, quiet spell-and-response reprise of the show's theme song. "M-I-C," Annette and the rest would sing in soft unison. "See you real soon," Jimmie would purr back. "K-E-Y," the Mouseketeers would continue. "Why?" asked Jimmie, looking directly into the camera and seemingly making electronic eye contact with every kid at home. "Because we like you!" And the Mouseketeers would bring it home with a lullaby-like, elongated "M-O-U-S-Eeeeeeeeeeeeeeee . . ."

In terms of content, *The Mickey Mouse Club* was one of the most dizzyingly diverse children's shows in the history of television. In terms of ethnic diversity, not so much: the cast was overwhelmingly, completely white, which in the 1950s, on TV, didn't appear that out of place. When the series would be updated for newer generations, that would change, and so would the level of young talent. The old Mickey Mouse Club might have given us America's sweetheart in Annette Funicello, who grew up to star in a series of *Beach Blanket Bingo* movies, but the Disney Channel's own 1989–94 *The All New Mickey Mouse Club* claimed such Mouseketeer future stars as Britney Spears, Justin Timberlake, Christina Aguilera, Keri Russell, and Ryan Gosling. But that was many ears later. In the 1950s, the original *Mickey Mouse Club* burned brightly for four years, then stopped. But like *Disneyland* in prime time, it upped the standards considerably for what was possible, and expected, in family TV programming.

By 1961, when Walt Disney's prime-time anthology series showcase moved to NBC as *Walt Disney's Wonderful World of Color*, it was to help spearhead the spread of color TV, which NBC's parent corporation at the time, the electronics manufacturer RCA, was pushing heavily, with such early full-color hits as 1959's *Bonanza*. Fewer than one million color TV sets had been sold at the time NBC acquired the Walt Disney prime-time series, but there were no more persuasive reasons to buy one, in 1961, than to watch vibrant, full-color cartoons, nature specials, and other offerings presented on Disney's newly evolved anthology show. "The world is a carousel of color," boasted the new show's theme song, and as Disney presented it, it was. Each week, an animated Tinker Bell would wave her magic wand and sprinkle fairy dust all over the place, and the place was Disneyland. Walt Disney died in 1966, but his vision, and series, kept going and kept growing in importance. Television in general, and Walt Disney in particular, are seldom given credit for helping spawn the environmental movement, but is it so far-fetched to imagine that the inclusion of all those nature-film excerpts and features, on *Disneyland* and its successors, infused a new generation with an enhanced sensitivity toward, and appreciation of, the world around them?

The Disney flagship TV show, over the decades, would switch networks and titles several more times, eventually settling at ABC, which had been bought by the Walt Disney Company, and settling for the same title it had on NBC from 1969 to 1979: *The Wonderful World of Disney*. It was canceled, finally, in 2008, but that was twenty-five years after the 1983 launch of the Disney Channel.

Meanwhile, quality children's TV kept maturing and metamorphosing. Just as *Disneyland* and *The Mickey Mouse Club* were starting out nationally, Josie Carey and Fred Rogers were starting out locally, in Pittsburgh, on *The Children's Corner*. And in 1955, CBS got into the children's TV business in a big way, by hiring Bob Keeshan to play an amiable, soft-spoken character named Captain Kangaroo—a role he would play, to generations of rapt pre-schoolers, for three decades.

CAPTAIN KANGAROO

1955–84, CBS; 1986–92, PBS. Creators: Bob Keeshan, Bob Claver. Stars: Bob Keeshan, Hugh Brannum, Cosmo Allegretti.

On *Howdy Doody*, as "Buffalo" Bob Smith's clown sidekick Clarabell, Bob Keeshan clocked several years as a silent second banana. But after watching the less antic, more central performances by the hosts of *Ding Dong School* and other shows, Keeshan set out to create a hybrid of the two children's TV approaches. His Captain Kangaroo, an almost timid fellow with a big mustache and bigger jacket pockets, used his jangling ring of keys to gain access to his Treasure House, a playhouse every bit as populated as those on *Howdy Doody* and *Andy's Gang*. The Captain's approach, though, was more like that of Miss Frances or Miss Nancy: soft-spoken, focused on preschool viewers at home, and more interested in educating and soothing than simply entertaining. The puppeteer Cosmo Allegretti did multiple duty, embodying everything from the silent, carrot-fixated Bunny Rabbit and the joke-telling Mr. Moose to the gentle giant Dancing Bear. Hugh Brannum, as the sidekick Mr. Green Jeans, brought a variety of common and exotic animals with which the host could interact—long before Johnny Carson did the same thing with San Diego zookeepers on *The Tonight Show*. The Captain also read picture books to children at home, decades before PBS's *Reading Rainbow,* hosted by LeVar Burton, did the same, and the popularity of those segments could be measured by surges in sales, and library demand, for *Mike Mulligan and His Steam Shovel* or any other book featured on *Captain Kangaroo*—like a preschool Oprah Winfrey book club.

There were also cartoons, but these were deliberately basic and non-violent, with Tom Terrific, and his faithful companion Mighty Manfred the Wonder Dog, having "adventures" that barely qualified as such but enchanted young viewers anyway, as did the Treasure House's talking Grandfather Clock and sudden hailstorms of Ping-Pong balls. Over its very lengthy run, *Captain Kangaroo* collected six Emmy Awards and three Peabodys and was eventually undone on CBS not because of falling popularity

Captain Kangaroo was played by veteran children's TV entertainer Bob Keeshan for more than thirty years, after a turn as Clarabell the Clown opposite Howdy Doody.

among the youngest TV demographic but because of a rise in deregulation regarding programming requirements for networks and local stations and a simultaneous rise in the value of network morning news operations. CBS cut back *Captain Kangaroo* from one hour to thirty minutes in 1981 and canceled it completely, after a thirty-year run, three years later. Keeshan and his show moved for an additional six-year run to PBS, which had proven itself, over the decades, much more fertile ground for serious-minded children's television.

MISTER ROGERS' NEIGHBORHOOD

1968–69, NET; 1969–2001, PBS. Creator: Fred Rogers. Host: Fred Rogers. Cast: Betty Aberlin, David Newell.

Fred Rogers, on and off camera, was intensely dedicated to children and, like the hostess of *Ding Dong School,* unusually qualified to appear on a TV show speaking to and about youngsters. While spending days producing one of public television's first local children's shows, Pittsburgh's *Josie's Corner,* Fred McFeely Rogers spent much of his downtime becoming ordained as a Presbyterian minister and taking classes at the University of Pennsylvania's Graduate School of Child Development. The same year he was ordained, he accepted a job offer from Canada's CBC to test his theories and approaches to children's TV, with a new show called *Misterogers.* In 1966, Rogers was wooed back to Pittsburgh, where he created another local show, this time, as in Canada, with himself as the host. That program went national in 1968, on public television's NET network (and, upon its formation, PBS), as *Mister Rogers' Neighborhood,* where it spanned six decades, winning four Emmy Awards and a Peabody.

The Rogers approach, to TV and to children, was to slow things down, be honest and intimate, and discuss and examine joys and fears with equal frankness and reassurance. He hit the airwaves just as concerns about televised violence and unchecked advertising tie-ins were attracting increased attention from watchdog groups and Congress. Rogers, in contrast, took the "Miss Frances" *Ding Dong School* approach to talking to the young viewer at home and extended it significantly. For Fred Rogers, as the host of *Mister Rogers' Neighborhood,* there was always time. Time to change, as he did at the opening of every show, from dress shoes and suit jacket to sneakers and a cardigan, while singing his all-inclusive invitation of a theme song: "It's a beautiful day in this neighborhood / A beautiful day for a neighbor / Would you be mine? / Could you be mine?" His home was open to an endless parade of guests, from everyday kids and his neighborhood deliveryman (David Newell's Mr. McFeely) to such world-class musicians as the cellist Yo-Yo Ma. Rogers went on field trips, to factories and theaters, to show how people made objects and made art. And, thanks to a quick trip following a toy trolley, there were visits to the Neighborhood of Make-Believe, where Rogers's childlike puppets would work their way through various problems. Most weeks were devoted to specific topics, which could be whimsical or serious, and addressed children's most basic concerns, as well as concepts fundamental to their development of a healthy self-image.

In 1968, the year he started with his national show, Fred Rogers asked for, and got, a prime-time special to discuss children's fears at a volatile time for the entire country. He addressed parents directly and encouraged them to watch, with their young children, a segment in which the whispery, childlike hand puppet Daniel Striped Tiger watched as Lady Aberlin (played by Betty Aberlin as a human interacting with puppets, as Fran Allison did on *Kukla,*

Mister Rogers' Neighborhood host and creator, Fred Rogers, got his start in children's television as an off-camera writer, composer, and puppeteer for a local Pittsburgh public TV children's show, *The Children's Corner,* hosted by Josie Carey.

Fran, and Ollie) inflated and deflated a toy balloon. After asking where the air inside the balloon had gone, and where the air inside Lady Aberlin went when she breathed out, Daniel Striped Tiger asked a question that no other children's show dared to ask: "What does assassination mean?" Robert F. Kennedy, running for president in 1968, had been shot and killed the day before, and Rogers was worried enough about the effect on preschoolers to address them, and their parents, directly. It was a stunning TV moment, and every time I rewatch it, showing it to my college students, it still is.

The following year, in May 1969, Mr. Rogers goes to Washington to testify in support of federal funding for public television. The Senate was considering cutting twenty million dollars in funding, and Fred Rogers appeared before Senator John Pastore, who had led an earlier investigation into violence on TV, to plead his case. He described to the Senate Committee chairman his *Mister Rogers' Neighborhood*, which Pastore had never seen, in terms as slowly, simply, and honestly as he addressed kids in his TV audience. "I give an expression of care every day to each child," Rogers told Pastore, "to help him realize that he is unique. I end the program by saying, 'You've made this day a special day, by just your being you. There's no person in the whole world like you, and I like you, just the way you are.' And I feel that if we in public television can only make it clear that feelings are mentionable and manageable, we will have done a great service for mental health." Pastore's response: "Well, I'm supposed to be a pretty tough guy, and this is the first time I've had goose bumps for the last two days." Rogers then sang a song to illustrate his point—his song that begins, "What do you do with the mad that you feel?"—and when he was through, Pastore, clearly touched, flashed a smile to Rogers and said quietly, "I think it's wonderful. Looks like you just earned the twenty million dollars."

On TV, on Capitol Hill, or in person, the Fred Rogers act was consistent— because it was no act. Much later in his career, in 1983, Rogers made a rare appearance on ABC's *Nightline* to discuss the possible effects on children of an upcoming ABC television movie, *The Day After*, dramatizing what might happen if the Soviet Union dropped a nuclear bomb on Middle America. Ted Koppel asked how old someone should be before watching such a potentially frightening film alone, and Rogers's reply, which appeared to charm and disarm Koppel as quickly as Pastore had gotten goose bumps decades earlier, was that Rogers hoped no one would watch it alone. When Fred Rogers came to Philadelphia the following year, to address a group of kindergarten students, *Nightline* invited him to appear on the show again, about another child-related issue. I was following Rogers around that day for a profile for the *Philadelphia Inquirer* and eavesdropped as he declined the offer. He told ABC, politely but firmly, that he owed the kindergarten students, with whom he was to meet the next morning, his full and rested attention. One classroom of preschoolers meant more to Fred Rogers than millions of adults watching on *Nightline*. That's when I got goose bumps.

Through one of the many and surprising ways my love of television has given back to me over the years, I have been lucky enough to serve, for the last several years, as a member of the Advisory Council of the Fred Rogers Center, an organization that strives to continue the legacy of Fred Rogers into a new millennium, by encouraging, as he did, the use of new media to benefit children, especially preschoolers. And through that connection, I was lent, for my New York art exhibit about television, a set of Fred Rogers's sweater and sneakers, which, displayed prominently under glass, was one of the biggest hits in the gallery.

SESAME STREET

1969–, PBS; 2016–, HBO. Creators: Joan Ganz Cooney, Lloyd Morriset. Cast: Jim Henson, Frank Oz, Caroll Spinney, Kevin Clash, others.

Mister Rogers' Neighborhood was one of the two most significant, groundbreaking, and invaluable children's TV programs to premiere in the late 1960s and maintain its influence and popularity for decades. The other was, and is, *Sesame Street.*

PBS, the Public Broadcasting Service, was born on November 3, 1969, replacing NET, National Educational Television, as the service providing noncommercial programming for viewers nationwide. One week later, on November 10, PBS presented its first episode of *Sesame Street,* a show that now ranks as one of the most important programs in TV history—a program that has taught preschoolers numbers, letters, words, and other valuable concepts long before they get a chance to step into the classroom but also introduces them to satire, allusion, and references, thanks to playful spoofs of nursery rhymes, fairy tales, and even popular movies and TV shows. The Children's Television Workshop, now known as the Sesame

Workshop, concocted all these ideas in advance, and more. The CTW was founded in 1968 by Joan Ganz Cooney, a public television documentary producer who conducted a formal study on the possibility of using TV as a teaching tool for the very young, attracted financial grants and like-minded artists such as Jim Henson, and crafted the CTW's first television series, *Sesame Street*.

Unlike *The Mickey Mouse Club*, the idea of *Sesame Street*, from the beginning, was to be all-inclusive and especially to resonate with disadvantaged young inner-city viewers. That's why the show's setting was a city street lined with stoops and dotted with garbage cans (the better to house Oscar the Grouch) and why the children seen playing on *Sesame Street*, and on Sesame Street, represented different races and ethnicities as well as gen-

Sesame Street, from its start as a public television show for preschoolers, has relied on the same mixture of comedy, numbers, vocabulary, guest stars, everyday children, music, and Muppets.

ders. When little kids watched *Romper Room*, they hoped the host would see them. On *Sesame Street*, they could tune in and see themselves, or at least a friendly approximation.

Sesame Street worked at a fast pace and packed in cameos by lots of playful celebrities as well as information about vocabulary, spelling, and mathematics. Most of all, *Sesame Street* had Jim Henson's Muppets, who used this pipeline to young viewers to create a loving, lifelong relationship with many generations of viewers. In any segment in which a young child is shown talking to a Muppet, there's no artifice, no pretense, no skepticism— just love. It's a formula that worked instantly and spread internationally: franchised, locally produced versions of *Sesame Street* soon appeared in other countries and languages, a global-village expansion of the concept of individually tailored local versions of Bozo the Clown or *Romper Room*. In Germany, it was known as *Sesamestrasse;* in Norway, *Sesam Stasjon*. And in every era, different Muppets would enchant, and resonate with, preschool viewers—first the happy awkwardness of Big Bird and the enduring friendship of Bert and Ernie, and on and on through the decades, up to the spin-off series *The Muppet Show* and the current childhood fascination with the squeaky-voiced Elmo. In recent years, *Sesame Street* has borrowed from the *Mister Rogers* playbook and addressed serious real-life events, such as the 9/11 terrorist attacks and the ravages of Hurricane Katrina, in hopes of informing and calming its young viewers. Since its launch in 1969, *Sesame Street* has won more than 150 Emmys, a Peabody, and eight Grammys and always remained true to its initial mission of giving disadvantaged kids an equal chance at early exposure to the basic building blocks of primary education. Always, that is, until January 2016, when it entered into a contract whereby new *Sesame Street* episodes would appear first, exclusively, on HBO for nine months before being shown on PBS. The new, shortened half-hour version, with a new opening and closing theme song, new digs for most of the characters, and an even more enhanced profile for Elmo, wasn't a betrayal of the *Sesame Street* approach, but by making poor families wait nine months before seeing fresh episodes, it sure seems to be a betrayal of its original ethos and mission. It took forty-six seasons, but there's reason to fear that *Sesame Street*, by moving to HBO, has been gentrified.

Other noteworthy children's series, of wildly different types, have appeared since the first days of *Sesame Street*, from such animated pop-culture phenomena as *Teenage Mutant Ninja Turtles, The Smurfs,* and *SpongeBob SquarePants,* and such popular children's sitcom series as *Saved by the Bell* and *Hannah Montana,* to more laudable educational fare: *The Electric Company, Where In the World Is Carmen Sandiego?, Blue's Clues,* even *Dora the Explorer* and *Word World.* Special credit is due to the occasional TV series that, like the reading segments on *Captain Kangaroo,* overtly championed reading. PBS's *Reading Rainbow,* hosted by LeVar Burton, was a standout example from 1983 on PBS, and there were others that, instead of just reading stories and providing animated visual accompaniment, acted out stories in freely adapted, cleverly inspirational versions. PBS's *Wishbone* (1995–99) did it with a dog imagining himself as the protagonist of classic stories, and Showtime's *Shelley Duvall's Faerie Tale Theatre* (1982–87), a brilliant anthology series for young children that drew inspiration from famous illustrators of classic fairy tales, cast the roles with the latest celebrities and had fun modernizing and playing with the familiar tales. These versions were so good, and so popular with children, that the Disney Channel ended up showcasing them on its own network, and in my household my kids watched *Faerie Tale Theatre* so much they could recite the best of them verbatim. For the record, these included *The Three Little Pigs,* with Billy Crystal as the smart pig and Jeff Goldblum as the Big Bad Wolf, and *Pinocchio,* with Carl Reiner as Geppetto and Paul Reubens, a.k.a. Pee-Wee Herman, in the title role. Every one of them is terrific and as much fun for adults to watch as they are for kids. And speaking of Reubens, he also presented one of the last great children's series in TV history—a show that recaptured the anarchy and energy of the earliest "clubhouse" TV shows but with a zany style and sensibility all its own.

PEE-WEE'S PLAYHOUSE

1986–91, CBS. Creator: Paul Reubens. Host: Paul Reubens. Stars: Laurence Fishburne, Phil Hartman, Lynne Marie Stewart, S. Epatha Merkerson, others.

Paul Reubens had created the character of Pee-Wee Herman, an overgrown kid of indeterminate age, back when he was a member of the Los Angeles improv troupe the Groundlings. An HBO special followed, then the big time: a 1985 movie, *Pee-Wee's Big Adventure,* directed by Tim Burton and featuring music by Danny Elfman. Within a year, CBS asked Reubens to create a children's show for the network hosted by his Pee-Wee alter ego, offering near-complete creative control. Presto: *Pee-Wee's Playhouse,* with a visual sensibility as vivid as anything from a Burton movie, and with a catchy, breathless theme song by Elfman, premiered on CBS as a Saturday morning kids' show in 1986 and ran for five successful years.

To produce and populate *Pee-Wee's Playhouse,* Reubens drew upon pretty much the entire history of children's TV. His Pee-Wee character, after all, had been modeled, in wardrobe even more than immaturity, on Pinky Lee from *The Pinky Lee Show.* Other shows from the 1950s and beyond generated such inspirations as talking furniture, mouthy puppets, stop-animation friends, and even the sort of vintage cartoons, from the Fletcher studios and elsewhere, first shown on TV's earliest children's shows. Friends dropped by, as they did on *Captain Kangaroo* and *Mister Rogers' Neighborhood—*

Pee-Wee's Playhouse was an antic children's show, as popular with adults as with youngsters, starring Paul Reubens as the agelessly immature Pee-Wee Herman.

except on *Pee-Wee's Playhouse*, they were gentle caricatures like Cowboy Curtis (played by Laurence Fishburne) and the glamorous beauty queen Miss Yvonne (Lynne Marie Stewart). The lengthy opening credits sequence was as bursting with energy and characters as *The Mickey Mouse Club*'s, and the playhouse itself—a magical nod to *Captain Kangaroo*'s Treasure House, only infinitely more surreal—left no inch untouched by some form of magical imagination. Ice cubes danced in the freezer, tiny dinosaurs lived in the mouse hole, and even the furniture and toys had minds and lives of their own. There were flying pterodactyls and big-headed door-to-door salesmen, disembodied genie heads, and even a self-appointed King of Cartoons. Anarchy, again, was the rule, but so was a special blend of creativity, freedom, and, at the center of everything, a positive self-image. That image proved quite durable, as Netflix presented in 2016 a comedy movie produced by Reubens and Judd Apatow, *Pee-Wee's Big Holiday*, in which Reubens reprised his ageless character, using CGI "airbrushing" effects to help maintain the illusion of youth.

One final, personal note about children's television: I watched *Pee-Wee's Playhouse*, and *Faerie Tale Theatre* and *Mister Rogers' Neighborhood* and other shows, with my daughter, Kristin, and son, Mark, when they were young. When I was young, I gobbled up such shows as *The Mickey Mouse Club* and *Captain Kangaroo* and was touched early by the spirit of Fred Rogers, thanks to Josie Carey's *Children's Corner*. And while the technology and the programming continue to change, the special magic of children's TV remains the same. While beginning this particular paragraph, I received via phone a video from Kristin, who had used her smartphone to film her daughter, Reina Ochoa, enjoying one of the only TV shows she's allowed to watch at six months old. The show is PBS's *Daniel Tiger's Neighborhood*, an animated continuation of the characters and camaraderie of *Mister Rogers' Neighborhood*. When Kristin was a toddler, one of the only TV shows I let her watch was the one hosted by Fred Rogers, and somehow, without my urging or recommendation, she had found the PBS cartoon continuation of the *Neighborhood* and happily showed it to Reina. Daniel Striped Tiger— the same sweet character who asked about the meaning of assassination in 1968—is presented on this animated series as a cartoon character, as are the other familiar residents of the old Fred Rogers show and the Neighborhood of Make-Believe. Rogers died in 2003, but *Daniel Tiger's Neighbor-*

hood, created under the auspices of those determined to carry on his legacy, premiered in 2012 and has succeeded in charming preschoolers just as Fred Rogers did half a century before. The new *Neighborhood* series opens with Daniel slipping on a comfortable sweater and shoes while singing, "What a wonderful day in the neighborhood," just as Fred Rogers did in the original. Then Daniel rides the trolley to the Neighborhood of Make-Believe, and as the opening credits end, Daniel greets the viewers at home. On the video sent by my daughter, my granddaughter watches all of this with rapt attention and warm familiarity, smiling a wide but toothless smile until the point when Daniel begins to speak, seemingly to her—at which point she squeals loudly, as if in the throes of some sort of baby Beatlemania. And according to Kristin, Reina reacts that way every time.

And then it hit me: Fred Rogers, as only one representative of an ambassador of quality children's television, has managed to reach three generations of loyal and grateful viewers in my family alone. That's not just evolution. That's a minor media miracle.

2 ANIMATION

KEY EVOLUTIONARY STAGES

Rocky and His Friends/The Bullwinkle Show	1959–64, ABC/NBC
The Flintstones	1960–66, ABC
A Charlie Brown Christmas	1965, CBS
The Simpsons	1989–, Fox
South Park	1997–, Comedy Central

Post–World War II baby boomers were the first official television generation—the first not only to grow up with television but to wake up to it as well. Starting with the early 1950s and continuing for decades afterward, children across America woke up on Saturday mornings in eager anticipation of their favorite cartoon and kids' TV shows—waking up so early, in many cases, that it would still be dark outside, with the only thing on television the unblinking TV test pattern and its accompanying electronic whine. In minutes or hours, though, the TV set would wake up as well, usually presenting a local weather or farm report before shifting to kids' shows. Waiting for Saturday morning TV to begin, especially the cartoons, was a familiar ritual for children my age in that era, whether you held vigil with siblings or all alone. In an era when most homes had only one TV set, Saturday morning meant one of the few times when kids had a chance of controlling the dial and selecting their own entertainment, as their grateful parents slept in or occupied themselves in other parts of the house. My personal ritual involved cereal, often of the individually sized "variety pack" boxes you sliced open on the perforations to make a self-contained rectangular "bowl." The milk almost always leaked out, but that just made you eat faster. And, somehow, it made the Sugar Frosted Flakes taste even better. Getting up before dawn to watch nothing, merely in anticipation of what was to come, may sound ridiculous . . . but I wasn't alone.

"I loved the idea of Saturday morning TV," confesses Matt Groening, whose love of cartoons would eventually spark him to create the longest-running cartoon series in history, Fox's *Simpsons*. "I would get up so early that there'd be a test pattern on the screen," he recalls, laughing, "and then you'd have to wait through *Farm Report*. There was a show in Portland [where Groening grew up in Oregon], it came on at like 6:30 a.m., 7:00 a.m., called *RFD 6*, which was about farms—farm news. And the only good thing about it, the opening title had a little diorama of a farm."

Others who went on to create TV of their own had different experiences of it as youngsters. "It was a pretty common thing to wake up and have breakfast and throw the TV on, yeah," recalls Louis C.K. "But actually, there's this one unique thing about the morning for me, which is that I lived in Mexico when I was little, until I was about seven. And I watched *The Flintstones* in Mexico—it was big in Mexico—and then *Sesame Street,* and I watched them both in Spanish. And there was a weird thing, of coming to the United States and seeing these shows in English."

Shawn Ryan, creator of the cop series *The Shield,* says, "I watched a lot of *Scooby-Doo,* and I remember all the songs from *Schoolhouse Rock*. I still can quote the preamble to the Declaration of Independence because of *Schoolhouse Rock*." Comic Amy Schumer's Saturday morning routine was programmed by her parents, who would preselect what she was allowed to watch. "I watched *Looney Tunes,* I watched the Muppets," she says. "They'd put on a tape for us, and we'd watch *The Muppet Show*." And Matthew Weiner, the creator of *Mad Men,* recalls, "We watched *Looney Tunes* and maybe the Jackson Five cartoon—things like that. *H. R. Pufnstuf.* It was such a weird fever dream, that Saturday morning TV stretch. It really was."

Those Saturday morning fever dreams eventually spread to prime time—first in the 1960s with *The Flintstones* and again a generation later with *The Simpsons*. But when television was as young as its child-age viewers, animation was the sole province of children's shows, with, at first, cartoons recycled after they appeared as pre-movie short features in theaters. The first animated cartoons had appeared in the first decade of the twentieth century, courtesy of Stuart Blackton's *Humorous Phases of Funny Faces* in 1906 and the *New York Herald* cartoonist Winsor McCay's wild visual experimentations in 1909's *Little Nemo*. Max Fleischer's first *Out of the Inkwell* cartoons, with KoKo the Clown emerging from the artist's bottle of ink, appeared in 1919, and Fleischer and his brother Dave continued to generate fluid, inventive, and memorable short and movie-length cartoons for decades, and played with synchronized sound years before 1927's landmark live-action drama *The Jazz Singer*. In 1928, Walt Disney popularized the sound cartoon, and his most iconic animated character, when Mickey Mouse starred in *Steamboat Willie*.

Only a year after his *Steamboat Willie* triumph, Disney released the first Silly Symphonies cartoon, 1929's *Skeleton Dance,* and the spectacularly blissful marriage of music and drawings sparked, within a few years, a shameless parade of competitors from rival studios. Warner Bros. struck its own mother lode, twice, with *Looney Tunes* and *Merrie Melodies,* and eventually all those cartoons would find their way to television, replayed prominently, and profitably, for decades.

The first Betty Boop cartoon, Dave Fleischer's *Dizzy Dishes,* appeared in 1930, showcasing one of the most outrageous and durable comic characters of the period. (One of them, a 1932 Dave Fleischer "Tarkartoon" featuring Betty Boop and the music of Cab Calloway, with skeletons and ghosts in electric chairs chanting and moaning to "Minnie the Moocher," completely creeped me out when I first saw it on TV. Still does.) In the 1930s, the Fleischer brothers kept their string running, introducing the first *Popeye the Sailor* cartoon in 1933 and ambitiously presenting the full-length *Gulliver's Travels,* an adaptation of the Jonathan Swift satirical novel, in 1939. But they were overshadowed, and eventually outlasted, by the Disney studio, which for a decade included an almost absurdly impressive string of advances and successes. Disney introduced color animation in 1932, in *Flowers and Trees* (the first cartoon presented in Technicolor), and won an Oscar for it. In 1933, Disney's *Three Little Pigs* introduced a catchy song that became a major radio hit in the 1930s, "Who's Afraid of the Big Bad Wolf?" And while cartoons were a welcome, and increasingly common, addition to movie theater schedules, serving as a light appetizer for the main course, Disney had greater ambitions. In 1937, Disney took top billing, and achieved another unprecedented accomplishment, with the release of the cinema's first full-length cartoon feature film hit—not the first full-length cartoon, but the first to use Technicolor, and the first to pack in audiences and garner rave reviews. Its title: *Snow White and the Seven Dwarfs.* You might have heard of it.

Though the Fleischers were able to produce and present *Gulliver's Travels* two years later, and launch a series of animated Superman adventures in 1941, Disney easily outdid them. In 1940 alone, Disney released *Pinocchio,* a stunning achievement of storytelling, visual artistry, and all-around excellence, and *Fantasia,* a boldly artistic attempt to present what amounted to classical music animated videos. (Most famously: Mickey Mouse casting a spell to have brooms come to life and carry water buckets to the tune of Paul Dukas's *Sorcerer's Apprentice,* the devil coming to life to Modest Mussorgsky's *Night on Bald Mountain,* and the beautiful ending set to Franz Schubert's angelic *Ave Maria.*) The more mainstream *Dumbo* followed in 1941, and *Bambi* in 1942, by which time Disney was, by far, the biggest cartoon game in town. Astoundingly, in retrospect, Disney was not the most financially successful operation, at least for its full-length animated efforts: despite their obvious technical and artistic merits, *Pinocchio, Fantasia,* and *Bambi* all lost money at the box office during the time of their original theatrical release.

But on the brand-new medium of television, replaying cartoons created for theatrical distribution was very cost-effective, and inventive animators soon learned how to cut costs and produce directly for TV. When World War II ended, television began in earnest, with NBC and the original "fourth network," DuMont, starting postwar operations in 1946. At the time, DuMont was technically the "second network," but when CBS and ABC began broadcasting their television programming in 1948, DuMont instantly went to second-class, fourth-network status. In the beginning, though, was DuMont, and in 1947 its *Small Fry Club* children's program on New York's WADB soon began offering a weekly program of film features, including a series of silent *Aesop's Fables* animated shorts from the 1920s—TV's first regularly scheduled cartoons.

At the movies, 1949 was the year the Road Runner and Wile E. Coyote made their first big-screen appearance, in the Chuck Jones cartoon *Fast and Furry-Ous,* and Mr. Magoo, the nearsighted old man voiced by Jim Backus, did the same in what became a series of Oscar-winning animated shorts. On television, the only cartoon addition that year was *Tele-comics,* a syndicated program that photographed nonmoving drawings of action comics, with offscreen voices reading the dialogue and providing narration. But TV's animated missing link was developed that year as well, though it wouldn't premiere in syndication until 1950. *Crusader Rabbit,* the first animated cartoon series made specifically for television, was created by Jay Ward and Alex Anderson. Episodes of the series, with continuing story lines presented in the manner of a movie matinee serial, were only five minutes long and cost only about five hundred dollars to produce. The animation was fairly static to keep costs down, but the writing was sharp and crafted to appeal to adults as well as their children—an approach Ward would continue, and perfect, with *Rocky and His Friends* and *The Bullwinkle Show.*

On television, the 1950s were boom years for animation—not visually, but economically. Even the crudest drawings could lead to lavish profits, from either syndication revenues or tie-in merchandising efforts. A perfect, though cynical, example of the latter was CBS's *Winky Dink and You,* the first interactive series in TV history. This children's program lasted four years, with a unique gimmick at its core that proved as lucrative as it was popular. The host, Jack Barry, later at the center of the quiz show scandals as the host of NBC's *Twenty-One,* presented and narrated a series of barely kinetic drawings featuring Winky Dink, a neighborhood kid whose natural curiosity got him into all sorts of trouble. To get out of that trouble, Winky Dink always lacked one key object—a footbridge, a rope, a rock, or some other easily drawn object. Barry would instruct his young audience members to place a special Winky Dink sheet of clear acetate over the TV screen and use the special Winky Dink washable crayons to draw the missing element. The animation would then show Winky Dink triumphing, thanks to the viewer's help, though youngsters who didn't play along watched Winky Dink with various levels of bafflement as he walked on thin air, threw an invisible rock, and so on. But for the producers of *Winky Dink and You,* what mattered wasn't the universality of the viewing experience but the money to be made by selling their Winky Dink "Magic TV Kits," available at toy stores everywhere for fifty cents a pop.

A more artistically ambitious form of TV merchandising occurred in 1954, when ABC and Walt Disney teamed up to present the new series called *Disneyland.* It brought many of the classic Disney animated shorts to prime time for the first time. Disney also recycled them effectively in the afternoons, once ABC's *Mickey Mouse Club* premiered in 1955, offering regular doses of vintage "Mousekartoons" from the Disney archive—more than a hundred of them in the first season alone. Others, like Disney, saw TV as a veritable gold rush and scampered to recycle old cartoons or generate new ones to cash in on this new medium. As *The Mickey Mouse Club* entertained kids weekday afternoons on ABC, CBS began entertaining them on Saturday mornings, that same year of 1955, with *Mighty Mouse Playhouse*. The program mostly repackaged the animator Paul Terry's old cartoons (the character, introduced in 1942 under the original name of Super Mouse, was a mash-up of Disney's Mickey and the animated Superman cartoons, which had come out the year before). But that didn't matter to youngsters, who made *Mighty Mouse Playhouse* a hit for twelve years and further established Saturday mornings as prime real estate for cartoon fare.

The first half-hour cartoon series whose content was created expressly for network television was *The Boing Boing Show*, which premiered on another TV beachhead, Sunday afternoons, on CBS in 1956. Based on the Oscar-winning 1951 film short featuring a character from a Dr. Seuss children's record, the Boing Boing series was promoted in 1958 and moved, briefly and less successfully, to prime time. Other cartoons were enjoying greater fortune in the mid-1950s: in 1956, old Popeye and Bugs Bunny cartoons began being sold to independent TV stations in major cities, in prominent time slots and with very competitive results. In 1957, a mixture of old (dating from the 1940s) and new, made-for-TV Woody Woodpecker cartoons were featured on ABC's *Woody Woodpecker Show*, which appeared on ABC's weekday afternoon schedule, sandwiched between *American Bandstand* and *The Mickey Mouse Club*. And weekday mornings on CBS, *Captain Kangaroo* proudly presented occasional short cartoons called and featuring Tom Terrific, made especially for the program.

Another significant animation event came in 1957 when MGM executives decided there was no future in cartoons and closed its animation unit, firing its recently appointed heads of animation, William Hanna and Joe Barbera. The duo started its own studio, Hanna-Barbera, and set out instantly to provide animation for television, using techniques designed specifically to keep costs down and artist manpower to a minimum. Theirs was the first major TV animated program, NBC's *Ruff and Reddy Show*, relying entirely on fresh content. The series, which made its debut in 1957, was rough all right: for an entire half-hour time slot, it required only twelve thousand cels—only two thousand more images than *Gertie the Dinosaur* had utilized more than forty years earlier, and Winsor McCay had drawn every one of those images himself.

Hanna-Barbera, though, wasn't interested in fluidity of artistic lines, just the straightest line between the two points of conception and completion. It was Hanna-Barbera, for example, that pioneered the use of specific body-part animation, splitting a body into several parts, on several overlaid cels, so that only the moving parts need be redrawn and replaced. If you ever wondered why, say, Yogi Bear wore a collar and cuffs, that's the reason: to give animators a clean dividing line between the moving face and hands and the static body.

Hanna-Barbera took its next project, *Huckleberry Hound,* directly to TV syndication, which meant greater profits, including in toy merchandising. (I must confess to carrying around, as a little kid, a Huckleberry Hound stuffed animal: hard plastic nose and face, stiff and un-cuddly barely furry body, but I carried it around anyway.) But that program, which premiered in 1958, was richer in other ways as well. It introduced, among its other short cartoon features, the aforementioned Yogi Bear, who was spun off into a successful show of his own. And by lacing in a bunch of parodies and punch lines and comic references that would go over the heads of young viewers but delight their parents, *Huckleberry Hound* established for television a dual-meaning "adult" approach to children's cartoons. Warner Bros. had done the same thing for years with its theatrical shorts, but doing it specifically for television meant that for animators producing cartoons for TV, all bets were off and all time-slot barriers crumbled.

Within a year, Hanna-Barbera had both *Yogi Bear* and *Quick Draw McGraw* in syndication, appearing in shows of their own, and another outfit, Cambria Studios, came up with an even cheaper way to isolate parts of its cartoons and reduce animation costs. Instead of drawing the mouth movements of its characters, it would film actors saying the lines of dialogue and superimpose their mouths onto the faces of the characters. The technique was called Syncro-Vox; it was unveiled in 1959's *Clutch Cargo* and was thoroughly creepy. It was also adapted, many decades later and much more entertainingly, by Robert Smigel on NBC's *Late Night with Conan O'Brien,* with Smigel's moving mouth superimposed over pictures of celebrities (Arnold Schwarzenegger, Bill Clinton, and so on) as he impersonated them, fielding O'Brien's playful questions. By far the biggest contribution to TV animation in the year 1959, however, was made by an ABC cartoon series called *Rocky and His Friends,* in which Jay Ward and company introduced the brilliantly comic characters of Rocky and Bullwinkle, the twisted stories of "Aesop & Son" and "Fractured Fairy Tales," and so on. *Rocky and His*

Friends wasn't shown in prime time, but when it moved to NBC two years later as *The Bullwinkle Show,* it would be.

ROCKY AND HIS FRIENDS

1959–61, ABC.

THE BULLWINKLE SHOW

1961–64, NBC. Creators and producers: Jay Ward, Bill Scott. Star voices: Bill Scott, June Foray, William Conrad, Paul Frees, Edward Everett Horton, Daws Butler, Hans Conried, Walter Tetley.

My love for "Rocky & Bullwinkle," the way these two TV series are linked in common vocabulary and memory, is lifelong. I was a loyal viewer of *Rocky and His Friends* on ABC, and *The Bullwinkle Show* was one of the first prime-time TV series, along with *The Twilight Zone,* that I made a point of staying up to watch as a little kid. In the 1970s, when I became a TV critic and started flying to Los Angeles for the semiannual press tours, one of the first places I visited, and what became a regular pilgrimage until it closed, was the Dudley Do-Right Emporium on Sunset Boulevard, run by the Bullwinkle co-creator Jay Ward's wife, Ramona. At the time, animated cels of Rocky and the gang were being sold for $50, which I rejected as too expensive—until a catalog arrived in 1988 saying the price had gone up to $250. I phoned the Emporium, spoke to Ramona, and frantically placed an order for one before the price rose again. But I confided to Ramona that I was a poor TV critic and that amount represented more than I had ever spent for a work of art. Because I considered it a work of art, I asked, could she get the artist to sign it? She laughed, put me on hold, came back, and said, "Sure." In the mail, a week or so later, I got a "Rocky & Bullwinkle" cel signed and dated by the reclusive and elusive Jay Ward himself. He died a year later, and an animation arts store appraised my cel at five figures, but I would never think of selling it. I did, however, proudly display it as part of my TV art exhibit at New York's apexart gallery in 2014, bringing my love of Jay Ward's cartoon series full circle. Others have loved it no less.

Rocky and His Friends/The Bullwinkle Show: Many cartoon characters broke things, but Bullwinkle J. Moose was fond of breaking the fourth wall and of speaking directly to TV viewers at home.

"'Rocky & Bullwinkle' was witty and fun to watch, and I was always happy when that show was on," says Matt Groening, who calls it "brilliant" and confesses it gave him a template to follow when creating *The Simpsons*—to worry less, at least initially, about the animation than the other elements. "You've got to get good writing, and you've got to get great voices, and you've got to get great music," he says, "and that meant success would follow." (There's also the middle-initial allusion, with Groening's Homer J. Simpson a fond nod to Ward's Bullwinkle J. Moose and Rocket J. Squirrel.)

On *Rocky and His Friends,* the music (composed by Fred Steiner) was vibrant, the voices were lively, and the scripts were as entertaining to adults as to children. The *Rocky* and *Bullwinkle* series both borrowed, for their central adventures of the flying squirrel and the bumbling moose, from the serialized format of *Crusader Rabbit* and were narrated, in frantic fashion, by William Conrad, formerly the voice of Matt Dillon on radio's *Gunsmoke* and later to provide the much slower and more somber narration for ABC's

Fugitive. (Conrad once told me his audition for the *Rocky* narration required him to double the speed when reading the lines, then double it again.) Sandwiched between the "Rocky & Bullwinkle" adventures were other, equally inspired elements: Edward Everett Horton narrating "Fractured Fairy Tales"; the silent-movie serial spoof, "Dudley Do-Right of the Mounties," with the villainous Snidely Whiplash; and a talking dog named Mr. Peabody taking his pet boy Sherman on time-travel adventures in "Peabody's Improbable History," which invariably ended with a groan-inducing pun, as did the skewed fables told in another segment, "Aesop & Son." (A typical "Aesop & Son" closing moral, to the fable "The Wolf in Sheep's Clothing," was "Always be alert, whether awake or a sheep.") And in the "Rocky & Bullwinkle" segments, there were the unforgettable Cold War villains Boris Badenov and Natasha Fatale.

Bill Scott, who co-created these series with Jay Ward, was no silent partner: in fact, he provided the voices of Bullwinkle J. Moose, Mr. Peabody, and Dudley Do-Right. June Foray was both Rocket J. Squirrel and Natasha Fatale, Paul Frees was Boris, and Hans Conried was Snidely. The plots were outrageous, the puns outstanding. I was in my twenties before I realized that the name Boris Badenov was a playful twist on the Mussorgsky opera *Boris Godunov.* And while young kids might have laughed at the silliness and unchecked greed of the prince coming upon the supine princess in the "Fractured Fairy Tales" version of "Sleeping Beauty," sharp-eyed adults would have noticed the resemblance, both physical and entrepreneurial, to Walt Disney, whose Disneyland theme park, like his *Disneyland* TV series, had been unveiled only a few years before. The Walt Disney–ish prince on "Fractured Fairy Tales" didn't just see a sleeping beauty; he saw a golden opportunity. "Awake," he says, "she's just another princess. Asleep, she's a gold mine! I can see it now: Sleeping Beauty comics, Sleeping Beauty hats, Sleeping Beauty bubble gum—and biggest of all, Sleeping Beautyland!"

Adult jokes, buried within shows aimed at children, had been seen earlier on children's TV shows, not only on Ward's *Crusader Rabbit* cartoon shorts, but on such live-action series as *The Soupy Sales Show* (out of Chicago) and Stan Freberg's *Time for Beany* (out of Los Angeles). But the "Rocky & Bullwinkle" TV shows pushed the humor to previously unexplored heights and depths. Puns and jokes were highbrow and lowbrow, often at the same time: for example, the jewel-encrusted toy boat called the *Ruby Yacht of Omar Khayyam.* Or the alternate title for one snowbound "Rocky & Bullwinkle" adventure, called "Avalanche Is Better Than None." Or my favorite bit of dialogue from the entire series, when, in "The Box Top Robbery" serial during the first season of *Rocky and His Friends,* Bullwinkle takes a wheelbarrow full of box tops into his local bank to open an account. "What kind?" asks the bank officer. "Just checking?" "No," Bullwinkle replies. "I really mean it." More than fifty years later, that joke still makes me laugh out loud.

While 1959's *Rocky and His Friends* was an afternoon show on ABC, with much of its humor being lost on younger viewers, the series, in 1961, would change networks, titles, and time slots, as *The Bullwinkle Show,* premiering in prime time on NBC. The reason? Another cartoon series, premiering in the evening the year before, had proven that adults, as well as kids, enjoyed watching animation on TV. In 1960, yet another new Hanna-Barbera series entered the TV landscape and became an unprecedented hit.

THE FLINTSTONES

1960–66, ABC. Creators: William Hanna, Joseph Barbera. Vocal stars: Alan Reed, Henry Corden, Jean Vander Pyl, Mel Blanc, Bea Benaderet, Gerry Johnson.

ABC launched *The Flintstones* in prime time at 8:30 p.m. eastern time, later than any other cartoon series before it had been scheduled, largely to try to capitalize on its potential appeal to adults. It was a Stone Age variation on *The Honeymooners,* a Jackie Gleason live-action sitcom that had premiered on CBS only five years earlier. It wasn't the most clever of animated comedies; like many cartoon and live-action series of the period, its most distinctive and memorable elements were its opening credits sequence and theme song. The most imagination was expended showing ways in which prehistoric animals, objects, and materials could approximate modern conveniences, but the plots were the same basic themes from *The Honeymooners.* On that familiar sitcom, Gleason's Ralph Kramden and his best friend and neighbor, Art Carney's Ed Norton, would hang out at the Raccoon Lodge. On *The Flintstones,* Fred Flintstone and his best friend and neighbor, Barney Rubble, were members of the Royal Order of Water Buffalos, and both sets of husbands would attempt, unsuccessfully, to get away with something without their wives getting wise to their scheme. Even loyal

Flintstones fans may be unaware that the show's vocal talents included the great Mel Blanc (the voice of Bugs Bunny and so many other wonderful cartoon characters) not only as Barney but as Fred's pet dinosaur, Dino, and the *Petticoat Junction* star Bea Benaderet as the first of two actresses giving voice to Betty.

Even without being written or drawn particularly well, *The Flintstones* deserves its proper recognition here as one of the key evolutionary stages in the animated TV series, and not only because it's so fitting, because this entire book is founded on the concept of those "five stages of man" textbook drawings depicting the evolution of man from prehistory to modern times. *The Flintstones,* though its premise was derivative, caught the public attention instantly and resoundingly. Ratings for *The Flintstones,* like certain passengers in Fred Flintstone's animal-skin-topped car, went through the roof. At the end of the 1960–61 TV season, according to the Nielsen ratings, *The Flintstones* was ranked No. 18 for the year, nestled between *Bonanza* and *The Red Skelton Show.* No cartoon series had ever ended a season in the Top 20

The Flintstones, the most popular animated series ever shown in prime time, featured caveman Fred Flintstone as a prehistoric version of Ralph Kramden on *The Honeymooners.*

before. And no other cartoon series—not *The Simpsons,* not *Family Guy,* not any other animated show in TV history—has done it since.

Clearly, TV animation in the 1960s was enjoying its own little Golden Age. Other characters popularized long ago on film made the transition to TV in 1960, led by Bugs Bunny (who started with ABC, then moved from network to network, but remained a television fixture for decades) and Mr. Magoo, whose syndicated success led in 1962 to television's first animated Christmas special, the delightful *Mr. Magoo's Christmas Carol.* And because television is endlessly (and tiresomely) imitative, the success of *The Flintstones* led to a predictable flooding of the market by other prime-time cartoons the following season. NBC premiered the best of them, *The Bullwinkle Show,* in 1961, while CBS countered with *The Alvin Show.* ABC, copying its own *Flintstones* formula as much as possible, presented *Top Cat,* an unofficial reworking of Phil Silvers's *You'll Never Get Rich* sitcom, only with animated alley cats as the fast-talking central schemers. None of those shows lasted more than a season in prime time, however, and were either relegated to weekend daytime slots or recycled as Saturday morning reruns. Hanna-Barbera and ABC kept trying, persistently, to have lightning strike twice, continuing to schedule prime-time cartoons after the other networks had given up—first *The Jetsons* in 1962, then *The Adventures of Jonny Quest,* another show using the *Clutch Cargo* Syncro-Vox trick, in 1964. Neither made it to a second season, though each had a long afterlife as Saturday morning repeats, and *The Jetsons,* especially, earned a place for decades in American cultural memory.

Prime time became less welcoming an environment for cartoon series, but producers found one other way to slip their product through the cracks: as holiday specials, which, if popular enough, could be repeated annually. *Mr. Magoo's Christmas Carol* had already demonstrated ample proof of this strategy, and other networks and sponsors followed suit, with equal or greater success, year after year: the first puppet-animation TV special, Rankin-Bass's *Rudolph the Red-Nosed Reindeer,* in 1964; the first Charles M. Schulz *Peanuts* holiday special, CBS's superb *Charlie Brown Christmas,* in 1965; and Chuck Jones's charmingly twisted CBS version of Dr. Seuss's *How the Grinch Stole Christmas* in 1966. No matter your age, it's a good bet you've seen all three, and one of them is an absolute, unqualified TV masterpiece.

A CHARLIE BROWN CHRISTMAS

1965, CBS. Creator and writer: Charles Schulz. Producer and director: Bill Melendez. Executive producer: Lee Mendelson. Music: Vince Guaraldi. Voices: Peter Robbins, Christopher Shea, Tracy Stratford, Kathy Steinberg.

A Charlie Brown Christmas, the first and still best *Peanuts* animated special, is more than fifty years old now and still a traditional part of the holiday TV season. CBS repeated it annually for decades, after which ABC purchased the rights and continued to showcase it. Not bad, for a holiday special that wasn't even expected to be seen again after its initial telecast, because both the sponsor (Coca-Cola) and the network thought the *Peanuts* creator, Charles Schulz, and animator Bill Melendez had delivered to them, on a very tight deadline, a Christmas lump of cartoon coal. All the elements on which Schulz insisted—including Charlie Brown's depression over the commercialization of Christmas, the absence of a laugh track, the exclusive use of the voices of actual children, and the inclusion of Linus's direct quotation from the New Testament—were initially hated by either

A Charlie Brown Christmas was the first and best *Peanuts* TV special, in which comic strip creator Charles M. Schulz managed to deliver a truly spiritual Christmas message.

the sponsor or the network, or both. Yet those same elements, as well as the jazzy music by Vince Guaraldi, were instantly beloved by viewers, and *A Charlie Brown Christmas* now stands as one of the most durable, and one of the few remaining, TV family viewing traditions. Guaraldi's "Linus and Lucy" instrumental is like a musical smile, and the recitation by Christopher Shea's Linus about "the true meaning of Christmas," quoting directly from the gospel of Luke, is an undiluted example of religious reverence of a type that's hard to imagine in any holiday special made in more modern times. "And there were in the same country shepherds abiding in the field, keeping watch over their flock by night," Linus began, bathed in a spotlight and reciting in a voice appropriately described as angelic. "And lo, the angel of the Lord came upon them."

A Charlie Brown Christmas, on its premiere telecast, was seen in 45 percent of all homes viewing TV at that hour—an estimated audience of more than fifteen million viewers. It won Emmy and Peabody Awards and has spawned numerous holiday sequels and spin-offs ever since, including the comparably excellent *It's the Great Pumpkin, Charlie Brown* in 1966 and, half a century later, 2015's *Peanuts Movie,* a full-length film true to Schulz's original content and style and presented lovingly in the new process of 3-D animation.

As the 1960s went on, animation, like just about everything else that decade, got a little stranger. Japanese anime was first imported and dubbed in 1963, with *Astroboy* from the Mushi Studios. In 1967, a dubbed version of a hit Japanese anime called *Mach GoGoGo* was presented in the United States under the title *Speed Racer*. In 1965, at the height of Beatlemania, King Features presented a syndicated cartoon show called *The Beatles,* in which the music was much more memorable than the animation, stories, or even the characters (unless the Beatles were heard on the soundtrack singing prerecorded songs, the voices of John Lennon and George Harrison were "provided" by Paul Frees, and the voices of Paul McCartney and Ringo Starr by Lance Percival). Also that year, a syndicated version of *The Adventures of Gumby* was launched, continuing the clay-animation adventures of Gumby and his equally spineless horse, Pokey. Other cartoon hits that decade included NBC's *Underdog* (another *Superman* spoof, with Wally Cox as the voice of Shoeshine Boy and his stronger alter ego) in 1964, Jay Ward's *George of the Jungle* (NBC, 1967), and *The Road Runner Show,* a 1967 CBS compilation presenting old and new cartoons.

The entertaining violence in those *Road Runner* cartoons, however, was about to be attacked by Congress—specifically, by Senator John Pastore, who in 1968 targeted TV content in general and what he found to be objectionable levels of sex and violence in particular. The networks were frightened enough of government interference to police their own shows rather forcefully, and producers of cartoon shows were told, very explicitly, to cut down on the violence. One of the first new shows to deal with Pastore's concerns head-on was a cartoon series that got around the violence issue by establishing, as part of each week's plot, that the violent and scary acts animated as part of the action turn out to be "faked" by some of the cartoon characters themselves. It sounds like a stupid way to get around the rules, and it was, indeed, a stupid show, but nevertheless, it worked, and the decade closed with CBS's *Scooby-Doo, Where Are You?* succeeding as the first in a long line of Scooby showcases. (Astoundingly, the main characters of *Scooby-Doo* were inspired by characters and actors from a live-action 1950s sitcom, *The Many Loves of Dobie Gillis.* Good-looking Fred was an animated version of Dwayne Hickman's Dobie, beautiful Daphne a cartoon take on Tuesday Weld's Thalia Menninger, plain and brainy Velma a two-dimensional approximation of Sheila James's Zelda, and the canine Scooby-Doo's owner, Shaggy, a variation on Bob Denver's *Dobie Gillis* beatnik, Maynard G. Krebs. Which explains, if nothing else, why Shaggy had a goatee in the late 1960s and beyond.)

By then, the Golden Age of TV animation had come and gone. What was left were sporadic and increasingly rare triumphs, often accompanied, each decade, by astoundingly clunky misfires.

On the good side—make that the great side—the 1970s brought us the 1971 animated musical *The Point* in prime time (story and music by Harry Nilsson, animation by Fred Wolf, and narration, for the initial ABC telecast, by Dustin Hoffman) and Bill Cosby's well-intentioned CBS cartoon *Fat Albert and the Cosby Kids* on Saturday mornings. On the awful side, Hanna-Barbera tried, in 1972, to syndicate an animated family sitcom that was a much tamer version of the then-provocative CBS prime-time series, *All in the Family.* Called *Wait Till Your Father Gets Home,* it starred, as the voice of the show's conservative patriarch, Tom Bosley. Two years later, Bosley would move on to much happier days, as the patriarchal Mr. Cunningham on ABC's nostalgic family sitcom *Happy Days.*

The 1980s started horrendously—with another Hanna-Barbera series, *The Smurfs,* in 1981—but ended gloriously with Steven Spielberg, working with Warner Bros. in 1989, presenting *Tiny Toon Adventures,* a clever reimagining of Bugs Bunny and other beloved cartoon characters as precocious tots. And, most gloriously of all, with Fox's *Simpsons* emerging from *The Tracey Ullman Show* (where it had begun as interstitial shorts, very tiny cartoons), and Matt Groening's spirited imagination, to usher in a new era for prime-time animation. In the evolutionary history of this genre, *The Simpsons* is the masterstroke.

THE SIMPSONS

1989–, Fox. Creators and writers: James L. Brooks, Sam Simon, Matt Groening. Writers: David X. Cohen, John Swartzwelder, Ian Maxtone-Graham, Bill Odenkirk, Greg Daniels, Conan O'Brien, others. Vocal stars: Dan Castellaneta, Julie Kavner, Nancy Cartwright, Yeardley Smith, Harry Shearer, Hank Azaria.

There may be no other series in this entire book that exemplifies the idea of television evolution so much as *The Simpsons.* The inspirations for its characters and setting came from previous TV shows. The series itself evolved from a "lower life-form," a series of interstitial shorts on a different program entirely. And once it premiered, *The Simpsons* not only continued to evolve, becoming more sophisticated and polished over the years in its style of animation, but became the evolutionary link that led to a whole new world of TV animation, including some shows, such as *South Park, Family Guy,* and *Futurama,* that would eventually refer directly to *The Simpsons* in their own programs.

On *The Tracey Ullman Show,* one of the first series on the fledgling Fox network in 1987, the *Life in Hell* cartoonist, Matt Groening, was hired to provide short little animated pieces to serve as bumpers between the live-action variety sketches. He created a dysfunctional family called the Simpsons—father Homer, mother Marge, and the kids, bratty Bart, sensitive Lisa, and baby Maggie. And though the Simpsons weren't able to do much beyond physical gags and quick wisecracks in the time allotted, their world nonetheless expanded over the three seasons they appeared in those short animated pieces. "The first season on *The Tracey Ullman Show,* the characters stayed in the house," Groening explains. "The second season,

The Simpsons has featured hundreds of special guest voices over its lengthy run, including an uncredited Michael Jackson playing a mental patient friend of Homer's who thinks he's Michael Jackson.

they went into the backyard. And the third season, they started to go into town."

Then, starting with a Christmas special in 1989, the Simpsons got their own half-hour series, stepping up to the big leagues, as Ralph and Alice Kramden had when Jackie Gleason "promoted" them from short skits on his variety series to a full-season sitcom of their own, called *The Honeymooners*. As a series, *The Simpsons* was co-created by Groening and the *Tracey Ullman Show* executive producers James L. Brooks and Sam Simon, who had worked together on *Taxi*. Brooks, who had greatly benefited from Grant Tinker's protective and tough negotiating tactics with the networks while working on such shows as *The Mary Tyler Moore Show* and *Lou Grant*, adopted a similar role, demanding that Fox give *The Simpsons* a full-season order, without a pilot, in order to give them time and freedom to develop it. "The idea of giving us an on-air commitment was anathema," Brooks recalls. "It took a while, but they did it. A drowning network going for a cartoon show."

In the beginning, neither the producers nor the network publicized who was providing the voices for the characters. But they deserve credit, especially here. Back in the days of *The Tracey Ullman Show,* Nancy Cartwright was hired as the voice of young Bart, and Yeardley Smith as Lisa. With those roles filled, the parts of the parents, Homer and Marge, were given to two members of the *Tracey Ullman Show* repertory cast, Dan Castellaneta and Julie Kavner, respectively, who retained those roles even after the parent program was canceled in 1990. Harry Shearer provided a number of voices (including Mr. Burns, Smithers, Ned Flanders, and Principal Skinner), as did Hank Azaria (who gave voice to Moe, Apu, Chief Wiggum, and others).

What was also amazing was that *The Simpsons* made all those characters seem so identifiable. "These were real people," Brooks insists. "We would not take advantage of the limitless nature of what you could do in a cartoon. We would be realistic; we would have relationships. And we did!" In time, the *Simpsons* writers would break those rigid rules, but not at first. "I would give a great deal of credit to Jim Brooks," Groening says, "because in addition to this high-velocity animated slapstick, he demanded that the show go for real emotion. He said the ultimate goal was that people would forget they were watching a cartoon. And he insisted on Lisa, for instance, being sensitive and talented and overlooked, and . . . Marge being frustrated, and he was always gunning for us to honor the female characters on the show." Also key to the early development of *The Simpsons,* once it became a series, was the music—the theme by Danny Elfman, and the consistently clever episodic music by Alf Clausen. From the beginning, Groening and company had succeeded in filling *The Simpsons* with what he admired so much about the "Rocky & Bullwinkle" cartoons: good writing, great voices, and great music.

After a quarter century of weekly cartoons and counting, *The Simpsons* is the longest-running scripted series in TV history. It's won more than thirty Emmy Awards, spawned a successful full-length movie in 2007, and generated an absurdly successful cottage industry—penthouse industry, really—of *Simpsons*-related merchandise. Guest stars providing voices have included Elizabeth Taylor, Johnny Carson, Dustin Hoffman, Michael Jackson, Thomas Pynchon, the Smothers Brothers, and, on separate occasions, Paul McCartney, George Harrison, and Ringo Starr. There have been so many outstanding episodes over the show's run, including the annual "Treehouse of Horror" anything-goes specials, that it's almost impossible to select an all-time best. Almost, but not quite: My favorite *Simpsons* episode ever, from 1990, is "Itchy & Scratchy & Marge," written by John Swartzwelder, in which Marge launches a crusade against the ultraviolent children's cartoon *Itchy & Scratchy,* which happens to be her children's favorite. Because of her write-in protest and subsequent notoriety, Marge is invited to appear on *Smartline,* Springfield's local version of *Nightline,* hosted by the sonorous news anchor Kent Brockman. "Are cartoons too violent for children?" Brockman asks as he opens his broadcast. "Most people would say, 'No, of course not, what kind of stupid question is that?' But one woman would say yes, and she's with us tonight." Her protests work, and the *Itchy & Scratchy* cartoons are rewritten to have the cartoon cat and mouse getting along nicely, sitting on the porch and happily sharing a pitcher of lemonade. Bart and Lisa and the other kids in Springfield respond to this newfound friendship by turning off their TV sets and going to the playground as Beethoven's *Pastoral* plays on the soundtrack. "That was fantastic," Groening agrees, laughing. He adds, "They sanitize *Itchy & Scratchy,* and the kids are so bored by them they go outside and play, and then the world does indeed become a better place." The real world, though, is a better place because of *The Simpsons.* In 1996, it became the first cartoon TV series to be given a Peabody Award.

Though Fox paved the way with *The Simpsons,* it wouldn't be until 1997, with Mike Judge's *King of the Hill*—a cartoon family sitcom about a propane gas salesman and his family and friends in small-town Texas—that broadcast TV enjoyed another prime-time success in the animation field. (When *King of the Hill* premiered on Fox in 1997, it ended the season ranked No. 23, the highest-rated prime-time cartoon series since *The Flintstones.*) Instead, it was cable that began to lead the way. In 1991 alone, Nickelodeon unveiled John Kricfalusi's *Ren and Stimpy Show,* as well as *Rugrats,* the adorable animated series by Arlene Klasky, Gabor Csupo, and Paul Germain, while MTV launched *Liquid Television,* an animation showcase that soon spun *Beavis and Butt-Head,* Mike Judge's first animated effort for the network, into its own very popular, briefly controversial MTV series. The 1990s were also the decade of USA Network's *Duckman* (1994), Comedy Central's *Dr. Katz, Professional Therapist* (1995), MTV's delightfully dour *Daria* (1997), and two wildly influential, wildly popular, wildly different cable cartoon series: Nickelodeon's ultra-gentle *SpongeBob SquarePants* (1999), and Comedy Central's super-sharp-edged *South Park* (1997), with the creators, Trey

Parker and Matt Stone, butchering sacred cows on a weekly basis. *Sponge-Bob* was intended for children. *South Park* definitely was not.

SOUTH PARK

1997–, Comedy Central. Creators: Trey Parker, Matt Stone. Vocal stars: Trey Parker, Matt Stone.

Before it was a TV series on Comedy Central, *South Park* was a bootleg: a five-minute foulmouthed holiday cartoon, with crude construction-paper animation and dialogue to match, called "The Spirit of Christmas." Brian Graden, then an executive at Fox, commissioned the University of Colorado film school graduates Trey Parker and Matt Stone to create a cartoon "Christmas card" he could send to friends for the holidays in 1995. "The Spirit of Christmas" featured prototypes of the characters we now know from *South Park*—Cartman, Stan, Kyle, and Kenny—who witness an expletive-filled fight to the finish between Santa Claus and Jesus. The irreverence and obscenity, combined, got lots of notice: Graden made scores of duplicates of the five-minute film on VHS and distributed them to friends. Those friends, including George Clooney, made copies for more friends, and even I received one—from someone at Fox, not from Clooney. Someone posted "The Spirit of Christmas" on this relatively new thing called the Internet, and it spread exponentially that way, too. In 1997, Comedy Central launched *South Park* as a series, and that series pretty much put Comedy Central on the map.

Parker has directed the vast majority of *South Park* episodes, and he and Stone continue to provide most of the voices. The production schedule is brutal, with episodes put together in a week rather than several months, but that allows for an unprecedented amount of timeliness and looseness. Whatever the process, it works: like *The Simpsons*, *South Park* has won the prestigious Peabody Award, as well as, at this writing, five Emmy Awards. The show skewers pop culture and current events in all directions, from the popularity of Apple products to the media introduction of Caitlin Jenner. One infamous *South Park* episode was 2005's "Trapped in the Closet," which took aim at Tom Cruise in general and Scientology in particular by animating a sequence in which a church official revealed the Scientology doctrine to Stan—a narrative of frozen aliens being dropped into Earth's volcanoes, subtitled "This Is What Scientologists Actually Believe." Two years earlier, Stan had learned about another religion in a 2003 episode called "All About Mormons," which eventually led to Parker and Stone collaborating, with the composer and lyricist Robert Lopez, on 2011's *Book of Mormon,* a brilliantly funny, and astonishingly good-hearted, smash-hit Broadway musical.

South Park stands right behind *The Simpsons* as the second-most-tenured cartoon in TV history. As with *The Simpsons,* a list of outstanding episodes could run into the dozens, and so could a list of oddball recurring characters, from Mr. Hankey (a talking piece of "Christmas poo") to Captain Hindsight (a hero who visits disasters after the fact to advise people what they could have done to avert them). *South Park,* more than any half-hour animated series before it, was both topical and envelope pushing yet knew its place in TV's cartoon canon. In 2002, *South Park* titled one episode "*The Simpsons* Already Did It" and had the character of Butters, as his trouble-making alter ego Professor Chaos, devising plan after plan to wreak havoc on the citizens of *South Park,* only to be informed by Dougie, his criminal sidekick, a.k.a. General Disarray, "They did that on *The Simpsons.*" Butters complains, perhaps echoing a common remark from the *South Park* writers'

South Park originated as a specially commissioned holiday-greeting VHS tape and expanded to become a hit TV series with a very large and funny cast of characters.

room, "Goddammit, how come every time I think of something clever, *The Simpsons* already did it?"

In 1999, Fox ended the decade, and the century, by unveiling two prime-time animated series that would prove so popular they eventually enjoyed a phoenixlike rebirth after they were canceled. One was Matt Groening's *Futurama*, co-created with David X. Cohen, one of the first futuristic prime-time cartoon series since *The Jetsons*. The other was Seth MacFarlane's *Family Guy*. *Futurama*, after four years on Fox, vanished in 2003 but was revived by Comedy Central in 2010, where it ran for three more years. And even after that, in 2014, the characters of *Futurama* made an appearance in a *Simpsons* crossover episode called "Simpsorama." *Family Guy*, the first of many prime-time cartoon series created by MacFarlane (who, like Parker and Stone of *South Park*, provided many of the lead voices as well), was pulled by Fox after three years. Yet it racked up such mammoth sales when released on the then-new format of home-video DVD that Fox reversed its cancellation decision, ordered new episodes, and welcomed Peter Griffin and family back to the fold in 2005, where they have remained as of this writing. In 2014, the same year *The Simpsons* did a crossover episode with characters from *Futurama*, *Family Guy* presented a special crossover episode with characters from *The Simpsons*: "The Simpsons Guy," in which Peter Griffin and family flee their neighborhood and end up stuck in a strange town named Springfield. "Don't drink the water," Peter warns his family. "Everyone around here looks like they have hepatitis." At the end of the episode, Peter Griffin and Homer Simpson sue each other and go to court—in a courtroom presided over by a very familiar judge: Fred Flintstone.

The new millennium managed, at first, to hold on to most of the groundbreaking recent stalwarts—*The Simpsons*, *South Park*, *King of the Hill*, *Futurama*, *SpongeBob SquarePants*, and *Family Guy* all reached the end of the first decade of the twenty-first century—while continuing the momentum of an animation renaissance. In 2001, Cartoon Network premiered Adult Swim, its prime-time and late-night showcase for more mature offerings. Adult Swim showed off-network reruns (*Family Guy*, *Futurama*), imported anime (the first, shown on its launch night, was *Cowboy Bebop*), and, starting in 2005, both Aaron McGruder's racially bold *Boondocks* and Seth Green's pop-culture-skewering stop-animation masterpiece, *Robot Chicken*. Even more recently, the audacity of FX's animated spy spoof, *Archer*, in 2009,

and HBO's laugh-out-loud animated versions of Ricky Gervais's freewheeling podcasts in 2010's *Ricky Gervais Show* (turning Gervais, visually, into a
modern-day Fred Flintstone), as well as 2011's Fox cartoon series *Bob's Burgers* and 2014's Netflix animated series *BoJack Horseman* (about the has-been
equine star of an old sitcom), suggest that the future of TV cartoons will be
just fine, thanks. The growth, in this new millennium, of manga and graphic
novels in bookstores, and live-action superhero movies in theaters, attests
to the continued appetite for stories told or inspired by illustrations. On
television, animation has come and gone and returned, with a vengeance.

BORN: 1954, Portland, Oregon.

FIRST TV CREDIT: *The Tracey Ullman Show*, 1987–89, Fox.

LANDMARK TV SERIES: *The Tracey Ullman Show*, 1987–89, Fox; Co-creator, *The Simpsons*, 1989–, Fox.

OTHER MAJOR CREDITS: Comic strips: *Life in Hell*, 1978–2012; TV: Co-creator, *Futurama*, 1999–2003, Fox, and 2010–13, Comedy Central; Movies: Producer and co-writer, *The Simpsons Movie*, 2007.

"I was obsessed with television," Matt Groening admits, looking back to his childhood and formative years. To stress the point, he clarifies, "It's not that there was any one show. There were a bunch of shows." When he begins rattling off titles, the enthusiasm stands out, as does the depth as well as the breadth. "Born in 1954, but I remember *Howdy Doody*," he says proudly. He recalls local children's TV shows just as vividly and spouts off a rapid-fire list. "In Portland, Oregon, where I grew up," Groening says excitedly, "there was a clown named Rusty Nails [played by Jim Allen]. Mr. Duffy [played by Frank Kinkaid], who was a circus ringleader and ran this show *Cartoon Circus*. There was Addie Bobkins [a.k.a. Bob Adkins], who had *The Addie Bobkins Show*; there were a whole bunch of them, and they showed various cartoons and Three Stooges shorts." Cartoons? The gamut, from *Crusader Rabbit* and *Spunky and Tadpole* to *Ruff and Reddy* and *Tom Terrific*. He and his brothers and sisters watched Saturday morning TV with great delight, and with sickly sweetened breakfast cereals. "One of my favorite jokes, very early on *The Simpsons*, written by John Swartzwelder," Groening says with a chuckle, "was that Krusty the Clown had his own cereal, Krusty Flakes, and the slogan on the side of the box was 'Only sugar has more sugar!'"

In time, young Matt's tastes developed, in breakfast foods as in television. He loved Jack Benny, George Burns, and Phil Silvers. He loved *Car 54, Where Are You?*, *The Adventures of Ozzie & Harriet*, *Leave It to Beaver*, and *The Andy Griffith Show*. He was a faithful viewer of the "Rocky & Bullwinkle" cartoons. He loved *Get Smart* and admits, "There are certain jokes from *Get Smart* that still run through my head. And I loved the secondary characters, like Hymie the Robot. And the cone of silence—every variation on the cone of silence made me laugh." Groening watched every episode of *The Smothers Brothers Comedy Hour* and identifies *The Avengers*, with Patrick Macnee and Diana Rigg, as his favorite show of the 1960s. He loved *Rowan & Martin's Laugh-In* ("at least the first season or two") and *Green Acres* ("the later seasons") and identifies *The Prisoner*, the metaphorical spy series starring Patrick McGoohan, as "just astounding." Groening and I are roughly the same age and, though we grew up on opposite sides of the country, seem to have gravitated to exactly the same shows, with precisely the same passion.

"Television was very important to me," he says. "The most important issue of *TV Guide* was the *Fall Preview*. I'm sure you must have been the same, right?" he asks me. Yes, he's right—no sense hiding it—but even I was caught by surprise when he name checked two of my favorite, yet most obscure, TV pleasures: the shows and specials of Ernie Kovacs (the amazing TV talent who died in 1962), and the short-lived 1971 PBS freewheeling anthology series *The Great American Dream Machine*. "It was a grab bag, and there was some very sly comedy on it," Groening says. "God, I can't think of the guy's name—the guy with the big mustache?" "Marshall Efron," I tell him, then tell him, though I could have answered his question regardless, that I was, at that very moment, writing gleefully enthusiastic liner notes for a first-time-ever *Dream Machine* compilation release on DVD. "David, I'm you. I'm you!!" Groening shouts. "I love this stuff!"

Yeah, he's me—if you attach about seven zeros to my bank-account balance, give me some talent as a cartoonist, and make me a whole lot funnier. But it's true: we both started off with an almost unchecked passion for television, and both figured out how to carve a lifelong career out of that passion. He just managed it a lot better than I did. But those connections run throughout *The Simpsons*, from Rusty Nails reflected in Krusty the Clown to so, so much more.

He imagined Homer Simpson as a cross between the affable Ozzie on *The Adventures of Ozzie & Harriet* and a grown-up Eddie Haskell from *Leave It to Beaver*, with Homer's son, Bart, being even more of a terror than Eddie Haskell ever was. He got the idea that his cartoon characters could watch TV, as when Bart and Lisa tune in to *Krusty the Clown* or *Itchy & Scratchy*, from the animated puppies who gathered around the television set in Disney's *101 Dalmatians*. Finally, the idea of a town full of characters—characters who could appear some weeks and not others—came to Groening from a surprising source indeed. "Another show I admired was *The Andy Griffith Show*," Groening says, "where you got to know the people in the town of Mayberry: Floyd the barber, and Barney Fife, and all the rest of those people. And I thought, 'Okay, I would like to do that with Springfield.' You know, have stores and bars and all the rest of that stuff. And we ended up, very quickly, building to about a population of three hundred secondary characters. It was amazing that you could do that."

The path to *The Simpsons*, for Groening, was relatively swift, though remarkably uncommon. In high school, he was already amusing himself drawing cartoons—carrying on the family tradition established by his father, Homer, who was a cartoonist, writer, and filmmaker. Young Matt's drawings were varied, but one set of recurring characters were crudely drawn rabbits—the precursors of Binky and Bongo in his *Life in Hell* comics. At the liberal and somewhat experimental Evergreen College in Washington, Groening worked for the school newspaper and even instituted a comics page. After graduating in 1977, he moved to Los Angeles and took a series of odd jobs, including one as a clerk at the Licorice Pizza record store, where he would sell his photocopied *Life in Hell* drawings for two dollars each. *Life in Hell* was his reaction to L.A., but it was also his ticket to success.

His hand-drawn comics soon became picked up by underground newspapers and magazines. The first was in 1978, in *Wet* magazine. Then, after Groening started writing articles and serving as a rock music critic (Hey, Matt, I did that, too, in high school—Matt, I'm you!) for *L.A. Reader*, that alternative paper published the first weekly version of *Life in Hell* in 1980. The first *Life in Hell* book collection followed in 1984, and the strip continued to be picked up in more and more publications, including New York's *Village Voice* in 1986. Groening's *Life in Hell* drawings were emblazoned on mugs, calendars, and shirts, and some of the original artwork was sold, suitable for framing. Some of those framed drawings found their way to the TV writer-producer James L. Brooks, whose company had just started work on *The Tracey Ullman Show,* a sketch variety series that would be among the early prime-time programs on the new Fox network. Originally, the idea was for Groening to provide short *Life in Hell* cartoons that would serve as divisions between the show's comedy sketches, but when Groening was wary of giving up a large percentage of his *Life in Hell* merchandising rights and profits, he was asked if he had other characters they might consider. Almost immediately, he did, and the Simpsons were born.

"I pitched the Simpsons to Jim Brooks and the other producers of *The Tracey Ullman Show,*" Groening says, "and they told me that I would have two minutes every episode to do a cartoon. And I thought, 'Oh, my gosh—what could we do in two minutes? That's not enough time to do anything!' And then they came back and said, 'No, no, I'm sorry. We said two minutes. We meant one minute.' And I was, 'Oh, no!' And then they come back," he says, laughing, "and said, 'When we said one minute, we meant four fifteen-second spots.' And then they pretty much left me alone. And I just thought, in fifteen seconds, the only thing you could do that would stay in people's minds was physical mayhem. They'd have to be sight gags . . . like variations on a theme where Homer would strangle Bart."

The Tracey Ullman Show premiered on Fox in 1987, with the interstitial, super-short Simpsons cartoons as part of the mix. Despite the time restrictions, and sometimes stretching them, Groening and company expanded the Simpson universe to something larger, moving outside the house and into the town of Springfield. By the second season, there was talk of giving the yellow-skinned family a spin-off series, or series of specials. Groening and Brooks fought hard for the former and a commitment from Fox to finance thirteen full episodes as an initial test. Before deciding, Fox executives conducted an experiment and collected some of the shorts from *The Tracey Ullman Show* to be shown as a surprise cartoon treat before the studio's special preview screening of its 1989 comedy *Weekend at Bernie's.* Groening was there and still remembers the crowd's reaction. "When the title card for 'The Simpsons' came on," he says, "the audience burst into applause. And I thought, 'Yippee! We hadn't even earned the laugh, and they were on board with it.' And it made me realize that a lot of people watch a lot more TV than the data shows."

The Simpsons got its first stand-alone, full-length TV exposure on Fox in a 1989 Christmas special, with the first season of regular shows unrolling in 1990. It's still going, more than twenty-five years later, and Groening remains exceedingly proud of it. "I can't emphasize it enough," he says, "but *The Simpsons* is a collaborative effort, and it is a shared vision, and the people involved with the show, to this day, make it what it is. And it's a bunch of inspired animators, and the writers, and of course the voice actors—I'm always astounded by them." He also credits Jim Brooks with injecting the characters with their initial, innate humanity and is thrilled that the success of *The Simpsons* led to an entire new generation of animated TV series, in prime time and in late night.

In 1999, a decade after that first Simpsons Christmas special, Groening tried his hand at prime-time animation again himself, teaming with the *Simpsons* writer David X. Cohen to create *Futurama,* a Fox cartoon series about a gawky pizza guy accidentally frozen in 1999 and revived one thousand years later to encounter a whole new world and universe. "There were a couple of reasons for doing the show," Groening explains. "One was just to see if I could do it again—if I could do another animated series but one that was nothing like *The Simpsons.*" The other reason was his love of the genre: "I couldn't believe that there hadn't been another cartoon since *The Jetsons* that was all about the future." Groening liked the science fiction stories of Arthur C. Clarke and Robert Heinlein, while Cohen "was a big fan of [the British sci-fi writer] Olaf Stapledon and some other, Russian science fiction writer." Groening and Cohen thought it would be fun to mix the ideas of literary science fiction with an animated comedy but found it harder than they thought, even though they protected themselves with the show's basic premise of a leap through time. "We decided to set the show a thousand years in the future," Groening admits, "so that the world wouldn't catch up. At least not in our lifetimes."

Asked for the source of the idea for all the disembodied heads kept in jars, one of the hallmarks of *Futurama,* Groening says he has no idea, then suddenly recalls it. "Oh. I know!" he says excitedly. "It was from the movie *Invaders from Mars!* Nineteen fifty-three. There's an alien with its head in a jar, with tentacles that—" And he stops, thinks for a moment, and laughs, conjuring up images of the slobbery, tentacled aliens so familiar from several "Treehouse of Horror" segments on *The Simpsons.* "It's also the inspiration for Kang and Kodos, now that I think about it." *Futurama* lasted four years on Fox, from 1999 to 2003, then was revived seven years later by Comedy Central, for an additional three-year run. Groening, Brooks, and company produced *The Simpsons Movie* in 2007 and, after the demise of *Futurama*, presented a 2014 crossover episode of *The Simpsons* called "Simpsorama," in which the characters from *Futurama* time travel back to the Springfield of the present, hoping to prevent a global disaster in which Bart accidentally unleashes a plague of mutant killer rabbits—rabbits who bear a striking resemblance to Binky and Bongo. Life in hell, indeed . . .

"What I do like about what's happening in the wake of *The Simpsons,* to kids' animation as well as adult animation," Groening says, "is that all of these shows don't look like each other. There's just this huge array of unique visual visions that are generally creator-driven, and I love it . . . I don't even have to like the writing on some of the shows, but I do like looking at them." Once again, Groening rattles off the names of shows he watches with enthusiasm—this time modern animated series, including *Adventuresome, Rick & Morty,* and *Pig Goat Banana Cricket* ("In my opinion," he says, "they should have lopped off one of the nouns in the title, but it looks amazing").

And Groening's opinions about current or recent TV programming, of course, aren't limited to animation. "*The Sopranos* seems like maybe the best show ever," he says. "And to me, *The Sopranos* is one of the great comedies. I know there's some very dark stuff in it, but to me it's still a comedy." He saw the British version of *The Office* on a plane coming back from London, before it was televised in the United States, and says he spread the word to friends, and even some TV critics, that it was "one of my favorite things." And even as our interview concluded, Matt Groening sent it into overtime, saying he had prepared a list of obscure or underappreciated TV shows he wanted to discuss. In forty years as a TV critic, I'd never had an interview subject come prepared with notes—so, sure. "From England, *The Book Group,*" he begins. "Did you ever see *The Book Group?*" When I say no, he reacts as if he's just won another Emmy. "Nobody knows *The Book Group,*" he says of the 2002–3 series. He describes it, accurately, as a book club that meets weekly to discuss the latest book they're reading ("I thought it was brilliant"). HBO's *In Treatment,* Groening loved so much he tracked down the Israeli original. Another British show, *The Royle Family,* also gets Groening's "brilliant" rating. "It's a sitcom that mostly takes place with the family sitting on a couch, watching the TV," he explains. "And the camera's situated in the position that they're basically staring at the camera." Closer to home,

Groening says he is "an absolute die-hard fan" of Canada's *Trailer Park Boys,* can watch any episode of *Reno 911,* and reserves special praise for a show that, at this writing, is on hiatus, taking a break from which it may never return. But when we spoke, it was still on the air on FX and was on Matt Groening's must-see TV list.

"Right now," he says, wrapping up his TV Critic for a Day Special Report, "the show that I absolutely cannot miss is *Louie.* Louis C.K. is pushing comedy even further, in that he goes for long stretches without a laugh. And to me, that makes the comedy even funnier when the laughs come, because he doesn't have a rhythm that a lot of comedy has, which is to grab as many punch lines as you can at as high a velocity as you can. He goes in a completely different direction. He's trying, he's experimenting, he's pushing himself," Groening concludes, "and it just feels very cinematic."

3 VARIETY/SKETCH

KEY EVOLUTIONARY STAGES

Toast of the Town/The Ed Sullivan Show	1948–71, CBS
Your Show of Shows	1950–54, NBC
The Smothers Brothers Comedy Hour	1967–69, CBS
The Carol Burnett Show	1967–78, CBS
Saturday Night Live	1975–, NBC

Of all the TV genres considered in this book, variety may be the hardest to define and pin down. What is a TV variety show? A parade of talented acts, presided over by a host such as Ed Sullivan? Sure. Then is *American Idol* a variety show? And musical showcases, from *American Bandstand* to *Shindig!* and *Hullabaloo*? What about sketch shows, like *Your Show of Shows* and *Saturday Night Live*? And late-night talk shows that feature comedy sketches, from Steve Allen to Jimmy Fallon? A strong case could be made for "all of the above," but let's narrow the focus. Sketch shows, whether or not they include musical guests, yes. Variety shows presenting a wide range of talent, whether or not they include sketches, yes. Competition shows, no matter how varied the type of talent, no. Talk shows with memorably funny sketches, yes. A few examples will be noted as contributing to the evolutionary development of the genre, but the focus here is on true variety. Ed Sullivan, yes; Ryan Seacrest, no.

Where to start? Actually, with vaudeville, because that's the major inspiration for the TV variety show. In the United States, the form grew out of two crude nineteenth-century entertainment forms: the minstrel shows (in which white people performed in blackface, imitating and usually making fun of black people) and the saloon song-and-dance routines, immortalized in many a Western movie (and satirized brilliantly by Madeline Kahn in Mel Brooks's *Blazing Saddles*). Tony Pastor, a veteran organizer of several touring minstrel shows, decided that attracting women to his shows could double his attendance figures, so he experimented by renting a theater in his native New York City in which to present a collection of more wholesome, family-oriented comedy and musical acts. He called these live theatrical programs "variety shows," and they proved so popular that imitators sprang up instantly, locally and across the country. The "variety show" took hold, becoming one of the dominant entertainment options by the 1890s and into the first few decades of the twentieth century. They became popularly known, though, not as "variety shows" but as "vaudeville." In time, the acts presented on the vaudeville circuit would be squeezed out of their theaters by motion pictures, but many of the acts would survive by appearing in some of those films or by taking their talents to newer venues for opportunity. Radio first, then television.

On television, the first regularly scheduled variety show was on NBC—a TV missing link back in the days when NBC as a network consisted of only three cities (New York, Schenectady, and Philadelphia). The year was 1947, the series was titled *Hour Glass*, and it was a ten-month experiment in staging for television a full-scale, one-hour program of variety acts, with various emcees (Helen Parrish being the most famous) and such acts as Peggy Lee and the TV debut of the ventriloquist Edgar Bergen and his wooden sidekick Charlie McCarthy. At the time, and until March 1948, the American Federation of Musicians refused to allow its members to perform on live television, so guest rosters were limited, but that's exactly how the DuMont network came up with another early variety show, one broadcast, in turn, by all four networks over the ensuing decade. Reasoning that the AFM ban applied only to professionals with union cards, DuMont sought and generated a TV version of a popular radio hit of the 1930s and 1940s: *Major Bowes' Original Amateur Hour*, whose most famous discovery had been a teen singer named Frank Sinatra (in 1935, part of a young vocal singing quartet called the Hoboken Four). The radio show had folded after its host, "Major" Edward Bowes, died in 1946, but DuMont persuaded Bowes's assistant, Ted Mack, to host a new incarnation for television. Mack's *Original*

Amateur Hour, an *American Idol* ancestor whose winners were decided by studio applause, premiered on DuMont in January 1948. Within a year, it had moved to NBC, which in the meantime had developed an even bigger variety TV sensation of its own.

Milton Berle was a comedian and master of ceremonies who was a vaudeville headliner in the 1920s and the above-the-title star of the Ziegfeld Follies in the 1940s. He had been a regular on half a dozen radio series when he was asked, in the spring of 1948, to be the new host of *Texaco Star Theatre,* a long-running radio revue that had premiered on CBS Radio a decade earlier. Almost immediately, he was asked by the sponsors to be one of a rotating corps of hosts for a new spin-off in an equally new medium: a show for NBC television called *Texaco Star Theater* (note the non-British spelling change), premiering June 8, 1948. By the time that first show was over, so was any consideration of hiring any other hosts. Berle had brought with him all his tricks from vaudeville—joking directly with the theater audience, doing a monologue of fast-paced jokes, and showcasing a wide range of talent, from Pearl Bailey to Señor Wences. He developed an instant trademark: dressing in an outrageous costume to open the show, getting laughs in a way that was impossible on radio. He also found a way to make the sponsor stand out from, and at, the start: by having a group of uniformed gas-station "attendants" singing the virtues of being serviced at a particular service station ("So join the ranks of those who know / And fill your tanks with Texaco").

Berle, on TV, was a pioneer not just for the variety series but for television itself. Days after his NBC debut, *Variety* raved that Berle was "one of those naturals," credited him with "a performance that may well be remembered as a milestone in television," and described that first *Texaco Star Theater* outing as "Vaudeo," which *Variety* defined as "the adaptation of old-time vaudeville into the new video medium." Berle was the first TV star and is credited with selling so many sets, as the first compelling reason to purchase a television, that he was given the nickname Mr. Television. The first year the A. C. Nielsen company began compiling audience ratings, for the 1950–51 season, Berle's *Texaco Star Theater* was No. 1—seen by a staggering 80 percent of all TV owners (at the time, there were only 500,000 TV sets in the entire country, but still . . .). But long before Nielsen began tabulating ratings, it was clear that whatever this "Vaudeo" thing was, with a host presiding over a variety of different acts, it was ready-made for TV. And it didn't take years for rival networks and producers to mount their own versions; it took weeks. The CBS Television Network had been providing programming for only three months, and NBC's *Texaco Star Theater* had been on the air only twelve days, when CBS presented the first edition of its own attempt at a variety series. It was a show that under two different names would last for twenty-three years and greatly affect not only television but the entire culture.

TOAST OF THE TOWN

1948–55, CBS.

THE ED SULLIVAN SHOW

1955–71, CBS. Creators: Ed Sullivan, Marlo Lewis. Host: Ed Sullivan. Guests: The Beatles, Elvis Presley, countless others.

The popularity and durability of Ed Sullivan's variety show on CBS is a marvel, considering how many competing variety shows sprang up during its lengthy tenure, but can be explained by two major factors. For the entirety of its run, which spanned from the late 1940s to the early 1970s, Sullivan's program existed in a now-quaint TV-viewing era during which families watched programs together on the same living room television set, and the competition elsewhere on the dial was limited to a handful of options at best. A variety show suitable for the entire family satisfied all the necessary requirements: wait a few minutes, and if you don't like the current act, you'll probably enjoy the next one, whether you're looking for stand-up comedy, rock music, or cute little animals. In time, the introduction and explosion of cable TV would subdivide those interests into separate networks—Comedy Central, MTV, Animal Planet—while TV sets would multiply around the house, encouraging viewers to watch only the programming they most enjoyed, without having to sit through anything else, and to watch it alone in the process. Variety shows waned in the late 1970s just as cable networks began to appear, but what was lost was the beauty of discovery, the joy of tuning in to see a familiar act and be equally excited by an unfamiliar one.

Many late-night talk shows still pull this off, as does *Saturday Night Live* (at least musically), but the best current example, and the most precious, is CBS's annual telecast of the Kennedy Center Honors, in which the saluted honorees regularly include rock singer-songwriters and ballerinas, opera superstars and great actors, jazz and classical musicians, and other artists from varied areas of popular culture. Watch the Kennedy Center Honors, become exposed to at least one artist with whom you were previously unfamiliar, and you'll experience the general feeling of watching *The Ed Sullivan Show* in its prime, except that Sullivan's show presented its variety of talent not annually but weekly. And, in what was another major component of its success and excitement, always, always live.

Ed Sullivan was selected by CBS to host its first variety series not because he was funny (he wasn't) or had an affable, easy manner that would translate well to television (he didn't) but because he was a well-connected news-

The Ed Sullivan Show, which started as *Toast of the Town* in 1948 and occupied Sunday nights on CBS until 1971, set ratings records when introducing the Beatles to American audiences on live TV in 1964.

paper columnist with great instincts for identifying gifted new talent. His column about New York nightclubs, which ran three times weekly in the New York *Daily News,* was called Toast of the Town—the name that also was used for Sullivan's TV show, until CBS acknowledged and rewarded his growing celebrity as host by renaming it *The Ed Sullivan Show* in 1955. Sullivan was laughably stiff and clumsy as a television host, but this only seemed to endear him with audiences, especially as he started to book impressionists who included imitations of Sullivan's vocal mannerisms and body language in their acts ("And now, a reeallly big shew"). His job, essentially, was as emcee and ringmaster, pointing out celebrities in the audience and introducing the next act, whether it be a frenetic plate spinner (the metaphor for my entire adult life, by the way), a taste of the new 1957 musical *West Side Story,* or Professor Backwards, a man whose entire act consisted of saying and spelling words in reverse order. Vaudeville wasn't dead—just transplanted to a new venue. Aside from introducing the acts, and sometimes talking briefly with them afterward, Sullivan rarely interacted with his guests, except to play straight man to a high-pitched, ten-inch, rubbery Italian mouse puppet named Topo Gigio, who appeared opposite Sullivan an astonishing fifty times, always ending the act by asking the host, "Eddie, keeees-a-me gooood night." Most of Sullivan's guests settled for a clunky intro and a few minutes in which to perform their best material. But if they did well, they could be literally accepted, famous, and successful overnight.

Sullivan's booking of acts, over the years, demonstrated not only great taste (his inaugural show in 1948 included the TV debut of the nightclub duo of Dean Martin and Jerry Lewis) but, in the context of the times, great bravery. He was insistent, from the start, on showcasing black artists, so long as they were talented, and gave valuable prime time to everyone from Fats Domino and Sammy Davis Jr. to Ella Fitzgerald and Lena Horne. So accepted and popular was Sullivan's show, which reached as high as No. 2 in the seasonal TV ratings (for 1956–57, the season Elvis Presley made three live appearances), that a performer's appearance on the show could be perceived, without exaggeration, as having made it into the mainstream of American culture. Elvis Presley had appeared on other TV shows, including ones hosted by Milton Berle and Steve Allen, by the time he got to Sullivan, but it was his first live Sullivan appearance that not only sold records but set them: an unprecedented sixty million viewers tuned in to see Presley sing, strum, and gyrate. And when the Beatles made their first appearance on live

U.S. television, on the February 9, 1964, edition of *The Ed Sullivan Show*, records were set yet again: that telecast was viewed by an estimated seventy-three million viewers (I was one of them), setting a TV audience record that would hold for three years, until 1967's final episode of ABC's *Fugitive*. But the Beatles on *The Ed Sullivan Show* can't be measured by audience figures alone. Because of its immediate and lasting cultural impact, it was one of the most important and indelible broadcasts in TV history.

The Ed Sullivan Show won only one Emmy Award for Best Variety Series Program, in 1956, but it was, and remains, as iconic as any other television program. In 1971, after twenty-three years and some ten thousand guests, Sullivan finally ended his "really big shew." His final guest, on that final hour, was the Italian mouse puppet Topo Gigio, who, one last time, requested (and received) from his host a special show of affection: "Eddie, keeees-a-me gooood night."

Decades earlier, back when Sullivan's show had premiered as *Toast of the Town*, the instant popularity of that show, on the heels of *Original Amateur Hour* and Berle's *Texaco Star Theater*, made the networks hungry for more variety formats and, once the AFM ban against live TV appearances was lifted, even hungrier. In December 1948, CBS blatantly copied *Original Amateur Hour* by presenting *Arthur Godfrey's Talent Scouts* (itself a TV spin-off of Godfrey's 1946 radio show, another *Amateur Hour* rip-off), and within a month CBS gave Godfrey another weekly prime-time variety showcase, 1949's *Arthur Godfrey and His Friends*, to run concurrently. Both shows lasted a decade and were remarkably popular: for the 1952–53 TV season, for example, Godfrey's *Talent Scouts* and *Friends* were ranked No. 2 and No. 3, behind only CBS's *I Love Lucy*.

The DuMont network was equally successful, at least at identifying and hiring new talent as headliners for its variety shows. DuMont was less successful at retaining that talent, because the other networks, with deeper pockets, would lure away any hot talent presented by the struggling network. Another of DuMont's variety shows introduced in 1949 was *Cavalcade of Stars*, but over its three-year stretch DuMont's rivals stole away as many hosts—the biggest theft being Jackie Gleason, hired away by CBS a few years before he made a season-long classic series called *The Honeymooners*. Yet another DuMont variety series that year, *Admiral Broadway Revue*, was simulcast with NBC—a rare occurrence—and became so popular that the sale of TV sets manufactured by the show's sponsor, the Admiral appliances company, surged from eight hundred per week to ten thousand. In a jaw-dropping case of corporate shortsightedness, Admiral executives opted to quit sponsoring their TV show so they could spend more money making TV sets instead. But the NBC executive Sylvester "Pat" Weaver, who would eventually create both the *Tonight* and the *Today* franchises, liked *Admiral Broadway Revue* so much that he made a deal with the show's producer-director, and two of its stars, to collaborate on a similar new show just for his network. DuMont, once again, got cut out of the deal, but *Revue*'s producer-director, Max Liebman, and stars Sid Caesar and Imogene Coca were about to team up on what may be the best variety series ever made.

YOUR SHOW OF SHOWS

1950–54, NBC. Creator and producer: Sylvester "Pat" Weaver. Director: Max Liebman. Writers: Max Liebman, Sid Caesar, Mel Brooks, Mel Tolkin, Lucille Kallen, Carl Reiner, Tony Webster, Joe Stein, Neil Simon, Danny Simon. Stars: Sid Caesar, Imogene Coca, Carl Reiner, Howard Morris.

When I teach my TV History and Appreciation class at Rowan University and get to *Your Show of Shows,* I begin by asking my twentysomething students what TV series comes to mind, based on the following clues: It's a weekly TV show broadcast live on NBC on Saturday nights, ninety minutes long, featuring different musical guests and guest hosts each week with a regular repertory cast of comic actors. The overwhelming consensus answer is *Saturday Night Live,* but the answer, because we're studying TV of the 1950s, is *Your Show of Shows,* which, I tell my students, was essentially *Saturday Night Live* more than sixty years ago but in prime time and without cue cards. They seem amazed by the thought, then, after sampling such sketches as "This Is Your Story" (a brilliant parody of the NBC ambush biography show *This Is Your Life*) and "The Clock" (the core acting quartet as mechanical figures in a malfunctioning Bavarian clock), they seem both amazed and amused. I was the same way when I was their age, a college student in the pre-*SNL* year of 1973, and a collection of kinescopes (including the ones described above) was released to movie theaters under the title *Ten from "Your Show of Shows."* I reacted then the way many of my students do today: Where did this blast of comedy brilliance come from?

Basically, it came from Pennsylvania's Pocono Mountains, where, from 1934 to 1940 and again in 1948, the writer-producer Max Liebman had created a weekly stage show for the Tamiment adult summer camp. Danny Kaye was a star of the early shows, before leaving to become a movie star. Sid Caesar and Imogene Coca became headliners of the 1948 version and went with Liebman when he created *Admiral Broadway Revue* for television, as did one of Caesar's personal gag writers, Mel Brooks. The four of them, along with the *Revue* writers Mel Tolkin and Lucille Kallen, migrated as a package deal to NBC's *Your Show of Shows* a year later and from 1950 to 1955 generated comic brilliance of a very high wattage: Caesar, Coca, Carl Reiner, and Howard Morris became the core repertory company, and Reiner, like Caesar, did double duty in the writers' room. It was a room populated, over the course of *Your Show of Shows,* not only by Caesar, Reiner, Liebman, Tolkin, and Kallen but by Neil Simon, his brother Danny, the future *Sgt. Bilko* writer Tony Webster, and Joe Stein. Together, they generated unprecedentedly ambitious and complicated parody sketches of subjects ranging from Italian operas

Your Show of Shows was a brilliant and influential early sketch and variety series, with a core company including Sid Caesar and Imogene Coca.

to *From Here to Eternity* (in their hands, "From Here to Obscurity"). One recurring comedy sketch, "The Hickenloopers," starred Caesar and Coca as an invariably feuding married couple and predated Gleason's first similarly themed "Honeymooners" variety-show sketch, on DuMont's *Cavalcade of Stars* in 1951, by more than a year. *Your Show of Shows* was an immediate hit, ranked No. 4 after its inaugural 1950–51 season, and won Emmys for Best Variety Show in 1952 and 1953. The comedy topics were smart, the acting was inspired, and everything about *Your Show of Shows* demonstrated what was possible in the variety and sketch formats. Others quickly took notice, including some of the most talented comic minds of TV's first generation.

The year 1950 was a boom time for innovation in TV comedy and not just because of *Your Show of Shows*. Even concepts and stars long established on radio migrated to the new medium with new approaches. And the NBC executive Pat Weaver (the actress Sigourney Weaver's father, by the way), who had helped germinate *Your Show of Shows,* had some other innovative ideas up his sleeve in the 1950s, including shows broadcast during usually dormant time slots, such as the late-night *Tonight Show* and the early-morning *Today* show. In 1950, he first tested the late-night waters with *Broadway Open House,* a vaudeville-style revue headlined by Jerry Lester, another of the freshly stolen hosts of DuMont's *Cavalcade of Stars.* Surviving kinescopes of *Broadway Open House* are pretty painful to watch, and not even the presence of TV's first sex symbol, a statuesque but stiff co-star called Dagmar (real name: Jennie Lewis), helps much. But *Open House* was television's first foray into late-night television and would lead to a much more successful NBC follow-up: Steve Allen's variety-heavy talk show, the original incarnation of *Tonight,* in 1954.

Weaver wasn't the only TV visionary working at, or aiming at, odd hours of the day: In 1950, a comic genius named Ernie Kovacs beat Weaver, and everyone else, to the early-morning punch by hosting a local show at NBC's Philadelphia station. Called *Three to Get Ready,* it soon expanded to two hours (7:00–9:00 a.m.) and included news and weather breaks, sandwiched between sketches and other live comedy bits featuring Kovacs. Even on a minuscule budget, Kovacs did so much with television that every network took notice, and over the next decade he worked for all of them. Kovacs played with the new medium as though he were one of its inventors, using crude but effective special effects, blackouts, and other effects never seen on

TV before. (In the 1960s, NBC's *Rowan & Martin's Laugh-In* would recycle most of them.) Those who remember Ernie Kovacs—and there are fewer of them every year—tend to recall him most for his visual special effects, such as everyday objects that defy gravity or seem to come to life as music plays. Kovacs, though, was so much more. He had a wide repertory of comic characters, including the effeminate poet Percy Dovetonsils, and was one of three players in gorilla costumes known as the Nairobi Trio, always pretending to play the same obscure Italian instrumental, "Solfeggio," and always regressing into slapstick violence. He was easygoing and natural as himself, acting as TV host and speaking directly to the camera. And finally, he was one of TV's first and best on-air TV critics, using sketches and spoofs, as *Your Show of Shows* did, to make fun of trends and programs in television. My absolute favorite of these came during his brilliant, lengthy deconstruction of the TV Western, in which one of his sarcastic and self-made samples of upcoming entries in the genre included an "iconoclastic" Western featuring a gun duel between an ordinary cowboy and an animal with an evil-looking mustache and a gun tied to his hoof: Rancid the Devil Horse. When you watched any episode of any Ernie Kovacs show, you had no idea what to expect, which made it a variety show in the truest sense of the word.

Other variety shows of the era were more traditional. The year 1950 saw one other memorable entry, NBC's *Colgate Comedy Hour,* which was quickly taken over by that high-energy team from Ed Sullivan's first *Toast of the Town* broadcast, Dean Martin and Jerry Lewis. Scheduled opposite Sullivan on Sunday nights, Martin and Lewis, on *Colgate Comedy Hour,* went so far as to do an extended spoof of Sullivan's show, called "Toast of the Colgate Town," with a bucktoothed Lewis as the variety-show host "Ed Solomon." As the 1950s progressed, other headliners eagerly agreed to host variety shows, sometimes for the second time around the track. Red Skelton, with NBC's *Red Skelton Show* in 1951, began a TV reign that, after moving to CBS in 1953, would last a total of twenty years. Jackie Gleason would also fare well after moving to CBS: starting in 1952, his *Jackie Gleason Show* would enjoy a healthy run in both the 1950s and the 1960s, interrupted by a one-year break so Gleason could spend the time expanding one of his show's popular sketches into a one-season sitcom called *The Honeymooners.* And in 1954, Sid Caesar (along with Carl Reiner and eventually Mel Brooks) went from *Your Show of Shows* to another NBC variety show, *Caesar's Hour,* where the writers included Larry Gelbart, later of TV's *M*A*S*H*. All three shows were classics and contained classic sketch elements, from Gleason's Poor Soul and Joe the Bartender to Caesar's lengthy silent-movie spoof, "A Drunk There Was."

And then there was, and still is, NBC's *Tonight Show*. Another brainchild of Pat Weaver, *Tonight!* (its original title) premiered in 1954, beginning with the host Steve Allen's prescient warning: "This program is going to go on forever!" (He was referring to the show's ninety-minute length, but give him points for an accurate prediction.) Each incarnation of the most tenured late-night talk show is distinctly its own, but let's pause to run down the major contributions by the show's initial hosts and eras.

Steve Allen was very interested in the talk part of his talk show and interviewed everyone from Richard Rodgers to Carl Sandburg, yet he loved the comedy bits of his show, too, especially the live remotes that took him outside the theater to try nonsensical stunts on the streets of New York. David Letterman, for one, got much of his inspiration from Allen, and not just for the stunts. Allen's *Tonight!* established the basic template for the TV talk show: an opening monologue, a sidekick announcer (in this case, Gene Rayburn), a desk and living room arrangement of furniture for guests, guest appearances, and a mix of sketch comedy, musical performances, and casual talk. Allen was so popular NBC called on him in 1956 to do a one-hour version of his late-night antics in prime time and scheduled *The Steve Allen Show* on Sunday nights, directly opposite *The Ed Sullivan Show*. It was on the Sunday evening *Steve Allen Show* that Elvis Presley sang "Hound Dog" to a basset hound and Allen conducted some of his funniest mock interviews with characters played by the repertory players Don Knotts, Louis Nye, Tom Poston, Bill Dana, and Pat Harrington Jr. To help out on *Tonight!*, NBC called in a temporary replacement host—Ernie Kovacs—then, in 1957, turned the franchise over to a new host, Jack Paar, so Allen could continue battling Sullivan in prime time.

Paar's version of the *Tonight Show* (no more exclamation mark), from 1957 to 1962, was the most conversational and unpredictable of all *Tonight Show* formats. Paar was very quick, highly attentive, and often temperamental. With him, it's not the variety sketches you remember but the honest, unfiltered talk. Well, not always unfiltered. Under Steve Allen, the *Tonight!* show was broadcast live, as it was in the early years with Paar. Once Paar adopted the practice of performing and recording his shows a few hours early, NBC executives stunned him one night in 1960 by objecting to what Paar thought was a harmless joke and cutting it out of that night's show. During the next night's taping, an angry Paar complained of the censorship and surrounding controversy and walked off the show, saying, "There must be a better way of making a living than this." Paar boycotted the show for a month until NBC apologized, then returned with a wonderfully phrased explanation. "When I walked off, I said there must be a better way of making a living," Paar told the studio audience. "Well, I've looked," he said, smiling through a long pause as the audience laughter built, "and there isn't."

The Tonight Show Starring Johnny Carson was next, arriving in 1962 and staying for thirty amazing, successful years. Not everything Carson did was original: his "Carnac the Magnificent" was a close relative of Allen's "Answer Man," and his desk-and-couch setup was a straight salute to his *Tonight* ancestors. But just as Carson's opening monologues were topical TV comedy of the highest order, feeding the audience's appetite for a humorous and often outraged take on the day's news the way Jon Stewart would do in the next century, his recurring sketches, like many of his guests, were pure variety. Take just one example of a classic sketch: Carson's slick, and slick-haired, "Tea Time Movie" host Art Fern, guiding viewers past the "fork in the road" of a Los Angeles freeway map as the shapely blonde Carol Wayne, frequent member of the Mighty Carson Art Players, stood nearby like a modern Dagmar. For generations of comics, getting a booking on Carson's show meant you had made it, and especially after the demise of *The Ed Sullivan Show* it was the biggest show in town.

Meanwhile, the traditional variety show, in prime time, kept appearing, but because of competition and a surplus of choices not every new variety show caught on. The few new successes in the late 1950s and early 1960s included CBS's *Garry Moore Show* (1958–64, featuring Carol Burnett), ABC's *Hollywood Palace* (1964–70, a vaudeville-type showcase with weekly guest hosts), and NBC's *Dean Martin Show* (1965–74, a welcoming, laid-back mixture of music, sketches, and basic silliness). Martin succeeded seemingly effortlessly, while his former partner, Jerry Lewis, flopped with his own variety series, ABC's *Jerry Lewis Show*, in 1963. Even talented people failed to attract enough viewers to survive, sometimes with very good variety shows. Frank Sinatra failed with two different variety shows, and neither NBC's *Bob Newhart Show* in 1961 nor CBS's *Judy Garland Show* in 1963 made it to a second season, though both shows were uncommonly good. By the time the variety and sketch format on TV was entering its third decade, it would take something unique, with a new approach and a different type of content, to stand out. And that's just what happened, in 1967, with *The Smothers Brothers Comedy Hour*.

THE SMOTHERS BROTHERS COMEDY HOUR

1967–69, CBS. Creators: Tom Smothers, Dick Smothers. Producers: Ernest Chambers, Saul Ilson, Allan Blye, George Sunga, Ken Fritz. Writers: Mason Williams, Rob Reiner, Steve Martin, Bob Einstein, Allan Blye, Hal Goldman, Saul Ilson, Carl Gottlieb, others. Stars: Tom Smothers, Dick Smothers, Pat Paulsen, Leigh French, Bob Einstein, Mason Williams.

The Smothers Brothers Comedy Hour showed up on CBS at mid-season in 1967 because the network was desperate: a 1966 revival of its formerly successful *Garry Moore Show*, scheduled opposite NBC's top-rated *Bonanza*, had literally bottomed out in the ratings, and CBS needed a mid-season substitution immediately. A variety series could be generated from scratch, unlike a one-hour drama, and CBS had worked with Tom and Dick Smothers before (on a 1965 fantasy sitcom, *The Smothers Brothers Show*, in which Tom played Dick's late brother and guardian angel), and so it offered them the opportunity. Tom, who had hated their lack of input on the silly situation comedy, stipulated that the Smothers Brothers be given creative control for the variety show. CBS agreed, informally but not contractually, setting the stage for three years of increasingly envelope-pushing television and behind-the-scenes tensions and battles. When the Smothers Brothers first took to their Tiffany-styled stage in 1967, they were satirizing folksingers, performing and lampooning traditional songs while wearing matching red blazers. By the time they were fired by CBS in 1969, they were satirizing presidents, political policies, and CBS censors and singing about how much their work had been diluted or cut outright by the network. Outside the current events news revue of NBC's *That Was the Week That Was*, no variety series in prime time had addressed such topical and controversial topics as integration, women's liberation, gun control, the Vietnam War, drugs, religion, and presidential campaign politics. *The Smothers Brothers Comedy*

The Smothers Brothers Comedy Hour was as popular with young artists as with young viewers, and hosts Tom (left) and Dick Smothers (right) once featured a surprise guest appearance by George Harrison.

Hour tackled it all, with more and more relish and conviction, while CBS became more and more tired of the show's messages and antics and pulled the show from its schedule after three seasons, even though it had already been renewed for a fourth. The Smothers Brothers were fired, not canceled, yet what they accomplished, and what they stood for, helped push CBS, and TV in general, into a more relevant programming era. Within a few years, the same network (and same executives) that jettisoned *The Smothers Brothers Comedy Hour* for being too controversial would reverse course and present such comedies as *M*A*S*H* and *All in the Family,* a show so incendiary its premiere was preceded by an on-air warning.

In the evolutionary chart of TV variety and sketch series, *The Smothers Brothers Comedy Hour* is a crucial pivot point. It leads directly to the rapid-fire topical humor of NBC's *Rowan & Martin's Laugh-In,* the rebellious sketches and faux news reports of NBC's *Saturday Night Live,* and the outspoken satire of Bill Maher, Jon Stewart, Stephen Colbert, and John Oliver. And yet all those other politically charged satiric voices emanate from late night, and most of them from cable. *The Smothers Brothers Comedy Hour* was on commercial broadcast television, right after *The Ed Sullivan Show* on CBS, and redefined what a variety show could and would address in its comedy sketches and monologues (or, in the case of the Smothers Brothers, dialogues). The musician and conceptual artist Mason Williams, one of the show's head writers, came up with the idea of running the series regular Pat Paulsen for president of the United States in 1968—a long-running, increasingly elaborate piece of performance art that laid bare the machinations of presidential politics and resulted in an estimated 200,000 protest write-in votes (and, for Paulsen, a special Individual Achievement Emmy Award). Another series regular, Leigh French, hosted a regular segment in character as a hippie named Goldie O'Keefe, giving advice to homemakers while throwing in all manner of counterculture drug references.

The beauty of it all, at least at first, was that the show introduced these elements without raising any ire from viewers, because the show, when it premiered, was designed on purpose to bridge the generation gap, not widen it. The weekly guest rosters were pointedly eclectic: Bette Davis and Mickey Rooney appeared on the same show as the first U.S. TV appearance by the Who. Another show featured both Kate Smith and Simon & Garfunkel. Still another made room for Don Knotts, Mel Tormé, and Ravi Shankar. And they didn't just do their respective star turns, as on *The Ed Sullivan Show*. They also appeared together in comedy sketches, which proved very popular: within ten months, *The Smothers Brothers Comedy Hour* was a Top 20 show, attracting thirty million viewers per week. Tom Smothers, the de facto prime engine behind the series, used that clout to try to comment more on politics and other issues and to champion such causes as getting the blacklisted folksinger Pete Seeger back to prime-time TV after seventeen years, and the more CBS censors resisted, the more Tom and his writing staff fought back. By the third season, it was out-and-out war, and the new staff writers included Steve Martin and Rob Reiner. By then, *The Smothers Brothers Comedy Hour* programmed to young viewers so aggressively, and was identified with the new generation so thoroughly, that when the Beatles chose to send exclusive homemade performance videos of their new songs "Hey Jude" and "Revolution" to one U.S. TV program, they chose *The Smothers Brothers Comedy Hour*, not *The Ed Sullivan Show*, which had launched them in America four years earlier.

Tom and Dick Smothers both say they, like their show, changed with the times and had an unprecedented opportunity to do so. They were the first members of the 1960s generation with a prime-time pulpit, and they used it aggressively, or tried to. Ironically, it was a prime-time pulpit, in the personage of the guest star David Steinberg and one of his comic sermonettes, that proved the proverbial last straw for CBS. And when I say "proverbial," I mean that literally. CBS stopped the series, and the Smothers Brothers were vindicated, both in court (for successfully suing CBS for breach of contract) and at the 1969 Emmys, where the third and final season of *The Smothers Brothers Comedy Hour* won for Outstanding Writing Achievement in Comedy, Variety, or Music. Steve Martin was among those onstage to accept that award, but Tom Smothers was not. Knowing how polarizing a figure he had become in the TV industry and across the country, he kept his name off the list when submitting the show for a writing Emmy, though he was a prime contributor. But in 2008, Steve Martin stood onstage at the Emmys again—this time to present his old boss Tom Smothers with a special commemorative Emmy, acknowledging his true contributions as a writer of the Emmy-winning final season of *The Smothers Brothers Comedy Hour*. Accepting the statuette and the honor, Tom Smothers memorably acknowledged the other members of his pioneering writing and producing staff. "I want to thank them," he said deadpan, "for all the great writing that got me fired."

THE CAROL BURNETT SHOW

1967–78, CBS. Producers: Bob Banner, Joe Hamilton, Ed Simmons. Writers: Gail Parent, Stan Burns, Barry Levinson, Arnie Rosen, Tim Conway, others. Stars: Carol Burnett, Harvey Korman, Tim Conway, Vicki Lawrence, Lyle Waggoner.

Carol Burnett launched her CBS variety show right on the heels of *The Smothers Brothers Comedy Hour,* later in the same year the Smothers Brothers had started theirs—on the same network, in the same Los Angeles studio facility, on an adjacent soundstage. Yet she wasn't following the trail they had blazed, for their two series couldn't be more different: *The Smothers Brothers Comedy Hour,* as it progressed, was out to provoke, while *The Carol Burnett Show* was out to entertain, avoiding controversy just as deliberately as the Smothers Brothers courted it. As a result, the Smothers Brothers lasted three seasons on CBS, while Burnett and company survived for eleven. And what company she had: Harvey Korman, Tim Conway, Vicki Lawrence, and Lyle Waggoner as her co-stars, and Bob Mackie behind the scenes, designing the most outrageous and inventive costumes. His design for Burnett's green velvet window-curtain dress in the show's spoof of *Gone with the Wind* made that sketch, "Went with the Wind," the most famous in its history. Other beloved elements included the audience Q&A with which Burnett would open each show; the tug at the earlobe with which she would end each program (a secret salute to her beloved grandmother, though she had died six months before *The Carol Burnett Show* premiered); and the ad-libs and other bits of business with which Tim Conway would catch the other players by surprise and, especially with Korman, crack them up. (Perfect example: "The Dentist" sketch, where Korman plays a patient, and Conway a dentist who accidentally shoots himself up with novocaine.)

The Carol Burnett Show was more a step backward than a step forward, echoing the laid-back, just-fun feel of *The Dean Martin Show* more than the variety shows that would follow the lead of *The Smothers Brothers Comedy Hour*. Its popularity and durability, however, gave momentum and impetus for variety-show producers and stars who would rather avoid issues as they sang, danced, and comedically carried on. Over its eleven years, *The Carol Burnett Show* certainly held up its side of the argument: the series won twenty-five Emmys, including five for writing, three for Outstanding Variety Series, four for Korman, three for Conway, and one for Lawrence. And Carol Burnett? Her career display case includes Emmy Awards for her performances in *The Garry Moore Show* in 1962, her *Julie and Carol at Carnegie Hall* special with Julie Andrews in 1963, and her guest appearances on *Mad About You* in 1997. But for acting on *The Carol Burnett Show,* she never won an Emmy. That's ridiculous.

Another surprising fact about *The Carol Burnett Show* is that it never finished a season in the Top 10, though stalwarts such as *The Red Skelton Show, The Dean Martin Show,* and *The Jackie Gleason Show* all scored multiple Top 10 rankings in the late 1960s. That seemed to bode well, in general, for the non-topical side of the variety-show fence, but then came NBC's *Rowan & Martin's Laugh-In* (1968–73), which burst onto the scene with a rapidly edited variety series that was part Smothers Brothers, part Ernie Kovacs, and filled with comic cameos by everyone from Sammy Davis Jr. and Frank Sinatra to Raquel Welch and Richard Nixon. Its jokes, both visual and verbal, flew by at almost subliminal speed and divided its targets fairly evenly among all points on the political and social spectrum, so *Laugh-In* got a reputation for being topical and cutting-edge without actually taking a position or saying much. The show won Emmys for Outstanding Variety Series in 1968 and 1969 and launched many comic careers. Dan Rowan and Dick Martin were the hosts, and the talent they discovered and made famous over their five-year TV voyage—an impressive list of rotating talent that populated the show's pop-art "joke wall"—included Lily Tomlin, Goldie Hawn, Ruth Buzzi, Jo Anne Worley, Gary Owens, Arte Johnson, Henry Gibson, Judy Carne, Teresa Graves, and the ukulele player Tiny Tim. One of the show's writers was Lorne Michaels, who would shortly create the most important variety and sketch comedy show in TV history. *Laugh-In* spawned a slew of catchphrases (starting with "Sock it to me!") and did get in some meaningful topical commentary while handing out (in absentia) its weekly "Flying Fickle Finger of Fate" Award to deservingly incompetent recipients, many of whom were from big business, the government, or the military. Before *Rowan & Martin's Laugh-In* premiered as a weekly series in

The Carol Burnett Show allowed Carol Burnett and company plenty of opportunity to present lengthy parodies of their favorite movies and TV shows, with lots of help from costumer Bob Mackie.

1968, it had appeared as a one-shot special in 1967, televised the same week as the first *Carol Burnett Show,* but *Rowan & Martin* leapfrogged way ahead in the ratings. By the end of the following season, *Laugh-In* would be the most popular show on all of television and would hold that No. 1 spot for another year. No other subsequent variety series to date would ever climb to that same TV mountaintop, but for a while plenty would try.

The late 1960s and early 1970s was a confusing era for the sketch and variety genre, with new entries in the genre pulling viewers in wildly different directions. There were the traditional, completely noncontroversial variety shows, such as *Hee Haw,* the countrified answer to *Laugh-In* that began in 1969 as CBS's replacement for *The Smothers Brothers Comedy Hour* (ponder that for a moment, please) before shifting to syndication in 1972 for an additional twenty-year run (ponder that, too, while you're at it). Also, there was 1974's *Tony Orlando and Dawn,* another utterly wholesome, utterly disposable CBS musical variety series.

Other shows, though, were meatier than they might have seemed at first glance. NBC's *Flip Wilson Show* (1970–74) was the first hit variety series headlined by an African-American, and Wilson managed to delight his viewers and guests (including an obviously tickled Bing Crosby) by taking on such comic alter egos as the sassy, liberated lady Geraldine Jones and the shady, fast-talking Reverend LeRoy of the Church of What's Happening Now. *The Flip Wilson Show* ranked as TV's No. 2 series two years running and won an Emmy as Outstanding Musical Variety Series, but Flip Wilson, like Carol Burnett, never won a personal statuette for being a variety-show headliner. CBS's *Glen Campbell Goodtime Hour* (1969–72), an actual spin-off of *The Smothers Brothers Comedy Hour,* delved into topical comedy on occasion, because of two young *Comedy Hour* writers who had continued there after the Smothers Brothers show had ended: Steve Martin and Rob Reiner. And after that, Martin moved on to another CBS variety series with some fellow *Comedy Hour* writing alumni, including Bob Einstein. This other series, *The Sonny and Cher Comedy Hour* (1971–74), slipped in some topical humor on occasion but was mostly a showcase for the singing and comedy talents of Cher and the glittery gowns and other costumes she wore, designed by the *Carol Burnett Show* veteran Bob Mackie. *The Sonny and Cher Comedy Hour* was a hit, ranked No. 7 for the 1973–74 season—the last time a variety series would end a season ranked in the Top 20, much less the Top 10. *Sonny and Cher* ended abruptly, but because of divorce, not declining ratings.

Where ratings didn't matter much—on public television—the variety show was undergoing a massive, thrilling transformation. In 1971, PBS presented the purest variety series ever made: *The Great American Dream Machine,* a mix of music, comedy, documentary, commentary, and interviews that folded together into a giddily eclectic "Anything Can Happen Day" for adults. Chevy Chase clowned around, Andy Rooney complained about everything (before his similar gig on CBS's *60 Minutes*), and Marshall Efron, the show's resident oddball and breakout star, addressed such questions as "Is there sex after death?" (His one-word answer: "No.") *Dream Machine* was something really new. And something even newer, which had begun on England's BBC1 in 1969, finally came to the United States in 1974, imported by individual public TV stations and in syndication. As a sketch show, it was brilliant, surrealistic, twisted, and immeasurably influential to the next generation of TV sketch comedy. It also, like its famous non sequitur segue between certain unrelated sketches, was something completely different.

In England, the spiritual antecedents of *Monty Python's Flying Circus* would have been familiar to young people of that culture, from radio's *Goon Show,* the *Beyond the Fringe* and Cambridge Footlights Revue stage shows, and several TV shows featuring individual members of the group that would band together as Monty Python: John Cleese, Michael Palin, Terry Gilliam, Eric Idle, Terry Jones, and Graham Chapman. But in the United States, the unheralded arrival of *Monty Python's Flying Circus,* to those who watched it from the start, felt almost like a second British invasion: What the Beatles had done to shake up rock 'n' roll, Monty Python did to TV comedy. Not since the early days of Ernie Kovacs was a sketch comedy series so freewheeling and free-range, and *Monty Python's Flying Circus* was even more chaotic and idiosyncratic. Gilliam's animated film shorts might, or might not, connect one sketch to another, and the cast members were equally inclined, for the sake of a laugh, to quote Proust, cross-dress, or slap each other across the face with dead fish. The "Dead Parrot" sketch, "The Lumberjack Song," the Ministry of Silly Walks—*Monty Python's Flying Circus* was sheer brilliance, and sheer idiocy, sharing equal time. It spawned movies, records, comedy stage tours, and Broadway musicals and greatly inspired the producer who was about to launch a new 1975 variety series called *Saturday Night Live.*

Actually, and almost unthinkably, there were two variety shows called *Saturday Night Live* scheduled to premiere on U.S. TV in 1975. One had Bill

Murray and Christopher Guest as regulars; the other one would as well, but not initially. The first show to arrive that year, in prime time on ABC, was *Saturday Night Live* with Howard Cosell. Hosted by the abrasive co-host of ABC's *Monday Night Football* and emanating from the same theater that until recently had housed *The Ed Sullivan Show,* this *Saturday Night Live* variety series counted Murray and Guest among its repertory company and premiered on September 20, 1975. Three weeks later, on NBC in late night, Lorne Michaels unveiled his new live weekend TV experiment, which, because of the title of Cosell's program, premiered under the name *NBC's Saturday Night*. By January, Cosell's live variety series was dead, and Michaels and NBC were free to change their show's title to the one they had originally intended to use.

SATURDAY NIGHT LIVE

1975–, NBC. Creator and executive producer: Lorne Michaels. Stars: Chevy Chase, Dan Aykroyd, John Belushi, Gilda Radner, Jane Curtin, Garrett Morris, Laraine Newman, Bill Murray, Al Franken, Eddie Murphy, Joe Piscopo, Julia Louis-Dreyfus, Billy Crystal, Christopher Guest, Martin Short, Pamela Stephenson, Damon Wayans, Robert Downey Jr., Nora Dunn, Jon Lovitz, Dennis Miller, Jan Hooks, Dana Carvey, Phil Hartman, Kevin Nealon, Mike Myers, Ben Stiller, Chris Rock, Chris Farley, Rob Schneider, Julia Sweeney, David Spade, Adam Sandler, Tim Meadows, Robert Smigel, Norm Macdonald, Sarah Silverman, Jay Mohr, Michael McKean, Janeane Garofalo, Chris Elliott, Molly Shannon, Jim Breuer, Cheri Oteri, Colin Quinn, Will Ferrell, Darrell Hammond, Chris Kattan, Ana Gasteyer, Tracy Morgan, Jimmy Fallon, Chris Parnell, Rachel Dratch, Maya Rudolph, Tina Fey, Amy Poehler, Seth Meyers, Will Forte, Fred Armisen, Kenan Thompson, Jason Sudeikis, Andy Samberg, Bill Hader, Kristen Wiig, Bobby Moynihan, Abby Elliott, Nasim Pedrad, Vanessa Bayer, Taran Killam, Jay Pharoah, Kate McKinnon, Cecily Strong, Colin Jost, Michael Che, Pete Davidson, Leslie Jones.

The list immediately above, of some of the talented repertory company members from *Saturday Night Live* over the years, is by no means complete. But it should be long enough to make the point that this long-running variety and sketch series has generated more comedy stars than any other program in TV history. That's indisputable. And that's not even counting the show's treatment of, and impact on, presidential politics over five decades. Or its movie spin-offs both large (*The Blues Brothers*) and small (the horrible *It's Pat!*). Or the gradual takeover by Lorne Michaels of the rest of NBC's late-night schedule, including the current incarnation of *The Tonight Show*. Or what would be an even longer list of the show's weekly guest hosts and musical guests—a list mixing the hottest current acts with others just about to make their mark. From the start of *Saturday Night Live* in 1975, Michaels chose his guest hosts and musical guests just as deliberately as he did the members, and name, of his original Not-Ready-for-Prime-Time Players. That name was intended to be defiant, not self-deprecating: the new late-night series wanted to distinguish itself from the mindless mush of mid-

Saturday Night Live has launched the careers of comedians and comic actors, as well as musicians, ever since it premiered in 1975, including the meteoric rise of Eddie Murphy in the 1980s.

1970s prime-time TV and signal from the beginning that *Saturday Night* was a new type of television show, aimed at a new audience—one that went to the movies, listened to records, and was younger.

"The network suggested, for the first show, that we use Rich Little and the Marine Corps marching band," Lorne Michaels told me back in 1991, revealing NBC's idea of the ideal inaugural guest host and musical act. "My hosts were Lily Tomlin, Richard Pryor, Paul Simon and Art Garfunkel, Rob Reiner with Penny Marshall, Candice Bergen, Robert Klein, and George Carlin. Those were the first seven, and they were all set before the show went on the air. So that was tremendously important to me, that credibility was established with the audience." The musical guests for those first shows made just as strong a statement: the list included Billy Preston, Janis Ian, Randy Newman, Loudon Wainwright III, Gil Scott-Heron, and ABBA. Also in that initial batch were short comedy films by Albert Brooks, the first appearance by the outlandish performance artist Andy Kaufman, and Chevy Chase, the first breakout star of *Saturday Night Live,* anchoring a news spoof segment called "Weekend Update." Chase left the show after one year to pursue movie stardom, but Bill Murray, the first cast replacement on *SNL,* fit in beautifully, establishing a tradition of succession, and success, that would falter only when Michaels walked away from the show temporarily after the first five years. His replacement executive producer, Jean Doumanian, presided over a single disastrous season (saved only by the emergence of Eddie Murphy and, to a lesser extent, Joe Piscopo). The NBC executive Dick Ebersol took over for the next four years, after which Michaels returned and has run *SNL* ever since.

The siren call from Hollywood, reaching out to *SNL* cast members and guest hosts, came almost immediately, signaling the generational entertainment shift that was just beginning in 1975, as Steven Spielberg's *Jaws* became a cinema blockbuster. Michaels said he had to threaten to resign in order to persuade NBC to allow Richard Pryor to host the seventh show (George Carlin, as host of the premiere, was a slightly easier battle). NBC was worried about Pryor's language and about offending network affiliates at this early stage of a new show, but after Pryor's episode aired and almost doubled the ratings established by the previous six shows, NBC offered Pryor his own NBC variety show, which appeared the following year. "In prime time," Michaels emphasized. "Which showed you how fast barriers came down."

Another early barrier that fell was the one that, until that time, was a fairly formidable one separating TV stars from working in motion pictures.

The 1978 film *National Lampoon's Animal House,* aimed at a new generation, made a movie star of the *SNL* regular John Belushi, for playing the human cartoon character (and pimple imitator) John "Bluto" Blutarsky, but in the movie's early planning stages other *SNL* players, according to Michaels, were set to appear also: Dan Aykroyd in a small part as the motorcycle rider (played in the film by Bruce McGill), and Chase in the starring role of Eric Stratton (played by Tim Matheson). Chase opted to star in another 1978 film, *Foul Play,* instead, then teamed with Bill Murray for 1980's *Caddyshack.* Michaels talked Aykroyd out of taking such a slight movie role, arguing that *SNL* was getting big enough to provide him, in time, with bigger cinematic opportunities. Michaels was right, and not just in that particular case. The history of *Saturday Night Live,* from the early cast members Chevy Chase and Bill Murray to such later crossover movie stars as Eddie Murphy, Mike Myers, Adam Sandler, Will Ferrell, and Tina Fey, is a story of Hollywood careers being made by a late-night variety sketch series. And there's plenty of TV history, too, from Coneheads and Samurais to "Wayne's World" and Fey's dazzlingly perfect imitation of Sarah Palin.

Saturday Night Live has presented a monumental array of talent and comedy since its 1975 premiere. I know, because I've seen every single show. That's not an idle boast or reckless hyperbole; it's simple gratitude. When I was a postgraduate college student at the University of Florida, I talked my way into writing a review of the first episodes of *Saturday Night Live* for the local newspaper, the *Gainesville Sun,* by arguing that it was a new series aimed at a new generation and that someone from that generation should review it for the paper. The review was a positive one ("well worth watching"), and afterward the paper's editor, Ed Johnson, called me into his office and offered me a deal: four more TV reviews of my choosing, at five dollars apiece. I was on my way and turned those clips and others into a full-time career as a television critic. I figure I have *Saturday Night Live* to thank for that, and once that first TV review was printed, I pledged to watch every episode of the show that gave me the chance to write about television as an actual television critic. Little did I know *SNL,* like my career, would chug along for more than forty years . . .

Yet while variety and sketch comedy found a welcome new environment in late-night TV, prime time was becoming a different matter. The broadcast networks had apparently decided, by the mid-1970s, that anyone could host a variety show, then set out to test the theory. Giving weekly shows to popular new music acts with precious little comic ability, as ABC did with *Donny & Marie* (1976–79) and CBS did with *The Jacksons* (1976–77), was bad enough. Giving them to one-shot music wonders utterly lacking in charisma, as ABC did with *The Captain and Tennille* (1976–77) and CBS did with *The Starland Vocal Band Show* (1977), was worse. And when the NBC executive Fred Silverman imported a popular music duo from Japan—two giggly young women who spoke almost no English—and paired the act with the comic Jeff Altman in a 1980 variety show called *Pink Lady*, it was the absolute worst. Its final indignity was adding to the supporting cast one of the legendary stars and pioneers of the variety and sketch TV genre: Sid Caesar of *Your Show of Shows*. On *Pink Lady*, he spoke nonsense Japanese to two Japanese women who couldn't understand him in that language, either. *Pink Lady* disappeared after five weeks.

Shows headlined by established stars fared no better. NBC's *Richard Pryor Show*, because of the star's increasingly busy movie schedule and the network's interference with his concepts and content (a form of Pryor restraint?), was canceled by mutual agreement after just five shows. And even after Mary Tyler Moore concocted a messy head trip of a musical special for CBS, 1977's legendarily unusual *Mary's Incredible Dream*, the network nonetheless gave her a weekly variety series called *Mary*. Its repertory company included both Michael Keaton and David Letterman, but it lasted only three weeks.

The variety show was clearly dying in prime time, but only on the broadcast networks. In syndication, three very clever series kept the genre, and the humor and inventiveness, alive as *Saturday Night Live* built its late-night empire. All three series, coincidentally, were built around the same concept: a behind-the-scenes look at a company of artists trying to put on a show—a concept that, on TV, goes all the way back to Jack Benny and George Burns. *The Muppet Show*, syndicated from 1976 to 1981, was a fabulous musical variety series for the whole family, a weekly look at a theatrical variety show run by the stage manager Kermit the Frog, with human guest celebrities performing alongside Miss Piggy and the rest and with the Muppet curmudgeons Statler and Waldorf heckling from the balcony. *The David Steinberg Show*, imported from Canada in 1976–77, was a syndicated series in which the former *Smothers Brothers Comedy Hour* guest star played the star of a TV variety show, which was shown in pieces, along with his backstage interactions with other cast and crew members, who included Martin

Short, John Candy, Joe Flaherty, and Dave Thomas, and such guest stars as Andrea Martin. All five of those actors also starred in *SCTV*, another syndicated sketch and variety series imported from Canada: Short joined the series midway through its run, while the other four were members of the original core company, along with Eugene Levy, Harold Ramis, and Catherine O'Hara. *The David Steinberg Show* and *SCTV* premiered in Canada the same week, and the actors in both shows simply pulled double duty, but *SCTV* is the show that made them stars.

The title was short for Second City TV, the Toronto branch of the improv company that had created the series (and, previously, had fed Dan Aykroyd and Gilda Radner to *SNL*), and the idea was perfect for a sketch show: It purported to show programs and promos from any time of day or night on a low-rent TV station, from the early-morning "English for Beginners" lessons to the late-night "Monster Chiller Horror Theatre" B-movie showcase, hosted by Flaherty's Count Floyd, moonlighting from his day job as Floyd Robertson, the station's news anchor. We also saw the personnel behind the TV station, so Flaherty also played the grumpy, wheelchair-bound station owner, Guy Caballero. Short and Rick Moranis joined the show in later years, and throughout *SCTV* presented the most ambitious, obscure, and complicated sketch ideas since *Monty Python's Flying Circus*. Best of all was "Play It Again, Bob," a parody mash-up of Woody Allen's *Play It Again, Sam* and the Bob Hope–Bing Crosby road pictures, in which Woody Allen (Moranis) teams with Bob Hope (Thomas) on a new movie. When their comic styles clash, Woody turns for advice to the ghost of Bing Crosby (Flaherty). Sheer brilliance.

SCTV, with title changes and eventual moves to NBC and Cinemax, survived until the mid-1980s. For most new variety and sketch series, though, the 1980s was a harsh decade, no matter where you looked, or in which time of day or night. In daytime, NBC's *David Letterman Show*, despite all its displays of Steve Allen–ish brilliance, came and went quickly in 1980. In prime time, NBC's *Big Show*, the network's first ninety-minute live variety series since *Your Show of Shows*, had various big-name guest hosts (including, on three occasions, Steve Allen himself) yet vanished after three months. And in late night, a challenger to *SNL* finally arrived when ABC programmed *Fridays*, a live variety sketch series emanating from Los Angeles. The series flopped after two years but was notable for at least two things: for staging a mock fistfight on camera between the guest host Andy Kaufman and the producer Jack Burns (one that many people took as real), and for being the show on which two cast regulars, Larry David and Michael Richards, forged a friendship that they would continue with NBC's *Seinfeld*.

By the time James L. Brooks presented *The Tracey Ullman Show* on Fox (1987–90), the variety sketch series had been dormant long enough, in prime time throughout the 1980s, that it was considered an official attempt to revive a dead genre. That show gave us not only Ullman's peerless gifts as a comic chameleon but also Matt Groening's *Simpsons*. And as *The Tracey Ullman Show* ended, Fox continued to fight for the cause with Keenen Ivory Wayans's *In Living Color* (1990–94), an equally daring and exciting sketch series—this one additionally notable for presenting comedy largely from a black perspective. It pushed the envelope, and the censors, more than any variety series since *The Smothers Brothers Comedy Hour,* and its earliest episodes went for the comedy jugular. In "Men on Film," Damon Wayans and David Alan Grier play the extremely effeminate gay movie critics Blaine and Antoine, rating movies based on their homosexual hotness. And in a particularly audacious and clever *Star Trek* parody, *In Living Color* series regular Jim Carrey plays a bombastic Captain Kirk who loses control of his bridge to a visiting Islamic leader, in a sketch called "The Wrath of Farrakhan."

Minority voices began to be heard, and their faces seen, much more frequently as one century led to another. It was mostly interviews and musicians, not sketches, on the syndicated *Arsenio Hall Show* (1989–94), but Hall's show was a potent pop-culture platform, and not just when the 1992 presidential candidate Bill Clinton showed up wearing shades to play the saxophone. The cast of Fox's sketch series *MADtv* (1995–2009) was roundly integrated and entertaining, while HBO's *Chris Rock Show* (1997–2000) was loaded with sketches as well as music and monologues. Comedy Central's *Chappelle's Show* (2003–6) was, famously, canceled not by the network but by the overworked and overwhelmed David Chappelle himself. Other Comedy Central shows, in recent years, have focused more on the sketch portion of the sketch and variety equation but with largely excellent results. *Key & Peele,* starring Keegan-Michael Key and Jordan Peele from *MADtv,* allowed those actors to find their own voice—or voices—in their very own, very shrewd sketch show, in which their best pieces, such as "President Obama's Anger Translator" and the "East/West College Bowl" preview (whose players sport such flamboyant names as Hingle McCringleberry and Sequester Grundelplith M.D.), went viral on the Internet.

And the Internet, in the Platinum Age of Television, is the great equalizer. Such currently running sketch series as IFC's *Portlandia* (2011–) and Comedy Central's *Inside Amy Schumer* (2013–) and *Broad City* (2014–) have their respective loyal TV audiences but reach millions more, at least in snippets, on YouTube and shared social media. Schumer's subversively funny, sex-appeal-questioning "Milk Milk Lemonade" music video has been seen, at this writing, more than seven million times on YouTube alone, attracting millions more viewers than watch her show on Comedy Central. This century's topical humor shows, discussed separately in another chapter, all use social media and streaming sites to build their audiences and reputations, but talk shows with variety components came to the game a bit more reluctantly. In the days before YouTube, the host's antics on NBC's *Late Night with David Letterman* (1982–93), like Carson's comedy bits and monologues on *The Tonight Show,* were shared and repeated only by local newscasts and *Entertainment Tonight*–type shows or in annual specials. Late-night fans, in that not-so-distant era, had two basic options: set their VCRs (or, eventually, their DVRs) and watch on their own schedule, or stay awake. Today, with the Internet, any really entertaining late-night segment is liable to be available the next morning on any number of venues and even sent and shared by friends. That's the good news. The bad news is that fewer people are making the effort to watch the shows themselves, which slowly but surely erodes not only the viewing audience levels but the habit of watching late-night TV at all.

When Jay Leno took over *The Tonight Show* in 1992, and when Letterman moved to CBS for *Late Show with David Letterman* in 1993, viral videos were not in the playbook. Letterman would stick around long enough to take advantage of the Internet a bit, but more with "Top Ten" lists than sketches or elaborate video pieces. CBS's *Late Late Show with Craig Ferguson* (2005–14), which inherited the post-Letterman CBS slot after Tom Snyder's all-talk show, was more adept at finding show segments ready-made for social sharing (singing puppets! talking skeletons!), as were most of the twenty-first-century broadcast network talk-show hosts. ABC's *Jimmy Kimmel Live!,* launched in 2003, gets an average audience of some two and a half million viewers, yet his show's infamous "F*@#ing Matt Damon" clip, with its in-your-face confessional sung defiantly by Sarah Silverman, topped over thirteen million YouTube viewers by early 2016. Jimmy Fallon, on both his *Late Night* stint replacing Letterman (2009–14) and his current post as the newest *Tonight Show* host, has a history of being aggressive and successful at circulating video clips, which makes sense, because his idea of a talk show is closest to an old-time variety show, with lots of things worth sharing. Videos of his imitating Bob Dylan and Neil Young reached much wider audiences on YouTube than when he first performed them, and a recurring segment called "Lip Sync Battle," featured on both *Late Night* and *The Tonight Show,* generated enough views, shares, and "Likes" on social media that it was spun off in 2015 into its own series on cable's Spike TV. And even more recently, the host of Ferguson's replacement series on CBS, *The Late Late Show with James Corden* (2015–), wasted no time in planting his flag in the viral video battlefield. His own recurring musical bit, "Carpool Karaoke," became an almost instant Internet phenomenon. The average viewership for Corden's show on CBS is slightly more than one million viewers, yet his 2016 "Carpool Karaoke" segment with Adele, once posted on the Internet, smashed all existing YouTube records for a video from late-night TV, drawing 42 million viewers its first five days and, as of June 2016, more than 106 million views overall. (And if you're not one of those more than 100 million, go watch it. It's magnificent.)

Corden's "Carpool Karaoke," in fact, might well evolve into a new species of talk show: a self-contained, highly concentrated version in which the host and guest interact informally and entertainingly under very limited time and space restrictions. Corden doesn't just duet delightfully with his carpool guests; he also has animated conversations with them, distilling the talk show into its purest elements, and into smaller, more conveniently digestible bites. The same goes for *Comedians in Cars Getting Coffee,* Jerry Seinfeld's long-running online series for Sony's Crackle streaming service. Seinfeld began that series in 2012 by driving his *Seinfeld* co-creator, Larry David, in a vintage VW Beetle to get breakfast. Since then, he's traded stories, reflections, and jokes with every comedian from Garry Shandling to John Oliver, with always engaging results. *Comedians in Cars* isn't a segment from a larger show, it *is* the show. And therein, perhaps, lies the future, not only for such popular talk-show segments as "Carpool Karaoke," but for all talk shows in general. Smaller. More focused. Self-contained.

But what of sketch and variety series? At this point, after all these years of TV history and evolution, the sketch comedy series seems to be alive and well, but true variety seems to thrive only in pieces and only on the Internet. I continue to believe, quite stubbornly, that with the right host and the right format, the TV prime-time variety series could make a successful comeback, but at the moment the most energetic signs of life are coming from late-night TV and in very small doses. NBC's *Best Time Ever with Neil Patrick Harris,* which came and went rather quickly in 2015, might have found the right host, but, based on a format copied from England, it wasn't a proper variety show—more like a combination stunt and game show. Much closer to the original formula was NBC's *Maya & Marty,* starring Maya Rudolph and Martin Short in a prime-time sketch variety series premiering in mid-2016. She was a veteran of *Saturday Night Live,* and he had spent time there, as well as several years on *SCTV.* Their new joint effort, a summer series produced by *SNL* creator Lorne Michaels, was a mixture of performances in front of a studio audience and taped segments, and first impressions were positive ones—the closest thing to a true TV variety show in many years. As I write this, I don't know whether *Maya & Marty* will earn enough acclaim and ratings to be renewed for a second summer season. But as you read this, you do know.

Maya & Marty is very close, but only in spots, to the variety series of old, in which everything was performed in front of a studio audience. I wonder if TV will ever give us the proper, old-fashioned variety combination again, and, if so, whether viewers will sit still for it. And I also wonder how big Johnny Carson would have been had YouTube been around during his three incomparable decades on the air. How many millions of views would he have gotten with, say, the Ed Ames tomahawk throw? Or the Bette Midler farewell song?

BORN: 1926, Brooklyn.

FIRST TV CREDIT: Writer, *Admiral Broadway Revue*, 1949, NBC and DuMont (uncredited); *Your Show of Shows*, 1950, NBC (credited).

LANDMARK TV SERIES: Writer, *Your Show of Shows*, 1950–54, NBC; *Caesar's Hour*, 1954–57, NBC; Co-creator with Buck Henry, *Get Smart*, 1965–70, NBC.

OTHER MAJOR CREDITS: Records: Co-creator and co-star with Carl Reiner, 2000 Year Old Man albums, beginning with *2000 Years with Carl Reiner and Mel Brooks*, 1961. TV: Co-writer, *The Sid Caesar, Imogene Coca, Carl Reiner, Howard Morris Special*, 1967, CBS; Voice actor, *The Electric Company* (as Blond-Haired Cartoon Man), 1971–77, and *The Simpsons* (as Mel Brooks), 1995; Recurring guest star, *Mad About You*, 1996–99, NBC, and *Curb Your Enthusiasm*, 2004, HBO; Star, *Mel Brooks: Live at the Geffen*, 2015, HBO. Movies: Writer and director, *The Producers*, 1967, *Young Frankenstein*, 1974; Writer, director, and actor, *Blazing Saddles*, 1974, *Silent Movie*, 1976, *High Anxiety*, 1977, *Spaceballs*, 1987, *Dracula: Dead and Loving It*, 1995; Writer and producer, *The Producers*, 2005; Actor, *The Muppet Movie*, 1979, *To Be or Not to Be*, 1983; Voice actor, *The Critic* (animated film short), 1963, *Young Frankenstein*, 1974, *Mr. Peabody & Sherman* (as Albert Einstein), 2014, and *Hotel Transylvania 2* (as Vlad), 2015; Producer, *The Elephant Man*, 1980, *My Favorite Year*, 1982, *Frances*, 1982, *84 Charing Cross Road*, 1987. Broadway: Sketch writer, *Leonard Sillman's New Faces of 1952*, 1952–53; Producer, book, music, and lyrics, *The Producers*, 2001–7, *Young Frankenstein*, 2007–9.

Mel Brooks's TV career began in 1949, but he was still producing and star-ring in TV specials for HBO in 2015. His varied and lengthy career has made him a member of the rarefied "EGOT" club—shorthand for those mul-tifaceted entertainers who have won at least one Emmy, Grammy, Oscar, and Tony. In the case of Mel Brooks, his awards have included Emmys for writing (as one of the writers of *The Sid Caesar, Imogene Coca, Carl Reiner, Howard Morris Special*) and acting (for a recurring role on *Mad About You*), Grammys for the Broadway soundtrack of *The Producers* and for the com-edy album *The 2000 Year Old Man in the Year 2000*, with Carl Reiner, Oscars for his 1963 animated short *The Critic* and for his original screenplay for 1967's *Producers*, and Tonys for Best Musical, Best Book of a Musical, and Best Original Score, all for Broadway's *Producers*.

But in television terms, he really was there from the start. The TV career of Mel Brooks began in 1949, when Sid Caesar hired him as a comedy writer for his live weekly variety series *Admiral Broadway Revue*, simulcast by NBC and the short-lived DuMont network. When the show's sponsor, Admiral, decided to stop producing the popular show to focus on making television sets instead, NBC snapped up its producer (Max Liebman) and two of its stars (Sid Caesar and Imogene Coca) and turned the concept into *Your Show of Shows*, one of the most ambitious variety and sketch series ever on TV. Mel Brooks came along for the ride, joining a writing staff that, working for Caesar over the years, included Neil Simon, his brother Danny Simon, Mel Tolkin, Lucille Kallen, and Carl Reiner, and, on later Sid Caesar shows, Larry Gelbart and Woody Allen. He co-created the spy spoof *Get Smart* TV series with Buck Henry in 1965, after which he broke into films by writing 1967's *Producers*, 1970's *Twelve Chairs*, and 1974's *Blazing Saddles* and (with Gene Wilder) *Young Frankenstein*. Thus began a lengthy career of film, TV, and stage work, which included, among many other impressive achieve-ments, jump-starting the director David Lynch's career by producing 1980's *Elephant Man*.

Mel Brooks was born in Brooklyn in 1926, as Melvin James Kaminsky. His love of comedy, drama, theater, and music all came to him early—thanks to the radio and his uncle Joe. Network radio was new then, and Brooks remembers the first show that caught his interest: an adventure drama, then broadcast by CBS, *Jack Armstrong: The All-American Boy*. "And then later, when I got a year or so older, I think it was *The Shadow*. Jack Armstrong, whatever he did, he triumphed. He never lost, whether it was a game or whether it was solving a problem. And he was an all-American boy, and I was a little Jewish boy in Brooklyn, and my greatest desire when I was six or seven years old was to be an all-American boy [laughs]. I just liked his title. I'm still aiming for his title. And I'm still a long way off."

Another thing Brooks remembers about that show, with fondness, was how he listened to it. "I think *Jack Armstrong* happened, like, at 5:30, you know? Just around dinner, just before dinner when you're a little kid. Very exciting. Except that he was pushing Wheaties, I think, and we were going to be eating tuna fish or salmon, so it was a little confusing because the way they describe the Breakfast of Champions, it made you want to eat the Wheaties. And sometimes I'd beg my mother, and she'd switch me out from a can of salmon to a bowl of Wheaties and some sliced banana. She would do that! My mother, she was a great person."

Radio also gave Brooks his love of music ("As I got older, when I got into my teens, it was Martin Block's *Make Believe Ballroom;* I got into swing then," Brooks says). But he was also influenced, as a youngster, by those around him. A neighbor taught him how to play drums, which doesn't sound all that noteworthy, except that this particular neighbor was Buddy Rich. And his uncle Joe sparked in young Mel Brooks a lifelong love affair with musical theater, by taking him to his first Broadway show in 1934: the new, original cast production of Cole Porter's *Anything Goes,* starring Ethel Merman.

"My uncle Joe drove a cab," Brooks recalls, "and he used to take the doormen at various theaters, who lived in Brooklyn, back home—for free, just because he was a Broadway cabdriver. So every once in a while, they'd get a couple of tickets and they'd give them to Joe." With free tickets to *Anything Goes,* Uncle Joe drove his cab into the city (with young Mel hidden on the floor of the backseat, because the meter wasn't running) and escorted his nephew to the back row of the second balcony. Even from that distance, young Mel was transfixed. "They start the show," he says. "And be still, my heart! I couldn't believe the joy, and the songs . . . And that was it. I was hooked." He loved it all: the wacky plots, the machine guns in violin cases, the tap-dancing production numbers, all of it—including the formidable voice of the leading lady. "They had no microphones in those days," Brooks says in amazement. "And even from the second balcony, I thought that Ethel Merman was a little loud."

As a teenager, he pursued a possible career in entertainment by working summers in the borscht belt in New York's Catskill Mountains, initially as a drummer and piano player. Eventually, he slid into stand-up comedy, where he became a successful tummler (master entertainer), working as a teen-ager entertaining the vacationing Jews poolside and onstage. After a year at Brooklyn College as a psychology major, he was drafted into the army and served as a corporal during World War II, defusing land mines. After the war, he returned to the much less intense environment of the Catskills and changed his name from Melvin Kaminsky to Melvin Brooks—to avoid con-fusion with another borscht belt entertainer, the trumpeter Max Kaminsky. Young Melvin Brooks was quite successful there, but wanted more. "I could have had a lovely career being a stand-up comic," he says, "but I wanted more. I wanted movies, and I wanted to write movies, and I loved theater, and I wanted to write musicals."

In 1949, thanks to another Catskills performer, Brooks found his entry point for his loftier ambitions, not onstage or in the movies, but in the newly established medium of television. Sid Caesar was starring in Max Liebman's *Admiral Broadway Revue* for NBC and DuMont and liked Brooks and his comedy material enough to pay him fifty dollars a week, out of Caesar's own pocket, for Brooks to supply him with jokes and sketches. A year later, when Liebman and Caesar started *Your Show of Shows* on NBC, Mel Brooks was invited along as one of the core members of the writing staff. Another writer, who had also worked on *Admiral Broadway Revue,* quickly became another major influence on Brooks's artistic tastes.

"Mel Tolkin, who was the head writer," Brooks says, "he came from Rus-sia. He went to McGill University, he went to Canada, and then he came down to Tamiment [the performing arts center in the Poconos], worked with Max Liebman, then came to New York and worked on the *Admiral Broadway Revue* first, and then *Show of Shows,* and he really influenced me." Until then, Brooks explains, his favorite books were *Ivanhoe, Robin Hood,* and *Robinson Crusoe,* which he still loves. "But he kind of guided me to real moving, emotional, complex, intellectual writing. And I read Tolstoy, and I read Dostoyevsky, and I read Andreyev, and I discovered my favorite author of all time: Nikolai Gogol, who wrote a beautiful, beautiful novel about the adventures of a character called Chichikov, and it was called *Dead Souls.*"

In fact, everyone in Brooks's circle of friends was devouring movies, music, and literature, and all of it would somehow emerge on national TV in the early 1950s, filtered through the twisted prism of *Your Show of Shows*—a

live, ninety-minute sketch variety show on Saturday nights, with a repertory company of comics, a weekly guest host, and musical guests. Sound
familiar, *Saturday Night Live* fans? And *Your Show of Shows* both broke and
established ground in terms of content as well as format.

"When we were writing *Your Show of Shows,*" Brooks recalls, "we'd have
fun with current movies like *From Here to Eternity*. We called it 'From Here
to Obscurity' . . . In 1952, we, on *Your Show of Shows,* were writing satires of
Japanese movies, where Sid was speaking in fake Japanese to Carl Reiner
and Imogene Coca. And they were talking to each other in this kind of
double-talk Japanese, or double-talk Italian or French . . . and maybe one
one-hundredth of America had even heard of foreign movies, let alone seen
one. And here we were—I mean, we were crazy. And Pat Weaver [at the
time, NBC's pioneering entertainment executive] said, 'Look. They're very
funny, but you shouldn't do these foreign movies.' And Sid said, 'We enjoy
doing them, so we're going to continue to do them.'

"We never wrote for the public. We wrote for us, and we prayed to God
that the public would get it. That's the only way things are good. You write
them for yourselves, to please yourself, to please big, bad portions of yourself, and you just have to pray that there'll be enough people out there."

Brooks also expresses pride about what he and his *Your Show of Shows*
colleagues didn't write: "We never did Bob Hope stuff. We never did political: we never talked about Democrats or Republicans, we never talked about
the president, we never talked about Congress, we never talked about world
affairs. We talked about human behavior."

Often, Brooks would marvel at how Caesar would wring even more
from a sketch than what was on the page. The famous "This Is Your Story"
spoof of *This Is Your Life,* in which Caesar played a hapless guy ambushed
with memories and people from his past on a national TV show, is one such
case. Brooks calls it "one of my favorite sketches of all time" (as does Reiner)
and reveals that there's a clear delineation point, in that famous piece of live
television, between the scripted and the improvised.

"After he gets on the stage," Brooks says of Caesar's initially unwilling
"This Is Your Story" participant Al Duncie, "almost everything is written . . .
But the pre-part, the ushers dragging him up, almost everything is ad lib.
He's swinging his coat, he's going down the wrong aisle, he's smacking the
ushers down, he's trying to escape, he's fainting when they mention his
name—that was Sid's idea. I would say the first third of it is all ad lib. And

the next two-thirds of it, [Howard Morris as the comically clinging] Uncle Goopy and all the people who come onstage as part of his life, it's all carefully written."

Exactly by whom, though, remains a mystery. Not because Brooks doesn't know, or recall, but because he won't tell, even though he's widely credited elsewhere as one of the authors of this classic sketch. "Listen to me carefully, Bianculli," Brooks says with a tone of mock menace. "Even if I remembered to the line, I would never tell you, because that is a secret code of comedy writers."

As for the possibility of doing double duty on *Your Show of Shows* as performer as well as writer, as his friend Carl Reiner was doing, Brooks says he never once lobbied for it. "Something in me said, 'Don't do it,'" Brooks admits. "First of all, honestly, as a performer, all my passions were completely fulfilled by Sid Caesar. He could do anything, and do it better than anybody who ever lived. So there was no need to play vocal ping-pong onstage with Sid Caesar. Privately, we used to do it," he adds, "because I was his stooge; we would hang around together twenty-four hours a day. I loved him."

Brooks also confesses being a bit frightened, of both the size of the national spotlight and the sheer number of performance hours required: thirty-nine shows per season for five years, with ninety minutes of live TV per show. Writing to help fill that demand was tough enough, but acting in the sketches as well? Reiner could handle it, but Brooks never wanted to try. "Had I done *Your Show of Shows*," he says, "it would have been the same thing as Sid Caesar. I mean, Sid Caesar was—I kind of hate to say this— used up. Thirty-nine shows a season, an hour and a half [each week]—can you imagine? Just even physically, how could you do that? But the world— Americans, anyway—got enough of Sid Caesar that he wasn't needed for anything else."

While Brooks worked with Caesar throughout the 1950s, on *Your Show of Shows* and eventually on *Caesar's Hour*, he also kept an eye on other Golden Age TV offerings. Milton Berle, the reigning king of sketch comedy known as Mr. Television and Uncle Miltie on NBC's *Texaco Star Theater*, Brooks considered a hit-or-miss proposition: "I loved Berle when he was good, and I hated him when he was bad." Some of the offerings by such dramatic anthology series as NBC's *Goodyear TV Playhouse* and CBS's *Studio One* and *Playhouse 90* also impressed him more than others; he cites, specifically, Reginald Rose's "Twelve Angry Men" and anything by Paddy Chayefsky ("Such great dramatic writers, such great talents writing for television"). Brooks also expressed special fondness for episodes of another anthology series, Rod Serling's *Twilight Zone* ("I thought they were really imaginative and extraordinarily well crafted").

Asked to identify the TV artist he feels has been most neglected by history, Brooks has an instant answer. "I thought Ernie Kovacs was a bit of a comedy genius and was thrilling, thrillingly funny," he says, "and there wasn't enough recognition for him. And another guy who's really witty and warm, and should've been much more appreciated, was Steve Allen [host of NBC's original *Tonight!* show in 1954] ... He was very self-sacrificing, and very loving, very giving. He was responsible for Carl Reiner and I doing our first album. He got us a place to record. I mean, took us down there [laughs], and he made us do an album of the 2000 Year Old Man. We didn't want to do it. He made us do it."

Brooks and Reiner had started concocting and conducting ad-libbed routines, for their own private amusement, back in the writers' room of *Your Show of Shows.* Eventually, it became an act their friends would request at parties: Brooks would adopt the persona of a world-weary, millennia-old guy who had seen and done everything, and Reiner would pepper him with questions and follow-ups. George Burns begged them to record their act, and Steve Allen basically forced them to, arranging for a 1960 date at a recording studio. The routines anchored an album, released the next year, called *2000 Years with Carl Reiner and Mel Brooks,* which caught on quickly. Almost immediately, Brooks and Reiner were performing their "2000 Year Old Man" act on television, on both *The Ed Sullivan Show* and the latest program by the man to whom they owed their success, *The New Steve Allen Show.*

Brooks likened their dynamic to that of Bud Abbott and Lou Costello, where Abbott would chase Costello into a corner, verbally if not physically, and never let him go. "That's what Carl did to me as the 2000 Year Old Man," Brooks says. "The son of a bitch always demanded proof of anything I said, which really forced me to be such an incredible, entertaining liar ... He is, if not the greatest, certainly one of the greatest straight men that ever lived. The work he did with Sid Caesar, and then later with me and the 2000 Year Old Man ... nobody could do that job better than Carl Reiner."

Ironically, though Brooks resisted performing on camera while writing for Sid Caesar, it was his teaming with Reiner on those improvised "2000 Year Old Man" sketches that made him a household name, got him on national TV, and opened the doors for him to pursue his dreams of working in the movies, and eventually Broadway. "I was never a big name to the public," Brooks was quoted as saying in the liner notes to the multi-CD *2000 Year Old Man: The Complete History* boxed set in 2009, "and then suddenly I surfaced. The record came out, sold maybe a million copies. Saved me."

Saved him, and made him and even his more outlandish ideas marketable. His first film script, and movie acting, were for his 1963 animated short film *The Critic,* in which only his voice was heard as, unseen, he watched an avant-garde cartoon and tried to make sense of it. The following year, *The Critic* won an Academy Award for Short Subject, Cartoons. Then David Susskind's company, Talent Associates, approached Brooks with an idea. The new James Bond movie franchise, starring Sean Connery, was fast becoming almost as big a part of the cultural British Invasion as Beatlemania, and TV was taking note: NBC had successfully launched its own Bond-like spy series, *The Man from U.N.C.L.E.,* in 1964, and shows already in the works for 1965 included *Secret Agent,* Patrick McGoohan's imported British series on CBS, and *I Spy,* the Robert Culp–Bill Cosby globe-trotting series on NBC. Brooks was asked if he could come up with a comedy spy series to cash in on the trend, and Brooks said sure. He brought in Buck Henry as his partner, and they played pool at Talent Associates every night, tossing out ideas until enough of them stuck. They shot a pilot, starring Tom Poston (one of Steve Allen's repertory company of comics, later a co-star of *Newhart*), but it got rejected. Rather than give up, they reshot the exact same script with a different actor: Don Adams, a stand-up comic whose vocally clipped impression of William Powell in *The Thin Man,* Brooks thought, might be perfect for the role of the inept but supremely self-confident Maxwell Smart, Secret Agent 86. It was. NBC's *Get Smart* premiered in TV's fall 1965 season and ran for five years. When the complete series of *Get Smart* was released on DVD, Brooks and Henry, in one of the accompanying extras, broke Brooks's writers' room rule about divvying up credit.

"Before we showed the pilot episode of *Get Smart,*" Brooks says, "I said [to Henry], 'Okay. I'm going to say something I think I created, and you're going to say something you think you created. Hands up first!' He put his hand up; Buck Henry did and said, 'The cone of silence!' And I was shocked. I said, 'Oh, my God, you're right! It was you. It wasn't me!' And then he stuck his hand up, and I said, 'Another?' And he said, 'No, yours! The shoe telephone.' And I said, 'Okay, I invented the cell phone. So we're even.' But that's the first and only time we've cut the pie up," Brooks adds.

While enjoying the success of *Get Smart,* Brooks got more good news: after he finished the first season of *Get Smart,* the screenplay he'd been writing on the side had finally been approved for financing and production, giving him a chance to make a full-length movie after all. But Joseph E. Levine, the moneyman and former motion-picture exhibitor, had one requirement: a title change.

"My screenplay was called *Springtime for Hitler,*" Brooks says. "And Joe Levine said, 'None of my network of exhibitors will put the word "Hitler" on the marquee. So any other title, you know? They don't mind it in the movie, but they don't want it on their marquee.'"

The Producers, starring Zero Mostel and Gene Wilder, came out in 1967—the same year Brooks and Reiner reunited with their old *Your Show of Shows* buddies for the CBS reunion special, *The Sid Caesar, Imogene Coca, Carl Reiner, Howard Morris Special.* Brooks won an Emmy for his work as a writer on that TV special, and the next year he also won an Academy Award for writing the screenplay to *The Producers.* He used his newfound clout to finance and realize a pet project, making a 1970 movie version of *The Twelve Chairs,* based on a comic novel by two more of his long-cherished Russian writers, Ilya Ilf and Yevgeny Petrov. That film didn't garner much notice at the box office, but his next two films, both released in 1974, were commercial as well as critical successes, and so audaciously brilliant they made Mel Brooks a top-tier filmmaker: the Western satire *Blazing Saddles* and the horror-film satire *Young Frankenstein.* Gene Wilder starred in both and co-wrote the latter.

"Gene was a combination of sweetness, sadness, and comedy you couldn't get from anybody else," Brooks says. "He's like a cello. It's beautiful, and yet it's deep. It has deep resonance. When he played the Waco Kid [in *Blazing Saddles*], he could make you cry. That's how good he was. And he never played for comedy. He just played the character . . . I think Gene is responsible for the 'art' part of my career. He started me on that track, he and Zero, in *The Producers*—not just crazy comedy, but comedy with character and purpose. I don't think *The Producers* would have been half as good without Gene and Zero, no matter who did it as a movie . . . When I spoke to Nathan Lane and Matthew Broderick [about starring in Brooks's 2001 Broadway musical version of *The Producers*], I said, 'Who are you going to play?' And they said, 'We're going to play Zero and Gene.' And I said, 'Okay. Good. Good.'"

Brooks has huge respect for talent and a very good eye for it, too. He wanted Richard Pryor to play Black Bart opposite Wilder's Waco Kid in *Blazing Saddles,* but the studio balked, so Brooks kept Pryor on the writing staff. Brooks adored the contributions of Madeline Kahn, whom he featured in both his 1974 comedies and beyond, and says proudly, "I actually stole Harvey Korman," and cast him in *Blazing Saddles* and other films, after watching him on *The Carol Burnett Show* on CBS. As a backstage veteran of *Your Show of Shows,* Brooks knew sketch comedy brilliance when he saw it.

"He was so fast and so furiously funny," Brooks says of Korman. "And Harvey was a splendid actor. A real actor. Once he was in character, he was in it, and he did it perfectly . . . That's why *The Carol Burnett Show* was so successful. I think he was the pillar that supported that entire show."

Understandably, once Mel Brooks tasted such major cinematic success, he largely left TV behind—especially after his next TV venture, ABC's 1975 Robin Hood satire *When Things Were Rotten,* lasted only three months. But he continued to watch for and appreciate talent wherever he could find it and was a particular fan of *Monty Python's Flying Circus.* He befriended Eric Idle, peppering him with fan-boy questions at weekly lunches ("How did you guys ever come up with the Ministry of Silly Walks?"), and noted with pride that London's Baker Street Cinema once ran a double bill of Monty Python's *Life of Brian* and his own *Blazing Saddles* for more than a year.

Perhaps his most unexpected talent find was the young director David Lynch, whose film output, up to that point, had been odd film shorts and the even odder 1977 cult movie *Eraserhead.* On the basis of that output, Brooks gambled and hired Lynch to direct and co-write the screenplay for what, for Brooks, was a major departure and equally major gamble: a black-and-white dramatic, biographical film called *The Elephant Man.* Without Brooks's believing in Lynch, and hiring him for that excellent 1980 movie, we might never have seen Lynch's *Blue Velvet* and other singularly artistic films—much less his TV masterpiece, ABC's *Twin Peaks.* ("I loved it!" Brooks says of that still-seminal, about-to-be-revived series. "I was amazed that they allowed it, you know? He did things that were really very bold, and he was a visionary of sorts.") And had *The Elephant Man* not been a success, audiences might never have been treated to any number of subsequent movies produced by Mel Brooks under his Brooksfilms production company banner.

"*The Elephant Man* allowed me to make this insane foray into drama," Brooks explains, "when, in all my life, I had been doing comedy—nothing but comedy . . . I used to keep my name assiduously off any of the posters, or any of the credits, for any of the Brooksfilms pictures . . . *The Elephant Man, 84 Charing Cross Road, The Fly, My Favorite Year,* I always kept my name off them."

But in comedies, Brooks became ever more prominent. He took leading roles in his own comedy films, such as 1977's *High Anxiety* (lampooning the films of Alfred Hitchcock) and 1987's *Spaceballs* (lampooning the Star Wars films of George Lucas). On television, he finally learned what it would be like to perform on a sketch comedy series opposite a Caesar-like force of nature, by guest starring on Fox's *Tracey Ullman Show* in 1990 and improvising with its very talented star. "It was heaven!" he recalls. "It was like, 'Okay! I'm glad I'm in show business, doing that sketch.' Because of the professionalism, the art, the energy, and the creativity that we both threw into that. Out of the blue, she started limping! That was her idea!"

For three seasons in the 1990s, Brooks guest starred on another series, NBC's *Mad About You,* playing the unpredictable relative Uncle Phil, and won Guest Actor Emmys three years running, from 1997 to 1999. Then, to start the new century, in 2000, Brooks mounted a Broadway musical version of his 1967 movie *The Producers* and was rewarded with his 2001 show winning an unprecedented number of Tony Awards, in a total of twelve different categories. *The Producers* ran on Broadway for six years, and the year it left New York, another Mel Brooks musical, based on another previous film, took its place: 2007's *Young Frankenstein.*

Brooks clearly loves the stage at this point in his life and has dabbled for the last few years compiling songs for a possible *Blazing Saddles* musical. But he's also dabbled more in television, doing several specials for HBO—including 2015's *Mel Brooks: Live at the Geffen,* his first true stand-up comedy act since his days in the Catskills—and, perhaps most daringly and memorably of all, appearing as himself in a season-long guest role on another HBO show, Larry David's *Curb Your Enthusiasm,* that played, brilliantly, off Brooks's phenomenal stage success with *The Producers.*

The plot, in the 2004 story arc of *Curb,* had Mel Brooks contacting Larry David and inviting him to become the latest actor to star as Max Bialystock in his long-running hit Broadway musical version of *The Producers,* even though Brooks's own friends don't think David can sing or act well enough to pull it off. But Brooks has an ulterior motive, which isn't revealed until the season finale: he and his wife, Anne Bancroft, were weary of dealing with the show after all those years, and hiring David is just the thing to finally close it down. "This guy will bury it," the real Brooks recounts. But in a twist ending worthy of, and intentionally echoing, *The Producers* itself, David proves to be a hit with the crowd because of his overacting and ad-libs, and Mel and Anne find themselves afterward foiled by their own success just as Bialystock and Bloom are in the original movie and play.

The brilliant twist ending came later (for that, see Larry David's interview profile later in this book), but the real Larry David's uncurbed enthusiasm ultimately persuaded the real Mel Brooks to give his blessing, and himself, to David's season-long story idea. And years after the *Curb Your Enthusiasm* surprise plot twist at the end, Brooks notes, "the punch line came later in real life"—in 2015, when Larry David made his Broadway debut, starring in *Fish in the Dark,* a comedy play he also wrote. "It was very successful! Never mind that the critics crucified him," Brooks said, chuckling at the irony. "You couldn't get a seat!"

One final Mel Brooks story related to comedians working in TV today: When I interviewed Brooks on NPR's *Fresh Air with Terry Gross* in 2013 and asked him about which modern comics he enjoyed, among those he mentioned was Amy Schumer. Subsequently, when Schumer was about to record her own *Fresh Air* interview, with Terry herself, Amy told Terry she was in the makeup chair getting ready to shoot a scene for her Comedy Central series, *Inside Amy Schumer,* and listening to my interview with Brooks on public radio, when he suddenly mentioned her name. She cried so hard, she told Terry, she had to have her eye makeup reapplied. When I relay that story to Mel Brooks, he says, very sweetly, "That's so beautiful." And when I ask why he was so impressed by her, Brooks returns with a comment that could just as easily be applied to his own sense of humor and his entire career.

"She's smart, and she's brave," Brooks says. "That's a great combination. So is Sarah Silverman . . . I think they're both beautiful, and fun, and smart, with the courage to actually say"—he pauses for a moment and laughs— "these crazy, dirty things. They're remarkable. Both of them. I wish I could marry them both." Another pause, for effect.

"But I'm not really going to marry them."

CAROL BURNETT

BORN: 1933, San Antonio.

FIRST TV CREDIT: Guest, *The Paul Winchell and Jerry Mahoney Show,* 1955, CBS.

LANDMARK TV SERIES: *The Garry Moore Show,* 1959–62, CBS; *The Carol Burnett Show,* 1967–78, CBS.

OTHER MAJOR CREDITS: Broadway: *Once Upon a Mattress,* 1959–60; *Putting It Together,* 1999–2000. Movies: *A Wedding,* 1978; *Annie,* 1982. TV: *Julie and Carol at Carnegie Hall,* 1962, CBS; *An Evening with Carol Burnett,* 1963, CBS; *Julie and Carol at Lincoln Center,* 1971, CBS; *Friendly Fire,* 1979, ABC; *Fresno,* 1986, CBS; *The Larry Sanders Show,* 1992, 1998, HBO; Recurring guest roles on *Mad About You,* 1996–99, NBC, and *Glee,* 2010, 2015, Fox.

Had UCLA offered a better journalism program in the 1950s, Carol Burnett might never have gone into comedy. She was born in 1933 in San Antonio to parents who lapsed into alcoholism, leaving her to be raised largely by her grandmother, who relocated with her to Hollywood and indulged young Carol's love of movies and other creative endeavors, including the convenient entertainment medium of radio. "My grandmother raised me," she says, "so the radio was it. Of course, there was no television. As a little girl, I loved *Let's Pretend.* That was a Saturday morning radio show that acted out fairy tales. And I must have been five or six when I started listening to Jack Benny."

When Carol Burnett was eleven, her earliest ambition was to be a cartoonist (at the time, she created, for her own amusement, a comic she called

"The Josephsons," about a teenage girl and her family). At Hollywood High School, she became editor of the school newspaper, then went to UCLA, where the university had a daily newspaper but no journalism major. She took theater arts as her major instead, planning to take courses in writing plays—until a mandatory acting class exposed her to the thrill of performing, and getting laughs, before a live audience. Her popularity and confidence at college increased, and she joined a musical comedy college workshop, because music was always a big part, and one of the brightest, of her childhood. "I can carry a tune," she says, "because my mother and grandmother and I used to sing in the kitchen all the time. Mama would play the ukulele." Her first assignment was to join the chorus for a number from *South Pacific,* a musical then in its original run on Broadway. Her job was to be one of several singers backing the leading lady on "I'm Gonna Wash That Man Right Outta My Hair," but, Burnett recalls with a laugh, "I sang so loud they took me out of the chorus." One of the directors, also a student performer, asked her to duet with him on a number from another then-current Broadway musical, *Guys and Dolls.* The song was the comic showstopper "Adelaide's Lament," in which the character sings about having a cold. Burnett was unfamiliar with it but instantly embraced its premise. "I thought, 'Well, I could do that!'" she recalls. "Because if I hit a bad note, I can sneeze and pretend that it's the cold." The reception to that one performance, combining her natural vocal and comic abilities, overrode any lingering dreams of cartooning, reporting, or writing. "That was the first song I ever sang in public, and that was at UCLA: 'Adelaide's Lament,'" she says, well aware of that moment's importance to her future career in show business. "I got great response from it. And I thought, 'Oh, now I know what I want to do. I want to be in musical comedy! And someday, be like Ethel Merman or Mary Martin.'"

From UCLA, Burnett pursued her dream by going to New York and moving into the Rehearsal Club, a hotel for young women interested in the theater ("Eighteen dollars a week, room and board," she remembers clearly). You had to be able to prove you were trying to land theater jobs, but you could hold other part-time work. What you couldn't do was fraternize with the opposite sex. "No gentlemen beyond the parlor," she remembers. But she also remembers the communal television set in that same parlor and that one of the shows she watched often then was *Caesar's Hour,* starring Sid Caesar, Nanette Fabray, Carl Reiner, and Howard Morris. "I just loved it," she says. She even got to attend a dress rehearsal once, and so enjoyed what she saw she gave up her ticket to that night's smash-hit performance of *My Fair Lady,* starring Julie Andrews as Eliza Doolittle, to return for the evening live telecast of *Caesar's Hour.*

By then, Burnett had already been on television herself. Her TV debut came in 1955, on the Saturday morning version of *The Paul Winchell and Jerry Mahoney Show,* starring a ventriloquist and his literally wooden co-stars. "I was the girlfriend of the dummy," she says. "The first show I did, I sang to Jerry Mahoney and Knucklehead Smiff; I sang 'Somewhere over the Rainbow' to the dummies." She called her grandmother, still living back out in California, to alert her to her upcoming TV appearance, and her grandmother asked her to say hello. "I said, 'Nanny, they're not going to let me say, "Hello, Nanny!"'" Burnett recalls. "So that's when we cooked up the idea of [my] pulling my ear." It's been her signature on-camera move ever since.

Burnett pursued stage and nightclub work wherever she could, including summer appearances in Pennsylvania's Pocono Mountains, at the Tamiment Playhouse shows produced by Max Liebman of *Your Show of Shows* fame. That connection eventually got her a recurring role on Buddy Hackett's 1956 sitcom *Stanley,* produced by Liebman and televised live from New York, with a writing staff that included Neil Simon and Woody Allen. Tamiment also introduced her to Mary Rodgers and Marshall Barer, whose *Once Upon a Mattress,* presented in workshop form at Tamiment, would eventually become Burnett's starring debut on Broadway.

Meanwhile, other club and TV spots followed, including occasional appearances on Garry Moore's daytime series and a 1957 appearance with Jack Paar on *The Tonight Show,* singing a comedy song, written especially for her by Ken Welch, that she had started singing in a nightclub act a few months earlier. A comedy love song to the then secretary of state, it gave Burnett another opportunity to sing well while acting funny, this time as a political groupie swooning over the cabinet member with a widespread reputation for being dull. The song was titled "I Made a Fool of Myself over John Foster Dulles," and after singing it on Paar's show and elsewhere, Burnett found herself with a hit novelty record and a suddenly hot reputation as a talented young comic singer. That was a major TV appearance for her, but even bigger, and more formative, was a last-minute guest spot on another of Moore's programs, the prime-time *Garry Moore Show,* when she was asked to fill in, with only forty-eight hours' notice, for the ailing guest star Martha Raye.

"It was a Sunday, and they were going to go live on Tuesday, and Martha got sick," Burnett recalls. "And Garry called me and he said, 'Can you come over and learn Martha's stuff?' . . . So I ran over to rehearsal, and they gave me all the stuff Martha was going to do, and I learned it. I was very nervous and very excited, and we went live on Tuesday night. And Garry, being the delightful human being that he was, at the end of the show brought me out and told the audience how I was filling in for Martha." She got a standing ovation and cried. And that fall, after beginning a starring run in the Broadway musical *Once Upon a Mattress*, she was asked to return to *The Garry Moore Show*—this time as a regular. "It was like *42nd Street*," she says.

From Moore, she says, she learned so much—about comedy, about collaborating, and even about how to maintain a friendly atmosphere on the set. "I had great training from *The Garry Moore Show*," she says, acknowledging without hesitation that she patterned her own variety series, *The Carol Burnett Show*, after her multiyear stint on Moore's program. For example, the way he doled out jokes to his co-stars, including Durwood Kirby and Burnett herself, was a practice she carried out with her own show's regulars, Harvey Korman, Vicki Lawrence, and (eventually) Tim Conway.

"I remember sitting with him at the table reading on Monday, the first time," Burnett says of Moore, "and we're reading a sketch, and Garry had a joke or a punch line in the sketch. And he looked up, and he said, 'You know what? Give this to Durwood. He can say it funnier than I can.' And another time he would say, 'Let Carol take this joke. She can do it.' He always said, 'It's the show that counts.' Even though he was the star, and this was *The Garry Moore Show,* he said, 'People are going to talk about how good the show was, and that's only good for me, you know?'" On her own show, she says, "they called Harvey and Vicki second bananas, but that's a term I never cared for. Because what I wanted—even though it was my name in the title—I wanted a true rep company. So you see sketches where I'm supporting Harvey, or I'm supporting Vicki, and Vicki and I are supporting Tim, or Tim is supporting us, or whatever. It was a true rep company, which is what I wanted, and that's what I got!" And on *The Garry Moore Show,* the host was generous enough, shifting the spotlight to others, that Burnett won an Emmy in 1962 for her supporting performances on the series.

During those years on *The Garry Moore Show,* Burnett got to meet and interact with a lengthy parade of talented guest stars, from Rod Serling (featured in a *Twilight Zone* parody written by Neil Simon) to Julie Andrews (whose duet with Burnett sparked a lifelong friendship). "I had a crush on

Rod Serling," Burnett admits, laughing. "Nothing ever came of it, of course. He was married and everything. But I just loooooved him!" As for Andrews, whom Burnett had met briefly when she came backstage to introduce herself while Burnett was starring in *Once Upon a Mattress,* she and Burnett bonded instantly when the show's just-hired special material writer— Ken Welch, the composer of Burnett's "John Foster Dulles" hit—wrote a cowboy-themed adaptation of the song "The Big D" from the musical *The Most Happy Fella.* "We were dressed as cowgirls," Burnett says. "Of course, Julie and I hit it off right away. It's as if we had always met." And the number got a standing ovation from the studio audience—a rarity for a production number in a TV variety show.

That's what gave Bob Banner, producer of *The Garry Moore Show,* the idea to sell a stand-alone variety special to CBS, starring the two young women. ("You know," Burnett remembers Banner telling them, "you guys really have great chemistry.") The network executives initially declined, arguing that viewers could already see Burnett every week on Moore's show and that no one west of New York could identify Andrews, who had starred on Broadway in *My Fair Lady* and *Camelot* but had yet to star in a movie. But after that conversation ended, those same executives, leaving a function with Burnett and others during a heavy rainstorm, witnessed Burnett catching a much-needed ride from a friendly truck driver (and obvious Carol Burnett fan) who had shouted a happy hello upon seeing her. By the time Burnett arrived home, her phone was ringing, and CBS had approved the special. Televised in 1962, *Julie and Carol at Carnegie Hall* was co-written by Mike Nichols and Ken Welch and produced and directed by the *Garry Moore Show* producer Joe Hamilton, whom Burnett would marry the following year. *Julie and Carol at Carnegie Hall* won two Emmy Awards (one for Outstanding Program Achievement in the Field of Music, and one for Carol Burnett herself), and a grateful CBS quickly offered Burnett a ten-year option contract with a highly unusual bonus provision: anytime in the first five years of the contract, if she wanted the network to commit for a Carol Burnett variety series, all she had to do was ask, and CBS was obligated to produce and broadcast the show for thirty weeks. Just as that five-year option was about to lapse, Burnett asked, and CBS, as promised, scheduled and launched *The Carol Burnett Show* in 1967.

In escalating from repertory player on *The Garry Moore Show* to star of her own series, Burnett brought with her not only the comic and generous sensibility of Moore but, because his series had ended, some of his staffers as well. These included the producer Joe Hamilton, by then her husband, and Bob Banner, who became the initial executive producer of *The Carol Burnett Show*. And there were others. "Several of the crew members—director, writer, so forth—who were on Garry's show [in New York] took the risk and moved out to California to be with us." She borrowed from other shows as well. From *The Danny Kaye Show*, she hired Harvey Korman. And from *Caesar's Hour*, Sid Caesar's follow-up to *Your Show of Shows*, as well as from *The Garry Moore Show*, she adapted a desired template. "I said I wanted what Garry had and what Sid had—the rep company and music, and this and that," she explains. "We had more music than Sid did, but that's about the only thing that I wanted more of." Her admiration for Caesar was obvious: in the first seasons of her own variety series, she showcased, as guest stars, Caesar's *Your Show of Shows* castmates Imogene Coca and Carl Reiner, as well as Caesar himself.

And from Garry Moore, she borrowed one other element directly—something that his TV audiences had never seen, but which his studio audiences experienced every week, and which Burnett made one of her signature bits. "Garry used to do his own warm-up, because he never wanted a comedian to come out and warm up the audience. He wanted to do it," she says. "And so he did it by doing Q&A with the audience. I remember," she continues, "I would sit backstage and listen to him, and how wonderful he was in connecting with his studio audience. But they never taped it." It was Bob Banner, the executive producer of *The Carol Burnett Show*, who suggested Burnett take questions from the audience to open her show each week. His argument was that before she showed up in sketches in outlandish costumes and obscured by fright wigs and makeup, people should get to know the "real" Carol—so, he advised her, let's do a Q&A each week, tape it, and use it to open the show.

"And I balked—big-time," Burnett recalls. She was too nervous and worried that the studio audience members wouldn't ask questions and also worried that her answers simply wouldn't be funny. "But he said, 'Just try it for three or four weeks, and if you're totally uncomfortable, and it doesn't work, we'll deep-six that idea.' Well, it worked! . . . After we had been on the air two or three weeks, the studio audience came prepared to have some fun and ask questions. And I started to enjoy it, because it was totally ad lib." Banner had even offered to start the experiment by putting a few "plants" in the audience, with show writers supplying both the questions and the host's answers, but Burnett vetoed that security blanket—reasoning, as she explains it now, "If I have egg on my face, at least it's going to be honest."

The Carol Burnett Show ran on CBS for eleven years, never cracking the Top 10 for any single season, but always gathering a large and loyal audience base. Topical and political humor was assiduously avoided, in favor of grandiose musical production numbers, comedy sketches, and elaborate film parodies of the type made famous on Sid Caesar's variety shows. And as with Caesar's parodies, it didn't matter whether the audience was in on the joke, so long as it laughed anyway. "What we used to say is," Burnett recalls, "they can get it on two levels. Either it's funny itself, even if you didn't know the movies, or it's even funnier if you do know the movie." That was certainly true of her show's most famous film parody of all: "Went with the Wind," a *Gone with the Wind* spoof in which Burnett, in the Scarlett O'Hara role, dons a hastily sewn green velvet gown made of her run-down plantation's curtains (complete with curtain rod across her shoulders, an especially inspired costume by the designer Bob Mackie).

Carol Burnett never won an Emmy for her acting on *The Carol Burnett Show,* though the show itself won three times as best variety series and was awarded twenty-five Emmys overall. Many of them went to Burnett's supporting cast, proving the wisdom of Garry Moore's belief in making those around you look good: Tim Conway, Harvey Korman, and Vicki Lawrence all won Emmys as supporting performers on *The Carol Burnett Show,* just as Burnett had on *The Garry Moore Show.* Another of Burnett's staunch comedy beliefs, that her TV show, as much as possible, should replicate the feel and pace of a live performance, also paid big dividends and became another *Carol Burnett Show* trademark element: mistakes and ad-libs that, instead of stopping the show, added to it.

"Unless the scenery fell down and knocked us out, we'll just keep going, as if we're doing a Broadway show," she remembers instructing the cast and crew. "I want that feeling of spontaneity. We don't have to be perfect." Even if boom microphones showed up in a camera shot, she says, "We'd just barrel through. And we never broke up on purpose. Ever. Ever."

But they did make each other laugh—a lot—and the chief culprit was Tim Conway, who took advantage of the way *The Carol Burnett Show* was taped to time his ad-lib attacks on his fellow cast members. Each week's show was performed and taped twice on production day, at 5:00 and

8:00 p.m., with different audiences. Conway would do the afternoon show according to the script, and if that taping went well, he would feel free, in the evening performance, to have a little fun. (One famous example, from a "Family" sketch, had Conway surprising his co-stars by launching into an unscripted, unexpected story about seeing a pair of "Siamese elephants," joined at their trunks, at a freak show.) "When he started doing it, he didn't ask permission," Burnett says of Conway's loose-cannon antics. She agrees that as the show's star she could have put a stop to Conway's ad-libs early, but didn't. "I thought, 'This is gold. This is just pure gold. Let him go and do it.' Because, if it didn't work, we had it in the can [from the afternoon taping]. And again, it's the whole thing: if people let him shine, it was only going to reflect how good our show is!"

After tugging her earlobe one final time to say farewell to *The Carol Burnett Show*, the comic actress and singer continued to rack up guest spots on other TV shows and embark on other projects of her own, as she had before, and during, the run of her series. Before *The Carol Burnett Show*, her guest star roles included appearances on *Get Smart*, on several of Lucille Ball's post–*I Love Lucy* sitcoms, and even on Serling's *Twilight Zone*. During the eleven-year run of her series, she reteamed with Julie Andrews for another musical special, reprised for TV her starring role in *Once Upon a Mattress*, and starred in Robert Altman's 1978 ensemble movie, *A Wedding*. And after her series ended, Burnett starred in both *Friendly Fire*, a dramatic ABC television movie about a grieving mother demanding more information about the mysterious death of her serviceman son, and *Fresno*, a comic CBS miniseries satirizing the style and content of such prime-time soap operas as *Dallas* and *Dynasty*. She also had a recurring guest role on NBC's *Mad About You*, for which she finally won an individual Emmy Award for acting, and a memorable guest spot, playing herself, on HBO's *Larry Sanders Show*, where she took full advantage of the relative freedom of premium cable television.

In the episode in question, Burnett had rehearsed an ultimately discarded Tarzan sketch with Garry Shandling's talk-show host Larry Sanders and was seated next to him at his desk, waiting between interview segments for the commercial break to end. In the script, Larry's loincloth in the sketch was described as notably skimpy, and Larry's producer, Artie, had informed him afterward, "I could see your balls." So Burnett, in the scene with Larry at his desk, decided to tap into her inner Tim Conway and surprised Shandling with an ad-lib echoing that loincloth exchange in the script. She leaned in to Larry and whispered, "I saw your balls," then stared straight into her host's eyes.

"I just threw that in," she says, laughing. "Garry loved it. It wasn't horribly dirty or anything. It was just kind of funny—for me, especially, to say that, you know? As opposed to if Joan Rivers, God rest her soul, said it, it would be funny, but not as shocking as hearing it come out of me, or Mary Tyler Moore, you know?"

TOM SMOTHERS

BORN: 1937, Governors Island, New York.
FIRST TV CREDIT: Talent show contestant, *Rocket to Stardom*, 1951, local TV, Redondo Beach, California.
LANDMARK TV SERIES: *The Smothers Brothers Comedy Hour*, 1967–69, CBS; *The Smothers Brothers Comedy Hour*, 1988–89, CBS.
OTHER MAJOR CREDITS: TV: *Pat Paulsen for President*, 1968, CBS.

Like many people who grew up to be professional comedians, Tom Smothers had a childhood visited by tragedy. He and his little brother, Dick, spent their early years in unusual surroundings. Because their father was a West Point graduate and career soldier stationed at Governors Island in New York, both Tom and Dick were born there—Tom in 1937, Dick in 1939. Shortly thereafter, the family relocated with him to the Philippines, where life on the army base was primitive. (Tom recalls that the legs of the beds were placed in pans of water "so certain things wouldn't crawl up.") When Tom's mother became pregnant with their third child, and with rumblings of danger in the Pacific, the family was sent back to California, while their dad remained stationed on Corregidor. The Japanese attacked Pearl Harbor and the Philippines in 1941, drawing the United States into World War II. Among the American troops fighting the Japanese on the Bataan Peninsula on Luzon Island was Tom and Dick's father, Thomas Bolyn Smothers Jr., who, after months of isolated fighting and a lack of supplies and reinforcements, was among the fifty thousand soldiers who surrendered en masse and were immediately herded into a sixty-five-mile forced march to a prison camp in

San Fernando. That forced relocation was so brutal, and claimed the lives of so many prisoners of war, that it became known as the Bataan Death March. Tom and Dick's father survived that march, and several more years of inhumane captivity, but died in the final months of the war when the Japanese POW ship imprisoning him was mistakenly bombed by Allied pilots. Tom was eight years old, and he and Dick and their sister, Sherry, spent the rest of their childhoods farmed out, together or separately, to live with relatives as their mother battled alcoholism and struggled through several tenuous marriages and relationships.

The first entertainment programs Tom Smothers remembers are from radio: Jack Benny for comedy, and, for drama and adventure, such shows as the rollicking Western *Red Ryder,* the scary *Inner Sanctum,* the suspenseful *Shadow,* and the action-packed *Captain Midnight.* "We didn't have TV until I was ten or eleven," Tom recalls. "When we saw television at all, it was at a neighbor's house. When I told my kids that, they couldn't believe it. They said, 'What did you do?' And I told them, 'We watched radio.'" When Tom was twelve years old, he was especially taken by *The Burl Ives Show,* a music program in which the host would play all sorts of folk songs, including, Tom Smothers remembers specifically, "Big Rock Candy Mountain." Ives's radio show was his musical inspiration ("That prompted me to want to play guitar," Smothers says), and young Tommy Smothers put together his first bands in grade school. "Clarinet, piano, drums, and me on guitar," he recalls of one sixth-grade effort, then laughs and adds, "And they all had to play in the key I knew how to play." A year or two later, he formed another group—a barbershop quartet, with his brother, Dick, as one of the other vocalists—and the Smothers brothers got their first television exposure as part of that group, on a live local TV talent program, *Rocket to Stardom,* sponsored by an Oldsmobile dealer in Redondo Beach. "We took second place," Tom says now, "to a marimba player who tap-danced."

Around that time, Tom saw someone on television who would change his life: George Gobel, the quiet, droll comedian, making a stand-up appearance on CBS's *Ed Sullivan Show* and telling a simple but funny story involving a bowling ball. "And I said," Smothers recalls, "that's what I want to be, and be able to do. I want to stand there and be funny . . . He didn't do jokes; he did attitude."

The folk music revival of the era, started by Burl Ives, by the calypso singer Harry Belafonte, and by Pete Seeger and the other members of the

Weavers, exploded in 1958 when a young, clean-cut collegiate group called the Kingston Trio had a No. 1 hit with "Tom Dooley." It exemplified, and codified, the new brand of folksinger: people who prefaced their folk tunes with lengthy, earnest stories about the origin and meaning of each song. Tom and Dick Smothers were studying at San Jose State University at the time, less than twenty miles from Palo Alto, where the Kingston Trio had emerged. The Smothers Brothers copied the same playbook. They auditioned at San Francisco's Purple Onion, where the Kingston Trio had broken out and become a featured act, and presented themselves as a trio (the third member, Bobby Blackmore, wasn't an actual relative but played guitar, sang lead, and knew some folk songs). The nightclub's manager liked the act, especially the way Tom joked and rambled between numbers, but suggested Dick get, and play, an upright bass, rather than just stand there and sing. He did, and the trio, billed irreverently as "Smothers Brothers and Gawd," opened at the Purple Onion in February 1959. By the end of the year, Gawd was gone, the Smothers Brothers were a musical-comedy duo, and they were on their way. In February 1960, Tom and Dick made their national debut on NBC's *Tonight Show*, where the delighted reaction of the host, Jack Paar, made them stars literally overnight. Comedy albums and years on the nightclub circuit and as variety-show guest stars followed, until the brothers, in 1965, hit what seemed like the big time: their own CBS situation comedy, *The Smothers Brothers Show*.

But they hated the entire experience and bowed out after one season. They had no input into the writing or content, and the sitcom reflected it. Copying the light fantasy premises of the time (talking horses, witches, genies, visiting Martians), this early series from Aaron Spelling cast Dick as a young playboy visited by his dead brother, Tom, now Dick's personal guardian angel. Tom considers the series a valuable lesson learned and vowed never again to do a TV show without having significant input. Meanwhile, another valuable lesson learned about that same time was a more brutal one. On Halloween night 1964, in Elkhart, Indiana, the Smothers Brothers played a show at a high school auditorium, then found their exit blocked by police, who had been summoned by the local promoter, demanding a percentage of the night's souvenir programs—the proceeds of which were earmarked for the American Cancer Society. Tensions escalated, and one of the police officers hit Tom over the head with his flashlight, requiring nine stitches. Ken Fritz, the Smotherses' manager at the time, was knocked out with a blackjack, and he, Tom, and Dick were all arrested. For Tom, it triggered an epiphany: He had heard tales of police brutality aimed at minorities and protesters but thought they were exaggerated or one-sided until that night in Indiana, when he, as a white celebrity performer, experienced his own taste of helplessness at the hand of the authorities. "I didn't think of myself as a privileged white guy," he says now. "I just thought life was fair for everyone. And when that happened, I changed a lot."

Almost as soon as *The Smothers Brothers Show* aired its final episode, CBS asked the Smothers Brothers to return to the network—this time as stars of a variety show. One of its new fall shows had failed miserably in the ratings, and a variety show was the fastest type of series that could be generated from scratch and thrown on the air. Tom, still smarting from the sitcom debacle, said he'd only do it if he had creative control. CBS, desperate to come up with some substitute programming, agreed, and in February 1967 *The Smothers Brothers Comedy Hour* premiered on CBS, becoming an instant surprise hit.

The program was designed, at least initially, to appeal to multiple generations—to present Bette Davis on the same show as a new rock group called Buffalo Springfield, premiering its new song, "For What It's Worth," which wasn't even in the Top 40 when the show was taped. "Society was changing so rapidly," Tom Smothers recalls. "'For What It's Worth'—we presented that thing, and I didn't even understand how important that song was, and now it just resonates. It should be a national anthem. The truth was, the whole social changes swept me along. I happened to be on television. I had a platform, and I didn't think that you were supposed to, all of a sudden, check your ethics or your creative efforts at the door. That was from growing up in the forties and fifties, and we believed everything we ever heard: every man has a voice, freedom for everyone, free speech, express yourself, and all that. I bought it completely. When it first became shattered for me, it was more of a battle. I just hated bullies. I didn't like to be pushed around."

When *Comedy Hour* began, Tom wasn't sure what sort of show he wanted it to be ("We didn't have any models"). But when the network resisted some of the early sketches and ideas, including an Elaine May sketch on film censors that itself was censored by CBS, the path of most resistance became the direction Tom wanted to pursue. "What drove us into it," Tom says, "was CBS saying, 'You can't say this, you can't say that.' Because they said I couldn't do it, I wanted to fight harder to be able to."

Those fights soon became legendary and the pivot point for meaningful entertainment television of the 1960s. When the Smothers Brothers succeeded in pushing the envelope of what was allowed on TV in an entertainment program, the results were important and often amazing. They broke the seventeen-year prime-time blacklist of Pete Seeger, by battling successfully to bring him on to sing his new antiwar song, "Waist Deep in the Big Muddy." At the urging of the head writer, Mason Williams, they ran one of their repertory cast members, Pat Paulsen, for president of the United States and embarked on a lengthy, brilliant bit of performance art. They gave early TV exposure to the Who, Simon & Garfunkel, George Carlin, Glen Campbell, David Steinberg, and others and presented lots of skits, songs, and artistic pieces that addressed such topics as race, politics, war, women's liberation, and the generation gap. And when they were prevented from presenting some of those elements, Tom would go to the press to complain. Ultimately, CBS tired of the constant friction, found an excuse to fire the Smothers Brothers, and did so in 1969. But every variety series or topical comedy series that's come since, from NBC's *Rowan & Martin's Laugh-In* in the 1960s to HBO's *Real Time with Bill Maher,* owes a major debt to the battles, the integrity, and the sacrifices of Tom and Dick Smothers and company.

I owe a major debt as well. I was a young teenager when *The Smothers Brothers Comedy Hour* premiered in 1967, and it's one of my fondest memories associated with TV—and with my father. My dad, Virgil Bianculli, would come home from his work as a pharmacist each Sunday in time for us to have a quick dinner and play a best-of-three series of chess games. Whoever won got to control the TV for the night, so the games were tense, but whichever one of us got control of the dial, the Smothers Brothers were part of the deal. We both loved watching them, and I loved watching them with him (my dad adored, and resembled, Pat Paulsen). So imagine my delight, little more than a decade later, when my job as a TV critic allowed me to interview Tom and Dick Smothers, for the first of what has become dozens of times over the years. You could write a book about the history and importance of *The Smothers Brothers Comedy Hour*—and I did, in 2009, with the cooperation of Tom, Dick, Mason, and so many others involved with that envelope-pushing variety series. (For the record, it's called *Dangerously Funny: The Uncensored Story of "The Smothers Brothers Comedy Hour."*)

"I'm seventy-eight years old now," Tom says, "and I look back at it all, and I remember how passionate I was. But it's so quaint, when you put it in today's structure of ultimate 'free speak.' Now everybody has a megaphone, a television show, an Internet blog, a tweet; you can say anything you want. It's way past the point of the Tower of Babel. But it's babbling and babbling so much it's much harder to get to the truth now than it was then, it seems to me.

"We were considered really rude at the time," Tom recalls. "We were so polite. It's all relative, isn't it? It depends what the restrictions are, and the society you live in at a certain time. It's always just trying to push the edges as much as you can."

AMY SCHUMER

BORN: 1981, Manhattan, New York.

FIRST TV CREDIT: Stand-up comic, *Live at Gotham,* 2007, Comedy Central.

LANDMARK TV SERIES: Creator and star, *Inside Amy Schumer,* 2013– , Comedy Central.

OTHER MAJOR CREDITS: Movie: Screenwriter and star, *Trainwreck* (2015).

Amy Schumer was born recently enough in the TV continuum (1981, the same year as *Hill Street Blues*) to be part of the first home-video TV generation, for whom Saturday morning TV, and TV viewing in general, meant watching not only what was shown at those hours by the broadcast networks (and, by this point, some cable networks as well) but whatever your parents fed into the family VCR. On "live TV," viewed as the networks presented it, young Amy watched *Looney Tunes* with glee and, when she was a little older, would be "freaking out" watching Saturday morning's *Saved by the Bell.* Another early TV staple was the Nick at Nite lineup of vintage TV shows; she cites reruns of *I Love Lucy* as her first major example of nighttime TV "appointment viewing."

But Schumer's TV diet, as a child, also included being spoon-fed videotapes from the family's home library of recorded favorites, including the syndicated late-1970s *Muppet Show,* which she pointedly differentiates from PBS's *Sesame Street.* ("I was not a *Sesame Street* lover," she admits, laughing.) Her parents also provided her, at a very young age, with her first prolonged exposure to televised sketch comedy: recordings of the original, 1975–80 cast of *Saturday Night Live,* where she fell in love with Gilda Radner.

"Gilda was a really big deal to me," Schumer says. "Her doing the queen of France [one of the imagined 'guests' in a highly imaginative young girl's pretend straight-from-her-bedroom TV program, 'The Judy Miller Show'] and all of her characters—I just felt I wanted to see more and more of her." Years later, as Schumer was just entering her teens, she remembers enjoying watching Sarah Silverman during her 1993–94 *SNL* season. "I was definitely kind of drawn to the women," Schumer recalls. And after growing up watching *Saturday Night Live*, Schumer would appear on the show herself, as a guest host in 2015.

Another early comedy influence for Schumer is Mel Brooks—not for his inspired writing for *Your Show of Shows*, which she never saw, or even *Get Smart*, but for his movies, which were in heavy rotation in the Schumer family's VCR. "I am a huge Mel Brooks fan," Schumer says. "*Blazing Saddles* was huge in our house. *Spaceballs* was insanely huge in our house. *History of the World* . . . It's the stuff that we still quote. I probably quote Mel Brooks by accident at least once a day . . . I feel very, very influenced by the smartness but also the real silliness of him."

When I interviewed Mel Brooks on *Fresh Air* and asked him which of the current comics he enjoyed, one of the names he mentioned was Amy Schumer. "He's a really big deal to me," she says. "Him even mentioning me on that NPR interview really made me cry."

Her sketch comedy tastes, Schumer says, were formed, in part, by watching old episodes of *The Carol Burnett Show*, then, eventually, MTV's *State*, Dave Chappelle's *Chappelle's Show* on Comedy Central, and *In Living Color* on Fox. She made her own TV debut as a stand-up comic on Comedy Central's *Live at Gotham* showcase in 2007 and soon began racking up guest spots on a series of impressive and influential comedies: *30 Rock*, *Curb Your Enthusiasm*, *Girls*, and *Louie*. That meant working, early in her career, with Tina Fey, Larry David, Lena Dunham, Judd Apatow, and Louis C.K., and some of those relationships would build over time. Apatow would collaborate with Schumer on her 2015 breakout film *Trainwreck*, while Fey would be there to hand Schumer her Peabody Award for *Inside Amy Schumer*, as well as guest star on that series in one of its most memorable sketches.

"These people that have been my heroes have just encouraged me the whole time," Schumer says appreciatively. She had to audition for her *30 Rock* and *Curb* roles, but winning those parts meant a lot to her, as did shows of support such as when Conan O'Brien came to see her backstage after she appeared on one of his late-night talk shows. "He said, 'I want you to come back, and I encourage you to keep going.' That kind of encouragement is really meaningful to me . . . It makes me think I do have all this potential, and I really want to do everything I can with it.'"

She sees a definite evolution in TV roles for women, so much so, she says paradoxically, that the best roles for women these days aren't necessarily women's roles at all. "With shows like *Girls* and *Broad City*, it's not so much about how we're portraying women," she says. "It's more—human. They're just people! For them to not make such a deal about it being women is really exciting to me. I think they do it on *Girls*. They're just human beings that happen to be women, and I think that's a huge step in the right direction."

When Schumer finally got her chance to do her own series for Comedy Central, she started with a focused premise ("We were going to make a talk show about sex," she recalls), but the show, eventually titled *Inside Amy Schumer*, quickly evolved into several shows in one: man-on-the-street interviews, guest star interviews, extended sketches, and stand-up. "That makes four shows!" she says. And the format is loose enough to allow for everything from music videos with a subtext questioning the cultural definition of sexiness ("Milk Milk Lemonade"), to a full-episode black-and-white parody of the Golden Age TV drama and movie *12 Angry Men*, with a dozen men—played by such guest stars as Jeff Goldblum and Paul Giamatti—deciding whether Amy Schumer was attractive and desirable enough to have her own TV series. The extended sketch was called "12 Angry Men *Inside Amy Schumer*," and it followed all the main dramatic beats, and character types, of Reginald Rose's original story but with a sexist twist.

"The season before," Schumer explains, "I had written a sketch called 'Focus Group,' where it's like an actual focus group of guys and they're supposed to be saying whether they think the TV show's funny or not. But they're just kind of voting on whether or not they'd have sex with me . . .

"I love *The Twilight Zone*, so I thought, 'What's the *Twilight Zone* version of this? What would be the ultimate deliberation?' And I love the movie *12 Angry Men*, and I thought, 'Wow, what if we shot in black and white, with really great actors?' And once I had the idea, I was very excited." Casting, she says, was so much fun ("I just couldn't believe everybody said yes"), and she's understandably proud of the final result. "I will really take credit for that episode," she says, "because I was really on top of those characters; I knew which of them was married and everything else. And I was pissed I didn't win an Emmy for directing that ... because I worked harder on that than I worked on anything."

Another Season 3 landmark sketch, "Last Fuckable Day," imagines Amy Schumer happening upon an outdoor picnic where Julia Louis-Dreyfus is being celebrated by Tina Fey and Patricia Arquette to honor the passing of—well, you've read the sketch's title. Schumer is asked to join them, and the actresses explain the unstated but obvious transition of movie actresses from leading lady roles to something ... other. "In every actress's life," Louis-Dreyfus explains with matter-of-fact bluntness, "the media decides when you finally reach the point where you're not believably fuckable any-more." Fey adds, by way of example, "You know how Sally Field was Tom Hanks's love interest in *Punchline*? And then, like twenty minutes later, she was his mom in *Forrest Gump*?"

"That was just one of the best days ever," Schumer recalls. "We kind of just sat around that table most of the day and talked shit and laughed and connected, talked about injustices, talked about silly stuff. And then, when we were punching up the scene, watching their minds work, coming up with what would be the funniest thing. It was just a really special, special day, in a surreal setting, and it was one of the best days of my life."

4 SOAP OPERAS

KEY EVOLUTIONARY STAGES

Peyton Place	1964–69, ABC
Mary Hartman, Mary Hartman	1976–77, syndicated
Dallas	1978–91, CBS; 2012–14, TNT
Desperate Housewives	2004–12, ABC
Empire	2015–, Fox

When I think of soap operas, my first thoughts aren't of the daytime serials, sponsored by detergent and bath care manufacturers, that gave the genre its name. I think of the onslaught of the prime-time soap, when CBS's *Dallas*, in particular, led a frenzy of copycats, competitiveness, and increasingly campy and absurd stories and characters. I think of Larry Hagman's ruthless and scheming Texas oil baron, J. R. Ewing, who made being a villain seem so much more fun (and, in TV terms, lucrative) than being the hero. I think of that show's "Who shot J.R.?," the global phenomenon and guessing-game obsession that drilled deeply enough to tap a vein of interest so huge and so devoted it would prefigure the trending topics and fan-based mania of the Internet age. And I think, also, of the time, during the heyday of *Dallas* and the height of popularity of Hagman's J.R., when TV critics were invited to a day-into-night press party, hosted by Hagman at his Malibu beach house. Stories and liquor flowed freely, but the toilets didn't—a problem that was solved when Hagman's next-door neighbor opened his doors to the over-flow crowd. That neighbor was Burgess Meredith, and it was one of the early nights on the TV critics' press tour when I discovered my chosen profession had occasional perks that were unimaginable and irreplaceable. At the same time, though, another discovery was made: a TV reporter for the *New York Post* was caught rummaging through Hagman's underwear drawer. So much, for the most part, for lavish parties hosted at celebrity homes. But everything has its moment, and that includes press parties and, it seems, soap operas.

On radio, the soap opera genre began in the 1930s, with a series of fifteen-minute weekday shows, both local (1930's *Painted Dreams,* on Chicago's WGN) and national (1931's *Clara, Lu, and Em,* on NBC)—equally forgettable and, by now, largely forgotten. Only one popular radio soap opera survived long enough to make a successful transition to daytime television: *The Guiding Light.* An NBC Radio soap launched in 1937, it moved to CBS Radio a decade later, then jumped to the CBS television network in 1952 and remained on the air until 2009, an overall run of seventy-two years. It was created and written by Irna Phillips, who also created the other super-tenured daytime soap, CBS's *As the World Turns,* which premiered on TV in 1956 and survived until 2010, a healthy life span of fifty-four years. These and other long-running daytime soaps were passed down like family treasures from one generation to the next: essay papers assigned to my college students, on their first favorite TV series memories, invariably contain examples of daughters being introduced to beloved soap operas by their mothers—a private little viewing ritual the daughters brought with them to college.

For daytime soaps on television, the genre began with NBC's *These Are My Children* in 1949 and peaked in number at the end of the 1960s, when nineteen different serials were shown weekdays on the three broadcast networks. One of those was ABC's *Dark Shadows,* a multiple-genre weekday series that managed to be a soap opera and a supernatural series, featuring vampires, witches, and time travel, all at the same time. Jonathan Frid starred as the conflicted vampire Barnabas Collins in a cult hit produced by Dan Curtis and eventually remade as a movie directed by Tim Burton, starring Johnny Depp. The daytime soap peaked in popularity in the 1980s, with the 1981 wedding of Luke and Laura on ABC's *General Hospital.* In an opulent ceremony, Laura (Genie Francis) married Luke (Anthony Geary), her former rapist, with the *General Hospital* fan Elizabeth Taylor in attendance (playing the evil Helena Cassidine, a role Taylor-made for the occasion). An estimated thirty million TV viewers witnessed that wedding, making it the most popular daytime soap opera episode ever televised. By 2016, the daytime soap opera had dwindled to the point that only four examples remained on the broadcast networks. The durable *General Hospital* was one, NBC's *Days of Our Lives* (which began in 1965 with the opening tagline "Like sands through the hourglass, so are the days of our lives") was another, and the remaining two, the relative newcomers, belonged to CBS: *The Young and the Restless* (begun in 1973) and *The Bold and the Beautiful* (begun in 1987). Prime time, however, was another (serialized) story entirely.

The first evening soap opera on television appeared back during network TV's infancy, on the long-defunct DuMont network. It was called *Faraway Hill* and was televised live, once a week, for the last three months of 1946. Scripts and still pictures survive (Flora Campbell played a New York widow who moved back to her family's small town and fell in love), but footage does not: The kinescope system of preserving TV images, the industry's only way of recording live TV shows until the 1956 advent of videotape, wasn't implemented until 1947, and it was barely acceptable, producing a murky recorded image that looked bleached out, partly out of focus, and partly underwater. (If you've ever seen old Golden Age recordings of *Marty* or *Requiem for a Heavyweight,* those are kinescopes.) Quite quickly, TV soaps became relegated to the daytime hours as other genres began to proliferate during the evening. After the 1940s, no soap opera would be televised in prime time until the mid-1960s, when the struggling ABC network, eager to attract viewers in almost any way possible, decided in 1964 to adapt a steamy Grace Metalious best seller that had already been made into a controversial 1957 movie starring Lana Turner and to present it as a twice-a-week prime-time soap opera, with new serialized installments shown every Tuesday and Thursday. That series, and its success, ended up changing the industry and having an eventual but meaningful effect on the evolution of quality TV.

PEYTON PLACE

1964–69, ABC. Creator: Paul Monash. Stars: Barbara Parkins, Ed Nelson, Ryan O'Neal, Mia Farrow, Dorothy Malone, Christopher Connelly.

Peyton Place came about because the TV writer-producer Paul Monash, whose credits had included the pilot for ABC's *Untouchables* and several Golden Age dramas for *Playhouse 90* and other anthology series, had noted the success in the U.K. of *Coronation Street*, a 1960 soap opera about working-class people in Manchester, England. *Coronation Street* was shown at night, twice weekly, instead of during the day, and was an instant hit. Monash, as an enterprising producer, suggested to ABC that the network import the series intact and televise it the same way. ABC was intrigued by the concept but put off by the thick British accents, so the network suggested Monash oversee the development of an American counterpart and proposed the Grace Metalious best seller, *Peyton Place*, as the source material. Monash had grander visions; he avoided or altered the more salacious parts of the original story line and refused to describe his series as a soap opera, preferring the loftier term "television novel." (Borrowed, no doubt, from other countries also, because the concept of the telenovela—a self-contained, limited-run soap opera—had been a popular Latin American TV genre since the 1950s.)

A soap opera by any other name, though, would attract the same target audience anyway. Denying the genre's roots and intent was ingenuous at best, for Monash even consulted Irna Phillips, the prolific writer-producer behind *Guiding Light, As the World Turns,* and *Days of Our Lives,* to help shape *Peyton Place* in proper form and tone for TV. Another thing he did, which was much more unexpected and meaningful, was to seek output from less credentialed writers as well. The *Peyton Place* writing staff included young writers, women, and, in time, writers of color, at a time when all of those subsets had difficulties finding steady writing work. (By the time *Peyton Place* left the air in 1969, its small town had been integrated on camera as well.) And *Peyton Place* was definitely steady work, because, as a prime-time soap, or "television novel," it was presented twice weekly without reruns and without a summer break. For a period, after it hit big, ABC greedily programmed it three times a week.

And *Peyton Place* did indeed hit it big, immediately. It was the first prime-time soap opera smash in TV history, and at its zenith all three weekly installments were planted firmly in the Top 5. Ryan O'Neal and Mia Farrow, as the show's initial young lovers, shot to stardom immediately. (Farrow left the show in 1966 to marry Frank Sinatra, proving that even in the soap opera genre, truth could be stranger than fiction.) But it wasn't the substance of *Peyton Place*, or its breakout cast, that was so important. It was the form.

Before *Peyton Place,* U.S. drama series, in the evening hours, were like individual playing cards. Episodes of *Dragnet* or *Perry Mason* could be watched and enjoyed in any order, without any regard to continuity or a continuing story arc. After *Peyton Place,* things were different. ABC repeated the same serialized, twice-a-week gimmick in 1966, just as successfully, with its campy *Batman* series. And fifteen years after that, in a bold experiment that would affect virtually all quality TV dramas to come, NBC incorporated the serialized prime-time story concept into a new, truly revolutionary cop series, *Hill Street Blues.* Fittingly, two of that show's stars—Daniel J. Travanti as Frank Furillo and James B. Sikking as Howard Hunter—had previously spent time as cast members on *General Hospital,* so they were familiar with the "television novel" approach.

Peyton Place brought the soap opera genre to prime time in attention-getting style, even if one of its breakout young stars, Mia Farrow, didn't stay around for long.

MARY HARTMAN, MARY HARTMAN

1976–77, syndicated. Developer: Norman Lear. Creators: Gail Parent,
Ann Marcus, Jerry Adelman, Daniel Gregory Browne. Stars: Louise Lasser,
Greg Mullavey, Mary Kay Place, Graham Jarvis, Dody Goodman, Dabney
Coleman, Martin Mull.

Norman Lear, by 1975, was in as powerful a position as a TV producer
could be. His breakout hit sitcom, *All in the Family* on CBS, had been the
most popular television show in the country for four years running. Two
other CBS sitcoms created by Lear—*Sanford and Son* and *Maude*—also
ended the 1974–75 season in the Top 10. Seemingly, Lear could do whatever
he wanted next, but even though the CBS executive Fred Silverman happily
financed Lear's next pet project, and loved the result, he told Lear there was
no way he could, or would, show it on CBS. So Lear, with all his connections
and clout, took the pilot of *Mary Hartman, Mary Hartman* to individual
TV stations and sold it locally, market by market, building his own ad hoc
network of more than a hundred stations willing to televise a late-night,
five-times-a-week soap opera spoof.

Lear's novel concept was to do for the soap opera form what *Married . . .
with Children* and *Roseanne* would later do for the family sitcom: take a
genre commonly set in middle-class homes or higher and put it, and lampoon it, in a working-class setting. Lear wanted to poke fun at consumerism
and chauvinism, and he and the comedy writer and novelist Gail Parent,
a staff writer for the first six seasons of *The Carol Burnett Show,* came up
with some intentionally outrageous opening stories: the suburban housewife Mary Hartman, living a life of quiet desperation in the fictional town
of Fernwood, Ohio, would obsess over the "waxy yellow buildup" on her
linoleum kitchen floors, while her neighborhood was being terrorized, separately, by a mass murderer and a flasher, and her husband, to her dismay,
was both lethargic and impotent. These very broad concepts were fleshed
out by the show's appointed head writer, Ann Marcus, who had formerly
served as a head writer on two actual soap operas: CBS's *Love Is a Many
Splendored Thing* (another Irna Phillips daytime soap creation), and ABC's
prime-time breakthrough, *Peyton Place.* Marcus contacted two other former writers from *Splendored Thing,* Jerry Adelman and Daniel Gregory
Browne, and together they fleshed out a guide for the first month's worth

Mary Hartman, Mary Hartman was Norman Lear's bold TV experiment: a satire of soap operas presented in the identical once-daily format, starring Louise Lasser and Greg Mullavey as a generally unhappy Ohio couple.

of proposed plotlines. The last core person to come aboard to realize Lear's vision was the actress Joan Darling, whom Lear was encouraging to try her hand at directing. When Mary Hartman was cast, with the Woody Allen featured actress Louise Lasser (*Take the Money and Run, Bananas*) in the leading role, Darling did just that. The finished *Mary Hartman, Mary Hartman* pilot didn't get picked up by CBS, but it was good enough to get Darling hired by James L. Brooks for her first televised directorial credit, helming what many have called the funniest sitcom episode of all time: the 1975 "Chuckles Bites the Dust" installment of *The Mary Tyler Moore Show*.

When Lear's cobbled-together "network" of local stations bought and broadcast his *Mary Hartman, Mary Hartman* series in 1976, it immediately generated national attention for its bizarrely toned lampoon. The show had no laugh track, and some of the scenes were almost uncomfortably tense, especially the intimate marital conversations between Lasser's Mary and her husband, Greg Mullavey's Tom. The real soap opera roots of the show's writers helped them play those notes and dare to talk about and show things that even actual soaps would not.

The writers of *Mary Hartman* also knew how to play, and play around with, familiar genre tropes, such as when Mary's country-music-singing neighbor Loretta, a happy housewife played by Mary Kay Place, got amnesia and ended up in another town, with a new identity as a flirtatious waitress named Lulu. Characters slipped into comas or discovered each other being unfaithful. Often these scenes, especially the ones about betrayal or being unfulfilled, were painted with an undercurrent of palpable pain or unhappiness. And then suddenly, for every genuinely touching moment of angst or existential dread, there followed a moment of pure, inspired absurdity, such as when a mildly sedated and drunken neighbor fell asleep, facedown, in a bowl of Mary's chicken soup and drowned. Or when Garth Gimble, a misogynist wife beater played by Martin Mull, met an untimely end by being accidentally impaled on an aluminum Christmas tree. There was more in store for Mull even after that, though: Lear liked the comedian so much that when *Mary Hartman, Mary Hartman* ended, he showcased Mull in a 1977–78 spin-off series sold in syndication to the same existing network of local stations. Initially, it was a summer replacement called *Fernwood 2Night*, conceived as a local talk show from and about Fernwood, Ohio. The host, played by Mull, was Barth Gimble, the smarmy but less violent twin brother of the late Garth, and his TV sidekick was the amiably clueless Jerry Hubbard, played by the hilarious Fred Willard. The following year, the same actors and characters starred on *America 2Night*, a "national" version of the same talk show. The two talk-show spin-offs, together, were direct ancestors of subsequent talk-show spoofs—most obviously and impressively, HBO's *Larry Sanders Show*. The parent program, though, opened up the soap opera to a new, late-night venue and, at the same time, to satire on a much higher level than even that classic recurring sketch on *The Carol Burnett Show*, portions of which were undoubtedly written by *Mary Hartman*'s co-creator Gail Parent: "As the Stomach Churns."

As for the idea of a full-bore, full-length continuing spoof of the soap opera genre, the concept of *Mary Hartman, Mary Hartman* was about to be continued, and in every sense broadened, by ABC's *Soap*, a controversial, laugh-track-laden Top 20 hit. It was an intentionally absurd, over-the-top soap satire about the families of two sisters—one wealthy, one working-class. Plots involved alien visitation, cloning, and demonic possession, as well as commonplace affairs, murder, and amnesia. Among the cast, notable standouts included Richard Mulligan as the working-class husband; Robert

Guillaume as Benson, the insolent and sarcastic African-American butler to the wealthy family, who eventually got his own spin-off sitcom, *Benson;* and Billy Crystal as Jodie Dallas, television's first openly gay character in a weekly prime-time TV series. Soap operas, though, were about to make an even bigger splash, not as spoofs, or by giving voice to minorities and alternative lifestyles, but by returning to prime time and taking the genre much more seriously.

DALLAS

1978–91, CBS. Creator: David Jacobs. Stars: Larry Hagman, Patrick Duffy, Linda Gray, Barbara Bel Geddes, Ken Kercheval, Victoria Principal, Charlene Tilton, Priscilla Presley, Mary Crosby.

Before CBS's *Dallas* burst onto the scene in 1978, the most recent prime-time soaps to end a season in the Top 10 were ABC's hit *Rich Man, Poor Man* miniseries in 1976 and, before that, *Peyton Place* in 1965. The popularity of the TV adaptation of *Rich Man, Poor Man,* which held the miniseries viewing record until the same network's *Roots* shattered it a year later, made the networks take another look at this long-neglected prime-time programming genre. One producer, David Jacobs, pitched an idea to CBS about a soap opera set in a suburban cul-de-sac. The network had another idea and pitched it back to Jacobs: the network had Linda Evans under contract and wanted to develop a modern Western for her about a poor young woman who marries the son of a wealthy Texas oil and cattle baron. Jacobs wrote a pilot script and called it *Dallas*—and even though Evans's part of sweet young Pam Ewing ended up going to Victoria Principal instead, the rest of *Dallas* arrived on CBS virtually intact—and by the end of its first season it was one of the most popular TV series in the country. Shortly after *Dallas* arrived, so did the Ronald Reagan presidency, and *Dallas* was such a resounding international hit that in many foreign countries importing the series, the United States was epitomized by Larry Hagman's J. R. Ewing, the villain you loved to hate: wealthy, ruthless, duplicitous, with excessive appetites and a paucity of scruples and conscience. And CBS couldn't get enough. Jacobs was asked if it were possible to revive his soap opera cul-de-sac idea as a spin-off of *Dallas* somehow, and presto: *Knots Landing,* starring

Ted Shackelford as the black-sheep Ewing brother Gary, premiered in 1979 and ran until 1993, outlasting even its parent program.

Back at the ranch, on that parent program, J.R. had an alcoholic wife (Linda Gray's Sue Ellen) and juggled several mistresses, including Sue Ellen's own sister, Kristin (played by Mary Crosby). J.R.'s primary adversary throughout the series, Ken Kercheval's Cliff Barnes, was about as cunning and credible as Wile E. Coyote on *The Road Runner* and, over the long run, about as effective. But to be fair, J.R. ran roughshod over just about anyone in his path, including his little brother Bobby, played by Patrick Duffy. Bobby, like his new bride, Pam, was as sweet as J.R. was scheming and was another easy target. It wasn't until J.R. himself became the target, though, that *Dallas* shot into the pop-culture stratosphere. To end the 1979–80 TV season, and the third season of *Dallas,* the writers had J. R. Ewing shot by

Dallas proved that the purported villain of a drama could be the most popular element. In this case, it was ruthless oil baron J. R. Ewing, played by Larry Hagman (right).

an unidentified assailant. Prime-time TV was no stranger to cliff-hangers: *Peyton Place, Batman,* and even the "Rocky & Bullwinkle" segments of *The Bullwinkle Show* had used them constantly. But this particular plot twist, coming at the end of a season, ignited an unprecedented amount of interest from the public and the media alike. During the summer months of 1980, with *Dallas* on hiatus, the national conversation turned to suspects in the "Who shot J.R.?" case: that August, *Time* magazine even put a drawing of Hagman's J. R. Ewing on the cover, with the all-caps headline "WHO-DUNIT?"

Whodunit turned out to be Kristin, his own sister-in-law, and when her identity as J.R.'s assailant was revealed, in the third episode of the fourth season of *Dallas,* it became front-page news, including the front page of my newspaper at the time, the *Fort Lauderdale News/Sun-Sentinel,* where I began my Saturday, November 22, 1980, story by writing, "Okay, okay, so Kristin shot J.R.," followed immediately by "Can we all go back to acting normal now?" and complaining, "The way the momentum of *Dallas* has been building, last night's culprit-revealing episode would have outrated a documentary disclosing *Who Shot J.F.K.*" (Probably not the most tastefully timed remark, considering, as I do now, that it was printed, by coincidence, on the exact seventeenth anniversary of John F. Kennedy's assassination.) When ratings were released later that week, the "Who shot J.R.?" episode of *Dallas* was estimated at having reached an unprecedented 53.3 Nielsen rating, meaning that more than half of all homes with TV sets were tuned to *Dallas.* And the audience share, measuring the homes whose TVs were in use at that hour, was even higher, at an estimated 76 percent. "CBS estimates its most recent *Dallas* installment was watched by approximately 83 million people," I wrote then, noting that this hour of *Dallas* was, at the time, the highest-rated program in the history of television. "Add one more million," I continued, "and you've got the total number of voters who participated in the 1980 presidential election."

The show's massive audience record was eventually toppled, three years later, by the series finale of CBS's *M*A*S*H.* From that point on, though, season-ending cliff-hangers became common, and all but required, on continuing drama series and even on a high percentage of comedies. Fox's *Simpsons,* in 1995, managed simultaneously to parody "Who shot J.R.?" and to reap big ratings rewards with a two-part cliff-hanger parody called "Who Shot Mr. Burns?" And while NBC's *Hill Street Blues* deserves credit for taking the *Dallas*-style episodic story line and applying it to a genre other than the soap opera, *Dallas* is the chief source for prime-time television's cliff-hanger mania. It's also responsible for the exponentially increased value of colorful TV antagonists, as well as the chief inspiration for something it might prefer not to claim: the infamous "dream season." At the end of the 1985 TV season, Patrick Duffy declined to extend his contract with *Dallas*, and writers obliged by killing his beloved Bobby Ewing character in a car crash, making Victoria Principal's Pam a widow. But after a year of sagging ratings, *Dallas* hit the reset button, by having Pam wake up to see Bobby, very much alive, lathering up in their shower. The entire 1985–86 season, including Bobby's death, had been a bad dream of Pam's, and now that she was awake, *Dallas* could go on the way it should have, with the previous year's events effectively wiped away. (Effectively, but problematically: There had been crossover characters and plots that season from the sister spin-off series, *Knots Landing*, whose narrative had not been rebooted.) The *Dallas* "dream season" was so absurd, and so instantly iconic, it was alluded to, playfully, in the final episodes of both *St. Elsewhere* and *Newhart*, in which those entire series were dismissed as dreams. Meanwhile, other shows, and networks, had dreams of following in the footsteps of *Dallas*, even though they proved to be very big boots to fill.

Once *Dallas* topped the ratings in 1980–81, other prime-time soaps were certain to follow, and did. The official spin-off, *Knots Landing*, was two years old by then, but new ones quickly joined it. In 1981 alone, three high-profile soaps joined the networks' evening schedules—one from each commercial broadcast network. NBC presented *Flamingo Road*, based on the 1949 Joan Crawford movie and featuring Morgan Fairchild in her breakout role as a sexy, villainous vixen. CBS added yet another entry in the genre with 1981's *Falcon Crest*, starring Jane Wyman as a wealthy matriarch, and ABC countered the same year with *Dynasty*, which eventually surpassed *Dallas* not only as TV's most popular soap but as TV's most popular series, period, in 1984–85. By the end of that season, four sudsy series ranked in the Top 10: *Dynasty* in first place, *Dallas* second, *Knots Landing* ninth, and *Falcon Crest* tied for tenth. A lot of their popularity was due to their attention-getting antagonists: J. R. Ewing had proven the value of that beyond doubt, and other prime-time soaps either began with or made room for their own utterly amoral bad guys or gals. *Knots Landing* surged even higher in the ratings once Donna Mills was added as the neighborhood home wrecker

Abby. Linda Evans, who had lost out on starring as the good girl in *Dallas*, got to play a similar role as one of the stars of *Dynasty* but saw her thunder stolen by the second-season addition of Joan Collins as the evil Alexis. Just as blatantly as presenting a female J.R. in Alexis, *Dynasty* also borrowed shamelessly from the *Dallas* playbook for season finale cliff-hangers and in 1986 presented a royal wedding, attacked by gun-toting revolutionaries in the Eastern European region of Moldavia, that ended the season by placing virtually all the leading characters squarely in the line of fire, as a hail of bullets from every direction riddled the church. Critics instantly dubbed it the "Moldavian massacre," but the next fall almost everyone walked out alive.

These prime-time soaps and others like them, just as their daytime counterparts, demonstrated a strong appeal among young adult viewers, who enjoyed, rather than recoiled from, the more over-the-top plotlines and characters. Naturally, the much-coveted young demographic got its own soaps, even in prime time, but when those shows arrived, they took the problems of their young characters seriously and showed that high schoolers and college students fell in and out of love and had other pressures just like adults. In the United States, the first and best of these arrived even before *Dallas*, with NBC's 1977 television movie and series *James at 15*, starring Lance Kerwin as James, a teenager whose inner thoughts and fantasies were visualized, an approach later employed by David E. Kelley on his unashamedly soapy law comedy-drama, *Ally McBeal*. For the record, because *James at 15* has been largely and unfairly forgotten, it should be noted that its protagonist was the first teenager on TV to lose his or her virginity. But eventually, after *Dallas*, youth soap operas became a subgenre of their own, commonly presented by fledgling fourth (and fifth) networks scrambling to survive by appealing to the young demographic.

In 1990, Aaron Spelling, the executive producer behind *Dynasty*, hired a young writer-producer named Darren Star to create a soap about teens going to school in the most impressive zip code in Southern California. That series, *Beverly Hills, 90210*, started the 1990s craze of teen soaps, which continued with an official Fox spin-off, 1992's *Melrose Place*. Not only was *Melrose Place* a "traditional" soap in title, by echoing the title *Peyton Place*, it was one in its emphasis on evil and bizarre behavior as well. *Melrose Place* went from interesting diversion to watercooler sensation once Heather Locklear, a *Dynasty* veteran, was added to the cast as the apartment-complex temptress Amanda. Later, when Marcia Cross's mentally unhinged Kimberly literally flipped her wig, *Melrose Place* became the latest soap opera media sensation. And there were other shows, each hitting its own patch of young-demo zeitgeist, including 1998's *Felicity*, starring Keri Russell as a college student, a series co-created by a then-unknown writer-director named J. J. Abrams. *Felicity* was shown by the WB, as was, the same year, another teen soap, *Dawson's Creek*, starring James Van Der Beek, Katie Holmes, Joshua Jackson, and Michelle Williams and created by Kevin Williamson. Those prime-time soaps were all the rage as the twentieth century ended, but shortly after the twenty-first century began, "adults" reclaimed the prime-time soap, with a surprise hit series from ABC that managed to be funny, sexy, relevant, addictive, relatable, and a Top 10 hit, often at the same time.

DESPERATE HOUSEWIVES

2004–12, ABC. Creator: Marc Cherry. Stars: Teri Hatcher, Felicity Huffman, Marcia Cross, Eva Longoria, Nicollette Sheridan, James Denton, Doug Savant, Ricardo Chavira, Jesse Metcalfe.

Before Marc Cherry wrote his *Desperate Housewives* script and sold it to ABC, he had written eleven episodes of NBC's *Golden Girls* sitcom, which served him well by teaching him not only how to write for very different, very vocal female characters but how to find and mine the humor in various conflicts and situations. It was the perfect training ground for *Desperate Housewives*, which somehow drew laughs, and struck chords, by presenting mothers who were worn out by raising their kids, single parents trying to restart their own lives, and a pampered married woman reclaiming her youth by flirting with the underage neighborhood gardener. It had the dark humor of *Mary Hartman, Mary Hartman*—so much so that its opening scene was of a truly desperate housewife, narrating and describing, in flashback, her own successful suicide.

Desperate Housewives had its male heartthrobs, like James Denton as the hunky neighbor Mike Delfino, and its female troublemakers, like Nicollette Sheridan's Edie, but the real strength and appeal of this show came from the quartet of beautiful, talented actresses playing loyal neighborhood friends:

Teri Hatcher as the insecure Susan, Felicity Huffman (the only star cast member to win an Emmy for her work on the show) as the harried Lynette, Eva Longoria as the spoiled Gabrielle, and Marcia Cross, formerly of *Melrose Place*, as the "perfect" homemaker Bree. *Desperate Housewives* was female empowerment on a grand scale, a series that, like *The Golden Girls*, was dominated by outspoken, interesting women who, in every conversation, would pass the Bechdel test with ease. The season it premiered, *Desperate Housewives* shot into the top tier of TV's most popular shows, behind only CBS's crime procedural *CSI: Crime Scene Investigation* and Fox's singing-competition reality series, *American Idol*. And more female-centric soaps, with and without a comic slant, followed right behind.

Desperate Housewives became an immediate hit for ABC, in no small part because of its initial company of leading ladies (from left, Nicollette Sheridan, Felicity Huffman, Marcia Cross, Eva Longoria, and Teri Hatcher).

. . .

ABC's *Grey's Anatomy,* created by Shonda Rhimes in 2005, was a medical drama (and will be discussed in that chapter), but one that, like NBC's massively popular *ER*—a hit from the mid-1990s that was still around a decade later—had large elements and plots that were pure soap opera. Rhimes, in fact, has since built an entire career, not to mention an entire night of ABC programming, around dramas of various genres that are part soap opera in both tone and structure and that feature at their center strong, resilient female characters. Ellen Pompeo's Meredith Grey fits that profile, as do several other prominent women on *Grey's Anatomy,* but it's also just as true, more recently, of other Rhimes-created heroines. And the leading ladies of her subsequent series would score points for race as well as gender, providing compelling, complicated roles, and role models, for African-American women. In ABC's *Scandal,* premiering in 2012, Kerry Washington plays Olivia Pope, a Beltway crisis fixer who, by the third season, had been publicly linked with the show's president of the United States, her former employer and longtime secret lover. And in yet another ABC drama with Rhimes as executive producer, 2014's *How to Get Away with Murder,* Viola Davis plays a brilliant criminal defense law professor, Annalise Keating, who's fiercely protective of her inner circle of law students, and just fierce, period. In 2015, Davis became the first African-American woman to win the prime-time Emmy Award for Outstanding Leading Actress in a Drama Series.

None of the Rhimes-generated ABC shows were purely soap operas, but other shows premiering since 2000 have a much clearer lineage, though sometimes those lineages are themselves surprising or unusual. *Ugly Betty,* starring America Ferrera as Betty Suarez, a smart but plain-looking young woman who works in the ultra-vain fashion industry, was a hit for ABC in 2006 but, before that, in 1999, was a hit in the country of Colombia, in its original telenovela incarnation as *Yo soy Betty, la fea* (I am Betty, the ugly one). The creator of *Desperate Housewives,* Marc Cherry, concocted another prime-time soap—this time a comedy-drama focusing on Latina maids who work for wealthy Beverly Hills employers. Called *Devious Maids,* it premiered in 2013 on the Lifetime cable network. Also premiering on cable, on TNT in 2012, was *Dallas,* a next-generation remake of the original CBS soap opera hit. It starred Josh Henderson and the *Desperate Housewives* teen hunk Jesse Metcalfe as the respective sons of J. R. and Bobby Ewing, and this new *Dallas* distinguished itself by reuniting, as series regulars, the original

J.R. and Bobby, Larry Hagman and Patrick Duffy, as well as Linda Gray, who played Sue Ellen. The new *Dallas* did not distinguish itself with its writing or directing, however, and after Hagman died in 2012, the series limped to the end of its third and final season. A more fitting testament to the memory of the original *Dallas* was ABC's *Blood & Oil,* a 2015 drama starring Don Johnson as a wealthy, somewhat unscrupulous oil-business patriarch in modern-day North Dakota—as clear a pure prime-time soap opera, and as close to a remake of the original *Dallas*'s conflicts and charisma, as you could get. But it didn't come close to capturing the public's attention, or surviving past its inaugural season.

However, if you were looking for stellar charisma and incendiary conflict, especially in a soap opera showcasing minority characters—and apparently, at this point in 2015, millions of people were looking for exactly that—there was one place to turn, and viewers turned there with quickly noted enthusiasm.

EMPIRE

2015–, Fox. Creators: Lee Daniels, Danny Strong. Stars: Terrence Howard, Taraji P. Henson, Bryshere Y. Gray, Jussie Smollett, Trai Byers.

The creators of *Empire*, Lee Daniels and Danny Strong, are an unlikely duo. The writer, producer, and director Daniels, who is black, comes from the world of cinema, with such sensitive and probing dramas, and African-American showcases, as *Monster's Ball, Precious,* and *Lee Daniels' The Butler.* The actor and writer Strong, who is white, played geeky Jonathan on *Buffy the Vampire Slayer,* among many other supporting roles, before turning to screenwriting. He wrote the excellent HBO election television movies *Recount* and *Game Change,* then wrote *Lee Daniels' The Butler,* which Daniels directed. After that, they reteamed to co-create *Empire,* the culmination of the entire history of prime-time soap operas.

Empire is set in the world of hip-hop, with music fueling the passions of its characters as well as the sales charts on iTunes. Terrence Howard plays Lucious Lyon, a music mogul with three grown sons vying for control of the family company and with a bitter ex-wife, out of prison and out for revenge. The wife, Cookie Lyon, is played by Taraji P. Henson, whose emotional outbursts are as colorful and entertaining as her wardrobe choices. Cookie was this show's early breakout character—its Alexis on *Dynasty,* its J.R. on *Dallas*—and viewers fell in love with her, and with *Empire,* in dedicated and almost unprecedented fashion. For the first season of *Empire,* the show's audience increased each and every week, which no TV series, new or old, has accomplished since they started tracking such things. Give the actors credit, because they all commit fully to their characters and situations—Howard and Henson especially. But credit, also, the fast and furious pace of the story lines: one reason to be such a loyal viewer is that you don't want to miss the latest Cookie outburst or shocking plot twist or have it spoiled on social media before you get a chance to see it for yourself. Credit, too, the music, which is produced with enough professionalism and talent to sell millions of downloads—as with such successful TV hits, in other genres, as *Glee, American Idol,* and *Nashville.* Celebrity guest stars, in cameo or recurring roles, are another key ingredient.

They all add up to a prime-time soap opera whose success means so, so much. Not only for Howard and Henson, who toiled for years before landing these juicy roles. (Henson was nominated for an Outstanding Lead Actress in a Drama Series Emmy in 2015, the year Viola Davis won for *How*

Empire was another instant hit in the soap opera genre, centered around the fiery performances of Taraji P. Henson as Cookie and Terrence Howard as Lucious Lyon.

to Get Away with Murder.) Not only for the soap opera genre, which will benefit from the predictable rush of other networks and producers to emulate its success. *Empire* is important, most of all, because it's a predominantly minority-populated drama series, telling often tricky stories about sexual identity and family loyalties and doing it in a way that makes race and racial identity an important element of the narrative and musical soundtrack yet invites in, rather than alienates, a wider audience. In drama genres across the board, the soap opera has given us two of the most significant elements of quality series in the Platinum Age of Television: novelistic narratives and compelling antiheroes. Diversity, in character and in casting, is another increasingly emerging key factor, and *Empire,* from day one, has proudly possessed and displayed them all.

CRIME

KEY EVOLUTIONARY STAGES

Hill Street Blues	1981–87, NBC
NYPD Blue	1993–2005, ABC
The Sopranos	1999–2007, HBO
The Shield	2002–8, FX
Breaking Bad	2008–13, AMC

No genre in television has a more complicated evolutionary history than the crime drama. It was present in the earliest days of TV, has been present throughout, and has undergone such a dynamic metamorphosis that basic elements of the form have been stretched, challenged, even reversed. What started as morality plays about good versus evil, with both sides clearly delineated, changed slowly but surely into gray areas, on both sides of the law: good guys with some bad traits, and bad guys with some identifiable and even laudable ones. Crime dramas went from focusing on the law-enforcement investigators to the criminals themselves, and the best of them, like AMC's *Breaking Bad*, dramatized their own studies of criminal evolution: How and why does a good person go bad and cross that line from model citizen to brazen lawbreaker?

The modern evolutionary chain in the crime genre begins with NBC's *Hill Street Blues* in 1981 and continues through *Breaking Bad* more than twenty-five years later—a period in which cops struggled to be good or didn't even try and sympathetic villains had as many problems with their real families as with their crime families. But decades before that, there was an earlier, more primitive evolutionary chain as well. It's one that started with the somber, no-nonsense case-files approach of NBC's *Dragnet* in 1951, spread to the on-location realism and dynamism of ABC's *Naked City* in 1958, glorified in the violence and villainy dramatized on ABC's *Untouchables* in 1959, established the continuing-narrative story form and the sympathy for the accused murderer in ABC's *Fugitive* in 1963, and presented a reversal of the mystery form, where the crime was solved at the start and the story was more of a character-driven chess match between detective and killer, in NBC's *Columbo,* first introduced in 1968. That's a lot of change in one genre, and in the crime genre that was only the half of it.

Arguably, TV's first crime drama emerged from the same place as many of the era's most notorious gangsters: the city of Chicago. In 1947, a local television series called *The Chicagoland Mystery Players* presented weekly stories in which the police officer Jeffrey Hall, played by Gordon Urquhart, investigated the case by examining the crime scene, questioning witnesses, and interrogating the chief suspects. But on that local Chicago TV show, he never solved a single case; viewers were instructed to refer to the next day's *Chicago Tribune,* the show's sponsor, in which the resolution of the story would be printed on the same page as the fledgling TV listings. The DuMont network picked up the series for a national run in 1949, but with the ending dramatized and included as part of the program. DuMont's *Chicagoland Mystery Players* lasted only a year but was quickly followed by one of the biggest, most influential crime dramas ever made.

Dragnet, created by Jack Webb, had begun as an NBC Radio drama in June 1949, a few months before *Chicagoland* made the move to the national DuMont TV network. Webb was a true auteur, a multi-hyphenate who not only starred in his radio show, as the Los Angeles homicide detective Joe Friday, but was director, producer, and lead writer as well. He carried that same work ethic, and those same duties, when he accepted NBC's offer to adapt *Dragnet* to TV in 1951—first as a successful pilot preview, then as its own series in 1952. The way Webb worked had lasting ramifications for the future of TV in general and crime shows in particular. His sources for most story ideas were the case files from the LAPD, which he dramatized with a by-the-book, "Just the facts, ma'am" staccato of dialogue-heavy exposition. Webb filmed in L.A., not New York, which occasionally allowed him to shoot exteriors, and set up a West Coast base of operations that, as with *I Love Lucy* for comedy, would blaze a trail followed by countless others. Webb was cost conscious and assembly-line-like in his approach to shooting, often photographing two-person scenes so each person could read cue cards rather than memorize dialogue and stockpiling random exteriors and traveling shots so voice-over narration (often replacing otherwise expensive dialogue scenes) could be inserted later. The postwar 1950s sensibility was perfectly attuned to, and accepting of, the reassuring workmanship, victories, and authoritative credibility projected by *Dragnet,* every episode of which ended with the narrator promising, "The story you have just seen is true. Only the names have been changed, to protect the innocent." *Dragnet* became the first crime series to land in TV's end-of-season Top 10, taking the No. 4 spot for the 1952–53 season. By this point in TV history, previous Top 10 entrants had represented variety and sketch shows, anthology shows, sports showcases, Westerns, musical competition shows, sitcoms, and quiz shows, but *Dragnet* was the first of its kind and won three consecutive Emmys as Best Mystery, Action, or Adventure Series. Its kind, by the way, would never be absent from television again.

In fact, another crime series, NBC's *Gangbusters,* made the end-of-season Top 10 that same year, ranked No. 8. It premiered a few months after *Dragnet,* shared the same time slot on a rotating bimonthly basis, and doubtless shared much of the same audience. *Gangbusters,* like *Dragnet,* began on radio (in this case, way back in 1937) and was based on cases culled from the files of local, state, and national law enforcement. The *Gangbusters* cases were open ones, dealing with criminals still at large, and each show concluded with a photograph and description of the fugitive and a request for viewers to contact officials if they had any helpful information. This TV version of the post office "FBI Most Wanted" bulletin board would be employed on other crime shows in successive decades, from ABC's *FBI* to Fox's *America's Most Wanted,* but it started with *Gangbusters.*

Other 1950s crime shows cropped up quickly, anticipating a new TV trend and strategically offering things *Dragnet* intentionally lacked—more action and violence, quirkier lead characters, and even some aspects that might seem astoundingly advanced for this early phase of crime TV development, such as moral ambiguity and the sudden, unexpected death of a primary heroic character. One prominent example was *Highway Patrol,* the 1955–59 syndicated drama starring Broderick Crawford as the head of a mobile police force somewhere in the West. Crawford's vocal delivery was even more clipped and rapid than Webb's, but *Highway Patrol* loaded its episodes with helicopter shots and on-location driving scenes to add action to the crime solving. Charismatic characters began coming to the fore in such 1958 series as NBC's *Peter Gunn*, a Blake Edwards series starring Craig Stevens as a suave private eye, and *77 Sunset Strip*, the first of a fast burst of ABC crime shows aimed at young viewers (the breakout star of *77 Sunset Strip* was Edd Byrnes as Kookie, a hair-combing, finger-snapping car-park valet working at the nightclub next door to the detective agency with a "ginchy" and "cool" vocabulary).

Yet the year 1958, for crime series on TV, was complex as well as Kookie. That was the year ABC premiered *Naked City*, a weekly crime series based on the 1948 movie, with a loud and proud determination to shoot on location in New York City—a concept so novel that the first-season narration bragged, "This story was not photographed in a studio. Quite the contrary, the actors played out their roles in the streets and the buildings of New York itself." It's a trick other crime shows, most notably NBC's *Law & Order*, would adopt decades later, and *Naked City* was a pioneer in other ways as well. It began most episodes by showing the villain commit the crime, as NBC's *Columbo* would later do. It devoted as much screen time to the villains as to the heroes, an approach employed much later by CBS's *Wiseguy* and *EZ Streets*, and, like those series, filled its guest roles with young talent that soon blossomed into stars. (Guest stars on *Naked City* included Dustin Hoffman, Robert Redford, Christopher Walken, and Gene Hackman.) And *Naked City* was one of the first TV shows to stun viewers with the unexpected death of a primary character. John McIntire, who starred as the veteran officer Dan Muldoon opposite a young cop played by James Franciscus, wanted out of the series, so the producers obliged him by ending a seemingly routine chase on the streets of New York City with Muldoon's patrol car plowing into an oil truck and erupting into flames. That was followed by the episode's opening credits, an unsettling and very unequivocal way of offing a primary character, then or now.

Two other markedly unusual crime dramas closed out the 1950s, just as Webb's original, pivotal *Dragnet* series was coming to a close. (It would resurface, before the next decade was out, in an all-color, politically reactionary sequel, initially titled *Dragnet '67*.) One of those crime dramas, a CBS summer series premiering in 1959, was called *Brenner* and starred James Broderick as a young cop working for his police lieutenant father, but working undercover against his own precinct mates, investigating corruption in the police vice squad. It was a rare admission and dramatization of cops policing their own, presented more than a decade before the fact-based movie *Serpico* and more than forty years before an undercover cop investigating an insular police unit sparked the deadly and controversial events of FX's *Shield*. The other police show worth noting from 1959, rather than being all but forgotten, remains one of the most famous, and even infamous: ABC's *Untouchables*. Set in the 1930s and starring Robert Stack as the federal Treasury agent Eliot Ness, *The Untouchables* ended the decade as Jack Webb's *Dragnet* had started it, by presenting a straight-arrow, straight-spined, no-nonsense, no-smiles lawman. Stories in this new series were allegedly based on real cases also and initially relied on such well-known villains as Al Capone, Lucky Luciano, and Frank Nitti—the types of characters who would surface again, half a century later, in another period crime drama, HBO's *Boardwalk Empire*. But where *Dragnet* avoided violence, *The Untouchables* reveled in it, with so many machine-gun drive-by shootings and literal hit-and-run killings that it drew even more attention, and congressional ire, than the then-ubiquitous TV Westerns. *The Untouchables* reached the Top 10 in its second season and immediately thereafter, in the summer of 1961, which, not at all coincidentally, was the year the Senate Judiciary Committee launched its hearings on the effects of TV violence on young viewers. Other watchdog and ethnic groups were incensed by the preponderance of Italian surnames and a series that seemed to stereotype and denigrate Italians—charges leveled again, at the end of the century, against HBO's *Sopranos,* a series that benefited greatly from the legacy of *The Untouchables,* which established the mob boss as a viable if controversial dramatic character.

The Untouchables ended in 1963, the year Quinn Martin, one of its executive producers (Desi Arnaz was another), bounced back with a crime series that was much less violent and even more focused on the person on the other side of the law. *The Fugitive* began on ABC in 1963, following the trail of David Janssen's Richard Kimble, a physician wrongly accused of murdering his wife. Convicted of the crime but escaping after a train wreck on his way to prison, Kimble searched the country for the one-armed man he saw leaving the crime scene as he arrived, and viewers went with him, watching him do various acts of kindness along the way. When ABC canceled the series in 1967, it was with enough advance warning for Martin to order and mount a series finale that summer, concluding the story and putting Kimble face-to-face with his wife's killer. Even though it was shown in the usually sleepy TV month of August, that *Fugitive* finale broke all viewing records at the time, outdrawing even the first 1964 appearance by the Beatles on *The Ed Sullivan Show,* and established, very early, the value and importance of a satisfying final series episode. And it wasn't just the ending that was popular: midway through its run, during the 1964–65 TV season, *The Fugitive* wound up in the Top 10—the last crime series from the 1960s to do so.

That may be because the U.S. television audience, at that time, was much more interested in pure escapism (the Top 10 that decade was filled with witches and Martians and wealthy hillbillies). But it may also be because the networks, in the 1960s and throughout the 1970s, treated the crime series like the Western before it and flooded the airwaves with too many thin variations on the same few basic themes. One of the few innovative efforts was *Arrest and Trial,* a 1963 ABC weekly drama that was ninety minutes long, divided in two just as the show's title suggests: half to the police investigator (played by Ben Gazzara) solving the crime and making an arrest, and half to the attorney (Chuck Connors) trying the case in court. It was the exact template eventually used for NBC's massively popular *Law & Order* series, with the singular but significant exception that in *Law & Order* the lawyers in the second half of the show were district attorneys, working with the arresting officers to convict the criminals. In *Arrest and Trial,* Connors played a defense attorney, so half of the show's protagonists were doomed to failure on a weekly basis.

Otherwise, most 1960s crime series fell into two familiar and comfortable categories. There were variants on Webb's *Dragnet* model of investigators who exhibited less personality than perseverance and went about their duties with a minimum of detours or distractions—in ABC's *FBI* in 1965, the official *Dragnet '67* reboot starring Harry Morgan and Webb himself, and NBC's *Adam-12* in 1968, a squad-car procedural co-created by the very busy Webb. Conversely, there were the shows in which the heroes had one thing, and usually only one thing, setting them apart from the pack. *Mannix,* a CBS private eye series from 1967, had its hero (Mike Connors) getting badly beaten up in the course of almost every investigation, while NBC's *Ironside* the same year starred Raymond Burr as a crime-solving consultant in a wheelchair. This trend would continue into the 1970s with shows devoted to an overweight investigator (CBS's *Cannon*), a blind one (ABC's *Longstreet*), a bald and brash one who sucked an omnipresent lollipop (CBS's *Kojak*), and also, in the case of Angie Dickinson's *Police Woman* on NBC, a cop who happened to be female. Sometimes, it was enough just to have a change of scenery, as when CBS presented *Hawaii Five-0*, starring Jack Lord, in 1968, or when ABC paired the veteran actor Karl Malden with the up-and-comer Michael Douglas in 1972's *Streets of San Francisco*.

One new "variation" emerging from this period was ABC's bold-faced attempt to attract a newly desirable demographic, young viewers, while still dealing with the police drama, at a time when young people and the police weren't entirely respectful of each other. It sounded like a hard sell, but the executive producer Aaron Spelling structured and promoted his 1968 crime series, *The Mod Squad*, as aggressively and brazenly as possible. The show starred a trio of attractive young undercover operatives, reporting to a veteran superior officer and working on cases involving illicit drugs and other illegal activities but always aiming to apprehend the (older) people pulling the strings. Michael Cole played a privileged kid thrown out by his Beverly Hills family, Clarence Williams III played an angry African-American street rebel, and Peggy Lipton played the flower-child daughter of an adrift and parentally absent streetwalker. Three youngsters with issues, and ABC promoted them, in that volatile year of 1968, as "One white, one black, one blonde." And it worked. Concerns were raised by some southern ABC affiliates uncomfortable with the integrated premise and with the pandering approach to the new generation, but *The Mod Squad* caught on immediately, and Spelling quickly tweaked his own formula to churn out other successes for ABC, from 1972's *Rookies* (young uniformed officers report to a veteran superior officer) to the mother lode, 1976's *Charlie's Angels* (beautiful young women work as private eyes for an unseen older employer).

These weren't quality shows, though, just popular ones. For quality, especially in the 1970s, viewers had to look for crime series built not on quirks or sex appeal alone but on character. More overtly character-driven crime dramas, in which the investigator's personality traits were part of the fun, included two NBC Mystery Movie franchises, *McCloud* (starring Dennis Weaver as a modern cowboy with a badge) and *Quincy, M.E.* (starring Jack Klugman as a medical examiner and the TV predecessor of all the *CSI* forensic scientists). David Janssen, who had thrived on TV as the angst-ridden protagonist of *The Fugitive*, returned to ABC in the early 1970s as *Harry O*, a former police officer who had been discharged after being shot in the back and put on disability. Harry worked cases as a private eye, but in pain, and often with so little profit that he often took the bus from place to place and from case to case. Great character, great actor, and the same can be said, even more fervently, of Peter Falk as Columbo. After being introduced in a pair of stand-alone dramas, Falk starred in his own series of rotating NBC *Columbo* television movies beginning in 1971, with an episode called "Murder by the Book." Its creators were Richard Levinson and William Link, with a series kickoff episode written by Steven Bochco (later to change crime TV forever with *Hill Street Blues*) and directed by Steven Spielberg (later to change just about all of pop culture). As the title hero of *Columbo,* Peter Falk played a disheveled, rumpled, mumbling police detective squaring off against the wealthy, pompous, privileged murderers who invariably underestimated Columbo and his comically persistent questions. Special guest stars, playing the murderer of the week and shown at the start of the show plotting and committing the crime, included Jack Cassidy and Patrick McGoohan, and the writing and acting were equally sharp, demonstrating how entertaining a mystery series could be when the killer and the investigator were evenly matched. Once again, the profile of the villain was upped, a trend that on TV kept going and growing. Conversely, the heroes started getting a little less heroic. In the crime genre, this happened with the delightful 1974 NBC series *The Rockford Files.*

James Garner, cast as the same kind of lovable rogue he had portrayed so wonderfully in the Western *Maverick,* played Rockford as a private eye who cut corners, forged his own cover-story business cards, was very diligent about collecting investigative fees and expenses, and was more cowardly than heroic, preferring to avoid both gunplay and fistfights, but seldom succeeding at the latter. This against-the-grain series protagonist was the brainchild of Stephen J. Cannell, who had written very formulaic shows for Jack Webb (beginning with *Adam-12*) and was delighted to play with and overturn crime TV's conventions, and was co-created with Roy Huggins, responsible for the original *Maverick* series. Cannell also worked with Huggins on 1975's *Baretta* for NBC, a series starring Robert Blake as an undercover detective that could have been one of those one-note quirky cop shows (he has a pet cockatoo!) but, with Blake's alternately laid-back and red-hot approach to the role and his improvisatory style of dialogue delivery, was instead, like *The Rockford Files,* another of the rare intelligent crime shows of the 1970s. But even the best of them, at that point, shared one significant trait with crime dramas of any other sort, whether the buddy-cop antics of *Starsky & Hutch,* the action-filled violence of *S.W.A.T.,* or the romantic investigative escapades of *Hart to Hart*—three shows premiering in the 1970s on ABC, all coming from the same Aaron Spelling TV factory. What even Starsky and Hutch and the Harts had in common with Rockford and Baretta is that all of their weekly adventures were interchangeable pieces of a very basic puzzle. Even when the characters were richly drawn and smoothly acted, as with Tom Selleck in CBS's 1980 hit *Magnum, P.I.,* a private eye series set in Hawaii, there was little or no character development. Columbo in Season 6 dressed, sounded, and acted the way he did in Season 1. Episodes could be watched in any order without affecting the continuity or understanding of the story—a great boon to the syndication market, where shows were not necessarily viewed or broadcast in sequence. That was the way crime shows had been at the end of the 1940s and still the way they were at the end of the 1970s. Then came the 1980s. Then came . . . *Hill Street Blues.*

HILL STREET BLUES

1981–87, NBC. Creators and executive producers: Steven Bochco, Michael Kozoll. Writers: David Milch, Jeffrey Lewis, Anthony Yerkovic, Mark Frost, Karen Hall, others. Stars: Daniel J. Travanti, Veronica Hamel, Michael Warren, Charles Haid, Bruce Weitz, Dennis Franz, Michael Conrad, Joe Spano, Betty Thomas, James B. Sikking, René Enríquez, Kiel Martin, Taurean Blacque, Barbara Bosson, Barbara Babcock, Robert Prosky, Jeffrey Tambor.

NBC's *Hill Street Blues* came to television only two months after the resolution to the "Who shot J.R.?" episode of *Dallas* on CBS, which set audience records at the time as the most viewed scripted program in TV history. Audiences, therefore, were quite acclimated to accept one of the significant innovations of *Hill Street,* the overlapping and continuing story lines that weaved through and among various episodes, as in daytime and prime-time soap operas. What viewers were less prepared to accept, though, was almost everything else. The handheld camera work. The frenetic blocking of scenes, with important action in both the foreground and the background. Overlapping dialogue. Broad humor and dramatic tension, sometimes in the same scene. And as the uniformed and plainclothes men and women of the precinct went about their daily duties, not only a sense of danger, but a sense of triage and futility—a sense that the odds were against them, and sometimes the best to be done was to hold the craziness at bay for another day's shift.

Hill Street Blues was generated by MTM Productions and pulled elements from several past, seemingly unrelated programs—for example, the comedy-drama mix of CBS's *Lou Grant* newspaper drama and the realism and unpredictability of CBS's *White Shadow* high school basketball drama. Its genesis was also inspired, in part, by influences as disparate as the documentary *The Police Tapes,* the movies of Robert Altman, and a film then in production but familiar to the then–NBC executive Fred Silverman, *Fort Apache: The Bronx.* The co-creators of *Hill Street* were Steven Bochco, whose writing credits included *Columbo,* and Michael Kozoll, one of the

Hill Street Blues changed the cop series immediately and indelibly. At its center from start to finish: Daniel J. Travanti and Veronica Hamel.

writers of *Quincy, M.E.* They had teamed previously on another MTM crime series, the James Earl Jones drama *Paris*, and this time presided over a writing team that, in time, would branch out to create additional triumphs on other groundbreaking TV series: David Milch (ABC's *NYPD Blue* and HBO's *Deadwood*), Anthony Yerkovich (NBC's *Miami Vice*), Mark Frost (ABC's *Twin Peaks*), Dick Wolf (NBC's *Law & Order*), and others. "It was an aggregate of really first-rate writers under one roof," Milch tells me, "and I think there was surprisingly little jealousy and self-proclamation involved. It really was more collaborative than I think one would expect it to have been. And a lot of that is a credit to Steven, who knew how to get the best out of each of us without necessarily wanting any of us to imitate any of the others. It was a little bit like a good baseball team."

And this team of writers, like the team of ensemble players headed by Daniel J. Travanti as Captain Frank Furillo, hit it out of the park from the very start. Nevertheless, viewership was depressingly low during the first season of *Hill Street Blues*, because its style and substance were so foreign that the series wasn't initially accepted: "Out of ninety-seven prime-time TV shows that season, *Hill Street* was ranked eighty-third," Bochco says now. "We put so much information on a frame of film. And I think that's probably the most remarkable thing about the show, particularly in its early years." But that summer, it drew an unprecedented number of nominations at the Emmys and racked up the first of four consecutive wins as Best Dramatic Series. *Hill Street* not only survived but drew millions more viewers from that point on, and its Thursday 10:00 p.m. eastern time slot became the cornerstone of what came to be known as NBC's all-quality night of Must-See TV. Once *Hill Street Blues* became an accepted form of storytelling, it became part of Hollywood shorthand, a quick way of describing, and even selling, another series: Bochco's subsequent *L.A. Law* series, for example, as "*Hill Street* set in a law office."

The history of TV crime series can be divided, cleanly and accurately, into "before" and "after" *Hill Street Blues*. There were a handful of exceptions, a few stubbornly old-fashioned crime shows that continued to appear throughout the 1980s and proved, on the whole, quite popular. There was the light romantic byplay of NBC's 1982 series *Remington Steele*, the Agatha Christie–style drawing room mysteries of CBS's *Murder, She Wrote* in 1984, the *Mod Squad*–style youth-appeal Fox series *21 Jump Street* (briefly starring Johnny Depp) in 1987, and the actual Agatha Christie drawing room mysteries in PBS's imported *Poirot* series in 1989. Most of the decade's new crime series, however, followed the lead of *Hill Street Blues* and tried to attempt something at least a little different and, sometimes, a lot different.

Consider how fast these post–*Hill Street* shows stacked up one after the other, gingerly testing or aggressively plowing new ground. In 1981, CBS's *Cagney & Lacey* presented a buddy-cop drama with a crucial distinction: both its buddies, played by Tyne Daly and (in the series version) Sharon Gless, were women. In 1984, the creator Anthony Yerkovich and the producer Michael Mann teamed for NBC's wildly influential *Miami Vice*, the Don Johnson series that, in the years just after MTV began, brought rock music to the foreground of the crime drama, along with a neon aesthetic and a pastel and linen fashion sense. Its soundtrack, fueled by such hits as "In the Air Tonight" by Phil Collins and Jan Hammer's propulsive *Miami Vice* theme, shot to the top of the album charts—the first TV soundtrack to do so since Henry Mancini's *Peter Gunn*. In 1985, Glenn Gordon Caron created ABC's *Moonlighting*, a private eye series so spirited, so comical, and so original it found room for everything from a full-episode Shakespearean spoof to a film noir mini-musical ballet. Cybill Shepherd and an unknown actor named Bruce Willis starred and sparkled, and while crimes were solved, it was the duo's flinty chemistry, and the comedy, that mattered most.

Two other crime series of the mid-1980s, while less flashy, proved more influential, and more widely imitated, at least in story structure. NBC's *Crime Story*, premiering in 1986, was the creator Michael Mann's next TV series after *Miami Vice*. Instead of modern Miami neon, *Crime Story* went for film noir and fedoras, telling a tale of crime fighters versus criminals in the 1960s. Essentially, it was a stylistic and narrative sequel to *The Untouchables*, starring Dennis Farina as the head of Chicago's Major Crime Unit. His job was to identify, target, and bring down the next generation of crime bosses, and his pursuit of a gangster named Ray Luca, played by Tony Denison, was so unrelenting that he joined a federal crime force just to follow Luca to Las Vegas. The show's setting, whether Chicago or Vegas, was less important than its focus, which followed the bad guy as much as the hero and with almost as much sympathy. It was a tactic amplified, the following year, in 1987's *Wiseguy* on CBS, a hugely influential series co-created by Frank Lupo and the prolific Stephen J. Cannell, whose crime and action series credits ranged from the sublime (*The Rockford Files*) to the ridiculous (*The A Team*). *Wiseguy* starred Ken Wahl as an undercover agent reporting to the Organized Crime Bureau, with Jonathan Banks (later of *Breaking Bad*) playing his steely superior, but the crime fighter of *Wiseguy,* like the one in TV's campy *Batman* series of the 1960s, was totally overshadowed by the villains he faced. On *Wiseguy,* actors playing the antagonists were hired for a dozen or so episodes and given time to develop their characters over a third of a season or more, in ongoing narrative stories the *Wiseguy* producers called arcs. Each arc brought a flashy new villain, writ large and played even larger. These included Ray Sharkey as the Atlantic City mob boss Sonny Steelgrave, Stanley Tucci as a mobster terrorizing a garment district manufacturer played by Jerry Lewis, and Kevin Spacey and Joan Severance as the incestuous brother-and-sister drug and munitions smugglers Mel and Susan Profitt. "That really, without question, put me on the map," Spacey says of his *Wiseguy* arc, but the arc idea itself turned out to be equally impressive.

The 1980s ended the same way the 1990s would begin, with the networks experimenting with new programming forms, or adapting old ones, underneath the overall crime TV umbrella. The new Fox network, in 1988, presented both *COPS* and *America's Most Wanted,* calling them "reality shows," though the former, with camera and sound crews riding along with patrol units in various cities, was more of a mini-documentary and the latter an update, with re-creations, of the audience-as-tipsters approach employed on TV as far back as *Gangbusters* and *The FBI.* Another old TV trick, the split-genre approach of *Arrest and Trial* (police investigation in the first half, courtroom prosecution in the second) was revived by the producer Dick Wolf in 1990 for NBC's *Law & Order,* sparking a sprawling, still-running franchise. And another prolific producer, David E. Kelley, took the split-genre approach to its zenith in 1992's *Picket Fences,* an excellent CBS series combining the crime, legal, medical, and family genres in a single one-hour drama. Steven Bochco experimented too, with his ABC musical drama series *Cop Rock* in 1990, and other programs explored the opposite end of the spectrum from the business-first, business-only approach of *Dragnet.* ABC's *Commish,* another crime series co-created by Cannell, was a 1991 comedy-drama series starring Michael Chiklis as a small-town police commissioner, whose home life was as prominent as his case work. And the same year, PBS's *Mystery!* series imported *Prime Suspect,* the first of a superb series of extended British crime-solving stories starring Helen Mirren as Jane Tennison—a woman in charge whose dealings with sexist colleagues were as important, and as riveting, as her masterfully conducted investigations and interrogations. Cases were becoming more and more complex, narratives longer and more subtle and daring, and the cops and detectives more human, flawed, and unpredictable. Then, in 1993, came two shows that elevated the crime drama even further.

The first was *Homicide: Life on the Street*, which NBC thought highly enough of to premiere after that year's Super Bowl. Its inspiration was a book by the *Baltimore Sun* crime reporter David Simon, who went on to create HBO's *Wire*, and its executive producers were Barry Levinson and Tom Fontana. Like *Hill Street Blues* a decade before, *Homicide* arrived on TV with a jarringly different look and feel. Its scenes would be performed and filmed several times, photographed from different angles and emphases each time by a single handheld camera, then edited together without concern for continuity lapses or viewer disorientation. *Homicide* was written and performed peerlessly, and its cast, without making any big deal of it, populated the squad room with enough minority characters so that they were often the majority. "We wanted the show to reflect the makeup of the population of Baltimore," Fontana tells me. "And it's a brown town. The white people are living in the suburbs; at least they were then," he says. "To be responsible, to be truthful, it only increased over the years, the number of African-Americans we had as regulars." From the start, the ensemble was amazing—Ned Beatty, Andre Braugher, Jon Polito, Melissa Leo, Kyle Secor, Yaphet Kotto, Clark Johnson, Richard Belzer, Daniel Baldwin—as were the individual story lines. Polito's Steve Crosetti ultimately committed suicide, leaving his squad mates behind to wonder why. Braugher's Frank Pembleton suffered a debilitating stroke. Secor's Tim Bayliss, who began the series as an idealistic newcomer to the homicide squad, ended it by committing cold-blooded murder as an act of revenge.

Guest stars were used brilliantly, too: Robin Williams as a Baltimore tourist whose wife is shot and killed as he watches helplessly, Vincent D'Onofrio as a commuter wedged between a subway train and a platform, and Moses Gunn as the prime suspect in an ongoing case investigating the rape and murder of the eleven-year-old Adena Watson. That last example resulted in a Fontana-written episode, "Three Men and Adena," devoted almost wholly to the suspect's lengthy interrogation by Bayliss and Pembleton, and an utterly remarkable hour of television. It was broadcast in March 1993. Six months later, an equally envelope-pushing, quality-seeking crime series would appear, this time with a self-imposed mandate to be as risky, and even as risqué, as possible.

NYPD BLUE

1993–2005, ABC. Creators and executive producers: Steven Bochco, David Milch. Executive producer and director: Mark Tinker. Writers: Steven Bochco, David Milch, Bill Clark, others. Stars: David Caruso, Dennis Franz, Jimmy Smits, Rick Schroder, Mark-Paul Gosselaar, James McDaniel, Gordon Clapp, Sharon Lawrence, Kim Delaney, Henry Simmons, Bill Brochtrup, Nicholas Turturro.

"Even in that early period of time," Steven Bochco says, talking of the early 1990s, when uncensored movies on such premium cable networks as HBO and Showtime were eating into the audience viewing totals for the broadcast networks, "we were having our lunch stolen every day by cable. And I thought, 'Well, what we need to do is, we need to grow up as a medium.'" Bochco, a TV producer who had moved to ABC with an exclusive ten-year contract, negotiated for the opportunity to present an "R-rated" cop show for adults in the final hour of prime time, then negotiated even more, for what he would be allowed to say and show. Actors had to sign nudity clauses agreeing to show certain portions of their anatomy if asked, and the last three words of the premiere episode's opening sequence, setting the stage for the entire series to come, were "pissy little bitch." Mark Tinker, an *NYPD Blue* producer who directed more than fifty episodes, recalls Bochco's comically specific negotiations with ABC: "He negotiated a whole set of words you could say, and body parts that you could show, and exactly how much, and it involved butts and side boob and . . . simulating sex in a way that hadn't been done before [on TV]." Tinker laughs and adds, "We had been given permission to say 'bullshit' twice a show." David Milch, co-creator with Bochco of *NYPD Blue*, says that "language was a big boundary to cross" and adds that because of all the envelope-pushing in *NYPD Blue* "those were exciting times to be in this racket."

The network branded *NYPD Blue* with a TV-14-LSV rating, meaning it was not suitable for viewers under age fourteen and that it came with special advisories for coarse language, sexual situations, and violence. Its startling-for-broadcast-TV sex scenes and shower scenes, and its much rougher language, were attention getting as intended but rarely gratuitous. Everything served the stories and the characters, and the leading characters were singularly drawn and portrayed from the start. The putative star, David Caruso as Detective John Kelly, and the co-star Dennis Franz as the troubled cop Andy Sipowicz were, like the creators of *NYPD Blue,* veterans of *Hill Street Blues:* Caruso had played the punk leader of an Irish street gang in that show's second episode, while Franz had played two different *Hill Street* roles. One was a cop so crooked he was known as Bad Sal Benedetto, and the other an only slightly more moral one, a viewer favorite named Norman Buntz. Franz had the ability to make the flaws of his characters not only acceptable but iden-

NYPD Blue was designed at the start with David Caruso as its star, but focus shifted to Dennis Franz once Caruso left the show early in its second season. The initial cast (from left) included Franz, Caruso, Amy Brenneman, Nicholas Turturro, and James McDaniel.

tifiable, which Milch, in particular, loved to explore—first on *Hill Street,* then even more so on *NYPD Blue.* When Caruso left *NYPD Blue* early into the second season, and Franz stood up to inherit the mantle of the series lead, it brought one of TV's most conflicted and flawed characters to center stage—a bigoted, short-tempered, shortcut-taking detective who nonetheless was easy to follow, and embrace, as a central hero. Over time, Franz won four Emmys for Outstanding Lead Actor in a Drama Series, and the series itself garnered sixteen others, including one for Outstanding Drama Series in 1995.

"Dennis was, for me, I think it's fair to say, a kind of surrogate," Milch says, "who really didn't fit exactly into the system and was kind of unapologetically and irreducibly himself. And there were aspects of my connection to the process that were similar to his, and I enjoyed, an awful lot, writing for him." The story arc of Franz's Andy Sipowicz, on *NYPD Blue,* was nearly mythic—happiness followed by searing tragedy, temptations and setbacks almost everywhere, and lessons learned, if learned at all, very slowly and painfully. Through all twelve seasons of the series, Sipowicz was forced to deal with loss and change. He went through several squad room partners, including Jimmy Smits as Bobby Simone, whose postsurgical death in the hospital was one of the show's emotional highlights. Sipowicz lost his grown son and his second wife but emerged at the end a more responsible and respected figure. The final episode of *NYPD Blue* had him promoted to squad room leader, and the series ended with a shot of Sipowicz working late at night at his desk, alone—a happy conclusion for a character who had struggled with so many demons, and so much adversity, for so long.

NYPD Blue introduced a new level of maturity to the crime genre, and other shows in the 1990s followed suit, one way or another. Another Bochco series, the 1995 ABC hybrid drama *Murder One,* was part police investigation, part trial, but told its story in a season-long, detailed, serialized fashion, spending the entire time on a single case (Bochco was inspired by the real-life televised murder trial of O. J. Simpson and sought a way to bring that level of detail to a scripted dramatic series). In 1996, Paul Haggis created the underrated CBS crime series *EZ Streets,* which, like *Wiseguy* and *Crime Story,* gave equal time to the cops and the criminals (in this case, Ken Olin and Joe Pantoliano represented the opposite sides of the law). And in 1997, Tom Fontana created the first great made-for-cable drama series, one that went where no crime series had gone before. The cable network was HBO, the setting was a prison, and the show was called *Oz*. It was a show so brutally honest—so brutal, period—that even the prisoners who appeared most sympathetic eventually did something heinous or horrifying, if only in self-defense. Once again, as with *Homicide: Life on the Street*, Fontana was working with an outstanding ensemble cast: on *Oz*, the prison staff was played by Terry Kinney, Rita Moreno, Ernie Hudson, and the future *Sopranos* co-star Edie Falco, and the prisoners were portrayed by, among others, Lee Tergesen, Harold Perrineau, Christopher Meloni, Eamonn Walker, Dean Winters, Adewale Akinnuoye-Agbaje, and, as the terrifying neo-Nazi Vern Schillinger, the future Oscar winner J. K. Simmons. Fontana went to HBO, he tells me, not because he was a visionary about the future of drama on cable TV but because he had no other choice.

"*Oz* on a broadcast network?" Fontana asks rhetorically. "There was no possibility." Beatings, brandings, rape—it was all part of the threatened and threatening environment of the prison, and even with inmates tending to divide among racial or ethnic lines for protection, no one was truly safe, whether or not the guards were watching. "In prison, there are no loyalties," Fontana says. "There is no way to relax with anybody that you're in contact with." HBO was interested precisely because *Oz* was so dark and unprecedented, because, like many cable networks following in its footsteps, it thought the fastest way to get attention, acclaim, and viewers might be to take big risks and encourage creative TV producers to pursue their most daring visions. "I remember saying to people, 'I'm going to do a TV series on HBO,' and they looked at me like I had gone to Mars," Fontana recalls. "They'd say, 'It's a movie channel. What are you going to do there?' And nobody believed me!"

Fontana and *Oz* took full advantage of the freedom allowed by HBO, and for two years *Oz* was the best crime series, and drama series, ever produced for cable. *Oz* continued on HBO, and was terrific, until 2003, but its reign as cable's best lasted only two years because of another crime series that HBO decided to produce and present in 1999. It was a series that, almost single-handedly, would usher in the Platinum Age of Television.

THE SOPRANOS

1999–2007, HBO. Creator: David Chase. Writers: David Chase, Terence Winter, Mitchell Burgess, Robin Green, Matthew Weiner, Todd A. Kessler, others. Stars: James Gandolfini, Edie Falco, Lorraine Bracco, Michael Imperioli, Dominic Chianese, Steven Van Zandt, Tony Sirico, Drea de Matteo, Steve Schirripa, Jamie-Lynn Sigler, Robert Iler, Nancy Marchand, Vincent Pastore, Joe Pantoliano, Steve Buscemi.

David Chase, by creating *The Sopranos,* changed all the rules for cable television, and TV in general, just as one century was giving way to another. In its initial season in 1999, it was the first cable drama to be nominated for an Emmy as Outstanding Drama Series. In 2004, after a four-year run by NBC's *West Wing,* HBO's *Sopranos* became the first cable show to win the Outstanding Drama Series. (It won again in 2007, for its concluding season.) By the time it was over, with a finale that still ranks as one of TV's most memorable and controversial, *The Sopranos* had collected twenty-one Emmy Awards—including three apiece for James Gandolfini (starring as Tony Soprano) as Outstanding Lead Actor in a Drama Series, Edie Falco (co-starring as Tony's wife, Carmela) for Outstanding Lead Actress, and Chase for his script writing—and a pair of Peabody Awards. Topping it all off, in 2013 *The Sopranos* was honored, by voting members of the Writers Guild of America, as the Best-Written TV Series Ever, heading a list of 101 shows.

How did *The Sopranos* come to be taken so seriously and praised so effusively? Because it had great scripts, directors, and actors, of course, but also because it broke all the rules and, in so doing, not only drew attention to itself like a magnet but proved that cable TV dramas could compete, for audiences as well as awards, with the biggest guns from the broadcast networks. *The Sopranos* had been pitched, initially, to the broadcast networks, starting with Fox, and had one of them scheduled and presented the series, it would have been different enough, no doubt, that it would have had much less of an impact on popular culture. But on HBO's unrestricted playing field, following the path paved by Tom Fontana's *Oz,* David Chase's *Sopranos* defied one convention, and set one new standard, after another.

Here was a series that, like *The Untouchables* (which Chase, as a child, had watched with his father), tapped into the allure of the inner workings and outer swagger of the mob, but in this case the wiseguys and bad guys were at dead center. Gandolfini's northern New Jersey mob boss, Tony Soprano, dealt with enough identifiable problems to seek help from a therapist. His marriage was troubled, his children were rebellious and often disrespectful, his aging mother was a constant responsibility and problem, and the power dynamics at work were shifting quickly, leaving him unsure of both his job status and his future. Oh, and he suffered anxiety attacks, sometimes so intensely that he passed out. If his "job" hadn't been that of a mid-level mob boss, Tony's problems could have been almost anyone's.

But Tony Soprano was a mob boss and, at bottom, a bad man. In case there were any doubts, *The Sopranos* erased them with an early Season 1 episode, "College," in which Tony, with his bare hands, strangled a mob informant. But we kept watching, liking, and even identifying with him anyway, because the performances and conflicts were so powerful. The organized-crime power struggles were riveting, but even they paled against Tony's biological family dynamics. Nancy Marchand, as Tony's bitter mother, Livia, was an amazingly compelling character, comic and chilling at the same time ("Oh, poor you!"), and when the actress died early on, *The Sopranos* had

The Sopranos was riveting, and much discussed by fans and critics, from start to finish. Especially the finish. Seen in the finale, minutes from the show's controversial ending, are (from left) James Gandolfini, Edie Falco, and Robert Iler, as Tony, Carmela, and A. J. Soprano.

to steer the spine of its story in other directions. Which it did, brilliantly, including a years-in-the-making drag-out fight between Tony and Carmela in which the intensity had me forgetting these were actors and frightened about the survival of the characters.

The Sopranos freed up TV writer-producers of other shows to put not just flawed heroes but flawed antiheroes and villains at the center of their own subsequent drama series. It was a change that opened up a vibrant, brand-new palette, allowing for such colorful lead characters as Walter White of *Breaking Bad,* and *The Sopranos,* over its run, popularized other meaningful changes as well, all influencing other TV writers and programs. Among the people I interviewed for this book, the two programs most cited as influential to them personally were *The Twilight Zone* and *The Sopranos.* That latter show had many other resonant, widely copied elements, in addition to its often villainous central character. *The Sopranos* adopted a less structured production schedule, doing fewer episodes per season and sometimes taking time between seasons merely to refresh and regroup. On occasion, it picked up the surrealistic dream sequence concept from ABC's *Twin Peaks* and injected even more astounding visual imagery into an already aggressively and imaginatively visual drama series. Its dialogue, both in its rawness and in its vagueness, was unusually realistic: Chase believed strongly that people seldom if ever said what they really felt, and he wanted those unspoken undercurrents dramatized and explored. Another way Chase wanted *The Sopranos* to reflect what he considered a truer reality was to avoid neatly wrapped scenes of closure from time to time. *The Sopranos* left certain plot points and story lines defiantly unresolved: the Russian in the tree, the rape of Tony's therapist (Lorraine Bracco's Dr. Melfi), and, most of all, that final episode, with its unexpected, unresolved, unexplained final scene.

About that finale . . .

"David, I'm not ever going to say another word about that finale," Chase says, laughing. "Honestly, I can't do it . . . No matter what I say, it just leads to something else." Fair enough. So I'll say some words about it, starting with the pressure I was under, as a TV critic, to deliver an instant analysis the night it was televised. Because the show's 2007 finale was considered front-page news—occupying the entire cover of the New York *Daily News*—it was one of the few times my newspaper editors required me to write an instant review, as had happened, earlier in my career, with the "Who shot J.R.?" episode of *Dallas* and the *M*A*S*H, Cheers,* and *Seinfeld* finales. The difference, this time, was that HBO had invited a few New York–area TV critics to its Manhattan headquarters to view a secret screening of the final episode about an hour before it premiered on HBO, to give us a head start on absorbing and reviewing it. Six or so of us spread out inside the network's comfy screening room to watch that last outing of *The Sopranos,* then were ushered to separate cubbyhole offices to write and transmit our respective reviews. As the Soprano family gathered for a meal at Holsten's ice cream parlor in Bloomfield, and Tony flipped through selections on the tabletop jukebox, selecting Journey's "Don't Stop Believin'," none of us were prepared for what came next. Or what didn't come next, as the lighthearted dinner scene, featuring a few menacing figures looming nearby, cut to black midway through. At least, because we were watching in a screening room, we didn't have the initial reaction of viewers at home—that our cable had just gone out. As final credits began to roll, the silent darkness of our screening room was broken by the brief but appreciative laughter of Alan Sepinwall, then of Newark, New Jersey's *Star-Ledger.* We all exchanged glances but no words as we divided to tackle our respective leads. Mine, which ran under the *Daily News* headline "One Whacky Ending," was "After all the hype and expectations about last night's final episode of HBO's *The Sopranos,* the mob drama series didn't end with a bang. It didn't even end. It just stopped."

Tom Fontana, who outraged millions of viewers and delighted millions of others with his infamous snow-globe ending to NBC's *St. Elsewhere,* loves that Chase's hotly debated ending to *The Sopranos* takes the heat off *St. Elsewhere* a bit but also loves Chase's ending, period. "I thought it was tremendous," Fontana says. "And courageous." He also thinks Chase was doing precisely the job that he, like Fontana and other TV drama writers, is supposed to do. "I don't think we're here to placate," Fontana says. "I think we're here to challenge. I think we're here to piss people off." For some viewers, mission accomplished. For others, the ending to *The Sopranos* ranks as an all-time TV high point. But from that moment on, for anyone writing and producing a TV series of quality, the finale would become supremely important—literally the final measure of a program's overall legacy.

After *The Sopranos* premiered, and caught fire, all bets were off. Even crime shows that revisited old formulas either did so with new twists (the high-tech microscopic-view visuals added to the otherwise standard forensic procedural of CBS's *CSI: Crime Scene Investigation* in 2000, or USA's

Columbo-with-OCD mystery series *Monk,* starring Tony Shalhoub, in 2002) or failed quickly (CBS's 2000 remake of *The Fugitive*). Notably, the year 2002 was a banner one for innovative TV, especially in and around the crime genre. NBC's *Boomtown* was a well-acted, well-written, multi-viewpoint crime series created by Graham Yost, later to create FX's *Justified.* HBO's *Wire,* David Simon's masterful dissection of the intersecting issues and problems of the city of Baltimore, began as a superb crime drama but, by the time it ended, had smartly examined so many city institutions, from education and city hall to the docks and the press, that it outgrew that narrow "crime" umbrella. (As a result, you'll find it saluted in detail elsewhere in this book, under general drama.) And FX's *Shield,* also launched in 2002, was a cop show with a definite difference. Its central cop, from the first scene and certainly by the end of the first hour, was a villain—badder than many of the perps he was targeting as part of his job.

THE SHIELD

2002–8, FX. Creator: Shawn Ryan. Writers: Shawn Ryan, Kurt Sutter, Glen Mazzara, Charles H. Eglee, others. Stars: Michael Chiklis, Walton Goggins, CCH Pounder, Catherine Dent, Benito Martinez, Glenn Close, Forest Whitaker, Natalie Zea, Reed Diamond.

Before he wrote the first five pages of his spec script for *The Shield,* Shawn Ryan's experience as a writer and producer of crime dramas had been limited to the Don Johnson CBS series *Nash Bridges,* and he was just about to add a season on Joss Whedon's *Angel,* a WB *Buffy the Vampire Slayer* spin-off about a vampire hero running an investigative private eye agency. A Fox executive, after asking Ryan to write a sample description and basic treatment of a college comedy she was looking to add to her schedule, declined to pursue it further but did ask Ryan what type of show he would like to write. It was a question he'd never been asked before in Hollywood, and it made him think. "And I thought to myself," Ryan tells me, "well, I guess what I'd really like to do is write a cop show that I'd like to watch. You know, I'd been writing *Nash Bridges* that had all these rules—that Nash always has to do the right thing, that Nash always has to be the hero in the end. I'd like to write something that doesn't have all those rules."

The Shield starred Michael Chiklis as rogue cop Vic Mackey, a protagonist with a self-protective evil streak that was evident from the start. And until the end.

That idea turned into the series that premiered on FX in 2002 as *The Shield,* providing the basic cable model for the playbook designed by HBO with such series as *Oz, The Larry Sanders Show,* and *The Sopranos:* launch one excellent, markedly different, potentially attention-demanding quality TV series, and build the network's reputation from there, one original show at a time. In *The Shield,* Michael Chiklis, who was much more cuddly and comedic in *The Commish,* played Vic Mackey, the alpha dog in charge of a Los Angeles police special strike force. In the pilot, not much but Mackey's badge, the shield, differentiates him from the criminals he pursues and arrests: he acts violently, deals ruthlessly, and traffics in the same drugs and money transactions as others on the street. The initial framing of *The Shield,* as a TV series, is that Vic Mackey is as tough as he needs to be to intimidate and subdue the bad guys around him—a twenty-first-century Dirty Harry. But that conceit lasts less than an hour: In the premiere episode, Mackey's unit is infiltrated by a colleague and friend of Mackey's, played by Reed Diamond of *Homicide: Life on the Street,* who is actually working undercover to expose Mackey's illegal tactics. At the climax of the episode, the squad raids the home of a drug dealer, exchanges gunfire, and kills him, whereupon Mackey takes the dead dealer's gun, points it at the officer Mackey knows is working to investigate him, and shoots him fatally in the face. It takes a few seasons for *The Shield* to confirm and confront what was established at the very start, that Vic Mackey is a psychopath with a badge. But that's the path, and the point, and, for TV crime shows, another major evolutionary development. Joe Friday on *Dragnet* was all hero, all the time. The cops on *Hill Street Blues* were humans first, police officers second. Andy Sipowicz on *NYPD Blue* was majorly flawed but not irredeemable. Tony Soprano was on the wrong side of the law but still at the center of his TV show. And Vic Mackey, arguably, was just as morally bankrupt as Tony Soprano yet was on the opposite side of the thin blue line. From Joe Friday to Vic Mackey— that's a measurable, startling change.

It wasn't the show's only daring difference, either. The FX executive John Landgraf, who joined the channel shortly after *The Shield* was launched, urged Ryan not only to think of introducing a new major character as Mackey's new boss but also, as Ryan says, "to think big" in terms of the casting as well as the writing. A full-season guest spot on a show as good as *The Shield*, he thought, might attract someone who rarely if ever appears on television. Ryan quotes Landgraf as saying, "You should just make a list of who you think are the best actresses in the world, and then let's see if we can get one of them." Ryan says that's exactly what he did and compiled a list including Meryl Streep, Holly Hunter, Judy Davis, and Glenn Close. As the writers broke out the story for the fourth season and fleshed out the character a bit, they decided Close was the ideal fit. She'd never seen the show, but her agent was a big fan and told her she had to consider it. Landgraf sent her the first three seasons and offered what was about the same time commitment as a movie contract: four and a half months. "When she showed up," Ryan says, "and after she'd done a few episodes, she goes, 'You know, this isn't so much like a TV show. This is more like summer stock theater, where you're playing one episode, but you're seeing the script for the next one, and you've got to play a different thing.' She really embraced it." So much so, in fact, that it led to her starring in her own FX series—the excellent legal drama *Damages*. And after Close left *The Shield,* the season-long guest role trick was tried again, very successfully, this time with Forest Whitaker.

And as *The Shield* neared its series finale, the intensity kept building. Walton Goggins, as Vic's second-in-command, Shane Vendrell, found himself in opposition to Vic in ways that he could neither reconcile nor accept, and Shane went down a hauntingly tragic path. (Goggins also gave a tremendous performance throughout.) As for Vic himself, the impact of the end of *The Sopranos* the year before had made Ryan quite conscious of the importance of the final episode of *The Shield*. The ending he selected for his series was, in its way, as daring as its beginning. In the final episode, Vic confessed to all his crimes, including the shooting of a fellow officer, in exchange for immunity and a continued job on the force. The job he got, though, was a desk job in a cubicle, and the final image of the series showed Vic Mackey alone at his desk, toiling alone at night rather than patrolling the streets. It was its own ironic punishment, its own type of prison, and yet, when the nearly identical scene and image served as the finale of *NYPD Blue,* with Andy Sipowicz doing paperwork as the head of an empty squad room, it was intended as a victorious, happy ending. Times had changed. So had TV's cops, and, for that matter, so had TV's criminals.

BREAKING BAD

2008–13, AMC. Creator: Vince Gilligan. Writers: Vince Gilligan, Peter Gould, others. Stars: Bryan Cranston, Aaron Paul, Anna Gunn, Dean Norris, Betsy Brandt, RJ Mitte, Bob Odenkirk, Steven Michael Quezada, Jonathan Banks, Giancarlo Esposito, Jesse Plemons, Laura Fraser, Krysten Ritter, Mark Margolis, Raymond Cruz.

Now that his series has concluded, and been hailed as one of television's all-time best drama series, Vince Gilligan's original shorthand pitch to AMC for *Breaking Bad* seems not only prescient but perfectly reasonable. "My pitch," he recalls, "was taking Mr. Chips and transforming him into Mr. Scarface." But back then, almost everything about that idea was somewhere between unprecedented and insane. Even though other networks had rejected the idea outright, pitching it to AMC, at that moment in TV history, made little sense. At the time Gilligan's agent sent over the pilot script, AMC was about to launch its first original drama series, Matthew Weiner's *Mad Men,* but was otherwise just a repository for old movies. Dramatizing a central character's slow trajectory from good guy to bad not only was very unusual but, to succeed, required several seasons to unfurl completely— seasons that would depend entirely on whether viewers found the concept intriguing, if, in fact, they found the show on AMC at all. And then there was the intelligence ingrained in the high-concept pitch itself: Scarface, as a ruthless gangster immortalized in movies in two different generations, was a readily accessible reference point, but the reserved British schoolteacher Mr. Chips? (That character was also featured in films from two different generations, but still.)

Yet that was precisely the vision Gilligan intended to follow: a story that, like a novel or a miniseries, had a beginning and an ending laid out from the start. It was a story arc with a colorful and glorious span, like a rainbow. Bryan Cranston played a high school chemistry teacher suddenly hit with a diagnosis of terminal cancer who decides to use his scientific knowledge to make a highly refined grade of crystal meth and team with a former student to produce and distribute it—all in a race-the-death-clock effort to raise enough money to leave a nest egg for his pregnant wife and their teen son. "I love the idea of a good character, a good man, doing arguably bad things for a good reason," Gilligan says. That distinction, to Gilligan, made his idea different—that the character not only would transform into an actual criminal but would start out as the opposite of one. "An everyman, you or me, not even a jaywalker," Gilligan explains. "If you motivated that character to become a criminal at age fifty, how would you go about that?"

The concept was bold and original enough, but the execution was even better. Gilligan and his team of writers, producers, and directors ensured that actions had consequences—that any act committed in one episode would have repercussions in the next. Seasons of episodes were plotted so thoroughly, and sometimes so far in advance, that hints and visuals could be dropped early in a season, with their meanings not evident until months later. The performances were sensational—not only Bryan Cranston as the central character, Walter White, who won four Emmys as Outstanding Lead Actor in a Drama Series, but Anna Gunn and Aaron Paul as, respectively, Walter's marital and meth-making partners, Skyler White and Jesse Pinkman. Both Gunn and Paul won multiple Emmys as well, and other actors, while not winning statuettes, were invaluable parts of the whole: Dean Norris as Walter's DEA-agent brother-in-law, Giancarlo Esposito as a quietly frightening drug (and fried chicken) magnate, Jonathan Banks as an even quieter and more frightening enforcer, and Krysten Ritter as Jesse's drug-addicted girlfriend, whose unexpected death was one of many unforgettable scenes *Breaking Bad* served up with astounding regularity.

The cinematography of *Breaking Bad*, the editing, the music—every element of it was integral and beautiful. The series was a masterpiece from start to finish and was increasingly recognized as such: *Breaking Bad* won the Outstanding Drama Series Emmy its last two seasons. Even the finale—by 2013, such a crucial part of any TV show's legacy—was a triumph, which Gilligan admits wasn't easy. "It weighed very heavily on my mind, and on the minds of all of the writers, this desire to satisfy," Gilligan says of planning that last episode. He and the other writers assiduously worked out every beat of every act, tacking detailed scene-by-scene note cards onto the writers' room corkboard, which Gilligan saved as a souvenir and, one year later, lent to me for display as part of my 2014 New York apexart exhibit. So thanks for that, Vince, and for *Breaking Bad*. And for its sequel-slash-prequel, AMC's *Better Call Saul*, a legal drama that established itself instantly as another superb example of quality television.

After *Breaking Bad*, you might think there was nothing left to say, or add. But there is.

Breaking Bad, one of the finest drama series in TV history, starred Aaron Paul (foreground) and Bryan Cranston as meth manufacturers Jesse Pinkman and Walter White.

In 2010, the executive producer and creator Graham Yost presented FX's *Justified*, starring Timothy Olyphant as Raylan Givens, a deputy U.S. marshal reassigned, as a punishment for trigger-happy rogue behavior, to his childhood stomping grounds in the coal-mining hills of Kentucky. Based on an Elmore Leonard short story, *Justified* had season-long story arcs and villains, delicious dialogue and characters, and yet another standout supporting performance by Walton Goggins, as Raylan's boyhood friend and now adversary Boyd Crowder. Leonard himself so liked the show's treatment of his work that he came aboard as adviser, suggested a story, and gave the show's writers an extra desire, and extra pressure, to try to do *Justified* Leonard's way. "We felt that pressure every episode," Yost admits, and especially so with the series finale, which, because of Leonard's reputation and body of work, was seen as the final chapter of a long novel and had to work as such, bringing everything to a fitting conclusion and, if possible, full circle. And it did, by making the final scene an honest, intimate conversation between Raylan and Boyd, with a sincere explanation for the bond between the two men, despite all other factors. "You want to stick the landing, you want people to love it, absolutely," Yost says of the finale. "But what you really don't want is for people to say, 'That was awful!'"

They didn't. *Justified*, from the day of its premiere in 2010, was one of the best shows of its decade and yet another sparkling jewel in the FX crown. Also in 2010, PBS and the BBC partnered on a series of newly adapted and updated Sherlock adventures, created by Mark Gatiss and Steven Moffat and starring Benedict Cumberbatch as Sherlock Homes and Martin Freeman as Dr. Watson. They're wonderful, and at this writing, they're still being produced, though only sporadically, and after long periods of hiatus—another beneficiary of the staggered scheduling of *The Sopranos*, perhaps, except that the British model of programming has been that way from the start. It's taken the United States about fifty years to catch up, but here we are.

TV has also given us several anthology series devoting an entire season to a single crime case, with varying results. In 2014, HBO presented a stellar first season of Nic Pizzolatto's *True Detective*, starring Matthew McConaughey and Woody Harrelson, then a wildly disappointing all-new second-season story. In 2015, ABC gave us an impressive first season of *American Crime*, starring Felicity Huffman and Timothy Hutton, followed in 2016 by an equally strong second season, with an all-new story featuring Hutton and Huffman in completely different roles. Also in 2016, FX pre-

sented *American Crime Story*, a new anthology series devoting one shortened season to a single story, and began with *The People v. O. J. Simpson*,
essentially a courtroom drama, but an outstanding one. And FX's *Fargo*,
inspired by the spirit and setting of the fabulous 1996 Coen brothers crime
film, presented an excellent season-long crime story in 2014, starring Martin
Freeman and Billy Bob Thornton, and followed that up with an even better, all-new story in 2015, featuring an all-new cast led by Patrick Wilson,
Ted Danson, Kirsten Dunst, and Jesse Plemons. The beauty of both seasons
of *Fargo* was that, as is possible with the miniseries form, any character in
mortal danger could die at any time, which made it extremely intense to
watch. And to the credit of *Fargo*'s TV creator Noah Hawley, many of those
characters did, and many of the others were as morally complex as characters in *The Shield* and *Breaking Bad* or as colorful as those of *The Sopranos*.
In the crime genre, stories have gotten longer, series have gotten shorter,
characters have gotten more complicated, and plots have become infinitely
less predictable. It's all part of the form's evolution, and it's all for the better.

BORN: 1943, Manhattan, New York.

FIRST TV CREDIT: Co-creator, *The Bold Ones: The New Doctors,* 1969, NBC.

LANDMARK TV SERIES: Writer, *Columbo,* 1971–74, NBC, and 1990, ABC; Co-creator, *Hill Street Blues,* 1981–87, NBC; Co-creator, *L.A. Law,* 1986–94, NBC; Co-creator, *NYPD Blue,* 1993–2005, ABC; Co-creator, *Murder One,* 1995–97, ABC.

OTHER MAJOR CREDITS: TV: Writer, *The White Shadow,* 1979, CBS; Creator, *Paris,* 1979–80, CBS; Co-creator, *Doogie Howser, M.D.,* 1989–93, ABC; Co-creator, *Cop Rock,* 1990, ABC; Co-creator, *Over There,* 2005, FX; Co-creator, *Murder in the First,* 2014–, TNT. Movies: Co-writer, *Silent Running,* 1972.

Steven Bochco may not necessarily have his childhood neighbors to thank for his career in television, but he certainly has to thank them for his family's television itself. His parents were in the arts—his father a concert violinist, his mother a painter—and Steven Bochco was born in New York City in 1943. It wasn't until after World War II that network television began to develop, but even then, Bochco recalls, his parents had "zero interest" in buying a TV set. "It was quite the contrary: they were in minus territory," he says, laughing. "We got our first TV when I was ten or eleven, something like that," he says, and that was only because friends and neighbors of his parents, knowing how hungry young Steven and his sister were to watch television, pitched in and bought them one. The first shows he remembers loving were *I Love Lucy* and the variety shows headlined by Red Buttons, Dean Martin and Jerry Lewis, Milton Berle, and Sid Caesar—especially

Caesar's *Your Show of Shows* on NBC. "Caesar, Imogene Coca, Carl Reiner, Howard Morris—I just remember how goddamned funny they all were!" Bochco says. He also adored the Mel Brooks–Carl Reiner 2000 Year Old Man albums, proclaiming, "He was the gold standard of comedy when I was a teenager." (A few years later, he got to meet Brooks up close and personal, when Brooks briefly dated Bochco's sister.) "I don't pretend to have a sophisticated sense of humor, as you can tell from *Hill Street* [*Blues*]," Bochco admits, laughing. "I was always a little prurient and juvenile. But I was raised on that kind of broad, slapstick, physical comedy, and I never got over it. It's why I loved Red Skelton; I loved performers who were clowns. And," he adds, jumping forward in his personal TV timeline, "Tim Conway on *The Carol Burnett Show* used to just kill me, he was so fucking funny."

In the early 1960s, into his Manhattan High School of Music and Art and Carnegie Institute of Technology years, young Bochco was drawn to drama as well. He lists such favorite high-profile anthology series as NBC's *Kraft Television Theatre* but also singles out two much more obscure, though equally impressive, weekly drama series. One was CBS's *East Side/West Side,* an atypically gritty 1963 show about a New York social worker, starring George C. Scott and, equally atypically for an African-American performer of that era, co-starring Cicely Tyson. The other was CBS's *Trials of O'Brien,* a 1965 legal drama starring Peter Falk as a New York attorney with a keen courtroom mind but a less organized private life. The show lasted only one season, but the actor, and the series, made quite a strong impression. "I watched the first episode of *The Trials of O'Brien,*" Bochco recalls, "and I just loved everything about it, and I loved Peter!"

Asked why that program in particular had hit a chord, Bochco says, "I hadn't specifically narrowed it to film and television, but I knew I wanted to be a writer by then. I mean, I really knew that I wanted to be a writer. And I think the thing that resonated for me so much with that show was that it just sounded right. It just sounded like real people in real situations . . . I loved everything about it." It wouldn't be long, just a handful of years, before Bochco would be writing for television and writing the premiere episode of Peter Falk's most famous TV role, as NBC's persistent, iconic Columbo.

At college, Bochco took advantage of a writing program connected with Universal Studios and leveraged it into a full-time job after graduation in 1966. Already married in college, he and his wife headed west for Hollywood, where he found steady work at Universal co-creating a new entry in

NBC's *Bold Ones* umbrella series, writing for the same network's *Name of the Game,* and taking whatever jobs were assigned to him. "I spent the first twelve years of my career at that place," Bochco says, "and that place was not a happy place. It was very corporatized, a lot of hierarchy, a lot of politics, a lot of shitheads . . . One of the great lessons I learned at Universal is how not to behave."

There was, however, at least one shining, stunning, happy exception: *Columbo,* the 1971 series created by the writing and producing team of Richard Levinson and William Link—creators not only of *Columbo* but of *Murder, She Wrote* and the important made-for-TV movies *That Certain Summer* and *The Execution of Private Slovik.* Bochco wrote the script for the introductory *Columbo* series story, "Murder by the Book," which played slyly with the dynamic of the writing team known as Levinson and Link: the plot had one member of a successful writing duo murder the other, with only Columbo being observant and intrepid enough to crack the case. Bochco got along great with, and learned a great deal from, Levinson and Link in those early days on *Columbo.*

"They were wonderful teachers and mentors to me," he says, then laughs. "Because they had to be. I wasn't just working for them; I was the staff. It was just the three of us. Just to sit in the room every day and listen to how their collective brain worked, in terms of constructing stories and characters," he adds, then pauses briefly to reflect. "When you're learning on the job that way—and I suppose it's the same for a college student, when you go to classes every day—you don't stop to reflect on how much you're learning. You're just too busy soaking it up." (One terrific anecdote Bochco soaked up: He once asked Levinson how he and his partner chose to be billed as "Levinson and Link" rather than the other way around. Levinson's reply: "We thought that 'Link and Levinson' sounded like a black writer." Bochco laughs and asks, "Isn't that great?" And yes, it is.)

Another great talent with whom Bochco worked on that 1971 "Murder by the Book" movie-length episode of *Columbo* was its director: a twenty-four-year-old up-and-comer named Steven Spielberg. Bochco, at the time, was twenty-seven. Both of them had made the Universal lot their home base and found each other quickly. "I was always sort of the youngest guy in the room [in those days], and Steven is a few years younger than I am," Bochco says. "So we were really boys on the lot, and when we worked together on that first episode I'd written, we became good friends. We went and had lunch every day." Their social lives were different: Bochco, by that time, was remarried, with a child from his second wife (the actress Barbara Bosson), while Spielberg was single and "really boyish in terms of his interests," in love with cars and gadgets. Bochco remembers Spielberg driving a two-seater Mercedes convertible and taking Bochco to the parking lot one day after lunch to show him a big box bolted into the console between the seats—"the first car phone," Bochco marvels, "I'd ever seen." Two months after their first *Columbo* episode hit the air on NBC, Spielberg's highly regarded, beautifully filmed made-for-TV movie *Duel* premiered on ABC, the first big stage in Spielberg's rocket to stardom. Bochco's career would have a rapid ascendancy also, but not until he left Universal in 1978 to work for Grant Tinker's MTM Productions.

"Nobody ever gave Grant enough credit for what that company was and what it became," Bochco says. "He was such a unique guy, in that he so honored writers; he had such a genuine affection and admiration and respect for writers that he created a company that was the first really writer-centric company in the history of the medium! And he empowered all of us to do what we wanted to do . . . I think anybody that worked at MTM when Grant was there, before he left for NBC, would say the same thing: it was just the best place to work at."

In the first half of the 1970s, MTM was known for its clever comedies, starting with its flagship series, *The Mary Tyler Moore Show*. But the company also began developing some ambitious, groundbreaking dramas, including the CBS *Lou Grant* newspaper drama spin-off in 1977 and the same network's *White Shadow* drama series in 1978, about a high school basketball coach (played by Ken Howard) and his young inner-city players. That series was created by Bruce Paltrow, who collaborated with Bochco on two MTM projects. "Brucie was one of my dearest friends," Bochco says of the writer-producer (husband of Blythe Danner, father of Gwyneth Paltrow) who died in 2002. "We were friends in our twenties, and we played tennis every week and our families were close, and his son and my son are still best friends in the world. And yeah, we did learn from each other. When I went over to MTM in 1978, he was already there, because he had just developed *The White Shadow*. I wrote one of the first ones [episodes] for him." The same year, he and Paltrow co-wrote a 1978 pilot for a proposed medical series called *Operating Room*. The drama series, about resident doctors at a Los Angeles hospital, wasn't picked up by a network, but the pilot—with its larger-than-usual ensemble cast, its story structure, and even a few of its cast members—hinted at what the two men would eventually present separately at MTM (Bochco with *Hill Street Blues,* Paltrow with *St. Elsewhere*).

Bochco's next projects for MTM were in the fantasy genre: a very short-lived comedy called *Turnabout,* Bochco's TV version of the Thorne Smith novel about a husband and wife who magically inhabit each other's bodies, and a made-for-TV vampire movie called, well, *Vampire,* co-written with another young writer at MTM, Michael Kozoll. Both those TV shows premiered in 1979, as did the first drama series Bochco created for MTM. That was *Paris,* a cop show starring James Earl Jones as the California police captain Woody Paris, showing him at work and as a family man at home. It was significant, even at that late date, for casting an African-American as the dramatic lead in a TV series, but not to Bochco himself, because of where and how he grew up. "I never thought of James Earl as a 'black actor,' and 'Ooh, I'm doing a show about a "black family."' That never occurred to me," Bochco insists. "Listen: I grew up in New York City and went to school with black kids and Puerto Ricans and everybody else. You know, it was the Upper West Side of New York! I had friends in Harlem, I had friends in the projects, where Lincoln Center is now, and I never really thought about it." Also, Bochco adds, Jones was a friend of the family's ("His agent was like my godmother"), and to Bochco, "I just thought he would be just a wonderful guy to do this show about. That's all!" *Paris* lasted only one season, but when it was canceled, Bochco and Kozoll were asked to collaborate once again, this time on a gritty big-city police series that would launch in 1981 as NBC's *Hill Street Blues.*

Hill Street Blues had different fathers and different inspirations. Fred Silverman, then president of NBC Entertainment, asked MTM to generate a cop show with the chaotic, visceral style of a movie still in production, whose energy had impressed him when watching dailies. (That movie was *Fort Apache, the Bronx,* which *Hill Street Blues* would beat to the screen by three weeks in 1981.) Bochco and Kozoll got the assignment, but they were less inspired by a Hollywood cop drama than by a new documentary: Alan and Susan Raymond's *Police Tapes.* Put those two influences together, add a strong dose of the visual and aural freedom of Robert Altman's 1970s films, and you have the basic, yet envelope-pushing, *Hill Street* template, which, when it arrived on TV, was nothing less than revolutionary. The show's most important advancement of all, Bochco says, was to "put so much information on a frame of film." Not only was *Hill Street* framed and photographed as though random actions were being captured, but those actions were anything but accidental.

"Most television, up to that point, was sort of east/west," Bochco says, then explains. "By that I mean, things moved from left to right and right to left. And with *Hill Street,* it became dimensional. It was also north/south." And what was going on in the deep "south," in the rear of the frame, was considered important also. "We used to write scripts with double columns of dialogue," Bochco says, "because we scripted everything in the background . . . We wanted to make sure that everything that went on the screen was relevant. And in doing so, it confused the shit out of the audience, initially, because there was just too much going on for most people to process." Bochco laughs. "Not because they were dumb, but because they just weren't used to it. It took a year or so for people to figure out what the hell we were doing!" By then *Hill Street* had survived low ratings, won multiple Emmys, and inspired other TV producers and networks to mount drama series with large ensemble casts and serialized, complicated story lines. Bochco, working with Terry Louise Fisher, even co-created his own "*Hill Street* in a law office" variation for NBC, 1986's very popular *L.A. Law,* for which he left MTM and started his own production company. He also hired, as a scriptwriter, the young lawyer and future TV writer-producer powerhouse David E. Kelley. "He was a hell of a student," Bochco says admiringly. "He just sucked it all up." Kelley, for his part, returns the compliment. "I think the first thing I learned, which is maybe the best thing," Kelley says of his days with Bochco on *L.A. Law,* "was just never underestimate the intelligence of the audience. There are a lot of studio and network executives that will preach just the opposite."

In 1989, Bochco invited Kelley to co-create, and collaborate on, another series, ABC's *Doogie Howser, M.D.* comedy-drama, starring a teenage Neil Patrick Harris as a young prodigy medical resident. When I interviewed Bochco, I mentioned I planned to classify *Doogie,* in my history of quality TV, under the medical show genre, but he disagreed with me, saying he considered it first and foremost a family drama. And he should know, so I reclassified it. "The medical aspects of it was the sort of organizing element of it, no question," Bochco allows. "But the concept, to me, was most interesting as a notion of 'How does a prodigy still manage to be a kid when he or she is possessed of some kind of prodigious ability?' . . . He was a sixteen-year-old boy who could write a prescription for morphine, but he couldn't go buy a six-pack of beer. And by the way, I meticulously researched all that stuff. And it was all true." *Doogie Howser, M.D.* lasted four seasons, but its success was anything but automatic. Harris was at that point an unknown, and the series was a then-unusual hybrid of comedy and drama, thirty minutes in length, with no laugh track. "A lot of the shows I did for ABC were a gamble," Bochco says, and laughs. "*Cop Rock*? Hello?"

Hello indeed. *Cop Rock* was Bochco's 1990 attempt to emulate the British TV writer Dennis Potter's 1986 miniseries period masterpiece, *The Singing Detective*, but to attempt a "drama with music" set in modern times, using the cop genre Bochco knew so well and getting Randy Newman to write new songs for each episode. It was an ambitious effort but an infamous flop. Bochco's next major TV effort for ABC was just as risky: another cop series, but this time designed, by the series co-creators Bochco and the former *Hill Street Blues* writer David Milch, to be as bold and risqué as possible, pushing the boundaries of what was permissible on commercial broadcast TV in subject matter, language, nudity, and sexual situations.

"For me, *NYPD Blue* was a completely defensive attempt to salvage my business," Bochco says, chuckling, referring to the onslaught of cable TV in general and the popularity of uncensored, uncut movies in particular at that moment in 1993. "It's the only time that I ever, ever, in all the years of all the shows I've ever created—which are in excess of twenty—where I didn't start with a concept for a show. What I did was," he explains, "I started with a construct. I said, 'What can I do to get eyeballs back?'" Pressure groups and advertisers boycotted the show at first, but once *NYPD Blue* began and the ratings and reviews came in, the new series became a twelve-year fixture on ABC, bare buttocks and frequent curses notwithstanding. And though Bochco and Milch were indeed able to redefine what was allowable on a broadcast TV prime-time drama, Bochco doesn't think *NYPD Blue* ended up blazing any new trails—except for the competition.

"I always thought that with the success of *NYPD Blue* we would bust open the door for broadcast television to really come into the twenty-first century properly," Bochco says. "And it never happened. And I was amazed then, as I am now, that it didn't seem to give broadcast television the license to get significantly more adult in their programming . . . But the interesting thing is, I think *NYPD Blue* created the cable drama world. I think that's the door that it opened. That's when cable started to realize that they could be in both businesses. They could be in the adult business and in the television business. So, the unintended consequences, as we say . . ."

A few seasons into the twelve-year run of *NYPD Blue*, Bochco tried one more highly experimental TV series concept for ABC. In 1995, he and two *NYPD Blue* writers, Charles H. Eglee and Channing Gibson, co-created *Murder One*, in which a single murder case was followed from start to finish over an entire twenty-three episode season, from initial booking and jury selection to courtroom strategy and deliberation. It had never been tried before on a scripted TV series, but Bochco admits to a specific reason he tried it then. "*Murder One* came out of a very simple observation on my part," he says. "I had just—and when I say 'I,' I mean 'we,' all of us—spent four months, five months riveted to our television sets, every single day, watching the O. J. Simpson trial. And what I realized was, you'd never be able to do a law show the same way again." Instead, he envisioned a lengthy drama as intricate and complex as the Simpson case and dramatized it in *Murder One*. Nearly two decades later, Bochco did it again, with 2014's *Murder in the First* on TNT, another series devoting an entire season to one lengthy crime story. Moving to cable, even for Bochco, might have been one of those "unintended consequences" of *NYPD Blue*, because cable TV, specifically FX, is where he went in 2005 to create and present, with Chris Gerolmo, *Over There*, a drama series about an army infantry division on its tour of Iraq. Not only was it Bochco's first series for basic cable, but it was television's first war series dramatizing a still-ongoing conflict. "I knew it would fail, I just knew," Bochco says, "because it was too soon." He also says, "But I thought it was an important effort, and I was just thrilled to do it, and I don't regret it. For a moment."

Finally, when I tell Bochco that I'm now a full-time tenured college professor and show many of his works in my TV History and Appreciation courses—from *Columbo* to *Hill Street* and beyond—he laughs and replies, "Boy, they've lowered the bar, haven't they, David?" And I'm fairly certain he wasn't referring to his shows . . .

BORN: 1945, Mount Vernon, New York.
FIRST TV CREDIT: Writer, *The Bold Ones: The Lawyers,* 1971, NBC.
LANDMARK TV SERIES: *The Sopranos,* 1999–2007, HBO.
OTHER MAJOR CREDITS: TV: Writer, *Kolchak: The Night Stalker,* 1974–75, ABC; Writer and producer, *The Rockford Files,* 1976–79, NBC; Writer and supervising producer, *I'll Fly Away,* 1992–93, NBC; Executive producer, *Northern Exposure,* 1993–95, CBS.

In 2013, the Writers Guild of America polled its members and released a list of the 101 best-written shows in TV history. Topping the list was David Chase's HBO series *The Sopranos,* which also figures as a pivotal starting point for my own definition of the Platinum Age of Television. Asked whether he agrees with that latter assessment, Chase replies, "Um . . . I'm not complaining," then speaks as objectively as he can about how his story of the mob boss Tony Soprano altered the evolution of TV as we know it.

"How influential we were, I can't say," Chase says. "I just know that things changed radically. Even the business model . . . doing fewer episodes, taking time in between—everything about it just changed. And I could also tell, from the amount of imitators, that something big had happened."

David Chase was born David DeCesare in 1945, in Mount Vernon, New York. Network television was born at about the same time, and young David's first TV memories were of watching NBC's *Howdy Doody,* which began in 1947. "It was funny, it was surreal, it was kind of violent," Chase recalls, laughing. "And the characters—Buffalo Bob, and Princess Summerfall Winterspring, and Clarabell the Clown—it was a hand grenade. It was just really great!" As he grew up, his tastes were eclectic but impressive: *The Twilight Zone* was his favorite TV show, followed by Jackie Gleason's variety show and *The Honeymooners*. He also loved Sid Caesar's variety shows ("Again, so bizarre, so surreal"), Richard Boone's *Medic* and *Have Gun, Will Travel,* and Alfred Hitchcock's suspense anthologies. "My favorite Alfred Hitchcock, without a doubt, is the one called 'An Unlocked Window' . . . I was probably eighteen or nineteen [he was nineteen, when it aired in 1965 on *The Alfred Hitchcock Hour*], and it scared the shit out of me." (It was about a murderer of nurses targeting some isolated caregivers.) Chase, significantly, also remembers watching one particular show each week with his father: ABC's *Untouchables*.

"I'm Italian-American," Chase says, "and my parents were somewhat defensive of the organized-crime aspects of the Italian-American culture. And so when my father would sit there with me, and watch these guys like [the early Mafia figures] Frankie Yale and Frank Nitti and those people, I felt encouraged, and I felt closer to him—my father. And I felt we were all part of the same . . . ethnicity."

Chase grew up wanting to pursue his love of music as a drummer and bass player in a rock band, but eventually gravitated to film studies, after years of devouring everything from classic gangster movies to French New Wave character studies. He studied at New York University, then at the graduate film program at Stanford University. That's where a teacher of his gave him his big break: She forwarded his sample feature film script to Roy Huggins, creator of *The Fugitive,* an occasional guest lecturer acquaintance of hers then working on NBC's rotating anthology "wheel" *The Bold Ones,* for the series called *The Lawyers*. Chase was given an assignment to write a script for *The Lawyers,* which became his first TV credit but not for a while. "It took me, I think, three or four months to write that, and I didn't realize that was a long time," he says, chuckling. "And they never called me and said, 'Where is it?' But I never worked there again, and I went for another two years without working at all." He did, however, have to join the Writers Guild because of that *Bold Ones* episode—the same Writers Guild that would later honor him as the best TV writer in history.

When Chase did find work again, one of his first jobs was on ABC's *Kolchak: The Night Stalker,* allowing him to pursue his love of *Twilight Zone*-style stories while working with quite a talented bunch—the series creator

Jeff Rice, the future *Hill Street Blues* co-creator Michael Kozoll, and others. It's a particular favorite of mine, and I was surprised and pleased to learn that Chase feels the same way.

"It's a favorite of mine, too," he says. "It's a favorite of a lot of people, I find out . . . I had a horrible time doing that, and I had a great time." The star was Darren McGavin, playing an old-school print reporter whose persistent investigations kept leading to the paranormal: vampires, zombies, mummies, and anything else that made him a sort of one-man precursor to *The X-Files*. "Darren McGavin hated all the producers, and they had what's called 'creative differences,'" Chase explains. "So Darren, as he got more burned out, and then sort of fed up with it, he began to treat it like a comedy. So we were able to do more than a little seditious humor within it. I knew how cheap and bad all these monsters were," he says, laughing, "and how cheesy they were . . . so I was amazed when I heard that kids watching were actually frightened."

While working on *Kolchak,* Chase often sat outdoors, on the studio lot, waiting to meet with one of the producers, and an executive producer of a neighboring show, Meta Rosenberg of *The Rockford Files,* would walk by and take note of him sitting there glumly. "She would always say to me, 'Smile, David, smile!' and we started talking." Those talks led to an offer for Chase to replace one of the departing producers on *Rockford.* By that time, one of the show's co-creators, Chase's college-professor contact Roy Huggins, had also left, but the other co-creator, the prolific TV writer-producer Stephen J. Cannell, was still aboard that genial James Garner private eye vehicle, and Chase learned a lot.

"There's so much teaching that goes on," Chase says. "It's just part of the process of making a show, because someone is constantly telling you, 'Then that's not going to work. You've got to do this. Or you could try that.' But it's not like you're in school. It's like on-the-job training." From *The Rockford Files,* and Cannell, Chase says he learned two crucial tricks: how to make even a non-heroic character appealing, and how to enliven a story by focusing on the bad guys. "He said Rockford could get his teeth knocked out, and all that stuff, and be a coward, but he needed to be the smartest guy in the room . . . And the other thing, which was even more important from a learning standpoint for me, was that Steve used to say all the time, 'What are the heavies doing?' . . . So if, at any time, the story would slow down, you could get the villains kind of pumped up, and they could enter the story and give it a shot of energy."

After *The Rockford Files,* Chase worked as an executive producer on two acclaimed series created by Joshua Brand and John Falsey: NBC's 1950s-era southern drama *I'll Fly Away,* and CBS's quirky set-in-Alaska character study, *Northern Exposure.* Chase is quick to clarify that neither of those shows was his. *Northern Exposure,* he says, "wasn't my favorite job, but it was fun," while *I'll Fly Away,* designed to show the incremental growth of the black maid and her white employer (played, respectively, by Regina Taylor and Sam Waterston), was canceled long before its characters could develop and change. "That show got short shrift," Chase says. "That show was treated abysmally by NBC. Abysmally."

And then came *The Sopranos.* Originally conceived by Chase as a movie idea about a mob boss in therapy, it was written and sold as a pilot script for Fox, which ultimately passed on moving forward. HBO picked it up, and Chase and company assembled the cast and the creative team, and *The Sopranos* premiered in 1999, changing the face of television. In 2004, it was the first cable production to win an Emmy as Outstanding Drama Series and ended up winning twenty-one Emmys overall.

"I think a lot of people who talk about their experiences in the entertainment business," Chase says, "don't give enough credence to luck." *The Sopranos,* he says, was the right show in the right place at the right time, with the right cast and collaborators. "We had a lot of luck," he adds. "At the same time, there was a tremendous amount of talent. And, I'll say it, including me."

The freedoms of writing a dramatic series for HBO, at the time, were more than the obvious ones of less restricted language, nudity, and sexuality. The freedom of language, Chase explains, was not only in the use of profanity but that "you could write English that sounded like really contemporary English, and people speaking it . . . You were free to depict human behavior much, much, much more realistically than you could on network television." Even at HBO, though, there were limits, or at least concerns. Though Chris Albrecht was the HBO executive who purchased and championed *The Sopranos* from the start, he balked after seeing a cut of the first season's fifth episode, in which the northern New Jersey mob boss Tony Soprano, played brilliantly by James Gandolfini, is on a college-tour road trip with his daughter. Tony comes upon a guy who had ratted on the mob and gone into hiding in the witness protection program and kills him.

"He said to me," Chase says of Albrecht, "'In five episodes, you've created one of the most compelling TV characters in history.' He said, 'And you're going to destroy him in the fifth episode.' And I just said to him, 'Chris, if he doesn't kill that guy, the show's over. He's not really a mob boss. He's not really true to himself. He's not a member of organized crime.' And I guess I won."

So did quality TV, because that daring move was noted by many other talented TV writer-producers, who saw it as a way to pursue their own darker, more complex characters and visions. (Matt Weiner, for example, saw that "College" episode as a TV viewer at home, sent his languishing *Mad Men* pilot script to Chase right afterward, and was hired, eventually amassing the clout to get *Mad Men* produced.) *The Sopranos* paved the way in other areas as well, such as doing fewer episodes per season and stretching the time between seasons when necessary. "The short season was welcomed by me," Chase admits, "because I'd had enough of television completely. But it was not welcomed by the [other] writers and producers, because it meant—seriously—you took a 50 percent pay cut. You went from doing twenty-two shows to thirteen, and it was reflected in your income tax form."

And finally (or finale . . .), *The Sopranos* made a major impact with the controversially abrupt ending to its closing episode. Not since the endings of *The Prisoner, St. Elsewhere,* and *Twin Peaks* had a drama series incited such heated conversations and analyses, but years after the dust has settled, Chase still refuses to add to that conversation.

"David, I'm not going to ever say another word about that finale," he tells me. "Honestly. I can't do it. No matter what I say, it just leads to something else."

Perhaps the only fitting way to conclude a profile of David Chase, therefore, is to embrace the spirit of the finale of *The Sopranos* and end it, unexpectedly and unexplained, in the middle of

BORN: 1959, South Orange, New Jersey, as Kevin Spacey Fowler.
FIRST TV CREDIT: Guest star, *The Equalizer*, 1987, CBS.
LANDMARK TV SERIES: Recurring guest star, *Wiseguy*, 1988, CBS; Star and executive producer, *House of Cards*, 2013–, Netflix.
OTHER MAJOR CREDITS: Movies: *Glengarry Glen Ross*, 1992; *Se7en*, 1995; *Outbreak*, 1995; *The Usual Suspects*, 1995; *L.A. Confidential*, 1997; *American Beauty*, 1999; *Superman Returns*, 2006. TV: Actor, *Long Day's Journey into Night*, 1987, Showtime; Actor, *The Murder of Mary Phagan*, 1988, NBC; Actor, *Recount*, 2008, HBO. Broadway: *Long Day's Journey into Night*, 1986; *Lost in Yonkers*, 1991–93; *The Iceman Cometh*, 1999; *A Moon for the Misbegotten*, 2007. London: Artistic director and occasional star, Old Vic Theatre Company, 2003–15.

As Kevin Spacey tells it, two people, above all others, might have been responsible for inspiring him, as a teenager, to pursue a career in acting. One was the real-life actor Jack Lemmon, who met and encouraged him early. The other was Artemus Gordon, the pretend actor played by Ross Martin in the CBS Western *The Wild Wild West*. That was the first television series young Kevin, born Kevin Spacey Fowler in 1959 in South Orange, latched onto as his own sort of Must-See TV. He and his family moved to California when he was four years old, and *The Wild Wild West* premiered just a few years later.

"I thought it was not only a great show and a great concept," Spacey says, "but Artemus Gordon, and the actor, Ross Martin, who played him, was one of the greatest characters ever. I thought the whole idea of being able to be 'The Man of a Thousand Faces' was such a cool idea—and all of the disguises he wore!" Artemus and his Secret Service partner, Jim West, worked as special agents for President Ulysses S. Grant, traversing the Old West in a tricked-out railroad car, embarking on special spy missions while working with the latest high-tech gadgetry, like tiny guns hidden in sliding wrist contraptions. "Jim West, whom Robert Conrad played, had a derringer that came down his sleeve and a knife in his boot," Spacey says, still sounding like the fan boy he clearly was. "He was like an 1800s MacGyver! He could do anything . . . And not only did I admire that show as much as I did, and was just hooked on it, but I was the guy who had the *Wild Wild West* lunch box," Spacey confesses. "I was a huge, huge fan of Robert Conrad's, to the point where I sought him out when I was in high school." Like Marcia inviting the former Monkee Davy Jones to her prom on *The Brady Bunch*, he invited the TV star to come watch him in his high school production of *The Sound of Music*, and, just like Davy Jones, Conrad, the action TV star with a tough-guy reputation, agreed to show up.

At that time, Spacey was attending Chatsworth High School in Los Angeles, which had a strong theater program, and starring as Captain von Trapp opposite Mare Winningham (another star of the future) as Maria. "Almost everyone in my drama class, when I told them that Robert Conrad said yes, and was going to come see us that Saturday night, thought I was completely full of shit," Spacey recalls, laughing. "Until he actually showed up and sat in the front row with his family and watched our production of *The Sound of Music*." That wasn't the only time Spacey interacted with Conrad, either. When Conrad and Martin reunited for a *Wild Wild West Revisited* made-for-TV movie in 1979, the nineteen-year-old Spacey visited the set, watched them film, and even got to strap the sliding gun on his own arm. "It was a dream come true," Spacey says. And it was a dream he never stopped embracing. "There was a period of time," he recalls, thinking of the years just after he won his first Academy Award (a 1996 Best Supporting Actor Oscar for *The Usual Suspects*), "where I tried desperately to convince Warner Bros. to let George Clooney and I do *The Wild Wild West* movie. Because I thought he would be a great James West, and I wanted to play Artemus Gordon. But needless to say," he says with a chuckle, "they went in a different direction." That direction was Will Smith and Kevin Kline, and the film flopped. "I can only say this: that I hope, one day, it's not too late to revive the franchise."

But there were additional influences, and from very early. His family took him to lots of live theater when he was young, and his mother loved to watch PBS, especially British drama, whenever she could, and the family often watched with her. Sometimes it was repeats of vintage TV productions, like Laurence Olivier directing Michael Redgrave in 1963's *Uncle Vanya*, but other times it was the latest miniseries from England, such as the 1990 multipart drama about political intrigue in Parliament, starring Ian Richardson and titled *House of Cards*. "I saw it when it first aired because my mother adored it!" Spacey says, and adds, "I was very aware of it, and I watched it." Other TV choices were more mainstream: as a youngster, Spacey enjoyed *The Dick Van Dyke Show, All in the Family, The Flip Wilson Show, Sanford and Son, The Carol Burnett Show, Columbo,* and especially *The Tonight Show Starring Johnny Carson,* on which he practiced his early gift for mimicry, imitating not only the show's host but some of his guests, including the endearingly hesitant James Stewart. (In 2015, Spacey would combine several of his childhood TV loves by imitating James Stewart for a surprised and delighted Carol Burnett on *The Late Show with Stephen Colbert,* reading a poem just the way Stewart used to do on *The Tonight Show.*) Spacey would stay up late to watch and study Carson and, on occasion, would go to his Los Angeles tapings. "I used to go to *The Tonight Show,*" Spacey says. "I'd stand in line at NBC and get tickets to watch him live." One time, one of the prop guys took him backstage, where young Spacey met Carson and got his autograph on an old *Look* magazine. Despite his celebrity encounters with Conrad and Carson, though, Spacey's most meaningful interactions by far with a Hollywood star were with the legendary actor Jack Lemmon.

"My relationship with Jack was a very lengthy one," Spacey says, "and it started when I was thirteen years old, at a workshop that he ran at the Mark Taper Forum that I went to with my junior high school class." Spacey describes himself as, at the time, "this shy kid who really wanted to be an actor," and after he enacted a scene with Lemmon watching, the movie star pulled Spacey aside and put his hand on the boy's shoulder. Spacey never forgot what Lemmon did next: "He said, 'You are a born actor, and you should go to New York and you should study. You are meant to do this for your life.'" Spacey took that advice and in time moved to New York, where he studied at Juilliard for two years before finding work at the New York Shakespeare Festival. Twelve years after Lemmon singled him out, Spacey auditioned to play Lemmon's son in a Broadway-bound revival of Eugene O'Neill's *Long Day's Journey into Night*. He got the part and toured the world with Lemmon and the production, which was captured as a televised stage production by Showtime in 1987. Spacey played opposite Lemmon again in NBC's 1978 *The Murder of Mary Phagan* miniseries and, in time, feature films as well, including 1992's stellar movie version of *Glengarry Glen Ross.* "He was my mentor," Spacey says. "He was my father figure. He taught me more about this business, and how to have a career that sustains, and how to be able to do comedy and drama . . . He was a remarkable man." Much of what Spacey has done since, including becoming artistic director of the Old Vic Theatre Company in London and starting his Kevin Spacey Foundation, has been dedicated to providing classes, grants, and other opportunities for young people hoping to pursue the theater arts. "I started my foundation four and a half years ago," Spacey says, "and it's very much driven by Jack's philosophy, which was: if you've done well in the business that you wanted to do well in, then it's your obligation to spend a good amount of your time sending the elevator back down. That was Jack's term." And that was why Lemmon was teaching at the Mark Taper Forum that day and putting his hand on Spacey's shoulder.

After he worked with Lemmon on Broadway, Spacey's next elevator stop was television. While still in New York, he did one-shot roles on both *The Equalizer* and *Crime Story* but hated both experiences. Then, on his first trip to Los Angeles to take meetings in Hollywood, Spacey arrived at his agent's office, totally exhausted, only to be asked to stop by a casting director's office to read for a role that had suddenly opened up, on a recently launched series by Stephen J. Cannell of *The Rockford Files* fame. Reluctantly, Spacey went, read, and was asked to come back later that afternoon for two different meetings: one with Cannell's team of writer-producers, and another with the CBS executives in charge of this new Cannell series, called *Wiseguy,* about an undercover agent infiltrating various criminal organizations. *Wiseguy* had recently completed its first season, an impressive full-season story arc guest starring Ray Sharkey as the hot-tempered mob figure Sonny Steelgrave, but Spacey had never seen the series and dismissed it as just another "cop show." Spacey left the casting director's office, sighing and muttering, got to where he was staying, and phoned his agent and manager to complain and explode.

"Look, I don't fucking want to do a TV show!" Spacey remembers yelling at them. "I just had a terrible experience doing the fucking *Equalizer;* it's so fucking stupid." They persuaded him to meet with Cannell and the network, but Spacey insisted that he'd do it only if it was all done in one single, all-purpose meeting with everyone in attendance. "At four o'clock, I walk into Stephen Cannell's office," Spacey continues, "and there's literally like a jury—twelve people, sitting in chairs. And I do this read through, and I meet everybody, and we have a little conversation, and I leave. At seven o'clock, I get offered this part. And at 7:05," Spacey says with a laugh, "I turn it down. And everyone is fucking flipping out on my team." Cannell asked if Spacey would come back that night so they could show him the end of the Sonny Steelgrave arc, because he'd never seen the series, and have a further conversation. Spacey was jet-lagged, tired, and at this point very negative, but he returned at nine o'clock as a courtesy, whereupon Cannell asked Spacey why he was so opposed to taking the job, a juicy recurring role as a drug-addicted, paranoid, incestuous crime lord named Mel Profitt. (The part was available, and Cannell and company were so interested, because the actor selected to play Profitt had unexpectedly gone into rehab.) Spacey told Cannell about the annoying network interference he experienced as a low-ranked guest player on *The Equalizer* and *Crime Story,* and Cannell promised him that if he took the *Wiseguy* job, he'd be left alone to create the role the way he wanted and would work only with the creative team, not anyone from CBS. Cannell then screened the finale of the first season of *Wiseguy*—a dynamic, intense, obviously different sort of television show.

"And I'm watching this thing," Spacey recalls, "going, 'Wow, this is really extraordinary.' And then, this is my favorite part of this story: I watch, like, maybe thirty or forty minutes of it," Spacey says, laughing, "and then I fall asleep." When he woke up, he apologized to Cannell for being so tired. Cannell thought he hated it, but the next morning, persuaded both by what he saw of *Wiseguy* and by Cannell's assurances, and after seeking counsel from his mentor Jack Lemmon (who encouragingly said his own early days in television were a place he was able to practice his craft with "total abandon"), Spacey accepted the role. That was on a Friday morning. "I flew to Vancouver [where the show was to start filming] on Saturday," Spacey says, "and I watched *Scarface* and *The Godfather* on Sunday, and I started shooting on Tuesday."

Spacey's performance as Mel Profitt was such an instant standout—so smart, spooky, creepy, and captivating all at once—that I arranged almost instantly to interview the relatively unknown *Wiseguy* guest star for a profile in the *New York Post,* where I was working as the TV critic. Because Spacey's

Profitt was such a cultured villain, we conducted the interview over high tea at the Helmsley Hotel as a harpist played from the balcony and waitresses brought us finger sandwiches and scones. Never before, and never since, have I interviewed anyone in such a setting, and I'm just as puzzled now about why that appealed to me as to why Spacey agreed to show up. But I'm glad he did, because *Wiseguy,* in terms of TV history, was both revolutionary and evolutionary, and the next time he appeared in a TV series, as the star of Netflix's *House of Cards,* it, too, was both evolutionary and revolutionary. And though it was more than twenty-five years later when I approached him for this book, he remembered our earlier interview and (perhaps despite that) graciously agreed to talk again—this time by phone. So, no scones.

In between, for Spacey, was a long string of successes in film and the theater, including winning a Tony for *Lost in Yonkers* in 1991 and Oscars for both Best Supporting Actor (*The Usual Suspects,* 1996) and Best Actor (*American Beauty,* 2000). How he came to do *House of Cards,* and how *House of Cards* came to Netflix, say volumes about how much television has changed, in both content and delivery, since Spacey guest starred on *Wiseguy.*

Spacey says he was on the set of *The Social Network,* the 2010 movie about Mark Zuckerberg and the origins of Facebook, adapted by Aaron Sorkin and directed by David Fincher. Spacey was the film's executive producer and began chatting with Fincher about doing something together. They'd both been offered a lot of television by that time and turned it down, but Fincher said he'd noticed the rights to this British series, *House of Cards,* had just become available. He hadn't seen it, but Spacey had, because of his mother's passion for British drama, and they agreed to see the original anew and regroup. "We came back together," Spacey says, "and both had decided that we thought it would translate incredibly well for a U.S. series, and that's how the whole thing began."

How it ended up on Netflix was another matter entirely and was due partly to Spacey's prescient view of the entertainment industry overall. "I had been thinking, and talking about, and looking at all of these companies, I would say literally for the past nine or ten years," Spacey says, referring to Netflix, Amazon, Hulu, and other companies that "had made a gazillion dollars being portals for entertainment." Spacey's gut instinct, he says, was that "at some point one of them, several of them, were going to step up and say, 'Hey, if we want to be in the game, we're going to have to start producing our own content.'" Spacey adds, "So it didn't surprise me that someone was going to step up and get serious and do it in a very serious way. What surprised me, ultimately, is that I was involved in it!"

That involvement came about because of how much Fincher and Spacey believed in an Americanized *House of Cards*. They hired Beau Willimon, who wrote the first two scripts, and then pitched the series to the networks based on those scripts. "Every single network was very interested," Spacey recalls, "and every single network insisted that we do a pilot first. David and I and Beau Willimon were not interested in doing a pilot." Spacey explains that a pilot is like an audition for the network, introducing all the characters, establishing the settings, and inserting arbitrary cliff-hangers, all to prove that the show was going to work. "And we believed it would work," he adds. "We had enormous faith in it. We thought it was a tremendously powerful series when it was originally done, and we thought that those two scripts [of Willimon's] were a really great runway to begin to establish the show and also to allow characters to be introduced in the time we wanted to introduce them." Netflix was the only place that didn't balk at the no-pilot demand.

Spacey says Netflix executives told him, "'Well, we've run our analytics, and people [in the Netflix subscriber base] would run David Fincher movies, and people would watch your movies, and people love that British show, so we don't need you to do a pilot. How many do you want to do?'" Spacey laughs, recalling how taken aback they were. "And we were like, 'Umm, uhh, two seasons?' And they were like, 'Okay.' And then we negotiated, and we were able to make a pretty remarkable deal." That deal, reported elsewhere, was estimated at $100 million for two thirteen-episode seasons of *House of Cards*. Netflix was widely criticized for what was considered, at the time, a high-risk, highly overpaid gamble, but Spacey didn't see it that way, from his side or from Netflix's. He and Fincher and Willimon got to make the show they wanted without either censorship or network interference, because, since Netflix had never done an original production before, no office even existed to give the creative team any notes. When Spacey was invited to give the prestigious James MacTaggart Memorial Lecture at 2013's Edinburgh International Television Festival, he asked, "Can you imagine the notes we would have gotten if we'd been at a network that didn't support us artistically?" Then he imagined them: "Umm, we are very concerned about the fact that Kevin strangles a dog in the first five minutes of the show. We are afraid we're going to lose half our audience."

Instead, the audience for *House of Cards*, and for Netflix, grew, and substantially, though Netflix guards aggressively all but the most basic numbers regarding internal measurement, other than the monthly subscription fee ($7.99 in 2016) and the overall subscriber totals (at the start of 2016, an estimated 44 million in the United States and another 30 million worldwide). But Spacey, privy to the inside numbers, is the first person I've ever gotten to reveal any of them. "When we made the deal, there were a lot of people running around saying it was crazy making a series with a streaming service, it made no sense," Spacey recalls, then adds, "Actually, when we sort of ran the numbers and thought about it—yeah, everything's a risk in this world, but in actuality, all Netflix had to do to break even was get 565,000 new members. And I'm pretty sure, by the time we got to Season 2, they had about 17 million new subscribers!" That makes Netflix's *House of Cards* a financial behemoth, but it was every bit as much an artistic monster as well. Once again, but in a different generation, Kevin Spacey had found himself in a TV series that changed all the rules and influenced countless quality shows that came in its wake.

When Spacey's *House of Cards* premiered on Netflix in 2013, unveiling all thirteen Season 1 episodes at once, my review as TV critic for NPR's *Fresh Air* raved about both the series itself and its probable importance to the future of television. "This isn't the first time, on the Internet or on Netflix, that an original production has been presented this way," I said, "but *House of Cards* is by far the best yet. It is to Netflix what *The Sopranos* was to HBO, what *The Shield* was to FX, what *Mad Men* was to AMC. It's an identity maker and a game changer."

My conclusion then, for *Fresh Air,* is the same conclusion I offer today: "And unlike all those others, *House of Cards* arrives all at once. If the broadcast networks, especially, aren't frightened by this, they should be. Netflix, this week, isn't merely making great television—it's making TV history."

VINCE GILLIGAN

BORN: 1967, Richmond, Virginia.

FIRST TV CREDIT: Writer, *The X-Files*, 1995, Fox.

LANDMARK TV SERIES: Writer, producer, and director, *The X-Files*, 1995–2000, 2002, Fox; Creator, executive producer, writer, and director, *Breaking Bad*, 2008–13, AMC; Co-creator, executive producer, writer, and director, *Better Call Saul*, 2015–, AMC.

OTHER MAJOR CREDITS: TV: Co-creator and writer, *The Lone Gunmen*, 2001, Fox; Writer, *Night Stalker*, 2006, ABC; Co-creator, executive producer, and writer, *Battle Creek*, 2015, CBS. Movies: Writer, *Wilder Napalm*, 1993; *Home Fries*, 1998; *Hancock*, 2008.

Most people interviewed for this book had no problem enumerating, and raving about, the TV shows they loved as youngsters, but *Breaking Bad*'s creator, Vince Gilligan, is the only one who paraded some of those old loves on television. In 2015, he hosted a personally selected programming block on MeTV: a four-hour special called *Vince Gilligan's Island of MeTV*. "Shows like *The Twilight Zone* and *The Honeymooners* made a big impression on me growing up," Gilligan said then. He also said, "I watched a lot of classic TV shows," and based on his curatorial choices, his tastes were superb: two relatively obscure episodes of *The Twilight Zone*, one strong episode each of *The Honeymooners* and *Taxi*, and "Murder Under Glass," a 1978 episode of *Columbo*, starring Peter Falk and directed by Jonathan Demme. With that kind of discerning taste and untiring enthusiasm as a youngster, and with a Spielbergian habit of borrowing a friend's Super 8 camera to film his own imaginative movies, it's no surprise that Gilligan, who was born in 1967 in

Richmond, Virginia, ended up attending, and graduating from, film school at NYU. What's more surprising is how he got his first big break and his second one.

His first break came shortly after graduation, when he entered a screenwriting competition in 1989 at the Virginia Film Festival and won. One of the judges was the producer Mark Johnson, whose credits included *The Natural* and *Good Morning, Vietnam* and who had just won an Oscar for *Rain Man*. Johnson was so impressed by Gilligan's "Home Fries" screenplay submission that he tracked down the fledgling screenwriter, befriended him, helped him get an agent, and soon made a movie based on another of Gilligan's scripts, 1993's *Wilder Napalm*. Eventually, they'd team up again, turning Gilligan's festival-winning submission into the 1998 film *Home Fries*, starring Drew Barrymore. In between, though, came Gilligan's second big break: tuning in to the premiere of Fox's *X-Files*.

At this point in his life, Gilligan was still living in Virginia, writing screenplays, and trying to get *Home Fries* turned into his second feature film. "*The X-Files* came on," he recalls. "I was home alone and watched the first episode, not expecting much. At the end of the first commercial break, I called my girlfriend and said, 'You've got to watch this.' After that, I watched every episode." A few months later, he was talking to his agent, telling her she had to check out this new series, when she replied, "Funny thing . . . ," and informed Gilligan that she was related to Chris Carter, creator of *The X-Files*, by marriage ("His wife was her cousin or something," Gilligan says). She offered to set up a meeting the next time Gilligan was in Hollywood, and she did. To Gilligan, it was just a casual visit to say how much he enjoyed the show, but Carter asked Gilligan if he had any ideas for an *X-Files* story. "And I did, because I was such a fan," Gilligan says. "About a shadow. What if it came to life and moved independently of you and had 'black hole' ability? I pitched that, and I was not even nervous, because I truly was not there to stump for a job." Carter gave him the freelance assignment to write that script, which turned into the second-season 1995 episode "Soft Light," starring Tony Shalhoub. Gilligan was invited to join the writing staff, and, he says, "Thus began a wonderful seven years. Chris Carter was the best boss I ever had. He was a wonderful mentor and teacher and taught all of us writers and producers how to write for TV and how to be a TV producer. He taught me. It was a wonderful film school, and I got paid a lot more than I deserved."

Asked what he learned the most from his *X-Files* university stint, Gilligan distilled it down to two major things: thinking cinematically, and not revealing too much through dialogue. "TV is tough," Gilligan says, adding, "Production is tight, and all of that tends to make television a very dialogue-heavy medium. What that tends to force you into doing is telling the story rather than showing it, and having characters speak their minds rather than reveal things by actions.

"In real life, we say the opposite of what we mean—the politically correct thing—and live something else," Gilligan continues. "Not to sound cynical, but it's human nature to say the opposite. I like that. And I first got a true taste of that on *The X-Files*." Also absorbed from *The X-Files* was pride in crafting a half-length movie every eight days of shooting and working to make it very visual and cinematic. When it came to *Breaking Bad*, Gilligan's intention was to "try to shoot it like a Sergio Leone Western" and to incorporate many *X-Files* visual tricks. "Go wider," Gilligan says. "Show more of the world around the characters. Show the character from head to toe. TV usually is tighter—more on the eyes. Try to frame wider."

One 1998 *X-Files* episode, written by Gilligan and directed by Rob Bowman, exemplified both those attributes. Called "Drive," it was about a paranoid, bigoted, severely agitated man named Crump, whose wife had suddenly died when her head exploded, and Crump feared the same thing would happen to him if he didn't keep moving in a certain direction at a certain speed, so he kidnaps the *X-Files* agent Mulder (David Duchovny) at gunpoint and forces him to drive, in hopes of alleviating the pain and pressure in Crump's head. Part of "Drive" is photographed and reported as if by a local TV station news helicopter, and the rest is from inside the moving vehicle, where Mulder tries to separate Crump's ramblings and diatribes from clues about what's really happening to him.

"We had a hard time casting that part, of Mr. Crump," Gilligan says. "You needed a great actor who could be scary and intense and deliver horrible, hateful lines yet, at the same time, have some sort of innate humanity, whereby the audience feels sorry for the guy. Not to spoil it," Gilligan says many years after the episode was televised, "but the guy dies at the end." Many actors were brought in—actors, Gilligan says, with "wonderful chops," but without "that extra something that made us want to root for them." And then, after several long days of auditions, the casting director brought in an actor who "just nailed it," according to Gilligan. "He was the guy, from the moment he sat down. I looked at the other producers and whispered, 'OTW,' our slang for 'Off to Work,' which is what we say when we know the guy is being hired." In this case, "the guy" was Bryan Cranston.

"And sure enough," Gilligan continues, "Bryan played the part wonderfully. His performance stuck with me, which is saying a lot, because I was with *The X-Files* for seven years, and did 202 episodes." Two years after Cranston's "Drive" episode of *The X-Files* was televised, Cranston showed up again on Fox, this time as the harried, childlike patriarch of a dysfunctional sitcom family in 2000's *Malcolm in the Middle*. "It took me a while to realize it was the same guy," Gilligan says, laughing. "Bryan is a true chameleon." He cites some of Cranston's pre-*X-Files* roles—such as the astronaut Buzz Aldrin in HBO's *From the Earth to the Moon* and the dentist Tim Whatley in NBC's *Seinfeld*—and marvels, "In everything, he does look like a different person. He immerses himself."

In time, that assessment would come in handy, but only after several more years of work, and a few years where the work wasn't as plentiful. In the latter years of *The X-Files*, Gilligan and Carter joined forces as two of the co-creators of an official spin-off called *The Lone Gunmen*, but it both came and went in 2001. Gilligan left *The X-Files* in 2002, and for a while nothing much followed. "The jobs were not coming quickly enough," Gilligan says of that period, and he remembers complaining on the phone to Tom Schnauz, his old NYU film school buddy who, like Gilligan, had worked on both *The X-Files* and *The Lone Gunmen*. "What should we do next?" they wondered, if no more Hollywood offers ever materialized. "We were just goofing and decided that we should go off and cook crystal meth or be a greeter at Walmart, joking that that was our Plan B. We didn't know what else to do." That desperation fantasy scenario resurfaced when Gilligan, meeting with Sony TV executives to discuss concepts for possible new series, pitched an idea that had sprouted from the "crystal meth" seed: the story of Walter White, a "straight-arrow, middle-class guy who decides to break bad." Surprisingly, the executives at Sony liked the concept and took it around town with Gilligan to pitch to the cable networks ("Just cable—we knew we had no shot with [broadcast] TV," Gilligan recalls). Less surprisingly, everyone turned them down. Gilligan fleshed out the *Breaking Bad* concept in a pilot script, but there were no takers. Then one of his agents sent the script to a cable network no one had considered as a player until that point: AMC, which was just about to launch its first scripted series, *Mad Men*. Executives there embraced *Breaking Bad* from the beginning, and it became the network's second salvo in a stunningly potent one-two punch. "That's the long answer of how *Breaking Bad* got on TV," Gilligan says. "The short answer is, I'm as amazed as you are that the show got produced."

It was the concept of following a lengthy, gradual character arc from one end to the other that drew Gilligan, he says, rather than the meth-making, meth-selling subculture. "I am a strange person to write this show," he admits. "I am neither a chemist nor a scientist, nor have I dabbled in drugs. What interested me about this show was Walter White . . . I love the idea of a good character, and a good man, doing arguably bad things for good reason, and watching this character devolve, and transform, into a bad guy."

About halfway through writing the pilot script, Gilligan remembered Cranston's performance in that *X-Files* episode and thought, "Bryan would be great . . . It was hard to try and rationalize the cooking and sale of meth as a life choice. We needed an actor the audience could sympathize with, even in his darker moments." Once AMC expressed interest in making *Breaking Bad*, Gilligan suggested Cranston as the lead. AMC executives were wary, because Cranston, by then, had just ended a long run as the dad on the *Malcolm in the Middle* sitcom—a far cry from the cancer-stricken, desperate, drug-dealing Walter White. "Just trust me," Gilligan told them, and showed them the "Drive" episode of *The X-Files*. Cranston was in, and the rest is TV history.

"I believe AMC was interested in it because it was unique," Gilligan theorizes. "I don't think they had a philosophy to be edgy. They just like a good story, and they'd not heard a story like this. That's what attracted them. That's a very smart corporate philosophy, trying to give the audience something they haven't seen before, which is hard to do."

The structure of *Breaking Bad*, with the corruption of its protagonist and a calculated end point of sorts, nonetheless allowed for all manner of variations between those broad outlines. "My original intention for Jesse Pinkman," Gilligan says of the former high school stoner (played by Aaron Paul) who partners with his former chemistry teacher to make crystal meth, "was that he was going to die at the end of season 1." Yet halfway through shooting the first episode, Gilligan continues, "It became clear to me that this actor, Aaron Paul, was a wonderful addition to the show." Consequently, Jesse Pinkman escaped death, though his junkie girlfriend Jane, played by

Krysten Ritter, did not. In season 2, Walter White came upon her passed out with an overdose and, to keep her from blackmailing him about his meth operation with Jesse, watched passively as she choked on her own vomit and expired. "That was the one moment where AMC called up," Gilligan says. "They did get me on the phone. But to their credit, they never said, 'You can't do this.' They just wanted to open up a dialogue." AMC executives warned Gilligan that once Walter walks through that door and essentially commits murder, he's not the same. If it takes the character somewhere bad, in relation to the viewers, you can't return. Gilligan thought the act was a necessary step in Walter's transition from good to evil and held firm, but not so firm that he didn't soften the scene somewhat. "To be honest," he admits, "the original version was, he actually shoots her up with more. He was more active in his culpability . . . and I'm glad I got talked out of that one."

Even as it was, it was akin to the first-season scene in HBO's *Sopranos* where Tony Soprano, the show's central figure, cold-bloodedly chokes a man to death. As AMC warned, there was no going back from that. And for *Breaking Bad*, going forward meant dealing with the ramifications of that death, up to and including an airline crash accidentally caused by the girl's grieving father, an air traffic controller.

"Actions do have consequences," Gilligan says insistently. "As a television viewer, that was something that always struck me as false about a lot of TV. In most TV shows, actions exist in a vacuum." Another complaint he has, about much of weekly television series, is this: "They're all about stretching it out for as long as they can—taking the character as far as they can, but then resetting everything to zero." With *Breaking Bad*, Gilligan intentionally set out to do something different. "It really wants to be a show truly about transformation," he says. "The character he turns into is a guy you would not recognize from the beginning . . . For good or bad, that is our franchise."

The end of the franchise, when it arrived, required a finale. And by 2013, when *Breaking Bad* presented its last episodes, expectations for a fitting finale, following in the wake of everything from *The Sopranos* and *The Shield* to *Lost*, were overwhelmingly high. "Somewhere along the line, as we created the final sixteen episodes of *Breaking Bad*," Gilligan recalls, "you start thinking to yourself, 'We've got to have a big, big ending. It's got to be big!' As Donald Trump would say, 'It's got to be huge!' Anyway, I came to realize, with the help of my wonderful writers, it doesn't need to be huge.

205 | VINCE GILLIGAN

It just needs to satisfy. It needs to be satisfying." Alternative endings were considered, in which Walter White would be carted off to jail in handcuffs or, perhaps worse, get away with all his crimes. "We even had a thought of ending the series with everyone else that he loves dying all around him, and he's the only one, perversely, that survives. Like a cockroach, and his hell, his torment, is that everyone else dies. But that seemed a little too consciously ironic to go in that direction. It just seemed fitting, and ultimately satisfying, to give the audience what we promised them sixty-one episodes before, in the very first episode: the fact that this guy was not going to survive the series." After the finale aired, Gilligan "breathed a big sigh of relief," not because *Breaking Bad* was over, but because "the general consensus was that folks were satisfied."

And though *Breaking Bad* was over, its overall narrative was not. Once *Breaking Bad* was completed, Gilligan and the *Breaking Bad* writer-producer Peter Gould began work on a spin-off series for AMC. The series, *Better Call Saul,* followed Bob Odenkirk's fast-talking, shifty attorney character of Saul Goodman but, like *Breaking Bad,* had a very unorthodox narrative structure. The opening of the show's premiere episode (and of its second-season opener as well), photographed in dreary black and white, begins in the time frame after the *Breaking Bad* story has ended, with Saul hiding under an assumed name as a Cinnabon manager in Nebraska. The rest of the episodes, though, are in color and in flashback, going back years before Saul Goodman existed. In Saul's place was Jimmy McGill, a low-rent lawyer with an agoraphobic brother, a struggling one-man practice, and an already somewhat slippery moral center. Odenkirk played him, too, and once again *Better Call Saul* was presented as a story about transformation, but this time one that could end up encompassing past, present, and future.

The credits for *Better Call Saul* include many, many members of the *Breaking Bad* crew and staff, including two collaborators Gilligan has known for decades: his NYU classmate Tom Schnauz (who inspired the original *Breaking Bad* meth-lab idea) and the producer Mark Johnson, who made Gilligan's first movie. Clearly, Gilligan is the loyal sort and makes sure to stress that when it came time to consider a spin-off of *Breaking Bad,* there were a "great many actors and actresses on *Breaking Bad* who could capably carry their own spin-off, starting with Aaron Paul." To prove his point, he rattled off several others, including Anna Gunn's Skyler, Walter's long-suffering wife; Dean Morris's Hank, the brother-in-law who pursued the drug kingpin who turned out to be Walter; Betsy Brandt as Marie, Hank's wife; and even Giancarlo Esposito's character, the smooth criminal Gus Fring.

"I like to stress no value judgment in regard to which actor was the best of the bunch," Gilligan says, "should be construed from the decision we made to give Saul Goodman the spin-off and not the other characters. Bob Odenkirk was, and still is, a pleasure to work with. He had the acting chops, as did the other actors . . . But Saul Goodman was always a treat to write for.

"We're very proud of the cinematic elements of *Breaking Bad* and *Better Call Saul*," Gilligan continues, "which is to say, we're proud of the visual, nonverbal storytelling. But sometimes as writers, and I think all writers share this, sometimes it's fun to just settle in and write reams of fun, snappy dialogue. And the character on *Breaking Bad* who consistently had the most fun dialogue—not counting Jesse Pinkman, I guess—was Saul Goodman."

Initially, the idea for *Better Call Saul* was to set that spin-off as a pure prequel, but one that didn't go back as far and began with Odenkirk in his familiar Saul Goodman persona and ornately tacky office. But then came a pair of inspirations that changed the new show's structure entirely. One was to take, quite literally, a toss-away line of dialogue uttered by Saul in one of the last episodes of *Breaking Bad* and use it to frame the new series by setting it in the post–*Breaking Bad* present ("If I'm lucky, a month from now," Saul had muttered as danger was closing in from all sides, "best-case scenario, I'm managing a Cinnabon in Omaha"). The other inspiration was to do the Saul Goodman equivalent of a superhero original story and learn who this character was before he adopted the alter ego who advertised on TV with the phrase "Better call Saul!"

Gilligan says of the brash, fully formed Saul character, "We thought we'd start out with that guy, and then we started to think, 'Well, maybe we should start off with the guy he used to be, before he became Saul Goodman.' And lo and behold, the realization that we've come to . . . is that we really like the guy he used to be far more than the guy he becomes. In other words, the show is a bit of a bait and switch, if you think about it. The show is titled *Better Call Saul,* and we have yet to see Saul Goodman! And not only that, but Peter Gould and I, and the other writers, realized that we don't want to see Saul Goodman.

"We have to. We are inexorably heading towards the time when Saul Goodman appears and Jimmy McGill [the character's real name] submerges and disappears. But we are saddened at the thought of that moment's approach, and, in fact, we've realized, more and more, that this show is a tragedy. And the tragedy comes when Jimmy McGill disappears and Saul Goodman appears. We want to put that day off as long as we can, but we can't put it off artificially . . . The day must come. So that's been a really interesting realization." And, for its first two seasons thus far, a really interesting series.

KEY EVOLUTIONARY STAGES

Perry Mason	1957–66, CBS
L.A. Law	1986–94, NBC
Boston Legal	2004–8, ABC
Damages	2007–10, FX; 2011–12, DirecTV
The Good Wife	2009–16, CBS

The courtroom drama series, it's generally believed, started with CBS's *Perry Mason* (1957–66), which is indeed a crucial early evolutionary stage in the development of the televised legal drama. But the roots of that genre, in fictional form and otherwise, in fact predate both *Perry Mason* and television. And in a book about television patterned in part after Charles Darwin's theory of evolution, it's fitting as well as fun to note that in this genre in particular the first real-life trial ever broadcast argued the legality of teaching Darwinism in public schools: the so-called Scopes "monkey trial" of 1925. Only four months after it began operations as a radio station, Chicago's WGN-AM dispatched reporters and equipment to cover oral arguments and the verdict in the trial of the part-time Tennessee biology teacher John Scopes, who had been arrested for violating the state law forbidding the teaching of evolution. The trial took five weeks in the summer of 1925 and featured, as its very high-profile courtroom combatants, the former presidential candidate and secretary of state William Jennings Bryan for the prosecution and the famed trial attorney Clarence Darrow for the defense.

In 1955, Jerome Lawrence and Robert E. Lee would write a play about the trial, called *Inherit the Wind,* which would be adapted as a theatrical film starring Fredric March and Spencer Tracy in 1960 and, in time, revisited in three different made-for-TV movies: an NBC Hallmark Hall of Fame presentation in 1965 (starring Ed Begley and Melvyn Douglas), another NBC remake in 1988 (Kirk Douglas, Jason Robards), and a Showtime cable version in 1999 (George C. Scott, Jack Lemmon). Interest in courtroom trials—whether actual or fabricated, scripted or reenacted—has been a constant throughout broadcast history, and some of the earliest examples on radio and TV, though largely forgotten, are surprising in both range and age.

Nearly a decade after WGN's coverage of the actual Scopes trial, the first dramatized legal series premiered on NBC Radio: 1934's *Court of Human Relations,* presenting reenactments of actual courtroom cases taken from the pages of the show's sponsor, *True Story* magazine. Another early radio effort was 1936's *Famous Jury Trials* on Mutual Radio, which restaged courtroom cases throughout history in an approach similar to CBS's *You Are There* (except that *Famous Jury Trials* came first, by about a decade). And on television, pioneers in the legal genre included shows with a wide range of approaches. ABC's *On Trial* (1948–52) was a debate on contemporary issues, including evidence and expert witnesses, and presided over by a real-life judge. Another ABC series, 1952's *Politics on Trial,* also used a courtroom setting and real-life judges, but in this case to hear arguments between Democratic and Republican representatives leading up to the 1952 presidential election. (This was before televised presidential debates became a reality, with Richard Nixon debating John F. Kennedy in 1960.) In 1949, the DuMont network adapted the aforementioned radio show *Famous Jury Trials* for television. And in 1954, CBS introduced television's first weekly series with an attorney as protagonist: *The Public Defender,* starring Reed Hadley as a lawyer taking the cases of destitute people charged with crimes.

That series didn't get much notice, but increasingly other scripted legal dramas did. The CBS anthology drama series *Studio One* presented two of the very best, and both of them spawned subsequent works. In 1954, *Studio One* presented "Twelve Angry Men," a live TV drama about a jury deliberating the verdict in a murder trial. The writer Reginald Rose, the director Franklin Schaffner, and the actor Robert Cummings (as the sole juror initially voting not guilty) all won Emmy Awards, and Rose subsequently adapted his teleplay into a full-length stage play (in 1954) and a movie (in

1957, starring Henry Fonda). *Studio One* also presented another excellent legal drama, 1957's two-part live production called "The Defender." Ralph Bellamy and William Shatner starred as father and son attorneys working at the same family law firm, and Steve McQueen played a young client on trial for murder. Reginald Rose wrote this drama, too, and four years later would find a way to recycle that *Studio One* program as well, turning it into one of the best courtroom dramas of the 1960s: CBS's *Defenders*. But before that, CBS had another courtroom drama series to introduce—one that, for years, would both dominate and define the genre.

PERRY MASON

1957–66, CBS. Creator: Erle Stanley Gardner. Stars: Raymond Burr, Barbara Hale, William Hopper, William Talman.

Perry Mason, as portrayed by Raymond Burr in the CBS drama series from 1957 to 1966, was considered—and, in some circles, still is—the quintessential, prototypical TV lawyer. Yet by the time the intrepid attorney got to television, it was the fourth medium in which this particular defense attorney had plied his trade. Erle Stanley Gardner, a lawyer himself, published his first Perry Mason novel, *The Case of the Velvet Claws*, in 1933. That first Perry Mason story featured no courtroom scenes, but more than eighty other novels would follow, and courtroom cross-examinations became more and more prominent. The character was snatched up by Hollywood almost immediately: *The Case of the Howling Dog*, the first in a series of Perry Mason movies made by Warner Bros. in the 1930s, appeared in 1934 (starring Warren Williams), only a year after Gardner's novel introducing the character was published. And after books and the cinema, the next medium to conquer was radio, where CBS introduced its new *Perry Mason* series in 1943. With Gardner involved behind the scenes, it ran for a dozen years, eventually featuring several different actors in the title role (most notably John Larkin), and was as much soap opera as legal drama—so much so, in fact, that when Gardner decided to make the move to television, his radio drama was essentially cleaved into two separate TV shows. The soap opera aspects were put into a new 1956 CBS serial, *The Edge of Night*, starring John Larkin, radio's *Perry Mason* star, as Mike Karr, a police officer studying to become a lawyer. The rest—the legal and investigative mystery portions—were put into CBS's *Perry Mason,* which premiered a year later in 1957.

Television's *Perry Mason* featured a different client each week and a constant three-against-one legal battle. On the one side, the defense, there was Perry Mason (Raymond Burr), who almost always extracted a climactic confession from someone testifying under oath; Della Street (Barbara Hale), his loyal and helpful secretary; and Paul Drake (William Hopper), the private investigator, whose evidentiary discoveries were such a crucial part of most episodes that *Perry Mason* could almost fall under the crime and private eye genre. On the other side, the prosecution, there was the district attorney Hamilton Burger (William Talman), whose success rate challenging Perry Mason in court was the equivalent of Charlie Brown's kicking Lucy's football or Wile E. Coyote's catching the Road Runner. Yet just as people eagerly gobbled up those respective formulas, they embraced the comfortable pre-

Perry Mason introduced millions of TV viewers to the vocabulary and tactics of the courtroom. William Hopper (left) played investigator Paul Drake and Raymond Burr (right) starred as the titular defense attorney.

dictability of *Perry Mason,* where the defendant was always wrongly accused and the hero of the show won every case. (Well, every case but one, but even that one ended with him exonerating his client afterward.) *Perry Mason,* on TV, depicted the defense attorney as noble, determined, shrewd, and victorious and gave millions of viewers, who had never stepped into an actual courtroom, the "inside jargon" of asking to approach the bench, requesting a sidebar, and yelling, "Objection!"

There were no objections, though, to the show's white-hat simplicity or structural repetition. *Perry Mason* was the first TV show about the law to end a season in the Top 20, ranked No. 19 in its sophomore year. The next year, it was in the Top 10, and by the 1961–62 TV season *Perry Mason* was ranked No. 5. Another courtroom series, though, premiered that season that would soon eclipse it in the ratings and steal its thunder by presenting a more nuanced portrait of the practice of law.

The legal drama that overshadowed *Perry Mason* was a spin-off of one that had preceded it. CBS's *Defenders,* premiering in 1961, was Reginald Rose's series version of his acclaimed *Studio One* teleplay "The Defender," about a father-son law firm. This time the experienced attorney father was played by E. G. Marshall and the fresh-from-law-school son by the future *Brady Bunch* patriarch, Robert Reed. These named partners at Preston & Preston fought vigorously for their clients but didn't always win and sometimes fought with each other, about courtroom strategies or even the issues being argued in court. And unlike the cases on *Perry Mason,* those on *The Defenders* often dealt with topical, controversial topics: one 1964 episode written by Ernest Kinoy, "Blacklist," guest starred Jack Klugman as a character actor unable to find movie work after being labeled a Communist sympathizer and was TV's first dramatic representation of Hollywood's Joe McCarthy–era practice of blacklisting. *The Defenders,* by the 1962–63 TV season, had usurped *Perry Mason* in the ratings, ending the year in the Top 20 at No. 18, while *Perry Mason* had slipped to No. 23. *The Defenders* also became, in 1962, the first show in the legal genre series to win the Emmy for Outstanding Drama Series, which it did, impressively, for three consecutive years. The law, on TV, was becoming more complex, as were its lawyers.

For the next two decades, attorneys on television were a reliable fixture, appearing in an increasingly disparate display of variations and subspecies. (Among them: the aforementioned ABC hybrid series *Arrest and Trial,* half police procedural, half courtroom drama.) Much more common was the legal series in the mold of *Perry Mason,* built around a sole, persistent lawyer, though even here, as with the various cowboys in TV's once-ubiquitous Westerns, seemingly endless minor differences sprouted from that central concept. Some lone-gun TV attorneys were brash and expensive, like Peter Falk in CBS's *Trials of O'Brien* (1965–66) and Carl Betz in ABC's *Judd, for the Defense* (1967–69). Others had oversized personalities often at odds with their surroundings, like Barry Newman's Harvard-trained attorney working in the sleepy Southwest in NBC's *Petrocelli* (1974–76) and Andy Griffith's cagey, drawling, also Harvard-trained attorney, defeating all city-slicker opposing counsel visiting him in Atlanta on *Matlock,* which had a combined nine-year run (1986–95) on NBC and ABC. And one barrister, literally an ocean apart from the rest, wore a powdered wig and argued his cases in England, in the long-running PBS *Mystery!* import *Rumpole of the Bailey* (1978–92).

Law firms and legal teams, as in *The Defenders,* remained big as well. NBC's rotating umbrella series *The Bold Ones* made room in 1969–72 for *The Lawyers,* with an older, experienced lawyer (played by Burl Ives) working with two brothers from a younger generation (played by Joseph Campanella and James Farentino). ABC utilized the same generation-gap ingredients, while chasing a younger demographic, with *The Young Lawyers* (1970–71), a one-season flop co-starring the veteran actor Lee J. Cobb as mentor to several freshly minted attorneys, led by Zalman King, a young actor who would find a second, more successful career producing Showtime's erotic anthology series *Red Shoe Diaries.* And while ABC's *Owen Marshall, Counselor at Law* (1971–74) may sound like a one-man legal series, the titular character, played by Arthur Hill, actually portrayed a respected professional whose practice included the mentoring of a young colleague, played by Lee Majors. In outline and in temperament, *Owen Marshall* was to legal dramas what *Marcus Welby, M.D.,* starring Robert Young and James Brolin, was to medical dramas: its father figures did no wrong and never lost a case. These two shows, interestingly, were linked more than just stylistically: they shared the same executive producer, David Victor, and occasionally did crossover episodes, with Marshall defending the father of one of Welby's patients on a murder charge and defending Brolin's Dr. Kiley in a paternity suit.

The TV audience's increasing familiarity and fascination with the law led to other types of programs in the 1970s and 1980s. *The Paper Chase,* a 1978

CBS spin-off of the 1973 movie, gave John Houseman a chance to reprise his Oscar-winning role of the dreaded professor Kingsfield, an imperious instructor of contract law. The excellent series lasted only one year on CBS, but old episodes were repeated by PBS, and new ones produced from 1983 to 1986 by Showtime, giving that cable network bragging rights at producing quality dramas long before its rival HBO got into the game. Meanwhile, after so many years focusing on young, old, and future lawyers, TV finally started paying attention to the judicial branch. Courtroom comedies focusing on the robed ones began to appear, starting in 1976 with ABC's *Tony Randall Show,* an MTM Productions comedy starring Randall as a Philadelphia judge. NBC's *Night Court* (1984–92) was a very successful workplace comedy, starring Harry Anderson as the Manhattan night court judge Harry T. Stone. He presided over a constant parade of oddballs (and that included his co-workers as well as the defendants, with such courtroom regulars as John Larroquette, Selma Diamond, and Markie Post).

Actual judges began to get screen time on TV, too. Reviving a "reality TV" concept from the earliest days of television, a syndicated show called *The People's Court,* premiering in 1981, got a retired judge to arbitrate cases otherwise headed to Los Angeles small-claims court and to have "plaintiffs" and "defendants" agree to the judge's decisions and be reimbursed, or not, by the TV show accordingly. Many people, it turned out, were willing and eager to air their grievances on television (huge surprise there), and the presiding judge, the former superior court judge Joseph Wapner, became a genuine TV star. *The People's Court* ran for twelve years and was immortalized by Dustin Hoffman's *People's Court*–obsessed Raymond Babbitt in 1988's *Rain Man* ("Four minutes to Wapner!"). A torrent of imitators followed over the decades, including a pair of *People's Court* revivals and another syndicated series about small-claims cases, starring the former New York judge Judy Sheindlin in *Judge Judy.* That series premiered in 1996 and was still in production twenty years later. Less manufactured, but certainly a portent of things to come, was an actual televised trial, broadcast live in 1977 in accordance with Florida's then-applicable "Sunshine Law" permitting cameras in the courtroom. The case, one of the first made available for national telecast, was the trial of Ronny Zamora, a fifteen-year-old charged with shooting and killing his eighty-three-year-old neighbor, Elinor Haggart, during a robbery. The defense by Zamora's attorney, Ellis Rubin, was that the boy, by watching so much television, was himself a victim of "involuntary subliminal intoxication" of televised violence. Unlike most of the fictional lawyers on TV, Rubin did not win his case. Before long, though, a very different TV courtroom series would appear, in which attorneys would lose cases regularly or, even when they won them, sometimes feel guilty afterward. The lawyers, in their private lives, were as much of a mess as they were when arguing cases. It was the polar opposite of the *Perry Mason* approach, but by 1986 the time was right for a series about flawed, yet fascinating, lawyers.

L.A. LAW

1986–94, NBC. Creators: Steven Bochco, Terry Louise Fisher. Writers and executive producers: David E. Kelley, William M. Finkelstein, others. Stars: Harry Hamlin, Jimmy Smits, Susan Dey, Corbin Bernsen, Jill Eikenberry, Alan Rachins, Michael Tucker, Richard Dysart, Susan Rattan, Blair Underwood, Michele Greene, Larry Drake, John Spencer, Amanda Donohoe, Diana Muldaur.

Hill Street Blues, the groundbreaking NBC cop series co-created by Steven Bochco and Michael Kozoll, paved the way for dozens of police shows to come but also blazed a path for NBC's legal drama *L.A. Law,* and in more ways than one. Co-created by Bochco and Terry Louise Fisher, *L.A. Law* featured a large ensemble cast, overlapping and serialized story lines, and characters whose behavior, personally as well as professionally, ran the gamut from laudatory to reprehensible. The shorthand description for *L.A. Law,* when it was unveiled in 1986, was "*Hill Street* in a law office" and when *Hill Street Blues* closed its doors for good a year later, NBC moved *L.A. Law* from Fridays to Thursdays, right into the old *Hill Street* time slot. It was a signal that *L.A. Law* was seen, at least internally, as a continuation of the network's carefully constructed Must-See TV Thursday lineup. It was seen that way externally as well: *L.A. Law* became the first courtroom series to win the Outstanding Drama Series Emmy in more than twenty years, since *The Defenders* in 1964. *L.A. Law,* from 1987 to 1991, won the top Drama Series Emmy four times out of five and climbed as high as No. 12 in the end-of-season A. C. Nielsen rankings.

L.A. Law set out to be so different from the get-go that its premiere episode began with a partner at the Los Angeles law firm being found dead at his desk after collapsing while working over the weekend. The scene was played not for dramatic value but for black humor: his rigor mortis made it difficult to get him out the door easily, and other associates at the firm were already claiming dibs on his office, and this was before the opening credits. The large cast of characters at the firm was established quickly, and cleverly. There was the distinguished patriarch, Richard Dysart's Leland McKenzie, presiding over a gaggle of lawyers who included Corbin Bernsen's unscrupulous and flirtatious divorce attorney Arnie Becker, Jill Eikenberry's ambitious feminist Ann Kelsey and her meek tax-attorney husband, Michael Tucker's Stuart Markowitz; Jimmy Smits as the smooth, passionate attorney Victor Sifuentes; Alan Rachins as named partner and cost-obsessed watchdog Douglas Brackman; and, as the initial "Will they or won't they?" romantic pairing of the series, Harry Hamlin's Michael Kuzak and Susan Dey's Grace Van Owen. (They did, then they stopped.) Key supporting play-

L.A. Law, like other large ensemble dramas inspired by *Hill Street Blues,* retained some actors while replacing others. Here, a later-season ensemble photo.

ers included Susan Ruttan as Becker's forgiving, responsible secretary and Larry Drake as Benny Stulwicz, the firm's endearing, mentally challenged office worker. Dysart, Smits, and Drake all won Emmys for their portrayals, and *L.A. Law* also won several Emmys for its writing. Bochco and Fisher won for "Venus Butterfly," an episode named after a mysterious, very effective, and sadly fictitious sexual technique, and David E. Kelley, who ran the show in its later years, won two. He also wrote the infamous episode in which Diana Muldaur, as the generally disliked attorney Rosalind Shays, was dispatched to her death unexpectedly when she stepped into an open elevator shaft. The episode's title was typical of the show's twisted wit: "Good to the Last Drop." Which, in retrospect, perfectly describes *L.A. Law* as well.

The 1990s heralded more change for the courtroom drama on TV, starting in 1990 with NBC's *Law & Order*, the "mother ship," as the creator Dick Wolf called it, for an entire series of related spin-offs. The structure of the original article, though, was *Arrest and Trial* done correctly, with detectives in the first half (played, at first, by George Dzundza and Chris Noth) collaring a suspect who was prosecuted by district attorneys in the second half (played, at first, by Michael Moriarty, Richard Brooks, and Steven Hill). By the time *Law & Order* won its Outstanding Drama Series Emmy in 1997, Jerry Orbach and Benjamin Bratt were playing the cops, and Sam Waterston and Jill Hennessy the district attorneys, and in time they, too, would be replaced, as the "mother ship" continued to fly until 2010. And even after it was gone, spin-offs such as *Law & Order: Special Victims Unit*, which began in 1999, remained on the NBC schedule. Another durable law-related series from the same period was *JAG*, an acronym for "Judge Advocate General," with David James Elliott starring as an attorney with the JAG corps of the U.S. Navy. The series premiered on NBC in 1995 but was canceled after one season. It was picked up by CBS, which ran it for another six years and launched a 2003 spin-off series, *NCIS* (the letters, in this case, stood for "Naval Criminal Investigative Service"), a perennial Top 10 series still in production as of 2016.

The biggest change of the decade in the TV legal genre, however, would be in the coverage and impact of real-life trials on television. The year 1991 saw the launch of Court TV, a channel dedicated to national coverage of local and high-profile trials allowing cameras in the courtroom (in 2008, the channel was rechristened and reconfigured as TruTV). The appetite for "actual" courtroom trials, as well as scripted ones, was obvious, and when O. J. Simpson was tried for murder in 1995, that appetite was voracious. CNN presented an estimated six hundred hours of Simpson trial coverage, Court TV provided some seven hundred hours, and E! Entertainment Television outdid them both, offering nearly one thousand hours of Simpson-related stories over the trial's duration. Simpson's celebrity and the story's appeal were such that when the verdict was announced on October 3, 1995, it was covered live not only by CBS, NBC, ABC, Fox, Court TV, and E! but by CNN Headline News, ESPN, ESPN2, Univision, CNBC, and even MTV. Estimates of the TV-viewing audience for the verdict went as high as 150 million, and television took note of the trial's massive viewership from the start. And that's not an exaggeration: one week after the prosecutors Marcia Clark and Christopher Darden presented their opening statements, the Fox TV network aired a reprehensibly exploitive and ill-timed made-for-TV movie called *The O. J. Simpson Story,* starring Bobby Hosea in the title role, the *One Life to Live* soap star Jessica Tuck as the murder victim Nicole Brown Simpson, and Bruce Weitz from *Hill Street Blues* as Simpson's attorney Robert Shapiro.

Watching early coverage of the Simpson trial, including jury selection, convinced the *Hill Street Blues* and *L.A. Law* co-creator, Steven Bochco, that he should try telling a fictional trial story in as detailed a fashion. Not hundreds of hours of coverage, but dozens, which is how ABC's *Murder One,* the season-long look at a single murder trial, came to premiere on the network in 1995. (The next year, the ambitious template was pulled back a bit, to make room for three different stories over the length of a season.) That would inspire later crime and courtroom shows to tell elongated, complicated courtroom stories, and decades later even the Simpson trial itself would be remade for television, as a ten-part miniseries drama.

As Bochco was trying something new in the legal genre with *Murder One,* his former protégé and production partner David E. Kelley had a few tricks up his sleeve, too. In 1997, he unveiled two series set in Boston law firms: ABC's *Practice* (starring Dylan McDermott as the head of a scrappy, low-rent Boston law practice), and Fox's much lighter *Ally McBeal* (starring Calista Flockhart as a fantasy-prone, romance-obsessed lawyer at a quirky, upscale law firm with unisex bathrooms and a cartoonishly eccentric staff). *The Practice* won the Outstanding Drama Series in 1998 and 1999, yet in 2004 Kelley retooled the series by introducing new characters in the final six shows of the season—characters who would end up starring in the renamed series that would rise from the ashes of *The Practice*. Those characters were Denny Crane and Alan Shore, played respectively by William Shatner and James Spader, and before 2004 was over, they'd be the stars of their own spin-off series. That series was *Boston Legal*, and from that point on the evolutionary changes in the legal genre arrived quickly and unmistakably, one on top of the other.

BOSTON LEGAL

2004–8, ABC. Creator: David E. Kelley. Stars: James Spader, William Shatner, Candice Bergen, René Auberjonois, John Larroquette, Julie Bowen, Betty White, Constance Zimmer, Rhona Mitra, Christian Clemenson, Saffron Burrows, Taraji P. Henson, Craig Bierko, Lake Bell, Kerry Washington, others.

James Spader and William Shatner both won Emmys for their roles as attorneys in *Boston Legal*, but the series itself never did, even though it con-

Boston Legal grew out of David E. Kelley's *The Practice* and refocused on attorneys Denny Crane (William Shatner) and Alan Shore (James Spader), seen here with Saffron Burrows as fellow attorney Lorraine Weller.

tained some of its creator David E. Kelley's very best work. In *Boston Legal,* he managed to combine, in one show, the anything-goes whimsy of *Ally McBeal* with the analytic and challenging legal arguments of *Picket Fences.* The silly antics of the lawyers in the first half of the show amused viewers, who then stayed tuned for the lengthy, often uncomfortable courtroom debates about freedom of religion, the right to bear arms, violence on television, and other perennially hot-button issues. Oh, there were murder cases, too, but even the accused murderers were multilayered and unpredictable. And, sometimes, guilty, regardless of the final verdict.

The final verdict on *Boston Legal,* though, was that it was a series that, like *St. Elsewhere* in the medical genre, made a remarkable effort to paint using every color on its palette. Denny Crane was a conservative Republican, so conservative he was like Archie Bunker with a law degree, a suit, and better cigars. Shatner played him with such gusto and range—from the comedy of inappropriate office conduct to the pathos of the early onset of senility—that he finally got a role to overshadow, or at least compete with, his iconic captain James T. Kirk from the original *Star Trek.* And Denny Crane's colleague and best friend, Alan Shore, was a litigating firebrand so intense that his closing arguments would often take up an entire act of a *Boston Legal* episode, from one commercial break to another. Spader was magnificent in these scenes, and Kelley, recognizing this, kept writing longer and longer monologues for Spader to deliver. And when Kelley wrote, he usually wrote alone—unlike his mentor Steven Bochco, who on *L.A. Law,* if he ran into a problem writing an episode, would convene the other staff writers to help him work it out. "If there's something in the story that's not working, and Steven couldn't figure it out, he'd call everybody into the room, because that's just the way he worked," Kelley says. Then he adds, "My process is just the opposite. If I can't figure out a story point, it's like, 'Everybody out!' I need to go into that world. If it's *Boston Legal,* then I have to be alone in a room with Alan Shore and Denny Crane."

One of the most original *Boston Legal* episodes—one in which he did work with a co-writer, Phoef Sutton—was 2007's "Son of the Defender," in which Denny Crane was forced to recount a murder trial he'd helped argue fifty years earlier, as a young lawyer working alongside his father in the new family firm. For flashbacks, the *Boston Legal* episode used kinescope footage from Reginald Rose's two-part "The Defender" episode from CBS's *Studio One*—the one where Ralph Bellamy played the father, and a young William Shatner the son. That live telecast was from fifty years earlier and was a uniquely clever use of a very old TV legal drama to tell a completely new story.

DAMAGES

2007–10, FX; 2011–12, DirecTV. Creators: Daniel Zelman, Glenn Kessler, Todd A. Kessler. Stars: Glenn Close, Rose Byrne, Zeljko Ivanek, Ted Danson, William Hurt, Tate Donovan, Marcia Gay Harden, Lily Tomlin, Martin Short, John Goodman, Dylan Baker, Judd Hirsch.

After accepting and playing a one-season role as a police captain on the FX cop series *The Shield,* Glenn Close let the network know she'd be interested in starring in a new FX series herself, and the network provided her with one that was similarly dark, challenging, and envelope pushing. It found *Damages,* which cast her as Patty Hewes, the head of her own New York law firm and one of the most powerful and feared attorneys in the city.

Damages starred Glenn Close as powerful litigator Patty Hewes, whose hunger for victory on all fronts drove her to cross all sorts of ethical and moral lines.

It was a meaty, morally ambiguous part, and Close won two Emmy Awards for playing the role. Opposite her in *Damages,* Rose Byrne plays Ellen Parsons, a recent hire at the firm whose relationship with Patty Hewes is similar to all those familiar older mentor/young lawyer pairings from classic legal dramas, except for two significant differences. For the first time on TV, both the powerful attorney and the novice are women. And also for the first time on TV, the former might have tried to kill the latter.

It's a plot unspooled in confusing, yet fascinating, flash-forwards, where we see Ellen Parsons, covered in blood, stumbling out of an apartment. Whose blood, which apartment, and the answers to dozens of other questions would take all season to unravel, as the story went back and forth in time, leading viewers slowly but surely to the climactic reveal, when the show's present narrative caught up with its future. The structure of *Damages* was as innovative as its focus on women, and the show also featured season-long legal cases and a wealth of superb guest stars willing to sign up to work with Close for a season. These included William Hurt, John Goodman, Lily Tomlin, Martin Short, and Ted Danson, who had co-starred with Close decades before in an outstanding 1984 ABC television movie about incest, *Something About Amelia.*

THE GOOD WIFE

2009–16, CBS. Creators: Robert and Michelle King. Stars: Julianna Margulies, Christine Baranski, Alan Cumming, Chris Noth, Matt Czuchry, Archie Panjabi, Josh Charles, Zach Grenier, Makenzie Vega, Graham Phillips, Matthew Goode, Michael J. Fox, Jeffrey Dean Morgan, Carrie Preston, Dallas Roberts, Stockard Channing, Mike Colter, Nathan Lane, Margo Martindale, Gary Cole, Denis O'Hare, David Hyde Pierce, Mamie Gummer, Dylan Baker.

My favorite moment of watching CBS's *Good Wife* came each week at a different time but arrived without fail. I'd watch the opening scene and get pulled in instantly by whatever story line I was being thrown into without warning or explanation. I'd keep watching, enthralled and utterly absorbed by what was happening, and then, eight or ten or twelve or more minutes into the show, a scene would end with a shocking revelation or plot turn, then shift to the opening credits sequence. That's when, each and every week, I'd suddenly remember, "Oh, that's right, they haven't played the opening credits yet!" And I'd laugh because they'd suckered me in all over again, like a carny rube who loses every week at the same rigged game of three-card monte.

And *The Good Wife* was rigged too—rigged by being overstuffed with a large ensemble cast, constantly reinforced by a revolving-door parade of absurdly talented and valuable recurring players. Forget the series regulars for a moment: when guest stars such as Michael J. Fox, David Hyde Pierce, and Margo Martindale pop in to play from time to time, you know you've got a special TV series on your hands. And *The Good Wife* is special, because from the very first episode, it confronted, and even specialized in, instability. In the premiere episode, Alicia Florrick (played by Julianna Margulies from *ER*) stood stoically next to her husband, the Illinois state's attorney Peter Florrick (played by Chris Noth from *Law & Order*), as he resigned his office after a sex and corruption scandal. Then she took responsibility for raising their two teen children alone and for finding a new job—using her long-dormant law degree to try to find work as a lawyer again. Which she does, joining a firm with both a female mentor (Christine Baranski as Diane Lockhart, another powerful woman lawyer in the manner of Glenn Close on *Damages*) and a former boyfriend (Josh Charles as Will Gardner, whose attraction to her remains strong, a vice that definitely is versa). But

The Good Wife starred Julianna Margulies as Alicia Florrick, a woman restarting her law career after her politician husband, Peter Florrick, resigns in disgrace. From left, Alan Cumming as political guru Eli Gold and Margulies and Chris Noth as the Florricks.

that's just the start of a long, somewhat unstable journey. Where most TV protagonists hold the same job for the length of the show, Alicia Florrick changes jobs, duties, and law firms repeatedly as she tries to find herself. In the process, former colleagues become vengeful adversaries, then reverse course again. All characters, even the apparent heroes and heroines, have ulterior, self-serving motives. Alicia has the same unsteady, always shifting relationship with her husband, whom she doesn't divorce and who, in time, stands by her figuratively as she runs for office, then stands by her literally as she, too, resigns in disgrace, in a years-later mirror image of the embarrassing opening moments of the series itself.

The series creators, Robert and Michelle King, weren't content merely to shake up Alicia's professional life. They also kept her private life in flux and in one of the show's most famous surprises had a lover of hers killed unexpectedly in a Chicago courtroom. Similarly major jolts were delivered almost weekly as the legal cases in each episode shifted perspective more times than a medical diagnosis on *House, M.D.,* and *The Good Wife,* more than any other courtroom show on television, prided itself on presenting cases dealing with the legal and moral issues surrounding the latest technologies, from Internet search engines to 3-D printers. In some ways, *The Good Wife* was an old-fashioned legal drama: Archie Panjabi's Kalinda Sharma, in the show's first five seasons, was used as an invaluable private eye asset unearthing key revelations at the last minute, just like William Hopper's Paul Drake on *Perry Mason.* But in many other ways, it had built on many shows and steps along the way. Serialized stories were mixed with stand-alone cases, as in *L.A. Law.* Closing arguments probed ethical questions in ways designed to inform and maybe even inflame the viewer, as in *Boston Legal.* And guest stars and regular cast members were mixed brilliantly together, as in *Damages.* And of all the rich characters and portrayals on *The Good Wife,* my favorite is Alan Cumming's Eli Gold, a political mover and shaker who, over the course of the series, often found himself moved and shaken. The politics, the romance, the courtroom arguments—in *The Good Wife,* none of it came easily to anyone. But all of it, up to and including the 2016 finale, was very, very easy to watch.

During the entire run of *The Good Wife,* I considered it the best drama series, and certainly the best law-related series, on broadcast television. Near the end of that show's trajectory, AMC presented a new legal drama that I considered its cable TV equivalent: *Better Call Saul,* the *Breaking Bad* combination prequel and sequel co-created by Vince Gilligan and Lance Gould and starring Bob Odenkirk as Jimmy McGill, the man who, in time, would become the sleazy lawyer known on *Breaking Bad* as Saul Goodman. *Better Call Saul* is a brilliant series and proof that the genre continues to evolve in a healthy and satisfying way.

Other recent developments worth noting are the reintroduction of exaggerated soap opera elements (in a 2014 series from the prolific executive producer Shonda Rhimes, *How to Get Away with Murder,* set originally in a *Paper Chase*–type law school classroom), sitcoms built around the law (in Fox's clever 2015 *The Grinder,* starring Rob Lowe and Fred Savage), and new shows taking the limited miniseries approach, or season-long anthology format, to dramatize a single legal case over ten episodes or more. ABC's *American Crime,* beginning in 2015, did this very successfully, and beginning in 2016, so did FX's *American Crime Story,* an anthology series whose inaugural ten-part, single-case subject was *The People v. O. J. Simpson.* It was a dramatization of a murder trial already presented on TV twice in 1995: once live, and once in a cheesy, quickie Fox television movie about the events leading up to the trial. That earlier made-for-TV movie was a travesty, the live trial coverage was a TV phenomenon, and *The People v. O. J. Simpson,* including behind-the-scenes strategy, intrigue, and infighting from both sides of the courtroom aisle, was outstanding. The cast included John Travolta as Robert Shapiro, Cuba Gooding Jr. as O. J. Simpson, Courtney B. Vance as the defense attorney Johnnie Cochran, David Schwimmer as the loyal Simpson friend Robert Kardashian, Nathan Lane as the Simpson "dream team" member F. Lee Bailey, and Sarah Paulson and Sterling K. Brown as the prosecutors Marcia Clark and Christopher Darden. Twenty-one years after presenting the original trial, television had matured enough to do justice to a lengthy, intelligent re-creation of it—a re-creation where questions about justice were at the very heart of it, just as they were of the best, most evolved TV series in today's legal genre.

DAVID E. KELLEY

BORN: 1956, Waterville, Maine.

FIRST TV CREDIT: Writer, *L.A. Law,* 1986, NBC.

LANDMARK TV SERIES: *L.A. Law,* 1986–92, NBC; *Doogie Howser, M.D.,* 1989–93, ABC; *Picket Fences,* 1992–96, CBS; *Chicago Hope,* 1994–2000, CBS; *Ally McBeal,* 1997–2002, Fox; *The Practice,* 1997–2004, ABC; *Boston Legal,* 2004–8, ABC.

OTHER MAJOR CREDITS: TV: *Boston Public,* 2000–2004, Fox; *Harry's Law,* 2011–12, NBC; *The Crazy Ones,* 2013–14, CBS; *Goliath,* 2016, Amazon. Movies: Writer, *From the Hip,* 1987; *Lake Placid,* 1999; *Mystery, Alaska,* 1999.

David E. Kelley was born in the small town of Waterville, Maine, in 1956. As a youngster, he was more interested in hockey than in television (his father was a professional hockey coach for the Hartford Whalers, among other clubs in his career). He remembers watching *Perry Mason* with his family but considered it "very old-fashioned" and admits, "I didn't watch a lot of legal shows growing up. But I liked the law, and studied the law." One of the first TV shows to which the young Kelley remembers being drawn was CBS's *Smothers Brothers Comedy Hour.* "That was an insidious and inspired show!" he recalls enthusiastically. "If there was a first show for me, at an early age, that taught me that something can tickle your funny bone and make you laugh, but also provoke you at the same time, *The Smothers Brothers* would be it."

It was a volatile mixture, of humor and ideas, to which he was naturally drawn. As David E. Kelley tells it, he didn't really have a favorite TV show, or get addicted to one, until he was in eighth or ninth grade, but when he did, he chose wisely. The program was Norman Lear's *All in the Family,* which was on the family TV set every week from the start. His siblings would drift in and out of the room, Kelley recalls, but he and his mother would stay put. "Sometimes I could see my mother squirming a little bit in the seat next to me," he says, chuckling, "and I'd go, 'Okay, they're talking about something that maybe I'm not meant to be seeing' . . . It wasn't *Gilligan's Island,* that's for sure." But from a quality TV standpoint, David E. Kelley was meant to be seeing *All in the Family,* because it gave him a love of vivid characters, and meaningful content, that he ended up presenting in his own television work.

"I loved the characters," Kelley says of Carroll O'Connor's prejudiced Archie Bunker, Jean Stapleton as his wife, Edith, and the rest of the *All in the Family* folks. "And I loved how provocative it was, the issues they took on with humor, how brave the show was. But I think, first and foremost, I fell in love with it as an entertainment vehicle. I sat in my chair and listened to these characters; I mean, Edith was so beloved, and Archie was lovable in his bigoted way. So I think, when I first saw *All in the Family,* that was maybe the first occasion it dawned on me that television really was a noble medium. That, in addition to entertaining, it could make people think and make people feel. And in all of our series," he says of his own TV output, "I've endeavored to do that. We don't get it right every time, but I think we accept that same challenge. If we can make people laugh, and make them think, and entertain them, and maybe, on a good day, even move them to tears, that's something. That's a pretty good day job."

Kelley also watched and loved two other ambitious CBS comedies of the 1970s, *M*A*S*H* and *The Mary Tyler Moore Show.* "Ed Asner's character [of Lou Grant], Mary Tyler Moore's character [Mary Richards]," Kelley says, "these are people who could make you laugh and, again, make you feel. Those were the kinds of shows that got to me." As the decade ended, though, Kelley wasn't thinking about a career in television. He was in law school, studying to be a lawyer, though he still found time to watch the best and most provocative TV shows, such as NBC's *St. Elsewhere* and, especially, the same network's envelope-pushing *Hill Street Blues.*

"*Hill Street,* I absolutely never missed it," Kelley says. "That was probably my first case of 'watercooler television,' because we would all talk about it the next day in class. Especially in civil procedure or criminal procedure class, because a lot of the shows on *Hill Street Blues* touched on criminal procedure, Fourth Amendment, and so forth. But it also was watercooler television because that show broke the rules in terms of the multi-story format, the subject matter, and the depth of character. I don't think it ever would have occurred to me to go into television as a vocation until I started watching that show." Even then, though, Kelley's sole focus was the law, and getting his law degree, and getting hired as a lawyer—all of which he accomplished before ever thinking seriously about Hollywood. Kelley graduated from Princeton University, then attended Boston University Law School. Studying for the bar exam, he remembers a professor telling the class there were three groups about to take the test: one group that saw the law in black and white and would do fine on the exam, a second group that failed to grasp the black-and-white concepts and probably wouldn't do well, and a third group that not only saw the black-and-white aspects of the law but recognized all the grays. "You people," Kelley remembers the professor saying with a laugh, "are in big trouble."

But those were the kinds of cases, Kelley realized quickly, that interested him the most, though he got little experience at trying them. Instead, for the first two years or so after passing the bar and joining a Boston law firm, he did what many young lawyers are obliged to do: motion practice, where fledgling attorneys argue in court for one small issue or another, waiting their turns to be called and heard among twenty or thirty other young lawyers there for the same purpose. "It's kind of grunt work," Kelley explains. "It's not intellectually exciting." That's when Kelley, at age twenty-nine or thirty, started whiling away the downtime, and channeling his nervous energy, by writing a screenplay as he waited. He wrote in longhand on legal pads—a necessity then, but a practice he still uses—and his first story was about a lawyer who got to do nothing but motion practice. Write what you know, even though, as the first thing he ever wrote, Kelley had no idea it would ever lead to anything. But it did.

By coincidence, the law firm for which Kelley worked had a client roster that included Howard Baldwin, who had started the New England Whalers in the World Hockey Association. Baldwin had once hired Kelley's father as the team's first general manager and coach, so the younger Kelley had known Baldwin for years when they crossed paths again at the law firm. By this time, Kelley says, Baldwin was breaking into entertainment as well as sports and heard of Kelley's script and said he'd be happy to read it. Baldwin liked it enough to pass it on to an agent in California ("It was, I guess, properly punctuated or something," Kelley jokes), who called Kelley and asked, out of the blue, "Have you heard of this guy named Steven Bochco?"

It wasn't the script that interested Bochco so much as Kelley's qualifications. "He was doing this new show about law," Kelley says, referring to what became NBC's *L.A. Law,* "and he was looking for lawyers who also wrote, because he wanted to be authentic." Bochco's name, by then, was one of the few TV names with which Kelley was intimately familiar, because *Hill Street Blues,* for Kelley, was truly Must-See TV. "I watched that show," Kelley says. "And also, if you remember, Steven was one of the first ones to stick his credit right at the end of the show, and usually it was right at a jaw-dropping moment where something had happened where you couldn't believe what you'd just witnessed. And before you were able to bring your lips back together, there's that name: Steven Bochco. Over black. So I knew the name, and I came out to meet with him . . . and we hit it off right away, and I basically never went back."

Getting the attention of Bochco, and being added untested to the staff of Bochco's next big TV hit, was a highly unusual path into show business, as Kelley readily admits. "I was lucky. Lucky, in so many ways, to land at all in the industry, but to have plopped into his lap," Kelley says of Bochco, "was really fortuitous. Because Steven, in addition to being a gifted producer and writer, was a great teacher." Kelley adds, "He's able to articulate the values of his writings, the targets of the storytellings. Something which I've never been good at, truth be told." Lessons learned from Bochco, Kelley says, included his work ethic ("His work habits were great") and his determination never to underestimate the intelligence of the viewing audience. "There are a lot of studio and network executives that will preach just the opposite," Kelley says. "You know: 'It's too complicated, dumb it down. We want this to appeal to a lot of people. We don't want it to go over their heads.' Steven never had that approach. He said, 'The audience is smart. Challenge them, and they'll respond to the challenge.'"

Bochco, from his perspective, is no less impressed with Kelley's work ethic or his talent. "He was really the first writer I'd ever known," Bochco says of Kelley, "who had this capability to this extent: I'd say, 'Well, we need a story about this.' And he'd say, 'Okay, I got it. Say no more. I'll figure it out and just do it.' And he would! He'd go away, and two days later he'd come back with half a script on that story, or the whole script. Whatever you asked him to do, he would do it, and 80 percent of the time it was perfect, first shot out of the box!"

Kelley spent six years on *L.A. Law,* contributing to such episodes as the one where Diana Muldaur's Rosalind Shays, a ruthless attorney at the firm, walks into an empty elevator shaft and falls to her death. "I didn't feel that we were breaking that many rules at the time," Kelley says of that show's writing staff, "because I was so new to the game that I was still trying to figure out what the rules were." He did another series with Bochco, ABC's *Doogie Howser, M.D.* in 1989, for which Kelley is credited as co-creator, but though he co-wrote the pilot, Kelley says *Doogie,* which starred a young Neil Patrick Harris as a teenage doctor, was "Steven's child—that was his baby." And Kelley credits much of that show's success to Harris, who was the only young actor to nail the role in auditions. "He was the only one we were prepared to go forward with," Kelley says—the only one who projected both the gravitas of a surgeon and the naïveté of a young teen. Harris surprised Kelley then and has surprised him with his career since. "I mean, who can do all that?" Kelley asks. "And I don't think he's done. I think he's got more in that magic bag of his."

Kelley's own magic bag, once he started his own TV production company, included a lot as well. CBS's *Picket Fences,* which premiered in 1992, was an unprecedentedly complex mixture of TV genres, braided together like a DNA strand: a family drama, cop drama, medical drama, and legal drama, all in one. In this particular family, the father (played by Tom Skerritt) was the small-town sheriff, the mother (Kathy Baker) was a respected doctor, and many of their respective cases wound up in court, where they were debated by a defense attorney (Fyvush Finkel) and a district attorney (Don Cheadle) and ruled upon by a judge (Ray Walston). "That is what I was endeavoring to do," Kelley says of the multi-genre concept, "but had I a better inkling of how hard it would be to do, I might have thought twice about it. I love that show. It's probably the one that's closest to my heart. But that was a very difficult show to do, for exactly what you say, and the town was very much a character in that series. So it was difficult, because you needed to find stories that could sustain through all those different worlds . . . That was a bear, that one. I loved every minute of it, but it was a hard one to do."

It's also the series in which he first displayed, to great effect, another approach, one that became a Kelley trademark of sorts. Most courtroom series from *Perry Mason* on presented their protagonist lawyers in court the same way: When they argued in court or cross-examined, their arguments were not only persuasive but definitive and final. They stood, they spoke, they won. Kelley, drawing on his love of the gray areas of the law, did something different when presenting the courtroom portions of *Picket Fences* and continued with all his subsequent legal series. When he was writing from the perspective of the defense attorney, the basic hero of the show, Kelley made his arguments as compelling, logical, and emotionally resonant as possible, then, when he turned around to write the prosecution's side of the case, he did the same thing, pretending as he wrote that the prosecutor was the star of the show. It made the courtroom adversaries more formidable, the drama more riveting and unpredictable, and the issues being debated, from gun control to assisted suicide, more nuanced and, for the viewing audience, more provocative. "I wanted for our best shows to have viewer participation," Kelley says. "And by 'viewer participation,' I didn't mean getting on the Internet or anything like that, but just for the show to occasion the viewer to say or think, 'What do I think about that?' or 'How do I feel about that?' and those cases that are close calls are the best ones to do that."

Before *Picket Fences* left the air, Kelley created another series for CBS: a medical drama starring Mandy Patinkin, *Chicago Hope,* that came to TV the same week as, and was quickly overshadowed by, NBC's *ER.* ("*Chicago Hope* certainly had a lot of medicine in it," Kelley says, "but it was, first and foremost, a character show.") And in 1997, with *Chicago Hope* still on CBS, Kelley created additional new series for two other networks: ABC's *Practice,* starring Dylan McDermott as a scrappy and fiery defense attorney, and Fox's *Ally McBeal,* starring Calista Flockhart as a fantasy-prone attorney whose internal thoughts, fears, and dreams were as much a part of the series as her courtroom arguments. These two series were set in Boston and mounted a very rare inter-network crossover story in 1988 (a two-part murder story in which the two legal firms teamed up for a murder case begun on *The Practice* and concluded, an hour later and on a different network, on *Ally McBeal*), yet they were, in tone and essence, two very different David E. Kelley legal series. "*The Practice,* you can pretty much lay out that show in outline form, because the plot is somewhat linear," Kelley says. "With *Ally McBeal,* it was a very different process. You were mining stories from the inside out of characters. And then, after you sort of told those stories and gave birth to them, then you went back and edited the scripts into a more linear form. So it's a very different way of birthing the episode, but that worked for that show."

Ally McBeal, Kelley says, he thought of as a musical romantic comedy, with the music of Vonda Shepard being prominent from the very start. "That show, I loved," he says. "It was different. It was a romantic comedy with a cauldron of very eccentric characters who were successful in their field but lonely in their hearts and trying to satisfy their lonely hearts. I think that was my best effort at, maybe, a *Mary Tyler Moore*–type show that could make you laugh and make you feel at the same time." *The Practice* was much darker ("Somebody usually was dead, and someone was on trial for it"), and Kelley shuffled between the two series, writing in longhand the scripts for the vast majority of both. "If I hadn't been doing both of them, I probably would have ruined each," Kelley says, then elaborates: "As hard as it was to do both shows, that worked for me, because while I was writing one show, I'd be in total escape from the other, and I'd actually feel refreshed when I went back to work on the other." That polarized approach also allowed him to confine many of the more somber stories and serious issues to *The Practice* while indulging in a bit more silliness—computer-generated dancing babies, holiday performance singing parties—on *Ally McBeal.* Robert Downey Jr. came aboard mid-run, giving Flockhart's Ally her most charming and quirky love interest, but long before that *Ally* had become part of the national conversation and added to Kelley's remarkable string of Emmy-winning successes. *L.A. Law* had won Outstanding Drama Series three times while Kelley was there, and he had won two personal Emmys for script writing. *Picket Fences* won Outstanding Drama Series two years running, as did *The Practice,* and *Ally McBeal* won Outstanding Comedy Series in 1999, the second year *The Practice* also won. That meant Kelley won Emmys for Outstanding Drama Series and Outstanding Comedy Series the same year, a feat unmatched before or since. And he accomplished that in 1999, the year that begins, in my mind, the Platinum Age of Television.

But Kelley wasn't through yet. In the year 2000, he created *Boston Public,* a high school series that melded issues and characters into a modern version of *Room 222.* "I tended to look at teachers as heroes," Kelley says of the 2000 Fox drama, and his series reflected that. "My biggest issue with that one was that I had two other shows going while trying to do that one. But at least I was lucky enough to get [as an executive producer, coming aboard in 2001] this young guy named Jason Katims, who knew what he was doing, to take that off my hands or do a lot of the heavy lifting. And obviously, Jason's gone on to do even more wonderful things. He's a terrific talent." Those wonderful things include, of course, *Friday Night Lights* and *Parenthood.* "He's brilliant, you know?" Katims says. "And it was an incredible situation for me to have access to him whenever I wanted it . . . but that he allowed me to sort of find my voice in the characters he created."

Kelley's best work of the new century, though, would come from a spin-off sequel to, and reworked continuation of, *The Practice.* In 2004, Kelley retooled that long-running law series, injecting a lighter tone and more fanciful characters now that *Ally McBeal* had been canceled. It was what Kelley had feared might happen to *The Practice* without *Ally McBeal* around to feed and satisfy his more comical side, but instead of ruining or diluting *The Practice,* the addition of such actors and characters as William Shatner's eccentric Denny Crane and James Spader's equally eccentric Alan Shore made the show seem fresh and new. So Kelley and ABC turned *The Practice* into a fresh new show, replacing the other supporting characters and calling the result *Boston Legal.* Premiering in 2004, it gave Shatner a late-career boost and the only Emmy wins of his career (for both *The Practice* and *Boston Legal*). More than two dozen actors have won Emmys for their roles in shows written by Kelley, and both Shatner and Spader won them for playing the same character on two different series. Spader won three Emmys in all for playing Alan Shore, and a good part of that had to be due to Spader's uncanny ability to perform, with infectious spirit in often long unbroken takes, the increasingly long courtroom monologues Kelley would write for him.

"He likes to talk, and I like to listen to him talk," Kelley says of Spader, "so it was pure synergy." The actor and the writer were on the same wavelength, Kelley says, from their shared "perverse sense of humor" to the delight in pivoting from broad comedy to serious ideas and keeping viewers along for the ride. "He would call me up," Kelley says about each time Spader received a new script and looked at the length of the closing argument he would have to deliver as Alan Shore, "and go, 'This is a joke, right? You're trying to see how far you can push this.'" But Kelley kept writing them longer because, on the set, Spader would not only memorize them but nail them. "We were in awe when he would do those," Kelley says. "He'd do the whole thing!" he adds. "Usually, you'd pick these things up [on film] in bits and pieces, but James would just do the whole thing, over and over again! And he'd be word perfect!"

After mounting another legal drama, NBC's *Harry's Law* starring Kathy Bates, in 2011, Kelley tried his hand at different genres—specifically, an unsold *Wonder Woman* pilot for NBC starring Adrianne Palicki in 2013 and *The Crazy Ones,* a CBS sitcom starring Robin Williams and Sarah Michelle Gellar as father and daughter, the same year. In 2016, he returned to the legal arena with a ten-episode series called *Goliath* but in an entirely new arena. Kelley is one of the few TV producers who have placed successful TV shows on all four networks, but *Goliath,* co-created with Jonathan Shapiro (who wrote *The Practice* and *Boston Legal*), is a David E. Kelley production for the Amazon streaming video service, starring Billy Bob Thornton.

"*Goliath* is kind of like almost a modern David and Goliath series," Kelley explains, "where you've got this down-and-out, sort of broken-down lawyer who's taking on big law. And law has become big law now; the law firms have exponentially grown." Kelley adds, "The fun of this show is, we're taking one case and playing it for the entire ten episodes . . . and everybody may have different heroes in this series. You'll go home with the judge and listen to him talking to his wife about what he's dealing with on a daily basis. You'll meet the lawyer on the other side. You'll get to go behind veils that I've never had the luxury to penetrate before in forty-three minutes." And writing for a solid hour without commercial time or interruption is, like working with Amazon at all, an invigorating experience for Kelley, whose first TV show and hit, *L.A. Law* for NBC, was thirty years ago.

"Amazon's been great," Kelley says partway through production of *Goliath.* "So far, it's been a joy. The most exciting thing about Amazon is, they really have a lot of ambition when it comes to content. Broadcast television, they don't necessarily aspire to make great television anymore. It's not that it can't happen on broadcast television, but the business tail very much wags that dog. They're looking for product that a lot of people will like. And Amazon, and some of the other outlets now, are looking for shows that a constituency will love. Does it have to be a huge constituency? Not necessarily. But they want to make product that viewers fall in love with. And when I started [at NBC], that was [the network programmer] Brandon Tartikoff's mantra. He said, 'Look, every show should be somebody's favorite show.' Not that they all were, but we should at least aspire to that."

These days, Kelley concludes ruefully, broadcast networks that once took big chances to please smaller audience blocs "would really rather make a show that a lot of people liked than a show that a fewer amount of people love."

ROBERT and MICHELLE KING

BORN: He: 1959, San Francisco. She: 1962, Santa Monica.
FIRST TV CREDIT: His: Playwright of source material, *Imaginary Friends*, 1983, BBC. Hers: Actress, playing a reporter in the Stephen King miniseries *The Stand*, 1994, ABC. Theirs: *In Justice*, 2006, ABC.
LANDMARK TV SERIES: Theirs: *The Good Wife*, 2009–16, CBS.
OTHER TV CREDITS: Theirs: *BrainDead*, 2016, CBS.

As TV creators working on the same successful TV series, Robert and Michelle King are triple rarities in Hollywood. One, they're married—to each other. Two, they're in their fifties, at a time when many television show runners are younger. Three, and these days most remarkably, they manage to produce one of television's best dramas on broadcast television, when most of the action, heat, and success has migrated to cable TV and streaming services.

They met in 1983, shortly after he moved to Los Angeles to pursue his dream of becoming a playwright. She was a senior at UCLA, and they met while working at the same athletics shoe store, called FrontRunners. (That same year, his play *Imaginary Friends* was produced as a television movie by the BBC, starring Peter Ustinov and Roger Rees.) She and Robert were married in 1987, and he wrote scripts for the next two decades before they finally teamed up as a writing duo. (Among Robert's solo credits was one more infamous than famous: he was one of six writers on the producer-director Renny Harlin's widely ridiculed 1995 Geena Davis swashbuckler, *Cutthroat Island*.) Their first successfully produced project together was the

ABC legal drama *In Justice* in 2006, starring Kyle MacLachlan of *Twin Peaks* as a wealthy attorney heading an organization of lawyers and investigators working pro bono to overturn wrongful convictions. That series, while generally well reviewed, didn't catch on, but their next joint effort, 2009's *Good Wife,* certainly did, as one of the best drama series on television.

Their respective TV influences growing up were, predictably, somewhat varied. Michelle "can recall getting up and being very eager to watch *Underdog,*" she admits, and was a loyal viewer of *The Flintstones.* Robert's first favorite TV cartoon was *George of the Jungle*—"There was a hip angle to the comedy," he recalls, adding, "It was really satire, more of a *MAD* magazine kind of satire of other cartoons"—and his first favorite prime-time shows were *Get Smart* and *I Dream of Jeannie,* which he remembers being shown as a combination block that made up an hour. And they were, on NBC's Saturday night lineup in 1965. "I can remember where I'm sitting!" Robert King says, thinking back on those childhood TV days. "Isn't that terrible? . . . We're not like Proust with madeleines. We're *George of the Jungle* and *I Dream of Jeannie!*"

As they matured, the shows they watched, individually and then collectively, had a strong impact on the kind of TV they would end up making. "Those Bochco shows!" Michelle says, rattling off the titles of the Steven Bochco drama series *Hill Street Blues* and *L.A. Law.* "I think I did poorly in several college courses as I spent my time watching Bochco."

"And this is slightly later," Robert adds, just as enthusiastically, "but *Twin Peaks. Twin Peaks!* I couldn't remember anything that grabbed me quite that way. Especially that third episode, where Kyle MacLachlan was throwing rocks." It was indeed a memorable scene, in the same astounding episode that also featured the first appearance of the Red Room and the oddly dancing Man from Another Place. MacLachlan's FBI special agent Dale Cooper gathered the local *Twin Peaks* police force outdoors, set up a blackboard with the names of suspects written on it, placed a glass bottle on a tree stump, stood far away with a bucket of rocks, and began throwing rocks at the bottle, one by one, after noting the name of the suspect and his or her relationship to the victim, Laura Palmer. If Cooper hits the bottle with a rock, it symbolizes . . . what?

"Wasn't it amazing?" Robert asks, still enchanted by that scene twenty-five years later. "It summarized every suspect in the show, so it played the function of reminding the audience where they were, and yet it was so quirky, and everybody there is taking it so seriously, as if it does mean something," he recalls, laughing. "It wasn't just the dream logic and everything. It was how they combined oddity, their kind of quirkiness, while still holding on to the whodunit framework." He also loved the pace of it, because that scene occupied the entire length of a TV act, from one commercial break to another. "It's kind of like when you read a good author," he says, "and they mix short sentences with long sentences. I loved the way it fluctuated your expectations." It's a trait you can see in later shows that are similarly artistic, Robert adds, specifically naming *The Sopranos, Mad Men,* and *Breaking Bad.*

The Kings would hire MacLachlan to star in their first joint series effort, ABC's *In Justice* in 2006, and bring him back years later as a recurring guest star on *The Good Wife,* playing a Department of Justice lawyer investigating Alan Cumming's Eli Gold. And their *Good Wife* series would play similar games with pace. Other tricks adopted or adapted from previous TV shows, the Kings reveal, include an eagerness to intentionally shake up their characters' status quo, both personally and professionally, and to have characters come and go, sometimes quite unexpectedly.

"The big predecessor," Robert says, "was probably *L.A. Law,* with having the woman [the ruthless attorney Rosalind Shays, played by Diana Muldaur] fall down the elevator shaft. And then, more recently, *The Sopranos.* Year to year, they just killed so many characters, not even with mob hits, but with cancer and so on."

Michelle widens the point to discuss not just sudden deaths of characters—which *The Good Wife* employed brilliantly in its unexpected death of Josh Charles's Will Gardner in a hotly discussed 2015 episode—but also the placing of established characters in new job situations, or against one another in new types of conflicts.

"There was one season of *The West Wing* where folks changed jobs. Do you remember that?" she asks. "I thought that was an interesting choice . . . It gave one the sense that, okay, a workplace drama doesn't need to look exactly the same every year."

"I remember *L.A. Law,* late in its run," Robert adds, "had a great episode where there was a struggle over the law firm, and it pitted people that you loved and embraced against each other. It was like a big argument within the family. And that obviously had a great influence on our fifth season, of just breaking up couples and relationships that you had come to count on." He explains, "Since you loved and embraced all these characters separately, it felt a little more like life—in that life doesn't always have a very easy go-to about what is right and wrong and who's right and who's wrong . . . I would say *L.A. Law* is the granddaddy on that front."

More recently, cable TV dramas have had their impact on *The Good Wife* as well, establishing and encouraging a complexity of both narrative structure and story line. Michelle King notes the evolution of the TV legal drama series and says, "We're allowed to tip the balance a little more towards serialized storytelling than some of the earlier law shows. It's not just personalities arguing a case. It can also be, how are those personalities doing with each other?" And Robert King observes, "Maybe cable has freed us up more to actually have our characters be wrong, not just misunderstood."

Another singular aspect of *The Good Wife* is its deep bench of recurring guest actors—many of whom portray judges on the bench, with their own personalities and idiosyncrasies. "The fact that we film in New York probably has benefited us in terms of getting talent," Michelle says, while Robert acknowledges that the presence of those often unpredictable judges is an important part of their show's overall design.

"We like that the courtroom fights are not binary," he explains. "That they're not either defense or prosecution, or plaintiff and defense . . . So it just makes it more complicated, a little more like 3-D chess, where you're not just up against one person. The judge may side with one person one day, and another one on the other. And also, it's a little bit of the show's take on the law, which is that the law is not impersonal. The law involves real people, who have their own little obsessions or crazinesses . . . This year, involving bond court, their bias is purely based on speed." The Kings have their own bias for speed, thanks to some early guidance from the CBS development executive Christina Davis. "We were shooting the pilot of *The Good Wife* and sat down with her between takes," Robert recalls. "And we asked her, 'What is the best advice you can give us?' And she said, 'Don't be stingy on plot. Just burn through it.' And she was exactly right. And we concluded that you can always create more plot. You can't create more audience. So that ethic is what we've lived by."

Writing and producing *The Good Wife* the old-fashioned way—on broadcast network television, generating twenty-two episodes a year—means burning through much more plot than their cable counterparts. And the smaller per-season episode order, not the censorial freedom allowed on premium or even basic cable, is what Michelle King envies most. "I never resent the parts of network television that prevent us from cursing or showing nudity," she says. "I don't think that harms our show at all." But in general, she points out regarding her cable competition, "They have to do thirteen episodes instead of twenty-two. Twenty-two is hard."

Yet on CBS, the oldest of old-school broadcast networks, *The Good Wife* thrived. As of the end of 2015, ten different actors on the series had been nominated for Emmy Awards, and four—all women—have won: the series star, Julianna Margulies, as Alicia Florrick, Archie Panjabi as Kalinda Sharma, and, playing attorneys as occasional recurring characters, Martha Plimpton (Patti) and Carrie Preston (Elsbeth). And in May 2016, *The Good Wife* ended its run with an intentionally open-ended finale. "The real point of it," Robert said when I checked in with him afterward, "was 'Who is Alicia going to be?' We kind of wanted to leave it a bit of a question mark, so the audience could kind of fill in either where they thought she would go, or where they wanted her to go."

The Kings continue to be loyal to broadcast TV, unveiling *BrainDead,* a playful sci-fi series about aliens consuming and controlling politicians in Washington, D.C., on CBS in the summer of 2016. "The last month and a half of *The Good Wife* overlapped the first months of shooting on *Brain-Dead,*" Robert recalls. "After I directed the first episode of *BrainDead,* there was a week off, and then I directed the last episode of *The Good Wife.*" The new show, he says, has a lineage traceable, in part, to TV's original Golden Age and Paddy Chayefsky, as well as a more recent auteur of high-energy, low-budget B movies.

"This meteor is sent to D.C. to be inspected," Robert explains, giving a verbal sneak preview of *BrainDead,* "and these bugs that come out of this meteorite crawl into politicians', and their staffers', ears and eat their brains out. It's very much about extremism and how it's creating dysfunction on Capitol Hill . . . We were creating it during the last government shutdown, where people just seemed to lose their senses." And as the presidential campaigns of 2015 and 2016 kept imploding or succeeding unexpectedly, the Kings had to adjust not only their stories, but their visuals, accordingly. Green-screen TVs were used on set so their images could be inserted in postproduction, which allowed for some subsequent replacement of what was planned to be on the TV screens in political back rooms and TV control rooms. Reflecting real-life events, that meant less Ted Cruz, more Bernie Sanders. As for the freedom offered by writing and presenting the political satire of *BrainDead* during the presidential campaign year of 2016, Michelle says, "You only feel as though you can never go too extreme. Nothing is off the table."

Robert King concludes, with a chuckle, "If it ends up being where we want it to be, it's somewhere between Paddy Chayefsky and Roger Corman."

And it was.

MEDICAL

KEY EVOLUTIONARY STAGES

Dr. Kildare	1961–66, ABC
St. Elsewhere	1982–88, NBC
ER	1994–2009, NBC
House, M.D.	2004–12, Fox
Grey's Anatomy	2005–, ABC

Like television's other major staples of weekly series genres, the crime and legal dramas, the medical drama has evolved from the most basic of procedurals into series in which the protagonist was unfailingly attractive and infallible, then more human and flawed, and finally abrasive as well as determined and gifted. Only in the medical drama, though, has there been a subsequent evolutionary shift backward—a sort of devolution. Heart surgeons persist through the TV ages on medical shows, but, once again, so do heart-throbs.

When television was young, whoever got to a genre first was able to set a standard, and make a stamp, simply by being a procedural and introducing to viewers the basic vocabulary and activities of a given profession. CBS's *Perry Mason*, starring Raymond Burr as a defense attorney with an almost perfect winning percentage, taught millions of people that lawyers said "Objection!" a lot. Jack Webb, as both producer and star of NBC's *Dragnet*, taught that patrolling the streets as a cop meant lots of legwork, lots of following leads and interviewing suspects, and little extraneous chatter. And while there were a pair of short-lived medical prime-time drama series introduced in 1952 (NBC's medical anthology drama series called *The Doctors,* dealing with different physicians and cases each installment, and CBS's live, somewhat soapy *City Hospital*), the real breakthrough came in 1954, when NBC presented *Medic.* It was a medical version of *Dragnet,* and though it didn't come from Jack Webb, it might as well have. It adapted Webb's just-the-facts-ma'am approach to a different TV genre and used the "inspired by actual cases" approach equally effectively.

Medic starred Richard Boone, later to play Paladin in the Western *Have Gun, Will Travel,* as Dr. Konrad Styner. Styner was in many but not all of the episodes, but Boone served as host and narrator regardless. *Medic* was created by James Moser, who had picked up Webb's feel for straightforward, fact-based storytelling as a writer on Webb's *Dragnet* radio series. Moser's interest in medical dramas had developed while he was working as a writer for another radio series, the 1949–52 audio-only continuation of the successful series of *Dr. Kildare* films, with Lew Ayres and Lionel Barrymore reprising their movie roles. For TV's *Medic,* Moser relied on actual case files for his story inspirations, getting the cooperation of the Los Angeles County Medical Association, which vetted scripts for realism and added to that realism by permitting *Medic* to shoot most of the series on location at actual hospitals and clinics, and using real medical personnel as extras and assistants during scenes of medical procedures. In the premiere episode, Boone's Styner is shown delivering a difficult pregnancy, in which the baby lives but the mother dies and the stillborn baby is revived only because the medical staff shocks its system into operating by bathing the newborn alternately in hot and cold water. The scene was intercut with footage of an actual delivery—a first for television and the type of verisimilitude that would make *Medic* the TV medical benchmark for many years. In 1957, Jack Webb tried his own medical series of sorts—NBC's *Noah's Ark,* starring Paul Burke as a veterinarian—but it didn't catch on. What did catch on, eventually, were a pair of ABC medical shows premiering days apart in 1961, starring very good-looking young men as very idealistic, compassionate, and effective doctors. One was *Ben Casey,* the next medical series created by Moser, starring Vince Edwards as a moody and sometimes rebellious physician instructed and inspired by a veteran administrator (Sam Jaffe's Dr. Zorba), and the other was the model on which the *Ben Casey* dynamic was based, focusing on the professional relationship between a young doctor and his elder mentor. That series was *Dr. Kildare,* which dramatized a medical partnership introduced on film decades earlier, before even the radio series, in 1938's *Young Dr. Kildare*—the first of nine films teaming Ayres as Kildare and Barrymore as the eccentric but wise Dr. Gillespie.

DR. KILDARE

1961–66, ABC. Executive producer: Norman Felton. Stars: Richard Chamberlain, Raymond Massey.

The Max Brand short stories that had inspired the *Dr. Kildare* films of the 1930s were adapted just as successfully three decades later, in a mini-medical craze ABC generated in 1961 by launching *Ben Casey* and *Dr. Kildare* the same week. This new ABC version of *Kildare* starred a young actor named Richard Chamberlain in the title role, with Raymond Massey playing the paternal yet persnickety Dr. Gillespie. Both shows ended their freshman

Dr. Kildare starred Richard Chamberlain (right) in the title role as young doctor James Kildare, with Raymond Massey (left) as his mentor, Dr. Leonard Gillespie.

seasons in the Top 20: *Ben Casey* at No. 18, and *Dr. Kildare,* becoming the first medical series to land in the Top 10, finishing at No. 9. The consensus, then as now, was that these shows succeeded primarily because of the matinee-idol looks of their respective stars. And though there's some truth to that—ABC was beginning to target a young demographic at that time, and Chamberlain, in particular, was prime bait—both these medical shows actually propelled the genre forward by examining not only medical issues but social ones and depicting power struggles between older and younger medical practitioners, at odds over established and new medical procedures. Both programs did stories involving the rights of minority and female patients, and hired writers, directors, and stars who would continue to do significant work. In the case of *Dr. Kildare,* the many writers, for example, included Bruce Geller (*Mission: Impossible*), Ernest Kinoy (*Roots*), Richard Levinson and William Link (*Columbo*), and Gene Roddenberry (*Star Trek*).

There's no denying *Dr. Kildare,* in particular, established the TV ideal of doctor as heartthrob—not with Chamberlain making the cover of so many teen and screen magazines. And Chamberlain would ride and amplify that popularity, about twenty years later, by becoming "King of the Miniseries," thanks to his outstanding, often romantically steamy, leading roles in NBC's *Shogun* and ABC's *Thorn Birds.* But *Dr. Kildare* was more than just a prime-time pinup show. In its final seasons, it even developed an overlapping story structure—with many patients and cases in a single episode, and with some plots carried over multiple episodes—that would be refined and multiplied in NBC's *Hill Street Blues* and even in another medical series, *St. Elsewhere.*

But not for decades. In the meantime, the soapier elements of the genre would find their natural level, and optimal habitat, in the daytime soap operas, exemplified by ABC's *General Hospital,* which launched on TV in 1963 (and, at this writing, remains part of ABC's daytime lineup). The basic template of old doctor/young doctor would be tried again, and once again successfully, by CBS with 1969's *Medical Center,* which starred James Daly as the experienced chief of staff and Chad Everett as a fiery young surgeon. *Medical Center* would peek into the private lives of its hospital staffers, but most of those subplots, like most of the operations, turned out positively. Simultaneously, the concept of physician as godlike, mistake-proof authority figure would reach its apotheosis in yet another ABC medical series from the 1960s: *Marcus Welby, M.D.,* in which the star Robert Young went from Father Knows Best to Doctor Knows Best. It was another obvious variation on the *Dr. Kildare* formula, with Young's Dr. Welby, a highly dedicated general practitioner in Santa Monica, teaching the ropes to the medical trainee Dr. Steven Kiley (played by the future film star James Brolin). Dr. Welby always made house calls, never made an incorrect diagnosis, and had the patient and loving bedside manner of a saint. Miraculously, perhaps, viewers ate it up: after premiering in 1969, *Marcus Welby, M.D.* was a Top 10 hit its first season, and its second season it became the first medical series to top the ratings, as well as the first ABC series in TV history, in any genre, to claim the No. 1 spot.

In the 1970s, a TV series finally dared to depict doctors as flawed human beings, no matter how gifted they might be in the operating room. That series was CBS's *M*A*S*H,* set near the front lines during the Korean War—a comedy including more death, and more blood, than many medical dramas before it. It'll be examined under the chapter on war, but it definitely blazed a new trail for medical series to follow. Some, like NBC's Jack Webb–produced *Emergency* series, appearing the same year as *M*A*S*H* in 1972, refused to follow a similar path and presented its protagonists as unvarnished heroes. Others, like NBC's *Medical Story* from 1975, attempted to tell more complex stories with more complex lead characters. The 1970s seemed to favor simplicity: *Marcus Welby, M.D.* and *Emergency* survived through most of the 1970s, while *Medical Story* lasted only one season. It appeared viewers preferred their heroes, especially their doctors, to be above reproach and without doubt, but then came the 1980s and the doctors and nurses of Boston's fictional St. Eligius Hospital.

ST. ELSEWHERE

1982–88, NBC. Executive producer: Bruce Paltrow. Creators: Joshua Brand, John Falsey. Developers: Mark Tinker, John Masius, Tom Fontana. Stars: Ed Flanders, Norman Lloyd, William Daniels, David Morse, Denzel Washington, Ed Begley Jr., Bonnie Bartlett, Christina Pickles, Howie Mandel, Eric Laneuville, Mark Harmon, Terence Knox, Ellen Bry, Barbara Whinnery, Ronny Cox, Kavi Raz, Alfre Woodard, Chad Allen.

Even though NBC's *St. Elsewhere* began with a good-looking young doctor at its center (Jack Morrison, played by David Morse), it was more the antithesis of *Dr. Kildare* than a modern variation. This young doctor didn't always know best, do the right thing, or even save the lives of all his patients. Some other staff members at Boston's underfunded, underappreciated St. Eligius Hospital (derisively called St. Elsewhere by others in the local medical community) were even worse: One, Terence Knox's Dr. Peter White, not only was addicted to drugs but ended up being the rapist who was terrorizing female staffers and patients throughout the hospital. A regular series character who devolves into a rapist and ends up being shot and killed by another unhinged regular series character (Ellen Bry's Nurse Shirley Daniels)? That sort of thing never happened on *Marcus Welby, M.D.* or, for that matter, on any other TV series at the time. Though its reputation was a reductive "*Hill Street* in a hospital," *St. Elsewhere,* in several aspects, pushed the TV envelope just as much, and often in different ways.

St. Elsewhere, overseen by the *White Shadow* creator, Bruce Paltrow, for MTM Productions, was created by Joshua Brand and John Falsey, who went on to co-create CBS's *Northern Exposure* and NBC's *I'll Fly Away* (more recently, Brand has written several scripts for the FX series *The Americans*). It was developed, early on, by John Masius, Tom Fontana, and Mark Tinker, all of whom went on to amass other impressive credits: Masius wrote for NBC's *L.A. Law* and CBS's period family sitcom *Brooklyn Bridge;* Fontana wrote and produced for NBC's *Homicide: Life on the Street* and created HBO's *Oz;* and Mark Tinker, the son of MTM Productions' founder Grant Tinker, was a producer and/or director on NBC's *L.A. Law,* ABC's *NYPD Blue,* and HBO's *Deadwood.* These talents, and their respective tastes, combined to make *St. Elsewhere* a very strange TV animal indeed. One week, it would tell its story through a series of MTV-style music videos. Another week, most of the episode would be set in a character's dream of heaven. And for two weeks running, the series would be built around an extended flashback, keyed to the hospital's golden anniversary. There were puns as bad—which means as good—as the ones on *The Bullwinkle Show,* as well as dramatic moments of memorable intensity. Even its most prominent characters could die suddenly or have their lives changed significantly, and that refers to the doctors and nurses as well as the patients. Not only did one doctor become a serial rapist, but another, Morse's Dr. Morrison, was a rape victim himself, taken hostage and brutalized while tending to male patients at a local prison. (Fontana's dry run, perhaps, for the brutality of *Oz.*) Regular characters died suddenly, committed suicide, became clinically depressed, lost their medical residencies, or suffered razor slashes to the face.

One doctor, Mark Harmon's Bobby Caldwell, became the first prominent TV character to contract AIDS, and that wasn't the first time *St. Elsewhere* had explored that particular subject matter. A story line in 1983, involving a secretly gay politician who tested positive for HIV, was the first mention and depiction of the AIDS virus on prime-time dramatic television. It occurred two years before Rock Hudson went public with his condition and two years before NBC's attention-getting made-for-TV movie about AIDS, *An Early Frost*.

Though *St. Elsewhere* itself never won an Emmy as Outstanding Drama Series, its actors, guest actors, writers, and directors were duly acknowledged, with a total of thirteen Emmys. Denzel Washington, David Morse, Ed Begley Jr., Mark Harmon, and Howie Mandel all got their big breaks here, and the veteran actors Ed Flanders, William Daniels, and Norman Lloyd did wonders with fabulous late-career roles. Daniels and Begley had particular fun subverting the long-established "older doctor as mentor to eager young doctor" formula, so familiar from *Dr. Kildare, Ben Casey, Mar-*

St. Elsewhere, one of the best TV dramas of the 1980s, set standards, broke rules, and made great use of a large ensemble cast, including William Daniels (left) as Dr. Mark Craig and Ed Begley Jr. as Dr. Victor Ehrlich.

cus Welby, M.D., and others. Begley's Victor Ehrlich was wide-eyed, coltish, eager to please, and sycophantic, but Daniels's Mark Craig, the hospital's widely respected heart surgeon, saw him as a constant irritation and disappointment. "The *St. Elsewhere* cast was so extraordinary," says Fontana, "that you really didn't want to give them a bad script, because they were too good to give a bad script to."

St. Elsewhere was my favorite drama series of the 1980s, because it was so brazenly unpredictable and its creators were so obviously enjoying themselves. Scenes that made you cry—like Morse's Dr. Morrison using his stethoscope to listen to the beating of his dead wife's heart, successfully transplanted into a St. Eligius patient—are still being "borrowed" decades later (a variation on that one was used, very recently, in NBC's 2016 series *Heartbeat*). And then there were things thrown in just for a laugh, like names announced randomly over the hospital loudspeaker. Some of the doctors being paged had a very funny, familiar ring: Casey, Kildare, Welby, Zorba. Others didn't ring any bells at all, except to a very select audience. Fontana says that while some of the names announced on the St. Eligius loudspeaker were indeed those of past TV physicians, others were culled from the eighth-grade class roll of the executive producer Bruce Paltrow's daughter, Gwyneth. The writers, it seemed, would do almost anything for a laugh, including having the three older doctors (Daniels's Craig, Flanders's Donald Westphall, and Lloyd's Daniel Auschlander) go out to a local bar for a drink and have it be a place called Cheers, where they swapped stories and dialogue with the barmaid Carla and the bar stool regulars Norm and Cliff (played, of course, by the guest stars Rhea Perlman, George Wendt, and John Ratzenberger from NBC's *Cheers*).

The biggest joke on *St. Elsewhere*, though, was saved for last. The 1988 *St. Elsewhere* finale was so self-aware of its final-episode status that it sprinkled several playful quick subplots throughout. In one scene, a missing one-armed patient is found on, and returned from, the roof's water tower to be delivered to an unseen but very concerned Dr. Kimble—a clear nod to *The Fugitive*, one of the most famous TV finales of all time. In another scene, cast members reenacted the "mass hug" scene from the finale of *The Mary Tyler Moore Show*. And in several scenes, Dr. Wayne Fiscus (Howie Mandel) treats a zaftig opera singer, who came to the emergency room in full Wagnerian regalia—breastplate, braided hair, horned helmet—complaining of laryngitis. Near the end of the episode, Fiscus is told to go home because his residency is over. "No, sir," Fiscus replies stubbornly. "It ain't over till the fat lady sings." At which point, of course, the opera singer belts out a sustained, triumphant note, and Fiscus smiles and leaves.

That could have been the ending to *St. Elsewhere,* but the show's creative team had something else in mind, something much more unexpected and controversial. Written by Mark Tinker (who also directed) and Bruce Paltrow (from a story also credited to Tom Fontana, John Tinker, and Channing Gibson), that ultimate *St. Elsewhere* ends with a stunner. After years away, Dr. Westphall (Ed Flanders) has returned to St. Eligius, with his autistic son Tommy (Chad Allen) in tow, to accept an invitation by his old friend Dr. Auschlander (Norman Lloyd) to come back and run the place. But by the time Westphall arrives, near the end of the finale, his old friend has died, collapsing suddenly at his desk. After the "fat lady sings" sequence, the action shifts to the late Auschlander's office, where Westphall is grieving silently, listening to one of his friend's cherished opera recordings, as his son Tommy stares silently out the window, looking at the unseasonable snowfall. Tommy turns away from the window, the scene switches to an exterior view of the hospital as it snows, and then, for seemingly no reason, the building shakes, as if in an earthquake. After that, the scene switches again—this time to an entirely different setting, where we see familiar faces in jarringly unfamiliar roles. Tommy, the autistic son, is seated on the floor of a cramped living room, engrossed by a round object he's holding. His father enters, arriving home from work, but even though he's still played by Flanders, he's a different character entirely. He's a construction worker with a hard hat (and without the beard he had in earlier scenes) and enters by saying "Hello, Pop," to the man reading a newspaper in the chair next to Tommy. That man is played by Norman Lloyd and is very much alive, even though his *St. Elsewhere* character of Dr. Auschlander is now dead. These are different people, in a different reality, and the point is driven home when the dad reaches down to the son and takes the snow globe the boy has been cradling and staring at. "He sits there all day long, in his own world, staring at that toy," the construction worker says. Then he asks his own father, "What's he thinking about?" He doesn't get an answer, but viewers do. The father returns the snow globe to its place atop the television set, the camera slowly zooms in on the globe, and in the last frames of the last episode of *St. Elsewhere* the inside of the globe is revealed to be a miniature of the exterior of St. Eligius Hospital, which explains both the unseasonable snowfall and the mysterious tremors. What it also suggests, though, is that the entire six seasons of *St. Elsewhere,* and all the events dramatized over that span, were nothing more than the idle imaginings of an autistic child. (There's a whole extended theory out there, tracing all the TV shows sucked into what's called "the Tommy Westphall Universe," but I'm juggling enough theories here already.) If that's a metaphor for watching television, it's a fairly bleak one. But, boy, is it a bold one, and until *The Sopranos* came along with its cut-to-black nonconclusion, *St. Elsewhere* was famous for having TV's most deeply polarizing final episode. I loved it. Many people hated it. And according to Tom Fontana, it could have been even more controversial.

He pitched the idea, he says, of having the *St. Elsewhere* globe returned, in the final sequence, to a display table covered with other globes, each of which contained a miniature exterior or set from another TV series from MTM Productions: the WJM newsroom from *The Mary Tyler Moore Show,* the precinct house from *Hill Street Blues,* the home or office from *The Bob Newhart Show,* and so on. As Fontana tells the story, laughing as he does so, Grant Tinker, then running NBC and still protective of the legacy of his former MTM company, squelched the idea outright, telling Fontana, in effect, that he could do whatever he wanted with *St. Elsewhere* in the finale, but he wasn't taking those other MTM shows down with him.

The next batch of prominent medical shows were genre benders, dealing with medicine in more unorthodox settings or styles than the straightforward medical series. ABC's *China Beach* (1988–91), set near the front lines during the Vietnam War, was, like CBS's *M*A*S*H,* as much a war series as a medical one and is discussed there instead. ABC's *Doogie Howser, M.D.* (1989–93), starring Neil Patrick Harris as a teenage medical resident, is split between scenes at the hospital and scenes at home, but the creator Steven Bochco says he considers the show, first and foremost, a family comedy-drama. CBS's *Northern Exposure* (1990–95), from the early *St. Elsewhere* producers Joshua Brand and John Falsey, was about a New York doctor repaying his massive student loan debt by tending to the citizens of a small town in Alaska but was much more about the townspeople than the medicine. CBS's *Diagnosis Murder* (1993–2001), starring Dick Van Dyke as a sort of crime-solving Marcus Welby, was primarily a mystery show, just as another inexplicably long-running CBS series, *Dr. Quinn, Medicine Woman* (1993–98), was primarily a Western, set in post–Civil War Colorado. But then, in 1994, came a return to the more traditional type of medical drama, represented by two excellent series premiering a day apart. On September 18, 1994, CBS premiered *Chicago Hope,* an ensemble show created by David E. Kelley, featuring such stars as Mandy Patinkin, Adam Arkin, Christine Lahti, Hector Elizondo, Peter Berg, Mark Harmon, and Rocky Carroll. *Chicago Hope* lasted six seasons and was quite good (Patinkin, in particular, was riveting) but never made the end-of-season Top 20. The NBC medical series that premiered the day after *Chicago Hope,* however, ended its first season ranked No. 2, right behind NBC's *Seinfeld,* and for three out of the four years after that, it was ranked as the most popular series on all of television. No medical series, before or since, has been as popular as NBC's *ER.*

ER

1994–2009, NBC. Creator: Michael Crichton. Executive producer: John Wells. Stars: Anthony Edwards, George Clooney, Noah Wyle, Laura Innes, Eriq La Salle, Julianna Margulies, Sherry Stringfield, Maura Tierney, Mekhi Phifer, Linda Cardellini, Goran Visnjic, Alex Kingston, Paul McCrane, Shane West, John Stamos, William H. Macy, CCH Pounder, Frances Sternhagen, Angela Bassett, Abraham Benrubi, others.

The concept for *ER* was truly ahead of its time. Michael Crichton, a young man who had attended Harvard Medical School and done a rotation in emergency medical care, wrote a movie script drawing on his experiences and observations there and tried to sell it to Hollywood in 1970 but got nowhere. In retrospect, it's not surprising: 1970 was the year the show about the perfect physician Marcus Welby, M.D., soared to the No. 1 spot in the ratings, so clearly it wasn't the time for a drama about doctors who drank excessively, had affairs with one another, and sometimes failed to save their patients. But a quarter century later, the time was just right.

In the meantime, Crichton wrote a string of very successful novels and screenplays. He wrote the novel on which 1971's *Andromeda Strain* was based. He both wrote and directed *Westworld,* the 1973 story about a robotic theme park run amok (an HBO reboot, from J. J. Abrams and company, is scheduled for late 2016). He wrote the screenplay for 1978's *Coma,* the novel and screenplay for 1979's *Great Train Robbery,* and the novel and screenplay

ER had many breakout actors over its lengthy run, including Julianna Margulies, who went on to CBS's *Good Wife,* and George Clooney, who went on to movie stardom.

for another little story about an out-of-control theme park, 1993's *Jurassic Park.* It was that film's director, Steven Spielberg, who heard about and ultimately read Crichton's decades-old medical movie script and suggested his Amblin Productions company produce it—but for television, with John Wells as the show runner. It was filmed with very few changes to Crichton's original script, save to pare it down to a two-hour pilot length for TV and alter the fate of one character. That character was Carol Hathaway, a nurse at the hospital who overdosed in a suicide attempt hours after completing her shift. In Crichton's original script, Carol was returned to the ER in critical condition and died. In the NBC version, she lived and eventually returned to work. Good thing, because the rocky romance between her character and the pediatrician Doug Ross became one of the show's most popular story lines. Carol was played by Julianna Margulies, and Dr. Ross by a then-unknown actor named George Clooney. She won an Emmy her first season; Clooney never won one, but *ER* itself did, as Outstanding Drama Series in 1996, a year after it was also awarded a Peabody.

ER borrowed a lot from *St. Elsewhere:* the chaotic hospital scenes, the flawed physicians and unsuccessful cases, the multiple and often serialized stories, the large ensemble cast of characters. But it also borrowed from older TV shows, with such proven formulas as the gruff veteran doctor (Peter Benton, played by Eriq La Salle) mentoring the good-looking youngster (the medical student John Carter, played by Noah Wyle) and the dedicated doctors coping with personal problems and overwhelming professional responsibilities (Dr. Mark Greene, played by Anthony Edwards). *ER* reached even more deeply into TV's past by mounting an episode, 1997's "Ambush," that was broadcast live—and performed twice, once for the East and West Coast audiences. Thomas Schlamme, soon to pair with Aaron Sorkin to perfect the "walk and talk" style on NBC's *West Wing*, directed. The original idea, he says, came from Wells, Clooney, and Edwards as a way to inject energy into the already top-rated show.

"It was just an incredibly smart idea, on John Wells's part," Schlamme says, "for esprit de corps. Here was a group of actors who were in the biggest hit TV show in years, and certainly the biggest hit that we'll ever see, I think. And it was the fourth year. What else could they do to challenge themselves, and how could they all work together?" The solution was to do an episode the way they used to do Golden Age TV dramas: rehearse extensively, then perform live, with no retakes and no safety net. And once the concept was approved, and the mechanisms put in place for a live transmission, the decision was made just days beforehand that if they were doing it for the East Coast, why not for another time zone, in the West, three hours later?

"Cut to the night we did it," Schlamme says, describing the end of the very first show, when all the actors were off camera while Edwards finished the episode with a silent solo scene. "Anthony's in a room by himself," Schlamme recalls. "Everybody's got to be quiet until we yell 'Cut!' and then they finally ran up there and rushed in. And I guess it's what live sports is all about. Both in the control room and on the set, people were just high as a kite that we pulled it off. It was so exciting." Schlamme laughs and adds, "And then it dawns on me: 'Shit, I've got to get everybody back into character in an hour, because we've got to do it again.'" Which they did, after which the cast and crew members were so pumped, Schlamme says, "They were like, 'Bring on Hawaii!'"

Schlamme, arguably the best director of dramatic TV working today, was surprisingly impressed, and excited, by the method of directing TV so many yesterdays ago. "The adrenaline and the energy of doing that show was, I think, as close to the idea of the Super Bowl," he says. "You've got one shot at it here, and it's not the same as doing theater," which, Schlamme points out, always has the promise of the next performance, and the one after that, to do things better. "This is it," he says of live TV. "It can go really wrong. But everybody stuck together. You're only as good as your weakest link, and everybody felt it. And I think it accomplished not only the idea of doing something rather great and interesting, but mostly how the actors and the crew, and the people involved in it, felt by just pulling it off."

Cast members came and went over the years, including Clooney, who bet on his future as a movie star and left *ER* in 1999. (Good bet, though he returned twice for brief surprise appearances.) And the movies paid attention to *ER* as well: the red-hot film director Quentin Tarantino directed an episode in 1995. But what *ER* did most notably and successfully of all was to lure viewers: for its entire fifteen-year run, *ER* occupied Thursday nights on NBC, capping its continuation of the network's Thursday night tradition, begun with *Hill Street Blues* and then *L.A. Law*, of that evening's acknowledged status as Must-See TV. *ER* also proved that a medical drama series with the proper mixture of medical procedures and soap opera could flourish for more than a decade, even with major turnover among its core cast. *ER* taught that lesson well. And before *ER* left the airwaves, another medical series, ABC's *Grey's Anatomy*, would begin proving it again.

Between *ER* and *Grey's Anatomy*, however, were a few other noteworthy advancements in the TV medical field. In 2000, the documentary producer Terry Wrong presented *Hopkins 24/7*, the first of many engrossing and educational nonfiction ABC series recording the lives, on and off duty, of professional doctors, nurses, and other caregivers. Other outstanding series by Wrong and his crew include *Boston 24/7*, *Hopkins*, *Boston Med*, and *NY Med*, and all of them adopted some of the techniques used by *ER* (and, later, *Grey's Anatomy*), including the use of rock music to hit certain emotional buttons and romantic subplots in which we look in as a doctor or nurse goes out dating, or getting married, or playing with kids at home. Bill Lawrence's medical comedy *Scrubs*, premiering on NBC in 2001, played the mentor–young doctor dynamic for laughs, with Zach Braff's young, fantasy-prone intern J. D. Dorian (in essence, a male, medical Ally McBeal) being both schooled and tortured by John C. McGinley's fast-talking, easily angered Dr. Perry Cox. And on the traditional drama side, there were advancements as well, thanks to FX's *Nip/Tuck*, Ryan Murphy's long-running (2003–10) series about two plastic surgeons, each of whom was equally insecure and, at bottom, fairly and ironically superficial. *Nip/Tuck*, even more so than *St. Elsewhere* and *ER*, proved that doctors need not be admirable, or even likable, to be watchable and interesting. And the year after *Nip/Tuck* premiered, another doctor walked onto the scene who tested that hypothesis pretty much to its limits. Actually, he didn't walk onto the scene: he limped.

HOUSE, M.D.

2004–12, Fox. Creator: David Shore. Executive producers: Paul Attanasio, David Shore, Bryan Singer, Katie Jacobs, others. Stars: Hugh Laurie, Lisa Edelstein, Robert Sean Leonard, Jesse Spencer, Jennifer Morrison, Omar Epps, Olivia Wilde, Peter Jacobson, Kal Penn, Amber Tamblyn.

The original concept for this series, about a team of medical diagnosticians tackling puzzling cases at a teaching hospital in Princeton, New Jersey, came from Paul Attanasio, the same TV producer credited with creating NBC's *Homicide: Life on the Street*. But just as that groundbreaking crime series, in reality, had many parents, so did *House, M.D.* One executive producer was Bryan Singer, director of the 1995 film *The Usual Suspects*, who also directed the *House* pilot. Another very influential executive producer was David Shore, who conceived the character of Gregory House. And, of course, major credit must go to the person embodying that character, the British actor Hugh Laurie, who made House's irascibility and brilliance not only believable but enjoyable to watch. Gregory House was the absolute antithesis of a Marcus Welby: he had no bedside manner whatsoever, was even more curt and cutting to his medical interns than Dr. Craig on *St. Elsewhere* or Dr. Cox on *Scrubs,* and was infinitely less interested in his patients than in their mysterious maladies. And mysteries were the key element of this particular medical series, though not in the crime-solving manner of *Diagnosis Murder.* Like *Columbo,* which started each episode by revealing the crime and the killer before letting Columbo slowly but surely work it out, most installments of *House* began by showing a person in sudden critical medical distress, with House and his team subsequently huddling to ascertain the cause.

The real mystery template at the core of *House,* though, was that of the adventures of Sir Arthur Conan Doyle's Sherlock Holmes. Like Holmes, House began each story confronted by a baffling mystery, distracted or fueled himself by taking drugs and playing music, eliminated all possibilities until whatever remained must be the solution, and had as his colleague and best friend a doctor who tolerated his sour mood out of respect for his undeniable brilliance. With House, it was a diagnosis, not a murderer, he was after; his drug of choice was Vicodin (because of chronic pain from a botched operation on his injured leg), an opioid not unlike the cocaine and morphine used on occasion by Holmes; House soothed himself by playing the piano, not the violin; and instead of enjoying the company of Sherlock's loyal friend, Dr. John Watson, he had his own best friend, Dr. James Wilson (played by Robert Sean Leonard). House genuinely liked Wilson but usually treated him miserably, as he did, even more so, the team of young doctors House was mentoring. These teams changed over the years but always featured interesting characters and talented performers, including Omar Epps,

House, M.D. borrowed from the Sherlock Holmes canon, and other inspirations, to present Hugh Laurie as a doctor whose bedside manner was more caustic than calming but whose ultimate diagnoses were brilliant.

Olivia Wilde, Kal Penn, Peter Jacobson, and Amber Tamblyn. And acting as both House's boss and, eventually, his lover was Lisa Edelstein as Dean of Medicine Lisa Cuddy, a perfect foil for House through the years, as was Leonard.

Another shared trait of *Columbo* and *House* was how rigidly structured they were, yet how that never seemed to detract from the enjoyment of watching them. With *House,* the correct diagnosis never comes at the beginning: a few red herrings have to be chased, and a few dead-end paths followed, before House and his team arrive at the actual medical solution. But *House* delved deeply into its main character's personal pain, emotional as well as physical, and, thanks greatly to Laurie, gave us another iconic, acerbic TV leading man. Laurie never won an Emmy for his role here, and *House, M.D.* never won as Outstanding Drama Series, but both were regularly nominated, and *House* did win a Peabody Award. Meanwhile, another medical series, one with a strikingly different tone and a much more endearing protagonist, would appear the season after *House* premiered and eventually change the dynamics of Thursday night television.

GREY'S ANATOMY

2005–, ABC. Creator: Shonda Rhimes. Stars: Ellen Pompeo, Chandra Wilson, James Pickens Jr., Justin Chambers, Patrick Dempsey, Sara Ramirez, Sandra Oh, Katherine Heigl, Kate Walsh, Kevin McKidd, Eric Dane.

ABC's *Grey's Anatomy* is the series that helped the executive producer Shonda Rhimes build her stable of popular, soapy prime-time dramas, which eventually monopolized the network's Thursday schedule and rebranded the night, taking advantage of NBC's fall from dominance. Instead of Must-See TV, once a specific term for NBC's Thursday lineup established in the early days of *Hill Street Blues,* Thursday in 2014 became touted by ABC as "TGIT," or "Thank God It's Thursday," because of the back-to-back-to-back pairings of three Rhimes-produced dramas: *Grey's Anatomy, Scandal,* and *How to Get Away with Murder.*

Grey's Anatomy was an advancement in some ways but not in others. Certainly it was significant in giving Rhimes unusual prominence and power as a TV executive producer who was both female and African-American. Also, her shows were populated by diverse casts and centered on women—usually women of color, though in *Grey's* the central protagonist was Dr. Meredith Grey, a white woman played by Ellen Pompeo. The core cast around her, from the beginning, was notably diverse, but in its fixation on romance in and out of the workplace *Grey's Anatomy* was unfailingly, unflinchingly obsessed. Attractive male doctors, in a throwback to the era of *Dr. Kildare,* were seen as heartthrobs and even given such nicknames as McDreamy and McSteamy. But the approach worked, and was accepted, and spread, not only to the 2007–13 ABC spin-off *Private Practice,* but to medical shows on other networks, including NBC's *Heartbeat,* starring Melissa George as a heart surgeon with a very active private life, in 2016.

In the wake of *Grey's Anatomy,* some medical shows, such as 2015's *Chicago Med* on NBC and *Code Black* on CBS, and 2016's *Heartbeat* on NBC, split the difference and included soap opera elements while focusing more on the medical aspect. The most revolutionary, and evolutionary, was Showtime's *Nurse Jackie* (2011–15), starring Edie Falco—who played Tony Soprano's wife on HBO's *Sopranos*—as a nurse who was very good at her job, but fairly bad at life, and addicted to drugs she stole from her own hospital or

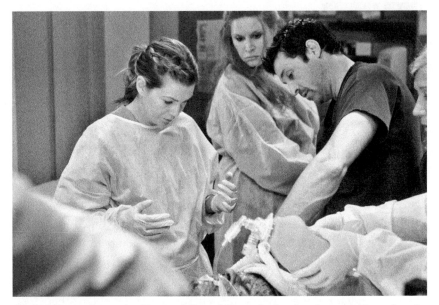

Grey's Anatomy, for much of its run, followed the professional and personal interplay of Ellen Pompeo (left) and Patrick Dempsey (right) as Dr. Meredith Grey and Dr. Derek Shepherd.

obtained from enabling colleagues and/or lovers. *Nurse Jackie* was carrying on in the tradition of *House, M.D.*, but most medical shows, at this point, were reverting to an earlier type. The prognosis for medical series, though, is a healthy one: like crime and legal shows, medical dramas come equipped with life-and-death story lines perfectly suited to their genre. By no means are they one of TV's endangered species.

KEY EVOLUTIONARY STAGES

I Love Lucy	1951–57, CBS
All in the Family	1971–79, CBS
The Cosby Show	1984–92, NBC
Roseanne	1988–97, ABC
Modern Family	2009–, ABC

It took a few years for drama series to appear on television, and when they did, they fell quickly into a few dominating categories, usually dealing with life-or-death issues: cop and detective shows, medical shows, lawyer shows, and so on. But on TV, the situation comedy, which, like the weekly drama series, had been a successful staple of radio for decades, caught on immediately. It also spread into so many varieties that classifying them all, as an evolutionary exercise, is like listing every species of ant. And there are more than ten thousand of those.

For a drama to work, the central character usually, though not always, has to do something . . . dramatic. In comedy, any profession works, and many work beautifully that have no matching counterpart in the dramatic series world. A bus driver? *The Honeymooners.* A cabdriver? *Taxi.* A garbageman? *Sanford and Son.* And no dramas are going to be built around sexy genies and flying nuns and talking cars (no, wait, there was a talking-car drama, *Knight Rider*), but for sitcoms, no problem. So long as it was comedy, the sitcom permitted almost any type of situation, from *My Mother the Car* to *Homeboys in Outer Space.*

For the purposes of this study, our analysis of the sitcom will be a bit more specific and by definition more limited. Sitcoms cut so wide a swath that attention could be paid—and, perhaps someday, will, if this volume sells well enough—to such subgenres as the "high concept" sitcom (the stranded societal microcosm of *Gilligan's Island,* the nonconformist free spirits of *The Addams Family*), nostalgia sitcoms (from *Mama* and *Happy Days* to *Brooklyn Bridge, The Wonder Years,* and *That '70s Show*), and ethnic sitcoms (from the CBS comedy *The Goldbergs* in 1949 to ABC's very different *The Goldbergs* in 2013). In this book, though, I'd like to focus on three specific types of situation comedies. In other chapters, I'll look at the workplace sitcoms, where the "family" is the one at work—typified by, say, *WKRP in Cincinnati, Cheers,* and *The Office.* And the hybrid, two-tiered sitcoms, which I call "splitcoms," where we spend time with the main character both at work and at home (*The Dick Van Dyke Show, The Andy Griffith Show, The Bob Newhart Show, Frasier*). Most central to the form, though, is the family sitcom. Whether the families are childless, like the couple on *The Honeymooners,* or dealing with lots of kids, like the parents on *The Cosby Show* and *The Brady Bunch,* the domestic situation comedy is the most common species of sitcom—as well as the first.

The term "situation comedy," it turns out, predates both television and radio and is first found in nineteenth-century British newspapers, used by reviewers of a particular type of theatrical farce, usually a domestic one. On network television, the first situation comedy was *Mary Kay and Johnny,* which premiered on the DuMont network in 1947 and eventually moved to CBS, then NBC, before being canceled in 1950. Years before Jack Benny and George Burns made it fashionable to play comically exaggerated versions of themselves on TV, a married couple named Mary Kay Stearns and Johnny Stearns did the same, in a domestic sitcom that was broadcast live. The show is all but forgotten, but certain of its "firsts" should be remembered. Because they were married in real life, the Stearnses were shown in the same bed, without any public outcry. And when Mary Kay and Johnny had a baby boy in real life in 1948, their TV counterparts reflected the same experience: her pregnancy showed, and was referred to, on television, and soon after the baby was born, it joined the show's "cast."

Other domestic sitcoms soon began to appear on TV, and because there were so few homes with TV sets, and because those TV homes were at that time exclusively in major cities, the networks started, in part, by targeting specific ethnic audiences by presenting shows reflecting, or at least acknowledging, their respective cultures and urban lifestyles. Some of these shows were adapted from existing radio hits or other sources and didn't focus primarily on family life: CBS's controversial *Amos 'n' Andy* from 1950, for example. Others, though, did. A show from 1949, CBS's *Mama* (based, in turn, on a novel, Broadway play, and 1948 movie, *I Remember Mama*), was a nostalgia sitcom as well, using the same framing device—an adult narrator looking back on childhood family life—that ABC's *Wonder Years* would employ forty years later. In *Mama,* which was performed live for most of its run, the setting was early twentieth-century San Francisco, and the family was Norwegian. Predating even that prototypical family sitcom was another 1949 ethnic comedy from CBS, *The Goldbergs,* presenting TV's first Jewish family.

The Goldbergs, starring Gertrude Berg as the talkative, nosy, but loving matriarch Molly Goldberg, was a spin-off of a popular radio hit that had begun in 1929 and was still running thirty years later when the show's star decided to try her hand at TV. And her hand was everywhere: Berg not only starred in both the radio and the television versions of *The Goldbergs* but wrote every script and demanded her artistic vision for the show be fulfilled and maintained, making her one of TV's first true auteurs and surely its first female show runner and power broker. Berg's Molly Goldberg was a good-hearted busybody, living in a crowded apartment building in the Bronx and dispensing advice to her children and neighbors as casually and frequently as she recommended freeze-dried Sanka instant coffee, and other products from the show's sponsors, to viewers at home. Berg stressed commonplace everyday events in every script she wrote, refused to include a laugh track, and provided a program in which mother knew best. *The Goldbergs* is the trunk of a family tree whose branches extend, over the years, to the "dramedy" sensibilities of *The Days and Nights of Molly Dodd* in the 1980s, the ethnic sensibilities of Gary David Goldberg's *Brooklyn Bridge* in the 1990s, and the minimalistic sensibilities of *Seinfeld* even more recently.

Not every family sitcom from TV's salad days was rooted in ethnicity. *The Life of Riley* had started on radio in 1941 and, like *The Goldbergs,* was still running successfully when a TV version was mounted in 1949—this time on NBC. But this time, because of contractual obligations to appear in movies, the show's radio star, William Bendix, was unavailable to make the migration to television, at least not initially. Instead, the role of Chester

A. Riley, the blue-collar husband and father whose working-class status and frustrations prefigured those on *All in the Family* and *Roseanne* (Riley's oft-quoted catchphrase was "What a revoltin' development this is!"), went to a young comic getting his first starring role in a TV series: Jackie Gleason. Gleason won an Emmy Award for his portrayal—the first ever given to a situation comedy—but with Bendix still playing the role on the radio each week, Gleason's TV version didn't catch on and was canceled after one season. Three years later, NBC revived *The Life of Riley*, with Bendix reprising his radio role, and it ran, as a hit, for five years.

Jackie Gleason, though failing in his first major TV showcase, was about to succeed wildly in another. In 1950, after *The Life of Riley* flopped on NBC, Gleason accepted an offer from the DuMont network to succeed the comedian Jack Carter as the host of its hour-long variety series, *Cavalcade of Stars*. In sketches, Gleason played several different characters on *Cavalcade*, and, as is still the case with today's *Saturday Night Live*, a character and bit received warmly by the studio audience was quite likely to be repeated—often. In October 1951, on live TV on DuMont's *Cavalcade of Stars*, Jackie Gleason played the Brooklyn bus driver Ralph Kramden for the first time, opposite Pert Kelton as Ralph's wife, Alice, in a new sketch called "The Honeymooners." Art Carney, a *Cavalcade* supporting player, also appeared, but as a neighborhood cop. Gleason's character of Ralph came more fully rounded, so to speak: he was blustery, stubborn, always chasing get-rich-quick schemes, and even threatening domestic violence with such empty threats, coupled with a clenched fist, as "Bang, zoom—right in the kisser!" and "To the moon, Alice!" Alice, by contrast, was smart, sarcastic, and completely unafraid, knowing that despite all his bellowing Ralph loved and needed her deeply. On *Cavalcade* that first season, the "Honeymooners" sketch kept recurring, and taking shape, adding and changing cast members and supporting characters. The fourth sketch—in which, notably, the Kramdens get a television set—introduced Carney in the now-classic character of Ralph's affable neighbor, Ed Norton. It also introduced Norton's wife, Trixie, who was played, that first time only, by the Broadway actress Elaine Stritch. The next time Trixie appeared, and from that point on, she was played by Joyce Randolph.

After two seasons on *Cavalcade*, and getting rave notices for his comedy work, Gleason moved to CBS, with a new variety series whose title, *The Jackie Gleason Show*, reflected his new star status. Network fights over intellectual property didn't exist then, so Gleason took his "Honeymooners" sketch concept, along with other familiar characters, with him. He also took Carney and Randolph along, but Kelton, his original Alice, had suffered a coronary thrombosis and needed to be replaced. Gleason hired Audrey Meadows, and the premiere episode of *The Jackie Gleason Show* on CBS included the first "Honeymooners" sketch with all four of the familiar players from the eventual *Honeymooners* TV series.

How it came to be a series is why it deserves so much space here, because the development of *The Honeymooners,* from brief sketch to season-long domestic sitcom, is a perfect illustration of the evolution of quality TV at its best. Through a combination of good fortune, strong artistry, and a kind of show-business natural selection, "The Honeymooners" kept changing, and growing. By the second season on CBS, the "Honeymooners" sketches routinely ate up more than half of Gleason's one-hour variety show, so spinning the characters off into a regular, full-length sitcom was an easy decision—especially given the money Gleason was offered to do it. He did it, though, for only one season, which at that time constituted thirty-nine first-run episodes per year. That's why CBS's single season of *The Honeymooners,* in 1955–56, came to be known as "the classic thirty-nine," though, eventually, surviving kinescopes of the variety-show "Honeymooners" sketches have surfaced and added to the show's overall legacy. No sitcom's legacy, however, is more celebrated, or its contributions and achievements more important, than that of a CBS series that premiered way back in 1951, the year of Gleason's first "Honeymooners" sketch.

I LOVE LUCY

1951–57, CBS. Creators: Desi Arnaz, Jess Oppenheimer, Madelyn Pugh, Bob Carroll Jr. Stars: Lucille Ball, Desi Arnaz, Vivian Vance, William Frawley.

I Love Lucy accomplished as much behind the camera as it did in front of the camera, which, if you've ever seen an episode of *I Love Lucy* (and who hasn't?), is an amazing statement. Desilu, the studio created in the 1950s to produce it, was TV's most influential independent production company until MTM Enterprises came around in the 1970s. The Desilu system of photographing sitcoms—filming the action with multiple cameras, resulting in a crisp, clear, final image and program that was easy to duplicate without any loss of visual clarity—not only changed the TV industry's way of doing things but had a lot to do with changing the epicenter of U.S. TV production from New York to Los Angeles and popularizing the concept of syndicated reruns. At a time when most minorities on TV were confined to ethnic comedies of their own or not visible at all, *I Love Lucy* proudly featured a marriage between the all-American redhead Lucille Ball and the heavily accented Latino bandleader Desi Arnaz, a singer and conga player from Cuba. And, though this final point may be absurdly obvious, the *I Love Lucy* shows produced by Desilu were as funny as they were popular, and for most of the time they were on the air, no TV series was more popular.

I Love Lucy, starring Lucille Ball and her husband, Desi Arnaz, as Lucy and Ricky Ricardo, was one of the most important and influential sitcoms in TV history, as well as one of the funniest.

The couple's, and the show's, unlikely success made for a true television sitcom original, yet many of the secret ingredients of *I Love Lucy* came from elsewhere—specifically, from radio, TV quiz shows, and movies. Lucille Ball had starred in a CBS Radio situation comedy called *My Favorite Husband*, which lasted from 1948 to 1951. She played Liz Cooper, and Richard Denning played her loving husband, George, but then Ball, now a radio star after a middling career in film, was asked by CBS to take her domestic sitcom act from radio to TV. She said yes, on the nonnegotiable condition that her husband on the TV show be played by Arnaz, who had been her real-life husband since 1940. CBS reluctantly agreed, and Ball and Arnaz brought along the major brain trust behind *My Favorite Husband*: the producer Jess Oppenheimer and the writers Bob Carroll Jr. and Madelyn Pugh, to create and write *I Love Lucy*. (Many of the first season's scripts, in fact, were reworked versions of plots from the old radio show.) Arnaz and Ball combined parts of their first names and came up with Desilu, the name of the production company they formed to produce *I Love Lucy*. He ran the company, and she was the star of its flagship show—the same arrangement Grant Tinker and Mary Tyler Moore had when they launched MTM Productions two decades later.

Before *I Love Lucy* even got into production, serious disagreements arose—not between Lucy and Desi, but between the showbiz power couple and the network and sponsor. The arguments were technical and logistical: At the time, the visual quality of what viewers saw on their TV sets depended on where they lived. If they resided on the East Coast, and were watching network shows emanating from New York, the images broadcast would be relatively crisp and clear. Other cities, especially in the West, would have to settle for the delayed delivery system of a kinescope—a film camera pointed directly at a TV monitor, resulting in a washed-out, barely watchable TV picture. CBS and the cigarette company sponsor, Philip Morris, wanted *I Love Lucy* to originate from New York, so the image received in East Coast TV homes would be a typically strong broadcast signal for those viewers, rather than a bleached, blurry kinescope image if the show were performed live in Hollywood and relayed back east. Lucy and Desi, as new parents with a comfortable home, wanted to stay in California and work from there, while Desi had the additional motivation of wanting his friends and relatives back in Cuba to see what he was about to do on American TV. (Shipping film prints of his series would be much easier, and more impressive, than cumbersome kinescopes.) Arnaz wanted to film *I Love Lucy,* yet he also wanted the energy and support of a live audience: His wife had blossomed on her radio show, playing someone else's wife, because she played so well to the laughter from the studio audience there. How to pull it off? By borrowing from the TV quiz show *Truth or Consequences,* which had come up with a method of using multiple cameras simultaneously to film the action before a live audience, and also by seeking out the master cinematographer Karl Freund, who had filmed part of the silent German classic *Metropolis* and photographed Greta Garbo in *Camille,* to figure out how to light a stage comedy so that the actors would be properly illuminated from a variety of angles. Why did Arnaz and Ball ask Freund? Because he was the cinematographer responsible for making Lucille Ball look so luminous in the 1943 film comedy *Du Barry Was a Lady.*

Eventually, a system was devised that Desilu thought would work, but neither CBS nor the sponsor wanted to pay the extra cost to finance a four-camera, 35-millimeter filming and editing process. (After the premiere episode, the number of cameras was reduced to three.) The difference, in total, was minimal, but CBS and Philip Morris both refused. Arnaz proposed a cunning counteroffer that ranks as one of the best deals ever made in Hollywood history. He would agree to reduce the salary he and his wife were owed weekly, from five thousand dollars to four thousand—a pay cut of 20 percent—if the multi-cam system was paid for. It was, split evenly between the network and the sponsor. That wasn't the brilliant business deal, though. This was: Desilu had been given 50 percent ownership of the finished *I Love Lucy* masters, and Desi Arnaz said that in exchange for their voluntary pay cut he and his wife would have to get 100 percent ownership from CBS. They did, and those crisp-looking *I Love Lucy* programs basically launched the TV rerun business (kinescopes, with their inferior quality, were seen as acceptable solutions before television networks were connected coast-to-coast in the early 1950s but never thought of as programming good enough to rebroadcast) and made a fortune for Desilu. It was a fortune spent immediately on land for studio space and for the production of additional TV series.

Using the *I Love Lucy* camera and tech crew on its down days, Desilu quickly doubled its output by producing *Our Miss Brooks,* starring Eve Arden as a schoolteacher, in 1952. Other series followed, and in another move MTM Productions would copy, the Desilu studio founded on comedy branched out into drama. For Desilu, the list was as impressive as it was unlikely and included both ABC's period crime drama *The Untouchables* and NBC's futuristic space-travel drama *Star Trek*. And in comedy, the three-camera system pioneered by Desilu became the industry standard, used by such iconic situation comedies as *The Dick Van Dyke Show, Happy Days,* and the MTM Productions flagship, *The Mary Tyler Moore Show.* Enough about the technology. Now about the comedy.

Lucille Ball's gifts, for both physical comedy and line delivery, were superb. Over its dominant run, *I Love Lucy* won five Emmy Awards, including two for Best Situation Comedy and one for Lucille Ball as Best Actress in a Continuing Performance. What's even more impressive about the show's universally loved set pieces and classic episodes is that they are spread so evenly throughout the show's six-season run, attesting to the overall comic consistency of *I Love Lucy.* My all-time favorite episode, "Lucy Does a TV Commercial" (in which she gets drunk on Vitameatavegamin), appeared in 1952, as did the equally classic "Job Switching" (in which Lucy and her best friend, Ethel Mertz, played by Vivian Vance, try to keep up with an ever-speedier conveyor belt at a candy factory). In 1953, *I Love Lucy* gave us "Lucy Goes to the Hospital" (in which she brought home Little Ricky), and 1955 gave us "Harpo Marx," featuring Harpo and his identically dressed hostess re-creating the mirror scene from *Duck Soup.* Finally, in 1956, Lucy stomped grapes in "Lucy's Italian Movie," eliciting a bunch of laughs in yet another timeless comedy triumph. The show was equally consistent, and triumphant, in the ratings: Its first year, *I Love Lucy* was No. 3 for the 1951–52 season, then topped the chart for the next three years. In 1955–56, the quiz-show phenomenon *The $64,000 Question* bumped *I Love Lucy* down to No. 2 for the season, but the next year, for the comedy's final season, *I Love Lucy* was back on top, and that's how it went out.

Another type of domestic situation comedy, in which the primary focus was parents raising children, also came from radio, and one of the most famous and long-lasting ones was a family sitcom that had started on CBS Radio in 1944 and shifted to NBC and ABC Radio before being adapted for television by ABC in 1952. That show was *The Adventures of Ozzie & Harriet,* starring the bandleader Ozzie Nelson and his wife, the singer Harriet Nelson, as themselves, raising their growing and good-looking sons, Ricky and David, who also played themselves on TV. *Ozzie & Harriet* lasted for fourteen seasons on TV (among live-action sitcoms, only *The Jack Benny Program* had a longer reign, at fifteen seasons) and was a pioneer in showing the power of scripted shows to boost tie-in music sales. A decade before NBC launched *The Monkees,* Ozzie Nelson put his younger son into the spotlight in a 1957 *Ozzie & Harriet* episode called "Ricky the Drummer," in which the teen TV star Ricky Nelson gets onstage to sing "I'm Walkin'," a song that had reached the Top 10 for Fats Domino earlier that year. After Ricky Nelson sang it on TV, his version, too, hit the Top 10 and launched the next-generation Nelson as a genuine pop star.

The biggest legacy of *Ozzie & Harriet,* though, was its early coalescence of what the family sitcom of the 1950s came to include and represent. Dad was the head of the household, going off to work somewhere, doing something, but always returning home in time for family meals and to deal with problems at home. Mom was there, always, and usually with an apron and a pearl necklace, handing out bagged lunches for school. And there were kids, going to school, getting into minor trouble, but always returning to the reassuring protection of their loving family. Most shows were set in the suburbs, at a time when the suburbs themselves were a new and shiny possibility. Also new and shiny possibilities were the state-of-the-art appliances featured so often on the shows, especially around mealtime: these were things, like new refrigerators and ovens, that the sponsors wanted TV viewers to covet. In retrospect, we tend to look at these vintage sitcoms as the way things were, but really they depicted the way many people wished things could be.

In the wake of *Ozzie & Harriet,* there was a sudden explosion of domestic sitcoms, and for every working-class, struggling TV family like the one in *The Life of Riley* there were many more tight-knit, middle-class TV clans who were more like the Nelsons: stable nuclear families in an unstable nuclear age. Danny Thomas—who, like Desi Arnaz and Ozzie Nelson, played a musical entertainer as well as a family patriarch—starred in ABC's *Make Room for Daddy* in 1953, which was soon rechristened *The Danny Thomas Show.* Then came a string of family sitcoms that, collectively, all but defined the genre in the 1950s: CBS's *Father Knows Best* in 1954, CBS's *Leave It to Beaver* in 1957, and ABC's *Donna Reed Show* in 1958.

Father Knows Best starred Robert Young, reprising his role of family man and midwestern insurance salesman Jim Anderson from his 1949–53 NBC

Radio show but as more of a domestic authority figure, because the title of radio's *Father Knows Best* ended, tellingly, with a question mark. *Leave It to Beaver* starred Hugh Beaumont and Barbara Billingsley as Ward and June Cleaver, with Jerry Mathers and Tony Dow as their young sons, Theodore (a.k.a. the Beaver, because of his buckteeth) and Wally, and Ken Osmond as Wally's unctuous neighborhood friend, Eddie Haskell. *Beaver* was more seditious, and less sanitized, because of what it showed behind closed doors in its suburban setting: the boys would misbehave, and the parents, in private, would express wonder and concern about both their parenting methods and the behavior of their children. And *The Donna Reed Show*, arguably the squeakiest of them all, featured Carl Betz as the pediatrician Alex Stone and Donna Reed, the program's titular star, as his patient and grounded wife, Donna. Problems were easily and lovingly solved, Donna Stone was an impeccable cook and housekeeper, and the series, like *The Adventures of Ozzie & Harriet*, managed to turn its teen actors into hit singers on the pop charts. And not just one TV teen, either, but two: in the 1960s, Paul Petersen, who played the family's son, Jeff, scored a Top 10 hit with the respectful "My Dad," while Shelley Fabares, who played Jeff's sister Mary, shot to the very top of the charts in 1962, weeks after singing "Johnny Angel" on *The Donna Reed Show*.

There were single-parent families around this time in TV sitcom history, but not many, and at first those parents were exclusively male. (It would be another decade before such single-women parents as depicted in *Julia* and *One Day at a Time* would appear.) John Forsythe starred in *Bachelor Father*, which premiered on CBS in 1957, as a well-to-do Hollywood attorney caring for his niece after her parents were killed in a car crash. Fred MacMurray presided over ABC's *My Three Sons* in 1960, playing a widower raising his boys as best he could. And in a hugely successful work-and-home hybrid sitcom spun off from an episode of *The Danny Thomas Show*, Andy Griffith played the small-town sheriff, and widower, Andy Taylor on CBS's *Andy Griffith Show*, keeping the peace in Mayberry while trying to do the same at home, raising his young son, Opie, played by the talented Ron Howard. Tellingly, because there were no female spouses around to cook and clean in these 1950s sitcoms, all these bachelor fathers had help at home: an "Oriental houseboy" (as he was then introduced) on *Bachelor Father*, an elderly housekeeping "uncle" on *My Three Sons*, and the blue-ribbon-baking Aunt Bee on *The Andy Griffith Show*.

Another hybrid sitcom—half workplace, half home life—premiered in 1961 and was one of the smartest, most influential sitcoms of the 1960s: CBS's *Dick Van Dyke Show,* created by Carl Reiner in 1961, starring Dick Van Dyke and Mary Tyler Moore as the TV-variety-show writer Rob Petrie and his suburban wife, Laura. It was one of the few modern, intelligent comedies of the 1960s—a decade that presented increasingly silly, fantasy-based situation comedies at a time when, in real life, everything from politics and war to music and film was getting increasingly relevant and revolutionary. "High concept" comedies became very popular, so much so that CBS's *Beverly Hillbillies* topped the TV ratings the season it premiered in 1962–63, the first sitcom to do so since *I Love Lucy. The Beverly Hillbillies* stayed there the next year as well, spawning a small raft of official and unofficial rural sitcom spin-offs. Fantasy was so big that two competing 1964 shows featuring families who happened to be "monsters," ABC's *Addams Family* and CBS's *Munsters,* could coexist comfortably. ABC's *Brady Bunch,* in 1969, injected the tiniest hint of topicality into the family sitcom by having the Bradys be a blended family, with a "bunch" of children from their previous marriages. But topicality, on entertainment TV in that era, wouldn't really arrive until 1970, when CBS purged itself of its older-skewing rural comedies and sought controversy by scheduling a family sitcom so different, so daring, it came with a warning label attached.

ALL IN THE FAMILY

1971–79, CBS. Creator: Norman Lear. Stars: Carroll O'Connor, Jean Stapleton, Rob Reiner, Sally Struthers.

"The program you are about to see is *All in the Family,*" ran the warning-label crawl preceding CBS's January 1971 mid-season premiere of its newest family sitcom. "It seeks to throw a humorous spotlight on our frailties, prejudices, and concerns. By making them a source of laughter we hope to show, in a mature fashion, just how absurd they are."

It was a complete change of pace for TV in general and for CBS in particular. This was the network that, in 1969, had fired the Smothers Brothers, and pulled *The Smothers Brothers Comedy Hour* from its schedule, largely in reaction to that show's persistent efforts to be topical, court controversy, and examine such third-rail issues as race, women's liberation, and the war. Now here was the same CBS, warning its own viewers that what they were about to see and hear, in that first telecast of *All in the Family*, might be a little rough.

And it was, but in a creatively exhilarating way. Norman Lear, anticipating by half a century the now-common TV trend of adapting successful shows from other countries, had been given a script of a current hit British sitcom, *Till Death Us Do Part*. The series, which had run in the U.K. for seven years before Lear brought the concept stateside, starred Warren Mitchell as Alf Garnett, a loudmouthed, opinionated working-class conservative with a deferential wife, flighty daughter, and liberal son-in-law. Something in the story resonated with Lear's own memories of his contentious relationship with his father, and based on the script alone, he set about casting the major roles and making a total of three pilots. The central character was now called Archie Bunker, and he was reimagined as a cabdriver living in Queens, with his wife, Edith, his daughter, Gloria, and his son-in-law, Mike, whom Archie referred to disparagingly as Meathead. Carroll O'Connor and Jean Stapleton were cast as Archie and Edith and remained through all three

All in the Family, starring Jean Stapleton and Carroll O'Connor as Edith and Archie Bunker, ushered in the new era of relevant sitcoms in the 1970s.

pilots. The younger characters were played each time by different actors, and the third time was the charm. With Rob Reiner, the son of Carl Reiner and a former staff writer on *The Smothers Brothers Comedy Hour,* as Mike, and Sally Struthers as Gloria, *All in the Family* hit the air, and by the end of the summer, thanks to word of mouth, it was not only a must-see show but the spearhead of a TV revolution. It won its first three Emmy Awards that first year, including Outstanding Comedy Series. In time, *All in the Family* would win a total of twenty-two Emmys, as well as a personal Peabody Award for Norman Lear.

O'Connor's deft acting helped give Archie a lovable core, which defused, if not excused, some of the abrasive things he would say and do. This, in turn, infuriated some viewers, who felt *All in the Family* was perpetuating, rather than ridiculing, racist and sexist attitudes. It was a dangerous line *All in the Family* was tiptoeing, but the series painted a more knowing and accurate portrait of its particular time, locale, and social class than any previous sitcom since *The Honeymooners.* But whether viewers laughed at Archie or with him, everyone seemed to be watching: for five straight seasons, it was America's most popular TV series. It sparked a national conversation whose flames only leaped higher with the popularity of the show's many hit CBS spin-offs, which were generated, on average, one per year. These included 1972's *Maude* (starring Beatrice Arthur as Archie's liberal feminist cousin), 1973's *Good Times* (starring Esther Rolle as Maude's former housekeeper, trying to make ends meet while keeping her family intact), and 1974's *Jeffersons* (starring Sherman Hemsley and Isabel Sanford as Archie's former neighbors, whose dry-cleaning business did well enough that George and Louise Jefferson could relocate to New York's exclusive Upper East Side). During the 1974–75 TV season, Lear and his production company partner Bud Yorkin saw all four of their *Family* sitcom spin-offs firmly in the Top 10: *All in the Family* in first place, *The Jeffersons* fourth, *Good Times* seventh, and *Maude* ninth. That's not a mere string of hits. That's a single-season empire.

All of Lear's shows courted controversy in one way or another. On *Maude,* for example, the title character considered getting an abortion and ultimately did. On *The Jeffersons,* one of the neighbors in the highrise was an interracial couple. Both concepts were TV firsts for a sitcom, as was everything on *All in the Family* from the sound of a toilet flushing to Archie's racial epithets of "spics," "spades," and so much worse. When his son-in-law, Mike, objected to Archie's use of the phrase "black beau-ties," Edith noted with a sigh, "It's better than when he called them coons." Archie was highly opinionated but rarely came out on the winning end of an argument, whether with a close friend who came out as gay or the celeb-rity Sammy Davis Jr., who, visiting the Bunker home to retrieve a briefcase left in Archie's cab, put his own stamp on a good-bye photograph by kissing Archie on the cheek just as the picture was taken. It was one of the series's most famous episodes, but from the very start, with a premiere episode that talked about religion and atheism, affirmative action, and several different minority groups, *All in the Family* was intentionally inflammatory. And according to creators of other groundbreaking TV series, it was influential as well.

"*All in the Family* was extraordinary," says James L. Brooks, whose own controversial sitcom, *The Mary Tyler Moore Show*, was part of a 1973–74 CBS Saturday night schedule that began with *All in the Family*, followed by *M*A*S*H*, *The Mary Tyler Moore Show*, *The Bob Newhart Show*, and *The Carol Burnett Show*. That astounding Saturday night lineup, it turns out, was required viewing for both Aaron Sorkin and Matthew Weiner, who went on to create *The West Wing* and *Mad Men*, respectively. And David E. Kelley of *Ally McBeal* and *Boston Legal* fame, who considers *All in the Fam-ily* the first show with which he ever fell in love. And Larry Wilmore, who wrote for several situation comedies before moving on to his *Daily Show* and *Nightly Show* duties on Comedy Central and who insists, "There are things on *All in the Family* you couldn't say on television today." That's cer-tainly the way my students at Rowan University feel when they're exposed to *All in the Family* in their TV History and Appreciation classes. Many of them, writing their reaction papers, are surprised *All in the Family* existed at all, much less in the 1970s.

Topicality was only one subgenre working its way through family sitcoms of the 1970s. Another was the idea of basing a sitcom on the essence of a comic's stand-up act and persona, which was started successfully by Bob Newhart for his *Bob Newhart Show* in 1972 and adopted thereafter, in later decades, by everyone from Bill Cosby and Roseanne Barr to Tim Allen and Ray Romano. Workplace sitcoms were popular, too, from the Korean War setting of *M*A*S*H* (1972–83, CBS) and the low-key police precinct of Danny Arnold's *Barney Miller* (1974–82, ABC) to the dispatching garage of the brilliant *Taxi* (1978–82, ABC; 1982–83, NBC). Norman Lear launched another successful and innovative family sitcom in 1975, with Bonnie Franklin playing a single working mother raising two teen girls in CBS's *One Day at a Time*. Yet as Lear's sitcoms pushed for relevance, another TV producer, Garry Marshall, opted instead for the warmth of nostalgia, which in 1976 knocked *All in the Family* off its perch atop the ratings: that season, Marshall's *Happy Days*, an ABC period family sitcom starring Ron Howard as the 1950s teen Richie Cunningham, was ranked No. 1, and one of its spin-offs, *Laverne & Shirley*, was right behind at No. 2. Two years later, *Happy Days* spawned a much more improbable sitcom, *Mork & Mindy*, starring the then-unknown Robin Williams as an antic alien visiting Earth, and it too caught on instantly. Yet another new sitcom subgenre was the salacious, sophomorically risqué comedy, lumped in with ABC's so-called jiggle TV movement of the time and typified by 1977's *Three's Company*, starring John Ritter and Suzanne Somers. For a brief time, all these types of comedies coexisted successfully, sometimes impressively so. At the end of the 1970s, the top four shows in the ratings were, in order, ABC's *Laverne & Shirley*, *Three's Company*, *Mork & Mindy*, and *Happy Days*. Except for the CBS newsmagazine *60 Minutes* at No. 6, all shows in the end-of-season Top 10 that year were sitcoms.

Sitcoms continued to develop and innovate in the early 1980s. One NBC sitcom, Gary David Goldberg's *Family Ties* (1982–89), successfully inverted the *All in the Family* formula with perfect timing for the Ronald Reagan era by having Michael J. Fox play the argumentative conservative son of a liberal suburban father (Michael Gross). Another NBC comedy, *Cheers* (1982–93), not only presented one of the best workplace sitcoms ever made but eventually spawned another, *Frasier* (1993–2004). But for a while, these situation comedies became increasingly overshadowed by prime-time soap operas, a new wave of action shows, and another type of TV revolution with NBC's *Hill Street Blues*. In less than five years, the ratio of sitcoms to other types of shows in TV's Top 10 had reversed: only one comedy, CBS's *Kate & Allie*, made the Top 10 in 1983–84, and many industry executives and TV pundits were declaring the situation comedy, especially the family sitcom, dead. And then, in the fall of 1984, came another show that changed everything.

THE COSBY SHOW

1984–92, NBC. Creators: Bill Cosby, Ed. Weinberger, Michael Leeson. Stars: Bill Cosby, Phylicia Rashad, Malcolm-Jamal Warner, Lisa Bonet, Sabrina Le Beauf, Tempestt Bledsoe, Keshia Knight Pulliam, Raven-Symoné.

When *The Cosby Show* premiered on NBC in 1984, my review in the *Philadelphia Inquirer* was an enthusiastic rave. I called it "the best sitcom since *Cheers*, and a good bet to become an instant classic." A little more than three decades later, my opinion of that series, especially its pivotally important first episode, hasn't changed. What has changed, because of all the charges, lawsuits, testimony, and controversies regarding Bill Cosby's alleged nonconsensual sexual misconduct toward women unknowingly drugged by him, is how his TV shows are seen by today's audience—if they're seen at all. As I write this in January 2016, Cosby has faced accusations from more than fifty women, some of whose stories of abuse date back several decades. He has been found guilty of no crime and has yet to face trial, but in the court of public opinion the sheer number of women coming forward with similar stories has been enough to impact Cosby's career and legacy substantially. TV projects in development were scuttled. Reruns of his TV series, including *The Cosby Show*, were pulled from cable networks and syndication. And in my college classes, when I get to the moments in TV history where Bill Cosby made invaluable contributions to quality television in general and racial equality in particular, the majority of my students, most of whom are between eighteen and twenty-two, now have an adverse and often vocal reaction to being shown even segments from *I Spy* and *The Cosby Show*.

This is tricky territory, for a professor and for an author. As a TV historian, I know full well what a monumental pivot point *The Cosby Show* was, and is, in the overall story of prime-time television. As a TV critic, I'm very aware of how purposefully, and responsibly, Cosby consulted advisers—including psychologists and educators—in an effort to fill *The Cosby Show* with the most socially progressive messages he and his writing staff could concoct, and how everything in his TV show's Huxtable household, from the professions of the parents (Cosby's Cliff Huxtable was a doctor, and his wife, Phylicia Rashad's Claire, a lawyer) to the artwork on the walls, was chosen deliberately to send a positive message. What Bill Cosby accomplished on, and with, *The Cosby Show* was remarkable. What he's accused of doing in his private life, by scores of women, is reprehensible, and the pall it casts upon his career body of work, unless it is refuted or diluted, may very well end up erasing his best accomplishments from popular culture and memory. Ken Burns, who had a documentary series on stand-up comedy in development when I spoke to him for this book, admitted to wrestling with the same problem about Cosby: not knowing the truth about the accusations, but not feeling right ignoring them, either.

"It's icky, you know?" says Burns, who, like me, devoured Cosby's comedy albums as a youngster. "It's really icky." But Burns has no problem imagining that today's headlines may have a lasting impact on how Cosby's career body of work will be received, and perceived, in the future. "People don't believe this," Burns says, "but I know this as an amateur historian:

The Cosby Show, starring Bill Cosby as family patriarch Dr. Cliff Huxtable (seen here with Malcolm-Jamal Warner, right, as son Theo), revived the sitcom form and brought acceptance to shows with minority casts.

time flows backwards as well as forwards, and it informs the past." Referring specifically to Cosby's TV shows and filmed stand-up acts, Burns says now, "It's hard to look at that stuff." He's far from alone. Jerrod Carmichael, the African-American star of the 2015 NBC sitcom *The Carmichael Show,* devoted an episode of his aggressively topical comedy series to the issues and emotions surrounding Bill Cosby and the allegations. The episode was called "Fallen Heroes," and was presented on NBC, the same network for which Cosby had achieved his most significant TV milestones as the star of *I Spy* and *The Cosby Show.* In this particular installment of *The Carmichael Show,* Jerrod was eager to see Cosby in concert, bought some tickets, and tried to talk his family and friends into attending: "Let's be honest: this is kind of his farewell tour," he argued. "Who knows how long he's going to be alive? Or free?" Jerrod's father, Joe, played by David Alan Grier, insisted Cosby was innocent until proven guilty ("Isn't that what you would want if you were accused of something? Or would you want the Internet to decide?"). Meanwhile, Jerrod's girlfriend, Maxine, played by Amber Stevens West, wanted no part of watching either Cosby's old TV shows or seeing his new stand-up act, given the number and severity of the accusations against him. "The ironic part is," she told Jerrod, "you would have to knock me unconscious to get me to go see Bill Cosby." The comedian, she insisted, is at fault for tarnishing his legacy and reducing the affection of his fans for his old shows and comedy albums. "He ruined his own reputation," she said flatly.

When I wrote my first book, a 1992 defense of television called *Teleliteracy: Taking Television Seriously,* Bill Cosby was one of the people I interviewed for it, a man whose work on TV I greatly respected. I'm on the record, over the years, of appreciating his work, but in the current context I find it all but impossible to watch it, much less enjoy it, the same way I once did. Here, though, is the legacy *The Cosby Show* once had, and why.

By the time *The Cosby Show* premiered in 1984, situation comedies were an endangered species on TV, and so were responsible, authoritative parents in family sitcoms. One unintended by-product of Norman Lear's *All in the Family,* and all its spin-offs and imitators, was that it came to be the usual comedy standard that the parents would be sillier and less intelligent than their children. *Father Knows Best* had devolved to "Children Know Best," and it was such an ingrained approach, by the mid-1980s, that you can hear its acceptance in the reaction of the studio audience witnessing the premiere episode of *The Cosby Show*, followed immediately by the stunned and delighted reaction as Cosby, with one line of dialogue, reverses course and reclaims the father figure as the one with wisdom and authority.

In the pilot, Cosby's Cliff is confronting his son, Theo (played by Malcolm-Jamal Warner), for bringing home a poor report card, riddled with Ds. Theo's defense was that he didn't need good grades to get a "regular job" and that not everyone could grow up to be as successful as his own father and mother, who should love him no matter what grades he got in school. The studio audience applauds Theo's sincerity and individuality, and then Cosby's Cliff, after a perfectly timed pause to let the applause die down and seep in, yells at his son, "That's the dumbest thing I've ever heard in my life! It's no wonder you get Ds in everything!" The response from the studio crowd, and from viewers at home, was almost cathartic. On TV, the adults were back in charge, and on *The Cosby Show* it was an African-American household with whom millions of viewers, regardless of race, could relate. So many millions of viewers related, in fact, that *The Cosby Show* became one of only three series in TV history to top the Nielsen ratings for five straight seasons. The others? Fox's *American Idol* and, before that, another family sitcom: *All in the Family*.

The Cosby Show, written by Michael Leeson, Ed. Weinberger, Matt Williams, and others, with constant input from Cosby, launched a successful spin-off, NBC's *Different World*, in 1987. *The Cosby Show* itself won six Emmys, including writing and directing awards for the pilot and Outstanding Comedy Series after its first season on the air. Cosby himself won no Emmys for performing, but that was largely his own doing: After winning five Emmys over the years for his other TV series and specials, including three straight Dramatic Actor Emmys for NBC's *I Spy*, Cosby declined to take part in the Emmys as an actor for the entire run of *The Cosby Show*. "I welcome nominations for other members of the cast," he explained then, "but I personally choose not to participate." Ironically, or at least fittingly, the Outstanding Comedy Actor Emmy that first year went instead to another African-American actor, Robert Guillaume, who had gone from a supporting role on ABC's *Soap* to the star of his own spin-off series, *Benson*. Guillaume had been nominated on six previous occasions but never won. When he did win, Guillaume's acceptance speech included the sly recognition "I'd like to thank Bill Cosby for not being here."

Workplace comedies, such as NBC's intentionally outlandish *Night Court* (1984–92), continued to find a place for a while, but the dominance of *The Cosby Show* meant that family comedies, for a while, were the sitcom du jour, and plenty more people than Robert Guillaume had Cosby to thank for it, in one way or another. Just as *The Cosby Show* had made its mark by presenting an upscale family that got along well, several sitcoms that followed went intentionally in the opposite direction, either as straight lampoons or as significant variations. Where *The Cosby Show* showcased an upper-class black family, the just-launched Fox network went for two very downscale versions of that theme: a broadly caricatured working-class white family in 1987's *Married . . . with Children,* and a seemingly dysfunctional but ultimately loving bright-yellow family in 1989's animated series *The Simpsons.* Both shows, taking polar opposite approaches, painted portraits of the same sorts of struggling, often arguing parents and offspring examined in *All in the Family* and spoke to a very different sort of American reality than had been depicted, earlier in the 1980s, by such opulent dramas as *Dallas. Married . . . with Children,* raucous and often raw, lasted a decade. *The Simpsons* is still running. But it took another stand-up comic, like Cosby, to spin stories of domestic life into a hit family sitcom while, in this case, taking the issue of living just above the poverty line seriously enough to comment, openly and overtly, on the trickle-down effects of the downside of Reaganomics. For this particular family sitcom, it took a woman. It took Roseanne Barr.

ROSEANNE

1988–97, ABC. Creator: Matt Williams. Stars: Roseanne Barr, John Goodman, Laurie Metcalf, Sara Gilbert, Sarah Chalke, Alicia "Lecy" Goranson, Michael Fishman, George Clooney, Johnny Galecki, Martin Mull, Sandra Bernhard.

The creation of ABC's *Roseanne* is credited to Matt Williams, who wrote for the first few seasons of *The Cosby Show,* co-wrote the pilot script for its spin-off *A Different World,* and would later be credited with creating ABC's *Home Improvement.* But just as that latter sitcom was based overwhelmingly on Tim Allen's stand-up act and persona, so *Roseanne* was actually "created" by the comic herself, the first time she stood on the stage of *The*

Roseanne revived the working-class sitcom, with Roseanne Barr and John Goodman as Roseanne and Dan Conner struggling to get by. They're holding hands here while watched by daughter Becky (Alicia Goranson, one of two actresses to play the part) and Roseanne's sister, Jackie (Laurie Metcalf).

Tonight Show Starring Johnny Carson and dryly declared herself a "domestic goddess." Carson roared with laughter at her routine, and once it was fleshed out in sitcom form, with John Goodman cast perfectly as Roseanne's working-class husband, so did America. *Roseanne* premiered at the start of the 1988–89 TV season and by the end of it was ranked as the No. 2 show in the country—right behind *The Cosby Show*.

Roseanne and Dan Conner, played by Barr and Goodman, both worked; they had to, to make ends meet. And even then, times were tough: they bought in bulk, came home exhausted, and, instead of revolving their lives around their children, were just as likely to sit there, sinking into the couch, while their children revolved around them. It was a cluttered household, and seldom a quiet one, but it was a loving one, and having a woman as the pivot point of all the action made *Roseanne* as significant as its proud fidelity to its working-class setting and sensibility. The sitcom benefited from unusually talented co-stars: Goodman was terrific, a perfect foil for Roseanne, and Laurie Metcalf, as her sister, Jackie, was just as lively and quirky. (Metcalf and Barr both won Emmys for their acting; amazingly, Goodman never did.) And George Clooney, before moving on to *ER* and stardom, played a recurring role on *Roseanne* for its first four seasons, as the foreman at the plastics factory where Roseanne and Jackie worked. The show's annual Halloween episodes were quite popular and imaginatively produced, allowing the cast members to wear increasingly complex and outrageous costumes every year. The final season of *Roseanne* betrayed its original vision, by having Roseanne win the lottery and live in a material world more suitable to the opulent prime-time soap opera *Dallas,* but at the very end that final year was dismissed as a season-long dream, another way in which it ended up copying *Dallas.* On its own terms and in its best years, though, *Roseanne* was the most popular situation comedy on TV—until it was usurped by two very different types of sitcoms, ABC's *Home Improvement* and NBC's *Seinfeld,* which were part of a TV sitcom renaissance.

For a genre declared endangered before *The Cosby Show* came along, the family situation comedy really exploded and expanded during and after the years when *Roseanne* was on the air. The working class was vividly represented in everything from ABC's *Grace Under Fire* (1993–98), in which Brett Butler starred as a struggling single mom in a modern-day counterpart to *One Day at a Time,* to the same network's sitcom *The Middle* (2009–), starring Neil Flynn and Patricia Heaton as working-class, overworked Ohio parents. And before moving to *The Middle,* Heaton had served as an overly patient TV mom on another classic, classically structured family sitcom, as Ray Romano's wife on Phil Rosenthal's long-running CBS hit *Everybody Loves Raymond* (1996–2005).

Other types of comedy did well, too. The year *Everybody Loves Raymond* left the air, Chris Rock presented and narrated a nostalgic family comedy based on his own childhood memories, in the cleverly named *Everybody Hates Chris* (2005–9). Married without children was a subgenre covered, for a while, by NBC's *Mad About You,* starring Paul Reiser and Helen Hunt (1992–99). There were sitcom adults raising the children of relatives, in both NBC's *Fresh Prince of Bel-Air* (1990–96, starring a teenage Will Smith) and Fox's *Bernie Mac Show* (2001–6, in which Bernie Mac, like George Burns, often turned to address the TV audience directly). NBC's *Friends* (1994–2004) found new excuses for a small circle of friends to keep hanging around as roommates and/or coffee mates, as did two crucially influential comedies that were important pop-culture steps in the increasing acceptance of gays on TV (and off, for that matter). Ellen DeGeneres made national headlines when her title character in ABC's *Ellen* (1994–98) came out as gay in 1997's "Puppy Episode," with the real Ellen to follow suit virtually simultaneously. And on NBC's *Will & Grace* (1998–2006), the likable gay characters portrayed by Sean Hayes and Eric McCormack also played their part in changing national attitudes on gay rights, simply because of the winning way they played their parts.

Two Top 10 CBS sitcoms co-created by Chuck Lorre, *Two and a Half Men* (2003–15) and *The Big Bang Theory* (2007–), juggled their characters around in various roommate configurations over the years—not quite as domestic comedies, but certainly as sitcoms with a strong sense of family. That was true even when family members didn't get along, as represented, most perfectly, by *Arrested Development,* which began on Fox in 2003 and had an eventual rebirth on Netflix in 2013. The finest, truest family situation comedy of the current era, however, managed to stay true to the form by breaking it apart into separate units, following different members of the same extended family in the same tightly intertwined and overlapping plots.

MODERN FAMILY

2009–, ABC. Creators: Steve Levitan, Christopher Lloyd. Stars: Ed O'Neill, Sofia Vergara, Ty Burrell, Julie Bowen, Jesse Tyler Ferguson, Eric Stonestreet, Sarah Hyland, Ariel Winter, Rico Rodriguez, Nolan Gould, Aubrey Anderson-Emmons.

In the premiere episode of ABC's *Modern Family,* the fact that the three households followed were related, not just thematically, but literally, was saved for a climactic revelation. From the second episode on, the show had lost the element of surprise, but that didn't matter. By then, viewers had already embraced these disparate but delightful characters—so much so that *Modern Family,* like *Will & Grace* but even more universally, is given partial credit for gently moving the national populace, and even the U.S. Supreme Court, toward a more accepting position on gay marriage.

The three households shown in *Modern Family* are markedly, intentionally different. Claire and Phil Dunphy, played by Julie Bowen and Ty Burrell, are the "nuclear family" representatives: married to each other since they were young adults, and still married as their kids get old enough to start leaving the nest. Jay Pritchett, a crotchety older guy played by Ed O'Neill, is on his second marriage, this time to a beautiful, much younger Colombian trophy wife named Gloria, played by Sofia Vergara. Together, they're raising her son from a previous marriage (then, in time, one of their own as well). And finally, there are Mitchell and Cam, played by Jesse Tyler Ferguson and Eric Stonestreet, who represent a family unit rarely seen on television: they're gay, and dedicated to each other, and before too long have become doting adoptive parents. And what we learned, at the end of the premiere, was that Jay was Mitchell's father and Claire was Mitchell's sister. Every character had a relationship with all the others, and even the children's roles were fleshed out, perfectly cast, and used to great effect. *Modern Family* borrowed, in one way or another, from several classic family comedies of the past: O'Neill, in a previous TV generation, played the even more dour Al Bundy on *Married . . . with Children,* while Claire and Phil Dunphy, like Roseanne and Dan Conner on *Roseanne,* treat Halloween as their favorite holiday. The faux interview sequences between scenes are nods to, if not outright steals from, *The Office,* and the culture-clash dynamic between Jay

Modern Family follows multiple related families at once, including the patriarchal Jay (played by Ed O'Neill) and his much younger second wife, Gloria (Sofia Vergara).

and Gloria, especially with her thick accent, mines a marital TV tradition that goes all the way back to *I Love Lucy*.

Other parts of *Modern Family*, though, are inarguably . . . modern. The multipart 2014 story line in which Cam and Mitchell decided to get married on *Modern Family* came one year after California legalized and recognized same-sex marriage and one year before the U.S. Supreme Court recognized those same rights under the Fourteenth Amendment. And the TV show took the wedding seriously—seriously enough to have Mitchell have a major argument with his father, Jay, who, at first, could neither approve of nor comprehend attending his own son's gay wedding. The pain and emotional turmoil were evident in both father and son, and in the rest of the family as well. When the issue was reconciled in time for the wedding, the ceremony itself was touching, all-embracing, and, in its way, instructive. Those viewers who had never attended a same-sex wedding, or had opposed the idea, suddenly had a new point of view to consider. Meanwhile, consider this: while *Modern Family* lost the Outstanding Comedy Series Emmy Award in 2015 to HBO's political workplace comedy *Veep*, starring Julia Louis-Dreyfus, before that, in its first five seasons on the air, *Modern Family* had won five consecutive Emmys in the top comedy category. The only other series to do that, so far in TV history, is NBC's *Frasier*.

And so the sitcom, like all program forms, continues to evolve. The openness, innovation, and call for tolerance exemplified by *Modern Family* are followed, on the Amazon Video streaming service in 2014, by the headline-grabbing, consciousness-raising series *Transparent*, starring Jeffrey Tambor from *The Larry Sanders Show* as a seventy-year-old patriarch who makes the momentous decision to live the rest of his life as a her, as a newly emergent transgender named Maura. Tambor won an Emmy for Outstanding Actor in a Comedy Series and deserved it, playing the part without any condescension or comedic exaggeration.

Finally, the latest evolution in the sitcom form has been a return to where it all began: with comedies intentionally focusing on, rather than overlooking, specific ethnic groups. NBC has provided a sort of updated *All in the Family* with the arguing-the-issues African-American clan of *The Carmichael Show*. ABC is a leader in this regard, giving us both 2014's *Black-ish*, starring Anthony Anderson as the head of a middle-class African-American household, and 2015's *Fresh off the Boat*, yet another family comedy that takes a nostalgic look at a previous era—this time the 1990s. Except this time, it's based on the very funny memoir by Eddie Huang, and it stars Constance Wu and Randall Park as a Taiwanese family experiencing a staggering culture shock after moving to Orlando. And there's one other nostalgic comedy presented by ABC, about a Jewish family in the 1980s, told from the point of view of the now-grown son. This period family sitcom premiered in 2013, and its title, by coincidence, takes us all the way back to the beginning of TV comedy, and the beginning of this chapter. The name of this particular sitcom is . . . *The Goldbergs.*

NORMAN LEAR

BORN: 1922, New Haven, Connecticut.
FIRST TV CREDIT: Writer, *Ford Star Revue*, 1950, NBC.
LANDMARK TV SERIES: *The Colgate Comedy Hour*, 1950–53, NBC; *All in the Family*, 1971–79, CBS; *Sanford and Son*, 1972–77, NBC; *Maude*, 1972–78, CBS; *Good Times*, 1974–79, CBS; *One Day at a Time*, 1975–84, CBS; *The Jeffersons*, 1975–85, CBS; *Mary Hartman, Mary Hartman*, 1976–77, syndicated; *Fernwood 2Night*, 1977, syndicated.

Norman Lear was born in 1922 in New Haven, Connecticut, and grew up when radio was young. By the time he came back after serving in the U.S. Air Force in World War II, Lear was in his twenties, with no clear indication about what to do with his life—except an interest in emulating his uncle Jack, a successful press agent. He found work as a joke writer, and ghostwriter, for various New York gossip columnists and eventually moved to Los Angeles, where he was inspired by another family member: his cousin's husband, Ed Simmons, already relocated to Los Angeles, and finding work as a comedy writer. They teamed up and had success selling parodies and jokes for nightclub performers, eventually crafting a bit that scored big with the nightclub entertainer—and future TV star—Danny Thomas. That led to an offer for the duo to move to New York in 1950 as staff writers for NBC's *Ford Star Revue*, a variety and sketch show on this new medium called television. At this point, very few people watched television sets, much less owned them. Lear remembers, on Tuesday nights, visiting yet another relative to watch Milton Berle on the new medium's most popular hot show, NBC's *Texaco Star Theater:* "We didn't have a TV set, so we would go over to my uncle Al's to watch." Before long, Lear was writing for an NBC variety series himself, and though audiences were much smaller for his *Ford Star Revue,* its viewership included two performers who were about to headline a TV variety show of their own: Dean Martin and Jerry Lewis. Hired to appear as recurring guest hosts for NBC's *Colgate Comedy Hour,* the young nightclub duo watched the sketches and monologues on *Ford Star Revue,* read the closing credits, and sought out Lear and Simmons to write for them, beginning immediately.

"In two or three weeks," Lear explains, talking about his stint with Simmons on *Ford Star Revue,* "we were suddenly not writers but 'television writers' . . . And they didn't exist anywhere! So we kind of fell into a title where we were pretty much alone." Brilliant writers for Jack Benny and others had moved to TV by 1950, "but they were radio writers," Lear adds, laughing. "We were 'television writers.' So we benefited enormously from it, because when Martin and Lewis saw that [*Ford Star Revue*] show, they said, 'I want those television writers!'" They learned on the job, and quickly, and also took inspiration from another NBC variety sketch series that started on TV in 1950: *Your Show of Shows.* "It was the smartest comedy," says Lear, who began a lifelong friendship with one of its writers and stars, Carl Reiner—a friendship forged by both being New York television writers when that was a very rare profession indeed.

After working with Martin and Lewis, Lear moved on to other TV variety series, including *The Martha Raye Show* and *The George Gobel Show,* and began the 1960s by teaming with the producer Bud Yorkin—a stage manager on *The Colgate Comedy Hour*—on well-received variety specials by Bobby Darin, Danny Kaye, Henry Fonda, and Andy Williams. They ended the 1960s producing movies, but Lear was nurturing another pet project: adapting, for American audiences, a British BBC-TV sitcom about a bigoted working-class grump and his family. That BBC series, *Till Death Us Do Part,* starred Warren Mitchell as the prickly Alf Garnett. Lear's show was of course *All in the Family,* which you have just read about along with its fabulously successful spin-offs *Maude, Good Times,* and *The Jeffersons.*

The Lear magic touch struck gold with unrelated projects as well. *One Day at a Time,* starring Bonnie Franklin as a single mother raising two daughters, premiered in 1975. *Mary Hartman, Mary Hartman,* starring Louise Lasser in an ambitious every-weeknight syndicated spoof of soap operas, followed in 1976. And a talk-show spoof spin-off of *Mary Hartman,* starring Martin Mull and Fred Willard and called *Fernwood 2Night,* was launched in 1977. (See the "Soap Operas" chapter for fuller descriptions.) In late 2015, Lear, at age ninety-three, was talking with producers of actual late-night talk shows, pitching Mull and Willard in a series of short segments featuring a modern-day *Fernwood 2Night,* which, in Lear's imagination, was still running as a local show in Fernwood, Ohio. "The guys are much older," Lear says, recounting his sales pitch to the network producers, "but they're still doing it locally. You ought to cut to it now and then." Lear laughs. "Isn't that a great idea?"

Yes, it is, except which real-life TV host would want to cut away from his own show for a clip of a pretend TV talk-show host who was likely to be funnier? At the time, the original *Fernwood 2Night* was as meta, and as giddily seditious, as its parent program, *Mary Hartman, Mary Hartman.* And Lear's other 1970s sitcoms, aggressively pushing liberal values and examining minority perspectives, were as important for their impact as for their financial and ratings success. One measure of that impact, Lear says he discovered, came when the Television Academy hosted an evening pairing him with a group of hip-hop artists and entrepreneurs. "The subtitle was 'What Do a 92-Year-Old Jew and the World of Hip-Hop Have in Common?,'" Lear recalls, listing such participants as Russell Simmons, Common, and Baratunde Thurston. All of them, Lear says, talked about specific moments from his shows that touched them.

"Russell Simmons, for example, talked about having seen a checkbook on George Jefferson's desk. And he, at ten or nine or whatever age he was, for the first time saw that a black man could have a checkbook, and he never, ever forgot that."

Lear's minority sitcoms gave voice, in the mid-1970s, to lifestyles, idioms, and concerns not seen before on television. Then, in 1977, came the ABC miniseries *Roots.* Written by, and based on the up-from-slavery family history of, Alex Haley, *Roots* shattered ratings records along with Hollywood preconceptions about what was acceptable, and possible, as meaningful mass entertainment. A few years later, to begin a new decade, the author of that landmark multigenerational narrative about race teamed for a new TV series with another pioneer of racially sensitive television programs: Norman Lear.

"Alex Haley and I were good friends," Lear says. "And we were having dinner one night, and he told me about his best friend, when they were nine or ten years old, who was this white kid. They were so close that their two families were closer than other families were comfortable with, in this small southern town. And then, when puberty set in, the culture called on them to separate . . . It would just move them to see less of each other, and eventually none of each other. And I said, 'My God! That's such a great show! That's a series! We follow these kids until puberty, and then we see how the culture ruptures their relationship.' And that's what we set out to do." But that ambitious and excellent series, 1980's *Palmerstown, U.S.A.*, lasted only one season on CBS, so, unlike such later character-evolving-over-time narratives as *Breaking Bad*, Haley and Lear's *Palmerstown* never got the chance to unfurl the transformative story it set out to tell. "I'd love to have seen that through six years or so," Lear says now. But even being asked about it brought a smile: "I'm so glad you remember *Palmerstown*!"

Lear's TV series did as much to spark conversation about women's issues as they did about race. *One Day at a Time* was about how hard it was, but also how possible, to raise children without a father figure. On occasion, special episodes or topics made national headlines: Edith getting cornered by a rapist on *All in the Family*, for example, or Maude considering, and getting, an abortion after becoming pregnant late in life on *Maude*. The furor over that latter story line, Lear says, was immense—but late, and orchestrated. When the two-part episode premiered during the show's inaugural season, according to Lear, "nothing happened," but when it reappeared during summer reruns, activists from the religious Right "knew it was coming, and then it was another matter entirely."

The network was uncomfortable with the controversies and the heat they attracted and battled with Lear on the subject matter and dialogue of his shows' scripts but loved the free publicity, and especially the ratings. "It was a fight every step of the way," Lear recalls. "They didn't want to do 90 percent of what we were doing, and their mentality didn't change." But CBS loved the results, so Lear kept getting mixed signals. "You know how Milton Berle used to, with his left hand, indicate, 'Come on, come on, give me more'?" Lear asks, referring to the way TV's first comedy star would milk his live audience for additional applause. "And [simultaneously] his right hand would be up in a 'stop' position? That's the network."

Despite the fights and controversies, or because of them, Lear is proud of his legacy of TV shows that, as he puts it, "presented the problems America faces every day, and has been facing for a long time . . .

"We've been a part of the cause of the conversation," he concludes. "And that's what we as a country were supposed to be all about: an informed citizenry talking about their problems."

WORKPLACE SITCOMS

KEY EVOLUTIONARY STAGES

Fawlty Towers	1975, 1979, BBC2; 1977, 1980, public TV
Taxi	1978–82, ABC; 1982–83, NBC
Cheers	1982–93, NBC
The Larry Sanders Show	1992–98, HBO
The Office	2001–3, BBC2; 2005–13, NBC

The "workplace sitcom" is one that takes place wholly, or primarily, at a place of work, unlike a domestic family sitcom (set mostly at home) or a hybrid "splitcom" (evenly divided between home and work). The first TV comedies set in a workplace environment, so far as I can tell, were two 1950 NBC sitcoms: *The Pinky Lee Show,* in which the future children's TV host played a baggy-pants stagehand at a vaudeville theater, and *Menasha the Magnificent,* in which the Yiddish comedian Menasha Skulnik played himself, but in a comedy set in a restaurant where he was the often befuddled manager. The first memorable one, also on NBC, was 1951's *Mr. Peepers,* starring Wally Cox as a meek high school science teacher. (Imagine Walter White of AMC's *Breaking Bad,* if he'd never broken bad.) *You'll Never Get Rich* (quickly renamed *The Phil Silvers Show*) was a workplace comedy but like other military comedies, including *M*A*S*H,* belongs in its own special category. Another, more properly defined early workplace comedy, from 1954, was *Duffy's Tavern,* a briefly syndicated TV version of the popular radio show, set in a New York bar.

Workplace sitcoms, over the years, have included everything from police comedies—NBC's *Car 54, Where Are You?* (1961–63), about two New York cops patrolling the Bronx in their squad car, and ABC's *Barney Miller* (1974–82), set in a low-key Greenwich Village police precinct house—to NBC's *Parks and Recreation* (2009–15), set in a low-key Indiana public works department. There was CBS's *WKRP in Cincinnati* (1978–82), set in a raucous Ohio radio station, and NBC's *30 Rock* (2006–13), set in a raucous New York TV show production office. All five of those shows were quality, significant additions to the genre: *Car 54* for its unchecked, unpredictable looniness, *Barney Miller* and *Parks and Recreation* for their droll tone and oddball characters, and *WKRP* and *30 Rock* for their even odder characters and plots. In this genre, though, there are five workplace sitcoms that stand above all others and influenced most of those that followed.

FAWLTY TOWERS

1975, 1979. BBC2; 1977, 1980, public TV. Creators: John Cleese, Connie Booth. Stars: John Cleese, Connie Booth, Prunella Scales, Andrew Sachs.

When the American comedian Jackie Gleason turned his "Honeymooners" variety sketches into a stand-alone situation comedy in 1955, he did it for only one TV season, and those shows became the "classic thirty-nine" episodes of CBS's *Honeymooners*—then and now, one of the absolute classic examples of the domestic sitcom. When the British comedian John Cleese turned an idea he had written for a 1971 U.K. sitcom called *Doctor at Large* into a stand-alone situation comedy in 1975, he and his co-creator, Connie Booth, did it for only six half-hour shows. Then, four years later, they made six more, but those "classic twelve," the entire canon of BBC2's *Fawlty Towers,* constitute one of the finest, and funniest, workplace sitcoms ever made.

To celebrate the millennium, the British Film Institute polled industry professionals to ascertain the best British TV shows of the twentieth century. Topping that 2000 poll—ahead of Cleese's previous TV triumph, *Monty Python's Flying Circus,* and even ahead of the brilliant Dennis Potter miniseries *The Singing Detective*—was *Fawlty Towers*. The setting for the series was a resort hotel in Torquay, with Cleese playing Basil Fawlty, the inn's preposterously rude, perennially besieged proprietor. Prunella Scales played Sybil, his bullying wife, with Connie Booth—Cleese's real-life wife at the time of the first batch of *Fawlty Towers*—as the levelheaded employee Polly and Manuel Sachs as Manuel, the hotel's porter and butler, who came from Barcelona and spoke very broken English, adding to Basil's many frustrations. These four primary characters rarely left the hotel but didn't need to: in this tightly wound workplace comedy, hilarious guests and situations would come to them, and the disagreements and disasters would escalate slowly until they exploded, with Basil always at ground zero.

Four years passed between the production of BBC2's first six *Fawlty* episodes in 1975 and the final six in 1979. In the interim, Cleese and Booth

Fawlty Towers presented only two six-episode seasons, but that was enough to establish an all-time comedy classic. Clockwise from top left: Connie Booth as Polly, John Cleese as Basil Fawlty, Prunella Scales as Sybil Fawlty, and Andrew Sachs as Manuel.

divorced, then reunited (professionally, that is) to write the second batch of episodes, which were even better than the first. Also in the interim, the first batch was sold and distributed internationally, including in the United States, where many public television stations picked it up (as they had with *Monty Python's Flying Circus*) and showed the six episodes, over and over, in 1977 and afterward.

Cleese based the character on a real-life innkeeper he had encountered while on location with some of the other Monty Python members—a character so rude, Cleese said, he was fascinating. But it's not just the idea that makes *Fawlty Towers* so fabulous. It's the execution. The plot elements start innocuously, and seem disconnected, yet always boil over into a climactic frenzy and an embarrassing crisis from which there is no escape. The closest modern analogue is Larry David's *Curb Your Enthusiasm*, in both character type and story structure, but *Fawlty* was there first. Cleese, as Basil Fawlty, was even more limber and loony a physical comedian than when he ran the Ministry of Silly Walks on *Monty Python's Flying Circus*. (One writer described Cleese, perfectly, as "playing Basil like a demented stick insect.") Sybil was a coldly frightening spouse—like Sapphire to Kingfish in *Amos 'n' Andy*—and whatever indignities Basil suffered (and he suffered many), he passed on to poor, barely comprehending Manuel. Polly tried to help Basil avoid trouble with Sybil and the hotel guests but never succeeded. The performances, however, always did, thanks to the show's core quartet of comic actors.

The all-out classic episodes of *Fawlty Towers* include "The Builders," "The Hotel Inspectors," "Gourmet Night," and "Waldorf Salad," with way too many brilliant bits of business to list. But I have to mention two. One is the way Basil gets out of that universally feared social moment of being asked to introduce someone whose name you've forgotten (Basil extricates himself by faking a heart attack and falling to the ground). The other is the "Fawlty Towers" hotel sign shown in the opening credits of every episode, because in each episode, the letters are rearranged. My favorite variations: "Farty Towels," "Watery Fowls," and, in the episode called "The Anniversary," one that's too rude to print here—but look for it.

TAXI

1978–82, ABC; 1982–83, NBC. Creators: James L. Brooks, Stan Daniels, David Davis, Ed. Weinberger. Stars: Judd Hirsch, Danny DeVito, Marilu Henner, Tony Danza, Jeff Conaway, Andy Kaufman, Christopher Lloyd, Carol Kane.

The year after *Fawlty Towers* finally made it to America, U.S. TV viewers were treated to another dazzlingly hilarious workplace sitcom with a rude and bullying, but ultimately ineffectual, authority figure trying to run things. In the case of *Taxi,* the temperamental tyrant was the New York taxi dispatcher Louie De Palma, played with feral ferocity by Danny DeVito, but instead of being the pivot-point center of the show, as John Cleese's Basil Fawlty was in *Fawlty Towers,* Louie De Palma was only one colorful character among many. In *Taxi,* the characters seemed to come from different universes, yet in this particular workplace melting pot they all found a way to get along and even understand and support one another.

Taxi was partly based on a *New York* magazine nonfiction article about New York cabbies, an article optioned by James L. Brooks and David Davis

Taxi managed to make room for several different styles of acting and comedy in one sitcom. Of the original cast, Randall Carver lasted only one season, but the others thrived. Clockwise from top left: Carver, Andy Kaufman, Judd Hirsch, Tony Danza, Danny DeVito, Jeff Conaway, and Marilu Henner.

while still at MTM Enterprises. Along with two other writers from *The Mary Tyler Moore Show* and other MTM comedy hits, they left MTM to start their own company, with *Taxi* as their inaugural effort. They also recruited a Who's Who, or Who Was About to Be Who, of TV comedy, including Glen and Les Charles and the director Jim Burrows (all of whom reteamed for NBC's *Cheers*), Glenn Gordon Caron of ABC's *Moonlighting,* Barry Kemp of CBS's *Newhart,* and Sam Simon of Fox's *Simpsons.* From the premiere episode on ABC to its final bow on NBC, where it moved for one last season, *Taxi* was a triumph—except in the ratings, where it started as a Top 10 show but never repeated that initial burst of popularity.

What *Taxi* presented on TV, though, was astounding, bending all the rules to allow so many different styles of comedy in one place—one workplace. Judd Hirsch's Alex was the quiet center, the Mary Richards of the Sunshine Cab Company, and just about the only cabdriver without grander aspirations. Marilu Henner's Elaine wanted to be an artist, Jeff Conaway's Bobby had dreams of Hollywood stardom, and Tony Danza's Tony wanted to be a successful boxer. "I related to that as a kid, trying to figure out, you know, what he wanted to do with his life," says Judd Apatow. "I felt like those people. I felt like it was hard to get noticed, it was hard for people to see my value. Would women ever like me? Was I good enough? And that's what that show is about."

These mostly insecure cabbies and their blustery boss, Louie, all existed on the same comic plane, but then there was Andy Kaufman as Latka, the "foreign" mechanic with his own language and wild-eyed enthusiasms. And joining the cast in the second season, after an enthusiastically received guest appearance, was Christopher Lloyd as the Reverend Jim Ignatowski, a former 1960s druggie and hippie whom the cabbies encouraged to come work with them. That all these characters could coexist on the same TV soundstage was unlikely enough, but what the cast and crew did with them was unprecedented and astounding. "Every minute we did it, it was great to be doing it," Brooks says now. "It was amazing."

"Reverend Jim: A Space Odyssey," the *Taxi* episode in which Jim takes his driver's test to become a cabdriver, was directed by Jim Burrows and written by Glen and Les Charles and is one of the most perfectly scripted, directed, and performed episodes in sitcom history. Even the application to take the test is a daunting challenge for the spaced-out Reverend Jim. Confronted with the question "Mental illness or narcotic addiction?" he thinks a moment and mutters, "That's a tough choice." And when it comes to the test itself, even the way Jim tries to cheat leads to one of the funniest misunderstandings ever filmed. It was a TV sitcom high-water mark, but Burrows and the Charles brothers, breaking off to create a new workplace sitcom of their own, would soon achieve another.

CHEERS

1982–93, NBC. Creators: James Burrows, Glen Charles, Les Charles. Stars: Ted Danson, Shelley Long, Nicholas Colasanto, Rhea Perlman, George Wendt, John Ratzenberger, Woody Harrelson, Kelsey Grammer, Bebe Neuwirth, Kirstie Alley, Dan Hedaya, Jean Kasem, Harry Anderson.

When *Cheers* was conceived by James Burrows and the brothers Glen and Les Charles, it was originally envisioned as a sort of American version of *Fawlty Towers*, but then, according to those producers, an even earlier inspiration took root: a workplace comedy built around a small group of employees and an endless parade of visiting strangers and regulars, but in a saloon, as in the radio and TV versions of *Duffy's Tavern*. So while the rudeness of Basil Fawlty remained, transferred to the character of Rhea Perlman's caustic Carla, the rest of the concept of what was to become *Cheers* was changed to a Boston bar—the unlikely setting of one of TV's most celebrated, durable, and popular workplace comedies.

But it wasn't always so popular. The sitcom that ended up running eleven years on NBC, and in 1990–91 topped the ratings as the season's most popular TV show, actually bottomed the ratings during its introductory season in 1982 as the week's least popular TV show. It wasn't the fault of the show's cast or writers: from the very first episode, *Cheers* was a confident, clever comic masterpiece. Ted Danson plays Sam Malone, the former pro baseball player (and former drinker) who now tends bar at his own Boston saloon, called Cheers. The rest of the initial core characters were either regular patrons (George Wendt's everyman Norm, John Ratzenberger's know-it-all Cliff), employees (Perlman's acerbic waitress Carla, Nicholas Colasanto's scatterbrained bartender "Coach"), or both (Shelley Long's Diane, a jilted customer whom Sam hired in the pilot). NBC unveiled *Cheers* on Thursday night in the fall of 1982, after the musical drama *Fame* and before *Taxi* (newly acquired from ABC) and *Hill Street Blues*. NBC's lineup was a strong night of television creatively, but not in the national ratings tabulated by A. C. Nielsen: *Cheers,* up against the Top 10 CBS crime series *Simon & Simon,* couldn't make a dent that first year, and one week that fall wound up dead last in the ratings.

As a TV critic at Ohio's *Akron Beacon Journal,* I couldn't stand that indignity. I wrote a column for the local Akron-Cleveland TV market but syndicated nationally, in which I made an offer directed at any readers whose home TV sets were attached to Nielsen's Audimeter computer boxes (at the time, some fourteen hundred of them were used to track viewing patterns and tabulate national ratings). If they'd come visit me on Thursday nights, I'd serve snacks and dinner and let them watch whatever they wanted on my TV set. "The only catch," I explained to those Nielsen families in November

Cheers was one of the most popular and durable workplace sitcoms of all, surviving several key cast changes. Ted Danson, as Sam Malone, starred throughout. Nicholas Colasanto, who played Coach the bartender, died three years into the show's eleven-year run.

1982, "is that you have to leave your own TV set tuned to NBC for the entire evening." The day that article was published, I got two phone calls at the office, but neither was from a Nielsen TV family. One was from a Nielsen company representative threatening a lawsuit; the other was from the then-NBC executive Grant Tinker, who had already renewed *Cheers* for the rest of the season, thanking me for the column and the sentiment behind it. The Nielsen folks never called again, but Grant Tinker did, and my outside-the-box defense of *Cheers* ended up sparking a long, warm acquaintanceship I was very honored to have. Two generations of Tinkers, Grant and his son Mark, have been very, very nice to me over the decades—one more bonus payback for my love of quality television.

Cheers finished that first season in seventy-fourth place out of ninety-nine shows—one notch behind *Taxi*, which NBC's Brandon Tartikoff, Tinker's now-legendary head of programming, had picked up after ABC had dumped it, then canceled it himself after one unsuccessful season. But he didn't cancel *Cheers*, and James Burrows, who describes the late Tartikoff as "a dear friend," confides why. "They had nothing to replace us with," Burrows says now. "They'll admit that. Brandon used to tell us that: 'I've got nothing to replace you with, so I might as well leave you there.'"

That patience, whatever its justification, paid off, slowly but very surely. That summer, against reruns, *Cheers* slowly began to get sampled as viewers grazed for programming they hadn't seen already. Also that summer, *Cheers* got a critical boost. The Television Critics Association, in what was a test-balloon precursor to the now-annual TCA Awards, polled its membership to vote in a single category: the best new show of the 1982–83 TV season. (I know, because I conducted and compiled the poll.) *Cheers* won handily, NBC put out a press release, and the first TCA Award was established. (The following year, the concept widened to a more complete roster of categories, and the TCA Awards as the industry now knows them were born.) Shortly after getting support from the critics, *Cheers* got some more—lots, really—from the Emmy voters, who honored the freshman workplace comedy with Emmy wins as Outstanding Comedy, as well as for writing (Glen and Les Charles), direction (James Burrows), and lead actress (Shelley Long). After critics and Emmys, all *Cheers* needed was an audience, and it got that, finally, when *The Cosby Show* arrived in 1984 and helped turn NBC's Thursday lineup into the first publicized lineup known as Must-See TV: *The Cosby Show, Family Ties, Cheers, Night Court,* and *Hill Street Blues.*

By 1985, *Cheers* was in the Top 10 and stayed there. Pivotal characters and actors left but were followed by intentionally different, equally dynamic replacements. When Shelley Long quit the show and took Diane with her, Kirstie Alley followed as Sam's new co-worker and sexual quarry, Rebecca. When Nicholas Colasanto died, Woody Harrelson was hired to play the new bartender, Woody Boyd. Kelsey Grammer showed up a few seasons in as Frasier Crane, Diane's latest love interest, but stayed around the bar long after she left—so long that after *Cheers* ended, Grammer reprised the character on a spin-off sitcom, *Frasier,* that lasted another eleven years and was one of the great hybrid "splitcom" comedies. *Cheers* won twenty-eight Emmys in all, including four as Outstanding Comedy Series (in 1984, 1989, and 1991, in addition to its first-year 1983 win). When *Cheers* presented an expanded final episode in 1993, it ended with Sam turning out the lights to the bar for one final time (a sly nod to the ending of *The Mary Tyler Moore Show*) and turning away a late-arriving customer at the door, telling him, "Sorry, we're closed." That finale earned a 45.4 Nielsen rating and 64 percent audience share, making it second only to CBS's *M*A*S*H* finale, shown three months earlier, in terms of overall audience reach for a sitcom finale. That night, the cast of *Cheers* reconvened for a celebration from the bar in Boston on which the show's set was based. The problem was, they did it on live TV, on NBC's *Tonight Show,* with its new host, Jay Leno, and the cast had celebrated so much they were drunk and borderline disorderly for the occasion.

A more fitting way to wrap up the *Cheers* run would be to recollect all the wonderful characters, situations, and punch lines the show provided over its lengthy span ("Norm!"). Or the extended narrative plotlines it slowly unfurled, or the trust it gave to its writers and actors to have spaces between the laughs, and even to go for deep, serious emotions. Or, perhaps, to reflect on what Kurt Vonnegut told me once when I interviewed him about television. "I would say that television has produced one comic masterpiece," he told me, "which is *Cheers.* I wish I'd written that instead of everything I had written."

THE LARRY SANDERS SHOW

1992–98, HBO. Creators: Garry Shandling, Dennis Klein. Stars: Garry Shandling, Rip Torn, Jeffrey Tambor, Wallace Langham, Penny Johnson Jerald, Janeane Garofalo, Linda Doucett, Scott Thompson, Jeremy Piven, Mary Lynn Rajskub, Bob Odenkirk.

There were times on HBO's *Larry Sanders Show* when we followed Garry Shandling's talk-show host Larry Sanders home, usually to lie with a girlfriend (or to a girlfriend) while watching his show on TV, but primarily this envelope-pushing series was a workplace comedy. And as a satire and examination of show business, specifically television, *The Larry Sanders Show* was

The Larry Sanders Show was Garry Shandling's expertly written, mounted, and performed dissection of the TV talk show. From left, Rip Torn played gruff TV producer Artie, Shandling played insecure host Larry Sanders, and Jeffrey Tambor was needy sidekick Hank Kingsley.

the best inside-baseball game ever pitched on network television. And by being such an early hit on HBO, and such a revolutionary one, it led to so much other great TV, in drama as well as comedy. "People forget how huge that was," Louis C.K. says of *The Larry Sanders Show,* and another comic, Denis Leary, agrees wholeheartedly. "There was nothing like that on television at all!" Leary says. "First of all, the behind-the-scenes aspect of looking at show business, but then the way they shot it, the reality they had going on. Amazing, right?" Aaron Sorkin calls *The Larry Sanders Show* "great" and "groundbreaking," and Judd Apatow, who worked on it as a writer, says, "I learned so much from Garry. And you know, Garry's whole thing was about truth—getting to the emotional core of people." Shandling's belief and approach, Apatow recalls, was that most people are "wearing masks all the time," projecting a carefully chosen and edited image of themselves into the world. "I remember him saying," Apatow says with a laugh, "'People never say what they're really feeling. And when they do, it's a really big deal.'"

It's the same honesty-seeking, groundbreaking way David Chase would approach his characters, scenes, and dialogue in *The Sopranos,* but when Shandling created *The Larry Sanders Show* in 1992, that other HBO series was still seven years in the future. And though *Larry Sanders* predates the official Platinum Age of Television, it's an instrumental predecessor, from the way it was photographed and acted to the way it ended and the way it elevated HBO as a destination for quality TV creators.

Garry Shandling had served as regular guest host for Johnny Carson on NBC's *Tonight Show* but was less interested in inheriting Carson's job than in deconstructing it in a situation comedy. The very year that Jay Leno took over *The Tonight Show* in 1992, Shandling moved to HBO and, with Dennis Klein, co-created a series about a fictional TV talk-show host, one whose insecurities and character flaws and overinflated ego were in full view. Klein was a smart choice as collaborator: He had written nine episodes of NBC's *Buffalo Bill,* the 1983 sitcom that, like *Fawlty Towers,* put a wholly disagreeable character at its center, and in *Buffalo Bill,* the title character, played by Dabney Coleman, was a local TV host in Buffalo, New York, whose behavior was too boorish and bullying to ever make a transition to the big time. Klein was also head writer for the second season of *Mary Hartman, Mary Hartman,* which not only featured Coleman as Mayor Merle Jeeter but spawned the spin-off series *Fernwood 2Night. The Larry Sanders Show* aimed to explore the same satiric ground, but on a major-league national level, and by following the host and his workplace colleagues off camera as well as on. Shandling played Larry Sanders, who cared about himself and his talk show and its ratings and little else; Rip Torn played Artie, Larry's pit bull of a producer; and Jeffrey Tambor played Hank Kingsley, Larry's on-air side-kick and off-air nuisance. Most on-air guests, including a memorable early appearance by Carol Burnett, played exaggerated versions of themselves on *The Larry Sanders Show,* and the guest list for its "pretend" talk show often featured bigger A-listers than the real late-night talk shows it was lampooning: Jim Carrey, Sharon Stone, Farrah Fawcett, Warren Beatty, and Howard Stern all sat between Larry and Hank on *The Larry Sanders Show,* and their interplay, not only "on air," but in the preinterviews, backstage visits, and commercial breaks, made for a workplace comedy that felt more like a documentary. Even the way these more intimate scenes were photographed, with a handheld camera, distinguished them from the show-within-a-show sequences, and from just about everything else on TV at the time.

When HBO gave Shandling the green light to make thirteen episodes of what he envisioned as his talk-show deconstruction comedy, it was without a clear sense of what it would look like, because not even Shandling knew for sure. "In its simplest form," Shandling says, "*The Larry Sanders Show* is a more cinematic series than was being done . . . I couldn't explain to them what that was going to look like. That's how new it was. I couldn't say, 'It looks a little like *The Dick Van Dyke Show* when they're in the writers' room,' because it doesn't. It doesn't look like *The Mary Tyler Moore Show* in there, it just doesn't . . . It was just a discovery, the first time I saw the handheld cameras just like I called for, and it just worked."

So did everything else about *The Larry Sanders Show,* which created its talk-show TV world so convincingly that players from the real world of TV talk could, and did, show up to play, and to play themselves. David Letterman showed up as he was about to transition from NBC to CBS, and when Sanders pushed for some inside info about who would get the post-Letterman slot at his new network, Letterman whispered, "Tom Snyder. But don't tell anybody." It was a punch line at the time, but a deliciously prescient one: that job, hosting the first incarnation of CBS's *Late Late Show,* did indeed end up going to the former NBC *Tomorrow* host Snyder. *The Larry Sanders Show* had a great eye for talent, too: Its supporting cast included Janeane Garofalo, Bob Odenkirk, and Jeremy Piven, and the three leading players—Shandling, Torn, and Tambor—were spectacular. All three were nominated for Emmys that first season, as were the writers, directors, and the show itself. No one won, but given the fact that *The Larry Sanders Show* was the first cable TV series ever nominated for an Emmy as Outstanding Comedy, it was quite a coup of recognition. And in the end, *The Larry Sanders Show* did win three Emmys, for writing, for directing, and for the supporting actor Torn.

The final episode—star-studded, supersized, and with a powerful emotional catharsis—not only provided a great ending for the show within the show (Jim Carrey was a memorably high-energy component) but also provided, to end the behind-the-scenes part of this workplace comedy, an angry outburst from Hank, after his final on-camera appearance alongside Larry, that revealed his true feelings about his relationship with, and treatment by, his longtime boss. "Peter Tolan wrote that Hank run at the end," Shandling recalls, "and it wasn't accidental. Pete and I talked for a solid year about that episode." When the show within a show is over, Shandling explains, there's no reason for either of them to be guarded or polite. "And then finally, when it's safe and it's over, the actual feelings come out." The power, and dramatic honesty, of that *Larry Sanders Show* finale, he insists, were all factors of letting things simmer, and be repressed and unsaid for years, until their ultimate, unexpected explosion. "If the actual feelings came out at the top of the series," he points out, laughing, "you'd have no series."

THE OFFICE

British version: 2001–3, BBC2. Creators: Ricky Gervais, Stephen Merchant. Cast: Ricky Gervais, Martin Freeman, Mackenzie Crook, Lucy Davis.

U.S. version: 2005–13, NBC. Creators: Greg Daniels, Ricky Gervais, Stephen Merchant. Cast: Steve Carell, John Krasinski, Rainn Wilson, Jenna Fischer, Mindy Kaling, Ellie Kemper.

The Office, the original British series made by Ricky Gervais and Stephen Merchant for the BBC, took the handheld documentary filming style established by *The Larry Sanders Show* and doubled down, adding interview segments to the action as well. In addition to the daily activities at a corporate paper manufacturing and sales company, *The Office* gave us "confessional" segments, where the characters would reveal their true feelings and perspective regarding what the "filmmakers" had captured while watching this particular workplace family in action. The same technique was replicated when *The Office* was remade for the U.S. market, then so widely copied by other sitcoms it was even adopted, while simultaneously being lampooned, by ABC's 2015 resurrection of *The Muppets*.

Just packaging itself as a mockumentary, though, wouldn't make *The Office*—both versions—as memorable as they managed to become. For that, you needed smart writing, nuanced acting, and situations that could make you cringe one moment and smile the next. And, in the case of the British original, even shed a tear or two.

The British version of *The Office* starred the series co-creator Ricky Gervais as David Brent, an office manager desperate to be liked, yet so odious and inappropriate with his approaches to jokes and to employees that witnessing his efforts to impress is both painfully comic and comically painful. Whether singing his own composition "Freelove Freeway" or telling sexist or racist jokes in an attempt to lighten the office atmosphere, David Brent was epically clueless yet, when rejected by a girlfriend or ignored by an underling, somehow pitiable. His employees had their own problems: the quiet everyman Tim (played by Martin Freeman) had an unrequited crush on the office secretary, Dawn (Lucy Davis), and David Brent's sycophantic underling Gareth (Mackenzie Crook) was simply too weird not to become the butt of office jokes, some of them extremely elaborate. Despite its lack of a laugh track, and its unusual faux-documentary format, the shenanigans in *The Office* could be laugh-out-loud funny, and yet the ongoing non-going romance between Tim and Dawn played out so beautifully, and so touchingly, that its final resolution, in a Christmas special episode that wrapped up the series, made me cry. No sense denying it.

The British version of *The Office*, like the same country's *Fawlty Towers*, succeeded superbly at concocting a workplace comedy revolving around a seemingly disagreeable, yet somehow strangely sympathetic, lead character. And the two shows had another element in common: *Fawlty Towers* produced two series of six episodes each, then called it quits. Except for adding a pair of stand-alone special episodes, BBC's *Office* did exactly the same thing, and when the entirety of the British *Office* was imported and shown by BBC America, it was hailed by many, including me, as an undiluted, finely crafted, smartly compressed masterpiece.

The Office had different bosses for its various international incarnations. Ricky Gervais, who co-created the original BBC series, played David Brent in that version, while Steve Carell played Michael Scott in the NBC adaptation.

When rights were sold for an American remake, though, the number of episodes quickly outstripped the original, and expectations by many, including me, were low. Six episodes were presented for the first NBC season in 2005—keeping pace with the British version—but once the American offshoot was renewed, it very quickly had to rely on its own writers to perpetuate the plots and spirit of the show. By the time it ended in 2013, a total of 175 episodes of NBC's *Office* had been produced for the States— more than fourteen times the number generated by the original BBC show. Overseeing the U.S. adaptation was Greg Daniels, a former *Saturday Night Live* writer who had moved into animation, writing scripts for *The Simpsons* and, with the animator Mike Judge, co-creating Fox's animated family sitcom *King of the Hill*.

Steve Carell, a correspondent on Comedy Central's *Daily Show with Jon Stewart,* was cast as Michael Scott, the U.S. equivalent of David Brent, and other major roles were filled by actors who approximated their British equivalents. The star-crossed Tim and Dawn were now Jim and Pam, played respectively by John Krasinski and Jenna Fischer, and the office oddball Gareth was now the even odder Dwight, played by Rainn Wilson. The setting was changed from the Slough branch of the Wernham Hogg paper sales company in England to the Scranton branch of the Dunder Mifflin paper sales company in the United States. Other characters came into their own over the years, played by such eventual breakout actors as Mindy Kaling and Ellie Kemper, each of whom eventually got her own sitcom. And NBC's *Office*, too, matured into its own rhythm and tone and won over many of its harshest critics—again, including me. By the end, the resolution of the Jim and Pam romance was almost as touching as that of the original's Tim and Dawn. The U.K.'s *Office* won six BAFTA Awards (the British equivalent of the Emmys), three for the series and three for Gervais as an actor. NBC's *Office* didn't win any Emmys for Carell, but it did win for editing, directing, and writing, and in 2006 it nabbed the big comedy Emmy prize for Outstanding Comedy Series.

While NBC's *Office* was still on the air, Greg Daniels co-created (with Michael Schur) another workplace comedy that was filmed documentary

style with "interview" segments edited in: NBC's *Parks and Recreation*, starring Amy Poehler as an idealistic public worker in the small Indiana town of Pawnee. It premiered in 2009, borrowing liberally from the *Office* format, and lasted six years. Meanwhile, the single-camera, behind-the-scenes showbiz workplace comedy, elevated to such high levels by *The Larry Sanders Show*, continued to thrive and evolve as well. Gervais and Merchant collaborated again, and got HBO and the BBC to collaborate as well, on a 2005 series called *Extras*, in which Gervais played a wannabe actor and Merchant his ineffectual agent. Like *The Larry Sanders Show*, it featured high-profile guest stars playing less flattering versions of themselves (in this case, the guest list included Kate Winslet, Patrick Stewart, and David Bowie) and did a great job satirizing show business.

So did Showtime's *Episodes*, a workplace comedy that, if possible, was even more meta than *The Larry Sanders Show*. Like *Extras*, it's an international co-production, teaming the Showtime cable network with BBC2. Created by David Crane and Jeffrey Klarik, it's about a married writing team, played by Stephen Mangan and Tamsin Greig, who are lured to Hollywood to write an American adaptation of their acclaimed British TV comedy about an elderly professor and his adoring prep school students. In the hands of the Hollywood TV executive, though, changes are forced on them that obliterate all artistic connections to the original. The portly, sweet old British gentleman portrayed in the original show within a show is now a high school hockey coach, played by Matt LeBlanc, who, in the behind-the-scenes portions of *Episodes*, carries on so terribly that he breaks up the couple by seducing the wife, even though she hates him and everything for which he stands. It's another excellent workplace comedy set in Hollywood, and it's funny because it has more than a hint of truth. Its premise has decades of precedent. For every successful U.S. adaptation of a British comedy, such as *All in the Family* from *Till Death Us Do Part*, there are scores of embarrassing failures. Hollywood, for example, tried on three different occasions to mount Americanized versions of *Fawlty Towers* and failed miserably each time. Remember Harvey Korman and Betty White as the innkeepers Henry and Gladys Snavely in ABC's *Snavely*, of which only the pilot episode was made and televised in 1978? Or Bea Arthur as an irascible seaside innkeeper in ABC's *Amanda's*, which ran for three months in 1983? Or John Larroquette as, no kidding, Royal Payne, a grouchy California innkeeper, in CBS's *Payne*, which lasted two months in 1999? I didn't think so. But by the time this is published, a less than faulty *Fawlty* may take the workplace comedy to new heights or, at least, to new countries and settings. In December 2015, John Cleese announced he had combined three of the old scripts from *Fawlty Towers* into a coherent whole and was premiering the result as a 2016 stage comedy in Australia and New Zealand. He would not be acting in them, but by adapting them to the stage, he was experimenting with TV evolution on a bold new playing field.

Well, not a new playing field at all, really. Way back in 1954, during the Golden Age of Television, Reginald Rose wrote an original drama for the CBS *Studio One* anthology series. Performed live and starring Robert Cummings, it was called "Twelve Angry Men" and proved so popular Rose adapted it for the stage the following year and adapted it again as a 1957 movie starring Henry Fonda. So why shouldn't some of the best episodes of *Fawlty Towers* be made into a stage play? Peter Falk once told me, shortly before he died, that he was thinking about taking *Columbo* to the stage in some form, and it's easy to imagine taking three great episodes of *Taxi,* or of *Cheers,* and turning them into a Broadway hit. It's easy for me to imagine, anyway . . .

JAMES L. BROOKS

BORN: 1940, North Bergen, New Jersey.

FIRST TV CREDIT: Writer, *Men in Crisis*, 1965, syndicated.

LANDMARK TV SERIES: Co-creator, *The Mary Tyler Moore Show*, 1970–77, CBS; Co-creator, *Lou Grant*, 1977–82, CBS; Co-creator, *Taxi*, 1978–82, ABC, 1982–83, NBC; *The Simpsons*, 1989–, Fox.

OTHER MAJOR CREDITS: TV: Creator, *Room 222*, 1969–74, ABC; Co-creator, *Rhoda*, 1974–78, CBS; *The Associates*, 1979–80, ABC; Co-creator, *The Tracey Ullman Show*, 1987–90, Fox. Movies: Screenplay adaptation, *Starting Over*, 1979; Producer, director, and screenplay adaptation, *Terms of Endearment*, 1983; Producer, director, and writer, *Broadcast News*, 1987; Producer, director, and co-writer, *As Good as It Gets*, 1997; Producer and co-writer, *The Simpsons Movie*, 2007.

Given that James L. Brooks flourished so early and impressively as a writer of quality, well-written TV series, it's more noteworthy than surprising that his earliest TV appetite was for quality, well-written TV series. Born in North Bergen, New Jersey, in 1940, Brooks remembers watching TV even before his family had a TV. "I don't think we owned a television set when *Your Show of Shows* was on," Brooks recalls. "But I remember seeing it on other people's television sets in some way, and that was extraordinary." He uses the same word to describe other Golden Age programs and writing talents, all of whom were among the best of the best: *Playhouse 90*, *The Honeymooners*, Paddy Chayefsky, *The Twilight Zone*, and Phil Silvers as Sergeant Bilko in *You'll Never Get Rich*, a military comedy written by Nat Hiken. "Bilko was perfect to me," Brooks says, and his enthusiasm led him to appreciate not just the show itself but specifically the writing. "They published a guide with eight [of Nat Hiken's] Bilko scripts in it that I ate up," Brooks says. It says something when a teenager, who was already writing for his high school newspaper, is pouncing on paperback collections of sitcom scripts back when almost none had been published—just as it says something that one of Brooks's favorite *Playhouse 90* memories, still vivid after more than fifty years, was of a 1959 Rod Serling drama called "The Velvet Alley," in which Art Carney starred as a singularly driven screenwriter. "It was about becoming successful as a television writer," Brooks says, "and becoming a shithead because of success. And I remember thinking, 'Oh, man! The inside stuff!'"

Brooks would have been eighteen years old then, a freshman at New York University with his eye on a career somewhere in the entertainment business. He didn't stay at NYU long enough to graduate but did remain in New York long enough to get a job as a copyboy, and eventually a news writer, for CBS News (the seed from which, eventually, would sprout his acclaimed 1987 movie *Broadcast News*). Next came a chance to move to Los Angeles to work for David L. Wolper Productions, writing and co-writing scripts for such TV documentaries as the syndicated 1965 series *Men in Crisis* (including the installment "Kennedy vs. Khrushchev") and the unsuccessful TV revival of the famous *March of Time* movie newsreels. That job with Wolper soon fell through, however, and young Brooks found himself alone in Hollywood with no work, no prospects, and no hope of pursuing his real dream, which was writing scripted fictional comedy or drama. "I mean, I had the ambition," Brooks says, "but I'd had zero expectations that I'd ever be able to sell a script. It wasn't the sort of thing that was going to happen to me." And then, at a party, Brooks ran into Allan Burns, a TV producer who was co-creator of a new NBC comedy series, and offhandedly mentioned both his dilemma and his dream. "He's such a totally good guy," Brooks says, "that when I even mentioned it, he said, 'Well, let me see what I can do.' And I got a shot."

That shot was actually a one-shot: a rewrite order, polishing someone else's existing story for an episode of what has become one of the most infamous sitcoms in TV history: *My Mother the Car*. It starred Jerry Van Dyke as a man whose dead mother is reincarnated as a 1928 Porter, her voice emerging from the car radio to talk to her son, the only person who can hear her. Brooks, given his work situation (or lack of it) at the time, saw the opportunity, and the paycheck, as the exact opposite of an insult. "I saw it as the Holy Grail!" he says, shouting. "Yes! As the shining gift from God that was never expected!" He remembers being pitched the story idea over the phone, the one they wanted him to rewrite, and thinking that it went against the entire series premise: the whole world finds out the car can talk. Asked if he knew how it ended, Brooks said, in a high-pitched, excited voice, "No—how could it possibly end?" And he was told, "It was all a dream!" Brooks says he replied, in a much lower and slower tone of voice, "Oh." And he laughs again at the recollection.

That job, though, gave Brooks a sitcom credit, another *My Mother the Car* assignment, and from there, in rapid succession, other jobs, including freelance writing assignments for some very well-regarded situation comedies. A few *That Girl* scripts in 1966–67. A couple of episodes of *The Andy Griffith Show,* and one of *My Three Sons,* in 1968. Followed, in 1969, by the chance to create his own comedy series, under the wing and auspices of a TV writer-director whose own career stretched back to the 1950s. The series was called *Room 222,* and it premiered in September 1969. That was four years after Bill Cosby broke the TV color barrier with NBC's *I Spy,* becoming the first African-American actor to star in a prime-time drama series, and one year after Diahann Carroll, with NBC's sitcom *Julia,* raised the profile for African-American actresses by starring not as a maid (as in *Beulah*), or as part of a minority ensemble (as in *Amos 'n' Andy*), but as a respected professional nurse and responsible single parent.

"The idea," Brooks says of *Room 222,* "was to do a show about a black schoolteacher." One innovation was that the show was thirty minutes long yet classified as a drama but was widely considered a comedy, because the dialogue and situations often stressed humor. Another innovation was that *Room 222* didn't have one African-American authority figure at its integrated inner-city high school. It had two: a history teacher played by Lloyd Haynes, and a guidance counselor played by Denise Nicholas. "We were certainly the first show that had more than one African-American [regular cast member] in it," Brooks says, "because that was something we really wanted to do, and not have the 'monolithic' African-American. There were two, and they were very different people. And Gene Reynolds [later of *M*A*S*H*] was the director and the man in charge, and he was the one who hired me to write the pilot. And he was the one who insisted I keep on going back and back and back to this [actual Los Angeles] high school to do research. Later, it became something that was my greatest friend—just doing research. It became one of the things I love most to do."

Allan Burns, who had gotten Brooks his first sitcom break on *My Mother the Car,* was called in to write several episodes of *Room 222,* and Brooks and Burns were paired yet again within a year, when the former advertising and network executive and 20th Century–Fox president Grant Tinker, then the husband of Mary Tyler Moore, handpicked them to create a new sitcom in which she would star. It would be the flagship offering of a new company, MTM Enterprises, which would largely succeed or fail on the basis of what Brooks, Burns, and company developed. No pressure. Fortunately for them, and for MTM Enterprises and the future of quality television, the result of that development was CBS's 1970 comedy series *The Mary Tyler Moore Show,* which would last for seven years and spawn not only a series of spin-offs but, through MTM, an entire roster of excellent, often groundbreaking TV sitcoms and dramas.

Their template, in creating a new show for Mary Tyler Moore, turned out to be her old show—Carl Reiner's *Dick Van Dyke Show.* "We admired *The Dick Van Dyke Show,*" Brooks says. "That was our gold standard. One way to describe that show was: people that you really liked, saying funny things frequently." Knowing that the audience would be equally enamored and aware of that show, though, eliminated some other possibilities for the new series. "We weren't going to have her be married again, after being Laura," Brooks says. "It'd be, like, too weird. So she was a single working woman." That simple fact, coupled with the concurrent rise of the feminist movement, infused the Mary Richards character, and the entire series, with a heightened sense of relevance.

"Not that she was a feminist," Brooks says of the show's protagonist, "because she wasn't. But being surrounded by the cultural change around us did somehow make us important, in a way we wouldn't have been at any other time doing the same show." Brooks pauses for a moment, then adds a qualifier: "I think." His hesitancy is understandable, even now, because everything about *The Mary Tyler Moore Show,* in those early days, was risky and uncertain. The premiere episode, written by Brooks and Burns, introduced Moore's Mary Richards by having her relocate to start a new life in Minneapolis, where the only people she knew were her friend Phyllis (played by Cloris Leachman) and Phyllis's young daughter, Bess. Phyllis finds Mary a vacant apartment, but someone else in the building tries to claim it for her own: the pushy and very independent Rhoda (played by Valerie Harper). In time, both these actresses would get their own CBS spin-off series—*Phyllis* and *Rhoda*, respectively—but when the pilot episode was first performed before a studio audience, there wasn't much feeling that *The Mary Tyler Moore Show* would survive, much less live to spin off other shows.

"Our first run-through was a disaster," Brooks recalls. "Nobody liked Rhoda, so the show just went in the toilet." With two days until the actual filming, and with so much on the line, suddenly the office was filled with concerned people ("Something I've never seen before or since, as if at a funeral," Brooks says, adding, "It was wildly upsetting"). No one knew how to fix whatever was wrong, until the script supervisor spoke up and said, "What if the little girl, Phyllis's daughter, says that she likes Rhoda?" Brooks smiles and concludes, "And I've always said that was the difference between success and failure—just that one note. Just that one great note."

The Mary Tyler Moore Show tackled sensitive and contemporary issues without ever being heavy-handed. One of Rhoda's dates came out to her as gay, making him one of the first openly gay characters on network TV, and in another episode, Brooks asserts, "I think the show was the first one to do any joke about birth control." By 1973–74, Mary Richards was paired on Saturday nights with Archie Bunker, Hawkeye Pierce, and other iconic standard-bearers of a new type of relevant, influential television. "It was the night," says Brooks, of a CBS Saturday lineup that consisted of *All in the Family, M*A*S*H, The Mary Tyler Moore Show, The Bob Newhart Show* (another great comedy from MTM Productions), and *The Carol Burnett Show.* "We always loved *All in the Family* and thought they were doing such amazing work," Brooks says, which made him proud to be part of the same TV evening. "I mean, I had a horse in the race, but as a viewer that was sort of like a great night for me."

The TV programming guru Fred Silverman was running CBS's entertainment programming at the time and was a big believer in the "divide and conquer" theory: when you have a hit show, take a supporting character or two and spin them off into their own shows. Two shows in CBS's Saturday lineup at the time were major beneficiaries of that practice: *All in the Family* spun off several hit shows, including *The Jeffersons* and *Maude,* while *The Mary Tyler Moore Show* led not only to *Rhoda* in 1974 and *Phyllis* in 1975 but to *Lou Grant* in 1977. But *Lou Grant,* co-created by Brooks, Burns, and Reynolds, was different—so different that it influenced most quality one-hour programs that followed. Though it was spun off from a sitcom, *Lou Grant* was a drama—one with some very funny scenes, but without a laugh track, and with some very serious dramatic content as well. "It was an amazing show to be able to do," says Brooks, who was very involved with *Lou Grant* the first year before turning the reins over to Burns and Reynolds. "It was just, 'When is a spin-off not a spin-off?' because we already had done those," Burns explains. "And the answer is, 'When you spin it off into another form.'"

After *Lou Grant,* Brooks spun himself off, away from MTM, and took three other MTM writer-producers with him to start a new production company. The others were Stan Daniels, David Davis, and Ed. Weinberger, and their departure was amicable—so much so that when Brooks realized the first property they wanted to develop as a sitcom was based on a magazine article he had optioned while still at MTM, Grant Tinker relinquished all rights to the property. "That was the rights to what became *Taxi,*" Brooks says, and repeats it for emphasis. "*Taxi.* And he gave it to us immediately. On one phone call . . . So that's Grant Tinker," he says appreciatively. "Certainly, the way he treated people is a model."

Taxi turned out to be a workplace comedy that worked beautifully, even though, or perhaps because, so many of its cast members came from so many different types of disciplines: Judd Hirsch was a serious Broadway actor, Andy Kaufman was pure performance art, Danny DeVito and Christopher Lloyd were wholly committed character actors. And yet all those worlds came together, from different orbits, to make a delightful comic universe all its own. "With *Taxi,*" Brooks says, "every minute we did it, it was so great to be doing it. It was amazing." And meshing many different acting styles into the same sitcom was something Brooks says he learned on *The Mary Tyler Moore Show,* where the supporting players included Cloris Leachman, Ed Asner, Valerie Harper, and Ted Knight. "*Mary* was absolutely my college," Brooks says, pointing out that the title star came from TV, Asner and Harper came from Chicago's Second City improv troupe, and Knight "was, like, the world's greatest circus clown," Brooks jokes, "just a fantastically talented man."

Brooks crossed over to movies, and after an early mega-success with 1983's *Terms of Endearment*—his adaptation of the Larry McMurtry novel that won Oscars not only for the stars Shirley MacLaine and Jack Nicholson but three for Brooks, for directing, adapted screenplay, and Best Picture—

never had to cross back, especially with the critical and commercial success of another major film venture, 1987's *Broadcast News*. Yet that very year,
Brooks returned to television as co-creator of *The Tracey Ullman Show,* a
variety sketch series that ran on Fox from 1987 to 1990. "Tracey Ullman is
a unique artist. You can't quite put a label on her of any sort," Brooks says.
She was capable of embodying original comic characters, anchoring major
musical production numbers, and singing and dancing with guest stars, and
the show, with its free-form structure, allowed her to do it all. "It was just the
hardest work imaginable," Brooks recalls. But he's proud now of what they
accomplished and treasures some specific memories, as when Mel Brooks
showed up as special guest star, to appear in a Hollywood sketch with Ullman. Brooks, watching from his usual off-camera perch, delighted in Mel
Brooks's antics and Ullman's improvisations. "I was on the floor!" Brooks
says. "For somebody like me, who loved *Your Show of Shows* [on which Mel
Brooks was a staff writer], it was one of the great joys of my life—just being
able to be on the stage with them."

The Simpsons emerged from *The Tracey Ullman Show* somewhat organically. The *Life in Hell* cartoonist, Matt Groening, had been hired to concoct
brief animated pieces that could run between, and separate, the various
Tracey Ullman Show sketches. Groening didn't want to give Fox the rights,
merchandising and otherwise, to his established *Life in Hell* characters, so
he came up with the Simpsons. The regular *Tracey Ullman Show* repertory
cast members Julie Kavner (from the *Rhoda* spin-off) and Dan Castellaneta
were cast as the voices of Marge and Homer Simpson, and Nancy Cartwright and Yeardley Smith were hired, respectively, to provide the voices of
the Simpson siblings Bart and Lisa—the same roles they would continue to
play for more than a quarter century.

When the idea of a spin-off was floated, Fox executives suggested a
stand-alone special to test the waters, but Brooks demanded a full-season
commitment so the writers and animators would have time and space to
find their way. "Fox was going broke," Brooks says of those early days, when
Married . . . with Children was the network's only early success. "The idea of
giving us an on-the-air commitment was anathema. They hated that gamble. But they did it—a drowning network going for a cartoon show," Brooks
says, marveling at it in retrospect. *The Simpsons* was the first cartoon in
prime time in decades, but it caught on immediately. Groening got the "created by" credit for the series, and Brooks shared the "developed by" credit

with Sam Simon, a *Tracey Ullman Show* executive producer whom Brooks had brought over from his writing and producing days on *Taxi*. Groening says where Brooks deserves the most credit, once *The Simpsons* became its own half-hour series, was for its tone and its heart.

Brooks, for his part, remembers the rigid rules they set down when establishing the new, wider world of the Simpson family. "At first, we never publicized who did the voices," Brooks says, explaining that the illusion the show's creators were after was that "these were real people!" Another early edict: "We would not take advantage of the limitless nature of what you could do in a cartoon." Brooks admits that everyone was "paranoid" about the rules initially, but "as the years went on, every once in a while, we'd break them."

Brooks laughs a hearty laugh. "And then," he concludes with a smile, "we finally realized, early on, that this show will take whatever kind of comedy you do, from burlesque to high; it'll take it. These creatures will do it. You can do romantic comedy with them, which we do. You can do farce. You can be all over the map, and eventually we started to breathe the freedom of that. But all of it started from paranoid, anal rules," he says, offering one final, hearty laugh.

GARRY SHANDLING

BORN: 1949, Chicago.
FIRST TV CREDIT: Writer, *Sanford and Son*, 1975–76, NBC.
LANDMARK TV SERIES: Star and creator, *It's Garry Shandling's Show*, 1986–90, Showtime, Fox; Star and co-creator, *The Larry Sanders Show*, 1992–98, HBO.

[NOTE: All interviews in this chapter were conducted, and the chapter written, before Garry Shandling died suddenly in March 2016 at age 66.]

Garry Shandling didn't originally intend to write TV, much less star in his own television series, but once he did, he produced nothing but ground-breaking comedies, both of them for cable networks just getting their feet wet in the original-programming business. First came Showtime's *It's Garry Shandling's Show*, a bold breaking-the-fourth-wall sitcom, in 1986. Then, in 1992, came HBO's *Larry Sanders Show*, in which Shandling played a somewhat neurotic talk-show host, with Rip Torn as his producer and Jeffrey Tambor his on-air sidekick. But when Shandling was young, he didn't watch much TV at all, except for the occasional *Adventures of Superman* or *Sky King*. For entertainment, he listened to comedy albums; Bob Newhart and the Smothers Brothers were special early influences, just as Woody Allen and George Carlin would be a few years later. Once Shandling was allowed to stay up to watch late-night TV, he was drawn early to the comedians on *The Tonight Show Starring Johnny Carson*, whose routines he would tape-record for his own amusement. Not on home video, which didn't exist yet.

On audiotape. ("I never thought of being a stand-up comedian," he recalls. "But I was writing funny things in school.")

His biggest hobby as a teenager, though, was amateur radio. In a small room the family built in their garage in Tucson, Arizona, Shandling, at age thirteen, had a ham radio license and a private place to connect with the world, sending and receiving signals from his rooftop antenna to wherever the radio wave signal landed after bouncing off the ionosphere.

"I was talking to people all over the world, sort of the way Twitter works," he says, "except I was talking to people, and I was sort of addicted . . . I would talk to someone in South Africa, and I would talk to someone in Australia, and I would talk to someone in Ethiopia, and someone in the Soviet Union. I was just a kid, and I had a big map of the world up on the wall, and . . . I was always interested in reaching a new place."

He attended the University of Arizona as an engineering major because of his interest in electronics and ham radio, but after his third year of designing circuit boards, he walked out and never went back. He decided writing comedy was the career path he wanted to take, even though there were no comedy clubs in Tucson and he knew absolutely no one in show business. Yet after taking nuclear physics and other challenging classes, Shandling reasoned, "Well, I seem to be able to learn," and he decided to teach himself, by doing something which he'd done very little of up to that point: watching television sitcoms.

He was told he had to write a "spec script," an example of an existing TV show that could be sent to agents to evaluate his writing level, and was advised to write spec scripts for CBS's *M*A*S*H* and *All in the Family,* two of the hottest comedies of the early 1970s. So he did, after which he got his first paid assignment, to write a script for NBC's *Sanford and Son.* "So," he says with a laugh, "I had to sit and watch *Sanford and Son.*" From there, he walked across the hall where *Welcome Back, Kotter* was filming, handed them a spec script, and got more work there and elsewhere, then stopped. "I didn't like being a staff writer," he says, so he told his agent he intended, at age twenty-seven, to try his hand at being a stand-up comic. Within three years, he made it to *The Tonight Show,* where Carson liked the young comic enough to ask him on repeatedly and eventually to think of him as an heir apparent, which Shandling ultimately declined.

Because of the *Tonight Show* exposure, though, Shandling was contacted by Michael Nesmith, who had already tasted major TV success as one of the Monkees in the 1960s. Nesmith, in the years since, was pushing lots of boundaries and envelopes, not only envisioning a pre-MTV music-video prototype, but also distributing one of the first home-video releases with his music-and-comedy anthology special, *Elephant Parts*. When Nesmith mounted a short-lived NBC experiment called *Television Parts* in 1985, one of its contributors was Garry Shandling, who Nesmith thought would be a good guy to star in another experimental form: short comedy videos. Shandling starred in a couple of them, and the gimmick was that in addition to playing the comic scene, Shandling would look into the camera and address the viewer directly—a conceit that Shandling liked and did well.

NBC, at that point, invited Shandling to come up with a sitcom idea for himself. Shandling, fresh off the talking-to-the-camera *Television Parts* experience, was eager to try more of the breaking-the-fourth-wall approach, especially because such films as Woody Allen's *Annie Hall,* in which Allen's Alvy Singer speaks directly to the audience in one hilarious bit after another, had so delighted Shandling the moviegoer. "I was never a more excited viewer than getting to those early Woody Allen movies," he recalls. "I really remember just thinking of them as diamonds."

Shandling's pitch to NBC was that he would play a stand-up comedian with a platonic girlfriend and a married male friend, and they'd talk about things and go about their daily lives, while Shandling—as a thinly veiled version of himself, long before Larry David played one on *Curb Your Enthusiasm*—would occasionally speak directly to the camera. George Burns had done it on TV as far back as 1950, with *The George Burns and Gracie Allen Show,* but to the networks, more than thirty years later, it was much too strange.

"There was silence in the room," Shandling says, laughing. And before addressing the fourth-wall issue, the network executives had another problem. "They said, 'Well, you know, the audience doesn't understand much about show business, and we don't really want to do a series that involves show business.'" Shandling shot back some obvious examples of classic TV shows that dealt with show business, from the programs of George Burns and Jack Benny to the bandleader husband of *I Love Lucy* and the TV comedy writer of *The Dick Van Dyke Show*. Besides, Shandling argued, "I'm not going to write a show business story. I'm talking about a guy in his home . . . dealing with relationships and everything in life. It's just that he happens to be a comedian." According to Shandling, the network's response was, "Could he be, like, in the hardware business?" Then they balked at the talking-to-the-camera idea, insisting that viewers felt uncomfortable and confused when spoken to directly. Shandling asked them about news broadcasters and why that seemed to work just fine, but the network's response was, "Instead of talking to a camera, could you talk to a dog?"

Amazingly, Shandling tried writing a pilot with the network's suggestions, but no one's heart was in it, especially Shandling's. "And now," he says, "we get into the lucky circumstance: that cable television comes along, and they're looking for programming that's different from what's on the network! So I'm in the right place at the right time, and Showtime comes to me and says, 'We'll let you do anything you want,'" and with a fifty-episode order. Shandling and Alan Zweibel created the *It's Garry Shandling's Show* pilot, fleshed out just as Shandling had originally pitched it to NBC, and the show was received as revolutionary, comedically daring, and, eventually, a precursor of the trend known as reality TV. A handful of episodes in, though, and Shandling was already a bit bored with the format, however envelope pushing it was.

"I found myself being a staff writer on my own show, and then I remembered why I didn't want to be a staff writer," Shandling says. "Because I don't like the formulas, or anything about cranking it out every week." As soon as the multi-season order was completed, Shandling walked away and vowed that his next TV project, if there was one, would reflect his maturation as an actor and a writer. He had been taking acting lessons, and what he calls "very, very, very personal psychological work, bordering on spiritual work," from the acting coach Roy London, whose other students included Brad Pitt, Michelle Pfeiffer, Sharon Stone, and Faye Dunaway. "Above all others," Shandling says, "he influenced and impacted me greatly, and gave me the freedom to learn about myself and put that into the work." Shandling told himself then, "If I do another show, it's going to be very grounded. It's going to be very real. It's going to be the complete opposite of *It's Garry Shandling's Show.*"

The thought Shandling kept coming back to was the world he knew so well from appearing on and guest hosting *The Tonight Show*. But while hosting the show for real, as the heir to Johnny Carson, didn't interest him, playing a talk-show host and showing the behind-the-scenes dramas and traumas seemed perfect. HBO's then-CEO, Michael Fuchs, offered Shandling a thirteen-episode series commitment without seeing any script or pilot and proceeded to give Shandling "98 percent freedom" to do the series, which became *The Larry Sanders Show*, exactly as he wanted. It was intentionally cinematic, aggressively realistic, and credible. (Shandling, he now admits, had his own "Deep Throat," the former Carson and David Letterman executive producer Peter Lassally: "I would occasionally call him and say, 'What would happen to the show if —,' and then I would tell him the story we were working on, and he'd say, 'Oh, that would cause this or this to happen.'")

The Larry Sanders Show had wonderful writers and a fantastic cast. Bob Odenkirk and Janeane Garofalo were but two of the relative unknowns who broke big after *Sanders,* and the central trio of stars—Shandling, Torn, and Tambor—meshed perfectly together, committing to the reality of the TV talk-show universe they created together. "It was like a lab," Shandling says. "It was like acting class. Rip and Jeffrey, of course, are such great actors that I was just giving them more and more freedom to be as grounded as they could go."

The guest stars, too, elevated *The Larry Sanders Show* to a stratospheric level, making it HBO's first major, standout, pay-attention-to-me comedy hit. By the time it was over, everyone from Letterman and Jon Stewart to Sharon Stone and Jim Carrey had shown up to play in this alternate TV world, and the show's first major guest star, in the third show of the first season, gave a performance that prompted HBO to tell Shandling his show was absolutely perfect: Carol Burnett. "I thought it was so great," Burnett says of Shandling's show, of which she was a fan, she says, from the very first episode. And she was far from alone.

"If you wrote a book that was just about *The Larry Sanders Show,*" Aaron Sorkin told me as I interviewed him for this book, "that would be good enough for me. I would read it. I would want to know everything about how that worked."

KEY EVOLUTIONARY STAGES

The Andy Griffith Show	1960–68, CBS
The Dick Van Dyke Show	1961–66, CBS
The Bob Newhart Show	1972–78, CBS
Seinfeld	1989–98, NBC
Louie	2010–, FX

In the science of TV taxonomy, the situation comedy "family" has at least three major subdivisions, and it doesn't take a "genus" to recognize them in broad terms. There's the domestic, or family, sitcom, revolving around a core family, usually at home; the workplace sitcom, where almost all action takes place on the job; and the hybrid sitcom, which I call the splitcom, in which both the home and the work arenas are represented and important. Classifying some sitcoms into these three groupings can be easy (CBS's *All in the Family* is a family sitcom, NBC's *Office* a workplace one) or can be tricky. CBS's *I Love Lucy* sometimes followed Ricky Ricardo to work on TV or at his nightclub, and ABC's *Roseanne* spent time with its heroine at her factory and diner jobs, but both those shows are primarily family sitcoms. And while NBC's *30 Rock,* on occasion, went home with Liz Lemon, the vast majority of the time was spent at the workplace.

Some comedies, though, spent equal time with characters at home and at work. ABC's *Home Improvement* (1992–99), for example, had Tim Allen clocking time both at home and at his *Tool Time* handyman TV show, and

NBC's *Frasier* (1993–2004), starring Kelsey Grammer, was just as funny when he was fielding calls on his radio talk show as when he was dealing with his brother and father, played so superbly by David Hyde Pierce and John Mahoney, in his upscale Seattle apartment. And while NBC's *Seinfeld* spent more time with Jerry Seinfeld in his apartment or at the diner chatting with friends than onstage doing stand-up, those solo comedy routines—his work—were a key component, and structural building block, of most episodes. And in its basic outline, in which the show was peeking in on the private life of an entertainer as he prepared for or relaxed between shows, *Seinfeld* had a lot in common with one of the earliest examples of the television sitcom: CBS's *Jack Benny Program,* which first came to TV from radio in 1950. One of the first clearly delineated examples of the TV splitcom, though, came a decade later, and though it was one of the first, it still ranks, more than half a century later, as one of the best. Here's a closer look at that one, and four others, that most exemplified and influenced the half-home, half-work splitcom genre.

THE ANDY GRIFFITH SHOW

1960–68, CBS. Creator: Sheldon Leonard. Stars: Andy Griffith, Don Knotts, Frances Bavier, Ron Howard, George Lindsey, Howard McNear, Aneta Corsaut, Jim Nabors.

Andy Griffith had been on TV only once, doing a southern-accent-drenched comic monologue called "What It Was, Was Football" on CBS's *Ed Sullivan Show* in 1954, when he learned the Theatre Guild was planning a live TV adaptation of a brand-new bestselling comedy novel by Mac Hyman. The book, *No Time for Sergeants,* was about a country bumpkin who goes into the military and wreaks havoc with his backwoods ways and syrupy drawl, and Griffith thought he'd be perfect for the leading role of Will Stockdale. He got an audition at the Theatre Guild, whose creative team agreed. The writer of the teleplay adaptation, Ira Levin (later the author of *Rosemary's Baby*), even inserted comic monologues to play to Griffith's established skill set. *No Time for Sergeants,* directed by Alex Segal, was performed live as a 1955 installment of ABC's *United States Steel Hour.* "He has not been on television before," the *New York Times* said (inaccurately) of

Griffith at the time, but attention was certainly paid. Griffith then starred in a long-running Broadway play adaptation, followed by a movie version in 1958, so by the time Andy Griffith guest starred on an episode of CBS's *Danny Thomas Show* in 1960, his unannounced entrance was enough to elicit a loud wave of applause from the studio audience.

The plot of this particular episode, titled "Danny Meets Andy Griffith," had Thomas—as the show's central character, the New York nightclub entertainer Danny Williams—driving through a small North Carolina town with his wife, Kathy (Marjorie Lord), and being cited, and then arrested, for running a stop sign. In Danny's defense, the sign wasn't at an intersection, but the sheriff explained that his small town hadn't raised enough money yet for the road—just for the sign. The town was Mayberry, the sheriff (played by Griffith) was Andy Taylor, and the episode was a back-door pilot episode for a spin-off series starring Andy Griffith. Ron Howard was featured as Sheriff Taylor's young son, Opie, and Frances Bavier (who would play their live-

The Andy Griffith Show spent a lot of time with Andy Griffith's Sheriff Andy Taylor at work, but nothing was more important than his time at home as a single dad with son, Opie (Ron Howard).

in relative Aunt Bee in the series) had a small role as a different character, a town resident. Sheldon Leonard, producer of *The Danny Thomas Show,* directed the episode, and CBS and the sponsor loved it. *The Andy Griffith Show* was immediately etched onto the network's planned 1960 fall schedule, and its missing ingredient surfaced during the show's planning stages, when Don Knotts, a supporting cast member from both the stage and the movie versions of *No Time for Sergeants,* called Griffith and suggested that on his forthcoming TV series Andy Taylor have a deputy. Griffith agreed, and Knotts came aboard as Deputy Barney Fife—a supporting comedy role for which he won five consecutive Emmys, though Griffith and *The Andy Griffith Show* never won top honors in their respective categories. The show did make quite an impact, however. One supporting character, the Mayberry auto mechanic Gomer Pyle (played by Jim Nabors), was spun off into his own CBS series, *Gomer Pyle, U.S.M.C.* (1964–69), in which he joined the marines and drove his sergeant crazy with his country ways and heavy southern accent—a virtual reboot of Griffith's original breakout vehicle, *No Time for Sergeants.* For a couple of years, *Gomer Pyle* even ranked higher than its parent program, but *The Andy Griffith Show* was firmly in the Top 10 for its entire run and said good-bye (in 1968) ranked as the No. 1 show on television. Only two other series in TV history have accomplished that: *I Love Lucy* in 1957, and *Seinfeld* in 1998.

The enduring core of *The Andy Griffith Show,* at least to me, was the quiet, credible, often moving relationship between the widower Andy Taylor and his young son, Opie. Even without a word, as they moseyed to the local fishing hole in the opening credits as Earle Hagen's whistling theme song played, there was a respectful bond between this TV father and son that couldn't be denied, or forgotten. The show's best episode, "Opie the Birdman," demonstrated Andy Taylor's brand of firm but thoughtful parenting back at a time when corporal punishment was still the accepted response to a child's misbehavior, at least on television. "You gonna give me a whippin'?" Opie asks his dad, after Andy discovers that Opie, playing outside with a new slingshot, has accidentally killed a bird. Instead, Andy opens Opie's bedroom window and orders him to spend the night listening to the cries of the baby birds orphaned by Opie's reckless act. "Listen to those baby birds, crying for their mother, who's never coming back," Andy says to Opie, and might as well have added, "Just as your own mother is never coming back." Tough love indeed, but it pushes Opie into an epiphany of responsibility, after which he collects, cages, and feeds the baby birds, raises them to the point where they can fend for themselves, then reluctantly but proudly sets them flying freely into the treetops. At work, Sheriff Andy dealt with Barney and all manner of Mayberry residents, visitors, and problems, but at home, with Opie, he routinely and quietly did his most important work of all.

THE DICK VAN DYKE SHOW

1961–66, CBS. Creator: Carl Reiner. Stars: Dick Van Dyke, Mary Tyler Moore, Morey Amsterdam, Rose Marie, Carl Reiner, Richard Deacon, Jerry Paris, Ann Morgan Guilbert, Larry Mathews.

The other most significant, revered, and durable splitcom of the 1960s, *The Dick Van Dyke Show,* had several things in common with *The Andy*

The Dick Van Dyke Show was equally funny whether Dick Van Dyke, as TV writer Rob Petrie, was shown at work in New York or at home with his wife, Laura (Mary Tyler Moore).

Griffith Show. Both were on CBS, both had theme songs composed by Earle Hagen, both were filmed at Desilu Studios (the production company owned by Desi Arnaz and Lucille Ball), and both had pilot episodes directed by Sheldon Leonard. Without Leonard, in fact, *The Dick Van Dyke Show* might never have existed at all. Carl Reiner had written thirteen scripts for a proposed sitcom called *Head of the Family,* based on his suburban family life in New Rochelle and his job in New York writing for a TV variety show, and filmed a pilot with himself in the leading role of Rob Petrie. Advertisers passed on the pilot, which also starred Barbara Britton (as Laura, Rob's wife) and Sylvia Miles and Morty Gunty (as Rob's fellow comedy writers, Sally and Buddy), but Leonard, after seeing the unsold pilot and reading Reiner's stack of unused scripts, suggested the show be revived, but with a completely new cast. Though Reiner's series was based on his own experiences on *Your Show of Shows,* Leonard thought another actor might make the difference, and when he found Dick Van Dyke starring on Broadway in *Bye Bye Birdie,* Reiner swallowed his ego and agreed. Every other major cast change was a similar upgrade: Morey Amsterdam as Buddy, Rose Marie as Sally, and especially Mary Tyler Moore as Laura were all perfect in their roles. And in time, Reiner got to join the company anyway, playing the variety-show star Alan Brady, his own comic version of his old boss Sid Caesar.

The Dick Van Dyke Show was one of the few smart sitcoms of the 1960s, a decade in which the genre was awash with flying nuns, talking cars, and subservient witches and genies. But *Dick Van Dyke* wasn't just good for its time; it's good anytime and still deserves to be considered one of the best situation comedies ever made. It was a Top 10 show for most of its tenure, ranking as high as No. 3. Overall, *The Dick Van Dyke Show* won fourteen Emmys, including multiple wins for Van Dyke, Moore, and the series itself. It also stood out at the time for showing a young married couple obviously attracted to each other (even though, per censorial restrictions of the time, they slept separately in twin beds) and for establishing the dual focus of the splitcom as a fully viable comedic approach. "This was the first situation comedy where, when the guy came home, you knew where he'd come home from," Reiner once boasted. And its classic episodes, from the parodies of *12 Angry Men* and *Invasion of the Body Snatchers* to the toupee and baby-delivery episode, were high-water marks of the form.

Two other episodes, in particular, demonstrated just how bold and intelligent *The Dick Van Dyke Show* could be. In "That's My Boy??," Rob feared the hospital had made a mistake and sent the Petries home with the wrong newborn, but when he expressed his fear to the Peterses, a similarly named couple who had been on the same maternity floor as the Petries and also just had a baby, and begged them to visit him and Laura at home, the delicate matter was settled instantly and hilariously—because the Peterses were African-American. This episode was televised in 1963, the year before the Civil Rights Act, and the idea of presenting whites and blacks as equals, getting the same care from the same hospital, was a quietly progressive thing to show on network television at the time. It was a brave move and a brilliant sight gag and generated a huge wave of laughter and applause from the audience. When Rob asked why Mr. Peters didn't just clear up the misunderstanding over the phone, a smiling Mr. Peters (played by Greg Morris, later of *Mission: Impossible*) replies, "And miss the expression on your face?"

Even more ahead of its time, perhaps—more positively *Seinfeld*-ian— was the series finale, in which Rob finally completes the memoir he's been writing for five years, and his boss, Alan Brady, options it, so he can play the role of Rob, which would, if the series kept going and followed the premise, allow Carl Reiner to play the role he wanted to play in the first place.

THE BOB NEWHART SHOW

1972–78, CBS. Creators: David Davis, Lorenzo Music. Stars: Bob Newhart, Suzanne Pleshette, Bill Daily, Peter Bonerz, Marcia Wallace, Jack Riley, John Fiedler, Oliver Clark, Amzie Strickland, Tom Poston.

The Bob Newhart Show was another early comedy triumph from MTM Productions, following on the heels of *The Mary Tyler Moore Show*, and, for the remainder of the years that latter sitcom was on CBS, following it on the network's Saturday night lineup as well. *The Bob Newhart Show* never won an Emmy as Outstanding Comedy Series, and its star was never even nominated, but *The Bob Newhart Show* was both popular (a Top 20 show its first three seasons) and respected.

The approaches to both the work and the home portions of this splitcom are what made it so appealing, so quietly revolutionary, and so durable. For the parts of *The Bob Newhart Show* focusing on his home life, Newhart was insistent that his character, Bob Hartley, have no children: he wanted the TV

Bob and his TV wife (Emily, played so winningly by Suzanne Pleshette) to have a happy adult marriage without having to cope with (or have the writers write mandatory scenes involving) kids. That was different for television at the time, when families were virtually synonymous with offspring. Also different was Bob Hartley's occupation as a psychologist. He shared office space on a floor with other businesses, which allowed constant contact not only with his receptionist, Carol (Marcia Wallace), but with the neighboring dentist Jerry (Peter Bonerz), both of whom were reliable comic foils. In the workplace part of this splitcom, though, no comedy foils were more reliable than the patients who came to Dr. Hartley's office for group therapy or, at times, individual consultation. It was an inspired idea to have Newhart, who built his stand-up comedy career on long pauses, deadpan reactions, and extended two-way conversations in which we heard only his side, play

The Bob Newhart Show was a shrewd ensemble comedy led by Bob Newhart and Suzanne Pleshette as Bob and Emily Hartley, who had a warm family life but no kids.

someone who listens for a living. And his patients were hilarious—so much so that a few of them ended up as guest stars on a wild episode of another MTM Productions series, *St. Elsewhere,* playing the same characters and being treated by the doctors of St. Eligius.

No crossover appearance connected to *The Bob Newhart Show* is more fabulous or more famous, though, than the one that served as the ending to Newhart's next TV sitcom, called, fittingly enough, *Newhart.* When that 1982–90 CBS series ended, Newhart and company served up a classic coda: after eight years of a series in which Newhart played the Vermont innkeeper Dick Loudon, the final episode ended with Newhart waking up in bed—in his old bedroom from *The Bob Newhart Show,* with Pleshette as Emily beside him—and proceeding to tell her about this crazy dream he'd had, about being an innkeeper in Vermont. It ranks as one of the best TV finales of all time, and it couldn't have happened if not for *The Bob Newhart Show,* a fairly memorable show of its own.

Between the departure of *The Bob Newhart Show* and the arrival of NBC's *Seinfeld,* the next barrier-busting entry in the splitcom genre, there was one other example of a splitcom that was written and acted superbly, popular from the start, and durable enough to last eleven seasons and amass a record number of Emmy Awards in its category (thirty-seven in total). That show was NBC's *Frasier,* the Kelsey Grammer spin-off of NBC's *Cheers.* As splitcoms went, *Frasier* did nothing new: Grammer's lead character had a workplace family at his radio station during the day and an actual family either residing in or constantly visiting his spacious Seattle apartment. There wasn't much that was new about *Frasier,* starting with its lead character: in his post-*Cheers* continuation, Frasier Crane was a psychologist on a phone-in radio talk show, allowing Grammer the same sorts of therapeutic comic conversations enjoyed by Bob Newhart as the psychologist Bob Hartley on *The Bob Newhart Show.* It's just that *Frasier* was so polished, so good, so funny. David Hyde Pierce was priceless as Frasier's fussy brother, Niles, another therapist, just as John Mahoney was wonderfully cantankerous as Frasier's live-in, ex-cop father Martin Crane, and Jane Leeves was deliciously loopy as Martin's live-in caretaker, Daphne, with whom Niles was hopelessly smitten. That was plenty for any situation comedy, but on *Frasier* it was only half the fun. There was also the radio station part of this splitcom, where Peri Gilpin, as Frasier's producer Roz Doyle, was only one of many larger-than-life co-workers. *Frasier* didn't expand the genre, but it did perfect it, and several years running, when both series were in competition at the Emmy Awards, *Frasier* beat *Seinfeld* as Outstanding Comedy Series. But while *Frasier* played by the rules and played brilliantly, *Seinfeld* broke them, and, thus, did more to evolve the TV splitcom.

SEINFELD

1989–98, NBC. Creators: Jerry Seinfeld, Larry David. Stars: Jerry Seinfeld, Jason Alexander, Julia Louis-Dreyfus, Michael Richards, Wayne Knight, Estelle Harris, Jerry Stiller, John O'Hurley, Patrick Warburton, Bryan Cranston, Bob Balaban, Peter Crombie, Jane Leeves, Teri Hatcher, Larry Thomas.

In one sense, *Seinfeld* changed so much over its massively successful run that it nearly evolved out of the splitcom category entirely. In another sense, though, *Seinfeld*, like its characters, stubbornly refused to change at all. On the one hand, Jerry Seinfeld's stand-up comedy routines that bookended each episode—the elements that initially qualified *Seinfeld* as a splitcom, showing him at work onstage—were phased out midway through the series. On the other hand, the last scene in the show's finale referred to, and continued, the identical conversation that had opened the series pilot nine years earlier, when NBC showed it in 1989 as a test balloon called "The Seinfeld Chronicles." In the interim, the characters hadn't changed or grown at all, but they had pursued a variety of different occupations, which we saw them attempt over the course of *Seinfeld*. George Costanza (played by Jason Alexander), for a while, had his job with the New York Yankees. Elaine Benes (Julia Louis-Dreyfus), for a while, had hers with different publishing companies, including the J. Peterman catalog. And Kramer (Michael Richards) always had some scheme going on, from selling a bra for men, called the Bro, to designing a coffee-table book that was big enough to change, *Transformers*-style, into an actual coffee table.

Some of the elements of *Seinfeld*—quite a few, in fact—go back to TV's earliest splitcoms, such as *The Jack Benny Program*. Here as there, the star of the series played a flawed version of himself, going about everyday life or putting on a show, and hanging around with a few close friends, encountering occasionally recurring acquaintances in the process. *Seinfeld* advanced the genre, and the sitcom, however, with an episodic structure made up of dozens of short scenes, intricate plotlines that usually brought everything together at the end, and characters that were almost universally selfish and conniving, yet somehow likable, even lovable. Attempting any one of those things in a weekly comedy would be impressive enough. Accomplishing them all, in the same series on a weekly basis, is an evolutionary quantum leap. Those achievements are general, but some of the specific achievements by *Seinfeld* are just as noteworthy. Certain episodes, as with the very best TV sitcoms, have risen to the level of iconic classics: "The Soup Nazi," "The Junior Mint," "The Puffy Shirt," and most of all "The Contest," in which Jerry and his pals bet on which of them could refrain the longest from masturbating (a word never mentioned in that episode, by the way). Catchphrases and comic concerns from *Seinfeld* became part of the national common vocabulary, from "double dipping" to "shrinkage"— not that there's anything wrong with that. And *Seinfeld*, one season, even got as self-referential as the finale of *The Dick Van Dyke Show*, by having Jerry and George pitch to NBC the idea for a TV series "about nothing"— the same basic pitch the real Jerry Seinfeld and Larry David had used to pitch *Seinfeld* to NBC.

Seinfeld won only one Outstanding Comedy Series Emmy, in 1993, and Richards and Louis-Dreyfus were the only regular cast members to win individual Emmy Awards. The show won several Emmys for writing, though,

Seinfeld, often described as "a show about nothing," had an impact on TV that was really something. It starred (from left) Michael Richards, Jerry Seinfeld, Julia Louis-Dreyfus, and Jason Alexander.

and when it signed off in 1998, its expanded final episode was viewed by an estimated 76.3 million people. The only series finales to attract more viewership than the last episode of *Seinfeld* were the TV farewells of ABC's *Fugitive* (78 million viewers in 1967), NBC's *Cheers* (80.4 million in 1993), and CBS's *M*A*S*H* (105.9 million in 1983).

LOUIE

2010–, FX. Creator: Louis C.K. Stars: Louis C.K., Hadley Delany, Ursula Parker, Pamela Adlon.

Many episodes of FX's *Louie* showed its comedian protagonist at work, onstage, reflecting on some of the events and emotions occurring elsewhere in the episode, which sounds, on paper, like a blatant rip-off of *Seinfeld*, down to the idea of the star playing a loose approximation of himself. Louis C.K., though, set out to do something entirely original with *Louie* and succeeded wildly. Louis C.K. has, to date, won two Emmy Awards for *Louie*, both of them for writing.

Louie, which premiered on FX in 2010, is one of the purest examples of auteur television in a very long time. Louis C.K. not only stars in *Louie* but writes, directs, and edits almost all of the episodes and shapes each one according to the needs of the story he's telling at the moment. Sometimes, in *Louie*, there are several vignettes presented in a single episode. Other times, plots can stretch out over many episodes, making them movie-length narratives rather than quickie short stories.

The splitcom elements of *Louie* are sometimes tough to identify, because the tales told are so fluid. The workplace portions are clear when we see *Louie* onstage, or interacting with his fellow comics Jerry Seinfeld and Marc Maron (who have guest starred as themselves), but his private life is a bit more slippery. Sometimes he's dating, or shopping, or impulsively traveling, which seems like a completely different type of sitcom, but other times he's caring for his two daughters, with whom he shares custody with his ex-wife, which absolutely qualifies as the nonwork half of the splitcom genre. As his daughters, Lilly and Jane, Hadley Delany and Ursula Parker act like real kids, and the relationship between the girls and their TV dad is as unassumingly believable, and often heartwarming or uncomfortable, as the one between

Andy Taylor and Opie on *The Andy Griffith Show*. Except that Ron Howard, talented as he was as young Opie, never played the violin in a way that took my breath away, as Ursula Parker did when she played a poignant duet with *Louie*'s recurring guest star Eszter Balint.

I consider this one of my favorite TV moments of the past ten years. It's a 2014 scene from Season 4, episode 6 of *Louie,* involving a man, a woman, a girl, and two violins. Louis C.K.'s TV alter ego of Louie has spent the last few episodes getting to know Amia, the visiting niece of another tenant in Louie's apartment building. They're getting along nicely, even though, or perhaps because, Amia (played by the guest star Eszter Balint) is from Hungary and speaks no English. In this scene, Louie is escorting his younger daughter, Jane (played by Ursula Parker), up the stairway to his apartment, when Amia opens her aunt's apartment door suddenly and encounters them. The language barrier makes things awkward, until Louie explains to his daughter that Amia is Hungarian, at which point the precocious Jane surprises Amia, and Louie, by greeting her in Hungarian. Then Amia notices the violin case Jane is carrying, retreats temporarily to her apartment, and returns with a violin of her own. She begins playing a beautiful song right there in the hallway, and before long Jane turns it into a duet as Louie looks on with

Louie stars Louis C.K. as a fictionalized version of himself in a series that explores both work and home life with a cinematic and freewheeling sensibility.

astonishment. The impromptu duet is a tune by the Hungarian composer Béla Bartók, based on a vintage folk song, and in both performance and context on *Louie* it's breathtakingly beautiful and resonant—a perfect piece of television.

"Moments like that," Louis C.K. explains, "are really created in the opportunities you create, and the people you bring together, and the elements that bring you together." He deconstructs the various elements that led to that gorgeous violin scene, starting with the initial idea, which was to have an elderly woman stuck in the elevator of Louie's building, talking to him through a narrow crack, and with him dispatched to her apartment to get her pills, and finding something surprising there. "That's what started the whole thing," he says. "I didn't know I was writing a six-part episode . . . I actually suspected that the idea was, I go into her apartment and I see a bunch of weapons, like AK-47s. That was my first idea." His next idea was to have Louie open the apartment door and find, instead of a cache of weapons, an attractive young woman sleeping on the couch in her underwear. That's as far as he got with the episode's plot, until he went to pick up his daughters from school and ran into his ex-wife, who pointed out the mother of one of the other students. It was Eszter Balint, the alluring young star of Jim Jarmusch's 1984 film, *Stranger Than Paradise*. The movie came out, Louis C.K. recalls, when he was about nineteen, "and everybody that age fell in love with her. She was the coolest chick in the world, the Hungarian girl from *Stranger Than Paradise*." His ex-wife suggested he cast Balint in his TV show, and suddenly all the pieces fit: the woman in the elevator would be Hungarian, Balint would play her visiting niece sleeping on the couch, Louie would come upon her in the old woman's apartment while retrieving the pills, and the language barrier would keep him from explaining his presence initially, so she would try to beat him up.

"That's what started the whole idea," Louis C.K. says, adding that the hallway scene with the violins came about because Louis C.K. and his ex-wife had seen Balint play violin at a concert in Brooklyn, and Ursula Parker, who plays Jane, has already displayed her violin skills on *Louie*. "So I thought, 'Okay, I've got two violins in the show,'" he says. "'I know that's going to work down the road.'" He hired Balint, who hadn't worked as an actress in years, and eventually wrote that scene, in which Amia and Jane connect both verbally and musically, playing violins while Louie just watches. Louis C.K. gives the credit for that scene's power not only to his female co-stars but to the cinematographer Paul Koestner, who shot several takes with a handheld camera. "We're like the last show in the world to do fucking hand-helds," Louis C.K. says, because it's so much easier to use a Steadicam. But I just love Paul's eyeball . . . Whenever I put the camera on his shoulder with a 25 or 35 mm lens, which is a nice size for a human perspective, like a person looking around the room—whenever I put a lens like that on Paul's shoul-der, I just tell him, 'You look where it's interesting.' That's the only direction I give him . . . And he takes a few cracks at it, and we have it." Louis C.K. sighs and agrees with my assessment. "Yeah, I'm very proud of that scene," he says. "I'm very proud of all that stuff we did that was like that . . . It let you feel like you were there, and it made the stuff feel like it was alive."

BORN: 1922, The Bronx, New York.

FIRST TV CREDIT: Performer, *Maggi McNellis Crystal Room*, 1948, ABC.

LANDMARK TV SERIES: Performer and writer, *Your Show of Shows*, 1950–54, NBC; *Caesar's Hour*, 1954–57, NBC; Creator, writer, and recurring actor, *The Dick Van Dyke Show*, 1961–66, CBS.

OTHER MAJOR CREDITS: Records: Co-creator and co-star with Mel Brooks, 2000 Year Old Man albums, beginning with *2000 Years with Carl Reiner and Mel Brooks*, 1961. TV: *The Sid Caesar, Imogene Coca, Carl Reiner, Howard Morris Special*, 1967, CBS; Guest star, playing Alan Brady, *Mad About You*, 1995, NBC. Movies: Director, *Where's Poppa?*, 1970; *Oh, God!*, 1977; *The Jerk*, 1979; *Dead Men Don't Wear Plaid*, 1982; *The Man with Two Brains*, 1983; *All of Me*, 1984.

Carl Reiner is the oldest person I interviewed for this book (when we spoke in 2015, he was ninety-three years old and claimed seniority on Norman Lear, also born in 1922, by four months). He co-starred in one of the very best and smartest TV shows of the 1950s (NBC's *Your Show of Shows*) and created one of the very best and smartest TV shows of the 1960s (CBS's *Dick Van Dyke Show*). And before all that, he got to television before anyone else included in this book. Living in New York after World War II, Reiner worked the borscht belt circuit as a performer and occasionally visited New York City to appear in experimental local broadcasts on this new medium called television. His first official network TV credit was on ABC in 1948, the very year that ABC began its TV operation—a small-scale variety show called *The Maggi McNellis Crystal Room*.

Here's one astounding measure of the man's importance and longevity: He's the only person in TV history to have appeared as a guest on every major incarnation of NBC's *Tonight Show,* chatting, over the years, with Steve Allen, Jack Paar, Johnny Carson, Jay Leno, Conan O'Brien, and, as of 2015, Jimmy Fallon. That's a measure of living not only a long life but, over most of a century in the public eye, a high-profile one.

Carl Reiner was born in the Bronx in 1922. Radio, not TV, was brand-new then, but his father, a watchmaker and inventor, was what would later be called an early adopter or a techie. "My father built the first radio we had," Reiner recalls. It ran on a storage battery, not electricity, and the whole family sat around to listen as his dad tuned in the elusive but exciting signals. "We heard Lowell Thomas and the news, and *Amos 'n' Andy,*" Reiner says, "and when I was a little older, a very big one was *The Fred Allen Show.* It was satirical, and I loved him, because he had a thing called 'Allen's Alley,' and he interviewed people who were very funny."

As a child, Reiner gravitated to the arts, performing in school plays and even, during the Depression, attending acting classes underwritten by the Public Works Administration. Immediately upon graduating from high school, he was appearing in off-Broadway plays and touring in summer theater. During World War II, he wrote and performed plays for servicemen, and when he came back from the war, there was this new thing around, called television.

"There was somebody in my sister-in-law's building [in the Bronx] who had a television," Reiner says. "We didn't even know the guy," he adds, laughing, "and I remember us all going up to his apartment and standing around looking. We didn't have seats and were just standing around looking at this fantastic thing that was going on . . . mainly it was a station identification; we waited for that to come on." He remembers *The Goldbergs,* Gertrude Berg's 1949–57 ethnic sitcom about a Jewish family living in a New York apartment building, as one of the first shows he ever saw on a TV set, and also remembers the first shows he considered what would now be called appointment television. "Nobody missed Milton Berle," Reiner says, referring to Berle's pioneering and phenomenally popular NBC variety series, *Texaco Star Theater.* "He sold more sets than anybody. We all watched Milton Berle, and we watched *Toast of the Town* with Ed Sullivan [on CBS]." Once he had his own TV set, Reiner "made sure we were home to watch all those shows," even when, on Saturday night with *Your Show of Shows,* he was appearing weekly on live TV himself. He could do it because he was on TV on Saturdays, while Berle was on Tuesdays and Sullivan on Sundays. And a bit later, he recalls, he "never missed an Ernie Kovacs episode. Ernie Kovacs was a genius." Reiner appeared on a couple of Kovacs's shows as a guest, but his TV career long predated even that.

His network TV debut, on ABC, came the same year as the debut of the network itself: in 1948, as a guest on the aforementioned *Maggi McNellis Crystal Room*. Almost immediately after that, he began landing network TV jobs as a regular cast member—first in another ABC series, 1948's *Fashion Story* (he played a photographer, providing comic relief between runway shows), then in a live CBS variety show, 1949's *Fifty-Fourth Street Revue*, also featuring Cliff Edwards and a young dancer named Bob Fosse. The CBS series was short-lived, but it lasted long enough for Reiner to be seen and appreciated by the producer Max Liebman, who was in the process of retooling his 1949 series *Admiral Broadway Revue*, which aired simultaneously on both NBC and the ill-fated DuMont network, into a new sketch and variety series for NBC alone. Liebman was retaining two headliners from the *Admiral* show and invited Reiner to join the *Admiral* veterans Sid Caesar and Imogene Coca in the 1950 launch of their new venture: *Your Show of Shows*. (Howard Morris, the fourth member of the core company, joined the following year.) Instantly, *Your Show of Shows* was a hit, ranked only a few notches behind Berle's *Texaco Star Theater* in the Top 10 and way ahead of Sullivan's *Toast of the Town*.

Performing on live TV in those days, Reiner made some enduring friendships—with Norman Lear, who was breaking into television as a writer just as Reiner was getting hired as a performer, and particularly with Mel Brooks, one of the *Admiral Broadway Revue* writers whom Caesar had brought along for *Your Show of Shows*. Reiner, in addition to co-starring, joined the writers' staff, working alongside such talents as Mel Tolkin, Lucille Kallen, Neil Simon, and Brooks. Reiner and Brooks got along so well, their downtime joking and ad-libbing led, eventually, to a series of hit comedy records in the 1960s and beyond, with Reiner as straight man, throwing questions to Brooks's "2000 Year Old Man."

"I've said this a number of times, and it's absolutely true," Reiner says. "Mel is the single funniest human being I know. 'The 2000 Year Old Man' proved that to me, when I was doing it with him. Every question I asked him, he had no idea I was going to ask it. I had no idea I was going to ask it. And the lines came out of him; I don't know where they came from, but he never ceases to amaze me, and he can do that to this day." And by "this day," Reiner is being astoundingly literal: as of this writing, he and Brooks continue a practice they started after the deaths of their respective wives of meeting for dinner every night.

More than sixty years earlier, when Brooks and Reiner worked together on *Your Show of Shows,* one of the absolute classic sketches was "The Clock," in which Caesar, Coca, Morris, and Reiner played malfunctioning parts of a giant mechanical Bavarian town square clock. "That's something Sid came up with," Reiner says of Caesar. "We didn't even know what he was talking about. He had seen a clock when he went to Europe, and he said, 'I'd like to do that.' And he showed us, and we all became parts of the clock." Another segment, an extended piece called "This Is Your Story," Reiner calls, after more than sixty years in show business, "my favorite thing I've ever done."

Much of the series, including those two sketches, was preserved on kinescope, which came in handy when Marlon Brando, after hearing *Your Show of Shows* had lampooned his movie *On the Waterfront,* stopped by. ("He loved the show and came to visit us," Reiner remembers, "and we showed him that particular episode.") Not everyone was so pleased by, or even used to, being satirized in such lovingly detailed fashion: when Caesar and Coca, in a sketch called "From Here to Obscurity," spoofed the film *From Here to Eternity* with a water-soaked love scene on the beach, NBC was sued by Columbia Pictures.

When *Your Show of Shows* ended in 1954, Caesar starred in a new sketch variety series for NBC, *Caesar's Hour,* with Reiner and Morris along for the ride, and with the writers' room including a new addition, Larry Gelbart, later to adapt *M*A*S*H* for television. And in 1973, Liebman dusted off those old kinescopes, compiled them in a movie-length sampler, and released them theatrically, for a new generation, in a film called *Ten from "Your Show of Shows."* Included among those sketches, as three of the ten, were "From Here to Obscurity," "The Clock," and "This Is Your Story." Reiner, having performed in all of those sketches live, had never gone back to see the kinescopes. When he finally saw *Ten from "Your Show of Shows"* on the large screen, in a movie house filled with the sound of laughter, he remembers watching the "This Is Your Story" sketch with particular delight. "I heard a woman laughing—screaming—with high-pitched laughter," Reiner recalls, "and I realized it was coming from me."

Long before that movie reissue revived the reputation of *Your Show of Shows,* however, Reiner had revived his own career. After *Caesar's Hour* ended, the variety hour as a genre was waning, so Reiner was being offered sitcoms, but not very good ones. Reiner's wife pointed out that he was a writer as well as an actor and said simply, "Why don't you write one?" So, as you just read, he did. Actually, he wrote thirteen—a baker's dozen episodes of a proposed comedy series called *Head of the Family.* And that led directly to *The Dick Van Dyke Show.*

It took years for Reiner to lend his face, not just his voice, to the character of the self-obsessed writer Alan Brady. "I tried to keep myself hidden," he admits, thinking viewers would identify him with his previous role as "a second banana to Sid" and wouldn't believe him as the star. In time, though, he felt comfortable playing Alan Brady as a fully visible character, which led to such riotous triumphs as his toupee-revealing episode, "Coast to Coast Big Mouth." Reiner did win an Emmy for the role of Alan Brady but not until he reprised that role, three decades later, and was awarded an Outstanding Guest Actor award in 1995 for appearing on NBC's *Mad About You.*

"By the way, there's one thing I'm most proud of," he adds. He says it's happened to him maybe forty times over the past fifty years: "Somebody will come up to me and say, 'My name is so-and-so. I'm a writer. And I wouldn't be a writer if it wasn't for *The Dick Van Dyke Show.*'" The person goes on to explain, Reiner says, that until he watched that show, he didn't know there was such a profession as a comedy writer and from then on that's what he wanted to be.

Reiner understands the desire to be a writer. And an actor. And a director, another profession in which he's excelled, directing George Segal and Ruth Gordon in the outrageous 1970 comedy *Where's Poppa?* and teaming with Steve Martin on a number of well-received comedy movies, beginning with 1979's *The Jerk.* Directing Steve Martin, Reiner says, was easy. "He's so well prepared that all you have to do is say, 'Is there anything left in this scene that you want to try?' And he'll try something that is absolutely amazing," he says, laughing.

Reiner, too, is drawn to trying new things. After his TV triumphs in the 1950s and 1960s, and directorial movie achievements in the 1970s, Reiner's subsequent résumé is sprinkled with something different, and impressive, every decade. In the 1980s, he starred on CBS in the dramatic television movie *Skokie* (about a neo-Nazi demonstration planned in a suburban Illinois town) and on Showtime as Geppetto in the "Pinocchio" episode of *Shelley Duvall's Faerie Tale Theatre,* opposite Paul Reubens in the title role. ("Hey! I loved that! . . . And Paul Reubens was so correct in that," Reiner says.) In the 1990s, Reiner won his Emmy for guest starring on *Mad About You* and also guest starred on HBO's *Larry Sanders Show* and NBC's *Frasier.* And in the twenty-first century, Carl Reiner not only landed parts in *Ocean's Eleven* and its sequel but had guest roles on different David E. Kelley TV shows: Fox's *Ally McBeal* and ABC's *Boston Legal.* "Anything that David E. Kelley writes is worth watching," Reiner says. "He's the best writer that ever worked in television."

Just as he did when both he and television were young, Carl Reiner continues to make a point of seeking out and watching good TV, and that even goes for the late-night shows, where he has been a staple since Steve Allen launched NBC's *Tonight* show in 1954. "By the way," he says, "we're in good hands with all the television late-night hosts. They're all good. And they've all taken from the masters and made it their own—from [James] Corden to [Jimmy] Fallon to [Jimmy] Kimmel to [Stephen] Colbert. They're all brilliant."

BOB NEWHART

BORN: 1929, Oak Park, Illinois.
FIRST TV CREDIT: Guest, *Playboy's Penthouse*, 1959, syndicated.
LANDMARK TV SERIES: *The Bob Newhart Show,* 1972–78, CBS; *Newhart,* 1982–90, CBS.
OTHER MAJOR CREDITS: Movies: *Catch-22,* 1970. TV: *The Bob Newhart Show,* 1961–62, NBC; Recurring guest roles on *ER,* 2003, NBC, *Desperate Housewives,* 2005, ABC, and *The Big Bang Theory,* 2013–16, CBS.

TV critics are geeky enough, when they get together for Television Critics Association press tours, to while away the lunch hours by concocting, and tossing out, tough trivia questions to one another. One of the all-time best asked which performers starred in the longest string of TV series over the most consecutive decades. James Garner, Betty White, and a few others came close but had brief holes in their résumés, so we eventually settled on a winner: Bob Newhart. He started in the 1960s, with a one-season variety series that won a Peabody after he closed it down, then went on to *The Bob Newhart Show* in the 1970s, *Newhart* in the 1980s, and both *Bob* and *George & Leo* in the 1990s. And when the new century came around, Newhart continued to show up on popular series, but as a recurring guest star on established hits. Among them: *ER* in 2003, *Desperate Housewives* in 2005, and *The Big Bang Theory* from 2013 on, playing the former TV science-show host Professor Proton, a guest role for which Newhart, after seven decades on television (his first appearance was in 1959, entertaining Hugh Hefner and guests on *Playboy's Penthouse*), finally won an Emmy. It was a long time to

345 | BOB NEWHART

wait, but Newhart had never planned on a career in show business in the first place. He was thirty years old, and a former accountant working as an advertising copywriter in Chicago, when he stepped onstage as a stand-up act for the first time, recording samples of the short comedy routines he had written and performed for friends at parties. He was, however, drawn to comedy from the start.

Bob Newhart was born in Oak Park, Illinois, in 1929. When he listened to the radio as a child, his first favorite entertainer was Jack Benny, whose long string of popular comedies began in 1932. Benny's exaggerated accounts of his everyday life as a famous entertainer were a precursor to *Seinfeld*, a similarly imaginative and character-driven "show about nothing." Newhart, even as a young boy, sought out Benny's radio show himself, rather than listen with the rest of his family. "We weren't that kind of family," Newhart says, laughing. "We had dinner, but then everybody kind of went off on their own, you know? And so I'd just go off on my own, and go into this little world of Jack Benny, and enjoy it, and then that was my night, which, to me, was very normal.

"I loved Jack," Newhart continues, laughing. "I loved that he didn't portray himself as a particularly lovable person. He was very cheap, never spent money, according to him, and always insisted he was thirty-nine. And, of course, I remember that famous show: He's confronted by a robber, who tells Jack, 'Your money or your life?' and he pauses. And it goes on and on, and Jack is timing the laugh, which is building. And the robber says, 'I guess you didn't hear me. I said your money or your life!' And Jack said, 'I'm thinking! I'm thinking!' One of the longest laughs ever in the history of radio, I think!" Newhart recalls, laughing again. "Because the audience was already ahead of the joke; they were laughing with him!" Newhart, from the very start of his own comedy career, would emulate Jack Benny, especially when it came to the pacing of his routines. "People have said that my timing and Jack's were similar, but you can't teach timing. Timing's something you hear in your head. If Jack taught me anything, it's not to be afraid of the silence. Just to wait—to have the courage to wait. And it is courage. The courage to wait."

A bit later, also from radio, another comedy act caught Newhart's attention, and held it: the comedy duo of Bob Elliott and Ray Goulding, better known as Bob and Ray. "They were an incredible, incredible influence on me back then. Especially in the deadpan part, though I hate that word,"

Newhart says. (Asked what he would prefer his own style of comedy to be called, Newhart offers, "Low-key, maybe?")

"Anyway," Newhart continues, "Bob and Ray, they were just—very formative. They would do these interviews, like where Ray interviews Bob, who is the head of the Slow Talkers of America." Newhart laughs loudly at the recollection. "You hear the setup, the premise, and already you're laughing. Which kind of tapped in to the routine I did on King Kong, which was built around the premise that I'd held a lot of jobs, which I had! I held a lot of part-time jobs, and they always had a week of orientation programs before you started the job. And then, I had recently seen the movie *King Kong* on TV, and I had the idea: What if the night King Kong climbed the outside of the Empire State Building was also the first night of a new guard who has gone through a week's orientation program, on what he could expect to face when he started work. And just saying the setup, that always gets a laugh. Then they're anticipating, and it's okay, go ahead, and it works. And that's pure Bob and Ray."

After becoming an accountant, then quitting, Newhart had moved into advertising, where he entertained friends and co-workers by conducting imagined one-way conversations. One, which hit very close to home (and was quite a hit) at his *Mad Men*–era ad agency, had him playing a press agent advising Abe Lincoln just before delivery of the Gettysburg Address: "You changed four-score and seven to eighty-seven? . . . Abe, that's meant to be a grabber." Newhart recorded some of his routines for the fun of it, and a tape made its way to a Chicago disc jockey, who sent it on to a record executive from a new label called Warner Bros. The label offered Newhart a contract and agreed to pay to have his next nightclub appearance recorded for the album. Newhart had no previous nightclub appearances, much less an upcoming one, but found an open date two weeks later at a club in Houston and stepped onstage for the first time, with audiotape rolling. Amazingly, that appearance provided the material for 1960's *The Button-Down Mind of Bob Newhart*—a comedy album from a complete showbiz unknown, which quickly became the first comedy album to hit No. 1 on the charts. A year later, Bob Newhart had his first network television series.

There, too, he had specific inspiration from a comic predecessor: George Gobel, whose 1954–60 variety series, *The George Gobel Show*, opened with a simple monologue, rather than the extensive makeup and costumes and physical buffoonery established as popular TV tricks by Milton Berle on

NBC's *Texaco Star Theater* at the dawn of network television. "He was so, so good in both stand-up and sketch," Newhart says of Gobel. "And my wife hates when I say this, but I have to say it: That's when I think I realized, 'Oh, oh, okay, you can do that and people will laugh. You don't have to put on a dress and walk on your ankles and black out a couple of your teeth to get laughs, you know? You can just stand there and talk.' Which is what George did," Newhart says, laughing. When it came time to mount *The Bob Newhart Show*—his 1961 variety series, not the subsequent hit sitcom that recycled the same title—Newhart even hired the *George Gobel Show* supporting cast member Joe Flynn, later of *McHale's Navy,* as one of his regulars. Flynn was good, Newhart recalls, but Newhart, by his own account, was not.

"I was very comfortable in the monologue," Newhart remembers. "I knew what I was doing—I'll script it, I'm going to deliver it, I'll work with the writers." Even so, the pace became too grueling, so he stopped making the show after the first season. "I just couldn't maintain the quality of the monologue, the opening of the show. Comparing it to my albums, which took years of preparation, and then trying to do that quality monologue every week, I felt was just impossible. And then we would do sketches, and I wasn't very comfortable with the sketches," he adds. "Which was another reason I quit after a year. I knew I wasn't very good, because I was watching really good sketch artists like Joe Flynn, who were good at sketches and really knew how to work it. So when *The Bob Newhart Show* came on after twelve years, in '72, I was kind of prepared. I had watched enough good sketch performances—not that we were doing sketch. We were doing situations, and character comedy."

The Bob Newhart Show, the first one, was hardly a failure. But by the time the comic was ready to headline another network TV series—this time produced by MTM Enterprises, home of *The Mary Tyler Moore Show*—he knew just what he wanted. He wanted, for one thing, a show where he played a married man with no kids. (It was a requirement also reflected in a later sitcom hit, *Newhart,* set in a Vermont inn.) Newhart got his wish: *The Bob Newhart Show* (a CBS sitcom this time), a mature comedy in which he played the married psychologist Bob Hartley, with no children, but with a beautiful and independently successful wife named Emily, played perfectly by Suzanne Pleshette. *The Bob Newhart Show* ran for six successful seasons and was part of what, arguably, was TV's best night of television ever broadcast.

One of Newhart's favorite moments from his first sitcom was an early-season scene that didn't even revolve around him. "The show started in '72," Newhart says, "and there was a lot of racial tension at that time, if you remember. And we did a show early on [in 1973] in which a patient, a large African-American man, was played by a large black fellow [Julius Harris], and his character has a large Great Dane named Whitey. And he's coming to me, as a patient, because he says he's having trouble selling insurance policies. And I try to politely tell him that his appearance may have something to do with it. And he says 'Thank you, thank you,' and he's coming into reception, and Jerry [the dentist sharing office space, played by Peter Bonerz] is there, and the guy shouts out the command 'Sit, Whitey!' and Jerry, looking frightened, instantly sits down. I'm so proud of it because, yeah, it's very quietly making fun of our tensions and saying, 'Why don't we all just get together, and look how ridiculous we are?' That bit got a lot of attention, and it's one of the biggest laughs we ever got."

In his next comedy series, *Newhart,* the comedian played Dick Loudon, who moves with his wife, Joanna (Mary Frann), from New York to run a small Vermont inn. *Newhart* premiered on CBS in 1982 and ran successfully until 1990, when it went out not with a whimper, or even a bang, but with what may be the most perfect final episode in TV series history. And according to Newhart, it was all his wife Ginny's idea. Six seasons into the show, when Newhart was becoming frustrated by the network's time-slot changes and lack of overall support for *Newhart,* he casually asked his wife, at a friend's Christmas party, whether she thought he should continue or quit. "With hardly a breath," he recalls, "she said, 'You should end the show, and you should wake up in bed with Suzy and describe that you had this weird dream about owning an inn in Vermont.' And I said, 'Oh, that's incredible! What a great idea!'" Suzanne Pleshette happened to be attending the same party, and they told her the idea. Immediately, she promised to do it. "If I'm in Timbuktu, I'll be back!" she told them. CBS and Newhart ironed over their differences and presented another two seasons of *Newhart,* but the star always knew how he wanted the series to end. When it came time, he told the writers, who embellished the idea, but not the crew. They were as surprised as the studio audience that night when, after a scene in which Dick Loudon was knocked unconscious by an errant golf ball, the setting for the next and final scene was revealed: the bedroom set from *The Bob Newhart Show,* with Bob Newhart in bed, awaking with a start from a bad dream. Under the covers in bed with him was Pleshette, reprising her role of Bob Hartley's wife, Emily. The second the old bedroom set was revealed, Newhart recalls, the studio audience began laughing, applauding, and shouting, "Yes! Yes!" and, Newhart adds, "They hadn't even seen Suzy herself yet." And when they did, the place went crazy. She listened, with increasing incredulity, as her bed-mate described his nightmare of running a remote inn, being married to a beautiful blonde, and dealing with such strange characters as two brothers named Darryl who never spoke. The more accurately he described the series that was moments from ending for good, the more absurd it sounded. "It almost had to be a kind of Monty Python kind of attitude of 'wink, wink, nudge, nudge' to the audience: You know what we're doing, right?" Newhart says.

More than twenty years later, Newhart got to take part in another well-orchestrated sitcom surprise. The executive producer Chuck Lorre had been after Newhart for years to guest star on one of his series, and Newhart agreed to appear on *The Big Bang Theory*, because he enjoyed the show, on two conditions. His scenes had to be performed in front of a live audience, and the part had to be written as a multiple-episode arc. Lorre had no prob-lem with either demand: *The Big Bang Theory* was filmed in front of a live audience anyway, and getting more Newhart was a bonus. But when it came time to shoot the first of his episodes, Newhart was thrown by the news that Lorre intended to block and film Newhart's initial entrance as a secret to the studio audience—having the door open for the arrival of his character, Professor Proton, and there was . . . Bob Newhart, with no prior announce-ment or hint to the studio audience.

"I said to him, 'Well, Chuck, what if they don't recognize me?'" Newhart recalls. "He said, 'They'll recognize you. Trust me.' So I walked out, and there was applause and standing ovations. It was crazy." It also was rewarding, both literally (Newhart won his first-ever prime-time Emmy as an actor for the role) and emotionally. "I wanted to do the show because I said, in my own mind, I still have my fastball," Newhart says, then laughs. "But it turns out I don't have my fastball. I have my slow curve, is what I have. It's more of a changeup. But it was a nice feeling. I still know how to do this! I want to do it! . . . I had a great time. And they got me an Emmy!"

With that *Big Bang Theory* experience, though, Newhart does notice one significant change in situation comedies from when he was starring in them in the 1970s and 1980s, or enjoying Jack Benny in the 1940s and 1950s.

"It may not mean a lot to people," Newhart notes, "but to comedians, it's important. It's the rhythm. We would sometimes take up to a minute and a half to set up a joke, where there weren't any laughs. It was just the setup for this punch line you'd eventually get to. You don't find that today. I'm not putting it down. I'm just—the rhythms are different. They are faster, and they pace it by the audience, and what they want. And they want it now. Although personally, I think those older jokes work. Jack Benny's joke worked fine."

BORN: 1947, Brooklyn.

FIRST TV CREDIT: *Fridays,* 1980, ABC.

LANDMARK TV SERIES: *Saturday Night Live,* 1984–85, NBC; *Seinfeld,* 1989– 98, NBC; *Curb Your Enthusiasm,* 2000–, HBO.

OTHER MAJOR CREDITS: Broadway: Writer and star, *Fish in the Dark,* 2015. Movies: Woody Allen's *Radio Days,* 1987, *New York Stories,* 1989, and *Whatever Works,* 2009. TV: *Clear History,* 2013, HBO; *Saturday Night Live* (guest starring as Bernie Sanders), 2015–16, NBC.

Larry David's television debut was as a founding member of the repertory company of *Fridays,* a late-night variety sketch series broadcast live by ABC in 1980. That's a surprisingly high board from which to dive into TV for your first experience—a live, national TV show—and even David himself was surprised to be there, or to be a part of the entertainment world at all. When he was younger, he had no grand plan to conquer show business. He had no grand plans whatsoever.

Larry David was born in Sheepshead Bay in Brooklyn in 1947, and his earliest entertainment memories were of television—a brand-new medium then, but one that was part of his daily life in Sheepshead Bay ever since he can remember. "One of my earliest memories, of course, is *Howdy Doody,*" David says. "And Uncle Miltie," he adds, referring to Milton Berle's *Texaco Star Theater,* television's first major hit show. "I remember really laughing hard at that show and enjoying it. And Sid Caesar, I loved," David recalls, referring to both *Your Show of Shows* and its follow-up, *Caesar's Hour.* By

that time, in the mid-1950s, young Larry David also enjoyed watching syndicated repeats of *Amos 'n' Andy* and his "all-time favorite," Phil Silvers's then-
new military sitcom, originally titled *You'll Never Get Rich.* Silvers played
Sergeant Bilko, a fast-talking schemer who tried to profit from everyone
else on his military base, including members of his own platoon. "He was
kind of morally reprehensible, in a way," David says, laughing. "He was a con
man! And he was a funny con man, and that seemed okay."

Asked if that persona, of a disagreeable man doing funny things, influenced the comic alter ego David himself later adopted on HBO's *Curb Your
Enthusiasm,* David doubted it. "I have a feeling I might still be doing the
same stuff had I never seen that," he says. And though he loved watching
movies (early Cary Grant films were "the greatest") as well as TV, he never
saw anyone who made him want to pursue a dream of being a comedian
or comic writer. "I just watched everything for entertainment purposes,"
he says simply. You can almost hear the shrug, and it's part of David's long-
standing let-it-roll attitude.

He graduated with a degree in history from the University of Maryland
but with no notion of what he planned to do with it. "I didn't have the
foggiest notion," he admits now. "And whenever anybody asked me what I
wanted to do, or what I wanted to be, I would just say—and honestly, this
was my stock answer—'I don't know. Something will turn up.' I was quite
confident that something would turn up. I don't know why."

After college, he returned to New York, had a series of odd jobs, and took
an acting class, but not because of a burning desire to learn and hone his
craft, or even because he thought that could be his craft. "I thought I needed
something to say," he admits, "to impress a woman. I thought saying 'I'm
an actor' might be a good thing. Might be helpful." But in class one day, an
exercise required the students to stand in front of the class, one by one, and
talk as themselves. David did it, he recalls, "and they laughed. And that was
it. It started me to do stand-up." But even as a stand-up comic, David was
uniquely, legendarily noncommittal. A famous story about him during his
early days turns out not to be apocryphal: he walked out onstage one night,
got to the microphone, looked the crowd over, didn't like the vibe he was
getting, and instead of introducing himself, said, "Naaaaah, I don't think
so," and walked off. That attitude might not have won over many audience
members, but it clicked with plenty of fellow comics, including another
then-struggling young comedian named Jerry Seinfeld. They became
friends, finding a common bond in being fascinated, and amused, by life's

everyday minutiae—a widespread comic obsession that would eventually pay enormous dividends. Meanwhile, Larry David found another genuine enthusiasm in those early days: improvisation.

"I remember taking an improv class, when I was a comedian in New York, from a guy named J. J. Barry," he says. "I took it with a bunch of comedians . . . and I remember that I really loved doing the improv. So much more than acting with a script. And that class kind of stayed with me." David got enough bookings as a struggling stand-up to qualify for residency at Manhattan Plaza, a federally subsidized housing project for performing artists. The rent was seventy-two dollars a month, and one of his neighbors in that building, an eccentric guy who became another good friend, was Kenny "Cosmo" Kramer. David held on to that apartment until 1980, when he moved to Los Angeles to co-star in the new ABC series *Fridays*, and moved back into it two years later, still down the hall from his buddy Kramer, after *Fridays* was canceled.

Fridays, broadcast live from Los Angeles, was ABC's attempt to emulate NBC's popular live, late-night franchise, which was about to say good-bye to its original producer, Lorne Michaels, and its original cast of Not-Ready-for-Prime-Time Players. "It was kind of a rip-off of," David says, then stops and corrects himself. "Not kind of. It was a rip-off of *Saturday Night Live*," he says. "So in that regard, it was kind of embarrassing." It was also uncomfortable, David admits, because of his own inexperience with television. "I really hadn't done any sketch acting, or anything like that, so it was kind of nerve-racking," he recalls, laughing. "I was riddled with anxiety before those shows. And I was doing characters and impressions, and wearing wigs . . ."

Fridays didn't last long, but for David it accrued plenty of benefits. The writing staff, of which David was a member, included Larry Charles, later a key contributor to both *Seinfeld* (as an early writer-producer) and *Curb Your Enthusiasm* (as an early executive producer and director). The on-air repertory company, of which David was also a member, also introduced him to his fellow cast mate Michael Richards—a friend of Seinfeld's who later played the neighbor friend named Kramer on *Seinfeld*, which Seinfeld and David co-created. "Jerry was a huge fan of Michael's," David remembers, "and when we were talking about [casting] Kramer, his name came up very quickly."

But first, in the interim, there was *Saturday Night Live*, where Larry David went to work for a season—specifically, 1984–85, the last season before Lorne Michaels returned as executive producer. Julia Louis-Dreyfus was there then as well, and the two of them—she as a cast member, he as a writer—were woefully underused. "Underused?" echoes David. "Fair statement, of course. I only had one sketch on the entire year." He even quit one week in frustration, loudly and dramatically, then reconsidered over the weekend and returned to work on Monday as though nothing had happened—a story line he later gave to his *Seinfeld* alter ego, George Costanza. The time on *SNL* introduced David to Louis-Dreyfus, another of his future *Seinfeld* stars, so it wasn't wasted. Nor was the last half of the 1980s, when David appeared in small parts in two Woody Allen movies, starting with *Radio Days* in 1987. (Much later, he would star in one, 2009's *Whatever Works*.) For *Radio Days,* he was called by the casting director to go to Allen's Park Avenue office to meet him. "I went in, and he looked at me and shook my hand, said hello, and that was it," David says. "Then I was in the movie." Asked if he has subsequently hired people that same way, David laughs and says, "No. No."

Hiring people for "The Seinfeld Chronicles," the 1989 NBC special that led to *Seinfeld,* was more than just a handshake deal but was a fairly smooth process nonetheless. The original concept was to show how a stand-up comic comes up with and develops his material. Once Seinfeld and David paired up to develop the show, with Seinfeld at its center, other pieces fell in quickly. Louis-Dreyfus, as Elaine Benes, was added after the "Chronicles" pilot, but Richards, as Kramer, was there from the start, as was Jason Alexander, then starring onstage in New York in *Jerome Robbins' Broadway,* who sent in a videotape audition for the role of George Costanza and got it. "Jerry and I were in L.A.," David says, "and Jason sent in a tape that he did with a casting director in New York. And after ten seconds, I looked at Jerry and I go, 'That's it. There he is!' I just knew it. I don't know why, but that's what happened."

The structure of *Seinfeld* mixed the very old with the very new. The conceit of Jerry Seinfeld playing an exaggerated caricature of himself, and retaining his real name, was as old as TV itself—older, because it came from radio—thanks to precedents set in their respective sitcoms by Jack Benny and George Burns. CBS's *Jack Benny Program,* like *Seinfeld,* had a large family of supporting characters, not all of whom would appear in every show, but which helped populate a wider, and even funnier, TV universe. Benny's plots, like those on *Seinfeld,* could be about the smallest bits of everyday life: one of the classic Benny episodes had him shopping for items on his

Christmas list, and that was it. Where *Seinfeld* was most different from any comedy that came before it was in the intricacy of its story structure, with seemingly disconnected plotlines coming together for a surprise, sometimes frenetic climax. At first, audiences responded slowly to *Seinfeld,* and so did some of the NBC executives, but others held firm, as did Larry David.

"In the first couple of years, there were some heated arguments about content and things like that," David says. "I had to quit a couple of times . . . And that worked out. So after that, we didn't have any interference at all. We sort of just had our way with it." Along with freedom came success: by 1994, *Seinfeld* was the top-rated series on television. David left the day-to-day operations of *Seinfeld* in 1996 but returned in 1998 to write the series finale, which ended exactly as the pilot episode of "The Seinfeld Chronicles" had begun, with Jerry and George discussing the proper placement of men's shirt buttons. In the pilot, they were discussing this at the luncheonette; in the finale, they were having the identical conversation nine years later but in prison. "It just seemed like a good bookend for the show," David says. "And it was for the fans who knew what was in the first one." The finale was seen by an estimated audience of more than seventy-three million viewers—less than the final episodes of *Cheers* and *M*A*S*H,* but more than any other scripted comedy series. After that triumph, David moved on to another, by shifting to HBO to create, and star in, *Curb Your Enthusiasm.*

Here, again, was an evolutionary step for TV comedy. Larry David's approach to *Curb Your Enthusiasm* was to combine the intricately interwoven plots of *Seinfeld* with the heady unpredictability and creative excitement of his improv classes back in New York. "It was all on the paper, really," David says of those early, pioneering *Curb* episodes. "It's all about the story. I wrote an outline, a detailed outline, and then we improvised it." The show's early directors (Robert B. Weide, Larry Charles, David Steinberg, and Bryan Gordon), like David's fellow founding cast members (Jeff Garlin, Cheryl Hines, Susie Essman, Richard Lewis, and others), were all on the same page, even if the page was just an outline. For David, playing a heightened, more verbal version of himself in an improvisatory atmosphere, with people he liked and trusted, was a joy, which, at times, made it a challenge.

"They were all my friends, who I had worked with, and who I knew, so I had a pretty good idea of what it should be," David says of *Curb,* adding that the experience was even better than what he'd dared to imagine. "It's pretty exhilarating," he says of improvising dialogue against a broad outline. "And

I can't even describe how much fun it is to do it. All those guys made me laugh so much it was hard for me to get through takes."

The platform of premium cable gave David other bonuses as well: more freedom, more time, and more flexibility. "There were no holds barred whatsoever in terms of language," he says, and also points out that a half-hour show on HBO, without commercial interruption, "was really a third longer," because the commercially broadcast *Seinfeld* episodes clocked in at around twenty-two minutes. "You could do a lot with that extra time," he says. And as the years wore on, David's stubbornly independent approach to signing up for new seasons—essentially, saying he'd do them if and when they were ready—paralleled a similar approach by David Chase on another contemporaneous HBO series, *The Sopranos*. It's an approach that has spread to FX's *Louie* as well, with Louis C.K., like Larry David, welcome to make more episodes if he so chooses but under no obligation to do so. Both men have struck deals where they commit to new seasons only when inspiration strikes, which, in both cases, has led to some inspirational seasons indeed. Most of them, despite their improvised feel, were densely structured and plotted not only within each episode but in an episodic manner, telling an ambitious overarching story across an entire season.

One example, from 2009, had David gathering the original cast of *Seinfeld* for a ten-year-reunion show. The season-long *Curb Your Enthusiasm* plot had the TV "Larry David" agreeing to the reunion special purely to cast his ex-wife (played by Cheryl Hines) in a supporting role, in hopes of getting back in her good graces. Jerry Seinfeld, Jason Alexander, Julia Louis-Dreyfus, and Michael Richards all show up to rehearse and take part in a reunion show that takes place not on NBC but on HBO. "First I got Jerry on board, and he was game right from the beginning," David recalls. "Then the others agreed, and we were off and running . . . It was fantastic. We had a blast."

As for NBC's reaction to its top-rated comedy staging a "reunion show" not on its network but on HBO? "I don't remember much of a reaction from NBC," David says. "I don't know if we had to run it by them, if we needed their permission or not, but if we did, and they gave it to us, and if I never thanked them, well, then, I'll thank them in this book. I'm sure I thanked them, by the way. It wouldn't be like me not to thank them."

Another standout *Curb* season, from 2004, had the TV "Larry" approached by Mel Brooks, who wanted him as the newest lead in Brooks's long-running Broadway hit, *The Producers*. Larry began rehearsing the role of Max Bialystock, alongside David Schwimmer playing Leo Bloom and Tony Award winner Cady Huffman, reprising her role of Ulla. The payoff, a surprise twist at the very end of the season, was that Brooks and his wife, Anne Bancroft (who also guest starred and was fabulously funny), had conspired to cast Larry in the Broadway play so he could ruin it, and it would finally close. I asked how that season-long plot came about, presuming David got Brooks's cooperation before embarking on it, but that wasn't the case.

"I made the mistake of writing the first three episodes," David says, chuckling. "I wouldn't say it was a mistake, but I wrote the first three episodes before I even spoke to him." David took Brooks out to lunch and pitched the idea, which, at the time, only involved Larry David getting cast in *The Producers* on Broadway. "He seems okay with it," David recalls, "but then he called me up and said, 'I just don't see why I would do this. I would put you in *The Producers*?' And he had a point. And I said, 'Oh, Jesus. This whole thing is going to collapse now. I've written three shows—what am I going to do? I'll have to do *Fiddler on the Roof*!' So then I thought of the idea, which was based on the [original *Producers* play and] movie, where he hires me on purpose to sabotage the show . . . He kind of forced me to come up with that." David pauses and adds, "And I can't even tell you what a thrill it was . . . to meet him and work with him, because he was certainly an idol. For sure."

Brooks had written some of the *Your Show of Shows* sketches David had watched and loved as a kid, so there was a certain symmetry to the connection. The same goes for the end of that *Producers*-inspired *Curb Your Enthusiasm* season, which ended with Larry David unprofessionally breaking the fourth wall during his *Producers* debut and ad-libbing his way to a standing ovation and rave reviews—becoming a Broadway hit when Brooks and Bancroft were sure he'd fail. Years later, in 2015, the real Larry David made his actual Broadway debut, starring in a comedy he'd written, *Fish in the Dark*. Critical reaction was mixed, but the show was a sold-out success from the start—so much so that when Larry David showed up, about the same time, on NBC's live prime-time telecast of its *Saturday Night Live: 40th Anniversary Special,* it was to crow over the popularity of his Broadway show, and his hit NBC and HBO sitcoms, at the on-air party for a show that didn't exactly welcome his talents thirty years earlier. David did a bit from the audience, talking with Seinfeld, who was taking questions from the stage, and managed to poke fun at his own short run at *Saturday Night Live* while noting his subsequent success—much to the delight of the studio audience. "I was actually surprised by the reaction to it," David admitted.

Here, too, there was one final twist ending. After that *SNL* special, later in 2015, Larry David returned to play the Democratic presidential hopeful Bernie Sanders—a live sketch comedy role bigger, better, and more warmly received than anything he'd done on *Fridays* or *Saturday Night Live*. It became a recurring role, and as the real Sanders maintained his presence deep into the primary season, so did his comic alter ego. Each time David appears as Bernie, he's greeted by a rousing ovation before he even begins speaking. "I have to say, they're really coming up with great stuff, so that's about 90 percent of the battle." I asked David how the *SNL* appearance came about, and he explained that after he had watched the first Democratic debate, his agent, Ari Emanuel, called, and David just picked up the phone and launched into an impromptu imitation of Sanders. His agent said it was so funny David should post it on the Internet, because it would get a lot of hits. "And I said, 'No, no, I'm not going to do that. It's more like a *Saturday Night Live*—,'" David recalls. "And before I even got the *Live* out of my mouth, he had hung up the phone. And ten minutes later, he was on the phone with Lorne Michaels, and Lorne told him that he had gotten texts, during the debate, from some of his friends, saying I should be doing Bernie Sanders." The facts that he and Sanders are about the same age, are Jewish, and grew up not that far from each other in Brooklyn of course contribute heavily to the success of the parody.

Finally, asked if he thinks *Saturday Night Live* will keep asking him back through the election cycle until November 2016, David replies (correctly, as it turns out), "Well, I assume they will. Yeah. It's fun to do." It's also more prominence than *SNL* ever gave him the first time around, and it better be fun. Because if there's one thing Larry David doesn't need, after changing TV comedy twice with *Seinfeld* and *Curb Your Enthusiasm*, it's the money.

PROFILE **LOUIS C.K.**

BORN: 1967, Washington, D.C., as Louis Székely.
FIRST TV CREDIT: Writer and comic, *Caroline's Comedy Hour,* 1989, A&E.
LANDMARK TV SERIES: Writer, *Late Night with Conan O'Brien,* 1993–94,
NBC; Writer, producer, director, and star, *Louie,* 2010–, FX.
OTHER MAJOR CREDITS: TV: Writer, *The Dana Carvey Show,* 1996, ABC;
Writer, *The Chris Rock Show,* 1997–99, HBO; Stand-up comedy special,
Louis C.K.: Shameless, 2007; Actor, recurring role, *Parks and Recreation,*
2009–12; Guest host, *Saturday Night Live,* 2012, 2014, 2015, NBC; Writer and
co-creator, *Baskets,* 2016, FX; Creator, writer, director, and co-star, *Horace
and Pete,* 2016, LouisCK.net. Movies: Writer, *Pootie Tang,* 2001; Co-writer,
Down to Earth, 2001; Co-writer, *I Think I Love My Wife,* 2007; Actor, *Blue
Jasmine,* 2013; Actor, *American Hustle,* 2013; Actor, *Trumbo,* 2015.

Of all the interviews and profiles I did for this book, the one with Louis C.K.
was the most surprising, because halfway through our interview, which was
the first time I'd ever talked to the comedian one-on-one, he told me he'd
been so upset by my negative review of one of his TV series that he'd written me an angry e-mail in response, which I'd never received. Yet the more
we talked about that, and my more positive reactions to his later work, the
more I learned about Louis C.K. as an artist and about myself as a critic, and
our respective relationship to each other. I'm grateful to every single person
who took time to talk to me about the evolution of quality television, but
I may be the most grateful to Louis C.K., because if I were in his shoes, I'm
not at all sure I'd be sufficiently well-adjusted to agree to talk to me. But

before we get to that part of our very personal conversation, let's revisit how he became a comedian, and Louis C.K., in the first place.

Louis C.K. was born Louis Székely in 1967 in Washington, D.C. His parents relocated the family to Mexico City after Louis was born and lived there until moving back to the United States, to the Boston suburb of Newton, Massachusetts, when Louis was seven. "My first exposure to television was in Mexico," he recalls. "*The Flintstones* was big in Mexico, and *Sesame Street,* and I watched them both in Spanish. And there was a weird thing of coming to the United States and seeing these shows in English. Never seemed right."

Once he returned stateside, young Louis began enjoying many of the popular sitcoms from the mid-1970s and at least one of the more esoteric ones. "*Barney Miller,* I just fucking loved," he says. Asked why, he explains, "I probably didn't know it at the time, but it was the writing. It was such a well-written show." He watched and enjoyed the popular sitcoms of the era ("I was with everybody else: you had to watch *Happy Days,* and you had to watch *M*A*S*H*") and even admitted to a TV crush or two. "*Laverne & Shirley* was a pretty big deal," he says. "I thought Shirley was cute, and I thought I really liked Laverne, for some reason." He loved *Taxi,* calling it "an amazingly written show." Just as much, though, he was drawn to the topical 1970s sitcoms produced by Norman Lear. "I went crazy for *All in the Family,*" Louis C.K. says, "and *The Jeffersons,* and *Good Times.* I liked *Good Times.* And I think I really wanted to be black when I was a kid, so I really liked the black shows." When he's reminded that he ended up writing for both Chris Rock and Cedric the Entertainer, Louis C.K. chuckles and says, "That's true. Well, I really wanted to be in *Good Times,* in that family. I really wanted to be poor, and black, and in that family." Growing up in Boston, he also identified sufficiently with the misbehaving Sweathogs on ABC's *Welcome Back, Kotter* to write a fan letter to Ron Palillo, who played the donkey-bray-laughing Arnold Horshack, and receive an autographed picture in return.

His comedy influences, more directly, were varied, but uniformly bold. Steve Martin was "a big, big influence," Louis C.K. says. George Carlin. Richard Pryor. Monty Python. The bizarre radio playlists of Dr. Demento. And, in the early 1980s, David Letterman's daytime show and late night's Eddie Murphy, whom Louis C.K. vividly recalls exploding his way to stardom in the 1980s. "When I was in high school, and Eddie Murphy got on *Saturday Night Live,* it didn't matter anymore what the sketches were. You just wanted to see Eddie Murphy; nobody else mattered. And then Eddie Murphy in his stand-up special, that was the first time I remember seeing HBO's raw, uncensored stand-up. A friend of mine had HBO, and I saw [1983's] *Delirious,* and I just couldn't fucking believe it. Even though I was exposed to Carlin and Pryor and everybody else, when I saw *Delirious,* I probably hadn't laughed that hard ever in my life."

Finally, there were the movies. Louis C.K. singles out two people who had a major influence on him when he was young and, in retrospect, had a good deal to do with the individualistic, different-drummer path he took as an adult. "Woody Allen was a huge part of that," Louis C.K. says, adding, "When you're a kid and you're watching TV, it's mysterious to you how it gets made. You just think these people are all geniuses, and they stand around and say all this great stuff. But Woody Allen was the first person that I knew about where he was identified as a writer, director, and actor, you know what I mean? That he made these things himself. And that was a special thing . . . And because you knew him as a personality, it reflected how he made the movie. You could tell you were watching a Woody Allen movie, and that this was all his invention, you know? That turned me on like crazy. That idea was really great, and I think," he concludes, talking of his own aspirations as a filmmaker, "that's why I first wanted to do it."

The other major influence was Steven Spielberg—not just because of such blockbuster 1970s movies as *Jaws* and *Close Encounters of the Third Kind* but because of some biographical details young Louis learned when watching the local Boston TV host Dana Hersey, of WSBK's *Movie Loft,* presenting and discussing Spielberg's 1971 made-for-TV movie breakthrough, *Duel.* "They showed it, and I was riveted by it," Louis C.K. says of the ABC television movie in which Dennis Weaver played a motorist terrorized by a homicidal truck driver on a desolate roadway. Young Louis was even more impressed, though, by Hersey's story about how Spielberg, who was fairly young himself, was ambitious and resourceful enough, while working as a messenger delivering packages, to set up shop at an empty office on the Universal lot and befriend someone into giving him a job and a chance. "That made me crazy," Louis C.K. says. "I think I knew, when I was a kid, that I was not going to go to college, and get a degree, and go about things the way most people did. So the idea that there are shortcuts was very exciting."

It turns out he pursued them and needed them. As a teenager, he worked at a photo-developing store and at a local TV station, and one of the things he developed was the desire, and skill, to make his own short films. He showed up for an admissions interview in hopes of getting into NYU film school, but he never completed the application process. Instead, he took a series of odd jobs, eventually pursuing his showbiz dreams as a stand-up comic. In Boston, he first took the stage in 1985 and worked his way up to full-fledged stand-up jobs alongside such hot local comics as Denis Leary. Any extra money he got, he spent on his self-made comedy shorts, a practice he continued after moving to New York in 1989. Whatever path he took to arrive, Louis C.K. got there—through shortcuts so effective he eventually ended up working at or with many of his early meaningful influences: acting in a Woody Allen movie, writing for David Letterman, guest hosting on *Saturday Night Live,* and doing his own uncensored full-length solo comedy specials like Eddie Murphy on HBO, starting with 2007's *Louis C.K.: Shameless.* Later, in FX's *Louie* and his even more recent, self-distributed 2016 *Horace and Pete* miniseries, he wrote, directed, and starred in comedy in a way that, as with Woody Allen, makes it very clear whose vision, and sense of humor, are being presented.

The first TV credit for Louis C.K. came on *Caroline's Comedy Hour,* an A&E series mounted by the comedy club now known as Carolines on Broadway. A well-liked comic at the club, Louis C.K. made a brief appearance as a stand-up comic, then was asked by the club's manager, Joe Falzorano, and the series host, Colin Quinn, about joining the TV show's writing staff. "He asked me for a writing sample, and I gave him short movies that I had made," Louis C.K. says. "That was rare for a comedian to have that . . . They weren't great, but they existed. And I gave them to him, and he hired me." The TV series didn't have much cultural impact, but for Louis C.K. it was invaluable. In addition to Quinn as the host, *Caroline's Comedy Hour* had a young Jon Stewart as the head writer and a writing staff that included Dave Attell and Susie Essman. "We had a ball," Louis C.K. recalls. "That was my first time, and I had sort of a thing where I got to go and shoot my own little things, because I had done that . . . And Jon, who couldn't have been a very old guy then, was a real leader. He was very wise, and he was a nice guy. And I loved Colin, so the whole thing was purely fun. And then, I had a little more of a [sample] reel, and now I had one credit."

His second credit, as member of a TV writing staff, came just as he was considering giving up comedy altogether, and even though it was a brand-new series built around a star who had never been on television, it exposed Louis C.K. to the highest levels of showbiz stress and to another extremely talented writing room. The show was the 1993 launch of NBC's *Late Night with Conan O'Brien,* and the inaugural writing staff, the two years Louis C.K. was there, included O'Brien; his sidekick, Andy Richter; the head writer, Robert Smigel; Bob Odenkirk; and the man who became Louis C.K.'s eventual officemate and writing partner, Dino Stamatopoulos. "Writing for Conan was an amazing thing," Louis C.K. explains, "because they gave us total control over our bits. If you wrote something that was funny, you got to really produce it. And I got exposure to being on high-stakes network television. The stakes were very high, because the show was in peril all the time." He considers O'Brien "a very inspiring guy to work with" and also a good friend and "a mensch," someone who really knows how to guide a show. Smigel was "an absolute mentor," and the entire *Late Night* experience, to Louis C.K., was "very exciting," especially to be playing at that level at a mere twenty-five years of age.

Smigel continued to mentor Louis C.K., giving him writing credit on some of Smigel's "TV Funhouse" animated shorts for *Saturday Night Live*—such memorable cartoons as "The Ambiguously Gay Duo," voiced by the future *Daily Show with Jon Stewart* correspondents (and future stars) Steve Carell and Stephen Colbert. Louis C.K. had moved on to writing for *Late Show with David Letterman* in the summer of 1995 ("I did it because I loved Letterman, way back to when I was a kid, very early in his tenure, watching his show"). He then reunited with Smigel in 1996 to co-produce ABC's *Dana Carvey Show,* whose writing staff and repertory company also included Carell, Colbert, and Odenkirk. "It was a bit of a mess," Louis C.K. says, chuckling. "We put together a now-legendary writing staff," he adds, describing a writers' room that also included Greg Daniels and the future *Being John Malkovich* and *Adaptation* screenwriter, Charlie Kaufman. And because Smigel wanted to perform and write rather than be the show runner, Louis C.K. was handed the reins.

"It was a lot of pressure," he says, especially because there were conflicting guidelines and interests from the start. ABC wanted an edgy comedy series as a lead-in to its intentionally irreverent and envelope-pushing *NYPD Blue,* which fit oddly with the comic persona Dana Carvey had established. "In Dana's heart, he loves edgy," Louis C.K. says, "but he's a very sweet guy . . . Dana's a great performer, and he's hilarious, but he's not a guy you look to to really unset the boundaries. That's not the kind of guy he is." The wholesome lead-in of *Home Improvement* didn't help, and when *The Dana Carvey*

Show was in preproduction, ABC was acquired by the even more whole-some Walt Disney Company. "I think that actually did happen," Louis C.K. recalls, laughing, and he's right. "So the ground shifted under our feet, and none of us were really prepared." *The Dana Carvey Show* premiered on ABC in March 1996. By May, it was gone.

Just before becoming head writer on *The Dana Carvey Show*, Louis C.K. had gotten several calls from his friend and comic contemporary Chris Rock, with a job offer to join him on his new HBO comedy series, which was still in the planning stages. "And I said, 'Nah, I'm going to ABC! It's a big fucking deal. It's Dana Carvey! It's bigger than you!'" Louis C.K. both laughs and groans at the memory. "I really should have taken the job."

After *The Dana Carvey Show* tanked so quickly, Louis C.K. went back to Chris Rock and asked for just a staff writing job—anything, just so he could help out. Rock made him a producer, even though *The Chris Rock Show* had already been created, and they started generating sketch and comedy ideas that both of them felt were different—especially for what HBO might have considered Rock's target audience.

"Chris is a visionary," Louis C.K. says. "He was a young man then, and he already knew that this was an opportunity. And he said, 'I don't want to give black people what everybody always gives black people. People believe that black audiences only like one thing. But the truth is, black audiences are only given one thing.' He said that he hired me because I was 'a weirdo Conan writer'—a strange, esoteric writer who came at it from a Monty Python kind of an angle." They also shared a love of Woody Allen's comedies, as well as the freedom that came from playing in HBO's uncensored TV sandbox, and a dedicated work ethic. "Chris was brilliant, how he worked on that show," Louis C.K. marvels. "He was always there when I got there, and he was there when I left. He worked extremely hard. And we all won Emmys."

The two of them worked next as two of four screenwriters on *Down to Earth,* the 2001 movie adaptation, starring Rock, of the 1978 Warren Beatty–Elaine May film, *Heaven Can Wait.* Louis C.K. also wrote his infamous *Pootie Tang* movie that year, then wrote for Fox's one-season *Cedric the Entertainer* variety series before devoting himself to a long, strong stretch of stand-up comedy tours. None of those projects caught fire, nor did Louis C.K.'s next project, a TV family sitcom recorded before a live audience, but for HBO, uncensored and uninterrupted. The 2006 series was called *Lucky Louie* and starred Louis C.K. and Pamela Adlon as parents of a young girl, living in a somewhat run-down apartment building surrounded by friends and wacky neighbors. The goal of the show, Louis C.K. explains, was to re-create the old way of doing multi-camera comedies but with a modern sensibility and vocabulary.

"You put a set in front of an audience," he says. "We dragged the set as close to the audience as we possibly could. We tried to find as honest an audience as we could. We went out and got people from church groups, and we tried to find stuff for retired people to do. We had the weirdest audience." The set design, he says, was based on the original blueprint for *The Honeymooners* set, as was the importance of the feel of a live performance before an involved studio audience—something that Louis C.K. loved not only from that classic Jackie Gleason sitcom from the 1950s but from the Norman Lear shows Louis C.K. adored so much growing up. "You had shows like *All in the Family,*" Louis C.K. recalls, remembering the potent performance of Carroll O'Connor as the bigoted Archie Bunker, "where he used to have to stop talking because the laughter was so raucous. And not only raucous, but shocked—and you could hear voices inside the laughs of those shows. And it mitigated the performances and brought out great performances in the actors."

Louis C.K. says now he always thought he would need two seasons for viewers to get comfortable with the tone and content of *Lucky Louie,* but HBO gave him only one, and Louis C.K. figures there were two major reasons why. One was that he deferred to the input from his writing staff, rather than staying fully faithful to his original vision. "I was headed towards the writing also being conventional, and letting there be real dialogue on the show, which I think would have made a difference," he explains. "But there's a striving for perfection that happens in a writing room, which was not the best way to do my show. I had a great group that was doing a job that should have been on another show." The other major reason, he recalls, was the critics. "We had some really good reviews, people that were saying, you know, this is worth looking at. This might work. I remember that's what a woman at the *New York Times* [Virginia Heffernan] said: this just might work. She was willing to give it a shot. But other people weren't," he continues, then hits me with a calmly delivered cannonball. "You weren't. You hated it."

At that point, my interview with Louis C.K., intended to gather information about his early influences and later artistic ambitions and decisions, turned into a very honest conversation between TV creator and TV critic—a conversation I'll never forget, and that I'll share in part here, because it was both so unexpected and so unguarded. It begins with Louis C.K. saying that he still remembers clearly the *Lucky Louie* review I wrote in the New York *Daily News* and the one the TV critic Tim Goodman wrote in the *San Francisco Chronicle*.

LOUIS: You both wrote the same thing, which was that they should cancel the show to show they knew they had made this [laughter] terrible mistake.

ME: Oh, man. Oh, Louis.

LOUIS: You have to know—sitting at a breakfast table in the morning and reading these things, it's a thrill. You're in the fucking fight, you know? I mean, take yourself back to obscurity days, when you're writing and you have no idea anyone's ever going to give you a chance to communicate what you say. And imagine: project yourself forward to a day where people are angry about what you're doing and writing in national papers. That's an amazing trip to be on . . . But I wrote you an e-mail, and I wrote and said, "Look—"

ME: I never got an e-mail from you.

LOUIS: Oh, you didn't?

ME: No.

LOUIS: I wrote it. I wrote you an e-mail, and I said, "I think you've overstepped your responsibility, because TV criticism is a great thing when you discuss the context and the intent behind a show and what your opinion is of it. But what you're doing now is talking about people who—I have hundreds of people who work for me. And they're trying to get through the fucking Christmas holidays without getting fired." And so I wrote you this angry letter—

ME: Oh, I never got it. Oh, damn. Okay.

LOUIS: You couldn't, because I looked at it—it was a very important moment. I read it on the screen in front of me, and I thought, "No, no, no, don't send this. You don't write this. You don't send this. This isn't how to respond to this. This is the water you're in, and this is an exciting time in television. Television is becoming an art form." I remember thinking that. Television is coming into a new place. *The Sopranos* . . .

I remember I talked to Norman Lear on the phone when I was making the show. And he talked to me about how when *All in the Family* came out, he was getting killed. But the *New York Times* wrote, like, a page-long review that kept the show floating. And I knew that this is what it's like. You're being shot at from all angles, and you're trying to shoot back, but you're trying to just do your job. It's heavy. It's heavy, heavy fire. And so, when I wrote that e-mail and didn't send it, I thought, "This is part of it. You've just got to defend the show the best you can, and it might not survive. And everybody is doing their job. Everybody's got a passionate voice because TV matters now, and you'll see how this turns out."

In the case of *Lucky Louie,* it turned out that Louis C.K. reorganized his writing team and wrote eight episodes of what would have been a very different approach for season 2, more along the lines of his original intent. But before those scripts could be produced, HBO pulled the plug. "I don't think I was good enough to do *Lucky Louie* as well as I should have," he says in retrospect. "I think the first season deserved what it got from critics. There's a lot of things I would have done differently. A lot. But you don't get to do those again. That's the great thing about TV: you have to learn in front of everybody." At the same time HBO canceled *Lucky Louie,* though, the network financed and scheduled the comedian's first full-length stand-up HBO special, 2007's *Louis C.K.: Shameless,* the first of an annual series of all-new comedy showcases produced and distributed by various networks (and, in time, via Louis C.K.'s own website). And then, in 2010, came Louis C.K.'s television masterpiece, FX's *Louie.*

"And the thing I had between those two projects," he says, "was a massively successful stand-up career—about two or three years. I'd gone through a divorce. I'd gotten even more hardened and grizzled through that. And I had been on the road, selling out large theaters." Everything that happened next, he figures, was due to the failure of *Lucky Louie* and the success of *Louis C.K.: Shameless.* "HBO had given me about as terrific a parting gift as you could get. *Shameless* was my first stand-up special, and when that went on the air, all of a sudden I was selling out stand-up clubs within minutes of putting them on sale, and I was starting to play theaters. And I was perfectly happy. I didn't give a shit if I ever did TV again." One time when he played Los Angeles, Louis C.K. was told by his manager that executives from the FX cable network wanted to meet with him about doing a show. "Going into it, I knew from *Lucky Louie,* and with the leverage of my current success at the time," he recalls, "I was able to say, 'There's no way I'm doing another TV show unless I do it exactly one way.' Because (a) I know how to do it now—I really knew how to make a show work. And (b) I know that if nobody lets me do it, it's not worth doing. But it's okay not to have a TV show. You know? If you need to be on the air, you're fucked right there. That's what kills every show ... The network executives have formulas for what they think works, but they will follow your lead if you're willing to not have a show. That's the only thing you need."

If he were going to do another TV show, it would be his way, and that meant eliminating the writers' room. "You don't need a roomful of people to write a TV show," he says. "It's ridiculous. And it takes it down. It ends up being necessarily diluted, because you've got twelve different people from twelve different pedigrees. It's going to sound like twelve different shows. And you also have to get some consensus from twelve people that something is a good idea, and anything that can please twelve people is not going to be that special. That's my feeling. And that's my prejudice, because there are amazing shows that are run by rooms. It's just not how I do it, and it's not the path that I have confidence in. And enough ground had been laid by other shows before me that you could do it." He cites HBO's *Curb Your Enthusiasm* by Larry David and *The Larry Sanders Show* by Garry Shandling ("People forget how huge that was"), as well as Ricky Gervais's BBC comedy, *The Office*. "The thing I knew going into *Louie*," he says confidently, "was that the American palate, the ear, was tuned better and that people were willing to go anywhere you wanted them to. People watching TV in the time I made *Louie*, whatever the fuck you wanted to try, they would want to watch it." Those were the preconceptions, and demands, he took into his discussions with FX, and even those were accompanied by Louis C.K.'s insistent assertion "I don't want to do a TV show." Then he pauses and laughs, and adds, "And you can hear about that, how that show got made, in other places."

My "other place" was John Landgraf, FX's president of entertainment, who revealed the unusual behind-the-scenes negotiations that led to *Louie*. The daringly free-form structure of the series Louis C.K. envisioned, with some episodes including multiple separate stories and other episodes being part of a larger and longer whole, didn't throw Landgraf. Instead of a sitcom, he saw it as "an existentially truthful show" that was more like a series of short films, like Woody Allen might make, with stand-up comedy providing a bridge when necessary. Harder to understand and embrace, at least at first, was Louis C.K.'s desire for rather unrestricted creative control. "Louis said, 'I can't do this and jump through a hoop. I have to do it as an auteur. I have to do it in a way where I just go out and make it, and I don't try to make it conform to some notion of what a well-made television show is. And so, therefore, I can't write a script. I don't want to have any [network] notes.' And I said, 'Okay,'" Landgraf recalls with a chuckle, but countered with a catch. Landgraf offered a smaller budget per episode, explaining that if costs were low enough, FX couldn't lose money so long as Louis C.K. delivered an acceptable finished product. Louis C.K. countered with a slightly higher figure as a compromise, to which Landgraf replied, "Okay, I'll give you that much, but then I've got to give you some notes." Louis C.K.'s decision, according to Landgraf: "I'll take the less money, and the no notes."

Landgraf wired the first-season estimated costs, five million dollars, into Louis C.K.'s company bank account, then waited. "Louis is one of the hardest-working and one of the most honest, decent people I've ever met," Landgraf says, "so I'm kidding here, but for all I knew, the next call I was going to get was from his business manager, saying, 'He's in the Bahamas, and you'll never hear from him again.'" Instead, the finished episodes began to arrive, ready to be televised, and more than exceeding expectations. "What we got," Landgraf says, "was *Louie*. It may not be everybody's cup of tea, but it was one of the most exhilarating experiences I've ever had, because, essentially, we really gave him a carte blanche to reinvent the notion of what a half-hour comedy could be. And he went out and did it, and he had the chops as a writer and a director and a producer and an actor and an editor. He edited every episode. And, by the way, he produced the music."

Landgraf loved *Louie* from the very start, and so did I. "This is such a change from HBO's *Lucky Louie*—such a welcome change," I wrote for my TV Worth Watching website when *Louie* premiered on FX in 2010, "I can't tell you. But I'll try." That column ended with an observation that was much more accurate, regarding the show's creation, than I knew at the time: "Louis C.K., by taking firm control of his new TV series, has converted me into a fan." As it turns out, Louis C.K. was aware of that review also.

"When I read your stuff about *Louie*," he says, "and Tim Goodman's, and other people who didn't like *Lucky Louie*, I didn't attach any emotion to that in terms of what had been written before. It's a different project. I was better at it." Even so, I apologized for not responding more positively to *Lucky Louie* and hoped my immediate embrace of *Louie* counted for something. Louis C.K. stopped me, then taught me.

"You can't apologize," he says. "Because that would be like Curt Schilling apologizing to the guy he struck out to win a World Series. It doesn't make any sense to apologize for it . . . I do not attach value to a good review or a bad review," he concludes. "I'm interested in what's actually being said—what actually was noticed."

Louis C.K. took a year off from *Louie* in 2013 to take a break and to make movies as an actor, working for his longtime idol Woody Allen in *Blue Jasmine* and for David O. Russell in *American Hustle*. After 2015, he suspended work on *Louie* entirely, focusing instead on co-creating another FX series, Zach Galifianakis's *Baskets,* and his own surprise Internet-delivered miniseries, *Horace and Pete,* with an even darker tone and an amazing cast. *Horace and Pete,* in which he starred opposite Alan Alda, Steve Buscemi, Edie Falco, and Jessica Lange, was set in a bar, filled with angst and dread and uncomfortably funny moments, and played like Louis C.K.'s personal interpretation of Golden Age TV drama and the plays of Eugene O'Neill. The comedian has hosted *Saturday Night Live* several times since 2012, loving every minute of it ("When I got to host *SNL,* every single part of it was fucking magic, and great, and just so meaningful," he says). As for returning to *Louie,* that timetable, like the series itself, is unstructured and impossible to predict.

"I wanted to stay with the original premise," he explains, "which was, 'I don't need this show. If I'm writing it out of need, it's going to mess everything up.'" He acknowledges his responsibilities, to both the actors and the crew members who choose to work with him as well as the employers who bet on him, to keep going, but he also feels a responsibility to be true to the work itself. If other projects such as *Baskets* and *Horace and Pete* excite him more, and if he's not inspired to start work on a season 6 of *Louie,* he won't.

To close the interview, I tell Louis C.K. one anecdotal story about the "violins" scene with Eszter Balint and Ursula Parker in *Louie* and get an even better response in return. I tell him that I visit Berlin each year to teach U.S. television history to international filmmaking and TV postgraduates of Europe's Serial Eyes program and for the past few years have shown that scene from *Louie,* which invariably resonates powerfully with people of very different nationalities and backgrounds and sparks discussions much longer than the scene itself.

"I'm telling you seriously," Louis C.K. says, "if you hadn't written the article you did about *Lucky Louie,* that scene would not have existed. So that's the truth."

KEY EVOLUTIONARY STAGES

The Mary Tyler Moore Show	1970–77, CBS
The Days and Nights of Molly Dodd	1987–88, NBC; 1989–91, Lifetime
Murphy Brown	1988–98, CBS
Sex and the City	1998–2004, HBO
Girls	2012–, HBO

In television's earliest situation comedies, the focus was squarely on family, starting with the modern New York Jewish family of CBS's *Goldbergs* and the period San Francisco Norwegian family of CBS's *Mama,* both premiering in 1949. Women in these shows existed either to feed and care for their families or to be on the lookout for men with whom they could start families of their own. "That is foolishness, all this education for girls," complains Ruth Gates's character, Aunt Jenny, in the 1950 "Queen of the Bee" episode of *Mama.* "All they need is to read the recipes and write their name on the marriage license." *Mama* was set at the turn of the twentieth century, but Aunt Jenny might as well have been speaking for women on TV at mid-century as well. Even Lucille Ball's Lucy Ricardo, who strove at every opportunity on CBS's *I Love Lucy* (1951–57) to break into show business and launch her own career, did so from the comforting confines of her home life, married to Desi Arnaz's Ricky, a successful bandleader and entertainer. Single working women in 1950s TV comedies? They barely existed. On *My Little Margie,* CBS's summer replacement show for *I Love Lucy* in 1952, Gale Storm played a twenty-one-year-old single woman, but she was hardly a role model for independence: she lived with her widower father and spent most of her time trying to disrupt his budding romances. And on the same year's *Our Miss Brooks,* Eve Arden played TV's first prominent single working woman: the high school English teacher Connie Brooks. But even Miss Brooks was depicted as man crazy and marriage obsessed, determined above all else to land her fellow teacher Philip Boynton, which she did, in a 1956 theatrical movie that premiered just as the TV series ended.

If it was an open question, in the 1950s, what many sitcom family dads actually did when they left the house to go to work, there were just as many questions—or should have been—about whether their spouses ever left home at all. From ABC's *Adventures of Ozzie & Harriet* to CBS's *Leave It to Beaver,* and from CBS's *Father Knows Best* to ABC's *Donna Reed Show,* the housewives on those series were precisely that: housebound wives, with a husband and children, but without an outside career or personal ambition.

With limited exceptions, it took another generation for single women to step forward and take center stage. Ann Marie, played by Marlo Thomas in the 1966 ABC series *That Girl,* took the big step—and, on TV, the virtually unprecedented one—of moving from the comfort of her parents' upstate home to the city of New York, in pursuit of her dream of becoming a successful actress. However, she met and attached herself to a boyfriend (Don Hollinger, a young magazine executive played by Ted Bessell) in the very first episode and stayed loyal to him throughout the series, so Ann Marie wasn't really alone in the big city. But it was a start, just as the women's liberation movement was beginning to percolate. And before the decade was out, on 1969's *Room 222* on ABC, Karen Valentine played a young high school teacher who was neither married nor frantically trolling for a husband. That half-hour show, as much drama as comedy, was created by James L. Brooks, who had written two scripts for *That Girl* and whose next television series, co-created with Allan Burns as the flagship inaugural program of a new independent TV company, MTM Productions, would be quietly, yet intentionally and proudly, revolutionary, a major evolutionary leap forward for the depiction of single working women on television.

THE MARY TYLER MOORE SHOW

1970–77, CBS. Creators: James L. Brooks, Allan Burns. Stars: Mary Tyler Moore, Ed Asner, Ted Knight, Gavin MacLeod, Valerie Harper, Cloris Leachman, John Amos, Georgia Engel, Betty White.

In the 1960s, the star of *The Mary Tyler Moore Show* had portrayed one of the most modern and beloved wives and mothers on television: Laura Petrie, wife of the TV variety-show writer Rob Petrie on Carl Reiner's classic 1961–66 CBS sitcom, *The Dick Van Dyke Show*. But in 1970, Mary Tyler Moore launched a new sitcom, as well as a new production company run by her real-life husband, Grant Tinker, that basically changed television, and all for the better. MTM Productions, the name given to the new company, injected sitcoms with a new maturity and cleverness, as with *The Bob Newhart Show*, and pushed the drama series to previously unrealized heights with such programs as *Hill Street Blues* and *St. Elsewhere*. And it all started with *The Mary Tyler Moore Show*, by having its star portray Mary Richards, a single woman who had moved to Minneapolis after ending a

The Mary Tyler Moore Show brought the actress from *The Dick Van Dyke Show* into the center of her own sitcom, which personified the emerging liberated woman. Ed Asner played Lou Grant, her WJM newsroom boss who eventually got his own show as well.

lengthy relationship with a boyfriend, intent upon starting a new life, professionally as well as personally.

"Grant, he's one of the great people," James L. Brooks says of the founder of MTM Productions, adding, "Everybody who ever worked for him loved him." Mary Tyler Moore trusted him with building both a production company for them both and a new situation comedy in which she could star. And Tinker, in turn, trusted Brooks and paired him with his fellow *Room 222* writer Allan Burns, whose other writing credits included *The Bullwinkle Show, Get Smart,* and the vastly underrated *He & She.*

"*The Dick Van Dyke Show* was our gold standard," Brooks admits. He and Burns, tasked with building from scratch a new vehicle for Mary Tyler Moore, knew one thing from the start: she would not be married.

That simple edict led to the groundbreaking aspects of *The Mary Tyler Moore Show*. Moore's Mary Richards dismissed her former boyfriend in the premiere episode and never looked back. Unlike Ann Marie in *That Girl*, Mary Richards never settled snugly with a steady boyfriend and was, in fact, the first female sitcom character known to take birth control pills. And while her first meeting with the WJM newsroom boss, Lou Grant, had its rocky moments ("You've got spunk," Ed Asner's Lou Grant told Mary in the pilot's most famous exchange, then, as she smiled and nodded proudly, snarled, "I hate spunk!"), she held her own, with Lou and with everyone else in the newsroom. One episode, "Chuckles Bites the Dust," relying on Moore's acting skills to giggle, laugh, and sob perfectly on cue, is widely regarded as one of the funniest sitcom episodes of all time and works because of the long-standing relationships among the characters. *The Mary Tyler Moore Show* was about the workplace as family—hardly a new conceit—and even underscored that point by ending, in the final episode, with a group hug. "I treasure you people," Asner's Lou told his WJM colleagues. As did we all. *The Mary Tyler Moore Show* won a total of twenty-nine Emmys, including three for Outstanding Comedy Series, four for Moore, and three for Asner.

The spin-offs for *The Mary Tyler Moore Show* were many, giving solo vehicles to three supporting characters: Phyllis, Rhoda, and Lou Grant. But where Rhoda, played by Valerie Harper, eventually married and divorced once she got her own series, Mary Richards stayed single, and independent, throughout. *Lou Grant* made TV history in a different way, by becoming a dramatic spin-off of a comedy series and paving the way for such subsequent MTM Productions hours, lacing comedy in with the drama, as *Hill*

Street Blues. *The Mary Tyler Moore Show,* however, made TV history merely by having its heroine be, and stay, happily single and professionally dedicated throughout.

After *The Mary Tyler Moore Show* advanced the cause of the independent working woman, another CBS sitcom put forth the proposition that working women could be even more formidable, and successful, by working together. *Designing Women,* which ran from 1986 to 1993, starred Dixie Carter as Julia Sugarbaker, a widow who teamed with her sister Suzanne (Delta Burke) and two female friends (played by Jean Smart and Annie Potts) to open an interior decorating firm in Atlanta. Many scenes had the women, in various combinations and often all together, discussing issues and problems, including, but not limited to, the men in their lives: *Designing Women* would have easily passed the Bechdel test (in a work of fiction, do two women conversing talk about anything other than men?), which was introduced by the cartoonist Alison Bechdel only the year before *Designing Women* premiered. And *Designing Women* was a feminist advancement behind the scenes as well: its creator was a woman, the writer-producer Linda Bloodworth-Thomason. Though, strictly speaking, you didn't have to be a woman to write a significant sitcom about working women, as Jay Tarses, the former writer for *The Bob Newhart Show, The Carol Burnett Show,* and *Buffalo Bill,* proved in 1987 with NBC's *Days and Nights of Molly Dodd.*

THE DAYS AND NIGHTS OF MOLLY DODD

1987–88, NBC; 1989–91, Lifetime. Creator: Jay Tarses. Stars: Blair Brown, Allyn Ann McLerie, James Greene, David Strathairn, William Converse-Roberts, Richard Lawson, Victor Garber, Jay Tarses.

In TV evolution terms, *The Days and Nights of Molly Dodd* could almost be considered a missing link. So few people remember it, it may not seem to deserve such prominent placement in the pantheon of single working women on TV, but it does. Molly Dodd, the thirtysomething character played by Blair Brown in this 1987 NBC series, was a single woman in New York, ultimately working in the publishing industry, and making her way through a slew of tumultuous romantic relationships, long before either

The Days and Nights of Molly Dodd starred Blair Brown as a divorced woman in New York making her way while surrounded by family, friends, and new lovers.

Carrie Bradshaw of HBO's *Sex and the City* or Hannah Horvath of HBO's *Girls*. And after NBC canceled *The Days and Nights of Molly Dodd,* the Lifetime network picked it up and produced additional episodes, making it one of the first TV series to move from broadcast to cable television. The real advancements of *Molly Dodd,* however, were that Molly Dodd, unlike Mary Richards, was divorced and that neither Molly nor her employment status was particularly stable. Molly kept reinventing herself, changing jobs, and checking out potential suitors with delightful unpredictability. More than forty years later, this approach to employers, and to relationships, still seemed fresh when applied to such drama series as CBS's *Good Wife*. On a sitcom in the 1980s it was bold enough to be almost brazen. On *Molly Dodd,* all this was presented in a markedly unusual way, especially on broadcast television: with no laugh track, with Molly's hovering mother (Allyn Ann McLerie) providing opening narration, and with Patrick Williams's jazzy theme song providing the perfect accompaniment to the evocative opening-credits images of Molly in and around New York City.

Over the course of the series, Molly had relationships with a few different men, demonstrating very good, yet very varied, tastes. She still got along well with her man-child ex-husband, an irresponsible jazz musician played by William Converse-Roberts. She had been the vocalist in his band but moved on to sell real estate, then books. She accepted a job, and became involved, with a meek but clever and quietly charming Greenwich Village bookstore owner played by David Strathairn. Then she found work as an assistant editor at a publishing house while dating a police detective named Nathaniel Hawthorne. She had an unplanned pregnancy with Nate, and after he died suddenly (not in the line of duty, but because of an allergic reaction to something he ate), Molly decided to bring the baby to term and raise it as a single mom. This was during the show's final season, on Lifetime, and is significant because it took place on TV in 1991—a year before the then vice president, Dan Quayle, denounced another single female sitcom character, the titular newswoman of CBS's *Murphy Brown*, for precisely the same decision. And Molly's late boyfriend was African-American, which might or might not have incensed Quayle even more. *The Days and Nights of Molly Dodd*, though, never got the attention it deserved, not even from a politician looking to position himself as a champion of "family values." *Murphy Brown*, though, was an entirely different matter . . .

MURPHY BROWN

1988–98, CBS. Creator: Diane English. Stars: Candice Bergen, Joe Regalbuto, Faith Ford, Charles Kimbrough, Grant Shaud.

The CBS comedy *Murphy Brown*, like *The Mary Tyler Moore Show*, was set in the world of television news: in this case, a weekly newsmagazine show called *F.Y.I.*, emanating from Washington, D.C., starring Candice Bergen as the veteran news interviewer and reporter Murphy Brown. Modeled partly after ABC's Barbara Walters in terms of celebrity status and CBS's Mike Wallace in terms of tenacity and clout, Murphy Brown had other attributes that made her stand out instantly as a sitcom character. For one thing, she was a woman who was clearly and indisputably in charge, often as tough on her staff as she was on her interviewees. For another, the premiere episode had her returning to the TV news operation after a stint in rehab at the Betty Ford Clinic for alcohol dependence. That, right there, is the sort of personality flaw that would never have been considered, much less approved, as a starting point for Mary Richards on *The Mary Tyler Moore Show*. Murphy was allowed to have a dark side and display some unlikable, less than role model tendencies. Here, again, was an evolutionary sitcom continuum in action, with *Murphy Brown* coming after another ill-tempered TV personality, Dabney Coleman on *Buffalo Bill* (1983, NBC), but before Garry Shandling's similarly bullying and self-absorbed TV host on HBO's *Larry Sanders Show,* starting in 1992. Television writer-producers and network executives were beginning to accept that viewers could embrace even centrally featured characters not only in spite of their flaws but sometimes because of them.

Not every viewer, however, was equally tolerant. *Murphy Brown* had premiered on CBS in the fall of 1988, just as a national election would hand the country's reins from the two-term Republican president, Ronald Reagan, to his second-in-command, George H. W. Bush. When Bush ran for reelection in 1992 (a contest that would eventually be won by the Democratic challenger, Bill Clinton), his second-in-command, Vice President Dan Quayle, made national headlines by targeting the *Murphy Brown* series and character during a May campaign speech in San Francisco. "It doesn't help matters," Quayle told the crowd and the country, "when prime-time

Murphy Brown was the story of a high-profile TV news anchor, fresh from rehab who was both dependent upon and caustic to her workplace family.

TV has Murphy Brown—a character who supposedly epitomizes today's intelligent, highly paid professional woman—mocking the importance of fathers by bearing a child alone and calling it just another 'lifestyle choice.'" When *Murphy Brown* returned with its season premiere that September, the series creator, Diane English, fired a return salvo by having Bergen's Murphy watch Quayle's speech on her own TV, then reply in kind on her own forum, the fictional *F.Y.I.* newsmagazine. "These are difficult times for our country," Murphy Brown told her audience. "And in searching for the causes of our social ills, we could choose to blame the media, or the Congress, or an administration that's been in power for twelve years. Or we could blame me." Overall, though, Murphy Brown got more praise than blame: Bergen won five Emmys for playing the role, and the series itself was awarded Outstanding Comedy Series twice.

The 1990s was a decade in which TV women, for some reason, were not only equated with social ills but discussed in terms more suited to flesh-and-blood newsmakers than wholly fictional characters. The Fox series *Ally McBeal*, starring Calista Flockhart as a young attorney, was a one-hour comedy-drama, not a half-hour sitcom, but certainly deserves mention in this historical and evolutionary context. Ally McBeal, in this playful 1997–2002 series created by David E. Kelley of NBC's *L.A. Law* and CBS's *Picket Fences*, was feisty in and out of court; like Mary Richards on *The Mary Tyler Moore Show*, Ally McBeal had "spunk." She also had an active imagination, vividly conveyed by a series of quick-cut fantasy images from Ally's point of view: arrows shot into her heart, animated dancing babies, and so on. Yet Ally, as a TV character, was also in some ways a throwback. She was as boyfriend obsessed as Eve Arden's Connie Brooks of *Our Miss Brooks* and as fond of short skirts and flattering, eye-catching outfits as Marlo Thomas's Ann Marie of *That Girl*. Rather than frame Ally McBeal in those contextual TV terms, however, *Time* magazine put her picture—Flockhart's picture, actually, though identified only as Ally McBeal—on its cover in 1998, as the last of four head shots arranged chronologically from left to right. The four women whose faces adorned that *Time* cover were, in order, Susan B. Anthony, Betty Friedan, Gloria Steinem, and Ally McBeal, under whose photograph was the cover story headline, "Is Feminism Dead?" The fictional Ally McBeal, sharing space with those three very real feminists, was a straw man—or, very pointedly, a straw woman—derided for her short skirts, her obsession with men and romance, and her often flighty personal fantasies. *Time* missed the point, but not television. Regarding the question "Is feminism dead?" the answer in TV terms, then and since, was no.

SEX AND THE CITY

1998–2004, HBO. Creator: Darren Star. Stars: Sarah Jessica Parker, Kim Cattrall, Kristin Davis, Cynthia Nixon, Chris Noth, John Corbett.

Here was a sitcom that, like *Designing Women,* specialized in putting a quartet of opinionated women together in one place and having them discuss their opinions. The difference with *Sex and the City,* inspired by the *New York Observer* Sex and the City columns by Candace Bushnell, was that much of the dialogue—like much of the action—was sexually related. Taking full advantage of the latitude provided by premium cable TV, HBO's *Sex and the City,* created by Darren Star, came out swinging and fixated as much on dating misadventures as designer shoes. Sarah Jessica Parker starred as Bushnell's fictional counterpart, the sex columnist Carrie Bradshaw, who, like her three best friends, began the series single and working in Manhattan. Miranda (Cynthia Nixon) was a lawyer, Charlotte (Kristin Davis) an art gallery manager, and Samantha (Kim Cattrall) an independent publicist.

Their adventures, misadventures, and reactions to life and love were undeniably and unprecedentedly modern, opening up a new world of possibilities to HBO and other unfettered comedy shows. In one episode, Carrie was in bed with a politician boyfriend, played by John Slattery (later and better known as Roger Sterling on AMC's *Mad Men*), when he revealed his secret fantasy to her: to take a shower together and have her urinate on him. In another episode, Samantha was babysitting Miranda's baby when its vibrating chair broke down, and Samantha resourcefully solved the problem, and soothed the infant, by activating her just-purchased vibrator and placing it next to him. Both plot points, in TV history terms, were absolute firsts.

When the four ladies were together, they mostly talked about men and sex and workplace inequities. And when they didn't, Carrie did, in voice-over narration quoting from her columns. *Sex and the City* gave voice to women in a literal and literary sense, by letting Carrie the writer have the last word on everything that happened to her and her friends (when she wrote about her politician boyfriend's unusual request, it was under the headline "To Pee or Not to Pee?"). Each character was different, ranging from Charlotte's prim shyness to Samantha's adventurous aggressiveness, but all of them supported, backed, and defended the others, consuming gallons of Cosmopolitans in the process. It's worth noting, too, that Candice Bergen, who played the proudly feminist Murphy Brown, guest starred on *Sex and the City* several times, in a recurring role as Enid, an editor from *Vogue*.

Some of the women in this sitcom did have ongoing or recurring relationships throughout the show's six-year run, most notably Carrie's on-again, off-again fixation with the wealthy gentleman she nicknamed Mr. Big. Played by Chris Noth, Mr. Big ended the series by following Carrie to Paris and revealing his love for her. They eventually married, but that event was saved for one of the subsequent *Sex and the City* theatrical movies. When the TV series ended in 2004, Carrie was still single but had shown a new generation of single working women how to conduct themselves, especially on TV, and especially in New York City.

Sex and the City was the story of four female friends in New York and how their careers and love lives changed over the years. Featured were (from left) Cynthia Nixon as Miranda, Kristin Davis as Charlotte, Kim Cattrall as Samantha, and series star Sarah Jessica Parker as sex columnist Carrie Bradshaw.

. . .

NBC's *30 Rock,* which premiered in 2006, wasn't so much about being a single woman in New York, though many plots and subplots centered on that, as it was about being a woman producing a live TV show in New York. Tina Fey, coming off her experience as head writer and cast member of NBC's *Saturday Night Live,* did what Carl Reiner had done after *Your Show of Shows* in creating *The Dick Van Dyke Show:* write what you know. What she knew was the crazy atmosphere of creating a live TV show in 30 Rockefeller Center, so she created and starred in a sitcom about precisely that. *30 Rock* starred Fey as Liz Lemon, executive producer of an NBC live talk-and-variety show. Alec Baldwin co-starred as her very corporate, politically conservative boss, and the co-stars on her live TV show were played by Tracy Morgan and, from *Ally McBeal,* Jane Krakowski. *30 Rock* won three Emmys as Outstanding Comedy Series, and Fey also won for both acting and writing. By both creating and starring in her own sitcom, Fey was carrying on in the tradition of Gertrude Berg in *The Goldbergs* but doing so in a much less traditional role: she might have been the matriarch who kept her family going, but in *30 Rock* it was a workplace family—like the WJM newsroom on *The Mary Tyler Moore Show,* only even more dysfunctional. Fey's Liz Lemon was as flawed and self-deluded as anyone around her, and her romantic relationships, while sporadic, were also laughably mismatched and ultimately doomed. Fey seemed to revel in the frequent uncomfortable embarrassment of the character she created and played, but she was soon to be outdone, in that regard, by yet another female sitcom creator who starred in her own series.

GIRLS

2012–, HBO. Creator: Lena Dunham. Stars: Lena Dunham, Allison Williams, Jemima Kirke, Zosia Mamet, Adam Driver.

Like *Sex and the City,* the HBO sitcom *Girls* is about a group of single friends in New York, wending their way through various jobs, triumphs, travails, and relationships. Specifically, it's about Lena Dunham's Hannah Horvath, a woman who hopes to use her writing talent and observational skills to become, as Lena boasts while high on opium in the 2012 premiere episode of *Girls,* "the voice of my generation—or, at least, a voice of a generation." The huge difference between Carrie on *Sex and the City* and Hannah on *Girls,* though, is that Sarah Jessica Parker was merely playing a generational voice. Lena Dunham, who created *Girls* and has written more than two dozen episodes to date, and directed more than a dozen, truly is a generational voice.

In *Girls,* Hannah and her twentysomething friends—Allison Williams as Marnie, Jemima Kirke as Jessa, and Zosia Mamet as Shoshanna—give voice, often loudly, to the particular aims, dreams, frustrations, and problems of their generation (broadly, the millennials). Mary Richards never had to worry about the cruelty of anonymously posted website comments or the particular rituals and occasional humiliations of online dating and casual texting and sexting, but Hannah and her friends do. In their private lives, they push the envelope beyond even what *Sex and the City* explored, and do so without worrying if it made their characters look insecure or unsympathetic. In fact, Adam Driver, as Hannah's sometime boyfriend Adam, is portrayed with just as much neediness and selfishness as Hannah, and their conversations, like their sexual encounters, can seem almost painfully intimate and awkward to witness. And friendships, on *Girls,* aren't locked in for

Girls not only tells the story of single women in New York but was created, and sometimes written and directed, by its star, Lena Dunham, who plays aspiring writer Hannah Horvath.

life: in another concession to reality, these girls disappoint one another at times, fight vigorously, and even hold grudges for a while. Such is life, and such is the evolution of the complex portrayals of women on television, even in situation comedies.

And the genre continues to evolve, with more female voices, and more unusual perspectives, being explored. In the year 2015 alone, several new sitcoms, and the entities presenting them, demonstrated the depth of both the concept and the market for comedies about independent, single working women. *Younger,* on TV Land, presented the Broadway star Sutton Foster as Liza Miller, a forty-year-old having no luck reentering the workplace until a friend gives her a makeover so she can pass for twenty-six, which she does, successfully, by lying on her job application. It's a comedy by Darren Star, creator of *Sex and the City.* Another series introduced in 2015 was CW's *Crazy Ex-girlfriend,* starring Rachel Bloom—who co-created the series with the *Devil Wears Prada* screenwriter, Aline Brosh McKenna—as a successful young lawyer who leaves her New York law firm impulsively, turning down an offer to become partner, to follow a former flame when he tells her he's moving back to his childhood home in West Covina, California. It runs counter to the directions taken by both Mary Richards and Ally McBeal, who changed cities to be away from their boyfriends and pursue professional careers, but it's all done from a decidedly female viewpoint and is a musical to boot.

And finally, also in 2015, there was the premiere of *Unbreakable Kimmy Schmidt,* a Netflix series co-created by Tina Fey and her *30 Rock* show runner, Robert Carlock. Ellie Kemper, from NBC's *Office,* stars in the title role, playing a twenty-nine-year-old who, like Molly Dodd and Liz Lemon and Carrie Bradshaw and Hannah Horvath, has ventured to New York in search of fame and fortune, or at least happiness. The difference with Kimmy Schmidt is her backstory: for the past fifteen years, she'd been held captive in Indiana, along with three other women, by a doomsday cult fanatic. She's determined to have a better and happier life and eventually finds employment in New York as a nanny, working for a flighty socialite played by Jane Krakowski, who's already co-starred in two other female-empowerment sitcoms, *Ally McBeal* and *30 Rock.* All three of these 2015 series demonstrate that on television, and especially on TV comedies, single working women have come a long way, baby.

JUDD APATOW

BORN: 1967, Queens, New York.

FIRST TV CREDIT: Stand-up comic, *Comic Strip Live,* 1988, Fox.

LANDMARK TV SERIES: Writer, director, and co-executive and consulting producer, *The Larry Sanders Show,* 1993–98, HBO; Executive producer, director, and writer, *Freaks and Geeks,* 1999–2000, NBC; Executive producer and writer, *Girls,* 2012–, HBO.

OTHER MAJOR CREDITS: Movies: Producer, *The Cable Guy,* 1996; Producer and actor, *Anchorman: The Legend of Ron Burgundy,* 2004; Producer, director, and co-writer, *The 40-Year-Old Virgin,* 2005; Producer, writer, and director, *Knocked Up,* 2007; Producer, *Superbad,* 2007; Producer and co-writer, *The Dewey Cox Story,* 2007; Producer, *Forgetting Sarah Marshall,* 2008; Writer, producer, director, *Funny People,* 2009; Producer, *Get Him to the Greek,* 2010; Producer, *Bridesmaids,* 2011; Producer, writer, and director, *This Is 40,* 2012; Producer, *Anchorman 2: The Legend Continues,* 2013; Producer and director, *Trainwreck,* 2015; Producer, *Pee-Wee's Big Holiday,* 2016. TV: Co-creator, writer, and actor, *The Ben Stiller Show,* 1992–93, Fox; Writer and consulting producer, *The Critic,* 1994–95, Fox; Creator, writer, and director, *Undeclared,* 2001–3, Fox; Guest writer, "Bart's New Friend" episode, *The Simpsons,* 2015, Fox; Executive producer and writer, *Love,* 2016–, Netflix.

When doing interviews for this book, I spoke with a couple of people who I felt could have saved me a lot of trouble by writing the book themselves. The FX programming executive John Landgraf was one, because he seemed so highly attuned to the evolution of quality TV shows, whether or not he played a part in developing them. Another was Judd Apatow, whose appetite for quality TV, like his appetite for Saturday morning sugarcoated cereal, was voracious. And Apatow did write a book, though it's his, not mine. In 2015, he published *Sick in the Head: Conversations About Life and Comedy,* a collection of interviews with comedians that he'd been conducting and recording since he was fifteen, on the pretense of airing them on a Long Island FM radio station—without mentioning that the station was based in his Syosset high school. He found, in these interviews, many patient kindred spirits. "My whole life," he writes in *Sick in the Head,* "I'd wanted friends who had similar interests and a similar worldview, people I could talk with about Monty Python and *SCTV*." And he found them, including many of the same artists I spoke to for *The Platinum Age of Television,* such as Mel Brooks and James L. Brooks, whose styles of comedy Apatow grew up absorbing and adoring.

"In my home, when we were kids," says Apatow, who was born in 1967 in Flushing, Queens, "what we were told from day one was that Mel Brooks was the funniest man in the world. It was never debated, you know? There was comedy, and then there was this strange man who was better at it than everybody." Apatow was too young to experience *Your Show of Shows,* the classic 1950s Sid Caesar sketch series for which Brooks wrote, until he saw kinescopes years later, and enjoyed *Get Smart* reruns without connecting them with Brooks, who had co-created the 1960s spy spoof comedy. "But I knew Mel," Apatow clarifies, "from his '2000 Year Old Man' appearances and his appearances on talk shows . . . And I always loved his confidence. He never looked like it was even possible for him to get nervous. There's no aspect of him that feels like he's going to melt down from nerves. He's on the attack the whole time." And to Apatow, watching Mel Brooks killing the audience on *The David Susskind Show* and *The Mike Douglas Show,* it was not only funny; it was inspirational.

"He was quicker than anybody," Apatow recalls. "And it was only later that I understood all that he had done as a writer, director, and producer, in addition to being a performer. And I looked up to that, because he was an odd Jewish man like myself, who found a way to make a comfortable living, you know, writing really silly things. And in a way, that was my dream: Oh! You can be the writer and the director, and be funny on talk shows, and occasionally act. It seemed like the perfect type of career to aspire to."

Apatow, in time, would achieve precisely that sort of career—producing *Bridesmaids* and *Superbad,* directing and co-writing *The 40-Year-Old Virgin,* acting in *Anchorman: The Legend of Ron Burgundy,* and making talk-show appearances with everyone from Stephen Colbert and Jimmy Fallon to Jon Stewart and Larry Wilmore. But before that, he wrote for and worked in television, and before that he watched television. A lot. And, like so many others interviewed for this book, he started watching early.

"When I was a kid," Apatow recalls, "you get up six thirty, seven o'clock in the morning, and you would watch TV till noon or one every Saturday and Sunday. I don't think I even considered leaving the house. I think my parents were very happy not to have to deal with me. Now that I'm a parent, I understand that." His weekend morning TV diet was the usual mixture of cartoons and old movies, but his actual diet, while sitting in front of the TV watching *Mighty Mouse* cartoons and all those Sid and Marty Krofft shows, was decidedly unusual. "When I look back on it now," he says, laughing, "the amount of sugar I was eating was just terrifying. I would have Rice Krispies. I would pour sugar over the surface, so the entire surface was covered with sugar. And then I would eat the top level of Rice Krispies. Then I would take the sugar, and I would create another surface, and then eat the next level of Rice Krispies. And I would continue to do that until the Rice Krispies were gone, and the milk sat over, like, two inches high of a sugar mountain—which I would then drink and eat."

Young Apatow's tastes in breakfast foods may be alarming, but his appetite for television, once he started watching prime-time TV, was more that of a gourmet. And that's when another Brooks, the comedy writer-producer James L. Brooks, became another prominent and significant early influence.

"I feel like my brain was programmed by James Brooks, Norman Lear, and Larry Gelbart, you know? That's what we watched at our house," Apatow tells me, singling out Brooks's *Mary Tyler Moore Show* as "the first bit of quality television that I watched and understood." Watching those MTM Productions of the 1970s, in the Apatow household, was nothing short of a family tradition. With *The Mary Tyler Moore Show,* he recalls, "We watched it as a family and laughed our asses off, and then we would watch *Rhoda* and all the spin-off shows—because, at one time or another, most of those characters had a show for a period of time . . . And I loved *Lou Grant.* I think I probably watched every single episode of *Lou Grant* as a kid in junior high school." He pauses and adds, "It was a very, very political show. It went for very serious issues. We need a show like that now," he says, laughing. He also recalls, quite fondly, watching *Kolchak: The Night Stalker* (an ABC precursor to *The X-Files*) and an early James Brooks show, *Room 222*. A particular family favorite was *Taxi,* yet another James Brooks series that, Apatow says, "really made us laugh." He recalls, in particular, an episode in which Christopher Lloyd, as the spaced-out former hippie Reverend Jim, attends a posh party with the other cabbies, sits down at a piano to play, bangs at the keyboard horribly, and then, as Apatow finishes the story, "he takes a beat, and then he plays the most difficult piano concerto. And then he pauses, and he looks up, and he goes, 'I must have had lessons!' And I don't know if I've ever heard my dad laugh harder."

That period of television viewing, Apatow admits, taught him two major lessons: to accept and pursue the idea of spin-offs, and to focus on a quieter, simple type of comedy. He's even done spin-offs of his own movies— taking supporting characters played by Paul Rudd and Leslie Mann in 2007's *Knocked Up* and focusing on them alone in 2012's *This Is 40*. "This is our *Lou Grant!*" Apatow proclaims proudly, adding, "And we did it with [2010's] *Get Him to the Greek,*" promoting a rock-star supporting character from 2008's *Forgetting Sarah Marshall*. "We liked Russell Brand's character, and we said, 'What if we do a spin-off?' And that was heavily influenced by all the James Brooks spin-offs," Apatow admits. "If you have a great character, well, why not tell their story? There's no reason why these things can't drift off. So when you see things like *Better Call Saul* [Vince Gilligan's spin-off of his *Breaking Bad*], that's my favorite thing in the world. I want every show to do that." Then, referring to one of his favorite James Brooks shows, *Taxi,* Apatow adds, "I'd love to see the Reverend Jim show!"

Apatow sees a straight line from the comedies he watched on TV as a youngster and the ones he made, on TV and in the movies, as an adult. "You know, I always liked stories about the underdogs," he says, "and in my work I think I was influenced to tell stories about people who are, like, the friends of the lead. And that's what I thought *Taxi* was. The whole show was filled with people who become friends with the star of the show, and I think that's what I've tried to do in my movies. These are the sidekicks, but what if you followed them?"

Taxi also exemplified the other comedy element Apatow took to heart from watching all those old James Brooks shows: its heart. "The thing I loved about those old James Brooks shows was, they were about life," Apatow says. "And it was honest and emotional and really funny. They weren't afraid to tear down the house, but they always had this grace note, at the end of episodes, where people would make a connection, or a lesson was learned, or something magical happened. And I thought, 'Oh, that's the type of writing I want to do.'"

So he did it. And he did it by studying comedy—first on his own, at an absurdly young age. At age fifteen, as a junior high student in Syosset, New York, he went to New York City in 1983 to record his first interview for his own school FM radio show, which he called *Club Comedy*. His first interview was with Steve Allen, a fairly lofty place to start. Three years later, he got a job as a dishwasher at a comedy club, with an eye on breaking in as a stand-up comic, which he did, briefly. He moved west to study film and screenwriting at the University of Southern California but also dabbled in stand-up, where he met Adam Sandler at the Improv and, after dropping out of USC, became his roommate and pursued stand-up comedy more aggressively. His first TV credits were doing stand-up, for Fox's *Comic Strip Live* in 1988 and Comedy Central's *Johnnie Walker National Comedy Search* in 1990, and writing comedy material for HBO's *Tom Arnold: The Naked Truth* special in 1991. But at the same time, he was continuing to learn about comedy writing, with his own self-taught syllabus, drawn from the TV shows he loved most growing up.

"I spent my whole life watching all these sitcoms," Apatow says, rattling off such names as *All in the Family, M*A*S*H,* and *The Bob Newhart Show,* "and I had never thought about how they were made . . . And then, when I decided to become a writer, the first thing I did was, I had someone hunt down a dozen episodes of *Taxi*—a dozen of the teleplays. And I read them, and I outlined them, and I tried to figure out how they worked. I studied them. It wasn't in a class; I just broke them down, created beat sheets. I tried to figure out, when do they move from the 'A' story to the 'B' story? How are they resolving these stories? How many scenes in each mini-arc are there? And I noticed that there was a structure that was pretty consistent in most of the episodes, so I wrote an episode of *The Simpsons* [then in its first season] on spec and an episode of [Fox's 1990 Chris Elliott sitcom] *Get a Life* on spec," he says, referring to the practice of writing an unsolicited, unpaid script of an existing series as a writing sample for prospective employers. "And I couldn't get anyone to hire me." (That *Simpsons* spec script from 1990, however, has an ultimately happy ending: decades later, when the then-successful Apatow mentioned that spec script once on a TV talk show, he was contacted by *The Simpsons*, and his rewritten script, twenty-five years later, was the basis of the 2015 episode "Bart's New Friend," in which Homer is hypnotized into believing he's ten years old and temporarily stuck at that age.)

So Apatow created an opportunity by teaming up with a fellow young comedian to co-create a new show for the Fox network: *The Ben Stiller Show*, a clever, ambitious 1992–93 sketch comedy series co-starring Stiller, Janeane Garofalo, and Andy Dick, with a writing staff that included Stiller, Apatow, Garofalo, Bob Odenkirk, and David Cross. "He did these high-end parodies," Apatow recalls, describing a couple of the still memorable ones: a monster-filled parody of Woody Allen's *Husbands and Wives* reimagined as Woody Allen's *Bride of Frankenstein,* or Oliver Stone showing off his new theme park, Oliver Stone Land, with such attractions as the Hall of Conspiracies. "We used to say some of these sketches are like *SCTV* if they had money," Apatow says, laughing, but *SCTV*, an obvious inspiration for Apatow and for *The Ben Stiller Show*, was great at mounting elaborate mash-up parodies of its own, as when *SCTV* crossed the Bob Hope–Bing Crosby road pictures with Woody Allen's *Play It Again, Sam* for a lengthy "Play It Again, Bob" sketch in which Allen is teamed with Hope and haunted by the ghost of Crosby. *The Ben Stiller Show* lasted only four months, but after its cancellation Apatow and the rest of the team won the 1993 Emmy Award for Outstanding Writing in a Variety or Music Program.

One of the guest hosts on *The Ben Stiller Show* had been Garry Shandling, who offered Apatow one of his two next jobs: working as a consultant and writer on Shandling's new HBO series, *The Larry Sanders Show*. The other job, offered simultaneously, was writing for *The Critic*, the animated comedy from the *Simpsons* writer-producers Al Jean and Mike Reiss, with Apatow's comedy idol, James Brooks, as one of the executive producers. Apatow desperately wanted to take them both, so he did. Because Jean and Reiss also worked for Shandling on *The Larry Sanders Show*, they all worked out a very unusual deal.

"So what I did was," Apatow explains, "two days a week I worked at *The Larry Sanders Show*, and two days a week I worked for *The Critic*. And that was the main year of education for me, because I was watching Garry rewrite scripts, and then I was watching Mike and Al rewrite scripts, and James Brooks give notes. And I did soak it up like a sponge." Apatow's approach was to always be as helpful as possible, contributing jokes and staying positive, and to learn. From Shandling, Apatow says he learned a lot, including a way to find humor through honesty. "Garry's whole thing was about truth—getting to the emotional core of people," he explains. "And asking, 'What would really happen in the situation?' If Hank [Larry's talk-show sidekick, played by Jeffrey Tambor] wants more money in his contract, would Larry [the talk-show host, played by Shandling] go to the network and say, 'Give him more money'? Or would he think that was unethical? And how would it affect Larry's relationship with him if he gets involved in this deal? And so, we had very deep conversations about human behavior, and when that was figured out, it was much easier to write the comedy."

Apatow managed to direct an episode of *The Larry Sanders Show* before it ended in 1998. He also found time, by then, to produce the Jim Carrey movie *The Cable Guy,* directed by and co-starring his old TV boss Ben Stiller, and to marry the film's female lead, Leslie Mann, whom he would later cast in such films as *The 40-Year-Old Virgin, Knocked Up,* and *This Is 40.* Before that, though, she appeared in one episode of the next TV series her husband produced for television: the 1999 NBC cult favorite *Freaks and Geeks,* created by Paul Feig (later the director of *Bridesmaids* and the dis-taff remake of *Ghostbusters*) and set at a suburban Michigan high school in 1980. *Freaks and Geeks* used period music perfectly and imaginatively, told its stories in an understated and intelligent manner, and managed to cast an impressive roster of future movie and TV stars, many of whom would come to prominence in films produced or directed by Judd Apatow. Cast members playing the high schoolers included Seth Rogen, Jason Segel, James Franco, Linda Cardellini, John Francis Daley, Samm Levine, Martin Starr, and Busy Phillips.

"We looked at *Freaks and Geeks* like they were little movies," Apatow says. "Paul wrote something that was very cinematic, and I was highly influenced by movies like *Fast Times at Ridgemont High* and *Welcome to the Doll-house,* and I had just come off *The Larry Sanders Show.* And I had learned so much from Garry [Shandling] that I felt like I had Garry's voice in my head when we did *Freaks and Geeks.* I had just spent so much time with him, and I really, intuitively understood what questions he would ask of scripts and how he would approach story problems. So the way I personally approached *Freaks and Geeks* was, I pretended I was still doing *The Larry Sanders Show,* except it was in high school." Another inside secret: the cast came first, the final script second. "Paul, [the director] Jake Kasdan, and I auditioned people with generic themes, and we had hundreds of people read the same themes," Apatow explains. "And then, when we found the people we liked, Paul went off and rewrote the whole pilot and tailored it to these actors and actresses that we had fallen in love with."

One of those actors was Seth Rogen, who at age sixteen, playing the character of the amiable misfit Ken Miller, expressed such natural ability and innate sensitivity that the show's creative team handed him a very daunting challenge near the end of the series run. After receiving its cancellation notice, the *Freaks and Geeks* team went for broke, and for one of its final episodes, titled "The Little Things," had Rogen's Ken contemplate breaking up with his girlfriend, Amy, after she reveals to him that she was born with both male and female genitalia. "It's a fascinating episode," Apatow says after I compliment it highly. "And how that episode happened was, I was listening to Howard Stern [on the radio], and they had someone on, talking about being born with ambiguous genitalia, and how the doctor had to choose the sex. This is before people talked about the transgender issue, and it sounded really interesting." Apatow suggested the idea to the writing staff, most of whom counseled against doing it ("They didn't think we could pull it off"), but they moved forward, Apatow admits, for two main reasons. "We wanted to do work we were proud of—provocative work," Apatow says, then reveals the other reason. "We knew we were about to be canceled," he says, adding, "So, in a way, it was confrontational with the network. 'Oh, you don't like our show? Well, now we're going to do this!' And we're really proud of it."

Apatow made only one other TV series, Fox's *Undeclared* in 2001, before embarking on his string of high-profile movie hits. In spirit, the series was *Freaks and Geeks* set at college, with Jay Baruchel starring as an incoming freshman and with Rogen, from *Freaks and Geeks*, along for the ride. It, too, was clever, very good, and criminally unnoticed. Like *Freaks and Geeks*, it lasted less than a season. After it was canceled, the R-rated comedy smash *Anchorman: The Legend of Ron Burgundy*, and a new phase of Apatow's career, were right around the corner. He wouldn't return to TV, and the sitcom form, for almost a decade, but when he did, it was a significant return, helping to bring HBO's *Girls*, created by Lena Dunham, to the small screen. Dunham, Apatow, and Jenni Konner are the show's executive producers, and the casting process, which yielded a strong group of markedly diverse personalities and talents, was similar to the open-ended one employed on *Freaks and Geeks*. The story of *Girls* tells of Hannah Horvath, a young woman and wannabe writer played by Dunham, and her circle of friends in and around New York, trying to succeed in various professions and relationships. The series is both emotionally honest and strikingly unpredictable, and, according to Apatow, a lot of that began in the casting sessions, looking for the actors who would end up interacting with Dunham's Hannah.

He explains his casting process, in general and in relation to *Girls*, this way: "We have an idea for the show and the characters, but we're willing to toss out a lot of it if we stumble upon an incredible actor or personality." Then he offers an example: "We didn't know we were going to find somebody exactly like Adam Driver [who plays Adam, Hannah's on-again, off-again boyfriend] when Lena and Jenni and I were looking at people for *Girls*. And, you know, he came in—it was supposed to be a character that might be on a few episodes, we didn't have a long-term vision for that character—and when we saw him, we all thought, 'Oh, this is what the show is about.' In addition to everything else, it's just a big part of this show. But that's only possible because the philosophy is that finding the right actors, and character, is as important as the thing you wrote alone, in your room, in your underwear."

As for the distinctive tone of the writing Lena Dunham established at the start of *Girls*, which premiered on HBO to great acclaim in 2012, Apatow concludes by noting, "Well, I think we were very aware of *Sex and the City* when Lena was writing the pilot. And then we were kicking it around, and certainly *Ally McBeal* was a show that, you know, was a major cultural event." Those shows, he notes, were about women with already defined career paths—a columnist, an attorney—but why not have a show about people who haven't made those choices yet, at least not successfully?

"I don't want to speak for Lena and Jenni," Apatow says, "but I feel like, in some sense, we were trying to flip all of that. So it would be the opposite of a show about, you know, a lawyer with some relationship problems, or a journalist and their personal life. For this person, the career thing is not working at all . . .

"What we were thinking about was, what is truthful for this moment in time and for this generation? And how is this generation of women different from other generations? And part of what we found fun about it, at the start, was writing about people that don't have their shit together in any aspect, personally or professionally. People who are lost. So at the start, what

Lena saw it as was that moment when you've been out of school for a few years, and things should be beginning to fall together properly, and they're just not." He points to the plot of the premiere episode, which begins with Hannah asking her parents for money to support her while she continues an unpaid internship in New York and ends with her reading samples of her writing to them in hopes of persuading them to invest in her future. Both times, they refuse.

"And then the pilot's over," Apatow says, laughing. "That's the whole pilot. 'Can I have money?' 'No.' Then, at the end, 'Can I have money?' 'No.' And that's what we thought set it apart from all of those other shows, which is: This is a generation of people who are both very smart, but a lot of them are very spoiled. They have a sense of entitlement. They see enormous things for themselves, but they don't necessarily want to do all the work it would take to accomplish those things. They're a scrambled mess a lot of the time—and their journey to figure themselves out might be a more complicated one than it has been for people in the past."

SCI-FI/FANTASY/HORROR

KEY EVOLUTIONARY STAGES

The Twilight Zone	1959–65, CBS
Star Trek	1966–69, NBC
The X-Files	1993–2002, Fox
Buffy the Vampire Slayer	1997–2001, WB; 2001–3, UPN
The Walking Dead	2010–, AMC

Approaching TV history as a Darwinian exercise gets you only so far. Charles Darwin had his clearly delineated taxonomic hierarchy, where every living subject fell into neat little categories and subcategories. But in television, even a particular species is hard to define, and pinning down a particular phylum or family is trickier still, even within the family sitcom. There's too much overlap, and nowhere, perhaps, is there more overlap among categories than in the realm of science fiction, fantasy, and horror TV. I believe, in fact, I can say that categorically.

Just try to pigeonhole a few particular TV pigeons, and see how quickly you get lost. Take, for example, ABC's *Lost*. Is it sci-fi? Yes, with its time-travel plots and mysterious underground bunkers and equipment. Is it fantasy? Sure, as the final episode makes clear, or at least semi-clear. And is it horror? Maybe that depends on how afraid you are of the Smoke Monster. Or try *The Twilight Zone* and *The X-Files,* where individual episodes fit neatly into any one of those descriptive classes. ABC's *Pushing Daisies,* pretty clearly, is a fantasy, but what the hell is ABC's *Twin Peaks*? Then and now, regarding the original and the reboot, there's no easy answer.

What I'm doing here, therefore, is taking the inclusive approach and a wider definition, closer in zoological circles to a kingdom or domain. Basically, if a TV show would qualify for entry at Comic-Con, the genre fan festival held annually in San Diego, it qualifies for discussion here. That means zombies, vampires and investigators of the paranormal, space explorers and living mannequins. And with so many subgenres intermingling, the evolutionary highlights singled out here are measured in terms of influence: Which TV shows most inspired and helped mold their successors? Which fantasy or sci-fi or horror shows, in short, altered TV the most, and for the better? And if you pose the question that way, there's really only one correct answer and one perfect place to start.

THE TWILIGHT ZONE

1959–65, CBS. Creator and host: Rod Serling. Writers: Rod Serling, Charles Beaumont, Richard Matheson, Earl Hamner, others. Directors: John Brahm, Douglas Keyes, Buzz Kulik, Lamont Johnson, others. Stars: Jack Klugman, Burgess Meredith, William Shatner, Bill Mumy, Agnes Moorehead, Anne Francis, William Windom, others.

It took Rod Serling five years of TV writing, and more than two dozen teleplays for live Golden Age anthology dramas, to become an overnight success. That occurred in January 1955, the evening NBC's *Kraft Television Theatre* presented *Patterns,* Serling's then-startling, still-relevant examination of modern corporations as exploiters of the working class, even within their own companies. At a time when the postwar American dream was still intertwined with the idea of working until retirement for the same monolithic company, *Patterns* presented a much different and darker picture. The morning after it was performed on live TV, Serling was suddenly a celebrity TV writer, and *Patterns* itself was so warmly reviewed after the fact (the only way to review TV shows then) that *Kraft Television Theatre* took the highly unusual step of gathering the cast and crew to mount a second live telecast a month later. *Patterns* earned Serling his first Emmy Award for Best Original Teleplay, starting him on an amazing streak. The next year, in 1956, he won another Emmy, for writing CBS's *Playhouse 90* presentation of *Requiem for a Heavyweight,* starring Jack Palance. And the year after that, in 1957, Serling won his third consecutive Emmy, for another *Playhouse 90* script—*The Comedian*, which starred Mickey Rooney in a drama clearly inspired by the TV career of Milton Berle. The following year, despite his unmatched success, Serling was so frustrated by the restrictions placed on him as a TV writer of dramatic anthology scripts, and other vagaries having to do with working for the television industry, that he wrote yet another *Playhouse 90* teleplay. This time it was a 1959 examination of the TV industry itself: *The Velvet Alley*, starring Art Carney as a television writer who suddenly hits it big and wins an Emmy, while betraying most of his loved ones, colleagues, and morals in the process. Serling didn't win an Emmy that year, but he didn't betray his own ideals, either. Instead, he pursued them, by finding a way to sneak the sensitive subject matter he most wanted to explore on

The Twilight Zone is one of the most iconic and influential shows in all of TV history, inspiring many of the artists interviewed for this book. One famous early episode, "Time Enough at Last," was adapted for TV by series host Rod Serling and starred Burgess Meredith as the lone survivor of a nuclear blast.

TV—bigotry, jingoism, paranoia, betrayal—into the more palatable guise of fantasy.

For four years, Serling had watched the film director Alfred Hitchcock become a TV star in his own right, hosting CBS's *Alfred Hitchcock Presents* and circumventing the censors while playing the droll host. Hitchcock's program was a weekly suspense anthology series; Serling, the three-time Emmy winner, pushed for a weekly anthology of a different sort. He wanted, and got, an anything-goes format that could make room for just about any type of story—each one with a moral, delivered by Serling himself. The new series was called *The Twilight Zone*, and it premiered later the same year as *The Velvet Alley*, with Serling writing an introductory teaser for *TV Guide*. "We want to prove," he wrote the month *The Twilight Zone* premiered, "that television, even in its half-hour form, can be both commercial and worthwhile." Commercial? In time, absolutely, but during its original broadcast run *The Twilight Zone*, like *Star Trek*, never ranked in the Top 25 for any given season. Worthwhile? Absolutely, astoundingly, from the very start. Its first year on the air, *The Twilight Zone* won Serling his fourth Emmy for writing. The year after that, he won again.

What made *The Twilight Zone* different from most of the genre shows that had preceded it—such radio carryovers as NBC's *Lights Out* in 1949 and the syndicated *Inner Sanctum* in 1951—was that, like *Alfred Hitchcock Presents*, it was aimed at and written for adults. Hitchcock's intent was solely to entertain, but the episodes presented by Serling came with both twist endings and lessons attached. Seeing and fearing Communists even in your friends and neighbors? Behold the dangers of paranoia in "The Monsters Are Due on Maple Street." Accepting too readily the aid and leadership of seemingly benevolent allies? Learn the translated warning behind the book cover of "To Serve Man." Too seduced by beauty or too eager to conform? Watch "Eye of the Beholder," or "Number 12 Looks Just Like You," or both. Horror, science fiction, fantasy—there was room for all of it in *The Twilight Zone*, and all of it delighted and inspired generations of viewers. Marius Constant's four-note musical theme is iconic, and the series spawned or inspired dozens of spin-offs, rip-offs, and homages from the start and is inspiring them still. More TV producers, writers, and actors interviewed for this book mentioned *The Twilight Zone* as a favorite and formative TV series than any other, and for several genres of television all roads lead straight back to Serling and *The Twilight Zone*. In Serling's *Velvet Alley*, the protagonist explains his questionable career choices by admitting to a new desire to be acclaimed for posterity. "I don't want to be forgotten," confesses the TV writer written by the TV writer Rod Serling. As for Serling himself, he won't be.

Even with anthology shows falling in and out of favor, *Twilight Zone* variations have regularly reappeared over the decades, from the 1983 movie to the official TV reboots in 1985 and 2002, and a BBC Radio version in 2016. As for shows that owe part of their DNA to the original *Twilight Zone,* that list begins with NBC's *Thriller* (hosted by Boris Karloff) in 1960 and ABC's *Outer Limits* in 1963 and keeps on going, down through Serling's own *Night Gallery* in 1969, NBC's *Amazing Stories* (created by Steven Spielberg) in 1985, HBO's *Tales from the Crypt* in 1989, and includes the most impressive recent entry, *Black Mirror,* which began on England's Channel 4 in 2011. Recently, that series has received global attention and distribution via Netflix, which has ordered a new season for 2016 and beyond, and its stories thus far have lived up to the imposing description of *Twilight Zone*–style stories for the digital age.

The *Twilight Zone* had succeeded artistically, and proven so durable and memorable, for the same reason as CBS's *Gunsmoke,* which took a more mature approach to a TV genre formerly reserved for children. *Gunsmoke* was TV's first "adult Western," just as *Star Trek,* with a franchise that has lasted for fifty years, was TV's first "adult sci-fi," and *Star Trek*'s creator, Gene Roddenberry, circumvented TV's then-current standards and restrictions the same way Serling did in *The Twilight Zone.*

STAR TREK

1966–69, NBC. Creator: Gene Roddenberry. Writers: Gene Roddenberry, Gene L. Coon, D. C. Fontana, David Gerrold, Theodore Sturgeon, Harlan Ellison, others. Stars: William Shatner, Leonard Nimoy, DeForest Kelly, James Doohan, Nichelle Nichols, George Takei, Walter Koenig.

Gene Roddenberry, a TV writer whose résumé at the time included many episodes of the CBS Western *Have Gun, Will Travel,* launched his NBC *Star Trek* series in the middle of the space race as Gemini missions were still being flown. "Space: the final frontier," the captain's narration intoned in the opening credits of every episode. "These are the voyages of the starship *Enterprise*. Its five-year mission: to explore strange new worlds, to seek out new life, and to boldly go where no man has gone before." The mission was for five years because that's how long it took, on average, for a successful TV series to amass enough episodes to strike a workable syndication deal. *Star Trek* was canceled after only three seasons, but it's done all right since then.

Like the BBC's *Doctor Who*, it's been around, in one form or another, for half a century. Unlike *Doctor Who*, which began as a children's show and morphed, through the many incarnations of its protagonists and production teams, into a clever series just as satisfying and meaningful to adult viewers, *Star Trek* began with adults, as well as youngsters, in mind. And while the space race was front and center in the mid-1960s, so was race

Star Trek remains a popular entertainment franchise fifty years after its TV debut, though the original NBC series lasted only three years and never was a hit. William Shatner and Leonard Nimoy starred as space explorers James T. Kirk and Mr. Spock.

itself, and *Star Trek* premiered just two years after the passage of the Civil Rights Act of 1964. Roddenberry's initial series gets credit for going where no futuristic TV series had gone before and for slipping allegorical pleas for racial harmony and planetary peace into prime time. The seventy-ninth and final episode of *Star Trek* was televised in June 1969—one month before Neil Armstrong landed on the moon. But the series thrived in off-network syndication and actually increased its pop-culture status and momentum. The space shuttle *Constitution* was renamed the *Enterprise* in 1976, and in 1979 the first movie spin-off, *Star Trek: The Motion Picture*, hit theaters.

In terms of race relations, *Star Trek* was commendably ahead of its time. It imagined a starship whose bridge was populated not only by earthlings of different races and ethnicities but also by a half-human, half-alien science officer, Mr. Spock (played by Leonard Nimoy). It encountered life on other worlds, and in other galaxies, that commented slyly on things much closer to home. The episode "Let That Be Your Last Battlefield," guest starring Frank Gorshin, pitted an alleged terrorist against a bigoted pursuer from his home planet. Both men had faces that were half-white and half-black, divided vertically, but they were racially biased because on one the white side was on the left, while the other's white side was on the right. A metaphorical examination of racism couldn't be more black and white. And in a 1968 episode called "Plato's Stepchildren," Captain James T. Kirk (William Shatner) and his crew found themselves prisoners of an alien race of telekinetic sadists who dressed and manipulated their captives like life-sized dolls. They even "forced" Kirk to embrace and kiss his African-American communications officer, Lieutenant Uhura (played by Nichelle Nichols)—the first interracial kiss on a U.S. television drama.

Star Trek was so influential some of its imagined hardware from the future ended up being emulated by future electronics designers. It wasn't by coincidence that early flip phones looked and opened like the communications devices on *Star Trek* or that early desktop and handheld computers accessed information the way they did. Most of all, though, *Star Trek* rises above most other genre shows because it spawned so many other successful sequels, prequels, and reboots. On TV, there was *Star Trek: The Next Generation* (1987–94, syndicated), starring Patrick Stewart as Captain Jean-Luc Picard, which was followed by *Star Trek: Deep Space Nine* (1993–99, syndicated), *Star Trek: Voyager* (1995–2001, UPN), and *Star Trek: Enterprise* (2001–5, UPN). In theaters, there were a total of six motion pictures starring the original TV *Star Trek* cast, four additional ones starring the cast of *The Next Generation,* and, beginning in 2009, a rebooted *Star Trek* film franchise overseen by J. J. Abrams, who also runs the rebooted *Star Wars* movie franchise.

Fantasy shows in the 1960s and 1970s were everywhere in prime-time sitcoms—with their witches, genies, Martians, flying nuns, talking cars—but the more serious fantasy dramas were few and far between, and even the best of them had a sizable percentage of tongue in cheek. ABC's daytime gothic soap opera *Dark Shadows* (1966–71), with its tragic vampire "hero," certainly served as a teaser for things to come in pop culture, as did the highly rated 1972 ABC vampire movie *The Night Stalker,* which spawned the single-season series *Kolchak: The Night Stalker.* That 1974–75 series starred Darren McGavin as a persistent newspaper reporter investigating cases that smacked of the paranormal—vampires, werewolves, zombies, witches, and the like—with a writing staff that included David Chase (later of *The Sopranos*), Michael Kozoll (later of *Hill Street Blues*), and Robert Zemeckis (later the director of the *Back to the Future* trilogy). Science fiction shows, after *Star Trek* and especially after the theatrical release of *Star Wars,* were in a fallow period, with such overblown efforts as NBC's *Buck Rogers in the 25th Century* and ABC's *Battlestar Galactica.*

Good science fiction was rare, but when you found it, it was very smart: the BBC's brilliantly satiric Douglas Adams 1981 miniseries *The Hitchhiker's Guide to the Galaxy,* for example, and ABC's *Max Headroom* dystopian series in 1987. And on the horror side, or the horror-comedy side, HBO took a 1950s EC Comics franchise and brought it to television, wickedly well, with its 1989–96 anthology series *Tales from the Crypt*—hosted, as were some of the original, outrageously violent and gruesome and pun-filled comics, by a skeletal wisecracker known as the Crypt-Keeper. In 1990, broadcast TV still took enough risks to lay claim to the best and most original genre show, even if it was impossible to pin down to one genre, or even two: that's the year ABC premiered the unique, brilliant, dreamlike, and imminently revisited David Lynch and Mark Frost genre-busting mystery series, *Twin Peaks*—one of my favorite TV shows of all time. But it was two of the older TV efforts, *The Twilight Zone* and *The Night Stalker,* that most directly inspired Chris Carter to create perhaps the most influential genre series of all from the 1990s.

THE X-FILES

1993–2002, 2016, Fox. Creator: Chris Carter. Stars: David Duchovny, Gillian Anderson, Mitch Pileggi. Writers: Chris Carter, Frank Spotnitz, Vince Gilligan, Howard Gordon, Glen Morgan, James Wong, Darin Morgan.

In *The Twilight Zone,* anything could happen from week to week: alien visitations, sightings of odd monsters, exercises in world-class paranoia, even stories laced with dark humor and eccentric characters. In *Kolchak: The Night Stalker,* the hero was the one believer in the paranormal, the one who faced shadowy demons and monsters directly as all around him proceeded slowly and skeptically. Chris Carter took those two series, mixed them with a dollop of the Sherlock Holmes stories and dynamic—an observant and

The X-Files brought the eerie mood and subject matter of *The Twilight Zone* into the weekly drama series format. David Duchovny (right) and Gillian Anderson starred as Fox Mulder and Dana Scully, FBI investigators of the paranormal.

quirky investigator paired with a pragmatic doctor—and came up with *The X-Files*. Like *The Twilight Zone* and *Star Trek,* it has spawned movies and sequels since its initial cancellation, including a six-part 2016 limited-series comeback that ended with a cliff-hanger, teasing fans with the probability of even more.

One advance made by *The X-Files* was its mixture of stand-alone stories with a continuing conspiracy-theory through line. The FBI agents Fox Mulder (David Duchovny) and Dana Scully (Gillian Anderson) were drawn to such one-shot investigations as parasites in the Arctic and human fluke worms in the sewers, yet were always swept back into the vortex of government secrets and secret plots that involved outer-space aliens and alien technology, government experiments and conspiracies, and alien abduction accounts that linked both to Mulder's past and to Scully's present. One 1993 story, "Drive," told of an uneducated bigot convinced that he and his wife had been tampered with by the government and implanted with devices affecting their behavior, and he was right, proving that you're not paranoid if they are out to get you, one of the major morals of the entire *X-Files* series. "Drive" was written by Vince Gilligan and guest starred Bryan Cranston, the first professional pairing of the men who went on to, respectively, create and star in *Breaking Bad*. Other stellar writers in the *X-Files* stable included Frank Spotnitz, who oversaw ABC's 2007 *Night Stalker* reboot and adapted Philip K. Dick's *Man in the High Castle* for Amazon in 2015, and Darin Morgan, who wrote some of the strangest and most unforgettable episodes in the history of *The X-Files*: "Clyde Bruckman's Final Repose" (which won an Emmy for Outstanding Drama Series Writing in 1996), "Jose Chung from Outer Space," and, from the 2016 revival series, the inventive "Mulder & Scully Meet the Were-Monster," which played with genre conventions in a delightful way while sneaking in a major visual nod to the hero's wardrobe on *Kolchak: The Night Stalker*. In fact, Spotnitz told me in 2016 that Morgan's *X-Files* script that year, the comically clever "Were-Monster" episode, actually was a slight rewrite of a script Morgan wrote for Spotnitz's *Night Stalker* ABC series remake in 2005. ABC had rejected it at the time, Spotnitz recalled, as being too weird.

The X-Files, much of the time—except for those riotous Darin Morgan episodes—took itself very seriously and set out to scare and disturb viewers and get them to think about the society and life around them. Decades later, *The Walking Dead* would do that, even more allegorically and successfully, but back in the mid-1990s the trend was toward fantasy shows, and lightly frivolous ones at that. Yet even they managed to lead to something more meaningful. The syndicated series *Hercules: The Legendary Journeys* began in 1994 as a series of television movies, starring Kevin Sorbo as the mythic hero but with a sort of laid-back, modern, Malibu sensibility. A weekly series followed the next year, as did a spin-off series that had the beneficial side effect of providing one of the strongest female TV roles in decades: *Xena, Warrior Princess,* starring Lucy Lawless. For two years on TV, there was no woman character quite as tough, heroic, and central to her television series as Xena. And then came Buffy . . .

BUFFY THE VAMPIRE SLAYER

1997–2001, WB; 2001–3, UPN. Creator: Joss Whedon. Stars: Sarah Michelle Gellar, Anthony Stewart Head, Alyson Hannigan, Nicholas Brendon, James Marsters, Emma Caulfield, Michelle Trachtenberg, David Boreanaz, Charisma Carpenter, Kristine Sutherland, Amber Benson, Eliza Dushku, Juliet Landau, Alexis Denisof, Julie Benz, Nathan Fillion, Danny Strong.

As a TV critic, I get advance access to most new television shows and see them even before the amazingly busy team at NPR's *Fresh Air,* and my current longtime producer, Phyllis Myers, has given me great trust, and great freedom, in selecting the shows I wish to review on air, even if she hasn't yet seen them. Only two times, in my thirty years as the *Fresh Air* TV critic, have I felt sheepish identifying the proposed subject of an upcoming piece. One was AMC's *Walking Dead* (more on that later), which I said was "a zombie show—but a really good one." The other was Joss Whedon's *Buffy the Vampire Slayer,* which I described as "a vampire show—but a really good one." As it turns out, there's so much to say about *Buffy the Vampire Slayer* that according to a review of academic journals and conferences it's the most studied TV show in history, written about and pored over even more than *The Sopranos, The Wire,* or *Breaking Bad.* And I might question that, except that I've attended academic conferences on both *Buffy* and *The Sopranos,* and, as keynote speaker of the first "Slayage" conference held in 2004, all I can tell you is that the *Buffy* academics are enthusiastic to an unmatched degree. In fact, there's been a "Slayage" conference every other year since then, opening itself up to all other sparkling bodies in the so-called Whedonverse, including the Buffy spin-off *Angel,* other Whedon TV series such as *Dollhouse* and *Firefly,* and his screenplays for the Marvel Comics movie franchise *The Avengers.*

There is, indeed, an awful lot to say about Joss Whedon, especially his approach to TV, and I'll let him say most of it. When I interviewed him in 2002 for *Fresh Air,* Whedon was very forthcoming about why his TV shows were the way they were. As I explained in my introduction to our conversation, "Viewers put off by the silly *Buffy the Vampire Slayer* title, or by monster dramas in general, are missing something really special here. Despite its paranormal situations and characters, and sometimes because of them, *Buffy* is turning out some of the best stuff on TV right now . . . The show is full of metaphors about how loved ones can turn into monsters, how high

Buffy the Vampire Slayer was series creator Joss Whedon's clever take on the monster and high-school genres, starring Sarah Michelle Gellar as the title character, the "Chosen One" destined to fight evil demons. David Boreanaz played Angel, an only occasionally evil vampire, who ended up getting his own spinoff series.

school and college life is a particular type of hell, and how everyone, to some extent, is haunted by his or her own demons. Characters grow, change, and sometimes even die."

Whedon first wrote *Buffy the Vampire Slayer* as a 1992 film starring Kristy Swanson, but the director Fran Rubel Kuzui went for a wildly uneven and much too cartoonish tone. When Whedon revived the idea as a TV series, he did so with the control he could exert as a show runner, and with Sarah Michelle Gellar cast as a vampire-hunting chosen one who could commit equally to the worlds of the normal and the paranormal. "What I wanted," he told me on *Fresh Air*, "was to create a fantasy that was, emotionally, completely realistic. That's what really interests me about anything." He's also interested in serialized storytelling, and though WB's *Buffy* began with self-contained monster stories, the series quickly shifted to longer, often season-long story arcs, like CBS's *Wiseguy* crime series, which also made a habit of hiring a guest star in a recurring role as the villain over a long stretch of episodes. Whedon even coined a now-familiar shorthand phrase for his season-long antagonists, calling them "the Big Bad," and relished the freeing, expanding format.

"I'm very, very much aware of it as being like a novel," Whedon said during our radio interview. "You know, the only equivalent of what you can do with a soap opera, to me, is what [Charles] Dickens was doing, and he happens to be my favorite novelist—the idea that you can get invested in a character for so long, and see it go through so many permutations. It's fascinating to me. The shows that I've always loved the best—*Hill Street Blues, Wiseguy, Twin Peaks*—have always been shows that did have accumulated knowledge." As to why, in all his shows and dramas, even leading characters suddenly die with no warning, Whedon explained that he does that to the audience because he's doing it for the audience. "I want to keep them afraid," he said. "I want to keep people in suspense. I want people to understand that everything is not perfectly safe." No, but in the hands of the *Buffy* team and its *Angel* spin-off, everything was perfectly entertaining.

As one century gave way to another, sci-fi returned to TV in both quality and quantity. *Farscape*, from 1999, presented on what was then called the Sci-Fi Channel, was a smarter variation on the *Buck Rogers in the 25th Century* theme. *Firefly*, from 2002, was Joss Whedon's next series for TV, essentially an outer-space Western that Fox failed to support (on TV, though the corporation's movie arm did release a big-screen companion film, *Serenity,* in 2005). And the Sci-Fi Channel burnished a lump of coal into a glittering diamond, by updating, and overwhelmingly improving, the post–*Star Wars* debacle that was ABC's *Battlestar Galactica* and turning it into a 2003 miniseries, and 2004 series, that served as a very adult allegory about occupied territories, armed conflicts, and the differences, if there were any, between terrorists and freedom fighters. And then there was ABC's *Lost* in 2004, which stylishly unrolled one of the most sustained and intriguing genre mystery stories since the "Who killed Laura Palmer?" story on *Twin Peaks.*

Conspiracy genre dramas, after *The X-Files,* grew and grew, embracing serialized story lines and all manner of sci-fi or fantasy elements. Sooner or later, it almost always seemed to get down to us versus them, and the them could be almost anyone, doing almost anything. Villains schemed to end the world in NBC's *Heroes* (which premiered in 2006); eradicate vampires in HBO's *True Blood* (2008); manipulate events from an alternate universe in Fox's *Fringe* (2008); turn people into mindless programmable playthings in yet another Whedon series, Fox's *Dollhouse* (2009); haunt the living, torture the infirm, and exploit the afflicted in various seasons of FX's *American Horror Story* (2011); and tamper with genetics and DNA for nefarious purposes in both BBC America's *Orphan Black* (2013) and FX's *Strain* (2014). In recent years on genre TV, the "Big Bad" battles have pitted monsters against monsters (Showtime's *Penny Dreadful,* 2014), replicants against humans (AMC's *Humans* in 2015 and HBO's *Westworld* in 2016), computer programmers against corporations (USA's *Mr. Robot,* 2015), and U.S. resistance fighters against victorious Nazis and Japanese in a postwar former America controlled by the enemy (Frank Spotnitz's *Man in the High Castle,* 2015, presented by Amazon). But of all these shows, the longest, most brutal battle, and the one taking the most toll on its characters, is the one taking place in an AMC series that, like more and more TV series this century, is inspired by and based on a graphic novel. It's a show that not only became the most popular series on cable television but manages to draw a larger audience than most broadcast TV series as well.

THE WALKING DEAD

2010–, AMC. Creator: Frank Darabont. Based on the comic book series by Robert Kirkman, Tony Moore, and Charlie Adlard. Stars: Andrew Lincoln, Norman Reedus, Steven Yeun, Chandler Riggs, Melissa McBride, Lauren Cohan, Danai Gurira, Scott Wilson, Sarah Wayne Callies, Lennie James, David Morrissey, Jeffrey DeMunn, Tovah Feldshuh, Chad L. Coleman, Emily Kinney.

My initial *Fresh Air* review of *The Walking Dead* in 2010 praised the show for its well-drawn characters, its inventive story structure, its beautiful photography, its graphic special effects, and its dramatic intensity. "You watch this," I concluded, "and there are times when you think, 'What would I do if this were happening to me?' My answer, way too often, is: I'd die. Your results may vary."

I showed that premiere episode of *The Walking Dead* to one of my Rowan University TV appreciation classes recently and marveled at the cast

The Walking Dead took the postapocalyptic zombie-filled world from a series of graphic novels and turned it into an intense, intelligent genre character study. Andrew Lincoln stars as Rick Grimes, with Norman Reedus as Daryl.

changes that have occurred in the subsequent six years. I didn't spoil things for my students, but as each name in the credits popped up, I made a mental checklist: alive, dead, dead, alive, dead, dead, dead . . .

The Walking Dead has taken every lesson learned from the evolution of genre television and, in each case, upped the ante. The allegorical lessons of *The Twilight Zone* are here, in a dystopian future overrun by zombies, asking its human survivors, at every turn, precisely what it means to be human. The hopeful undercurrent of *Star Trek* is here, too, in a determination to find something better on every voyage, despite the odds and obstacles. *The X-Files* is reflected in the well-earned wariness: "trust no one" is a clear lesson here, too, until and unless they prove otherwise. The "walkers"—this show's name for the zombies—can prove fatal if they get too close and manage to bite or wound, but *The Walking Dead* makes it clear, time and again, that nothing in this postapocalyptic world is more dangerous to humans than other humans. And as with *Buffy the Vampire Slayer,* the only way the scrappy heroes in *The Walking Dead* can survive is to work together and, often quite literally, have each other's back.

When most aspects of everyday society are taken away, what's left? And, from that point on, what matters? Those are the big questions of *The Walking Dead,* and it poses them all the time, but not vocally or overtly. At the center of the story, instead, is the Kentucky deputy sheriff Rick Grimes (played by Andrew Lincoln), who, in the opening episode, is shot, is hospitalized, and falls into a coma, whereupon, weeks later, he literally awakens to a scary new world. And boy, is it scary. Showtime's *Penny Dreadful* and FX's *Strain,* in recent years, have managed to stage some truly spooky set pieces, but as horror TV series go, *The Walking Dead* packs more horrifying moments per hour than any show on television. And that includes *Fear the Walking Dead,* the less compelling AMC companion series launched in 2015 that dramatizes the initial zombie outbreak that occurred while the hero of *The Walking Dead* was comatose. *The Walking Dead* is riveting because the characters are so strong, and so vulnerable. And it's frightening, deliciously so, because so many of them do indeed fall victim—to walkers, human outsiders, or their own stupidity.

Another major genre show with a fierce body count, and an almost perverse delight in offing even its most popular characters on occasion, is HBO's *Game of Thrones,* the ambitious fantasy epic bringing to life the novels of George R. R. Martin. Danger and intrigue are everywhere, and so are fire-breathing dragons, in a story of warring fictional kingdoms filmed on several continents, with a lavish budget and an attention to detail and production design to match. The popularity of this series, which began in 2011, is great enough that variations on *Thrones* are in the works, or about to premiere, at several competing networks.

13 WESTERNS

KEY EVOLUTIONARY STAGES

Gunsmoke	1955–75, CBS
Maverick	1957–62, ABC
Rawhide	1959–65, CBS
Lonesome Dove	1989, CBS
Deadwood	2004–6, HBO

No genre exemplifies the theory of TV evolution so much as the Western. Its earliest hits arrived to the new medium as hybrids, adapted from radio shows or old B Westerns, or both. It caught on so wildly with youngsters, and later with adults, that at one point in the 1950s seven of TV's Top 10 series were Westerns. And then, like dinosaurs after the ice age, they virtually vanished. Unlike the dinosaurs, however, TV Westerns managed to return in later years, for one or two grand resurrections. And in characterization, themes, violence, and just about every other aspect, the TV Western had evolved, and matured, considerably.

Television's first Western, *Hopalong Cassidy,* was an exercise in inventive recycling. William Boyd, as the silver-haired, black-garbed hero, had starred as Hopalong (Hoppy to his friends and fans) in his first B movie Western in 1935, eventually filming sixty-five additional adventures. As early as 1945, when only a few hundred TV sets had been produced for general consumption, some of those Hopalong Cassidy films were being shown on New York television. In 1948, Boyd launched two different syndicated *Hopalong Cas-*

sidy programs: a new radio show, and a newly packaged TV show, featuring edited versions of the old Hopalong Cassidy films, with new narration and occasional bits of new footage. Local TV stations snatched up the series, and radio play and promotion, including a daily *Hopalong Cassidy* comic strip, helped the television show become so popular. Boyd filmed a new series of Hoppy adventures specifically for TV in 1952—in his late fifties. These Westerns were for kids, and kids loved them. They also loved *The Lone Ranger,* an ABC series that followed *Hopalong Cassidy* to TV in 1949. Its pop-culture roots also originated in the 1930s, the series having begun as a radio drama in 1933, but with their trusty steeds, their straight-shooting pistols, and their trusty companions both *The Lone Ranger* and *Hopalong Cassidy* became the first Westerns to land in TV's Top 10, ranking seventh and ninth, respectively, for the 1950–51 season. Another carryover from the movies was NBC's *Roy Rogers Show,* a lighthearted contemporary Western starring the singing cowboy and his wife, Dale Evans. Except for *The Lone Ranger* and *Hopalong Cassidy,* though, no other Western series would make another appearance in the seasonal Top 10 for several years, although a miniseries of *Davy Crockett* adventures, shown in monthly installments on ABC's then-new anthology series *Disneyland,* demonstrated the widespread appeal of Westerns, especially to kids. Millions of pint-sized replicas of the character's coonskin caps were sold across America, the "Ballad of Davy Crockett" theme song was a No. 1 hit, and, though the third monthly installment killed off Davy Crockett at the Alamo, Walt Disney kept the franchise alive by following up with a pair of prequels. The *Davy Crockett* miniseries made everyone aware of the potential of Westerns to reach children, but it would take another mid-1950s TV Western to prove that adults could be attracted as well and to start an avalanche of copycats and variants, all trying to cash in on the same Western stampede.

GUNSMOKE

1955–75, CBS. Creator: Charles Marquis Warren. Stars: James Arness, Amanda Blake, Milburn Stone, Dennis Weaver, Ken Curtis.

Gunsmoke, which ran for twenty years on CBS, isn't just the longest-running TV Western of all time; it's also the longest-running TV drama of all time, period. It's credited as television's first "adult Western" and often cited as continuing the vein of such serious and influential Western films as 1952's *High Noon* and 1953's *Shane*. The problem with that particular theory of "adult Western" evolution is that *Gunsmoke,* as a radio program, predated both those classic movies. Three months before *High Noon* appeared on the big screen, *Gunsmoke* premiered on CBS Radio, starring William Conrad (later the narrator of the "Rocky & Bullwinkle" adventures) as the U.S. marshal Matt Dillon. Three years later, in 1955, *Gunsmoke* made the transition to television, starring James Arness as Dillon. The premiere TV episode, famously, was introduced by the biggest star of Western movies, John Wayne, who encouraged his fans to watch *Gunsmoke* and give Arness and the series a chance. Less famously, that first TV show let viewers know

Gunsmoke, the original "adult Western," starred James Arness as imposing Dodge City marshal Matt Dillon. Arness played the role for twenty years. At left, Dillon's original deputy, the limping Chester, played by Dennis Weaver.

they were in for something different: Matt Dillon got into a shoot-out with a visiting, quick-drawing wanted gunman, lost and got shot, and spent most of the episode recuperating, nursing his wounds, and gearing up for a rematch. Rarely did a TV Western dwell on the effects of gun violence, and it was even rarer still for the hero to be shot and nearly killed. By having *Gunsmoke* start out on TV that way, and having Matt Dillon tended by his concerned friends (Milburn Stone's Doc, Amanda Blake's Kitty, and Dennis Weaver's Chester, Dillon's limping but loyal deputy), *Gunsmoke* said everything about what was of interest, and importance, to the makers of this new small-screen Western.

By 1957, *Gunsmoke* was the top-rated show on television, a position it maintained for the next three years. It used its period setting the way *Star Trek,* in another TV genre, used its futuristic one: to explore themes of bigotry, violence, loyalty, responsibility, and so on, and to get away with addressing such potentially volatile current issues precisely because the conflicts being dramatized occurred in a distant time and place. Actually, the comparison between *Gunsmoke* and *Star Trek* is an apt one: The stoic, heroic characters of Marshal Dillon and Captain Kirk are quite similarly motivated and presented, as are their physician sidekicks, Stone's Doc and DeForest Kelley's Bones. And *Star Trek*'s creator Gene Roddenberry, long before pitching the science fiction series he sold as "*Wagon Train* in space," wrote dozens of episodes of CBS's *Have Gun, Will Travel*—a stylish "adult Western" that caught on almost as quickly as *Gunsmoke*. During the 1958–59 TV season, the four most popular series on television were all Westerns: *Gunsmoke,* NBC's *Wagon Train, Have Gun, Will Travel,* and ABC's *Rifleman,* in descending order. The genre was so popular, in fact, that three more Westerns occupied the bottom half of the Top 10 that season: ABC's *Life and Legend of Wyatt Earp* was ranked No. 10, NBC's *Tales of Wells Fargo* was ranked No. 7, and another significant evolutionary step in Western TV history, ABC's *Maverick,* was ranked No. 6.

"*Gunsmoke* was high water," says the TV writer-producer David Milch, recalling the TV Westerns he enjoyed when he was young. "And I liked *Maverick* an awful lot." In time, Milch would create a TV Western of his own: HBO's *Deadwood.*

MAVERICK

1957–62, ABC. Creator: Roy Huggins. Stars: James Garner, Jack Kelly, Roger Moore.

Maverick was another game changer, and not just for the Western genre. In the character of James Garner's Bret Maverick especially, this Western differentiated itself from the others by presenting a protagonist who was not, by definition, heroic. Bret Maverick would rather draw to an inside straight than draw his gun, would avoid confrontation whenever possible, and disliked both fisticuffs and gunplay but loved to gamble, especially poker. Bret's brother Bart, played by Jack Kelly, was a bit more noble and heroic, but only by comparison. *Maverick* had such a light tone, compared with the

Maverick had several characters with that last name, each a relative, each a gambler, and each played by a different star. The most famous of these was Bret Maverick, played by James Garner, seen here with guest star Connie Stevens.

other Westerns dominating TV at the time, that it even blatantly lampooned its less playful counterparts. When NBC's *Bonanza* became an instant hit after premiering in 1959, it wasn't long before *Maverick* worked a full-scale *Bonanza* parody into the plot of one episode, meeting the patriarch and his three sons at a ranch called the Subrosa. The quintessential episode of *Maverick,* no doubt, is "Shady Deal at Sunny Acres," in which Bret literally whittled away most of the hour while surreptitiously plotting to retrieve his money from the clutches of an unscrupulous banker. Roy Huggins created *Maverick* and reteamed with Garner on another series, NBC's *Rockford Files,* which did for the private eye genre what *Maverick* had done for the Western. Garner, meanwhile, left *Maverick* after a few seasons because of a contract dispute, at which time Roger Moore, as his cousin Beauregard Maverick, joined the cast, but for *Maverick* fans the star of the show, and the antihero to remember most, was James Garner as Bret.

RAWHIDE

1959–65, CBS. Creator: Charles Marquis Warren. Stars: Clint Eastwood, Eric Fleming, Paul Brinegar, Steve Raines, Sheb Wooley.

By the 1958–59 TV season, there were thirty-one different Western series in prime time—an astounding number, given that there were only three broadcast networks at the time. *Rawhide* joined their ranks in 1959, ostensibly as a sort of cattle-rustling variation on the *Wagon Train* theme of roving adventurers. Except that the cowboys on the cattle drive in *Rawhide* were less like happy campers than cantankerous co-workers: the trail boss Gil Favor, played by Eric Fleming, had a bunch of rowdy cowhands on his hands—including Rowdy Yates, Gil's right-hand man, played by a young and often shirtless Clint Eastwood. Driving the cattle to market on the long and dusty trail from northern Texas to Kansas, these cowboys faced all sorts of dangers and problems, from a lack of water and grazing land to the temptations, along the way, of women, saloons, and recruiters for various armies, communities, and religions. *Rawhide* was considered one of the most realistic of the TV Westerns, which made sense, because its creator was Charles Marquis Warren, who also brought *Gunsmoke* to television. *Rawhide* acknowledged that cattle, as well as men, got tired and hungry and that even in a close-knit undertaking like a cattle drive, folks didn't always get along or act heroically. Even the two lead characters, Gil and Rowdy, could and did fight with each other, fists flying. That unpredictability and complexity extended to everything and everyone encountered on the trail. The Indians whose territory they crossed could be hospitable as well as hostile, and the same went for the land barons, local sheriffs, and area women. Rowdy would get angry and quit early but would always return before the end of the episode. Eastwood stayed on *Rawhide* to the end but used his summer hiatus periods wisely: he traveled abroad and starred in "spaghetti Westerns" for Sergio Leone, becoming an international movie star in such films as 1964's *Fistful of Dollars* and 1966's *The Good, the Bad, and the Ugly.*

The single most memorable element of *Rawhide* was neither the realism nor Eastwood but the show's theme song, which contained loud yells, whip cracks, and such lines as "Rollin', rollin', rolling / though the streams are swollen / keep them doggies movin' / Rawhide!" Ned Washington wrote the infectious lyrics, and Dimitri Tiomkin, composer of the score for *High Noon,* wrote the music. The song was sung by Frankie Laine, with so much energy and enthusiasm that more than fifteen years later Mel Brooks tapped him to sing the title song of his big-screen Western spoof, *Blazing Saddles.*

Like dramatic anthology series before them and variety shows and reality shows after them, the Western genre grew almost exponentially for a while, with new entries whose series premises ranged from the tiniest of tweaks to the most inventive of variations. Some shows were content to feature a different type of weapon: a bowie knife for ABC's *Adventures of Jim Bowie,* a modified Winchester for ABC's *Rifleman,* or a sawed-off carbine for CBS's *Wanted: Dead or Alive.* Other shows focused on different types of loners— not only Richard Boone's Paladin, the black-clad gun for hire in the moody *Have Gun, Will Travel,* but also Nick Adams's former Confederate soldier, wandering the Old West in ABC's *Rebel,* and Brian Keith's Dave Blassingame, a man with a faithful dog, meandering through the territory near the Mexican border in NBC's *Westerner,* a quirky Western created in 1960 by a pre–*Wild Bunch* Sam Peckinpah. And, of course, for the ranch owners on the prairie, there was *Bonanza,* a male-driven family Western that proved so popular that by 1964 it ascended to the No. 1 spot in the Nielsen ratings.

By the mid-1960s, though, most Westerns, except for *Bonanza* and the still beloved *Gunsmoke,* had faded, either from the glut of imitators or from growing concerns over televised violence. CBS's *Wild Wild West* premiered in 1965, with a genre-blending premise that helped it stand out from the pack: Robert Conrad and Ross Martin played James West and Artemus Gordon, post–Civil War secret agents reporting directly to President Ulysses S. Grant and roaming the country in a lushly appointed steam engine and passenger car full of the latest weapons and gadgets. *The Wild Wild West* managed, simultaneously, to spoof Westerns, spy stories, and science fiction fantasies while anticipating other TV trends. The show's recurring and entertaining villains, most notably Michael Dunn as the evil dwarf Dr. Miguelito Loveless, paved the way for a focus on scene-stealing guest star villains on ABC's *Batman*, which appeared the following season. Also appearing a season later was CBS's spy series *Mission: Impossible*, featuring Martin Landau as Rollin

Rawhide was another "adult Western," this one starring Eric Fleming as Gil Favor, Sheb Wooley as Pete Nolan, and Clint Eastwood, who achieved movie stardom overseas, as Rowdy Yates.

Hand, a spy with a thousand faces—very similar to the Artemus Gordon character in *The Wild Wild West,* who adopted so many accents and disguises that he inspired at least one young viewer to become an actor: Kevin Spacey. "I don't think there's any doubt," Spacey says when asked if there was a direct influence.

The Wild Wild West was done in not by low ratings but by a new congressional examination on televised violence—the first since the days of *The Untouchables* in the early 1960s. Westerns were so full of violence that networks found it easier, in many cases, to cancel them than defend them. *Gunsmoke,* in 1973, was the last Western series ever to appear in the Top 10. Ever. And by then, any new prime-time Western had to be strikingly different from what had come before—like the 1972 ABC series *Kung Fu,* starring David Carradine as a Buddhist monk who toured the West. It was another variation on the loner theme, but Carradine's stranger in a strange land was a pacifist who spouted Buddhist philosophy and used martial arts only as a last defense.

On television, as in the movies, the Western was a dying breed. But the genre itself, on television, still had two marvelous comebacks, and high points, in store.

LONESOME DOVE

1989, CBS. Writers: Larry McMurtry, William D. Witliff. Director: Simon Wincer. Producer: Suzanne de Passe. Stars: Robert Duvall, Tommy Lee Jones, Danny Glover, Anjelica Huston, Diane Lane, Rick Schroder, Robert Urich, Steve Buscemi.

By 1989, when CBS presented *Lonesome Dove,* the TV Western had been dead for decades, and the miniseries format was fading fast. Yet Larry McMurtry's story and script demonstrated, stunningly and inarguably, the major strengths of the miniseries form: the ability to put even its leading characters in credible dramatic jeopardy and to develop those characters with the depth and subtlety that only a long-form narrative can allow. In the *Lonesome Dove* miniseries, Robert Duvall, as the former Texas Ranger Augustus McCrae, gave one of television's all-time best performances, and Tommy Lee Jones, as his quiet but ultimately explosive partner, Woodrow

Call, matched him with another. Anjelica Huston, as the rancher Clara, added a third.

On television, the Texas Ranger as protagonist goes all the way back to *The Lone Ranger,* but neither Gus nor Woodrow was a typical Western hero. Gus, much closer to Bret Maverick than to the Lone Ranger, loved the ladies and hated hard work, while Woodrow was so tightly wound and taciturn he refused to acknowledge the paternity of his own son. Yet Gus and Woodrow were clearly dedicated to each other, and the eight-hour miniseries followed them as they traversed territories, seasons, and years. The scenery was breathtaking, and so was the jarringly unanticipated narrative. The Wild West earned its name because danger, and even death, lurked around every corner (even when there were no corners). Even the leading characters in *Lonesome Dove* could die at any time, and some of them did, adding

Lonesome Dove, one of TV's best miniseries, was an epic Western about former Texas Rangers, starring Robert Duvall as talkative Gus McCrae and Tommy Lee Jones as taciturn Woodrow Call.

to the drama's overall impact. *Lonesome Dove* was the most viewed mini-series in years and was at the cutting edge of a short but significant Western revival. In the movies, *Dances with Wolves,* starring and directed by Kevin Costner, followed in 1990, and Clint Eastwood's *Unforgiven,* starring and directed by the former co-star of *Rawhide,* was right behind in 1992. Both *Unforgiven* and *Dances with Wolves* won Oscars as Best Picture, as well as for their respective directors. *Lonesome Dove,* on the Emmy front, won for its director, Simon Wincer, as well, but was beaten in the miniseries category by ABC's *War and Remembrance.* On television, other than the eventual *Lonesome Dove* sequels, prequels, and spin-offs, there were no other noteworthy Westerns in sight for years. Not, that is, until . . .

DEADWOOD

2004–6, HBO. Creator: David Milch. Stars: Timothy Olyphant, Ian McShane, Molly Parker, Keith Carradine, Brad Dourif, John Hawkes, Kim Dickens, Dayton Callie, Anna Gunn, Powers Boothe, William Sanderson, Gerald McRaney, Ray McKinnon, Sarah Paulsen, Brian Cox, Keone Young, Garret Dillahunt.

In 2005, midway through the run of HBO's *Deadwood,* I was one of many TV critics invited to tour the set at the Melody Ranch in Santa Clarita, California. I went, eagerly, because this was no ordinary set: the series creator, David Milch, had demanded such authenticity that his re-creation of the frontier town of Deadwood was built fully to scale and at the same pace at which the original town had developed. Touring the set during a brutally hot summer, you could (and I did) stroll down dusty streets, enter saloons and hotels and private homes, and walk up the stairs and examine the upper floors. Everything existed in three dimensions, in relation to everything else, adding to the amazing overall illusion of verisimilitude. "It was really like being transported into another world," Milch agrees. And that world, constructed specifically for *Deadwood* in the Santa Clarita hills, was built on the same back-lot ranch once owned by the singing cowboy star Gene Autry and was where, over the years, many classic Westerns were filmed, including *Hopalong Cassidy, The Lone Ranger,* and *Gunsmoke.*

Milch's *Deadwood,* however, was a very different animal from any Western that had come before it. It was the first successful Western on premium cable TV, which meant Milch could take advantage of HBO's unrestricted freedoms and include lots of nudity, sexual situations, violence, and obscene language—all of which he did, liberally and gleefully. And because Milch stuck fairly true to the actual historical record of the actual Deadwood's main characters and events, he was able to be colorful, outrageous, and artistic while still honoring the memory of the town and its people. These were, after all, the lawless, rough-and-tumble Black Hills of South Dakota.

Gold, a series of rich veins of it, was discovered in the Black Hills in 1874. Two years later, miners established the town of Deadwood, which almost immediately grew into a boomtown attracting all manner of hopeful prospectors, as well as opportunistic gamblers, outlaws, and prostitutes. Many of the key characters in Milch's *Deadwood* were taken straight from the historical record, including Sheriff Seth Bullock, the town boss, Al Swearengen, and the now-legendary Western figures Calamity Jane and Wild Bill Hickok.

Deadwood was David Milch's version of a Western, with a town full of superbly written and acted characters led by Ian McShane as Deadwood town boss Al Swearengen.

But as Milch fleshed out the story, his fidelity to the facts allowed him to expand, and explode, the genre conventions. He cast and promoted Keith Carradine, for example, as the star of *Deadwood*, portraying the best-known character, Wild Bill Hickok. Only those who knew, or reviewed, their Western history were prepared for the shocking moment, just a handful of episodes into the series, when the recently arrived Deadwood visitor Wild Bill was shot and killed while playing poker, just as he was in real life. Watching at home, and having the ostensible hero eliminated suddenly before your eyes, was like seeing Janet Leigh's character stabbed to death in the shower partway through *Psycho*. What next? With *Deadwood*, what was next was to follow the new town sheriff, played by Timothy Olyphant in a star-making role. Bullock was often in direct opposition to the powerful town patriarch, Al Swearengen, played so ferociously by Ian McShane that he became one of the best Western villains of all time. Except that he wasn't an outright villain, any more than Olyphant's Bullock was a pure hero. Westerns, and Western audiences, had gotten too sophisticated for the black-hat-white-hat approach, and Milch, on ABC's *NYPD Blue*, had already crafted one of the most complicated antiheroes on television in Dennis Franz's Andy Sipowicz. In *Deadwood*, he would create several more. "The performances were extraordinary," Milch says of his *Deadwood* cast. And not just from the leading players: Garret Dillahunt, as the man who killed Hickok, was so mesmerizing Milch brought him back as an entirely different character. And all the supporting players were wonderful, from Brad Dourif and William Sanderson to Kim Dickens and Molly Parker. You could have followed any of them for an entire episode, or even a spin-off series, without any complaints or restlessness. The complexity of the plots, the language, the characters—all of it was unparalleled in the Western TV genre, a major evolutionary step forward. *Deadwood* lasted only three seasons before it left the HBO schedule, with much more story left to tell. And as this book goes to press, it appears that story will be continued.

BORN: 1945, Buffalo, New York.

FIRST TV CREDIT: Writer, *Hill Street Blues*, NBC, 1982.

LANDMARK TV SERIES: Producer and writer, *Hill Street Blues*, NBC, 1982–87; Co-creator, executive producer, and writer, *NYPD Blue*, ABC, 1993–2005; Creator and writer, *Deadwood*, HBO, 2004–6.

OTHER MAJOR CREDITS: TV: Writer, *L.A. Law*, NBC, 1992; Writer, *Murder One*, ABC, 1995; Creator, executive producer, and writer, *John from Cincinnati*, HBO, 2007; Creator, executive producer, and writer, *Luck*, HBO, 2011–12.

David Milch, a key contributor to the evolution of TV protagonists from admirable heroes to flawed ones, and to the acceptance of villains as just as central and even relatable, was born in Buffalo in 1945—just in time to be among the first generation to be born with televisions already in their homes. And even the first TV show he remembers watching, which began in 1947 on NBC as a children's series called *Puppet Playhouse,* Milch insists shaped his later love of, and fascination with, blustery bad guys.

"I watched a lot of *Howdy Doody,*" Milch says, laughing at the memory. "And I thought that Mr. Bluster was a very funny character," he adds, referring to the marionette Phineas T. Bluster, the entrepreneurial mayor of Doodyville and the ongoing grumpy nemesis of Howdy Doody, for whom *Puppet Playhouse* was quickly renamed. "And I'd like to think," Milch adds, "that most of the villains that I've worked with subsequently have really just been derivative of that character." When I tell Milch of my delight in learning that Al Swearengen, the town despot of HBO's *Deadwood* played so menacingly yet charmingly by Ian McShane, had his origins in Mr. Bluster, Milch laughs deeply. "His roots are in Mr. Bluster," Milch confirms. "Yeah."

Growing up, Milch watched more TV, with just as much enthusiasm for the shows he viewed regularly. Milch liked variety shows, leaning toward both Jackie Gleason (both his variety series and *The Honeymooners*) and Milton Berle, TV's first superstar, who appeared in many sketches wearing women's clothing ("You never can go wrong seeing a man in a dress," Milch jokes). Milch also devoured dramas, particularly ones with wandering heroes—*Route 66* (1960–64, CBS), *The Fugitive* (1963–67, ABC), and *Run for Your Life* (1965–68, NBC)—and was loyal to some of the era's more singular and adult Westerns, such as *Maverick* and *Gunsmoke*.

From the time he was a young boy, Milch would accompany his father, a surgeon with a taste for gambling, on summer trips to the Saratoga racetrack, a place of reliably happy childhood memories for young David. It began a fascination he would never outgrow and that, at times, would cost him dearly. Another fascination was literature, and Milch, early on, aspired to be a novelist. He graduated summa cum laude from Yale University, where he sought and attracted the attention of the novelist and poet Robert Penn Warren. Despite a series of drug and alcohol addictions and other problems throughout undergraduate college and after, Milch not only excelled at Yale but landed a teaching fellowship at the Writers' Workshop at the University of Iowa, from which he eventually got his master of fine arts degree. Eventually, after some hazy and sordid adventures in both the United States and Mexico, Milch returned to Yale to teach as a lecturer and assist Warren and the respected faculty members R. W. B. Lewis and Cleanth Brooks on a history of American literature. "That had taken up a good deal of my time," Milch says in retrospect, "and all of my conscience." Milch was toying with script writing at the time—working on a story set at the racetrack—and toying with other things as well. "That about covers the parts of my activities that were legal, at that point," Milch admits. It was then that he was contacted by his former undergraduate Yale roommate, Jeffrey Lewis, who was on the writing staff of a new NBC series called *Hill Street Blues*. It was during the 1981 Writers Guild of America strike, when guild members were prohibited from discussing projects with other guild writers but not writers without guild credentials. Lewis had recommended Milch to Steven Bochco, co-creator of *Hill Street*, who invited the Yale professor to come out and talk. Milch was invited to pitch story ideas, and though he wasn't even aware of *Hill Street Blues* at that point, Milch says he "regarded it as an opportunity" and accepted the challenge. When the three-month strike was over, Milch had rolled the dice—a natural reaction, given his gambling nature—left Yale, and joined Bochco's *Hill Street* staff and got his first script-writing assignment.

"I read several *Hill Street* scripts," Milch says of his preparation method, "and I very much benefited from the collaborative process." Not only the input from Bochco and Lewis, but also that from Anthony Yerkovich, another staff writer, who was a few years away from leaving the show to create *Miami Vice*. "It was a much more collaborative effort than the fact that I was given sole credit [on his first script] would indicate." That first script featured a plot inspired by a recent incident read about by Milch in the *New York Post*, "in which," he recounts, "a nun was attacked, robbed, and sexually assaulted. And it seemed to me that it was the type of crime which galvanized a city, to the extent that a city like New York could be galvanized. So I adopted that story line as the kind of overarching organizing principle of the storytelling." Milch's script won him the Emmy in 1983 for Outstanding Writing for a Drama Series, an award he would win two other times, for ABC's *NYPD Blue*. He also wrote scripts that year featuring a truly rough-guy cop on the squad, a break-the-rules, break-some-laws detective so heinous his nickname was "Bad Sal" Benedetto. "Bad Sal" was played by Dennis Franz, and the character was so reprehensible he had to be killed after five shows, but Milch thought the actor, and the chance to explore a less than noble cop character, were too good to sacrifice. "I enjoyed an awful lot writing for him," Milch says of Franz, who returned to *Hill Street* as a new, only slightly less compromised character named Norman Buntz, then reteamed with Milch as the eventual star of *NYPD Blue*. Milch saw Franz as "a kind of surrogate who really didn't fit exactly into the system," and the more he saw of Franz on-screen, the more he wanted to write for him—a kind of symbiosis between actor and writer that Milch loved about the TV process. "That's exactly the right word," Milch says when I ask him about it. "It's a symbiotic process, and you begin to get the sense that something of value is being generated. And there's this small voice that says, 'Don't louse this up.' Not 'Don't louse it up for *yourself*,' but 'Don't louse up the end result.' And if you have even an ounce of character, that begins to generate a kind of humility, so that it's not an exercise in self-proclamation, but of subordination to the larger task. And *then,*" Milch adds with enthusiasm, "you got a game."

Milch played the *Hill Street Blues* game until the series ended in 1987, at which time he and his Yale college buddy Lewis collaborated on an oddly toned, mostly comic half-hour spin-off, *Beverly Hills Buntz,* transplanting Franz's colorful Norman Buntz character to Los Angeles. That series didn't work, and didn't last, but a handful of years later Milch's old boss Bochco asked him to team up as co-creators of a show intentionally designed to push the envelope, challenge the censors, and change the face and direction of broadcast television. The show, premiering in 1993 on ABC, was called *NYPD Blue,* and Milch, who had come to TV not even knowing the rules, was now being asked to deliberately break them. Language, nudity, violence, mature themes—*NYPD Blue* challenged them all, early and consistently, in search of more vibrant characters and resonant stories, not just for the original objective of competing with cable TV's uncensored movies. "Those were exciting times to be in this racket," says Milch, who won two more Emmy Awards for his *NYPD Blue* scripts. And with its twelve-year serialized story following the trials and occasional triumphs of Franz's bigoted, boozing, loose-cannon detective, Andy Sipowicz, and his slow but sure development into a reliable and respected leader of his precinct, the series won the Emmy for Outstanding Drama Series in 1995. The story line in which one of Sipowicz's many partners, Jimmy Smits as Bobby Simone, died in the hospital of a postoperative infection was a more realistic and resonant portrayal of death and grieving on TV than most TV series had even attempted to approach.

After experiencing the unprecedented broadcast TV freedom of *NYPD Blue,* Milch went to a place, and a show, allowing even more freedom: HBO's *Deadwood* (2004–6), one of the finest dramas of TV's Platinum Age. "It was a whole new world," Milch says with wonder. "What was a battle in network dramaturgy was a given in cable storytelling, and it was a kind of laboratory experiment in the possibilities of freedom." Milch recalls one of the actors referring to the acting ensemble as "the '27 Yankees," and Milch felt a bit of that as he wrote for them. This Western series, set in the 1870s in the lawless mining camp known as Deadwood, South Dakota, starred Timothy Olyphant, later of FX's *Justified,* as the lawman Seth Bullock, and Ian McShane as his main adversary but occasional ally, Al Swearengen, the bullying *Dead-*

wood town boss Milch insists is connected somehow to Mr. Bluster from *Howdy Doody*. Other superb players in the *Deadwood* cast included Molly Parker, Brad Dourif, John Hawkes, William Sanderson, Robin Weigert, Kim Dickens, Garret Dillahunt, Powers Boothe, Gerald McRaney, and Ray McKinnon. "It was a very rare instance," Milch says, "in which you got quite a substantial collection of artists working at the top of their game." True enough: Many scenes in *Deadwood* were not only among Milch's very best but among television's as well. Many of the characters in *Deadwood* spoke with fiery bursts of profanity—a defense mechanism, Milch explained in a Television Critics Association press conference just before the show's premiere, to startle and intimidate potential attackers, just like animals in the wild who puff themselves up to look larger and more threatening. That helpful explanation, by the way, was elicited by my all-time favorite question in TCA press tour history, when Hal Boedeker, then of the *Orlando Sentinel,* opened the Q&A session with Milch by praising the show, then posing a question: "What the fuck is it with all the fucking fucks?"

After *Deadwood,* Milch made two more series for HBO: the religious allegory *John from Cincinnati* (2007) and the racetrack series *Luck* (2012), a salute to and examination of all the characters Milch encountered all those decades of attending and betting on horse races. Dustin Hoffman starred in *Luck,* and the director Michael Mann was Milch's collaborator, but the series was plagued with bad luck of its own, with three horses dying during production. Combined with backstage conflicts between Milch and Mann, *Luck* was deemed impossible to continue and was scratched after a single season. "That was a show that was *steeped* in bad luck," Milch says now. "The collaboration was not as constructive as it might have been between author and director, just because we were two different personalities, and we worked in two different ways, and the different ways in which we worked did not constructively influence the others." Milch pauses. "So that happens," he adds. "It was regrettable, but it was a fact . . . and in particular, the opportunity to work with Dustin was great. And so many of the supporting actors were terrific, and Nick Nolte was a pleasure to be with."

About the difference between the broadcast networks and HBO, Milch says, "HBO is very brave," and credits all the administrations with whom he's worked there with backing him and his visions. "Finally, all you can ask is to go to bat," he says, "and they get you to the plate. And after that," he says, laughing, "to recklessly mix a metaphor, it becomes a roll of the dice."

When we spoke in late 2015, Milch hinted about a roll of the dice that appears destined to come up a winner. "They're talking about doing a '*Deadwood* ten years later,'" he says. "It's not true of any other show I've ever worked on, but that's one I would very much like to see what had happened to those characters ten years hence. And just between you and me," he adds, "I think it's a much more realistic possibility than those kind of rumors usually are." In January 2016, HBO executives confirmed that a television movie sequel to *Deadwood* was indeed in the planning stages—good news for Milch and *Deadwood* fans everywhere.

KEY EVOLUTIONARY STAGES

The Avengers	1961–69, ITV/Thames (U.K.); 1966–69, ABC
Mission: Impossible	1966–73, CBS
Alias	2001–6, ABC
Homeland	2011–, Showtime
The Americans	2013–, FX

Every generation of TV viewer, like every generation of radio listener used to, gets hit hard—perhaps hardest—by the entertainment to which he or she is exposed during the preteen and young teenage years, when everything seems new and intense. I consider myself fortunate, as a baby boomer, to have come of age in the 1960s, when the British Invasion brought us the Beatles. But it also brought us James Bond and the spy craze, and a lot of TV secret agents, including—sigh—Diana Rigg as Emma Peel, on an imported British series called *The Avengers*. Modern TV viewers may know her as Olenna, the crafty old matriarch of House Tyrell on *Game of Thrones*, and 007 enthusiasts might recall her as the one Bond "girl" to become a Bond bride, briefly, in 1969's *On Her Majesty's Secret Service*. But before that, Diana Rigg's Emma Peel was the most formidable, modern, independent, liberated, and alluring female character on television. Mrs. Peel, as she was known, wore formfitting one-piece jumpsuits, was equally quick with deft one-liners and incapacitating martial-arts moves, and made a lasting impression that far outlasted the 1960s.

As a TV critic, I was fortunate enough to meet Dame Diana Rigg twice. The first time was in the summer of 1989, when she was starring in the *Mother Love* miniseries on PBS's *Mystery!* anthology show. At the PBS party event in Los Angeles that year, she was the star attraction, with TV critics, many of them male and approaching middle age, either assaulting her with endless *Avengers* questions or hovering nervously nearby. Mark Dawidziak, a TV critic friend of mine, and I were determined to stand out from the pack somehow and devised a strategy. Instead of discussing how much we adored her as Mrs. Peel when we were younger, we complimented her on her recently published book, *No Turn Unstoned,* a collection of unkind (and amusingly wrong) critical responses to individual performers and works of art through the ages. That particular conversational icebreaker did the trick, and our conversation turned out to be memorable for me as well. I soon learned, thanks to a late-night phone call, that while I was talking to Diana Rigg that night, my home, back in New Jersey, had been hit by lightning and burned halfway to the ground. There may be a lesson there somewhere.

The other time I encountered Diana Rigg was eight years later, when she was doing the publicity rounds for another PBS miniseries import, a remake of Daphne du Maurier's *Rebecca*. I was writing for the New York *Daily News* then and met her at her room at the Rihga Royal Hotel (now the London). We conducted an amiable interview, and as I was putting away my notepad and recorder, she asked if I wanted to use her phone to call home—to see if it was still standing. Obviously, someone had told her what happened to me the last time we'd talked, and I thought it was sweet of her to remember. Then she asked me if I wouldn't mind following her into the bedroom so she could show me something. Take a moment to let your imagination run wild—because I did. But when we got there, she pointed to her TV set, which was on, and said excitedly, "What is this?" She'd been watching Turner Classic Movies, a recently launched cable channel unfamiliar to her back in the U.K., and wanted to know all about it. There may be a lesson there somewhere, too.

During American television's Golden Age, there were virtually no spies to be found—certainly not with series of their own. Significantly, and somewhat amazingly, one of the earliest instances of a James Bond type on U.S. television was James Bond, eight years before he got to the big screen, played by Sean Connery in 1962's *Dr. No*. The first appearance of Ian Fleming's suave spy character was for a CBS anthology series called *Climax!*, courtesy of a 1954 adaptation of the novel *Casino Royale*. It was a live TV production, and the gunplay special effects were laughable, but not as laughable as the Americanization of 007. He was rewritten as a CIA agent, played by Barry Nelson, who identified himself as Jimmy Bond. The villain Le Chiffre, played by Peter Lorre, was much better, but though this was the first dramatized Bond adventure, it wasn't the one that spawned countless imitators. Nor was another pre–*Dr. No* TV spy offering, a 1960 British series called *Danger Man*, starring Patrick McGoohan as the secret agent John Drake. Episodes of that series were shown in the United States as a CBS summer replacement series in 1961, under the *Danger Man* title, but vanished without notice. When another spy series was launched in the U.K. in 1962, no U.S. network initially picked it up for stateside viewing. That series was *The Saint*, the latest revival of a series and character, already portrayed on radio and in the movies, based on the Simon Templar stories written in the 1920s by Leslie Charteris. This time, for England's ITV, the title character was played by a young actor named Roger Moore, but in the United States there were no takers. Not at first.

Yet only a few years later, after the annual cinematic salvos of *Dr. No* (1962), *From Russia with Love* (1963), and *Goldfinger* (1964), American TV was poised to bet on the international spy genre in a big way, starting with a show that, like the *Climax!* offering, had an Ian Fleming connection.

NBC's *Man from U.N.C.L.E.*, starring Robert Vaughn as the secret agent Napoleon Solo, originally included the involvement of Fleming, who suggested plotlines and character traits and even gave Napoleon Solo his name. The growing popularity of the Bond films, though, led Fleming to sign away his affiliation as an adviser, so the series premiered in 1964, and continued, without him. It caught on quickly, thanks in no small part to Vaughn and his co-star, David McCallum. McCallum played Illya Kuryakin, Solo's partner at U.N.C.L.E., who had a Russian background and a blond Beatles haircut—personifying both the spy and the Fab elements of the British Invasion, with a little Cold War intrigue thrown in as a bonus. The headquarters for U.N.C.L.E. (an acronym for United Network Command for Law and Enforcement) was hidden behind a tailor shop's false front in New York's garment district, and the agents were outfitted with nifty communications devices, weapons, and other gadgets, just like James Bond in the movies. *The Man from U.N.C.L.E.* eventually inspired a spin-off, *The*

Girl from U.N.C.L.E., starring Stefanie Powers, but that *Girl* lasted only one season. Other spy series proved more durable.

NBC's *I Spy*, launched in 1965, was the story of secret agents who traveled the world, hiding behind cover identities as a top-tier tennis pro and his personal trainer. (No one ever explained how every international crisis or assignment dovetailed so perfectly with the pro tennis travel circuit.) *I Spy*, starring Robert Culp and Bill Cosby, was significant because it filmed on location globally and important because, by hiring and showcasing Cosby, it gave American TV its first African-American leading man in a weekly dramatic series. The same year, 1965, also gave U.S. television several other spy-related series as the secret agent craze became official. There was NBC's *Get Smart*, the Mel Brooks–Buck Henry comedy that spoofed both *The Man from U.N.C.L.E.* and the Bond films, with Don Adams as Maxwell Smart talking on his high-tech "shoe phone." There was CBS's *Wild Wild West*, a post–Civil War Western with gadgetry fit for a nineteenth-century U.S. special agent, and a slight tongue-in-cheek approach as well. All these shows enjoyed early momentum: The 1965–66 TV season was the first time a spy series made it to the Top 20, with *Get Smart* ranked No. 12, and *The Man from U.N.C.L.E.* right behind at No. 13. Even *The Wild Wild West*, with its odd mixture of Western and spy genres, made it to No. 23.

Then there were the British imports, for which U.S. networks unashamedly went back to the source of the British Invasion for more, ready-made spy-related programming. Though CBS had tasted no success when presenting Patrick McGoohan's *Danger Man* as a British import in the summer of 1961, the intervening four years, and three James Bond hit movies, prompted the network to reconsider and try, try again, this time repackaging the series with a new title, *Secret Agent*, and a new theme song performed by Johnny Rivers, "Secret Agent Man," which quickly became a hit record. Aside from those changes, though, *Secret Agent* offered the same *Danger Man* character of John Drake, played by the same actor, and subsequent episodes of the same *Danger Man* series, but this time it worked. And what worked even better was another British import, which was brought to the United States midway through its run, beginning with full-color episodes starring the aforementioned Diana Rigg as the secret agent Emma Peel.

THE AVENGERS

1961–69, ITV/Thames (U.K.); 1966–69, ABC. Producers: Leonard White, John Bryce, Julian Wintle, Albert Fennell, Brian Clemens. Stars: Ian Hendry, Patrick Macnee, Honor Blackman, Diana Rigg, Linda Thorson.

Like *Danger Man,* which had premiered in the U.K. in 1960, *The Avengers* had begun on TV overseas before Sean Connery first appeared as 007. As a black-and-white spy drama, *The Avengers* starred Patrick Macnee as John Steed, whose entire demeanor was an exaggerated caricature of the refined, old-fashioned British gentleman: bowler hat, bumbershoot, vintage car, impeccable manners, refined tastes. Steed's first partner in crime solving was Ian Hendry's Dr. Keel; his second, beginning with Season 2, was Cathy Gale, played by Honor Blackman, who, after leaving the show, would play

The Avengers, imported from England, came to the United States with Diana Rigg as the wildly emancipated Emma Peel and Patrick Macnee as her very proper British spy partner, John Steed.

Pussy Galore in *Goldfinger*. Neither of these partners was seen by U.S. viewers, whose exposure to *The Avengers* began with Diana Rigg's Emma Peel episodes, televised in the States beginning in 1966. And eventually Mrs. Peel, too, was replaced, by Linda Thorson as Tara King, beginning in 1968.

But it was the John Steed–Emma Peel stretch that made *The Avengers* so iconic and so fascinating. Theirs was a "will they or won't they?" chemistry in which they never did—or, perhaps, did all the time, but never so viewers could see. They certainly flirted like lovers. But they conversed, and related, as equals, and this was where *The Avengers* moved not only the spy genre but all of television forward a notch. Emma Peel not only represented the liberated female but reveled in it. The show, during their era, veered more toward humor and science fiction, with a cleverness and playfulness that was delightful to watch, as was Mrs. Peel's wardrobe. Cybernaut robots, silent-movie villains, body swappers—you never knew what you might encounter on *The Avengers,* except that it was bound to be the wittiest, strangest, and sexiest action series on the air at the time. Many other spy series, though, were playing it much straighter.

MISSION: IMPOSSIBLE

1966–73, CBS. Creator: Bruce Geller. Stars: Steven Hill, Peter Graves, Greg Morris, Barbara Bain, Martin Landau, Peter Lupus, Leonard Nimoy, Lynda Day George, Lesley Ann Warren.

Cast members came and went on the CBS series *Mission: Impossible,* but the show's structure remained the same: each episode opened with the head of the Impossible Missions Force getting his directives via an audio recording that would then self-destruct, leading to a fast-paced montage of almost subliminal scenes from the program to come, as Lalo Schifrin's energetic theme music propels the sequence forward. The show's unsettling lack of accountability remained the same, too: Each week, the voice on the recording would remind the mission's mastermind (Steven Hill's Daniel Briggs the first season, Peter Graves's Jim Phelps thereafter), "As always, should you or any of your IM Force be caught or killed, the secretary will disavow any knowledge of your actions." Then the recording would self-immolate, destroying the evidence of governmental culpability. If that ethical vacuum bothered viewers, it didn't show up in the ratings: by the end of its second season, *Mission: Impossible* was ranked No. 11, making it the most popular spy series televised to that date.

Martin Landau's Rollin Hand, like Ross Martin's Artemus Gordon on *The Wild Wild West,* had fun with his master-of-disguise duties. So did Leonard Nimoy as Paris, when he joined the show after Landau's departure. Peter Lupus's strongman Willy wore good sweaters, while Greg Morris's Barney was a good sweater. And Barbara Bain's Cinnamon was the show's first and best sex symbol; others to follow included Lesley Ann Warren's Dana and Lynda Day George's Lisa, but Cinnamon was the spiciest.

Many spy series, and movies, since *Mission: Impossible* have relied on this show's basic formula, which, of course, didn't exactly originate here in the first place. But the *Mission: Impossible* approach has proven especially durable, first with a 1988 ABC remake also starring Graves as Jim Phelps, then, beginning in 1996, as a series of movies starring Tom Cruise as the IMF

Mission: Impossible had different teams of spies, and spy bosses, all getting their marching orders from self-destructing recordings. Here, Peter Graves stars as IMF leader Jim Phelps.

agent Ethan Hunt. Brian De Palma directed the first, and other directors have included John Woo and J. J. Abrams. Cruise's first *Mission: Impossible* movie, while it revived the franchise and set the big-screen, big-budget standard, also betrayed the original series by having Jon Voight, playing the old IMF head Jim Phelps, revealed at the climax as a murderous traitor. Based on the character established by Peter Graves in the TV series, that never, ever would have happened. The spies in TV's *Mission: Impossible* never doubted their missions, much less their motives and loyalties. That type of spy, however, was just around the corner.

The late 1960s was the last big burst, for a while, for TV spies. In 1967, NBC affiliates in the United States, stricken by James Bond fever, finally began importing *The Saint*, starring Roger Moore, who, before too long, would play James Bond. A brief run on the entire network followed in 1968, a year that also gave us Robert Wagner in ABC's *It Takes a Thief*, playing a reluctant master thief forced by the government into acting as a one-man *Mission: Impossible* force or going to prison. No TV spy was more reluctant, though, than the one played by Patrick McGoohan in a still-controversial one-season British drama series, *The Prisoner*.

Imported and televised as a summer series by CBS in 1968, the same year it was produced, *The Prisoner* was actually more of a lengthy miniseries: a story with a beginning, middle, and end, though its allegorical narrative was open to multiple interpretations throughout. In the premiere episode, and the opening credits of every episode to follow, McGoohan's unnamed British secret agent was shown resigning his post angrily. Why? We don't know. Who is he? We don't even know that. He could be John Drake, the secret agent McGoohan played in *Danger Man* (renamed, for the U.S. market, *Secret Agent*), or not. But it matters little, because he's captured and whisked away to a remote place, surrounded by water and mountains, called only the Village. He's given the dehumanizing name Number 6, and it's the job of the Village's second-in-command, Number 2, to crack Number 6 and learn the real reasons for his resignation. Which country or spy agency is behind the Village? Number 6 doesn't know, and neither do we. But each episode, as McGoohan's stubborn and resourceful character resists interrogation, the unsuccessful Number 2 vanishes, to be replaced by another, until, in a bizarre conclusion as unconventional as later finales for *St. Elsewhere* and *The Sopranos*, Number 6 is awarded with the opportunity to meet, and unmask, Number 1, who turns out to be . . . himself. Hey, it was the 1960s. If you accept the trappings of a certain type of occupation, you become, in effect, your own jailer and your own prisoner.

Reluctance in secret agents, especially a justifiable reluctance to trust even those on their own side, was enhanced even further by *Tinker, Tailor, Soldier, Spy,* a 1979 British miniseries shown in the United States a year later. Based on the novel by John le Carré, it starred Alec Guinness as George Smiley, a retired British spy brought back to uncover the identity of a suspected mole slipping secrets to the Soviets. Instead of the gadgetry and flash of most spy shows riding in the wake of 007, *Tinker, Tailor,* like its 1982 sequel *Smiley's People,* was almost all about talking, listening, observing, and reasoning. It was cerebral, mature, difficult to predict, and more than a little melancholy. Smiley, like Number 6, was a different breed of spy: he questioned not only his suspects but also his own motives, assumptions, and associates. That would evolve, eventually, into the new breed of secret agent, one who, rather than blindly follow orders from above, would decide what to do, and whom to trust, for himself. And, in time, herself.

One of the most troubled and conflicted secret agent heroines arrived on TV courtesy of a spin-off from the 1990 French movie *La femme Nikita,* starring Anne Parillaud as a convicted felon taken from jail and given a new identity, and new responsibilities, as a secret agent ordered to kill on command. A TV version, starring Peta Wilson as Nikita, was made by USA Network in 1997 and remade by the CW network in 2010, starring Maggie Q as Nikita. Both versions retained the idea of their protagonists being coerced into doing the bidding of others, as in *It Takes a Thief,* but in *It Takes a Thief,* Robert Wagner's character never plotted to bring down and cripple the organization that had "recruited" him, as both Nikitas did in their respective series. And that's also the career path, from recruitment to betrayal to revenge, followed by the era's most famous and popular female spy, beginning the twenty-first century in an ABC series called *Alias.*

ALIAS

2001–6, ABC. Creator: J. J. Abrams. Stars: Jennifer Garner, Victor Garber, Bradley Cooper, Ron Rifkin, Michael Vartan, Lena Olin.

Before J. J. Abrams directed 2015's *Star Wars: The Force Awakens,* before he directed 2013's *Star Trek Into Darkness,* before he directed 2006's *Mission: Impossible III* (the one with Philip Seymour Hoffman as a particularly sadistic villain), and before he helped develop ABC's *Lost* in 2004, his first TV credit was as the creator of 1998's *Felicity,* a WB drama starring Keri Russell as a college freshman dealing with life, love, and midterm exams. At some point, Abrams began dreaming of a more dynamic alternate reality for

Alias starred Jennifer Garner as a young spy who was dressed to kill, or at least for serious espionage, in a J. J. Abrams series that balanced character development with an array of gadgets and costumes.

his heroine—"What if Felicity were a spy?"—and pitched that oddball idea, about a young woman with a secret life as a secret agent, to ABC. The network said yes to the new series idea immediately. Abrams cast Jennifer Garner, who had played Hannah Bibb in three episodes of *Felicity*, and presto: *Alias* was born. Garner played Sydney Bristol, a college graduate student who, for a few years, had lived a double life as a spy for SD-6, a covert division of the CIA. Except that, as Sydney very quickly learned, the SD-6 was not a CIA operation at all, but a rogue outfit that had targeted and recruited her under false pretenses. She went to the real CIA to offer her services as a double agent, which led to all sorts of trust issues—even Freudian ones, because her own father, played by Victor Garber, was a spy also, but for which side?

Alias was injected throughout with paranoia, betrayals, and uncertainty, but also with love interests (Bradley Cooper was one, for the first few seasons), increasingly *Avengers*-like sci-fi elements, and an eye-popping series of disguises, wigs, and costumes for Garner's Sydney. On one level, *Alias* was a graphic novel come to life, all images and attitude, but on another level it was a spy series deeply concerned about responsibility, loyalty, and the dangers of accepting orders, and even people, at face value. On TV, for secret agents, times had changed. Before long, so would perspectives. In 2010, fresh off the successes of *Mad Men* and *Breaking Bad*, the AMC cable network presented *Rubicon*, a brooding spy series about code breakers and information trackers. It didn't last long, but it presented an internal spy structure where it was unclear who, exactly, was the hero of this particular story, and that was a bold narrative concept that would soon come to full fruition, thanks to another cable TV offering.

HOMELAND

2011–, Showtime. Creators: Alex Ganza, Howard Gordon. Stars: Claire Danes, Mandy Patinkin, Damian Lewis.

Homeland was based on an Israeli series called *Prisoners of War*, about various POWs and their often awkward returns to society. Retooled for the United States and renamed *Homeland*, it became a modern variation on *The Fugitive*, with Claire Danes playing Carrie Mathison, the indefatigable

CIA investigator on the heels of Nicholas Brody (played by Damian Lewis), a returning POW she suspects of being a sleeper agent working for a Middle Eastern terrorist and determined to strike on U.S. soil. In this Platinum Age series, though, nothing is quite as linear, or simple, as it was in *The Fugitive*.

The central investigator, Carrie, is a woman in power and with responsibility, which would be evolutionary enough. But she's also bipolar, which makes her potentially unreliable as both an analyst and a protagonist. And Brody, the man in her sights, is initially portrayed so tightly wound, and so inscrutably, that we don't have access, at first, to his true motives. *Homeland* began with a complex, rarely seen approach to a TV series: there were two main characters, seemingly on opposite sides, but it wasn't clear who was right and who deserved the audience's sympathy and allegiance. And by the time it was revealed, late in the first season, that Brody was indeed planning a traitorous act and donning a bomb vest to target a highly ranked elected official, our viewing loyalties were split regardless. On *The Fugitive*, the accused murderer Richard Kimble was innocent, but on *The Sopranos* Tony

Homeland looks at spies and spying through a much more complex lens, questioning motives as well as actions. Claire Danes stars as CIA agent Carrie Mathison, with Mandy Patinkin as her boss, Saul Berenson. Their relationship, like their job status, has been quite fluid over the course of the series.

Soprano actually was guilty of being a New Jersey mob boss. On *Breaking Bad,* Walter White really was a murderous meth dealer. And on *Homeland,* Brody really was the sleeper terrorist Carrie suspected he was, but she ended up loving him anyway, as did viewers. The world of espionage, like the world of TV spies, had become a very complicated place. In retrospect, maybe it was always that way, though it would take a period spy series to drive that point home, from a very different point of view.

THE AMERICANS

2013–, FX. Creator: Joseph Weisberg. Stars: Keri Russell, Matthew Rhys, Noah Emmerich.

The innovation, as well as the beauty, of the FX series *The Americans* is that it turns the conventions of spy dramas inside out. Instead of watching secret agents in action as we infiltrate them, we watch as they infiltrate us. In the Reagan-era Cold War, with the Berlin Wall still standing and dividing,

The Americans stars Keri Russell and Matthew Rhys as Soviet spies in the early 1980s posing as a married American couple and gathering information about government secrets while raising their two teenage children.

Keri Russell—the actress who, as the star of his *Felicity* series, J. J. Abrams mused might be an interesting college-age secret agent—now played Elizabeth Jennings, an American wife and mother, working part-time at the travel agency operated by her husband, Philip (Matthew Rhys). Both of them are longtime Soviet sleeper agents, paired by the State and shipped to the States, where they had two children, now teenagers. Their children, like their suburban neighbors, were completely unaware of their status as secret agents, and one of those neighbors, Stan Beeman (played by Noah Emmerich), is an FBI agent working some of the very cases Philip and Elizabeth are tasked by the KGB with carrying out. Stan is to his neighbors what Hank is to Walter White on *Breaking Bad*: a dogged investigator who has no idea his quarry is so close, so familiar, and so trusting. Yet trust, in *The Americans*, is the biggest issue of all, across the board, and is explored here in several different uncomfortable and unpredictable permutations. Stan, whose marriage is disintegrating for various reasons, falls in love with a Russian consulate worker named Nina (Annet Mahendru) while coercing her into working as a double agent. Philip, in one of his undercover disguises and aliases, seduces an FBI worker in Stan's office and goes so far as to marry her, while his own "real" marriage to Elizabeth—itself a sham of sorts, a government-arranged pairing—is strained by their missions, their efforts to maintain their cover as a "normal" family, and their increasingly differing political philosophies. Elizabeth remains fiercely loyal to all Soviet ideas and ideals, while Philip has come to enjoy, if not embrace, much of what the West has to offer. And when their teen daughter, Paige, embraces a local church group and is earmarked by Philip and Elizabeth's handlers as being old enough to be told the truth and recruited to the cause as they were, *The Americans* becomes all about identity and loyalty, responsibility and trust. Whose daughter is Paige? Philip and Elizabeth's, or the KGB's?

The Americans has the disguises and missions of *Alias*, and the shifting and confusing loyalties of *Homeland*, but played out in a way where we're incongruously and uncomfortably rooting for these Soviet spies to prevail, at home and at their missions. The entire spy craze, in the 1960s, was ignited by such James Bond movies as *From Russia with Love*, and some fifty years later that title serves as a perfect summation for the viewpoint, and the motivation, of *The Americans*. The series was sufficiently aware of TV history, as well as general history, to set one episode against the controversial telecast of ABC's 1983 telemovie *The Day After*, which frightened United

States viewers by presenting a fictional drama in which the Soviet Union dropped a nuclear bomb on Lawrence, Kansas. All the characters in *The Americans* were watching, as well they would have been, and their respective reactions were appropriately complicated. Moral ambiguity, and seeing conflicts and even enemies from both sides, have become the province, and the specialty, of Platinum Age TV spy series.

15 GENERAL DRAMA

KEY EVOLUTIONARY STAGES

Twin Peaks	1990–91, ABC
The West Wing	1999–2006, NBC
Six Feet Under	2001–5, HBO
The Wire	2002–8, HBO
Mad Men	2007–15, AMC

Elsewhere in this book, we've isolated and covered some of the specific subgenres that have been most prevalent and dominant throughout television history. Crime. Medical. Legal. But in the field of drama, that doesn't account for everything, and there are shows, whether they be family dramas, shows examining occupations less commonly dramatized on TV, or just defiantly unclassifiable ones, that elude the dominant classifications. Every decade starting with the 1960s has them, and some are exceptional exceptions indeed. CBS's *East Side/West Side* (1963–64) starred George C. Scott as a committed social worker dealing with the New York slums. Period dramas looked at family life in CBS's *Waltons* (1971–81) and racism in NBC's *I'll Fly Away* (1991–93). Modern family dramas about everyday life were depicted, using very different approaches in different decades, in ABC's *Family* (1976–80), ABC's *thirtysomething* (1987–91), ABC's *Life Goes On* (1989–93), NBC's *Friday Night Lights* (2006–11), and NBC's *Parenthood* (2010–15). Of those, *thirtysomething, Friday Night Lights,* and *Parenthood* were all superlative, as were three other dramas, over the years, that stand out more or less alone.

There's CBS's *Lou Grant* (1977–82), a drama about people putting out a major metropolitan newspaper; CBS's *Picket Fences* (1992–96), a David E. Kelley drama that managed to be at least four genres in one; and ABC's *Lost* (2004–10), a mystery parable drama that got more complicated, and less classifiable, every season.

Perhaps they, and others like them, require and deserve more of a catchall category, something along the lines of "general drama." And along those lines, here are five evolutionary steps deserving of longer separate mention—five TV drama series that are as singular as they are spectacular.

TWIN PEAKS

1990–91, ABC. Creators: David Lynch, Mark Frost. Directors: David Lynch, Lesli Linka Glatter, Caleb Deschanel, Tim Hunter, Todd Holland, Mark Frost, Stephen Gyllenhaal, Diane Keaton, others. Stars: Kyle MacLachlan, Michael Ontkean, Sheryl Lee, Sherilyn Fenn, Madchen Amick, Richard Beymer, Dana Ashbrook, Lara Flynn Boyle, Peggy Lipton, James Marshall, Everett McGill, Jack Nance, Joan Chen, Piper Laurie, Kimmy Robertson, Harry Goaz, Eric DaRe, Wendy Robie, Ray Wise, Russ Tamblyn, Don S. Davis, Grace Zabriskie, Catherine E. Coulson, Kenneth Welsh, David Patrick Kelly, Miguel Ferrer, Heather Graham, David Lynch, Frank Silva, Michael Parks, Michael J. Anderson, Clarence Williams III, Julee Cruise, David Duchovny.

Less than a year after this book is to be published, the Showtime cable network is scheduled to present its 2017 revival of *Twin Peaks,* with the series creators, David Lynch and Mark Frost, teaming up once again, as they did on their short-lived, long-influential 1990–91 ABC series. I'm very excited by the prospect of *Peaks* returning, especially in the right hands and on a premium cable network, where virtually anything goes, mostly because, in the twenty-five years since ABC presented *Twin Peaks,* there has still been nothing quite like it. Not even close, and not because other producers and networks haven't tried to copy it. And in a series that embraced illogic and dream states, there's even a logical justification for revisiting it now: Early in the original *Twin Peaks,* the FBI agent Dale Cooper (Kyle MacLachlan) visits the odd northwestern town of Twin Peaks to investigate the murder of a high school girl named Laura Palmer and has a dream—a vision—in which older versions of himself and someone who looks very much like Laura are seated in a mysterious Red Room, hosted by a dancing dwarf who speaks cryptically (and so oddly he requires subtitles). After Cooper awakens, he describes the strange scene as taking place twenty-five years in the future. Later in the series, as weirdness piles upon weirdness, we learn that the Red Room is part of the Black Lodge, and it's all part of a *Twin Peaks* mythology that could well be picked up on in our present, which is the former future of the ABC version. Weird? Incomprehensible? Fun to watch, and hear, and ponder? Welcome to *Twin Peaks*, whatever its current population. (And in March 2016, after principal photography was completed, Showtime released the full cast list for the new *Twin Peaks* program, which included MacLachlan and many more of the show's original players.)

In 1990, *Twin Peaks* began with a feature-length TV pilot, directed by Lynch and co-written by Lynch and Frost. One of the opening scenes has a

Twin Peaks, created by David Lynch and Mark Frost, was and remains an astoundingly different approach to the TV drama. The original ABC version starred Kyle MacLachlan (left) as FBI agent Dale Cooper, Michael Ontkean as sheriff Harry Truman, and lots of doughnuts.

character, just about to do some early-morning fishing, discover the body of a young woman. He calls the local sheriff and makes an initially vague report: "She's dead. Wrapped in plastic." The corpse in question was that of the high school student Laura Palmer (Sheryl Lee), seen thereafter in flashbacks, dream sequences, or as a doppelgänger relative. The identity of her murderer became the biggest pop-culture obsession since the "Who shot J.R.?" mystery on CBS's *Dallas* a decade before, and "Who killed Laura Palmer?," like the J. R. Ewing phenomenon, intensified over the summer and became the cover story of several national magazines. In fact, in those pre-Internet days, the "Who killed Laura Palmer?" mystery, and *Twin Peaks* in general, generated their own national magazine, which analyzed episodes and plotlines, encouraged letters from other *Twin Peaks* fans, and interviewed virtually anyone associated with the series. The magazine's name: *Wrapped in Plastic*.

The Red Room dancing dwarf scene in *Twin Peaks* came two episodes after the movie-length pilot and also included another jaw-dropping, lengthy scene—one in which Dale Cooper walked the local Twin Peaks law-enforcement team through an exercise involving throwing rocks at a bottle. It was an exercise he said was inspired by a dream, and by Tibetan philosophy, and it was one of the strangest things I'd ever seen on television. Until, that is, the end of that very same episode, in which the whole Red Room thing happened and left me wondering what in the hell I'd just witnessed. That week, I did something I had never done before, and haven't done since, as a TV critic for NPR's *Fresh Air:* two weeks after broadcasting a review of a new series, I returned to review it again. Back then, *Twin Peaks* was that special. And it still is.

The show's partly or wholly surrealistic plots and characters made *Twin Peaks* the most unusual and puzzling TV drama since CBS's *Prisoner* miniseries in 1968. Its hefty helpings of playful allusions, especially to movies (*Laura* and *Double Indemnity* in particular) and TV shows (the look-alike-cousin concept from *The Patty Duke Show*, the one-armed man from *The Fugitive*), made *Twin Peaks* the central topic of conversation everywhere from the watercooler to the classroom. Lynch directed only a handful of episodes, but all the most resonant, unshakable set pieces were his, including the Red Room, the rock-throwing exercise, and the disturbing death of Laura's identical cousin, Madeleine. The actors on the show were amazing to watch and inventively cast: Lynch and company pulled from old movies and TV shows (Russ Tamblyn and Richard Beymer from *West Side Story*,

Peggy Lipton and Clarence Williams III from ABC's *Mod Squad*), hired a small squadron of beautiful young vixens (Sherilyn Fenn, Madchen Amick, Lara Flynn Boyle, Sheryl Lee, Heather Graham), showcased dynamic and idiosyncratic actors (Kyle MacLachlan, Ray Wise, David Duchovny, Miguel Ferrer), and even tossed out meaningful roles to chauffeurs and crew members (Harry Goaz and Frank Silva, respectively, as Deputy Andy and "Killer Bob").

More than any other series on TV before or since, *Twin Peaks* was intensely visual and just as intensely aural. Lynch paid more attention to the way things sounded than anyone else had or would, and the show's memorable images—from traffic lights swaying in the darkness to those opening-credit shots of waterfalls displaying their awesome natural power and sawmill blades being sharpened robotically—are much too numerous to cite. But the musical director of *Twin Peaks*, Angelo Badalamenti, deserves an individual citation, because his haunting and jaunty contributions, as much as anything else, made *Twin Peaks* what it is today. And, it appears, what it will be tomorrow: the composer Badalamenti, like the co-creators, Lynch and Frost, and the actors Kyle MacLachlan and Sheryl Lee, have returned for 2017's *Twin Peaks*. Just as Michael J. Anderson's dancing-dwarf Man from Another Place predicted in Cooper's Red Room dream: "That gum you like is going to come back in style!"—which was the cryptic phrase Lynch tweeted in 2014 to hint at a probable *Twin Peaks* revival. And this time, we'll have social media . . .

THE WEST WING

1999–2006, NBC. Creator: Aaron Sorkin. Stars: Martin Sheen, Allison Janney, John Spencer, Bradley Whitford, Richard Schiff, Janel Moloney, Dulé Hill, Joshua Malina, Rob Lowe, Stockard Channing, Jimmy Smits, Kathryn Joosten, Lily Tomlin, Kristin Chenoweth, Alan Alda, Timothy Busfield, Elisabeth Moss, Moira Kelly, Gary Cole, Mary-Louise Parker, John Amos, Tim Matheson, Anna Deavere Smith, Ron Silver, Janeane Garofalo, Oliver Platt, Danica McKellar, Lisa Edelstein.

I consider Aaron Sorkin's *West Wing* one of the pivot points of the Platinum Age of Television. Along with HBO's *Sopranos* in the same year of 1999, it aimed higher, and got there, just as TV was heading into a new century of fresh possibilities. Even now, the premiere episode of NBC's *West Wing* crackles with wit, intelligence, energy, and simple inspiration. Or perhaps it's complex inspiration, because it's not easy to do a successful drama series, much less a riveting one, about politics. That's why this show is in this catchall category: perhaps it's the dramatic equivalent of a workplace comedy, or drama's version of a family sitcom. Except that on *The West Wing*, the Bartlets just happen to occupy the White House, so it'd be more like a First Family sitcom. And make no mistake, portions of *The West*

The West Wing, created by Aaron Sorkin, presented an idealized view of political operatives, showcased an outstanding cast, and popularized the "walk and talk" method of filming often expository scenes. Martin Sheen, as President Josiah Bartlet, is shown here flanked by his White House staffers in an early episode.

Wing are indeed laugh-out-loud funny. Other portions, though, are weep-silently sad. *The West Wing,* especially the first few years of its seven-year run, reset the gold standard for dramatic TV series. Reset it, as I see it, to platinum.

The closest thing to *The West Wing,* in TV drama history, is *The Senator,* a 1970–71 edition of NBC's *Bold Ones,* starring Hal Holbrook as Hays Stowe, a first-term U.S. senator trying to navigate his way through Beltway politics. The time was pre-Watergate, but *The Senator* was ahead of its time in identifying and dramatizing a political schism: the idealism of its main character versus the cynicism of those entrenched in power positions around him. *The Senator* lasted only a shortened season but probed such then-incendiary topics as industrial pollution, assassination threats, and—reacting to the shooting of Kent State University students by the Ohio National Guard in 1970—a two-part TV episode, later that same year, in which Senator Stowe convenes a hearing to investigate the shooting deaths of college students by members of the National Guard. *The Senator* won the Emmy for Outstanding Drama Series in 1971, as well as Emmys for writing, for direction, and for Holbrook's portrayal of the idealistic senator.

On *The West Wing,* Martin Sheen never won an Emmy as President Bartlet, though so many actors around him were awarded theirs: Allison Janney won four times, and Richard Schiff, John Spencer, Bradley Whitford, Stockard Channing, and Alan Alda (as one of the politicians running to replace Bartlet in the Oval Office) all won once. And *The West Wing,* like *The Senator,* earned the Emmy for Outstanding Drama Series, but *The West Wing* did it four years in a row, while ranking as high as No. 10 in the ratings, and while its competition most years included *The Sopranos.* More currently, TV shows about politicians have tended more toward the soapy (CBS's *Commander in Chief,* ABC's *Scandal*) or the severely cynical (HBO's *Veep* and Netflix's *House of Cards,* both of which are excellent but tonally quite different). *The West Wing,* especially as Sorkin wrote it, presented a presidential administration in which staffers tried their best to do the right thing. Their best was usually better than anyone around them: characters talked fast and moved faster, usually doing them both at the same time (in what became known as "walk and talk" extended takes). And the right thing, in most cases, was humane, not partisan. *The West Wing* showed politicians—most of them, anyway—as passionate and involved representatives of the people. It was meant to be more fantasy than documentary, but it did manage to ask meaningful topical questions and tackle hard national issues, two things that hadn't been done much on prime-time TV since, well, *The Senator*.

Sorkin left the show after four seasons, the first few of which were spectacular, but even after he left, *The West Wing* achieved something quite exciting, when it mounted a live presidential "debate" in 2005 between the show's fictional Republican and Democratic candidates, played respectively by Alan Alda and Jimmy Smits. The debate was scripted, but the performance was live, and a very exciting throwback to the days of live Golden Age TV.

SIX FEET UNDER

2001–5, HBO. Creator: Alan Ball. Stars: Peter Krause, Michael C. Hall, Frances Conroy, Lauren Ambrose, Freddy Rodriguez, Mathew St. Patrick, Rachel Griffiths, Richard Jenkins, Jeremy Sisto.

Without fear of contradiction, I feel free to assert that HBO's *Six Feet Under*, created by Alan Ball, is the best TV show ever made about a family-run funeral home. It's also like another HBO series, Tom Fontana's *Oz*, which took place in a maximum-security prison. Until Netflix's *Orange Is the New Black* came along, there weren't a lot of other prison shows out there, either. Yet even though *Oz* and *Six Feet Under* don't have much competition thematically, both of them, right out of the blocks, burst forth with original, effective ways of telling their stories.

The premiere of *Six Feet Under* opened with the patriarchal owner of the Fisher & Sons Funeral Home, played by Richard Jenkins, going about his day when he was killed in a car accident. Viewers wouldn't know until the following week to recognize that string of events as a reliable storytelling pattern: an opening death scene, then an episode dealing, in part, with the decedent's memorial service, loved ones, and leftover baggage. And some, like the newly dead Nate Fisher Sr., decide to hang around for a while and haunt the place and some members of his family.

Said family members include Peter Krause as Nate, who returns for his father's funeral and is reluctantly talked into staying to help; Michael C. Hall as David, the younger, more responsible brother, whose homosexual-

Six Feet Under was a family drama dealing with existential questions of mortality and life's meaning housed in the unusual setting of a family-run funeral home. The core cast included (from left) matriarch Ruth Fisher (Frances Conroy), daughter Claire (Lauren Ambrose), sons Nate (Peter Krause) and David (Michael C. Hall), and funeral-home employee Federico Diaz (Freddy Rodriguez).

ity is only one of the things he's repressing; and Lauren Ambrose as the youngest child, Claire, who, like their mother, Ruth (Frances Conroy), has little idea what she wants to do next. Every episode explores the concepts of death, grief, loneliness, and the meaning of life, and *Six Feet Under* is a series where no character is either noble or safe from stress. Yet they do, sometimes despite themselves, learn to support one another as family, even though there are plenty of confrontations, misunderstandings, deceptions, and disappointments along the way. And at the end of their journey, in the final moments of *Six Feet Under,* the series ends with one of the most beautiful, organically perfect TV finales ever presented. As one character drives away from the family and the funeral home and looks behind in the rearview mirror, we begin to reflect, so to speak, on the future and see the year and circumstances of each major character's death, a flash-forward version of the way each show had opened. It's one amazing way to end a series, by killing all the main characters. It was also a foolproof way to torpedo the possibility of a sequel.

THE WIRE

2002–8, HBO. Creator: David Simon. Writers: David Simon, Ed Burns, George Pelecanos, Richard Price, Dennis Lehane, David Mills, others. Stars: Dominic West, Wendell Pierce, Lance Reddick, Deirdre Lovejoy, Sonja Sohn, Clarke Peters, Michael Kenneth Williams, Idris Elba, Reg E. Cathey, Peter Gerety, Michael B. Jordan, Callie Thorne.

If the central thread of *The Wire,* David Simon's brilliant examination (and part autopsy) of a crumbling American city, is indeed the titular eavesdropping tool with which police listen in on a surprisingly sophisticated Baltimore drug-running operation, then *The Wire* is a cop show and could be housed snugly under the TV drama subdivision of crime. But *The Wire* is so, so much more than that. It's the study of a city's problems—drugs, violence, the crumbling of infrastructure and neighborhoods, political corruption, and more—as seen through a different perspective, or prism, each season. The last time a TV drama looked at a city's institutional problems this empathically and critically might well have been *East Side/West Wide*

The Wire looked at Baltimore from the perspective of a different city institution each season. The first season of David Simon's complex drama looked at street drugs and the city police effort to corral the dealers and drug traffic. Some of the investigators were played by (from left) Sonja Sohn, Wendell Pierce, and Dominic West.

more than fifty years ago. No series, though, has ever done it the way David Simon and his determined and gifted collaborators did it, by focusing on a different part of the city each season and leaving it to the audience to pay attention and weave it all together.

The first season of *The Wire* seemed to be a straightforward police investigation into drugs, a longer version of the sort of case Simon might have dramatized on NBC's *Homicide: Life on the Street,* the series that pulled the former Baltimore police reporter into the orbit of television production. But as the season went on, we learned at least as much about the drug kingpins and street hustlers as we did about the cops. We got to know the detectives, all right, especially Dominic West's Jimmy McNulty and Wendell Pierce's Bunk Moreland. But we also got to know, quite well, the drug kingpin Stringer Bell (played by Idris Elba), the street-level drug dealer Wallace (Michael B. Jordan), and the opportunistic street thief Omar Little (Michael K. Williams). Breaks in the case were made methodically and slowly, and given the bureaucracy and obstacles in place, the odds were against them making much of a dent at all. In the dramas singled out in this chapter, the political staffers of *The West Wing,* the morticians of *Six Feet Under,* and the cops on *The Wire* have something in common with McNulty and his partner, and with the squad members of NBC's *Hill Street Blues:* everyone is struggling against overwhelming forces, where there's always someone or something new demanding your attention, and every day seems like an impossible task just to break even.

Future seasons of *The Wire,* using some but not all of the cast members from previous years, focused on various other aspects of Baltimore's city institutions. The docks and dockworkers. The drug world again, but this time filtered through the prism of city hall and the politicians. The public school system. And finally, the media, as deconstructed through Baltimore's once-thriving, now-struggling newspapers. That sounds less like a TV series than a series of monographs, but in the hands of Simon and the other writers and producers *The Wire* was fascinating, unpredictable, and, yes, educational. As drama, it was an ambitious, multilayered study of crime and punishment, actions and consequences. *The Wire* was a total success artistically but failed, over its six years and five seasons, to win a single Emmy. That's a crime that it may take a wiretap to solve, but Emmys or no Emmys *The Wire* emerged with the reputation of being one of the best TV dramas ever made. It's a reputation the show very much deserves.

MAD MEN

2007–15, AMC. Creator: Matthew Weiner. Stars: Jon Hamm, Elisabeth Moss, Christina Hendricks, John Slattery, Vincent Kartheiser, January Jones, Kiernan Shipka, Robert Morse, Jessica Pare, Rich Sommer, Aaron Staton, Alison Brie, Jared Harris, Maggie Siff, Harry Hamlin, Talia Balsam, Linda Cardellini, Julia Ormond, Ray Wise.

A few other hard-to-classify drama series mentioned at the top of this chapter are set in the past—*The Waltons, I'll Fly Away*—but *Mad Men*, even among shows dealing with a previous era, is in a place all its own. The Depression-era *Waltons* was primarily pure nostalgia, ultimately as warm and cozy as the sweet "Good nights" that bounced around the walls at bedtime. *I'll Fly Away* was much more clear-eyed in its examination of the past, but its 1950s story was concerned almost entirely with the topic of race, as seen through a white southern attorney (Sam Waterston), his African-American housekeeper (Regina Taylor), and their families. *Mad Men*, which premiered on AMC in 2007, dealt with race too, but seldom overtly, and never as the single focus of an episode. On Matthew Weiner's *Mad Men*, set against the world of Madison Avenue advertising, people were glib and gifted at speaking in flowery and seductive tones and phrases, but rarely, if

Mad Men was a period drama about Madison Avenue advertising agency owners and employees, centering on Don Draper (played by Jon Hamm) as an inventive ad agency executive with a gift for reinvention, as in the show's famous finale.

ever, did they expose themselves by telling the truth or revealing their true thoughts and desires. And when they did, in this repressed era of the 1950s and 1960s, things seldom went well.

The central character of *Mad Men* was Jon Hamm's Don Draper, a man so adept at creating alluring advertising slogans and campaigns that he had once sold himself as a complete, and completely false, bill of goods. He had adopted another man's identity during wartime, a secret that ultimately surfaced, but bore few measurable consequences, except on Don's own conscience. Appearances may be deceiving, but they also just might be more important than reality.

Individually, each episode of *Mad Men* was a richly detailed character study, decorated with lavishly detailed set designs and costumes, that let us know the quirks, joys, and frustrations of these colorful characters. And as the years progressed, in the series and in the timeline of the narrative, the characters, like their wardrobes, got even more colorful. During the late 1950s, the men appeared to have it made: each man seemed to be issued a matching fedora, a bottomless supply of triple martinis, and a tag-team complement of adoring and forgiving women. But by the time *Mad Men* moved into the mid-1960s, after the assassination of John F. Kennedy, the foundations of their world had shaken, if not fallen. It was no surprise, but it was a delight, when the advertising firm's women, Elisabeth Moss's Peggy Olson and Christina Hendricks's Joan Harris, stood tall at the end. And it was both a surprise and a delight when Don Draper, who had spent much of the latter seasons spiraling out of control and out of relevance, ended the show by having an epiphany during a visit to a seaside hilltop religious retreat—an epiphany not about his soul, or the meaning of life, but about how to turn his feel-good surroundings into a potent new ad for a soft drink. And *Mad Men*, in an incredibly inventive end to its final episode, went out not with a bang or a blackout but with a full-length Coke commercial. The ending of *Mad Men* was as perfect as it was risky and allowed the series, like Don Draper, to go out on top—not with a cliff-hanger, just on a cliff.

DAVID SIMON

BORN: 1960, Washington, D.C.

FIRST TV CREDIT: Series based on book by him, *Homicide: Life on the Street,* 1993, NBC.

LANDMARK TV SERIES: *Homicide: Life on the Street,* 1993–99, NBC; *The Corner,* 2000, HBO; *The Wire,* 2002–8, HBO; *Generation Kill,* 2008, HBO; *Treme,* 2010–13, HBO; *Show Me a Hero,* 2015, HBO.

"I was not really much of a TV person," David Simon admits, making him different from most of the other baby boomer TV artists interviewed for this book. Born in Washington, D.C., in 1960, Simon missed the so-called Golden Age of TV, so his inspirations as a dramatist came later. "I was too late for *Playhouse 90,*" he says. "I was too late for the first real, sort of provocative, dramas of television . . . I'm not seeing any of that stuff, not even in reruns. The only stuff that made it to reruns were sitcoms." Well, sitcoms and action series—Simon recalls watching *Combat!* reruns, then playing army outside as a little kid. "The only time when you controlled the set, when you were a little kid, was during the day, right after school," he says. He also remembers loving, for a brief time, military-related sitcoms: *McHale's Navy* and *Hogan's Heroes,* and repeats of Phil Silvers as Sergeant Bilko in *The Phil Silvers Show* (originally titled *You'll Never Get Rich*), though he tired of them all after a time. One sitcom running in repeats on those childhood afternoons, however, never lost its appeal. "I fell in love with *The Honeymooners,*" Simon says, "and stayed in love with *The Honeymooners.* To this day, I can't walk out on a *Honeymooners* episode. If I walk through the room, and I'm going somewhere and *The Honeymooners* is on, I've got to sit down."

As Simon reached adulthood, he remembers being underwhelmed by most TV drama series ("It was all so bad") but catching enough episodes of two new NBC series, starting with *Hill Street Blues* in 1981, to be impressed by what he saw as a new direction and seriousness. "I wasn't an appointment television guy," Simon says, "but I saw enough of *Hill Street,* and then of *St. Elsewhere,* to realize some of this is really good writing!"

Simon's main interest growing up was journalism, an interest inherited from his ex-newspaperman father. At the University of Maryland, College Park, he edited the school newspaper, became a college stringer for the *Baltimore Sun,* then became a staff writer there after graduating in 1983, working the police beat. Within a decade, he had turned his experiences covering the city's Homicide Unit into a nonfiction book, 1991's *Homicide: A Year on the Killing Streets.* The book was optioned for television by the production partners Tom Fontana and the Baltimore native Barry Levinson and within two years was the inspiration for a new NBC series, called *Homicide: Life on the Street,* with Paul Attanasio credited as creator for adapting the book to television. Simon was invited to propose story ideas, then write scripts, and was eventually brought on as a producer, changing his career path markedly and irrevocably. His first teleplay, based on a story by Tom Fontana and co-written with his former college friend and fellow journalist David Mills, was presented as the Season 2 opener—a 1994 episode called "Bop Gun," about a distraught tourist to Baltimore who watched helplessly as his wife was shot and killed by a robber. Robin Williams, in an Emmy-nominated performance, played the tourist, and Simon and Mills won a Writers Guild of America Award for their teleplay. Mills got a job working for David Milch on another pioneering cop show, ABC's *NYPD Blue,* and helped Simon land a freelance story assignment there. Simon remained in Baltimore, at both the city and the newspaper, to work on his second book, about life in the inner city as seen through the microcosmic focus of a single urban street corner. Simon eventually finished that book, co-written with the former Baltimore cop Ed Burns, but not before learning his newspaper was offering buyouts to reporters to leave the paper voluntarily and help cut staff budgets.

"And to my great astonishment," Simon says, "I had job offers from *NYPD Blue* and *Homicide* at the moment that my newspaper was offering a buyout. I really didn't want to go to television, but I wanted to finish the second book. And you can't go to another newspaper when you're finishing a book manuscript because, when you go to a new newspaper, you've got to kick ass for a couple years." Simon didn't think he could jump to another newspaper and immediately ask for a leave of absence to edit his manuscript, so he decided to stay in Baltimore, take the *Homicide* staff job, and finish the book in his spare time. "I thought, 'Well, I'll do this for a while. And it's a show based on my book, and I'll learn how to do it; it'll be a good skill set. And then I'll go to a real newspaper.'" Simon pauses and chuckles. "And that was twenty years ago."

At *Homicide: Life on the Street,* Simon did indeed learn a good skill set and a lot more. For starters, he learned, from Fontana and the co–executive producer Jim Finnerty, how to manage money and allocate resources on a TV production, something Simon has done proudly ever since. "Jim taught us to respect the budget and to respect money, because in the Fontana/Levinson world, you never went over your budget. And if you went over for the day, you had a good reason, and you made it up somewhere else . . . Jimmy Finnerty's great phrase was: Have a conscience. It's not your money . . .

"You'd be amazed," Simon adds, "how unlikely an ethic that is on television."

As for what he learned about writing TV from *Homicide* in general, and Tom Fontana in particular, Simon replies, "Oh, just about everything. I mean really. Tom's my mentor." What sorts of writing tips did Simon pick up during his time there? "Every line justifying itself. Forward motion. Don't come in on the beginning of a conversation if you can help it . . . Try to get in and out faster. Pacing!" Simon says, shooting off quickly summarized lessons like rounds from an automatic rifle. "Pacing is what I didn't have any of when I came in as a prose writer. And then, there was something that was very much admired in the Fontana camp, which was . . . don't write exactly to what you're trying to say with a scene, because human beings don't talk that way."

Simon remembers, when he first landed in the *Homicide: Life on the Street* writing room, the writer-producer James Yoshimura handing him a book on Chekhov and a quick, valuable lesson on writing dialogue. "Every play by Chekhov," Simon says, distilling the lesson, "is people not saying what they mean. Or saying what they mean, but only in the most roundabout and incomplete ways. And the more that human beings do that onstage, the more believable the drama can be. If they do it too much, there's no there there. But if they don't do it enough, it's like a Clifford Odets play. They're all there for a reason, and they're going to demonstrate it too quickly and too obviously."

As Simon was learning and practicing the ins and outs of television, he was also finishing his second book. This one, co-written with the former Baltimore police detective Ed Burns, was published in 1997 as *The Corner: A Year in the Life of an Inner-City Neighborhood.* It, too, was optioned for television—this time by HBO, which hired Simon and his Homicide "Bop Gun" writing partner, David Mills, to adapt the book as a six-part miniseries. Televised in 2000, the story of a poor family living in poverty, in a neighborhood dominated by drug dealers and addicts, won several Emmy Awards, including for Outstanding Miniseries and for the teleplay by Simon and Mills. HBO encouraged Simon to do whatever he wanted next, and what he wanted to do was a complex sociological drama series called *The Wire,* in which each season would look at Baltimore's people and problems through the prism of a different institution, including the police, the docks, the schools, and the media. *The Wire* was Simon's undisputed masterpiece, and from that point on he produced all his TV work for HBO. The 2008 Iraqi war miniseries *Generation Kill* was co-written with Ed Burns of *The Corner* and Evan Wright, who wrote the original nonfiction book. The 2010–13 series *Treme,* examining life in New Orleans after Hurricane Katrina, was co-created with his fellow *Homicide* and *The Wire* writer-producer Eric Overmyer. And his 2015 miniseries *Show Me a Hero,* based on a case of a young politician in Yonkers dealing with racism and politics concerning a desegregation housing ruling, was co-written with Lisa Belkin, author of the original nonfiction book of the same name, and the *Wire* staff writer and story editor William F. Zorzi. All these dramas were excellent. None of them came easily.

"Listen," Simon says, describing his long-term relationship with HBO. "It would be completely smooth sailing for me if I could've acquired an audience. But I never really have." After the fact, when you add in DVD boxed sets and downloading and streaming sites, people do find his stuff eventually, and continue to do so, he adds—"So that stuff still has value to whatever the grand lending library that modern television now is." That's why, Simon figures, he can continue to be seen as of value to HBO.

"But it's been a long, strange trip," he says, "and I've gone through a lot of years begging to finish shows, and begging to complete narrative arcs, because I come from the prose world. It's a little surreal, and I never cease to be exhausted by it . . .

"I never heard of anybody coming in with five book chapters and having people say, 'This is really great, but we tried selling these already, and we didn't get the number that we were hoping for on the book list, so don't bother with the last seven. We're only going to put out half the book.' What the fuck? It's terrifying! Because who wants to waste time delivering half a story? And that's the terror that I live with. Even at HBO.

"It would have been easier if I'd landed some *Sopranos* or *Game of Thrones* or *Walking Dead*–like numbers early on, and I could run on those fumes. But I never did, so everything is still an argument. But to credit HBO, I come in with six hours on public housing, or three seasons on the culture of a city and how it might resurrect in the wake of great distress, and they listen more than they otherwise might, because they know whatever I'm talking about, at least I'm going to execute at a certain level . . .

"But when you do something like *Generation Kill*, there's a ceiling. *Generation Kill* had a ceiling because it was an unpopular war, and we were in the midst of it, and most of the country would not go there. *Treme* has a ceiling because it doesn't have any of the currencies we know work in television: it wasn't overtly violent, it wasn't hyper-sexualized, and it didn't have the stakes of the Oval Office or anything like that."

One answer, Simon has discovered, is the same one discovered and embraced by other ambitious TV producers of late: a rebirth, if not redefinition, of the television miniseries. By painting on a smaller canvas, Simon says, he solves the fear of having his narrative stopped prematurely and gains another major benefit as well.

"I know I'm going to get to the end right away," Simon says of the miniseries form, "so right away, I'm not fighting that fight. How many hours do I have? Okay, I'll plan six . . . and that's healthy. About six is right for this," he says of *Show Me a Hero*, "just as I would say seven or eight were all we needed for *Generation Kill*." And then, he adds, there's the bonus of casting a miniseries, as opposed to a regular series. "You can start pulling actors that you wouldn't otherwise pull. Despite the rising quality of television, there are many, many actors from the feature world who are not going to sign for three or four or five years, and you can't get them." But for the tense and impressive *Show Me a Hero,* Simon was able to cast Oscar Isaac, fresh from *Inside Llewyn Davis* and *A Most Violent Year,* as his Yonkers politician leading man and also book such supporting players as Alfred Molina, Catherine Keener, and Winona Ryder. And not only because of the work schedule, but because of the content and the acting challenge.

"If you're an actor," Simon points out, "doing long form is a revelation. Nobody gets to shape a story over six hours if all you do is features . . . How do you pull people like this, except by the fact that the work is not a comic-book movie, and they're making too many comic-book movies? . . .

"People want the work to matter," Simon concludes. "I profess a certain amount of astonishment that I was able to pull these actors, but that's the miniseries format. You're asking for what you're asking for, and no more. I thought, 'Yeah, I'd be happy to keep doing miniseries, one a year, for the rest of my time.' At HBO, they want me to try for series still. I'm going to try, but it's harder. And it's more stressful."

AARON SORKIN

BORN: 1961, Manhattan, New York.

FIRST TV CREDIT: Creator, executive producer, and writer, *Sports Night,* 1998–2000, ABC.

LANDMARK TV SERIES: *Sports Night,* 1998–2000, ABC; *The West Wing,* 1999–2006, NBC; *Studio 60 on the Sunset Strip,* 2006–7, NBC; *The Newsroom,* 2012–14, HBO.

OTHER MAJOR CREDITS: Broadway: Playwright, *A Few Good Men,* 1989; *The Farnsworth Invention,* 2006. Movies: Screenwriter, *A Few Good Men,* 1992; *Charlie Wilson's War,* 2007; *The Social Network,* 2010; *Moneyball,* 2011; *Steve Jobs,* 2015.

Aaron Sorkin admits he wasn't much of a Saturday morning TV kid, getting up early to watch cartoons, even though he was a full-fledged member of the baby boom generation. "But I sure was a Saturday night TV kid, with that CBS lineup," he says. The lineup to which he's referring, from the 1973–74 TV season, was arguably the best regularly scheduled night of television in the history of television—Must-See TV a decade before that term was coined, with one Saturday night treasure following another, on a night long since consigned to reruns and rejects on broadcast television: *All in the Family, M*A*S*H, The Mary Tyler Moore Show, The Bob Newhart Show,* and *The Carol Burnett Show.* Watching those shows, Sorkin wasn't just getting laughs; he was getting inspired.

"I was growing up wanting to be a writer," says Sorkin, who triumphed on Broadway with his play *A Few Good Men* (later made into a movie star-

466 | THE PLATINUM AGE OF TELEVISION

ring Tom Cruise and Jack Nicholson) and in Hollywood with his screenplay for *The American President* before coming to TV with ABC's *Sports Night* and NBC's *West Wing*. "And the first two writers I wanted to be, before I was sort of old enough to discover Arthur Miller and Tennessee Williams and David Mamet and some others, were Jim Brooks and Larry Gelbart."

Jim Brooks was co-creator of *The Mary Tyler Moore Show*, which Sorkin calls "fastball, right down the middle, world-class comedy writing." Larry Gelbart, who had written with Mel Brooks and Carl Reiner on *Caesar's Hour* before developing *M*A*S*H* as a television series, had such a profound effect on Sorkin that, as Sorkin says, "*M*A*S*H* is the show that has informed everything that I've ever written. And it's not just me," he adds, suggesting that every TV writer who followed in the 1980s and 1990s, including Steven Bochco, David E. Kelley, and David Milch, "all are walking in the footprint left by Larry Gelbart."

As Sorkin got older and went to college, he kept watching and enjoying quality TV—loving NBC's *Hill Street Blues, Cheers, L.A. Law,* and *Seinfeld* and ABC's *NYPD Blue*—but never considered it as a career option. "My intention was to be a playwright," he explains. "I loved television and movies as much as anyone else but for some reason never related to them as a writer the same way, when I would go to see a play or read a play, that I would kind of connect to the playwright." But once he saw Jim Brooks's *Broadcast News* movie in 1987, and linked the name back to some of the great TV shows he had enjoyed over the years, Sorkin had an epiphany.

"You know what? Television and movies," he says, laughing now at his long-overdue realization, "they're written by writers, too! And there might be a place for me there, if I can get good enough. And that's really what did it."

When he got his opportunity, after the success of *A Few Good Men* on-screen, Sorkin wanted to make a TV comedy series imagining the behind-the-scenes workings of a real-life TV show he watched avidly, ESPN's *SportsCenter*. But even when making a TV show about the making of a TV show—a theme to which Sorkin would return in both NBC's *Studio 60 on the Sunset Strip* and HBO's *Newsroom*—Sorkin insisted on following what he considered Larry Gelbart's golden rule, which was to keep it real.

"Take *M*A*S*H*," Sorkin explains. "I have no idea what an army hospital in the Korean War looked like, but I believed that's what it looked like, and plainly they wanted me to believe that. Before Larry could do anything, before he could do jokes, he nailed down the reality of this place. That was a half-hour comedy that had blood in it, okay? And so what it allowed him to do was, he could tell stories that were funny, emotional, tense, thrilling—not just in the same series, not just in the same episode, but oftentimes in the same scene, because he nailed down the reality of it.

"And that's what I took with me when I did my first half hour, which was *Sports Night*. Before anything else, I wanted the place to seem kind of real. I didn't want to do it on a comedy set with a lot of doors, and it wasn't written in a three-jokes-a-page structure." Coincidentally, if not ironically, the first season of Sorkin's *Sports Night* suffered the same fate as Gelbart's *M*A*S*H*: The network demanded that a laugh track be inserted in post-production to make it less "confusing" for the audience. Gelbart forced a compromise, allowing for all operating room scenes to be presented without canned laughter, while Sorkin, after season 1 of *Sports Night*, was able to drop the laugh track entirely.

Sorkin launched NBC's *West Wing* while still working on *Sports Night*, making him one of the few TV writer-producers in history to have prime-time comedies and dramas running simultaneously (another, famously, is David E. Kelley, with Fox's *Ally McBeal* and ABC's *Practice*). Common to both shows: realistically designed, complex workplace sets ready-made for all those patented Sorkin long-take "walk and talk" scenes, and ensemble casts populated by impressively gifted actors. "I look for actors, real actors, who generally have a lot of stage appearances on their résumés," Sorkin says. "I've been very lucky in casting. And whoever said casting was 90 percent of the battle was dramatically undervaluing casting."

Sorkin walked away from *The West Wing* after four seasons—and four straight Emmy Awards for Outstanding Drama Series. (The following year, HBO's *Sopranos* won its first Emmy.) While writing movies, Sorkin also created two new TV series, both set in fictional TV worlds: the making of a weekly live comedy-variety show on *Studio 60 on the Sunset Strip*, and a nightly cable news show on *The Newsroom*. (The former was less successful, creatively and in terms of audience response, than the latter.) He also wrote an excellent, undervalued 2006 play about the creation of television, Broadway's *Farnsworth Invention*, that he's now thinking about trying to mount for television. As we spoke in late 2015, he's also contemplating a film biography of the iconic *I Love Lucy* star, Lucille Ball, and has even grander dreams about televised drama—a return to the glory days, and the live TV drama anthology format, that gave us Paddy Chayefsky's *Marty* and Rod Serling's *Requiem for a Heavyweight*.

"I'm very interested in bringing live theater back to television," says Sorkin, who admits to having had exploratory talks with executives at NBC and HBO. The appetite demonstrated by the success of recent live televised musicals, he says, is a good sign, and, he says, "If you gather a group of diverse and interesting writers, from Tina Fey to Jim Brooks, and say, 'Write a ninety-minute play' . . . it can be thrilling! . . . And I think we can do the same kinds of plays that Rod Serling and Paddy Chayefsky were doing back when our business was young."

MATTHEW WEINER

BORN: 1965, Baltimore.
FIRST TV CREDIT: Writer, *Party Girl*, 1996, Fox.
LANDMARK TV SERIES: *The Sopranos*, 2004–7, HBO; *Mad Men*, 2007–15, AMC.

"I wasn't allowed to watch TV as a kid," says Matthew Weiner, who was born in Baltimore in 1965 and grew up to create AMC's *Mad Men*. "That's an important part of it." His parents encouraged reading instead and restricted their children from watching TV on school nights, which included Sundays ("*The Wonderful World of Disney* was a Sunday night thing that I missed out on," he says"). On the rare occasions when TV was available, though, young Matt was an eager and voracious consumer. On Saturday mornings, there was NBC's live-action *H. R. Pufnstuf* and similarly antic cartoon series ("It was such a weird fever dream, that Saturday morning TV stretch," he recalls with a chuckle). On Friday nights, there was ABC's *Brady Bunch* and *Partridge Family*. Weiner was five years old when the Partridges hit the road in their psychedelic rock tour bus. "Like all boys that age," he says, "I wished I was Danny Partridge." With Saturday evenings fair game for TV viewing, the Weiner family opted for the shows in CBS's now-legendary Saturday lineup—*All in the Family, M*A*S*H, The Mary Tyler Moore Show, The Bob Newhart Show, The Carol Burnett Show*. While he wasn't able to watch much prime-time TV as a child, what little he saw was among the very best.

And when he was eleven years old, Matt's book-loving parents made a grand exception to the family's strict TV-viewing rules, letting the kids stay up to watch prime-time television for an entire week: ABC's massively influential, hugely viewed 1977 miniseries adaptation of Alex Haley's *Roots*. "If you can imagine being starved for television," he says, "and being allowed to watch, on your stomach, in the middle of the week, some of the greatest acting and greatest writing . . ." His sentence stops there, but not his memories. Though he hasn't seen *Roots* since that initial telecast, he describes in startling (and accurate) detail specific scenes that got to him and, in retrospect, gives it some credit for inspiring his eventual career choice. "You know, I never imagined that I would be a dramatist," he says. "I didn't know that there was such a job as TV writing. I don't know why. But I can tell you that *Roots* was something that I always, always aspired to."

Weiner attended Baltimore's then all-boys Park School, which, he says, self-deprecatingly, gave him "plenty of Saturday nights alone" to watch TV. He attended college at Wesleyan and was inspired to pursue filmmaking after seeing a moody, spooky, surreal 1986 David Lynch movie that bowled him over. "I applied to film school within, like, three months of seeing *Blue Velvet*," Weiner says. He got accepted into the prestigious film program at USC, where he had another, this time studies-related excuse to watch TV, much of it for the first time. "Because TV was this forbidden fruit," he explains, "when I watch TV, I really watch TV. I do not glaze over." He found his way to some classic series late but discovered binge watching very, very early. "I discovered *Star Trek* when I was in film school. I'd never seen *Star Trek* before. And *The Twilight Zone* was the gold standard. They would run, you know, one hundred of them in forty-eight hours on New Year's and on the Fourth of July, and that was exciting TV for me. I could not get enough of that."

Newly produced and televised shows caught Weiner's attention as well, and he was particularly taken by two ABC series: the sitcom *Roseanne*, and the drama *thirtysomething*. Weiner says admiringly, "*Roseanne* was just a gift to me. *Roseanne* was everything *The Cosby Show* wasn't. There was the marital relationship, the relationship with the kids, the hostility, the poverty. These were things, where all the humor was coming from, that you literally couldn't believe it was on TV." And *thirtysomething*, which Weiner also watched loyally, had a basic framework with similarities to the eventual structure of *Mad Men*: a handsome protagonist (in *thirtysomething*, Ken Olin's Michael Steadman) works for a successful advertising agency, then quits to start his own. "It was coincidentally about an advertising agency, and I was way younger than those people," Weiner qualifies. "And I found it to be unnecessarily morose at times. But I love the problems those people had, and their inability to communicate, and the moments of honesty that were kind of new [to TV]."

In 1991, Weiner got married, graduated from film school, and . . . nothing much happened for a while. "I spent four years—some of it without any employment at all—writing at home while my wife supported us. I was home, writing. And my life revolved around, for the first time, my own television." One of the high points of TV viewing during that period, for both Weiner and his wife, was ABC's *Twin Peaks,* co-created by Weiner's inspiration for pursuing filmmaking, David Lynch. "*Twin Peaks* came on, and it was absolutely so exciting . . . I loved every minute of that." And it came from television, not the movies, which might have been a sign of sorts. Television was about to become Weiner's path into show business, but not before he tried making it in the movies. His student documentary film had attracted attention but nothing else, and after three years of postcollegiate struggling, Weiner and his wife took a low-budget trip to Paris, saw Kevin Smith's low-budget *Clerks* there, and returned with the resolve to make their own bare-bones, independent, "Here I am" movie. The result, shot for twelve thousand dollars in twelve days with all his friends pitching in, was 1996's *What Do You Do All Day?,* a black comedy that Weiner himself describes as "sort of like an Albert Brooks movie." Weiner played a character named Matt, a repugnant version of himself (this was a few years before Larry David's *Curb Your Enthusiasm*) who was supposed to be at home writing but had gambled his wife's money away and gotten kicked out of the house. "If there was a message," Weiner says, "it was to myself, which was: You cannot postpone your life because your career is not happening . . . I was bitter and unhappy, and making the movie exorcised all of that."

And then, finally, came a break. Daisy Mayer, a college friend from Weiner's days at Wesleyan, directed and co-wrote a 1995 independent film comedy called *Party Girl,* starring Parker Posey. It became a cult hit, and the Fox network ordered a pilot for a TV spin-off, starring Christine Taylor. Mayer and Weiner spoke about the pilot order, Weiner recalls and says that he spontaneously "gave her a joke over the phone." It led to an invitation to visit the writers' room. "She brought me in to just sit at the table and tell jokes, 'cause they love this joke. And they hired me the same week that I screened my movie." Nothing happened with *What Do You Do All Day?,* but

Party Girl, the TV spin-off, "got picked up . . . and that was my first job. I didn't understand how the room worked. I didn't know that comedies were written in rooms like that . . . I didn't know any of those things."

Nor did he get much of a chance to learn. *Party Girl* premiered on Fox in September 1996 and was canceled, and gone, before the month was over. But with a sitcom writing credit, Weiner was able to find other work, however brief, first on *The Naked Truth* (starring Téa Leoni as a free spirit), then on another short-lived comedy, *Living in Captivity*. "You don't choose," Weiner explains, putting into context that point in a writer's career. "You will take any job and, you know, you're lucky to have it. It's Major League Baseball: you'd like to be on the Yankees, but you would gladly play in Arizona because you're in Major League Baseball." From *Living in Captivity*, Weiner landed a staff writing job on CBS's *Becker*, Ted Danson's post-*Cheers* sitcom. "At that point," Weiner says of his own TV career, not Danson's, "you're just trying to get a job. And to get on a Paramount show with Ted Danson in it, that has an order—that was a big job. I wouldn't say I was drawn to it. I would say that that was my profession." Weiner stayed with *Becker* for three years and, during one of the hiatus periods, wrote the pilot episode for what would become, many years later, *Mad Men*. When he described the concept to people in advance—a period drama series based in the world of 1960s Madison Avenue—even his friends either balked or said it was "execution dependent." So Weiner figured he had to write it, and did. "I just pulled the trigger and wrote the pilot, gave it to my agents," Weiner says, "and nothing happened. I couldn't get a meeting." Weiner begged to get just a pitch meeting with HBO, where he could "leave the script as a surprise at the end," but no luck.

But Weiner was lucky back at home—because his wife, watching HBO in 1999, steered him toward a new series she thought her husband would enjoy. He didn't much like the pilot, because he wasn't that much into violence. But his wife kept watching and after a few more episodes told him he had to watch the current episode. The series was David Chase's *Sopranos*, and the episode was the now-famous "College" episode.

"I just turned to my wife, and I said, 'You do understand what's going on here,'" Weiner recalls. "'This has never been done, that you would take this hero and father of this TV show . . . and he's going to strangle this guy with his bare hands. And we're going to have to watch him next week and act like we care about what's going on with him. That is revolutionary.'"

For Weiner, it was more than Tony Soprano just being an antihero. "It's way more complicated than that. He is not just the antihero. He is a representative of the lead in a TV series. And that's not what they do. They always do the right thing. They don't get their hands dirty. They find a way to be the moral center, even in an immoral universe. Tony strangling that guy—I was talking out loud during it. My wife had already seen it. She was like, 'No shit, that's why I wanted you to watch it!' . . . And I was like, 'This is a sea change. That this is commercially successful is a joy; this is hope for everybody!'"

Yet for Weiner, there seemed no hope of selling his *Mad Man* pilot script, even though the success and complexity and originality of *The Sopranos* seemed like such a positive omen. After three years on *Becker,* Weiner quit of his own volition to work on a less orthodox sitcom, Fox's *Andy Richter Controls the Universe,* in 2003. Shortly after starting there, Weiner demanded "at gunpoint" that his agents finally get his unproduced *Mad Men* pilot script to two HBO talents he admired, Alan Ball of *Six Feet Under* and David Chase of *The Sopranos,* hoping one of them would recognize a kindred spirit and "be my rabbi or something." The script got to David Chase's agent, who gave it to Chase, "and a week later, I'm in New York," Weiner says, still sounding incredulous. "I'm on the show!"

Chase was impressed by Weiner's *Mad Men* script and very complimentary. "I forgot that people talked this way," Weiner recalls Chase telling him, then giving him more praise, and a warning, at the same time. "When I got there," Weiner recounts, "he said, 'I don't know if you can write this show. That is, I might fire you. But this is the next show that HBO should do. This is a whole world,'" he said, referring to the 1960s era of *Mad Men*. Matthew Weiner didn't get fired. He joined *The Sopranos* in its fourth season and stayed until its instantly iconic finale. While he was there, he freely admits, he learned so much and tapped that knowledge when finally getting the chance to develop his long-dormant *Mad Men* pet project.

"*The Sopranos* didn't lie about human behavior, which is really a high compliment," Weiner says. "The writers, and David in particular, had a standard—that if he understood it, the audience would understand it, and that things didn't have to be explicit. And that things could be visual. And the subtleties, the repressed desires . . . anything you see like that in *Mad Men* is because, though I naturally felt that way, I would never have had the confidence to do it if I had not seen David doing it, and if I had not seen it work. And those similarities are exactly what you think they are. It's me taking that from *The Sopranos*," Weiner admits, laughing. "It's not a coincidence."

Also not coincidental is another shared trait between *The Sopranos* and *Mad Men*: on these two TV dramas in particular, characters rarely express or reveal their inner feelings and motivations or say anything close to what they're really thinking. "It's a different way of writing," Weiner acknowledges. "It requires some bravery, because you're asking the audience to pay attention, because they're going to have to put it together in their head. And the duplicitousness of the characters—if you are educated only in the language of TV or popular entertainment, all of these things can pass by unnoticed. And you'll just be bored. And somebody walking into a room and lying will not be as entertaining, right?" Weiner laughs, and turns to Shakespeare for an example. "Iago flattering Othello is not something that would get by in traditional television." Weiner ended up writing or co-writing a dozen scripts for *The Sopranos* and winning Emmy Awards as a co–executive producer. When Chase announced his intention to end the series after two more seasons, Weiner dusted off his *Mad Men* script and shopped it around again, this time as a writer-producer with a white-hot current credit. HBO, the first stop, passed. So did every other network, broadcast and cable, except for AMC, which was interested in attempting original series production again for the first time in years. "I received a lot of pity about taking my 'dynamite script' to a place where no one would ever see it," Weiner says. "But at a certain point, everybody was like, 'Well, this script is old. There's no heat on it. HBO doesn't want it. Maybe we don't want it.'"

Even AMC's executives were unsure and required Weiner to meet with them, before they would commit to *Mad Men,* and tell them where he saw the series going. From one of his old unsold scripts from his post-film-school days, Weiner lifted the story of a war veteran who had stolen the identity of a fallen fellow soldier and grafted it onto the backstory of his Don Draper protagonist in *Mad Men*. In addition to fleshing out his character's past, Weiner looked way into the future. He suggested the first season could end with the 1960 Kennedy-Nixon election and with Don's black-mailer, Pete, outing him to his company's founder, Bert Cooper, who would respond with a shrug. And Weiner had plans, and visions, even beyond that. "When I pitched it to the network," he says, "I actually told them about trying to do the whole decade [of the 1960s] and ending with Don on a bluff in the lotus position at an ashram or something."

AMC decided to finance a pilot, and Weiner went with AMC, he says bluntly, because "it was the only offer I got." Even then, he wasn't optimistic *Mad Men* would go beyond the pilot. His rather practical approach: "If worst comes to worst, let's try and make the best pilot ever made. That was our goal."

Between the final two seasons of *The Sopranos,* Weiner secured the services of almost the entire crew, while they were otherwise on a lengthy hiatus, to shoot the *Mad Men* pilot. As auditions began, Weiner got nervous. "When I first went in to hear it at an audition," Weiner says of his then-dusty pilot script, "I was terrified that it wasn't going to play, that it was just good on paper." But as cast members began to accumulate, led by Jon Hamm as Don Draper, those fears were assuaged. AMC gave Weiner a series order and a 2007 launch date, and Weiner and his freshly assembled writing staff began working on follow-up scripts. "There's seven years between finishing the pilot [script] and writing the second episode," Weiner says, pointing out that both he and his perspective were markedly different from so many years before. That altered the direction of future *Mad Men* scripts substantially, as did the talents, and inspiration, brought to the show by various cast members.

"Christina Hendricks—her character, Joan, that wasn't a series regular," Weiner says. "That's the best example I can give. She was just going to be in the pilot to introduce Peggy [played by Elisabeth Moss] to the office. I always saw her like Eve Arden or something, you know? She's just sort of the best friend. And when Christina read for it, we changed it and made her a series regular. I'm like, 'I'm not doing this show without that woman!' Imagining her and Elisabeth Moss walking down the hall together—that's a series!" Weiner was not interested, however, in taking these workplace women in any sort of traditional TV direction. "Joan is not that nice," Weiner says. "She's not Peggy's friend. That, in itself, was in contrast to the traditions of television. On a network TV show . . . Joan and Peggy would have been living together by episode 4. And Peggy would have gotten a makeover. And they would have been fighting over the same man." Instead, while their relationship, like their power within the industry, evolved over the course of the series, it ended with Joan's offering Peggy a partnership position at her own firm and Peggy's declining. "That was kind of fun," Weiner says, savoring that particular series-long story arc.

Discovering the characters, and letting their stories unfold naturally and unpredictably, were other things Weiner learned from *The Sopranos*—as a viewer, years before he joined the show as a staff writer. "That was a *Sopranos* thing, too, that every character has their own story and that you shouldn't be afraid to put them on hiatus. A little goes a long way. Pete Campbell [played by Vincent Kartheiser], he's not in the second episode [of *Mad Men*]. That's probably one of the biggest fights I had with the network. He's the villain." But Weiner wanted to emulate *The Sopranos* by not making every episode the same, tonally or in terms of content. "Really try and make every episode different," Weiner says, summarizing the ethos. "And part of that means, sorry, but there's no formula. Don's not going to pitch the Carousel every week."

One more thing Weiner learned from direct observation of *The Sopranos* was how passionate viewers and critics can get about a series finale and how important that final episode can be. "Well, the good thing is, I didn't have to think of that," Weiner says, laughing, referring to the hugely debated cut-to-black ending with which David Chase, writer and director of that last outing, concluded *The Sopranos*. But knowing the cultural weight given that finale and others like it, Weiner did have to come up with one for Don Draper and *Mad Men* and did it, he reveals, between the fourth and fifth seasons, three years before the series ended in 2015.

"I knew I was going to end with him on this bluff," Weiner says. "And just to get pretentious for a second, I wanted to give Don the journey of Siddhartha. I wanted to have him renounce his earthly life and have some form of enlightenment that would allow him to return with substance. Especially because he was so self-hating, and he could not get over his past, wouldn't that be interesting? So I imagined him leaving the agency, and all these things that would cost a lot of money. But when I imagined the ending . . . I did the 'Ommm, ommm' chant in my head, and out loud, and I heard the beginning of the Coke ad. And I was like, 'I think this is the same note!' And I was bummed because I was like, now I've got to get all the way to 1971? And I was like, 'You know, I don't, actually. I just have to get close.'"

To those old enough to remember, the 1971 commercial, in which a crowd of happy young people on a hilltop sing, "I'd like to buy the world a Coke," was a feel-good anthem, an after echo of the already dissolved 1960s. Ending a TV drama series about advertising with a climax that is itself a full-length commercial—in its own way, that's as audacious as the fill-in-your-own-blank conclusion to *The Sopranos*. But it wouldn't work, couldn't work, without the advance cooperation of the Coca-Cola company, so I asked Weiner how and when he got it. "I knew this was going to be it," he says of the "Buy the World a Coke" ad—the perfect ending for *Mad Men*. Through his agency, he spoke to Joe Tripodi, head of marketing for Coca-Cola, and asked, a bit indirectly. "I didn't tell him it was the last episode, but told him I wanted to use it. What would I have to do to make that happen? And could he keep it a secret?" His first response was a noncommittal "Let's see what we can do," and Weiner began to worry that "it would have been better to beg forgiveness than ask permission." But Lionsgate demanded official permission from Coca-Cola, so Weiner went all out to do things correctly. He got rights to the song sung in the commercial. He explained that Coca-Cola could neither be paid for the use of the spot (so it couldn't be seen as product placement), tell anyone, nor advertise anywhere during commercial time on the final *Mad Men* episode. Weiner went beyond even those restrictions and suggested to AMC, whose executives agreed, that no other beverage company should be allowed to buy ads during the finale, either. "Let's not punch them in the face," Weiner said of Coca-Cola. "They're doing us a favor." Everything was agreed to, and Weiner felt fine, until, before the paperwork was signed, Tripodi retired from Coca-Cola, and Weiner had to renegotiate from scratch with his successor. He got the permission, again, and *Mad Men* was history—his way.

"This is probably one of the last conversations I'm going to have about *Mad Men*," Weiner says. "And honestly, it's a pleasure to talk to you about it."

KEY EVOLUTIONARY STAGES

Combat!	1962–67, ABC
M*A*S*H	1972–83, CBS
China Beach	1988–91, ABC
Band of Brothers	2001, HBO
Generation Kill	2008, HBO

Television, for the most part, has been much better at documenting and analyzing wars than at dramatizing them. The list of excellent documentary series about warfare is long and impressive, starting with three twenty-six-part TV productions: 1952's *Victory at Sea,* NBC's detailed account of World War II naval battles and other key conflicts; and two equally ambitious British series, 1964's *Great War,* BBC-TV's largely oral history of World War I, and 1973's *World at War,* a thorough overview of World War II presented by Great Britain's ITV, which appeared in the United States via syndication in 1975. PBS gave us the unblinkingly honest *Vietnam: A Television History* in 1985, and the documentarian Ken Burns chose war as his subject for PBS nonfiction series on several occasions, including 1990's *Civil War* and 2008's *The War* (about World War II). On the fictional scripted side, though, television wasn't as quick or eager to depict war, especially whichever was the current or most recent one.

For years, comedy was the easiest way in. Nat Hiken's *Phil Silvers Show,* which began on CBS in 1955 under the original title *You'll Never Get Rich,* lasted for four seasons, during which time it earned three Emmy Awards as TV's best comedy series. Larry David identifies it as "my all-time favorite," citing the stories, the characters, and the cast as being "amazing." Matt Groening, creator of *The Simpsons,* remembers watching it with his older brother and his parents ("That was a really great show"), and James L. Brooks, co-creator of *The Mary Tyler Moore Show, The Simpsons,* and many more TV classics, considers *The Phil Silvers Show* one of television's most underappreciated television gems, with Hiken leading "one of the great writing staffs."

In *The Phil Silvers Show,* Silvers played Master Sergeant Ernie Bilko, a man who finagled both his superiors and his squad members with one moneymaking scheme or card game after another. But Silvers and company were safely ensconced in the motor pool at the fictional Fort Baxter in Roseville, Kansas, and the only action they saw was when they got weekend passes into town. The Bilko formula, and character, were essentially re-created, though less cleverly, in ABC's *McHale's Navy* (1962–66), in which Ernest Borgnine's scheming lieutenant commander, Quinton McHale, with help from Tim Conway's ensign, Charles Parker, maneuvered their way around the navy's rules and regulations as easily as they maneuvered their PT boat around the Pacific during World War II—for the most part avoiding, rather than seeing, any action. Another military comedy that avoided actual combat was 1964's *Gomer Pyle, U.S.M.C.* on CBS, a 1964 spin-off of *The Andy Griffith Show* starring Jim Nabors as the slow-talking, slow-thinking Gomer, who went from pumping gas in Mayberry to being a Marine Corps private in California, stationed at Camp Henderson. That series lasted five years, but Gomer never advanced past boot camp. Had he shipped out, anytime during the show's 1965–70 run, he would have most likely ended up in Vietnam, and neither the comedies nor the dramas of the time had any interest in going there.

World War II was a different story, and there was one very successful comedy, running on CBS from 1965 to 1971, that I still have a problem imagining how it was ever sold in a network pitch meeting, even with Billy Wilder's 1953 film, *Stalag 17,* as partial precedent: *Hogan's Heroes,* starring Bob Crane as a U.S. Army colonel who runs a highly sophisticated resistance operation during World War II while incarcerated in a Nazi POW camp. ("Yes, there are Nazis," I imagine the meeting going, "but they're cuddly Nazis.")

At first, TV dramas were less willing to explore the war angle. The Korean War was occupying hearts and minds in the early 1950s, and it wasn't until the Western genre began to wane, after peaking in the late 1950s, that World War II dramas swiftly replaced it as the primary source of violence on television. It was violence that, for a while, was accepted as being wrapped in the cloak of patriotism and/or historical "accuracy." Though even then, there was no appetite to dramatize the most recent war with U.S. involvement, the "police action" in Korea; that conflict wouldn't be represented on a scripted TV series until CBS presented its version of *M*A*S*H* in 1972, long after the Korean War had been supplanted in national consciousness and international headlines by the Vietnam War. On television, one of the first World War II dramatizations was on a 1960 Season 1 episode of CBS's *Twilight Zone,* written by Rod Serling himself. Titled "Purple Testament," it was about a lieutenant, stationed in the Philippines, who suddenly developed the ability to discern, simply by looking at his men and sensing an eerie glow emanating from their faces, which of them would be the next to die in battle. It was a subtle Serling allegory about death and duty and the costs and fears of war, and in 1960 the only way to address those issues was through the protective make-believe filter of *The Twilight Zone.*

In the 1960s, though, as war dramas began to replace the Westerns, there was a sudden shift, propelled chiefly by a flurry of ABC dramas set during World War II. There was *The Gallant Men* (1962–63), one of Ken Burns's favorite shows as a kid, following a frontline infantry division as it fought its way through Italy. And *Twelve O'Clock High* (1964–67), based on the 1949 movie, about an air force bombardment group stationed near London and flying missions across enemy territory. And *The Rat Patrol* (1966–68), whose focus was North Africa, where a ragtag group of Allies, driving in jeeps around the desert, fought the tanks and other armored vehicles of General Rommel's Afrika Korps. And *Garrison's Gorillas* (1967–68), a *Dirty Dozen* variation that dispatched a quartet of stateside convicts to use their particular skills to fight the enemy in various secret missions across Europe. All of these shows were on ABC, but none were as popular or durable as the ABC war series that basically started it all, and the one that still, all these years later, ranks as the longest-running war drama series ever to run on television.

COMBAT!

1962–67, ABC. Developer: Robert Pirosh. Stars: Vic Morrow, Rick Jason, Pierre Jalbert, Jack Hogan, Dick Peabody.

Combat! was developed by Robert Pirosh, a World War II veteran who wrote the premiere episode and set the tone of the series. A master sergeant in the infantry, he fought in the Siege of Bastogne during the Battle of the Bulge and later won an Academy Award for his screenplay dramatizing that battle in the 1949 movie *Battleground.* Also setting the tone was Robert Altman, who was just starting out in television at the time; it would be years before he directed 1970's *MASH,* the counterculture movie hit that would spawn an even more popular CBS comedy series, but he was already dabbling in war stories. Altman had directed the premiere episode of another 1962 ABC war series, *The Gallant Men,* then moved on to *Combat!* because he thought he could do more with a show that, while telling a different story each week, also focused on a larger military campaign, taking half a season to dramatize a single grueling wartime objective. Altman was fond of injecting the reality of war into *Combat!* by introducing a supporting

Combat! starred Vic Morrow (far right) as a sergeant in a World War II infantry squad fighting on the front lines across several European battlefields.

character in one episode, having him reappear in the next few episodes, then killing him, suddenly and unexpectedly, as part of a minor subplot in a later episode. "That was unorthodox," Altman told me once, with a smile, when I interviewed him. "I used to get fired for it." And he did but not before directing ten episodes of *Combat!*, showcasing his penchant not only for random story surprises but for handheld camera angles, unusually detailed wide shots, and moodily lit, semi-obscured scenes.

Combat! starred Vic Morrow and Rick Jason as Sergeant Chip Saunders and his lieutenant, Gil Hanley. They led their U.S. Army platoon across Europe, in adventures that began with D-day, but throughout, and notably, the series presented at least as much inaction as action. The men were as apt to be shown waiting to be deployed to fight as actually engaging in battle; much of what they fought against, as they joked or bickered among themselves, was anxiousness or boredom. Some tension was of the noncombat sort, as they came upon, and had to defuse, unexploded bombs dropped by the enemy. And when they did do battle, there was a lot of the rolling-in-the-dirt, crawling-on-your-stomach maneuvering, with soldiers on both sides dying demonstratively but usually bloodlessly—the sort of theatrics that spawned copycat play behavior from millions of young viewers, just as the adventures of Davy Crockett had on *Disneyland* the decade before. Ironically, though *Combat!* and shows like it tended to glorify war even as they dramatized its tension, tedium, and high stakes, it would take another decade, and a different type of TV war series, to become television's first, most famous, and ultimately most popular antiwar show. It would take a comedy—an expansion, and different interpretation, of Robert Altman's 1970 black comedy. It would take *M*A*S*H*.

M*A*S*H

1972–83, CBS. Creator: Larry Gelbart. Stars: Alan Alda, Wayne Rogers, Loretta Swit, Larry Linville, Gary Burghoff, McLean Stevenson, William Christopher, Jamie Farr, Harry Morgan, Mike Ferrell, David Ogden Stiers.

Larry Gelbart had started writing for TV when both he and it were young. Born in 1928, he wrote for NBC's *Colgate Comedy Hour* the same season as Norman Lear in 1950 and wrote for NBC's *Caesar's Hour* in 1954–

57, alongside Mel Brooks and Carl Reiner. In 1962, he co-wrote, with Burt Shevelove, the book for the hit Broadway musical *A Funny Thing Happened on the Way to the Forum,* with music and lyrics by Stephen Sondheim. For the movies, he wrote such boldly structured comedies as 1978's *Movie Movie* and 1982's *Tootsie.* For television, he wrote 1979's far-ahead-of-its-time marital comedy-drama *United States* for NBC and, late in his career, a series of excellent HBO television movies, including 1993's *Barbarians at the Gate* and 1997's *Weapons of Mass Distraction.* Nothing else in his résumé, though, had anywhere near the impact of the long-running CBS series *M*A*S*H,* which he developed for television from Robert Altman's equally brilliant 1970 movie *MASH.* (Which, in turn, was based on the 1968 novel *MASH* by Richard Hooker, the shared pen name for the writer W. C. Heinz and the former military surgeon H. Richard Hornberger.) In reshaping for television this black comedy about a Mobile Army Surgical Hospital unit working near the front lines during the Korean War, Gelbart and company did a lot more than merely add asterisks.

M*A*S*H ended its lengthy, artistic run as an antiwar comedy with a final episode that was, and most likely always will be, the most-watched scripted TV episode in history. Alan Alda (right) starred throughout as Hawkeye Pierce; Mike Farrell joined the cast midway as B. J. Hunnicut, another doctor serving during the Korean War.

On television, *M*A*S*H* lasted for eleven years—nearly four times as long as the Korean War itself, a North-South conflict stretching from 1950 to 1953. It was a Top 10 show for most of its run, and won eleven Emmys, including one for Outstanding Comedy Series (in 1974) and several for its star, Alan Alda, and other cast members. Alda played Hawkeye Pierce, the role played by Donald Sutherland in the Altman film: a gifted surgeon, assigned to the 4077th, who shared Groucho Marx's screen tendencies of a quick wit, a fondness for women, and a contempt for authority. Hawkeye reserved even more contempt for the war itself and complained about its futility even as he stitched up its boyish victims, helicoptered in straight from the front.

That was what made *M*A*S*H* so different and so important. When it premiered in 1972, the United States was still embroiled in the highly divisive Vietnam War. But because it was set two decades in the past, in Korea, *M*A*S*H* was able not only to dramatize war but to speak out against it, making it an antiwar comedy, and a very popular one, even as the country was fighting yet another war. Exteriors were shot at Malibu Creek State Park, where an extensive series of tents and helicopter landing sites was constructed, adding to the overall verisimilitude. The show's many acknowledgments of the seriousness of its wartime subject included the subtle yet significant fact that whenever Hawkeye or any of the other doctors or nurses were tending to a patient in the operating tent, there was no laugh track, no canned laughter. Death was serious business and, in the medical tent scenes especially, so was comedy.

Without any prompting, several artists interviewed for this book cited *M*A*S*H* as a seminal show in their own viewing history.

"I loved *M*A*S*H*," David E. Kelley says. "You had to watch *M*A*S*H*," Louis C.K. concurs. "*M*A*S*H* was extremely moving and intelligent." (In his own series, FX's *Louie*, the comedian did his own stand-alone variation on *M*A*S*H*: an episode called "The Duckling," in which he unknowingly transports his daughter's pet duckling to a USO tour of Afghanistan.)

"*M*A*S*H*," Aaron Sorkin adds, "is the show, I think, that has informed everything I've ever written. And it's not just me . . . Steven Bochco, David Kelley, David Milch—all of us are walking in the footprint left by Larry Gelbart, and here's why." He goes on to explain that *The Mary Tyler Moore Show* and *Murphy Brown*, while fantastic comedy shows, were not realistic depictions of how a local or national news show was done. *M*A*S*H*, Sorkin insists, was different.

No one ever died on *McHale's Navy* or *Hogan's Heroes*. War was fun, even in a POW camp. But on *M*A*S*H*, patients died from time to time. So did doctors. One stunningly unexpected moment came at the end of McLean Stevenson's final appearance as Lieutenant Colonel Henry Blake in 1975. All the other members of the 4077th had waved good-bye as Henry's helicopter whisked him off to his plane to return home, only to have Gary Burghoff's Radar O'Reilly, the colonel's loyal assistant, enter the operating tent in the episode's closing scene to announce that Blake's plane, en route to the United States, had gone down in the Sea of Japan, with no survivors. The doctors and nurses absorbed the news wordlessly, devastated, then returned sadly and silently to their tasks at hand. The news stunned viewers at home just as much. The scene, because it was in the operating room tent, had no laugh track, and no reason for laughter.

My favorite *M*A*S*H* episode, though, and the one I consider the most dramatic and daring, was "The Interview," a 1976 episode written and directed by Larry Gelbart. It was fashioned after the fabled CBS reporter Edward R. Murrow's 1952 visit to the Korean War for "Christmas in Korea," a special installment of his *See It Now* newsmagazine. In Gelbart's version, the actor Clete Roberts played a Murrow-like reporter visiting the 4077th and asking the doctors, nurses, and other personnel about their wartime experiences. The entire episode, except for the credits, was filmed in black and white, in documentary style. Actors were given leeway to improvise answers to some of the questions posed to them by the reporter, while other answers were carefully and powerfully scripted. The best of the latter, taken from an actual army doctor's recollections, was uttered by William Christopher's Father Mulcahy, the army chaplain. "When the doctors cut into a patient—and it's very cold here, you know—steam rises from the body," Mulcahy quietly and somberly tells his interviewer. "And the doctor will warm himself over the open wound. Could anyone look on that and not feel changed?"

With characters, episodes, and writing like that, it's no wonder *M*A*S*H*, by the time it decided to pull up its tent stakes and present an expanded final episode in 1983, had generated an amazing amount of national anticipation. Many critics, including myself, predicted it would become the most viewed scripted TV event of all time, which it was. I was fortunate enough, because of one of those unpredictable perks of being a TV critic, to be among those critics invited to the *M*A*S*H* set on the 20th Century–Fox studio lot in January 1983 to witness the cast film its last scene of the series, then talk to them. It was a month before the finale would be televised, but that episode had already been shot. The scene we critics were witnessing was from the penultimate episode, held back for this purpose precisely because it included all the main characters, placing items into a time capsule before the war ended officially. There was an air of reverence as the scene was shot, and everyone was drawn into the solemnity of the occasion. Afterward, Alan Alda spoke for everyone when he said, "Like *M*A*S*H* itself, I'm sad and happy at the same time. I'm very sad to be leaving my friends and collaborators, but I'm very happy because I'm so proud of what we've done. We've really accomplished something."

A month later, the final episode, "Goodbye, Farewell, and Amen," presented the typical (but only for *M*A*S*H*) mixture of sad and happy. Alda's Hawkeye suffered a nervous breakdown because of the death of an infant, while Jamie Farr's character, Corporal Klinger, who had spent the show's first few seasons wearing a dress in hopes of getting sent home on a psychological discharge, ended up falling in love with a Korean girl, marrying her, and deciding to stay. That final episode attracted 77 percent of all TV viewers that night and earned a Nielsen rating of more than 60—something no Super Bowl has yet done. The A. C. Nielsen audience estimates for the finale approach 125 million viewers, making it the most watched series finale, and most watched scripted TV show period, in television history. Because of audience fragmentation, it's a record that will never be broken.

During the eleven years *M*A*S*H* was on the air, and in the years that followed, other war-related dramas appeared, almost all of them about World War II, rather than the more recent Korean or Vietnam War. In 1981, PBS presented a superb adaptation of Mark Twain's Civil War story, *The Private History of a Campaign That Failed*, along with an epilogue, starring Edward Herrmann, dramatizing another Twain work, *The War Prayer*. Like Twain's story itself, it was one of the most searingly honest antiwar statements ever presented. But in this period of television, World War II was the war of choice: each network had a World War II drama series or miniseries, some more successful than others.

NBC had Robert Conrad's forgettable *Baa Baa Black Sheep*, his 1976–78 series about the exploits of the Marine Corps flying ace Pappy Boyington, but also had 1978's *Holocaust*, a bravely serious and detailed miniseries account of Nazi persecution (starring Meryl Streep, James Woods, and many others), and 1979's *From Here to Eternity,* a miniseries remake of the 1953 movie, later made into a weekly series. (The miniseries, starring Natalie Wood, William Devane, Steve Railsback, and Joe Pantoliano, was quite good.) ABC had the massive miniseries *Winds of War* in 1983, followed by the even bigger (and much better) *War and Remembrance* sequel in 1988. Its account of the Holocaust was even more unflinching and unforgettable than that in NBC's *Holocaust.* Even PBS's *Masterpiece Theatre* got into the action in 1981, by importing a superb 1979 ITV British series called *Danger UXB.* Here was not only a thirteen-part World War II series about the same subject, unexploded bombs, once explored in *Combat!* but a weekly series that had the emotional intensity of 2008's *Hurt Locker.* Even the leading characters in *Danger UXB,* risking their lives to defuse dangerous bombs dropped by Germans in and around London, could die while carrying out their duties, and several of them did—another move forward in the wartime TV genre. And in addition to showing us the Allied point of view, TV gave us World War II from the German perspective, when the Bravo cable network, in 1985, imported a claustrophobic, character-driven, relentlessly compelling 1981 German TV miniseries, Wolfgang Petersen's *Das Boot.*

Das Boot was brilliant television—even better as a six-hour miniseries than when it was chopped down to movie length and distributed to cinemas internationally. But for a TV drama about the Vietnam War, viewers had to wait until the mid-1980s. ABC was first, in 1984, with *Call to Glory,* a quality period drama series about an air force pilot (played by Craig T. Nelson) and his family. The series touched on Vietnam, but only in its nascent form as a military concern, before it was escalated to outright war: the narrative of *Call to Glory* began in 1962, with the Cuban missile crisis. CBS made it official in 1987 with *Tour of Duty,* starring Terence Knox as Sergeant Zeke Anderson, a platoon leader during the Vietnam War. It was a solid series, very much in the spirit and with the flavor of *Combat!,* with some of its regular characters doomed to die unexpectedly, as had become the accepted norm. And ABC made the Vietnam War drama series not only official but outstanding with its 1988 effort and did it with a woman at the show's center, an unprecedented and very welcome distinction.

CHINA BEACH

1988–91, ABC. Creators: William Broyles Jr., John Sacret Young. Stars: Dana Delany, Robert Picardo, Marg Helgenberger, Brian Wimmer, Michael Boatman, Jeff Kober, Chloe Webb.

The movie-length pilot of ABC's *China Beach* was a beautiful thing to behold. It took what *M*A*S*H* had brought to the TV comedy—realistic settings, life-and-death stakes, painfully realistic operating rooms—and transplanted them to the TV drama. The operating rooms in this close-to-the-action seaside medical outfit were in sheds, not tents, and the setting was Vietnam, not Korea, but otherwise these two series were very close spiritual relatives. And at the center of *China Beach*, instead of a wisecracking doctor, you had a young but world-weary nurse: Colleen McMurphy, played with empathy and a haunted resignation by the beautiful Dana Delany. As *China Beach* began, Delany and Chloe Webb, playing a visiting first-time USO performer, bonded in such believable fashion it made their respective wartime epiphanies that much more credible and emotional. And by the end of the

China Beach was a dramatic war series with two key distinctions: It was set during the Vietnam War, and its story was told through the eyes of a female protagonist—nurse Colleen McMurphy, played by Dana Delany (seen here with Robert Picardo as a doctor also assigned to the China Beach medical base).

series, three years later, *China Beach* had advanced its narrative in so many ways—including making room, in one episode, for first-person accounts by actual nurses who served at similar military outfits in Vietnam—that it was a solid successor to what *M*A*S*H* had accomplished in a comic framework, dealing with an entirely different war. It took a dozen years after the Vietnam War ended in 1975 for TV to deal with it directly in a drama series and only one year after that, with *China Beach,* to deal with it magnificently.

After that show ended, though, TV reverted to more World War II nostalgia. First came ABC's *Homefront* in 1991, which dealt with World War II but from the perspective of loved ones back in the United States. And then, in 2001, came a miniseries that brought frontline war action back to the TV war drama and did so with an intensity, and a military fidelity, the genre had not yet seen.

BAND OF BROTHERS

2001, HBO. Executive producers: Steven Spielberg, Tom Hanks. Stars: Damian Lewis, Ron Livingston, Donnie Wahlberg, Scott Grimes, Neal McDonough, Michael Fassbender, David Schwimmer, Colin Hanks, Tom Hardy, Simon Pegg, James McAvoy, Jimmy Fallon.

Steven Spielberg and Tom Hanks had teamed as director and star on 1998's *Saving Private Ryan,* a war movie elevating the "you are there" experience of a drama about the terror, brutality, and overwhelming sensory overload of battle. Spielberg won an Oscar as Best Director that year, and he and Hanks reteamed to tell another complicated, intense war story—this time as executive producers, and this time on a TV miniseries. HBO's *Band of Brothers* was a major gamble for the network, unprecedentedly expensive and expansive: ten episodes, with an estimated budget of $125 million. *Band of Brothers* followed, rather faithfully, the real-life narrative told by the historian Stephen E. Ambrose in his 1992 book of the same name, following "Easy" Company (Company E, Second Battalion, 506th Parachute Infantry Regiment, 101st Airborne Division) as it trained for parachute jumping and combat, landed in Normandy, and took part in battle after battle until the end of the war. *Band of Brothers* ended up winning six Emmy Awards, including one for Outstanding Miniseries.

The opening episode of *Band of Brothers* began the same way as had

Band of Brothers was a fact-based miniseries following members of a specific army division as it worked its way across key battles during World War II. Stars included Damien Lewis (center foreground) as Richard Winters.

ABC's *Combat!* almost forty years earlier: with troops nervously awaiting orders to participate in that evening's planned top secret D-day invasion of Normandy—weather permitting. And when weather didn't permit, they waited, even more nervously, for the next night, and the next opportunity. On *Band of Brothers,* the rest of the first episode was devoted to flashbacks, showing how the Easy Company recruits went through basic training and found themselves on the precipice of war. In the second episode, they descended upon Normandy by air, whereas the *Combat!* soldiers had arrived by sea. Both groups found themselves immersed in incomprehensibly hectic and hellish battle conditions and were lucky, in both cases, to make it to dry land and plant their boots on the ground. And that was just the start of it. For *Band of Brothers,* technical innovations in special effects, coupled with the skills of the various directors and other collaborators, allowed them to depict the sheer scale of the invasion, and its attendant horrors, in ways comparable only to Spielberg's *Saving Private Ryan.* To comprehend the evolution of war dramas on TV, there's no better way than to compare the respective D-day episodes of *Combat!* and *Band of Brothers.*

The cast of *Band of Brothers* was gifted enough to make you care about their characters deeply: the central figure, Richard D. Winters, was played by Damian Lewis, years before he became a well-known star in America as the suspected terrorist sympathizer in Showtime's *Homeland*. Other players included many whose careers would rise significantly in the next few years, including Michael Fassbender, Tom Hardy, Neal McDonough, Colin Hanks, and James McAvoy. Even David Schwimmer and Jimmy Fallon took on dramatic roles here and did very well.

And as with *Danger UXB*, the miniseries form ensured that the sense of danger, even to central characters, would be palpable. Easy Company's route through World War II was almost Zelig-like (or, given the Tom Hanks connection, Forrest Gump–like): the men fought their way from D-day to Adolf Hitler's mountain retreat at Berchtesgaden. In between were such pivotal European engagements as street-by-street fighting in Carentan, Operation Market Garden in Holland, enduring the German offensive at Bastogne, and the explosive German attack in the Ardennes Forest, when hell seemed to rain down on them from every direction. That episode was written by Graham Yost and equaled the opening of *Saving Private Ryan* in its unrelenting barrage of overwhelming confusion, carnage, and deadly danger. *Combat!* and *The Gallant Men* might have prompted millions of games of make-believe among young viewers to whom war seemed glamorous and exciting, but no one watching this miniseries, no matter how young and imaginative, was "playing" *Band of Brothers* afterward.

At the beginning of each installment, real-life veterans were shown giving testimony about the war and their memories and experiences—as they had on a special episode of *China Beach*. But at the end of *Band of Brothers*, for the first time, those veterans were identified by name, and they turned out to be the surviving Easy Company members who had been portrayed by actors during the length of the miniseries itself. It was a wonderful final touch, topped only by a sequel that extended that finale. In 2010, nine years after *Band of Brothers* was televised, HBO, Spielberg, and Hanks presented *The Pacific*, which told the story of World War II again, this time from a different part of the world and the conflict. If anything, it outdid *Band of Brothers* in emotional intensity and followed a few marines through their respective wartime exploits and in one case after, following a war veteran home, like the focus of *Homefront*, to dramatize what we now know as post-traumatic stress disorder. As with *Band of Brothers*, the battlefield action was raw and brutal, the sense of mortality and danger was unavoidable and unforgettable, and at least one prominent cast member, Rami Malek, would later ride his intense style of acting to a higher level of stardom as the troubled protagonist of USA's *Mr. Robot*. *The Pacific* would cost even more to

492 | THE PLATINUM AGE OF TELEVISION

make than *Band of Brothers* and won eight Emmy Awards, including, as had *Band of Brothers,* for Outstanding Miniseries.

In the years between those two World War II miniseries, however, television had finally dared to dramatize a war even more recent in U.S. experience and memory than Vietnam: the Iraq War. One was a series co-created by Steven Bochco; the other was a miniseries co-created by David Simon. Both were outstanding.

Over There, a one-hour drama series co-created by Bochco and Chris Gerolmo, premiered on the FX network in 2005, telling of the U.S. Army's Third Infantry Division's first tour of duty in Iraq and the effect of the war on relatives and loved ones back home. It was the first time in TV history that a television program dramatized a still-ongoing military conflict, and *Over There* did so with violent scenes shockingly faithful to the Iraq War itself. One stunning example: Mark-Paul Gosselaar, who had co-starred for Bochco in the final years of ABC's *NYPD Blue,* guest starred in two episodes as an embedded TV reporter traveling with the army. In the second episode, his character was captured by the enemy, prompting a search-and-rescue mission, but just as they stormed the location, one of the kidnappers beheaded the reporter. "I knew it would fail," Bochco says now. "Because it was too soon. We were still in the goddamn thing, and when you turn on the six o'clock news and you get an eyeful and an earful of that tragedy, it's not something you were going to curl up on the couch and spend an hour with at nine o'clock, or whenever it was. But I thought it was an important effort," he adds, "and I was just thrilled to do it, and I certainly don't regret it for a moment." And then, three years later, came another drama about that same war, co-produced by another bold TV pioneer.

GENERATION KILL

2008, HBO. Executive producers: David Simon, Ed Burns. Based on the book by Evan Wright. Stars: Alexander Skarsgård, Lee Tergesen, Stark Sands, Chance Kelly.

For a 2008 HBO miniseries called *Generation Kill,* David Simon hired a writer, Evan Wright, whose war reporting in Iraq had been published in an

article in *Rolling Stone*, which led to a book, which led to Simon's option-
ing the book and working with the writer. Simon and Ed Burns, who had
worked together on both *The Corner* and *The Wire*, co-wrote *Generation
Kill*, which tells of Wright's experiences while working as an embedded
reporter with a marine battalion in the opening days and weeks of the Iraq
War in 2003.

Generation Kill opens with what seems to be a battle scene in progress
but turns out to be a training maneuver for the marines of the First Recon
Battalion. After that, it's briefings and boredom as the uniformed men do
what they did in other TV dramas, in other wars: wait, often impatiently,
for the order to advance, while superior officers berate them for dress code
violations and violent windstorms rip their tents from their moorings. It
takes a while for these marines to be tested under fire, but once they are, it's
not long before they get the shot to be the "tip of the spear" for Operation

Generation Kill was another fact-based miniseries about war, this time about the assault
on Baghdad by Marines in 2003. Lee Tergesen (left) stars as Evan Wright, the reporter on
whose book the miniseries is based. Stark Sands (right) plays a young lieutenant who is
part of the assault force.

Iraqi Freedom. The Alpha Team leader, Sergeant Brad "Iceman" Colbert, is played by Alexander Skarsgård, who would shortly be cast as one of the lead vampires of HBO's *True Blood*. Here, he plays a marine concerned about the safety of his men, especially in the face of risky and/or ridiculous missions ordered by his superior officers. Another of his concerns is an embedded reporter, Evan Wright, who will write the book that will inspire *Generation Kill* and who is played in this miniseries by Lee Tergesen.

After a lengthy, episode-long period of waiting, the First Recon Battalion takes off and finally gets the first of many missions that are both important and dangerous. "From now on," Colbert tells his men, "we have to earn our stories." And they're off—all the way, eventually, to Baghdad. As part of their circuitous and risk-filled journey through Iraq, these marines see sudden death and serious injury, inflicted both on them and on others. They suffer not only the pervasive dangers of battle but the sometimes absurd commands and behaviors of the officers outranking them. Simon, on *The Wire* and elsewhere, always specialized in the rules and frustrations of bureaucracy, whether on a street corner or in city hall. The military is an ideal subject to explore those same concerns, and by combining the realism of the war scenes, the detail of Wright's observations and reporting about the way the marines related to one another, and the often maddening military protocols, procedures, and loose cannons, *Generation Kill* advanced the war drama, especially the miniseries, to its most timely setting and fact-based battlefield story yet.

MINISERIES

KEY EVOLUTIONARY STAGES

Roots	1977, ABC
The Singing Detective	1986, BBC; 1988, public TV (U.S.)
Lonesome Dove	1989, CBS
The Civil War	1990, PBS
Downton Abbey	2010–15, ITV (U.K.); 2011–16, PBS

Television in this century has rediscovered, and revived, the long-form TV drama—a fairly recent rebirth due to a combination of two key factors.

One, TV programs that envision themselves as what used to be called miniseries—shows with a finite number of hours, telling a single story from beginning to end—can now lure top-tier talent that would otherwise be unlikely to commit to TV for a longer-range contract. That's how HBO's *True Detective* landed Matthew McConaughey for its first stand-alone season, how Martin Freeman managed to co-star almost simultaneously in both FX's *Fargo* and PBS's imported *Sherlock* series, and how Jessica Lange and Lady Gaga traded leading roles on successive years of FX's *American Horror Story*.

Two, in today's increasingly fractured and competitive TV universe, programs must do anything and everything they can to stand out. Back in the golden age of the TV miniseries, these long-form productions were considered "event television," generating lots of buzz as well as many millions of loyal viewers. Increasingly in the Platinum Age of Television, even weekly series, as well as miniseries, are adopting more of the standard British model, which is to produce a small number of hours, call it a season, and, after a suitable waiting period, perhaps make some more. It's a more civilized way of making television, rather than cranking out dozens of episodes per season, yet only in the past twenty years, with the advent of HBO's *Sopranos* and other cable shows, has the American model slowly shifted to making fewer episodes, with longer breaks in between. Is Fox's *24: Live Another Day* sequel a twelve-hour series or a twelve-part miniseries? It depends on semantics and on where the producers would like to enter the show and its actors come Emmy nomination time.

There's no question, though, that the miniseries is back and that TV is even better for it. The 2016 History channel remake of ABC's 1977 classic *Roots* proved that all by itself. What's surprising is how this potent form of television nearly vanished in recent years, and what's even more surprising is, when tracing the true beginnings of the miniseries genre, how far back you can go.

The television miniseries, in fact, was an experimental form first attempted in the earliest days of the medium, performed live in local TV productions, with cast and crew forced to reunite several times to complete their multipart stories. One of the first, and certainly the first to be reviewed, was a three-part adaptation of Robert E. Sherwood's Pulitzer Prize–winning play *Abe Lincoln in Illinois,* broadcast in 1945 over a two-month period by the NBC-owned WNBT-TV in New York. It was the inaugural offering of an ambitious local TV anthology series called *NBC Television Theater,* produced and directed by Ed Sobol. After the first installment was televised, *Variety* deemed it "one of the most ambitious shows since the advent of video." And after Sobol left the series the following year, his assistant, Fred Coe, took over and was at the helm in 1947 when *NBC Television Theater* attracted a sponsor and was renamed, shown on the brand-new network of NBC stations as *Kraft Television Theatre.*

Kraft Television Theatre was the first, and most durable, of TV's prestige dramatic anthology series. It ran for eleven years on NBC, and its hundreds of presentations included Rod Serling's 1955 masterpiece, *Patterns.* In television's early years, anthology shows, rather than continuing series with returning stars, were the dominant method of presenting scripted dramas in prime time. This meant each show had to be promoted from scratch, instead of being built around a recurring leading actor. However, those early anthology dramas, because of that very liability, also boasted some very potent dramatic assets. One was that the characters on these shows, even the leads, could be placed in actual jeopardy, and even die; no one had to survive to return the following week. Another built-in advantage was that these single-night dramas, like their later limited-episode miniseries counterparts, offered viewers something that weekly TV series would, by and large, not provide for decades: actual, concrete endings to the stories they told. Those same assets are being exploited, superbly, by the likes of such modern miniseries, or "single-season dramas," as FX's *Fargo* and ABC's *American Crime*.

But to return to the beginning, and to the form's evolutionary roots, we have to travel long, long before ABC's *Roots* in 1977. The pre-network experiment of *Abe Lincoln in Illinois* was no isolated aberration. Quite the contrary. The story of Honest Abe was tapped again for a long-form storytelling venture in those early TV years in 1952, when CBS, on the distinguished arts anthology series *Omnibus,* presented five thirty-minute bimonthly installments of *The Birth and Death of Abraham Lincoln,* written for television by James Agee and directed by Norman Lloyd. (Royal Dano starred as Lincoln, with other players including Joanne Woodward, Jack Warden, and Agee himself.)

Other fledgling multipart dramatic TV productions in the 1950s, among the first steps in the evolution of the miniseries genre, included a three-part adaptation of Henrik Ibsen's *Peer Gynt* on NBC's *Cameo Theatre* in 1952 and another multipart *Omnibus* historical presentation, a four-part examination titled *The Adams Family*. Notably, that same Founding Father and his relatives would inspire subsequent miniseries biographies in two different generations: PBS's *Adams Chronicles,* a thirteen-week drama starring George Grizzard in 1976, and HBO's *John Adams,* an Emmy-winning miniseries starring Paul Giamatti in 2008.

But if there was one early miniseries that demonstrated both the appeal and the potential of the genre, it was the prime-time Western that launched one of the biggest pop-culture crazes of the 1950s and prompted the sale of millions of toy rifles and, yes, coonskin caps. Over a three-month period in 1954–55, ABC's new *Disneyland* anthology series presented its three-part *Davy Crockett* adventure, starring Fess Parker as the intrepid trapper, adventurer, and congressman. Everything about the show was a success: the theme song became, at the time, the fastest-selling record in history, toy stores couldn't stock enough merchandise to meet the demand, and by the time *Disneyland* presented the third and final episode, *Davy Crockett at the Alamo*, Walt Disney knew he had a major hit on his hands. But in the true spirit of the miniseries form, *Davy Crockett*, like its hero, had a very finite ending: the final episode led to Crockett's death at the Alamo. Yet in wanting to keep cashing in on the Crockett craze, Disney, before the year was out, produced and presented two additional episodes, dealing with earlier points in Crockett's life. Disney, by necessity, had invented the TV prequel.

Other noteworthy pioneers—of the miniseries genre, not the Old West—included the director Alfred Hitchcock and the actor Patrick McGoohan.

Hitchcock embraced the anthology series form early by hosting *Alfred Hitchcock Presents* on CBS in 1955, four years before Rod Serling stepped in front of the cameras to host *The Twilight Zone*. And in 1957, Hitchcock devoted three consecutive episodes to the same continuing story: an Agatha Christie–type mystery called *I Killed the Count*. The twist in this particular story was that there were not only multiple suspects but multiple confessions, with the Scotland Yard inspector, played by John Williams, having to make sense of the overabundance of clues and motives. By the end of the first episode, two different suspects had admitted to killing the same man, and neither the confessions nor the story was over at that point, which Hitchcock, returning in his role as host, addressed in his delightfully droll fashion.

"Well, this is embarrassing," Hitchcock says. "Our time is running out, and here we are with an unfinished story on our hands. I'm afraid you'll just have to wait until our next show to find out more about just who killed the Count." At the end of the second *I Killed the Count* episode, Hitchcock returned and shrugged his shoulders apologetically.

"Well, we've done it again," he said. "We still haven't finished the story. How extremely careless of us. But I promise you, on my honor, the truth will be out next time." And it was, but in the meantime Hitchcock managed to sneak a ninety-minute narrative into his half-hour weekly time slot, essentially presenting a full-length movie mystery on television in small weekly doses.

Back in England, Hitchcock's native land, others were making strides in the evolution of the TV miniseries as well. Science fiction, it seems, was especially ripe for multipart presentations. Among England's very first miniseries was 1953's *Quatermass Experiment,* which spawned a pair of popular sequels, and arguably the limited-episode story arcs of *Doctor Who,* which began in 1963 and at this writing is still going strong, are a connected series of miniseries, even presenting different actors, more than a dozen of them, in the title role.

And in 1968, the U.K. produced, and the United States imported, one of the most surrealistic TV dramas ever made: the single-season, seventeen-episode futuristic drama series called *The Prisoner,* starring Patrick McGoohan. *The Prisoner* was a strange, strange TV show—the strangest thing to come along until David Lynch and Mark Frost unveiled *Twin Peaks* on ABC more than two decades later. In the U.K., it premiered in the fall of 1967 on the ITV channel. In the United States, it was broadcast the following year, as a summer replacement series for *The Jackie Gleason Show.* Viewers making the transition from Gleason's variety show to McGoohan's allegorical study of paranoia, persecution, and rebellion could be forgiven for being as disoriented as the future Number 6, awakening groggily in the unidentified seaside village (filmed, actually, in the storybook-like North Wales village of Portmeirion). But what *The Prisoner* offered at the start was nothing compared with how it ended, with a bizarre climax whose meaning is still being debated.

The point, though, is that it ended. It went out with a bang and with an actual conclusion. CBS demonstrated, as ABC had in 1967, once again the value of providing a final chapter, however inscrutable or controversial.

The next significant steps in the development of the miniseries were British imports as well. TV producers in the U.K. began adapting classic literary properties for the small screen and enjoying great success almost instantly. One of the earliest efforts, a twenty-six-part 1967 prime-time serialization of John Galsworthy's *Forsyte Saga,* became a major hit in England, and when PBS imported it in 1969, it became public television's first must-see costume drama. In the States as well as abroad, it was that era's equivalent of *Downton Abbey:* an upstairs/downstairs melodrama affording not only a peek behind the closed doors of the wealthy but a peek below, to the servants' quarters, as well.

Novels for television became big business very quickly—overseas at first, with the United States importing rather than producing. In 1971, giddy with the success of *The Forsyte Saga,* PBS established an umbrella anthology series to showcase these multi-hour imports and tapped Alistair Cooke, the host of the miniseries-pioneering *Omnibus,* to sit back in a plush arm-chair and introduce these long-form stories as well. The new series, called *Masterpiece Theatre,* hit some home runs early: 1972's *Elizabeth R* starring Glenda Jackson, and another *Downton*-type global phenomenon, *Upstairs, Downstairs,* beginning in 1974.

But by this time, PBS and even the commercial U.S. networks had become convinced of the potential power and popularity of the miniseries form. CBS, at the urging of its founder, William S. Paley, used some of its summer hours, normally reserved for reruns and replacement variety shows, to present *The Six Wives of Henry VIII* in 1971 and *The Life of Leonardo da Vinci* in 1972. By 1973, other networks had joined the game as well: NBC with its four-hour adaptations of *Frankenstein: The True Story* and Joseph Wambaugh's *Blue Knight,* and ABC with seven hours of *The Strauss Family* and three hours of *Divorce His/Divorce Hers,* a split-perspective drama starring Elizabeth Taylor and Richard Burton.

As with any Darwinian cycle, the strongest survived and led to another generation of even fitter and more dominant species. In 1974, NBC mounted the latest miniseries to tap the Lincoln legend with the six-hour *Sandburg's Lincoln,* starring Hal Holbrook and Sada Thompson as Abe and Mary Todd Lincoln. That same year, CBS devoted six hours to *The Lives of Benjamin Franklin,* and ABC slightly more than that to its version of the Leon Uris novel *QB VII,* starring Anthony Hopkins and Ben Gazzara. By 1976, the miniseries had become one of TV's ruling classes, with every network devoting lots of money and airtime and reaping big rewards, both financially and artistically.

In 1976 alone, PBS, while continuing to import British miniseries for *Masterpiece Theatre,* also produced its own: the thirteen-hour *Adams Chronicles.* CBS did a great job with a four-hour version of Vincent Bugliosi's *Helter Skelter,* about the Charles Manson murder spree. NBC presented the nine-hour *Captains and the Kings,* launching its own miniseries-embracing *Best Sellers* franchise, and triumphed with Sally Field and Joanne Woodward in an excellent four-hour dramatization of the psychological drama *Sybil.* Meanwhile, ABC soared above them all with its superb four-hour drama *Eleanor and Franklin,* starring Jane Alexander and Edward Herrmann as those most famous of Roosevelts, and with its twelve-hour hit version of Irwin Shaw's *Rich Man, Poor Man,* which launched the careers of Nick Nolte and Peter Strauss.

For ABC, especially, the miniseries was a way to gain prestige as well as viewers, and considering that in 1976 the ABC lineup included *Charlie's Angels, Donny & Marie, Starsky & Hutch,* and *The Captain and Tennille,* prestige was rather lacking in the weekly series department. It seemed, back then, that as ABC's series department kept aiming lower, its miniseries department, run by Brandon Stoddard, aimed higher. And a year later, in 1977, with Fred Silverman aboard as ABC's new entertainment president, ABC and the miniseries shot into orbit, with a record-setting, twelve-hour adaptation of Alex Haley's *Roots.*

ROOTS

> 1977, ABC. Based on the novel by Alex Haley. Producers: David L. Wolper, Stan Margulies. Stars: LeVar Burton, John Amos, Louis Gossett Jr., Ben Vereen, Leslie Uggams, Olivia Cole, Ed Asner, Chuck Connors, Vic Morrow, Sandy Duncan, Lynda Day George, Carolyn Jones, Ralph Waite, Moses Gunn, Maya Angelou, O. J. Simpson.

In the 1970s, a TV miniseries dramatized slavery in such personal and evocative terms that it caused an entire nation to reflect upon racial pride and prejudice and either embrace or confront its own past. The nation was England, the year was 1975, and the miniseries was *The Fight Against Slavery,* a six-part BBC and Time-Life dramatization that had a substantial impact in that country. And it happened again, on an even larger scale, in the United States in 1977, when ABC televised its miniseries adaptation of Alex Haley's *Roots* over eight successive nights, striking both a nerve and a vein. The story of Haley's purported family tree, beginning with the birth of his African ancestor Kunta Kinte (played by LeVar Burton), was, at twelve hours, the first lengthy drama in American TV history to be televised on consecutive evenings. Partly because of intrigue about the new best seller, partly because of a vicious winter storm that left much of the country snowed in, and partly because there was little significant TV competition over that particular January stretch of nights, viewers watched *Roots* in record numbers. (Silverman had scheduled *Roots* to play consecutively not to maximize its impact but to minimize damage if it failed, which was why it wasn't shown in the more lucrative and competitive February sweeps period.)

Over its eight-day telecast and multigenerational narrative, *Roots* followed the succession of Haley's maternal ancestors. In the opening sequences, audiences saw the birth of Kunta Kinte in West Africa in 1750, his capture by slave traders as a teenager, and a harrowing three-month journey aboard a slave ship, where he's taken to colonial America and sold to a southern plantation owner. In time, John Amos takes over the role of the slave (now named Toby), and the rest of *Roots* follows the story to the late nineteenth century, presenting such vibrant characters as Lou Gossett Jr.'s Fiddler, Leslie Uggams's Kizzy, and Ben Vereen's Chicken George. Familiar and beloved white TV actors, from Ed Asner to Sandy Duncan, were cast in supporting roles, many of them unsympathetic, to keep viewers interested and tuned in to what seemed like a demanding and often depressing nar-

Roots broke viewing records when it premiered on ABC in 1977, starring LeVar Burton as Alex Haley's enslaved ancestor, Kunta Kinte. In 2016 the History network mounted a remake aimed at a new generation of viewers, with Burton as one of its executive producers.

rative, but it was the story of the practice and costs of slavery and racism, not the supporting cast, that carried the day and started a TV phenomenon. *Roots* won a Peabody and nine Emmy Awards, including Best Limited Series, and, to this day, remains the highest-rated miniseries ever broadcast. Its final episode ranks third on the list of all-time top-rated TV programs, behind only the finale of *M*A*S*H* and the resolution to the "Who shot J.R.?" mystery on *Dallas*. *Roots* was to television what, a century earlier, *Uncle Tom's Cabin* was to literature: a dramatic work of fiction reaching an impressively, almost amazingly large audience, sparking national discussion and reevaluation along racial lines.

Haley's account of his ancestral history was questioned by some, supported by others, but seen and debated by seemingly everyone. According to audience estimates from A. C. Nielsen, the finale of *Roots* drew a 51.1 rating and a 71 share, meaning that half of all homes with TV sets, and more than 70 percent of those watching TV that evening, were tuned to *Roots*. Not at all surprisingly, given its massive popularity, *Roots* sparked its share of sequels and remakes, starting with ABC's even more dramatically impressive *Roots: The Next Generations* in 1979, carrying the story to the modern day. In it, James Earl Jones played Alex Haley, and Marlon Brando, a major fan of the original *Roots,* made himself available to play one of the journalist Haley's interview subjects, the neo-Nazi leader George Lincoln Rockwell. Brando won an Emmy, as did this *Roots* sequel, like its parent program, for Best Limited Series. Other sequels and spin-offs, in time, included 1993's *Queen* on CBS, starring Halle Berry as Haley's maternal grandmother, and 1988's *Roots: The Gift* on ABC, in which Burton and Gossett reprise their original *Roots* roles of Kinte and Fiddler in a "missing chapter" from that first miniseries.

The most significant *Roots* offspring of all, perhaps, is the May 2016 remake by the History cable channel, starring Laurence Fishburne as Alex Haley, Forest Whitaker as Fiddler, Anika Noni Rose as Kizzy, and Malachi Kirby as Kunta Kinte—a new production bringing the old issues and stories to a new generation and acknowledging history, and TV history, at the same time. It was compelling enough, and added enough new storylines while condensing others, to more than justify its presence as a major TV miniseries remake.

The telecast of *Roots*—the original one, from 1977—is the production that led directly to the golden age of TV miniseries. That golden age tarnished in just a few years, but until about the mid-1980s television busied itself by tapping into the full potential of long-form drama, presenting ambitious stories with finite endings and concentrated narratives.

From 1977 to 1983, the period when miniseries exploded on American TV in both quantity and quality, there were many outstanding imports on public television: Ingmar Bergman's *Scenes from a Marriage,* Dennis Potter's *Pennies from Heaven,* and presentations of *I, Claudius* with Derek Jacobi, *Rumpole of the Bailey* with Leo McKern, *Tinker, Tailor, Soldier, Spy* with Alec Guinness, *Danger UXB, Edward and Mrs. Simpson,* and that costume-drama high point, *Brideshead Revisited.* NBC offered, among others, *Jesus of Nazareth, Holocaust,* a six-hour *From Here to Eternity,* Ray Bradbury's *Martian Chronicles,* the similarly sci-fi alien-invasion story *V,* and the network's personal best of the era, a twelve-hour adaptation of James Clavell's *Shogun,* starring Richard Chamberlain. CBS, while not as competitive, presented the Watergate memoir *Blind Ambition* and Stephen King's four-hour *Salem's Lot.* ABC, continuing to lead the charge, boasted not only *Roots* during this period but, in rapid succession, *How the West Was Won* (six hours), *Roots: The Next Generations* (fourteen hours), *Masada* (eight hours), *The Winds of War* (eighteen hours), and *The Thorn Birds* (ten hours). Other, new competitors entered the programming fray as well, as ad hoc syndicated networks and just-emerging cable networks began presenting their own acquisitions and independent productions, as well as importing even more daring works from abroad.

If the barrage of titles begins to blur into one confusing lump, that's the way it felt watching TV in the 1980s and why the miniseries form, like the Western and the variety-show formats before that, went all but extinct because of prime-time overpopulation. During competitive ratings sweeps months especially, when viewing levels were used to set advertising rates for the following fiscal quarter, networks began pitting opening nights of high-profile miniseries against one another. The winners in these prime-time games of chicken wound up with a top-rated miniseries, but the losers limped off with many hours of expensive TV that went largely ignored. Before long, the risks began to far outweigh the rewards, and after a decade of fierce competition the broadcast networks in the United States all but ceded the territory to cable networks and PBS.

Despite this, the miniseries has continued to achieve greatness from time to time, and from all around the globe. England, one of the original champions of long-form TV, continued, in the first years of the post-boom miniseries era, to provide such gripping works as 1985's *Edge of Darkness* and, a year later, an unqualified masterpiece.

THE SINGING DETECTIVE

1986, BBC; 1988, public TV (U.S.). Writer: Dennis Potter. Director: Jon Amiel. Producers: Kenith Trodd, John Harris. Stars: Michael Gambon, Patrick Malahide, Joanne Whalley, Jim Carter, Janet Suzman, Bill Paterson, Alison Steadman, Imelda Staunton, David Ryall, Gerard Horan, Janet Henfrey, Lyndon Davies.

Dennis Potter's *Singing Detective*, produced for England's BBC in 1986 and shown by certain U.S. public TV stations two years later, remains the single best scripted drama ever written expressly for television—especially given the era in which it was presented. Yet as of 2016, no U.S. television network has ever televised this masterpiece nationally. If you've seen it at all, it's because of the taste and bravery of your local public television station or because of your own impeccable taste in purchasing it once it finally became

The Singing Detective, starring Michael Gambon, is Dennis Potter's 1978 miniseries masterpiece, one of the most ambitious, audacious, and original TV dramas ever concocted.

available on DVD in 2006, twenty years after it was broadcast in the U.K. Part of the reason it was never broadcast on PBS's *Masterpiece Theatre* or *Mystery!*, or on advertiser-supported cable networks such as A&E and BBC America, is that Potter was powerful enough a force in the U.K. to demand, and get, a clause in his contract stipulating that any telecast of *The Singing Detective* be wholly uncensored and unedited. Because of its language, nudity, and sexual situations, that made it untenable to televise under national PBS and basic cable standards. That was part of the reason. The rest of the reason was that *The Singing Detective* is uniquely, amazingly, gloriously bizarre.

Viewers in Potter's home country had long been acclimated to his adventurous and unpredictable styles of storytelling. In England, they first had the opportunity to sample Dennis Potter dramas in 1965, when the former political aspirant and TV critic burst upon the scene with four different teleplays. These included two semiautobiographical dramas, *Stand Up, Nigel Barton* and *Vote, Vote, Vote for Nigel Barton*, about a youth from a rural mining town who attends Oxford and runs for public office. None of Potter's first twenty-five TV productions, however, were exported to the United States, so the daring and different dramas that British audiences had come to accept, embrace, and even expect were wholly unknown in America. The first Potter-written TV production to reach the States was an adaptation, not an original: a seven-part 1978 miniseries version of Thomas Hardy's *Mayor of Casterbridge*, starring Alan Bates and shown on *Masterpiece Theatre* later that same year. Potter's next TV production, also from 1978, was an original—so original it got him noticed in the United States when it arrived here a year later, presented on public TV stations in an ad hoc syndication arrangement. It was his six-part miniseries *Pennies from Heaven*, starring Bob Hoskins and described as "a drama with music," which was so remarkable in both concept and execution. Hoskins played a sheet music salesman in the 1930s, a sad man with a stifling marriage and a longing dream that life, even his life, could and should be like the happy love songs he struggles so hard to peddle to shopkeepers in and around London. Period recordings of hit and lesser-known songs are utilized throughout *Pennies from Heaven*, with characters lip-synching them in drab but meaningful fantasy sequences. (Steve Martin, working with Potter, made a more lavish, less successful movie version in 1981.)

The Singing Detective, premiering on the BBC in 1986, employed the same technique as *Pennies*, allowing characters to express their deepest emotions by lip-synching in fantasy sequences to old recordings, but as part of an even more complicated, interwoven, and challenging story line, one with all sorts of echoes of Potter's own past. Even a concise description of this six-part miniseries seems almost comically complex. *The Singing Detective* stars Michael Gambon (Dumbledore in the later Harry Potter movies) as a writer who, like Potter, has struggled for most of his adult life with a psoriatic arthropathy, a disfiguring and somewhat crippling skin condition. The writer, in *The Singing Detective,* is named Philip Marlow (like the famous Raymond Chandler gumshoe, but without the *e* at the end of the surname) and has a past similar to Potter's: a childhood spent in the Forest of Dean, a remote mining village where his father worked the mines and sang songs at the local pub and where the one-room schoolhouse felt more like a prison. In a narrative that gets more and more meta, the adult Marlow is admitted to the hospital for medical and psychiatric treatment because of another full-body flare-up of his flaky and raw skin and aching joints. The experimental drugs make him hallucinate, and he tries to keep his brain active and alert by reworking one of his old pulp novels—called *The Singing Detective* and featuring a healthy, handsome version of himself, also named Marlow—into a movie screenplay. The only problem is, because of his drug-addled imagination, he starts seeing characters from his book and screenplay popping up in his hospital ward, and vice versa. He is also paranoid that his wife, and her lover, may be conspiring to steal the screenplay out from under him—a scheme that may, like the boyfriend, be wholly imaginary as well. And then there are the therapy treatments, which force Marlow to remember his childhood, and its deepest darkest secrets, in hopes of unlocking the mental origins of his physical problems. Confusing? Absolutely. But brilliant.

   The Singing Detective finally arrived in the United States two years later, broadcast by individual PBS member stations who bought and showed the miniseries on their own, after the PBS network's umbrella anthology series all rejected it as something that couldn't be broadcast unedited, as was demanded by contract. New York's WNET was one of the TV stations showing it, albeit after prime time, and when it premiered, my January 7, 1988, review in the *New York Post* began, "*The Singing Detective,* the latest import from England's Dennis Potter, is almost impossible to describe, yet blissfully easy to praise." Four years later, Potter made his way to the United States, and New York, as the invited guest of what was then called the Museum of

Television and Radio, for a career retrospective exhibition of his work. The museum presented a series of seminars in January 1992, one of which paired Potter, and a *Pennies from Heaven* clip, with the American TV producer Steven Bochco, and a clip from his 1990, Potter-inspired series *Cop Rock*. After seeing a taste of *Cop Rock* for the first time, Potter looked at Bochco and playfully punched him in the arm. "Was that homage," Potter asked him, "or plagiarism?" It felt like a tense moment at the time, but decades later Bochco tells me he was such an admirer of Potter's work he wasn't bothered at all by Potter's combative attitude.

"First of all, he was dying," Bochco says (Potter died of pancreatic cancer in 1994). "Second of all, he was a drunk. And third of all, he was Dennis Potter!" Bochco laughs. "But honestly, I didn't care. I have a thick skin," he adds. "I was just so thrilled to be on a stage with this guy he could have shit in my coffee cup and I wouldn't have cared."

As TV critic for the *New York Post,* I met Dennis Potter during that visit, interviewed him a few times, and even got to go out drinking, dining, and talking with him one night—a treasured memory indeed. Not as treasured, though, as my first meeting with him, which ranks among the very best moments of my professional career. He was at a pre-exhibition luncheon held by the Museum of Television and Radio for TV critics for the major New York papers. Imagine my surprise and delight when Potter suddenly called my name and asked whether I was in attendance. Then he remarked, so all my newspaper TV critic rivals could hear, that he thought my writings on him were the best he'd read in the New York papers. Life doesn't get much better than that—at least not for me.

England wasn't the only country producing quality miniseries in the 1980s. Domestically, we had ABC's *War and Remembrance,* the lavish sequel to *The Winds of War* that was not only longer (spread out over twenty-nine hours in 1988 and 1989) but darker and better. Even more impressively, CBS in 1989 presented a flawless version of Larry McMurtry's *Lonesome Dove,* a miniseries so good it should have single-handedly revived the TV Western, but didn't.

LONESOME DOVE

1989, CBS. Writers: Larry McMurtry, William D. Witliff. Director: Simon
Wincer. Producer: Suzanne de Passe. Stars: Robert Duvall, Tommy Lee Jones,
Danny Glover, Anjelica Huston, Diane Lane, Rick Schroder, Robert Urich,
Steve Buscemi.

In the late 1970s, pondering the artistic and popular success of ABC's
Roots, the author Larry McMurtry published an essay extolling the virtues
and possibilities of the TV miniseries, especially when it came to adapting
novels. "There are many stories with extended time spans," he wrote, "that
simply cannot be told adequately within the roughly three-hour duration of
a movie. Obviously, the miniseries is ideal for such books. The five- or six-
episode format allows writers to keep rhythms and textural details that are
usually lost in the cuttings and budgetings of movie scripts." He concluded,
quite presciently, that "the fact that *Roots* so firmly established the format's
commercial viability is surely going to freshen the prospects of dozens of
overlong properties."

What McMurtry didn't know then was that within a decade he would
write a book perfectly suited to the miniseries form. It would end up being

Lonesome Dove ranks not only as one of the best TV Westerns ever made but also as one
of the finest miniseries. Here, Robert Duvall as Gus McRae (left) has a quiet moment
with ranch hand Newt, played by Rick Schroder.

his most famous novel, *Lonesome Dove*—an epic Western about two best friend former Texas Rangers who embark on a lengthy cattle drive to the rugged lands of Montana—and would gain that stature at least partly because CBS presented McMurtry's story as a stunningly good eight-hour miniseries in 1989 (see the discussion of *Lonesome Dove* in the chapter on Westerns for the details).

Given the quality and popularity of 1989's *Lonesome Dove*, you'd think the miniseries genre would thrive well into the next decade, but it didn't. The glut of competing projects, a tightening of network budgets, and other factors all led to a quick culling of the herd. On broadcast television, only PBS continued to present quality ambitious long-form dramas into the next decade. The commercial networks largely abandoned their efforts, though they had made occasional significant strides in toying with telling longer, more involved stories under the increasingly flexible weekly series format. CBS introduced multiple-episode story "arcs" in *Wiseguy* in 1987, following the same case and featuring the same guest-star antagonist, over several hours. Steven Bochco, whose NBC series *Hill Street Blues* had changed prime-time dramas forever in 1980 by introducing multiple continuing subplots, attempted another sea change in 1995 with ABC's *Murder One,* a series in which all twenty-two first-season episodes told the continuing story of the same murder case. And in 2001, Fox introduced the daring real-time concept of *24,* in which twenty-four hours of TV time were used to dramatize as many hours in the life of the government agent Jack Bauer's very busy, nonstop day. All of these were called TV series; all of them, by design, were actually miniseries at heart. And one of the biggest successes in PBS history, garnering unprecedented amounts of viewers and praise, appeared in 1990 to prove just how massive an impact a well-made miniseries could have—though, at the time, it was called a series, a special, an eleven-hour "film," anything but a miniseries. Yet a miniseries, even though it was a documentary, was exactly what it was.

THE CIVIL WAR

1990, PBS. Director: Ken Burns. Writers: Ken Burns, Ric Burns, Geoffrey C. Ward. Producers: Ken Burns, Ric Burns. Narrator: David McCullough. Voice actors: Sam Waterston, Jason Robards, Julie Harris, Morgan Freeman, Arthur Miller, Paul Roebling, Garrison Keillor, Horton Foote, Kurt Vonnegut, George Plimpton.

The Civil War premiered over five successive nights in late September 1990, in direct and defiant opposition to TV's fall premiere week on the commercial broadcast networks. Like the previous six Ken Burns documentaries televised on PBS, beginning with 1981's *Brooklyn Bridge*, this new production was labeled "A Ken Burns Film" yet occupied nearly a dozen hours

The Civil War was a documentary miniseries by Ken Burns and company that transformed nonfiction filmmaking and its presentation on public television. Here, Burns (right) is seen with Shelby Foote, the most vivid of the historians interviewed on camera.

of prime time in a single week. *The Civil War,* though not called one, was a miniseries, pure and simple. And its success as a nonfiction narrative, luring to PBS an unprecedented thirty-one million viewers over its initial run, vaulted the form to a new level. There had been mammoth long-form documentaries on TV before, but *The Civil War* made it not only fashionable but potentially lucrative. Ken Burns himself was the greatest beneficiary, getting the clout, and the backing, to pursue whatever subjects interested him and to devote to them the time he deemed necessary—to research as well as televise them. The results, over the decades, have included one spectacular long-form history lesson after another, all presented by PBS: *Baseball* in 1994, *Jazz* in 2001, *The War* in 2007, *Prohibition* in 2011, and *The Roosevelts: An Intimate History* in 2014.

When Ken Burns decided on the Civil War as a subject, his original plan was for a five-hour documentary, with one hour devoted to each year of the conflict. Instead, the project more than doubled in scope, and the narrative was crafted as a five-part documentary instead, with each part taking two hours or more. The more he and his team researched, interviewed, and filmed, the bigger and better *The Civil War* got. "It was in my wheelhouse," Burns says, explaining that his previous documentaries all touched upon or led to that war in some way. "I was biting off more than I could chew, and learning how to chew, but also tackling something that was at the essence of who we are."

The first reels of film shot were interviews with the historian Shelby Foote, who gave *The Civil War* its most authoritative and memorable voice—other than, that is, the super "Honourable Manhood" section that closed part one of *The Civil War,* using every one of the patented Ken Burns tricks, including haunting period photographs, examined and swooped over slowly with a detective's eye for detail and meaning. And when I say "patented Ken Burns tricks," I'm being more literal than figurative, because on current Apple software programs, a process that focuses in and out of, and pans slowly across, still photographs is called "the Ken Burns effect."

Cable and PBS, meanwhile, have to this day carried on the miniseries tradition with more traditional, and fictional, presentations. The British dramas imported by PBS, on one umbrella anthology series or another, have included several particularly durable or inspirational offerings. *Agatha Christie's Poirot* starred David Suchet as the pompous Belgian detective Hercule Poirot, a role he began playing on TV in 1989 and didn't stop until all the Poirot stories were filmed, some twenty-five years later. In 1991, Helen Mirren starred as Detective Chief Inspector Jane Tennison, a deliciously complicated character, in the first of several fabulous, multipart *Prime Suspect* miniseries. Other imports spawned remakes rather than sequels: 1989's *Traffik* miniseries was remade as a 2000 movie starring Michael Douglas, and 1990's *House of Cards,* starring Ian Richardson as a scheming British politician, was reinvented as a Spacey vehicle, with a Washington, D.C., setting, for the Netflix streaming service in 2013.

PBS also imported *The Lost Prince,* an outstanding period drama written and directed by Stephen Poliakoff, in 2004; *Bleak House,* starring Gillian Anderson as Lady Dedlock in a flawless version of the Charles Dickens novel, in 2005; and, beginning in 2011, *Downton Abbey,* the lavish miniseries that brought the whole genre full circle, back to the earliest days of *The Forsyte Saga* and *Upstairs, Downstairs.*

DOWNTON ABBEY

2010–15, ITV (U.K.); 2011–16, PBS. Creator and writer: Julian Fellowes. Stars: Hugh Bonneville, Elizabeth McGovern, Maggie Smith, Michelle Dockery, Jim Carter, Brendan Coyle, Joanne Froggatt, Dan Stevens, Lily James, Lesley Nicol, Rob James-Collier, Sophie McShera.

The appeal of soap operas built around servants and the ruling class was proven persuasively in the early days of TV and the miniseries, thanks to the widespread, unexpected international appeal of *The Forsyte Saga* in the 1960s and *Upstairs, Downstairs* in the 1970s. In the cinema, the director Robert Altman demonstrated the durability of this fascination with the upstairs and downstairs folk in his 2001 film *Gosford Park,* a movie set in an English country house in the 1930s. That film was written by Julian Fellowes and starred not only Michael Gambon of *The Singing Detective* but Maggie Smith, who would act out the words and actions of Fellowes again, nine years later, when she was featured in his newest TV costume drama, *Downton Abbey.*

By the time *Downton* came to television, the once-ubiquitous period dramas were all but a thing of the past, in more ways than one. But *Down-*

Downton Abbey caught on with the viewing public the same way *Upstairs, Downstairs* had several decades earlier. Class differences, superb acting, and elements of soap opera still carried the day. One of the regular scene-stealers, Maggie Smith (left) as Violet Crawley, the Dowager Countess, is seen here with guest star Shirley MacLaine as visiting American Martha Levinson.

ton Abbey, whose narrative began in 1912 with news of the sinking of the *Titanic* and ended six TV seasons later with the arrival of New Year's Day 1926, was an instant, constant, and talked-about hit, on both sides of the Atlantic. Once again, it tapped into all the genre's biggest strengths, presenting sudden deaths, crushing tragedies, quiet victories, and lavish settings. Its cast, headed by Hugh Bonneville upstairs and Jim Carter downstairs, was a large TV ensemble with no weak links in its chain. It won the Emmy for Outstanding Miniseries or Movie after its first season and held on to both ratings and quality until its last, when it presented a finale that served almost every character fittingly, ending the lengthy story with a tear, a smile, and a song.

BORN: 1953, Brooklyn.

FIRST TV CREDIT: Producer, director, and cinematographer, *Brooklyn Bridge*, 1981, PBS.

LANDMARK TV SERIES: *The Civil War,* 1990; *Baseball,* 1994; *Thomas Jefferson,* 1997; *Jazz,* 2001; *Mark Twain,* 2001; *The War,* 2007; *Prohibition,* 2011; *The Central Park Five,* 2012; *The Dust Bowl,* 2013; *The Roosevelts: An Intimate History,* 2014; *Jackie Robinson,* 2016 (all on PBS).

Ken Burns has had a profound influence and impact as the most popular TV documentarian in PBS history. His landmark 1990 miniseries, *The Civil War,* was so successful it allowed him to spend decades pursuing his historical and artistic interests—interests that were stoked, and in many ways shaped, by Jerome Liebling, one of his photography professors at Hampshire College, an alternative school in Massachusetts. But Ken Burns, in an amazingly frank and self-reflective conversation, traces his love of history, and his obsession with race relations, to emotional moments from his own childhood and from his personal relationship, when he was very young, with television.

Ken Burns was born in Brooklyn in 1953, but his family moved several times when he was young, residing in France, in Ann Arbor, Michigan, and in Newark, Delaware, where Burns first recalls seeing television as a child. "The first thing I got into as a kid, before *The Man from U.N.C.L.E.,* before *Mission: Impossible*—before even *The Smothers Brothers [Comedy Hour],* if that's possible—was ... *The Gallant Men,*" Burns recalls, referring to a

1962 ABC World War II drama series. "I loved everything about it," Burns admits, remembering afternoons and weekends spent playing *Gallant Men*–inspired army games outdoors with his friends and brother (Ric Burns, who also grew up to become a lauded documentarian). Ken Burns would have been nine years old at the time, and he dismisses both the style of play and his understanding of wartime history as "corny," but it was, he says, "a way for me to fully invest in my father's war." Their father, Robert Kyle Burns, was an anthropologist, a film and photography enthusiast, and a World War II veteran. That was the war Ken Burns would eventually bring back to life in *The War,* his excellent 2007 World War II documentary miniseries. But when he and his brother were young, war was child's play. "My mother was yelling at us, 'Don't dig out my flower bed!,' you know," Burns recalls, laughing at the vividness of his childhood imagination, "because we were throwing grenades and killing Germans."

There was one shadow of death around the Burns household, though, that was anything but make-believe. "My mom had been dying from cancer from the moment I was an aware human being," says Burns. She died in 1965, when he was twelve. And during his childhood, when seeking solace in the company of television, he developed an aversion to situation comedies but an almost unhealthy fascination with the news.

"I wasn't a huge fan of comedy," Burns says, "because they all hinged on misinformation. So at the heart of all the stories was anxiety, right? And my mom was dying of cancer. I had enough anxiety." Especially because, though he had no problem avoiding most sitcoms, he couldn't stop watching, or seeking out, newscasts showing the most eye-opening and disturbing images of the early 1960s. "I remember lying awake having unbelievable anxiety," Burns recalls. "Stomachaches where my parents even sent me to a doctor, and I had all these tests. And what it was, was just anxiety." Young Ken would watch footage of the civil rights protests in Selma, and the fire hoses and police dogs, and go into his parents and cry. "They'd say, 'Oh, you shouldn't worry about that,'" Burns says. "And it took me a long time to realize—and maybe it's why I am who I am right now—that I had transferred from the sheer terror of the cancer that was killing my family to the cancer that was killing my country."

Burns considers his early awareness of race and civil rights seminal to his personal story, as well as to the stories he's driven to tell. But some stories, even his own, are too complicated and nuanced to share easily. For example, the story of the day in the summer of 1963 his family prepared to move from Newark, Delaware, to Ann Arbor, Michigan, stopping briefly to say good-bye to the African-American woman who had helped take care of the house, and the Burns children, for years.

"I've never told this to anybody," Burns confesses. "We rented a station wagon . . . and when we packed up the thing and were heading out, we went across the tracks, literally, to Cleveland Street, and went to see Mrs. Jennings. And she came out, and I was in the back part of the station wagon, and I wouldn't come forward to give her a kiss good-bye. And my father looked at me with such disappointment, and I remember it to this day." Burns explains that he was nine years old, about to turn ten, and had heard kids in the neighborhood using racial slurs. Burns hadn't, but he "felt the pressure" to keep distant at that moment, so he stayed put.

"You know how you regret, particularly with people who are gone, things you may have said or done?" Burns asks, and pauses and sighs. "I just always wish I could go back and hug Mrs. Jennings, and tell her how much I loved her, and how much she meant to me." Burns notes that "in a few short months, the president would be shot, and all that other stuff would come to a head."

Television would continue to relay that change and turmoil to Ken Burns, who kept watching and absorbing the news. He did, though, have more typical viewing habits throughout his childhood but usually for entertainment programs he would watch with his father and delight in doing so. *The Smothers Brothers Comedy Hour* and *Rowan & Martin's Laugh-In*, and before that *Hootenanny*, and well before any of those the animation of Chuck Jones, and also Jay Ward's pun-filled cartoons on *Rocky and His Friends* and *The Bullwinkle Show*, which often featured a "Dudley Do-Right" segment and wordplay that Burns recalls fondly to this day.

"I can still remember my dad walking across the room on a Saturday morning," Burns says, "when [the cartoon villain] Snidely Whiplash had decided, in quotes, to 'go straight,' to 'go legitimate.' And he opens up a demolition company called Edifice Wrecks. And my father cracks up!" That moment, Burns insists, was an important one, and an educational one as well. "I learned about the pun," he explains, "before I knew what *Oedipus Rex* was. My father explained it to me, and in a way he pulled me into a larger consciousness. He laughed, I didn't know why he laughed, he told me why he laughed, and that meant that was something that I then had to learn about. Like watching *Jeopardy!* with my dad; he knew all the answers. Now my ten-year-old daughter, Olivia, and I watch *Jeopardy!* every night, and I get all the answers. And she sits there, and every once in a while she gets an answer, and you can see her being pulled, like it's opening up doors . . . For me, that's what it was. Whenever my dad knew something, I thought, 'Oh, I need to know about that stuff, too, because my dad knows.'"

That inquisitiveness, as well as an aversion to scripted comedy antics, led Ken Burns to a steady diet of watching documentary and news shows. He recalls watching with his dad, the day after Thanksgiving, Edward R. Murrow's landmark *Harvest of Shame* 1960 CBS documentary on migrant workers. And the early years of *60 Minutes,* which began on CBS in 1968, as well as all those breaking news reports from the tumultuous 1960s. "All of the things that *60 Minutes* does so well," he says, "I think came out of an absolute hunger, borne of the periodic relief of the intentionally good pieces like *Harvest of Shame.*"

At college, where he was pursuing his interests in fictional filmmaking, an eye-opening photography class reawakened his love of nonfiction and the stories that could be found in, and unlocked from, vintage photographs. Documentaries became his new direction, and in 1976 he and a trio of similarly minded friends founded Florentine Films, the production company presenting the first Ken Burns documentary, a 1981 film called *Brooklyn Bridge.* Financed partly by money from New York and Washington, D.C., public TV stations, *Brooklyn Bridge* had a brief theatrical run and was nominated for an Oscar, then was shown on public TV the following year—the beginning of a lifelong relationship between Ken Burns and PBS. And even in his first full-length documentary, Ken Burns was displaying the tools, and storytelling moves, for which he would soon become famous. *Brooklyn Bridge* made photographs of the construction of that mammoth structure come alive, adding sound effects and slowly gliding across photos to reveal key details, and expressive faces, in effectively dramatic fashion. Original and period music added to the emotion, while off-camera celebrities, reciting the words of the movie's biographical subjects, added to the poetry. David McCullough, the author of the book *The Great Bridge* (whose rights Burns had secured from McCullough himself as the spine of the documentary), narrated, and other voices included Arthur Miller, Kurt Vonnegut, Paul Roebling (a direct descendent of the Brooklyn Bridge designers John and Washington Roebling), and Julie Harris. Not bad, especially for a first effort from a filmmaker not yet thirty years old.

Burns's earliest works were stand-alone films on such subjects as religious sects (1984's *Shakers: Hands to Work, Hearts to God*), southern politicians (1985's *Huey Long*), American iconography (1985's *Statue of Liberty*), and American government (1988's *Congress*). All of them led, chronologically and conceptually, to 1990's multipart nonfiction epic *The Civil War*, though not even Burns saw that coming at first. He had long recognized and appreciated the Civil War as "the most important event in American history," but only after making a handful of his early films did Burns recognize where they were headed and what they shared.

Burns begins to reel off the connections, starting with the subject of his very first film. "The Brooklyn Bridge was sponsored by this new metal called steel, which the Civil War helped to promote," he begins. Other connections? "That the guy who built the Brooklyn Bridge got his practical training as a bridge builder during the Civil War. That the Shakers declined precipitously during the Civil War. That Huey Long came from a North Louisiana parish that thought the Confederacy was a rich man's cause, and so refused to secede from the Union. That the Statue of Liberty was a gift from the French to commemorate the survival of the Union despite Lincoln's ultimate sacrifice. That the Congress's greatest challenge was when they were two Congresses." And once Burns saw the common thread that ran through his work, he realized the Civil War had to be his next subject. "For me, personally, it was just sort of realizing, 'Oh, my gosh! I am being kind of ordered to do that.'" He laughs.

On the eve of the 2015 PBS silver-anniversary rebroadcast of his most famous documentary, Burns reflects, "There's something extraordinarily topical about showing *The Civil War* right now. Because whether we're debating the Confederate flag, whether we're debating 'Black Lives Matter,' whether we're debating 'Driving While Black,' it's all there." Scheduled over nine episodes on PBS in 1990, *The Civil War* set ratings records for public television and won Emmy, Peabody, and Television Critics Association Awards. The writer-producer-director, Ken Burns, the writer-producer Ric Burns, and the writer Geoffrey C. Ward established a new standard and spent the next decades of their careers doing more ambitious and impressive work. For Ken Burns, that would mean both smaller, focused studies (such as 2001's Mark Twain biography and, with his daughter Sarah, 2012's very recent historical analysis, *The Central Park Five*) and more epic-length nonfiction miniseries (1994's *Baseball*, 2001's *Jazz*, 2007's World War II history *The War*, 2014's *Roosevelts: An Intimate History*).

Nothing in any of Ken Burns's other works, though, has had anything near the impact of the sequence with which he chose to close the opening installment of *The Civil War*: the love letter sent by the Civil War soldier Sullivan Ballou to his wife shortly before he was killed at the Battle of Bull Run. When a researcher found it and passed it on to Burns, Burns knew he had something great in his hands. He saved it for the climax of the first night and commissioned the musician Jay Ungar to record the haunting version of "Ashokan Farewell" that plays as Paul Roebling reads so passionately the words that Ballou sent home, a week before he died on the battlefield. "Sarah, do not mourn me dead," Ballou tells her. "Think I am gone and wait for me, for we shall meet again."

"When it took off in the country," Burns says, recalling its reception after that initial telecast, "there's something I can still remember: That kind of vivifying experience, the way you remember yourself in the face of a sunset." To Burns himself, the impact of that letter was so touching and personal that ever since he's kept a copy folded in his wallet, as a kind of talisman.

"Somewhere at a memorial service today, somewhere at a renewal of vows, somewhere at a wedding," Burns says, with what sounds like as much amazement and gratitude as pride, "people are playing that song and reading that letter—the Sullivan Ballou letter. You have this marriage of music, the fastest way to your heart, and this just utterly gut-wrenching prose—another good way to your heart . . . Every man wishes he could say those things to the woman he loves."

TOPICAL COMEDY

KEY EVOLUTIONARY STAGES

That Was the Week That Was	1962–63, BBC; 1964–65, NBC
The Daily Show with Jon Stewart	1999–2015, Comedy Central
The Colbert Report	2005–14, Comedy Central
Last Week Tonight with John Oliver	2014–, HBO
The Nightly Show with Larry Wilmore	2015–16, Comedy Central

During the earliest years of broadcast television, the opportunities to be topical were everywhere, because all television was live. Those opportunities were largely squandered, at least in the United States, where thoughtful satire on TV was exemplified by NBC's *Your Show of Shows,* which devoted its energies largely to parodies of popular culture. Comic reflections on news of the day were found mostly in monologues in Bob Hope specials and occasional comments by the NBC *Tonight Show* hosts Steve Allen and Jack Paar. It wasn't until Johnny Carson took over the late-night *Tonight Show* reins, in 1962, that viewers began to anticipate and eagerly devour a regularly scheduled comic take on current events, delivered by Carson's expert hand for the next thirty years.

Carson, of course, was the champ, doling out sharp jabs and swift knock-out punches to politicians of all parties and reacting swiftly to headlines, from the space race to Watergate. Carson's nightly monologues, though, were only a few minutes long and safely nestled in TV's late-night schedule. In prime time, there were few places where political satire could take root. In the late 1960s, CBS's *Smothers Brothers Comedy Hour* and NBC's *Laugh-*

In successfully injected political comedy and commentary into portions of their variety-show formats, but only in spots and, in the case of the Smothers Brothers, not without severe repercussions. By the time NBC's *Saturday Night Live* introduced "Weekend Update" as a regular news parody feature in its 1975 debut show, topical humor on TV had been pushed back to late night. On broadcast TV, that's pretty much where it has remained ever since, and most topical comedy has migrated to the freedom of cable television. And even there, most of the best, most meaningful topical satire shows over the years have been held back until after prime time is over. There was one early TV show, however, that dared to present unfiltered, though not always uncensored, doses of topical, political satire weekly in prime time. Based on a British series, it lasted only two seasons in the 1960s yet gave spirit, and voice, to all such TV efforts that followed it.

THAT WAS THE WEEK THAT WAS

British version: 1962–63, BBC. Host: David Frost. Writers: Christopher Booker, John Cleese, David Frost, Tony Hendra, Bernard Levin, Dennis Potter, others. Cast: Millicent Martin, Roy Kinnear, others.

U.S. version: 1964–65, NBC. Hosts: Elliott Reid, David Frost. Writers: Buck Henry, Herb Sargent, Gloria Steinem, Calvin Trillin, others. Music: Tom Lehrer. Cast: Nancy Ames, Paul Sand, Alan Alda, Buck Henry, Phyllis Newman, others.

In England, *That Was the Week That Was* premiered in 1962, the same year Johnny Carson inherited *The Tonight Show* on this side of the Atlantic. Its reign was short but significant; it was gone by the end of 1963, but not before planting its seed, in the form of a spin-off series, in the United States. In England, *That Was the Week That Was*—known widely as *TW3*, the abbreviation hereafter used here as well—held court on the dominant BBC-TV channel, with David Frost as host, Millicent Martin as the featured singer of memorably topical tunes, and John Cleese, pre–*Monty Python's Flying Circus,* as one of the writers. Another writer who contributed sketches was Dennis Potter, hired after writing a positive and encouraging review in his job as TV critic for the *Daily Herald*. Potter not only would provide some of the British show's best pieces but in time would become his country's most famous TV writer, penning such miniseries classics as *Pennies from Heaven* and *The Singing Detective*.

A month before the final show was broadcast in the U.K., NBC experimented with an Americanized special, hosted by Henry Fonda and featuring the singer Nancy Ames. It led to a full-fledged weekly NBC series two months later, hosted by the journeyman actor Elliott Reid. Ames and Phyllis Newman shared singing duties, and other regulars included Buck Henry and the *Kukla, Fran, and Ollie* puppeteer Burr Tillstrom, who won a Peabody Award for his silent piece, using just hands, to comment on the recently erected Berlin Wall. By the second season, David Frost had taken over as host, and Alan Alda and Tom Bosley had joined the cast. Writers included Herb Sargent (a pivotal early writer-producer of *Saturday Night Live* a decade later), Gloria Steinem, and Calvin Trillin. The show's most valuable contributor of all, though he never appeared on camera, was the songwriter Tom Lehrer, whose biting satirical songs—"Pollution" and "Vatican Rag," to name just two—were series highlights.

That Was the Week That Was was a short-lived NBC version of a weekly British satirical variety series of the same name, originally produced by the BBC (shown here, with cast).

The U.S. telecast of *TW3* was the most topical, and edgy, live comedy show seen on American prime-time TV for a generation. It was controversial, it was often preempted, and it rankled and lost advertisers. Commercials from tobacco companies were absent from the show's constantly hard-hitting finale, which included a segment built around the just-released health warnings linking cigarette smoking to cancer. As the song "Smoke Gets in Your Eyes" was performed, scenes of smokers and cigarette ads were intercut with scenes of patients being wheeled into operating rooms. Close-ups of cancer-riddled chest X-rays were shown to accompany the lyric "Something here inside / Cannot be denied." That last, brilliant *TW3* show began with Frost holding up a *New York Times* headline announcing the show's impending demise and ended with the entire company performing an ode to the threat of global nuclear annihilation, Lehrer's "We Will All Go Together When We Go." Sample lyrics: "You will all go directly to your respective Valhallas / Go directly, do not pass go, do not collect two hundred dollahs." Brilliant, brave, and, as a TV series, already destined to die.

When *Saturday Night Live* brought its "Weekend Update" TV news satire to late-night TV, it introduced a comedy element, and a television tradition, that continues to this day. Over the decades, "Weekend Update" anchors, each with his or her unique take on the news, have included Chevy Chase, Jane Curtin, Bill Murray, Dan Aykroyd, Norm MacDonald, Amy Poehler, Seth Meyers, Jimmy Fallon, and Tina Fey. Topical comedy, especially in political years, became and remained an *SNL* hallmark, but elsewhere, for a while, *SNL* had little competition in the political satire TV arena. More than a decade after *TW3* had been canceled, American television got another topical comedy series, and it, too, was based on a popular British model. *Not the Nine O'Clock News,* featuring Rowan Atkinson, Mel Smith, and the eventual *SNL* player Pamela Stephenson, ran from 1979 to 1982 on BBC2, the parent network's alternative channel. The show lampooned TV news and public affairs, and public figures, but spent much of its time also doing more typical character-comedy bits. Its biggest innovation was the use of edited news clips, marrying them with unrelated footage for comic effect, such as when Prince Charles shoots an arrow, followed by a jump cut to Nancy Reagan falling down as if hit. That technique was borrowed, quite liberally, when HBO produced its own version, *Not Necessarily the News,* from 1982 to 1990. Its repertory company, over its eight-year run, included the *SNL* players Jan Hooks and Rich Hall, but HBO was young then, and the satire was fairly toothless, so *Not Necessarily the News* never got much notice or traction. HBO fared much better with a subsequent topical show, this time a live comedy current-events discussion program. The comedian Bill Maher's *Politically Incorrect* roundtable series had begun on Comedy Central in 1993, moved to late-night ABC in 1997, and been canceled in 2002 when Maher was fired after a firestorm erupted surrounding his post-9/11 remarks that whatever the terrorist pilots who steered into the Twin Towers were, they weren't cowards. HBO hired Maher and backed him on a live Friday night program called *Real Time with Bill Maher*—an excellent show, often as serious as it is funny, and still thriving on HBO more than a dozen years later.

But Maher, good as he is, didn't change the TV satirical-comedy landscape as much as another comedian from Comedy Central, who is indirectly or quite directly responsible for all the remaining shows in this particular evolutionary chain: Jon Stewart.

THE DAILY SHOW WITH JON STEWART

1999–2015, Comedy Central. Host: Jon Stewart.

Jon Stewart's first crack at hosting a TV talk show was in 1993, when he presided over MTV's short-lived *Jon Stewart Show*. His final-show guest on that series, in 1995, was David Letterman, a few years after he had shifted from NBC to CBS. Many years earlier, Letterman had lasted only a few months in a daytime series that was his own first attempt at a talk show. "You're a smart man," Letterman told Stewart in the finale of Stewart's MTV talk show, and offered some very personal words of encouragement: "Cancellation should not be confused with failure."

Twenty years later, Stewart hosted another talk-show finale—the farewell episode of Comedy Central's *Daily Show with Jon Stewart*. He had hosted the show for sixteen years, taking over in 1999 from the previous *Daily Show* host (a much snarkier and more superficial Craig Kilborn) and putting his mark on it from day one, when he clicked with the carryover correspondent Stephen Colbert. Stewart's interests were wide-ranging and smart. When he interviewed guests, adding as many authors as Hollywood celebrities, his questions were designed to root out information as well as laughs. When he worked with his comic correspondents, there were serious points to be made, and wherever hypocrisy could be found, they'd expose it. And *The Daily Show,* under Stewart's long and inspired reign, paid as much attention to the media as to the news makers, exposing all of them to the simple yet withering trick of repeating what they had said and done in the past, using file footage to point out patterns, inconsistencies, and outright errors. On occasion, serious TV shows such as NBC's *Meet the Press* did that sort of thing, but for Stewart's "comedy news" operation it was part of the daily routine.

Louis C.K. showed up on Stewart's penultimate *Daily Show,* that August night in 2015, to tell Stewart, jokingly, "I represent all comedy, just to say, you know: nice job." Then Louis C.K. elaborated, much more seriously: "I'm really amazed by what you did here. It's really impressive that you did this show for this long, and kept it this good for this long. And you stayed with the world's events, and you were a voice of reason, and you were funny.

The Daily Show with Jon Stewart was a fake news show that often delivered more real substance, context, and commentary than many of its serious cable TV counterparts. Here, President Barack Obama visits Stewart, one of seven appearances made before or during the Obama presidency.

It's really, like, one of the great comedy accomplishments of all time that you did."

The next night, on his final show, Stewart made room for virtually all of his correspondents, past and present, as well as a nod to the future—a roll call that included not only the *Daily Show* alumni Steve Carell, Samantha Bee, Lewis Black, John Oliver, and Larry Wilmore but the next *Daily Show* host, Trevor Noah, who took over later that year. And, of course, there was Colbert, who made Stewart squirm by going off script to say some heartfelt thank-yous that weren't in the prompter. "We owe you," Colbert told Stewart, speaking on behalf of all his fellow *Daily Show* contributors. "And not just what you did for our career, by employing us to come on this tremendous show that you made. We owe you because we learned from you. We learned from you, by example, how to do a show with intention, how to work with clarity, how to treat people with respect. You were infuriatingly good at your job, okay?"

Yes, he was. All of that put together, along with Stewart's equally valuable arsenal of playful accents, cartoonish double takes, and incredulous straight-man setups to his correspondents, made him a fabulous host for a satirical comedy TV show. But add to that, as a bonus, Stewart's undiluted passion—his fury at the government's treatment of returning war veterans, his anger at the empty babble of many cable news programs—and he was more than just a political comic. At times, he was a political activist, as much Edward R. Murrow in *Harvest of Shame* as a simple seeker of laughs. Louis C.K. was exactly right: *The Daily Show with Jon Stewart* is, indeed, "one of the great comedy accomplishments of all time."

During Stewart's sixteen-year tenure, *The Daily Show* won multiple Peabody Awards and a total of twenty-three Emmy Awards, including a ten-year streak as Outstanding Variety, Music, or Comedy Series. It may be the Television Critics Awards won by Stewart, though, that are the most telling of all. In 2003, Stewart and his *Daily Show* won TCA Awards for Comedy. The following year, *The Daily Show* won another TCA Award—this time for Outstanding Achievement in News and Information. For Jon Stewart, current-events comedy is not exclusively a laughing matter. He takes his work, even his jokes, quite seriously, as do those who work for and with him.

Just look at the shows, from his former correspondents, that have followed in his wake, and also rank as important stops on the evolutionary scale of political TV comedy programs: Comedy Central's *Colbert Report,* HBO's *Last Week Tonight with John Oliver,* and Comedy Central's *Nightly Show with Larry Wilmore.* All of these hosts, like Stewart, work very hard not only to craft and land their jokes but to project and crystallize their viewpoints. And with laughter as their not-so-secret weapon, people are listening. And watching.

THE COLBERT REPORT

2005–14, Comedy Central. Host: Stephen Colbert.

On his very first show, playing the role of a pompous, conservative, Bill O'Reilly–esque TV pundit also named Stephen Colbert, the host introduced a new vocabulary word, "truthiness." A linguistics society honored it as the 2005 Word of the Year, and it was soon included in actual dictionaries, with Colbert credited as part of the etymology. That's an example of language in evolution, but in TV terms *The Colbert Report* was evolving as well. Colbert was playing a blowhard TV host who never broke character over the course of the entire series. That's a tough trick, but one that's been accomplished before: Martin Mull did it by playing the smarmy small-town Ohio talk-show host Barth Gimble on Norman Lear's syndicated 1977 *Fernwood 2Night,* and Garry Shandling did it, with even more depth and dexterity, by portraying the self-absorbed, insecure late-night TV host Larry Sanders on HBO's 1992 sitcom *The Larry Sanders Show.* But where *Fernwood 2Night* targeted low-rent community TV programming, and *The Larry Sanders Show* the entire talk-show universe, *The Colbert Report* was interested in everything from politics and the media to science and industry—all filtered through the bizarrely uninformed prism that was the TV character of "Stephen Colbert."

The Colbert Report was mounted with the encouragement, input, and audience lead-in of Jon Stewart, whose company produced it. On Comedy Central, the weeknight combination of *The Daily Show* and *The Colbert Report* was a potent one, especially popular among young viewers, but television alone could not contain Colbert or his ideas. Like Pat Paulsen of *The Smothers Brothers Comedy Hour* decades before him, who ran for president in 1968 to make comic yet valid points about political campaigns and prac-

The Colbert Report was a spinoff from *The Daily Show* in which Stephen Colbert, in the guise of a pompous conservative pundit, held court, dispensed opinions, and interviewed and debated guests, and managed to keep the joke fresh for many years.

tices, Colbert delighted in a type of political performance art that exemplified thinking outside the box—with TV being the box. In 2007, he took preliminary steps to be added to the South Carolina presidential primary ballots but backed off after that state's Democratic Party executive council denied him a space on the ballot. His taste for "extracurricular" political humor and satire, however, only increased. In 2010, with Jon Stewart, Colbert co-hosted the "Rally to Restore Sanity and/or Fear" on the Mall in Washington, D.C., drawing hundreds of thousands of enthusiastic supporters. (I was there, about halfway back from the stage—the guy in the Hawaiian shirt.) In 2011, Colbert officially and legally founded a super PAC, which he called Americans for a Better Tomorrow, Tomorrow, Inc., and raised over one million dollars. Most of that money, financial disclosures showed, was funneled to charity, including Habitat for Humanity and the Yellow Ribbon Fund. The fans he addressed as "Nation" supported him, it seems, wherever he went, and where he went, in 2015, was to replace David Letterman as the new host of the CBS *Late Show,* where he unveiled, finally, the "real" Stephen Colbert. Turns out he, too, was a smart, funny, very watchable TV host. Big surprise there . . .

LAST WEEK TONIGHT WITH JOHN OLIVER

2014–, HBO. Host: John Oliver.

John Oliver was another *Daily Show* correspondent who rose from the ranks to get his own show—though not, like Stephen Colbert or Larry Wilmore, at Comedy Central. As a *Daily Show* reporter and interviewer, referred to as the show's Senior British Correspondent, Oliver's droll delivery, and his willingness to do even the silliest things, endeared him to Stewart quickly and obviously: over the years, Stewart probably spent more screen time unsuccessfully stifling laughter while doing back-and-forth chats with Oliver than with any other *Daily Show* staffer. When Stewart took

Last Week Tonight with John Oliver is yet another satirical comedy show with its roots nestled firmly in *The Daily Show.* Oliver was a correspondent there, and Stewart's summer replacement host, before moving to HBO for his own series, which quickly found distinction, as well as laughs, in looking at a few topics in depth each week.

a sabbatical in the summer of 2013, to direct his dramatic film *Rosewater*, he selected Oliver as his summer replacement host. They were big shoes to fill, but Oliver filled them nicely. When Stewart left permanently two years later, or when Colbert departed for CBS, Comedy Central doubtless would have considered John Oliver as the top pick to replace either of them, but by then HBO had already pounced and given Oliver a show of his own: *Last Week Tonight with John Oliver,* a refreshingly intelligent and informative topical comedy series that premiered in 2014.

Taped only a few hours before its telecast late each Sunday night, *Last Week Tonight* was, and is, the final satirical word on the week's news. Many weeks, it follows not only new editions of Comedy Central's *Daily Show with Trevor Noah* and *The Nightly Show with Larry Wilmore* but also fresh installments of Friday's *Real Time with Bill Maher* on HBO and NBC's *Saturday Night Live*. But even though he's last in line, Oliver has found an innovative, unexpected way to stand out. After covering the week's top and breaking stories, *Last Week Tonight with John Oliver* devotes a large chunk of its program to coverage of a single, in-depth story. No other TV topical comic has ever done that, and it requires a delicate mixture of journalistic fact-finding (and fact explaining) and comedic timing and one-liners. Oliver took on FIFA, the world governing body of what Americans call soccer, in an early piece ranting about the corruption of its president, Sepp Blatter, who, soon after being reelected, was forced to resign. Each week focuses on another topic at length, and many chosen subjects, like the adoption of Sharia law in Brunei, are anything but sexy or simple. Oliver's long examination of net neutrality, and how that concept was under attack and why it should be preserved, gave me a better understanding of the issue than I had before tuning in—and I'm a TV critic.

After learning how to do Jon Stewart's job very well on *The Daily Show,* John Oliver learned how to do his own job just as well, but a bit differently, on *Last Week Tonight*. Like a giraffe on the plains, reaching for the food few other animals can reach, he's managed to adapt, and thrive, by going longer and reaching higher.

THE NIGHTLY SHOW WITH LARRY WILMORE

2015–16, Comedy Central. Host: Larry Wilmore.

Larry Wilmore spent eight years, from 2006 to 2014, as the "Senior Black Correspondent" on *The Daily Show with Jon Stewart,* covering everything from police shootings and race riots to the Barack Obama presidency and the removal, by one publisher, of the so-called *N*-word in Mark Twain's *Adventures of Huckleberry Finn.* When Stephen Colbert opted to replace David Letterman at CBS, the post–*Daily Show* slot opened on Comedy Central, and Stewart decided Larry Wilmore was the person to fill it. Almost immediately, as the new host made his viewpoints about certain current events memorably and quotably clear, Stewart's faith in Wilmore was more than validated.

As an actor, Wilmore's career goes all the way back to a few episodes of NBC's *Facts of Life* in the 1980s; as a writer, his lengthy résumé includes several seasons on Fox's *In Living Color* and creating Fox's *Bernie Mac Show.* Being "Senior Black Correspondent" and trading lines and jokes with Stewart on *The Daily Show,* and crafting those pieces with Stewart behind the scenes, allowed Wilmore to both perform and write and to find his own comic voice. And when he stepped out into the solo spotlight, as star of Comedy Central's *Nightly Show,* it was Stewart, most of all, who encouraged Wilmore to talk straight and swing for the fences.

"He said, 'Stop being a fucking host! You've got to be you!'" recalls Wilmore, who told Stewart he was just trying to do a good job and think of the guests first. Stewart had other advice. "He says, 'I know what your passions are, what your points of view are. Don't be afraid of that. Just embrace it!'" So he did. And right about that time, news broke about the mass shooting at a historic black church in Charleston, South Carolina, where a white gunman shot and killed nine people, including a pastor. Calls went out for the Confederate flag to be taken down from the South Carolina statehouse, and when local officials initially resisted, Wilmore stepped in—with an excoriating, incendiary barrage of facts and opinions.

"For the record," Wilmore said, "the Confederate flag is not a proud symbol of tradition or heritage. It's a symbol of oppression and intimidation. That's not my opinion. That's an objective fact. On March 21, 1861, the vice president of the Confederacy, Alexander H. Stephens, stated that the

Confederate government was based on the great truth that the Negro is not equal to the white man. That speech is now called the Cornerstone Speech, because that idea is the cornerstone of the Confederacy. You don't get much clearer than that . . .

"And for the record, South Carolina," Wilmore continued, "you don't get to make the heritage argument, because the Stars and Bars hasn't been flying over the statehouse since the Civil War. It went up in 1961 to mark the centennial of the Civil War—and, coincidentally, right around when the black people started with the wanting of the civil rights.

"In 1961, it was a reminder to black people that they should know their place. It has always been used as a symbol of intimidation and terror, and that's what it remains today. In fact, because displaying the swastika is illegal across much of Europe, skinheads and neo-Nazis often adopt the Confederate flag in its place. It's such a racist symbol that it does double duty as the backup racist symbol for another racist symbol!"

That's just one example, but it's a powerful one. It demonstrates, all by itself, how topical comedy has developed on television and made room for more diverse and outspoken viewpoints. It has cultivated such quick-witted

The Nightly Show with Larry Wilmore starred another former *Daily Show* correspondent, who, like Stephen Colbert and John Oliver, was given a platform to air his own perspective on the news and the media. With Wilmore that perspective often, though not always, dealt with issues of race.

comics as Wilmore, comics with the inclination and willingness to be honest, specific, passionate, and bold, while never forgetting about how to be funny.

"I watch it whenever I can, and I think he's been fantastic," the documentary filmmaker Ken Burns says of Larry Wilmore's *Nightly Show*. "His timing, when he's on, he's so razor sharp. And I think, in a kind of comic's way, he skewers just like [Ta-Nehisi] Coates does in [his memoir] *Between the World and Me*."

But not everyone was as fervent a fan of Wilmore's, even at his own network. In August 2016 Comedy Central president Kent Alterman announced the sudden cancellation of *The Nightly Show,* citing a drop in ratings compared to what Colbert had achieved in the same time slot as well as a Comedy Central perception that the show "hadn't resonated." Wilmore's initial reaction was to thank the network and executive producer Jon Stewart for the opportunity but also to regret not being able to cover the final months of the 2016 presidential election. "I'm also saddened and surprised," Wilmore said in a statement, "we won't be covering this crazy election, or 'The Unblackening,' as we've coined it. And . . . I guess I hadn't counted on 'The Unblackening' happening to my own time slot as well."

Wilmore's *Nightly Show* swan song was appropriately amusing, reflective, and even cyclical. On the first show of his final week he joked that "on the plus side, our show going off the air has to only mean one thing: Racism is solved." But things got serious on his final program when Jon Stewart showed up as a special guest—just as David Letterman had showed up on Stewart's short-lived MTV series. Stewart even quoted Letterman, though not by name, echoing the exact same words of encouragement.

On that final show Stewart told Wilmore, "A very wise man said to me, 'Do not confuse cancellation with failure.' And I took that to heart. So I would say this: What you, my friend, were tasked to do, you have done, and done beautifully. You gave voice to underserved voices in the media arena . . . It was a show that was raw and poignant and funny and smart, and all those things, and you did it from scratch."

And at the very end of the same program Wilmore made a vow I hope he keeps. "I'll just say this," he said, "I'm not done yet."

BORN: 1961, Los Angeles.
FIRST TV CREDIT: Actor, *The Facts of Life,* 1983, NBC; Writer, *Into the Night Starring Rick Dees,* 1990–91, ABC.
LANDMARK TV SERIES: Writer, *In Living Color,* 1991–93, Fox; Writer and on-air correspondent, *The Daily Show with Jon Stewart,* 2006–15, Comedy Central; Star and executive producer, *The Nightly Show with Larry Wilmore,* 2015–16, Comedy Central.
OTHER MAJOR CREDITS: TV: Creator and writer, *The PJs,* 1999–2001, Fox; *The Bernie Mac Show,* 2001–2, Fox; Writer, *The Office,* 2005, NBC.

When Larry Wilmore hosted the White House Correspondents' Association dinner in April 2016, presiding over the last "official" televised political roast of Barack Obama's administration, it was an event for which he had been preparing, in one way or another, his whole life. As a political satirist, he'd earned his credentials, and honed his performing skills, as the "Senior Black Correspondent" on Comedy Central's *Daily Show with Jon Stewart* and as host of his own series, *The Nightly Show.* As a TV writer, he'd contributed comedy scripts for series as wide-ranging as Fox's *In Living Color* and NBC's *Office* and forged his own comedy creations with Fox's animated *PJs* and live-action *Bernie Mac Show.* As a performer, he had his first regularly scheduled gig as a stand-up comic when he was still in high school—at his high school. And even before that, young Larry Wilmore wasn't just watching TV and movies. He was devouring them.

"I was a TV-aholic when I was a kid," admits Wilmore, who was born in Los Angeles in 1961. "I had the complete *TV Guide* memorized. I could tell my parents when any show was on and what channel it was on." He remembers whatever TV station he was watching signing off for the night and switching to a test pattern with an oscillating tone. "I mean, that's something people can't relate to these days," he says. "I remember watching that thing for a couple of minutes and just looking at it and going, 'What? What?? Why is my TV not working?'" Wilmore laughs. "God! That's such an odd concept now!"

Early TV favorites, all from prime time, included cartoons that broke the fourth wall, such as *The Bullwinkle Show* ("As a kid, I didn't quite get all the layers of it; I didn't appreciate those until later") and *The Flintstones.* "They were tearing that fourth wall down," Wilmore says of that ABC cartoon series, laughing at the memory of the prehistoric cartoon animals used as primitive record players or vacuum cleaners who would look directly into the camera and say with a shrug, "It's a living." This method of addressing the audience directly was something Wilmore enjoyed whenever he encountered it throughout childhood, whether it was George Burns talking privately to viewers on *The George Burns and Gracie Allen Show* or Groucho Marx shooting glances and one-liners directly at the movie screen. "A big revelation to me at a young age," Wilmore says, "was seeing the Marx Brothers for the first time and just thinking, 'What the hell is this? This is fantastic!' They had re-released *Animal Crackers* on the big screen, and my dad took us, and it was on a bill with *Duck Soup* and [the W. C. Fields film] *My Little Chickadee.* And I just couldn't believe how funny these guys were . . . And that was transformational to me because of the whole rhythm of Groucho and all that stuff, and so I immediately immersed myself in the Marx Brothers and just learned as much as I could about them. I found every book I could find on them, I would memorize the movies, and I still know some of the movies almost by heart."

Wilmore appreciated anarchy on TV too, citing the prank-staging *Candid Camera* as one early favorite and mentioning two comedies that were the first with which he was "completely in love." One was NBC's pioneering 1971–74 *Flip Wilson Show,* a variety show Wilmore calls "one of the most influential to me as a comedian." (He would have been nine years old when it premiered.) The other was NBC's *Get Smart,* the Mel Brooks–Buck Henry spy spoof starring Don Adams as Secret Agent Maxwell Smart ("I just couldn't believe how funny this guy was"). As a teen, he expanded his tastes to Monty Python, and beyond comedy altogether, in particular to the French New Wave films of François Truffaut and Jean-Luc Godard.

The shift from watching comedy to performing it occurred when Larry Wilmore was a young teen, and it wasn't his idea. Wilmore went to a Catholic school where the classes ranged from first to eighth grade, and in seventh grade Larry had a teacher from Peru who, with his wife, were the lay teachers at the Catholic school. Larry was a good student who wanted to learn, but he also wanted to cut up in class and make his friends laugh. "I just couldn't keep my stupid mouth shut," he admits, "but it was always a witty comment; it wasn't just a silly one, you know?" Weary of the constant interruptions and disruptions, the teacher pulled Larry aside—not to reprimand him, but to negotiate. "He came to me one day," Wilmore recalls, "and said, 'Okay, Larry, I'm going to make a deal with you.' He said, 'You are talking way too much in class, and that has to stop. But here's what I'll do. When we come back from lunch, there's fifteen minutes where the kids are just settling down, and I can't really get anybody's attention. I'm going to give you fifteen minutes where you can have comedy time, and you can get up in front of the class, and you can do whatever you want.' Then he says, 'But for the rest of the day, I don't want to hear a peep out of you.' And I said, 'Deal! Are you kidding me?! That is a deal!!'"

Every day, young Larry would get up and do his fifteen minutes in front of a tough audience—great training for the White House Correspondents' Association dinner. Impressions, sound effects, reactions to whatever had happened that morning were all part of Larry's quickly developing comic persona. "This teacher believed in me," Wilmore says now, "and he turned something which could have been a negative into a positive."

Wilmore was a theater major at California State Polytechnic University, studying the classics while doing a little stand-up comedy on the side and going on auditions as an actor—a two-pronged approach to finding a career, and one he maintained even after leaving the university shy of graduation. He was less fortunate pursuing acting auditions, he says, because "they'd be looking for a 'street type,' as they would call it then," and then reject him for being "too smart," in favor of someone who looked and acted "more urban." Wilmore says, "It's so ridiculous it's funny. You go, 'I think I'm offended, but not really? I can't tell. Thank you?'" Wilmore chuckles. "That's why I've always had a very funny, contrary relationship with race." His first steady job and credit came off camera, when a friend who had just started writing for a midnight ABC talk show, *Into the Night Starring Rick Dees,* told Wilmore they were hiring writers. Wilmore fired off some jokes, and they brought him in for the comedy writing equivalent of a one-day stress test. "I had to do that thing," Wilmore says, "where you write jokes in twenty-four hours, because they want to make sure you didn't just store those jokes [you sent in to apply] over the course of a year or whatever." He got the job, then left it, six months later, when he got what he calls his "big break," joining the writing staff of Fox's *In Living Color* in 1991, its second year on the air as Keenen Ivory Wayans's envelope-pushing, attention-getting sketch variety series.

"The writers' room was as entertaining as the television show, if not more so," Wilmore recalls, adding, "And it was one of the best experiences of my life. I said, 'It was the worst of times, it was the worst of times,' because it was the hardest thing to do." Wilmore laughs. "You thought you were going to get fired every single day, but that's kind of what made me fearless as a writer, to go through that. You had to pitch every single day. Keenen was a really tough boss, but he was wildly entertaining as well, so it was a real interesting experience." Wayans and his funny family members Damon, Kim, Marlon, and Shawn were all showcased on *In Living Color,* as were such young, explosive talents as David Alan Grier, Jamie Foxx, and Jim Carrey. The latest hip-hop music was on display too, performed by guest artists and danced to by an in-house dance troupe known as the Fly Girls. Rosie Perez was house choreographer the first four seasons, and members of the Fly Girls over the years included Carrie Ann Inaba and Jennifer Lopez, later to resurface on prime-time TV as judges on, respectively, ABC's *Dancing with the Stars* and Fox's *American Idol.*

Whatever was presented on *In Living Color,* the audience at home, and especially the studio audience at the taping, responded to not only enthusiastically but often incredulously—laughing, applauding, and sometimes even gasping at what they were seeing. That was true of Damon Wayans and Grier as the flamboyantly gay "Men on Film" movie critics Blaine and Antoine; of Keenen Ivory Wayans as a high-pitched Mike Tyson; of Damon Wayans as the angry and uncooperative Homey D. Clown ("Homey don't play that!"); and of an extended *Star Trek* spoof, with very unexpected overtones, called "Star Trek: The Wrath of Farrakhan." You not only heard the studio audience at those moments; you felt them.

"I know exactly where you're going," Wilmore tells me. "You're absolutely correct. And I've never experienced it since, by the way. It was a combination of joy, excitement, titillation, and just unbridled exuberance—like they were watching something they couldn't believe was on television. And they were privileged to a moment, too. It was all that stuff wrapped up in one." All that, and more.

"*In Living Color* was one of the shows, I think, along with *The Arsenio Hall Show,* to kind of introduce hip-hop culture to America," Wilmore says. "You can't really say it was a black show, or it was 'this.' It was really hip-hop culture, which was embraced by black and white alike. It was the movement of music and style and bravado, and all kinds of stuff which now everybody takes for granted. And music was the first entry into that, but no one had quite seen the humor of that movement yet. And whether it was 'Men on Film,' or the guys selling stuff out of the back of the truck [the 'Homeboys Shopping Network'], or whether it was Jim Carrey doing Fire Marshal Bill, it was so outrageous, and it was so much fun to be a part of it. It was really amazing."

Wilmore's next series was Fox's *PJs,* a stop-animation prime-time comedy series he co-created with Eddie Murphy and Steve Tompkins. The Will Vinton Studios provided the stop-animation, which centered on the disagreeable superintendent of a building in the projects and all his inner-city tenants. *The PJs* ran for two years on Fox and another on the WB, but never without controversy, including complaints from Spike Lee and protests from the NAACP. "Some people were protesting the show, and they didn't like the fact that there were characters drinking forty-ouncers in one episode," Wilmore recalls. "And I said, 'Well, I remember in *Family Guy,* the father gets dead drunk and passes out on the table in the pilot, for Christ's sakes!' And they said, 'Yeah, but your characters are real.' I said, 'They're puppets! They're not real!' . . . We did a lot of hard, satirical humor that we were really proud of," Wilmore says. "Some that you couldn't do in other ways. But sometimes with television, it depends what era you're writing in. There are things on *All in the Family* that you can't have on television today."

Wilmore was the sole creator of his next TV series, *The Bernie Mac Show,* which premiered on Fox in 2001. It starred Bernie Mac as a broad caricature of himself, with a premise taken from the comic's true-life stand-up routine about raising the children of his drug-addicted sister. The style of the show, though, had been decided upon before the star or the premise and drew from inspirations ranging from the obvious to the stunningly arcane. Because of Wilmore's longtime love of Groucho Marx and classic TV, it's easy to trace the influence of Groucho, and George Burns, in the breaking-the-fourth-wall approach that had Bernie Mac looking directly into the camera to address the audience with "Hello, America!" Wilmore freely acknowledges those predecessors as part of the inspiration for *The Bernie Mac Show* but reveals others that are wholly unexpected—most of all, an obscure 1999 British reality series and "social experiment," quickly imported by PBS, called *The 1900 House*. In it, participants tried to live in period conditions from a century earlier, with hidden cameras tracking their every move and with a "confessional" booth where they could reveal their true emotions, and transgressions, to the TV audience.

"I was looking at how the reality shows were starting to take hold," Wilmore explains. "*The Real World* [on MTV] was a big show at that time, and there was a new show that had just started, called *Survivor*. And I'm like, 'What's going on with this? What's happening there?' And I'd wanted to do a show that felt kind of like it was real—like we were eavesdropping on it. And the biggest influence for me, at the time, was a show called *The 1900 House* . . . Because they had these cameras put around the house, and it was all about behavior. And you know I'm a big behavior guy.

"So I thought it would be interesting," Wilmore continues, "to have a show where it felt like we were observing this family, rather than having a show where all the jokes are pushing at us, and it's more of a performance thing. I was after more of an observational show, where it looked like we were eavesdropping. And even when Bernie was in the confessional—and I called it a confessional, based on *1900 House*—it wasn't to advance the plot but to reveal his hidden feelings, as when *1900 House* participants tried to justify eating a smuggled-in candy bar. That was what I wanted with Bernie in those 'talking to America' scenes," he adds. "It's not an expositional tool. It's a confessional tool."

Wilmore further enhanced the "reality" feel of the series by working with Ken Kwapis, who directed the pilot, to establish a visual look and editing pace that seemed more frantic and unplanned than carefully choreographed and photographed. Again, the primary inspiration was an unexpected one. "As part of our preparation for it, we watched French New Wave films together," Wilmore says. "I know. It's so ridiculous . . . But we talked about people like Truffaut, and Godard's editing style, I was really drawn to a lot." Action would happen just out of frame, or pull Bernie Mac out of frame to investigate what the kids were up to—all with the intent of showing that these kids he was raising were a handful, and a lot of responsibility, but that he wasn't about to lose the battle. "I was drawn, at the time, to the whole notion that kids were kind of taking over the role of the parents," Wilmore says, adding that it was a notion he resented and wanted to counteract. "So the theme of *The Bernie Mac Show,*" Wilmore says simply, "is: Children are terrorists. I don't negotiate with terrorists."

Wilmore took the pilot of *The Bernie Mac Show* with him to England, to show at a seminar on sitcoms. Also shown there, by a producer named Ash Atalla, was an episode of a new BBC comedy called *The Office,* starring and co-created by Ricky Gervais and using a faux documentary format, yet another new way of breaking the fourth wall. Wilmore and Atalla loved each other's shows so much Atalla made an unrealistic but passionate request. "He goes, 'Larry, just promise me one thing, if you will,'" Wilmore recalls. "I said, 'Sure.' He says, 'Please don't let them take this to America and ruin it.' I said, 'I'll give you this promise: If it does go to America, I'm not going to work on it!'"

But it did, and he did. Wilmore was fired from *The Bernie Mac Show* after its first season ("It was one of those Hollywood stories," he says diplomatically) and moved to NBC with an overall deal to develop TV shows. Greg Daniels, one of the writer-producers tasked with adapting the British *Office* for an American audience at NBC, was a longtime friend of Wilmore's ("He had done [Fox's animated] *King of the Hill* when I was doing *The PJs,*" Wilmore explains, "and we kind of had similar careers") and invited him to help launch the U.S. adaptation. Wilmore needed the work, so despite his earlier pledge he accepted and found himself working, briefly, on a show where even after the pilot was shot and waiting to air, its reputation was that of a rip-off version doomed to failure, even among those who had seen it in advance. "Everybody hated the pilot," Wilmore recalls of the period before the Americanized *Office,* starring Steve Carell, premiered on NBC. "I remember getting the 'stink eye' from all these writers, and I was going, 'Guys! It's going to be good!'" The pilot had stayed faithfully close to the British original, which was revered, but beginning with the second episode, "Diversity Day," NBC's *Office* began staking out its own territory. The staff writer Wilmore was cast as a sensitivity trainer in that episode, a part Daniels urged him to take after Wilmore read the role at the first table read. (It was a good writers' room for career advancement: that episode's writers, B. J. Novak and Mindy Kaling, became even more familiar faces on NBC's *Office* over the years.)

"We decided not to think about the English version and just do our own thing," Wilmore says. "Greg Daniels really led that charge. He has his own take on things, and the combination of him and Steve Carell just really made it interesting." Carell had come from Comedy Central's *Daily Show with Jon Stewart,* where he'd been a comic correspondent since 1999. NBC's *Office* premiered in 2005, and the following year Wilmore was hired by Carell's old boss and became "Senior Black Correspondent" on *The Daily Show,* a post he held until 2015.

"Jon Stewart," Wilmore says, stopping for emphasis before summing him up. "I would say he is the smartest person I've ever worked with and collaborated with, in terms of knowing how to investigate what is really important about a topic." Wilmore says the type of writing required by *The Daily Show,* and later by his own *Nightly Show,* is vastly different from the playwriting he studied in college, where it's all about characters and conflicts and dramatic obstacles. "Editorial writing," he says, "has to be about something very specific. You have a passion, and an idea, and you're extrapolating that idea. You have to get that idea across to the audience in a very clever, dynamic way. There's really nothing quite like that . . . and Jon is a master at that. He really perfected it in his first few years on the show."

Stewart's role as Wilmore's mentor is one that was established just as a "very nervous" Wilmore was about to make his inaugural appearance as a *Daily Show* correspondent. "And Jon, I remember," Wilmore says, "he looked at me and said, 'Larry, just look in the camera. Just fucking give it to America!' And it really just made me relax. And I was like, 'Okay, great!' And I started getting laughs. It was kind of the best advice anybody can ever give you. My relationship with Jon has just been great. And the fact that he's now a producer on *The Nightly Show,* and really made that happen, and pitched that show to me . . ."

Wilmore, by that time, was already supplementing his *Daily Show* correspondent duties with work as executive producer of Anthony Anderson's new ABC family sitcom, *Black-ish,* but saw *The Nightly Show* for the opportunity it was and jumped aboard. He was entertaining from the start but, he admits freely, not as good initially as when, once again, Jon Stewart stepped in to give some advice that made all the difference.

Wilmore says, "I remember Jon being—I'll use the word 'angry,' but it's not quite the right word, because it's a patrician type of nudging and encouragement . . . From my point of view, I was still involved with all the juggling of doing a TV show. I was kind of leaving myself last, you know? I was putting the interests of the guests first. And Jon said, 'Larry, you have to reverse that. You can't put their interest first. You have to lead and then let them comment on your point of view.' So it was very instructive."

Wilmore was a quick study. Initially, he was reluctant to focus so aggressively on issues touching on race ("I was a little reticent, I'll be honest with you, with wanting to do that full on," he says), but between Stewart's goading and a rash of headlines about racially motivated mass shootings and the Confederate flag, he went for it. "When those things started happening," he says, "I realized, 'You know what, Larry? It may as well be you to really attack these and really talk about them. Why shouldn't it be you?' And Jon and I had some really great conversations about that also."

And he was off: giving a history of the Confederate flag that left no doubt he considered it "a racist symbol," and giving his opinion in short, blunt bursts that, on occasion, elicited oohs and gasps, then fervent applause, from his studio audience, just as some of the envelope-pushing characters and skits used to back in his *In Living Color* days. But to be fair, he'd done that with his very first joke on the premiere episode of *The Nightly Show,* opening with an incendiary opening teaser about the Bill Cosby controversy, in which he'd been accused of sexual misconduct by dozens of women. "We'll ask the question, 'Did he do it?'" Wilmore said, launching his premiere telecast, then followed with the audience-rattling capper "The answer will be yes."

"Well, that's because nobody was saying that on television," Wilmore says, recalling the studio audience's high-decibel excited reaction. "Everybody was kind of dancing around it. Respectability was taking the place of authenticity . . . and when you drop respectability and you're just honest about something, it's refreshing to an audience."

Next stop: the April 2016 White House Correspondents' Association dinner, at which Wilmore insulted many of the high-profile journalists in attendance, did the same to almost all the remaining presidential wannabes, and signed off by saluting President Barack Obama with a warm embrace and an exit line, "You did it, my nigga," that the website Deadline Hollywood described as "gasp-inducing" . . .

CONCLUSION

In 1988, an independent British TV production company and a pair of U.S. public television member stations got together to make the first serious documentary series to look at the history and development of its own medium. It was called *Television,* and it arrived on PBS just after *Hill Street Blues* had ended, *The Wonder Years* had begun, and BBC-TV had delivered one of television's greatest masterpieces, Dennis Potter's musical miniseries *The Singing Detective.* You can understand why the host of that *Television* documentary, the respected TV news journalist Edwin Newman, concluded the series by asking, "Can television change for the better, or is it as good as it will ever be?"

That question, actually, is a craftily wielded two-edged sword. On one side of the blade, Newman is asking, by implication, whether the business structures and commercial requirements of TV will allow it to focus more on quality than profit than it has in the past. On the other side of the blade, he's asking, with no apparent sarcasm or irony, whether TV in 1988 is as good as it gets. I understand both the perspective and the argument. Edwin Newman's *Television* question came out four years before my first book as a TV critic and historian, 1992's *Teleliteracy: Taking Television Seriously.* In that book, I argued that television had matured to the point where it was the equal of other art forms. What I call TV's Platinum Age was still a few years in the future, but once it arrived, television generated so many amazing programs so quickly that the argument of TV artistic equality to other forms of narrative art became a given. The debate, these days, is more often about which visual medium, television or film, is superior.

In some very obvious positive ways, TV has indeed matured and gotten even better. In the past few years, U.S. television finally adopted the model of British programming that was part of that culture from the start: allow-ing series to be however long, or short, they need to be to tell their story properly. As we've read, Aaron Sorkin used to joke with the director Thomas Schlamme, when they worked together on "episode 14 of twenty-two" of a season of *The West Wing*, "If we lived in the U.K. and this was on the BBC, we'd be done already." Sorkin laughs and adds, "And he'd say, 'Yeah, but we'd all be living in smaller houses.'" What may make them a little poorer, though, may make TV a little richer. Once again, the FX executive John Landgraf explained, also supporting the more flexible model of episodes in a TV show's season, "Television is now figuring out how to support sto-rytellers better. And I think that's one of the reasons television has gotten better, because the business model has morphed into something that is bet-ter able to support the writer making the better choices for the story, rather than having to subvert those choices into the business model."

What writers, producers, directors, and actors are finding in the cur-rent TV climate, though, is that sacrificing part of a salary for the right rea-sons—a stronger role, a limited production schedule, the chance to pursue or generate a pet project—can be not only acceptable but preferable in the long run. TV characters, as well as serialized story lines, have become deeply complex and delightfully unpredictable, making them more attractive to the likes of Glenn Close and Jessica Lange, who formerly worked exclusively in films or onstage. With more networks and distribution platforms than ever before, and with most of those networks and streaming sites looking for distinctive new ideas and programs to attract attention and viewers, there's never been a better time, at any point in an artist's career, to pursue a career in television or to attempt to make better TV.

Throughout TV history, the times when the ground was most fertile for innovative new shows were when a network was most supportive, which usually came when it was also the most desperate and/or when someone at the very top decided to give writers and producers the freedom and resources to pursue their most personal visions. That's what happened when Grant Tinker launched MTM Productions in the 1970s, and his "mired in third place" NBC network rallied behind *Hill Street Blues* and *St. Elsewhere* in the 1980s, and HBO launched the Platinum Age by trying to call attention to itself with *The Sopranos* in the late 1990s. All those shows and eras were jump-started because certain production companies and networks had faith in individual creators, and in the twenty-first century things are continuing to evolve for the same reason, and also because certain creators, such as

Louis C.K., are being brave enough to have faith in themselves and find new ways to produce and even distribute their own works.

"It seems to be way better!" Larry David says, comparing today's TV with when he started on *Fridays* in 1980. "I think there's so much more creative freedom now. Cable has changed everything. And I think there are so many writers who would be in other mediums if not for this freedom that they have in television."

Tom Fontana, a writer-producer from NBC's *St. Elsewhere* and *Homicide: Life on the Street,* may be the only person who pioneered in two different TV arenas. After those NBC shows, he created the first original drama series for HBO with *Oz* in 1997, then went abroad to create one of the first original drama series for Netflix, with *Borgia* in 2011. "What's wonderful about that," Fontana told me, "is that I had virtually no idea, either time, what I was getting myself into, because I am such a techno-dinosaur. Both times, I literally went where the door was open." And when, in both cases, Fontana's friends expressed bafflement at his career move, his explanation was the same, and is critical to the future, as well as the history, of quality TV. "Al I know is," Fontana says he told them, "they're going to let me do what I want."

The future of television, I believe, will continue to encourage quality TV to thrive. I just have no idea where. It took me a few years to fully grasp and accept the idea that for a TV show to succeed more impressively in social media than in the Nielsen ratings didn't mean it was failing in its mission—just reaching fans a different way. My students at Rowan University watch TV not primarily on a television set but on portable devices such as their smartphones and may not even know the network of origin. But they're still watching, and not only watching, but sharing. Larry Wilmore has observed this phenomenon—not only the wealth of options available, but the viewing methods—with his own seventeen-year-old daughter.

"She just started watching *Jane the Virgin,* and she said, 'Dad, this is a really great show!'" Wilmore says. "And I said, 'Oh, yeah, it's on the CW, right?' And she goes, 'Um, uh, I don't know.' So there's no brand identification with a network. For me, when I was a kid, I *knew* if a show was on CBS or NBC," he says, laughing. "That *meant* something. But she doesn't know. It's on Netflix. What does *she* know? She finds it somewhere on her phone, or on Tumblr she'll see a clip from something."

But the point is, she's finding it and watching it, and it's getting made. And if, say, in the case of late-night talk-show hosts, they're tailoring parts of their TV shows to make content more likely to be shared on social media, that's not so much abandoning the old rules as recognizing, and adapting to, the new ones. Garry Shandling, in one of his last interviews before he died in 2016, talked to me about precisely that.

"There's an evolution," Shandling said of the talk-show genre. "Things don't stand still." He liked a lot of what's out there in the current generation of hosts: Shandling saluted Jimmy Fallon as being "extraordinarily talented," called Seth Meyers "a spectacular writer," and said Stephen Colbert was "fantastic." But he was aware of the differences in terms of overall content, compared with the era of *The Tonight Show with Johnny Carson.* "Some people—not me—are a little uncomfortable [with the new talk shows], saying, 'Oh, there's no conversation like there was with Johnny,'" Shandling said. "But before that, they were saying, 'With Johnny, there's no conversation like there was with Jack Paar,' right? So it's going to speed up. The interview parts are tight, and there's an evolution! Jimmy Fallon is really *playing* with the guest. The guest comes on and becomes part of that show in a new way that sort of hasn't been done." And on CBS's *Late Late Show with James Corden,* the affable host does his best work with his guests *outside* the studio, taking them on "Carpool Karaoke" runs that have become viral videos on YouTube. They're among the most joyous and infectious entertainment segments I've ever seen on television—even if most of the more than 100 million YouTube viewers of his sing-along-with-Adele video saw it on their phones or laptops instead.

The evolution of late-night talk shows, by the way, would have been a fun one to explore fully (in terms of its variety aspects, you'll find it in the "Variety/Sketch" chapter), along with plenty of others. If you're missing individual evolutionary chapters on TV superheroes, science shows, ethnic comedies, made-for-TV movies, reality shows, game shows, anthology series, and so on, well, so am I. But even Darwin, in the Galápagos, limited his study to one chain of isolated islands. TV is too vast, too encompassing, to nail down comprehensively, even in a volume as large as this one, so the focus was, at times and by necessity, narrowed and limited. It is my fervent hope, though, that this book contains enough examples, analysis, and voices to spark the conversation and make a case for just how vast, interconnected, and wonderful so much of TV, past and present, really is. One thing I discovered while researching *The Platinum Age of Television,* and interviewing the artists I did, was how beautifully interwoven the entire history becomes. You might almost say "You are what you watch," and some of what today's best creators of TV shows watched, when they were young, fed both their tastes and their ambitions. Today there are more scripted shows produced each year than ever before, and more places than ever to see them, but one of the final unresolved questions, and problems, as we move forward into TV's future is this: How best to preserve, and present, its past?

"There always will be a place for the network," *Breaking Bad*'s creator, Vince Gilligan, says assuredly. As a person who makes edgy TV, he says, he's also grateful there are shows like *The Andy Griffith Show* and cable networks and streaming sites to repeat them. "I'm no prognosticator, but that, it seems to me, is the future," Gilligan says. "A place where the scroll-through list goes on for thousands of entries, and you, the viewer, decide." That's nice—and truly, when it comes to TV choice, "the more the merrier" is indeed the ideal—but just because everything is available doesn't mean people will find it, much less sample it. Despite their widespread availability on nostalgia networks and streaming sites, such classic TV shows as *The Andy Griffith Show, The Honeymooners, I Love Lucy,* and *The Twilight Zone* are familiar to fewer of my students in 2016 than they were at the turn of the century, and the majority of my students are majoring in television and film. As all these new shows are coming in, some of the old ones are getting lost, and not even all of the new ones are being found and enjoyed, either. It's a problem: so much great TV, so little time to watch it. But honestly, what a wonderful dilemma, especially for a career-long television critic. It was hard enough deciding when the Platinum Age of Television began. Imagining when it will end, right now, is beyond my comprehension, as well as my pay grade.

Matt Groening, when I interviewed him for this book, began with a comment that I'll borrow to end this entire exercise. He was thinking not about his own decades-long TV output with *The Simpsons* but about the television he's been watching, and enjoying, all his life. He was imagining what it was like to be a TV critic at this point in TV history, and he was very enthused by the idea.

"What a great time to be writing about television. It's absolutely an amazing time in TV, and I never would have predicted that TV would get this good," Matt Groening says.

He's completely correct—on both counts.

ACKNOWLEDGMENTS

This book—a study of TV evolution—itself has evolved from a number of sources and inspirations, so I have many people to thank. My TV criticism, my radio work, my college teaching, my seminars and lectures abroad, even my art gallery exhibit in New York all fed, like streams into a river, to make this study both an idea and a reality. And my agent and my editor encouraged and improved it from the start, while scores of publicists, friends, transcribers, and others helped greatly along the way.

Laurie Fox, my book agent for *Dangerously Funny: The Uncensored Story of "The Smothers Brothers Comedy Hour,"* urged me to write a book that would plant my flag atop the history of TV, reflecting both my opinions and my decades of experience as a TV critic. She paired me with Gerry Howard, my editor at Doubleday, who kept challenging me to make my interviews more substantive and my evolutionary chapters more informative (and who reacted with saintly patience as both the manuscript and the delivery date kept expanding). The people who helped me reach my interview subjects deserve special thanks, as do the artists themselves, who gave generously of their time and memories to walk down TV memory lane with me.

Those who spoke with me specifically for *The Platinum Age of Television,* and earned my sincere gratitude, include Judd Apatow, Steven Bochco, James L. Brooks, Mel Brooks, Carol Burnett, Ken Burns, Jim Burrows, David Chase, Louis C.K., Larry David, Tom Fontana, Vince Gilligan, Matt Groening, Jason Katims, David E. Kelley, Michelle King, Robert King, John Landgraf, Norman Lear, Denis Leary, David Milch, Bob Newhart, Carl Reiner, Phil Rosenthal, Shawn Ryan, Thomas Schlamme, Amy Schumer, Garry Shandling, David Simon, Tom Smothers, Aaron Sorkin, Kevin Spacey,

Frank Spotnitz, Mark Tinker, Matt Weiner, Larry Wilmore, and Graham Yost. The book wouldn't be the same, and perhaps wouldn't be, without them.

Their respective assistants and publicists, and many network executives and staffers and personal assistants dealing with promotion and publicity, deserve thanks also. Executives and longtime friends Tobe Becker at HBO and John Solberg at FX, in particular, were absurdly helpful and patient with my many requests, and other generously accommodating gatekeepers along the way included Jordan Anthony, Jeff Apple, Philip Arnold, Lily Bedrossian, Maya Brooks, Jenn Carroll, Antonia Coffman, Lea Cohen, Chris Connor, Stephen Day, Allesandra DiMona, Sheena Eustice, Joy Fehily, Barbara Fillon, Sam Fishell, Leslie Fradkin, Brittany Gilpin, Lauren Kamm, Greg Longstreet, Katherine Macpherson, Laura Mandel, Michelle Margolis, Jane McKnight, Kerry Meehan, Jeff Peisch, Morgan Pesante, Todd Pfeffer, Katherine Pongracz, Reena Rexrode, Michele Robertson, Kent Rotherham, Bess Scher, Britney Scott, Laura Streicher, Sheila Feren Thurston, Elli Vacca, Shelby Van Vliet, Lisa Walder, and Scott Wilson.

My teaching TV, through the years, had a lot to do with shaping my own perspective on television history, so thanks are due to Mike Donovan, who drew me back into academia after a three-decade run in daily newspaper journalism. We not only designed Rowan University's first TV History and Appreciation course together, but the question he suggested we ask of our students from the start—about their first favorite personal entertainment choices—provided the jumping-off point for all my interviews in this book. I'm also indebted for his partnership on our almost-annual Broadcast Education Association–Rowan University presentations, "A Conversation with . . . ," a Las Vegas event giving us the opportunity to interview, and present a career overview of, some of the participants in this book, including Vince Gilligan and David Simon. (A very special thanks goes to BEA executive Heather Birks for facilitating all these talks, and so graciously and charmingly, too.) Back at Rowan—and that's literal—later on, George Back came aboard to co-teach that first TV history course, adding insight and enjoyment as well. Among the courses I developed solo is The Evolution of Quality TV, which I designed as my book began to take shape—road testing some of my ideas on my Rowan University students. Special thanks, therefore, go to my radio/TV/film department chair, Keith Brand, for shepherding me through the hoops to present special-topics courses, as well as all the committees and promotion processes; my dean, Lorin Arnold, for always being supportive, friendly, and a wise counsel; and Rowan University president Ali Houshmand and interim provost James Newell, for putting up with me, and even being friendly while doing so.

Another teaching platform that shaped the book significantly was Serial Eyes, Europe's first postgraduate TV serial writing and production program. Run by the German Film and Television Academy, it's an intense eight-month seminar taught by dozens of writers, producers, and lecturers, drawing international mid-career professionals aiming to expand their global reach. Thanks to Serial Eyes writing coach Frank Spotnitz and program head Lorraine Sullivan, I was asked to teach a concentrated series of lectures on U.S. drama and comedy history—which led me to think in broad, evolutionary terms, as well as to identify key specifics—and have been returning to Berlin to repeat and refine those lectures ever since. Thanks so much, everyone at Serial Eyes.

Also forcing me to think in both broad and specific terms were the makers of the CNN documentary *The Sixties* and its sequel series, *The Seventies* and *The Eighties*. As an interview subject for the installments devoted to television, and as a consultant for the latter series, I had to remember, and wrap my head around, what did and didn't matter most during those respective decades. My thanks for that experience extend to Gary Goetzman, Mark Herzog, and Tom Hanks at Playtone, and to my scarily well-prepared interviewer, Stephen J. Morrison.

I've always been grateful for the part I've been able to play as TV critic for NPR's *Fresh Air with Terry Gross,* but never more so than in the past few years, when I was challenged and given the opportunity to do special "TV history" segments with Terry on such topics as the history of late-night TV talk shows and of interactive television. And I should thank Terry, my producer Phyllis Myers, and executive producer Danny Miller not only for those opportunities and their perpetual support, but also for continuing to put up with me as part of the *Fresh Air* team and for giving me the necessary time off to work on and complete this book. Other *Fresh Air* teammates who helped me get through this include producers Lauren Krenzel and Sam Briger, who provided contact information for some of the artists I was targeting, and contributor Dave Davies, who without complaint augmented his own duties filling in for Terry Gross by subbing for me subbing for her as well, giving me much-needed time off to work on the book. Even Terry herself substituted for me substituting for her one Friday on *Fresh Air,* which was both absurd and much appreciated.

When the founder of apexart, Steven Rand, offered me the opportunity to curate an exhibit on TV history at his New York City gallery space, I had just begun formulating the idea for this book. The result, a 2014 exhibition called "Bianculli's Personal Theory of TV Evolution," taught me a lot about how to organize and present my thoughts on the topic and also, at Steven's urging, to inject the personal from time to time. So thanks for that, Steven—and thanks also to his apexart staff at the time, especially to Julia Knight for all her help and to Ryan Soper, who turned my video display ideas into three-dimensional reality. (Thanks, too, to my former student Joe Ponisi for editing my final video selections into properly timed and segmented shape.)

Double thanks go to Linda Donovan—first, for continuing, along with Eric Gould, to post writers' articles to my TV Worth Watching website so I didn't have to; and, second, for transcribing so many of my interviews for this book. (Thanks to Jim Davis on the TVWW front as well.) And when Linda fell ill, others stepped up to finish the onerous task of transcribing. Thanks in that regard to Jessica Barry and her colleagues at BTS Software Solutions; to Colin Heindel; to my TV-savvy former students Damien Andre, Valerie Balock, and Joseph Block; and to Chris Sandell, who transcribed interviews for my first book decades ago and surfaced like a guardian angel to help complete the task this time around.

The final few thanks are widespread and largely personal. While I tried not to overuse Jane Klain of New York's Paley Center for Media as a trusted and intrepid resource, she was my final go-to source whenever I was hopelessly stumped—she and her colleague Ron Simon have been good friends of mine for years, helping with whatever research projects are on my plate. *Cleveland Plain Dealer* TV critic Mark Dawidziak has been a great friend even longer and not only was my pace car for this project, lending me guidance and encouragement throughout, but he also loaned me many TV photos from his personal collection.

Last, I thank my family and friends for tolerating all the excuses and rain checks generated by "the book." I thank Ed Johnson and Diane Chun, my editors so long ago at *The Gainesville Sun,* for allowing me to embark on a career in TV criticism. And, most of all, I thank my late father, Virgil Bianculli, for watching TV with me during his rare time away from work. And watching all the right TV, too . . .

BIBLIOGRAPHY

BOOKS

Alley, Robert S., and Irby B. Brown. *Love Is All Around: The Making of "The Mary Tyler Moore Show."* New York: Delta/Dell, 1989.
Andrews, Bart. *The "I Love Lucy" Book.* Garden City, N.Y.: Dolphin/Doubleday, 1985.
Apatow, Judd. *Sick in the Head: Conversations About Life and Comedy.* New York: Random House, 2015.
Bianculli, David. *Dangerously Funny: The Uncensored Story of "The Smothers Brothers Comedy Hour."* New York: Touchstone/Simon & Schuster, 2009.
———. *Dictionary of Teleliteracy: Television's 500 Biggest Hits, Misses, and Events.* New York: Continuum, 1996.
———. *Teleliteracy: Taking Television Seriously.* New York: Continuum, 1992.
Bloom, Ken, and Frank Vlastnik. *Sitcoms: The 101 Greatest TV Comedies of All Time.* New York: Black Dog & Leventhal, 2007.
Bright, Morris. *"Fawlty Towers": Fully Booked.* London: BBC Worldwide, 2001.
Brooks, Tim, and Earle Marsh. *The Complete Directory of Prime Time Network and Cable TV Shows, 1946–Present.* 9th ed. New York: Ballantine Books, 2007.
Carrazé, Alain, and Hélène Oswald. *"The Prisoner": A Televisionary Masterpiece.* London: Butler & Tanner, 1990.
Castleman, Harry, and Walter J. Podrazik. *Watching TV: Six Decades of American Television.* 2nd ed. Syracuse, N.Y.: Syracuse University Press, 2010.
Cotter, Bill. *The Wonderful World of Disney Television: A Complete History.* New York: Hyperion, 1997.
Dawidziak, Mark. *The "Columbo" Phile.* New York: Mysterious Press, 1988.
———. *Night Stalking: A 20th Anniversary "Kolchak" Companion.* New York: Image, 1991.
Dunning, John. *On the Air: The Encyclopedia of Old-Time Radio.* New York: Oxford University Press, 1998.
Evenson, William K. *The Hollywood Western.* 2nd ed. New York: Citadel Press, 1992.
Fischer, Stuart. *Kids' TV: The First 25 Years.* New York: Facts on File, 1983.
Greenfield, Jeff. *Television: The First Fifty Years.* New York: Crescent Books, 1981.
Grossman, Gary H. *Saturday Morning TV.* New York: Dell, 1981.
Ilson, Bernie. *Sundays with Sullivan: How "The Ed Sullivan Show" Brought Elvis, the Beatles, and Culture to America.* Lanham, Md.: Taylor Trade, 2009.

Lenburg, Jeff. *The Encyclopedia of Animated Cartoon Series*. 2nd ed. New York: Da Capo Press, 1986.

Marc, David, and Robert J. Thompson. *Prime Time, Prime Movers: From "I Love Lucy" to "L.A. Law"—America's Greatest TV Shows and the People Who Created Them*. Boston: Little, Brown, 1992.

McCrohan, Donna, and Peter Crescenti. *The "Honeymooners" Lost Episodes*. New York: Workman, 1986.

McNeil, Alex. *Total Television: The Comprehensive Guide to Programming from 1948 to the Present*. 4th ed. New York: Penguin Books, 1996.

Mitz, Rick. *The Great TV Sitcom Book*. New York: Richard Marek, 1980.

Okuda, Ted, and Jack Mulqueen. *The Golden Age of Chicago Children's Television*. Chicago: Lake Claremont Press, 2004.

O'Neil, Thomas. *The Emmys: Star Wars, Showdowns, and the Supreme Test of TV's Best*. New York: Penguin Books, 1992.

Ortved, John. *"The Simpsons": An Uncensored, Unauthorized History*. New York: Faber and Faber, 2009.

Perlmutter, David. *America Toons In: A History of Television Animation*. Jefferson, N.C.: McFarland, 1980.

Sabin, Roger. *Cop Shows: A Critical History of Police Dramas on Television*. With Ronald Wilson, Linda Speidel, Brian Faucette, and Ben Bethell. Jefferson, N.C.: McFarland, 2015.

Sackett, Susan. *Prime-Time Hits: Television's Most Popular Network Programs: 1950 to the Present*. New York: Billboard Books, 1993.

Sander, Gordon F. *Serling: The Rise and Twilight of TV's Last Angry Man*. Ithaca, N.Y.: Cornell University Press, 2011.

Scott, Keith. *The Moose That Roared: The Story of Jay Ward, Bill Scott, a Flying Squirrel, and a Talking Moose*. New York: St. Martin's Press, 2000.

Snauffer, Douglas. *Crime Television*. Westport, Conn.: Praeger, 2006.

Sterling, Christopher H., and John Michael Kittross. *Stay Tuned: A History of American Broadcasting*. 3rd ed. Mahwah, N.J.: Lawrence Erlbaum, 2002.

Thompson, Robert J. *Television's Second Golden Age*. Syracuse, N.Y.: Syracuse University Press, 1997.

Waldron, Vince. *The Official "Dick Van Dyke Show" Book*. 2nd ed. Chicago: Chicago Review Press, 2011.

Winship, Michael. *Television*. New York: Random House, 1988.

Zicree, Marc Scott. *The "Twilight Zone" Companion*. 2nd ed. Los Angeles: Silman-James Press, 1989.

AUTHOR INTERVIEWS

Apatow, Judd. Sept. 29, 2015.
Bochco, Steven. Aug. 26, 2015.
Brooks, James L. Aug. 12, 2015.
Brooks, Mel. July 29, 2014; Oct. 7, 2015.
Burnett, Carol. Oct. 7, 2015.
Burns, Ken. Aug. 31, 2015.
Burrows, Jim. Oct. 6, 2015.

Chase, David. Sept. 17, 2015.

C.K., Louis. Nov. 5, 2015.

David, Larry. Nov. 11, 2015.

Fontana, Tom. April 14, 2010; Sept. 11, 2015.

Gilligan, Vince. *Fresh Air*. National Public Radio, March 9, 2010, plus recorded radio out-takes; Jan. 27, 2016.

Groening, Matt. May 27, 2009; July 31, 2015; Oct. 23, 2015.

Katims, Jason. Oct. 13, 2015.

Kelley, David E. Aug. 17, 2015.

King, Robert, and Michelle King. Sept. 28, 2015; May 26, 2016.

Landgraf, John. Oct. 21, 2015.

Lear, Norman. Aug. 31, 2015.

Leary, Denis. Oct. 13, 2015.

Milch, David. Oct. 20, 2015.

Newhart, Bob. Sept. 24, 2014; July 13, 2015.

Reiner, Carl. Oct. 2, 2015.

Rosenthal, Phil. Sept. 23, 2015.

Ryan, Shawn. July 24, 2014; Nov. 4, 2015.

Schlamme, Thomas. Nov. 12, 2015.

Schumer, Amy. Oct. 2, 2015.

Shandling, Garry. Sept. 18, 2015.

Simon, David. Aug. 4, 2015.

Smothers, Tom. Nov. 12, 2015.

Sorkin, Aaron. Sept. 9, 2015.

Spacey, Kevin. Sept. 29, 2015.

Spotnitz, Frank. Nov. 11, 2015.

Tinker, Mark. Oct. 2, 2015.

Weiner, Matt. Oct. 23, 2015.

Wilmore, Larry. Oct. 27, 2015.

Yost, Graham. Oct. 15, 2015.

INDEX

Page numbers in *italics* refer to illustrations.

A&E, 359, 362, 506

ABC, 4, 5, 15, 17, 18, 19, 20, 21–22, 24, 28, 29, 36, 40, 41, 42, 43, 44, 46, 48, 49, 51, 73, 79, 88, 92, 93, 95, 107, 110, 117, 129, 130, 131, 132, 133, 134, 136, 137, 140, 142, *143*, 144, 145, 148, 149, 150, 152, 153, 154, 156, 158, 159, 160, 162, 164, 168, 176, 178, 181, 183, 184, 185, 186, 187, 199, 208, 209, 212, 213, 214, 218, 219, 225, 226, 230, 231, 233, 235, 236, 237, 241, 242, 243, 244, 245, 246, 250, 254, 257, 258, 260, 262, 268, 270, 271, 275, 279, 280, 282, 283, 285, 286, 289, 291, 292, 295, 296, 298, 299, 305, 308, 310, 323, 324, 334, 338, 340, 343, 344, 351, 353, 359, 360, 361, 363–64, 372, 377, 388, 395, 399, 402, 408, 412, 413, 415, 416, 418, 419, 420, 422, 424, 425, 426, 427, 428, 431, 435, 438, 439, 440, 441, 444, 446, 447, 448, *448*, 450, 452, 460, 465, 466, 467, 469, 470, 471, 478, 479, 480, 481, 487, 488, 489, 490, 492, 495, 496, 497, 499, 500, 501, *502*, 503, 504, 508, 509, 510, 516, 525, 535, 536, 537, 538, 542

Abe Lincoln in Illinois (miniseries), 496, 497

Aberlin, Betty, 26, 27

Abrams, J. J., 142, 251, 402, 438, 440–41, *440*, 444

Adam-12, 153, 155

Adams, Don, 105, 434, 536

Adams, Douglas, 402

Adams Chronicles (miniseries), 497, 500

Adams Family, The (miniseries), 497

Addams Family, The, 261, 271

Addie Bobkins Show, The, 60

Adelman, Jerry, 134

Adkins, Bob, 60

Adlon, Pamela, 334, 364

Admiral Broadway Revue, 73–74, 75, 98, 99, 101, 340

Adventures of Gumby, The, 50

Adventures of Jim Bowie, 418

Adventures of Jonny Quest, The, 48

Adventures of Ozzie & Harriet, The, 61, 62, 268–69, 270, 372

Adventures of Spin and Marty, The (serial), 22

Adventures of Superman, 318

Adventuresome, 65

Agatha Christie's Poirot series, 159, 512–13

Albrecht, Chris, 189–90

Alda, Alan, 370, 450, 452, 453, 482, *483*, 484, 486, 522, 523

Alexander, Jane, 500

Alexander, Jason, 332, *333*, 354, 356

Alfred Hitchcock Hour, The, 187

Alfred Hitchcock Presents, 398, 498

Alias, 431, 439, 440–41, *440*, 444

Allen, Chad, 245, 249

Allen, Steve, 67, 72, 76, 78, 79, 93, 104, 105, 339, 343, 389, 521

Allen, Tim, 274, 280, 323

Allen, Woody, 93, 99, 112, 135, 318, 320, 351, 354, 361, 362, 364, 368, 370, 390

Alley, Kirstie, 297, 300

All in the Family, 5, 51, 81, 134, 193, 227, 260, 263, 271–74, *272*, 275, 278, 279, 280, 285, 287, 288, 290, 308, 314, 319, 323, 360, 365, 366–67, 389, 465, 469, 539

Allison, Fran, 16, 27

All New Mickey Mouse Club, The, 23

Ally McBeal, 5, 141, 218, 220, 226, 231–32, 233, 274, 343, 379–80, 382, 384, 393, 467

Altman, Jeff, 92

Altman, Robert, 117, 157, 182, 481–82, 483, 484, 513

Alvin Show, The, 48

Amanda's, 308

Amazing Stories, 399

Amazon, 10, 11, 196, 226, 234, 285, 404, 408

Amblin Productions, 252

Ambrose, Lauren, 453, 454, *454*

AMC, 2, 5, 8, 148, 173, 175, 198, 199, 202–3, 204, 205, 224, 291, 380, 395, 405, 408, 409, 410, 441, 446, 457, 469, 474–75, 477
America 2Night, 136
American Bandstand, 41, 67
American Crime, 176, 225, 497
American Crime Story, 177, 225
American Horror Story, 9, 408, 495
American Idol, 67, 143, 146, 279, 538
Americans, The, 246, 431, 443–45, *443*
America's Most Wanted, 150, 160
Ames, Nancy, 522, 523
Amick, Madchen, 447, 450
Amos, John, 373, 450, 501, 502
Amos 'n' Andy, 262, 294, 312, 352
Amsterdam, Morey, 327, 328
Anderson, Anthony, 285, 542
Anderson, Gillian, 403, *403,* 404, 513
Anderson, Harry, 214, 297
Anderson, Michael J., 447, 450
Andrews, Julie, 84, 112, 113, 114, 117
Andy Griffith Show, The, 6, 61, 62, 261, 270, 312, 323, 324, 325–28, *325,* 335, 479, 548
Andy Richter Controls the Universe, 473
Andy's Gang, 17, 24
Angel, 170, 406, 407
Animal Planet, 70
Apatow, Judd, 5, 7, 34, 126, 296, 302, 385–94
Archer, 58
Arden, Eve, 3, 267, 372, 379, 475
Armstrong, Jack, 99–100
Armstrong, Neil, 401
Arnaz, Desi, 9, 152, 264, 265, *265,* 266–67, 269, 328, 371
Arness, James, 413, 414, *414*
Arnold, Danny, 274
Arquette, Patricia, 128
Arrest and Trial, 153, 160, 212–13, 217
Arrested Development, 283
Arsenio Hall Show, The, 94, 539
Arthur, Beatrice, 273, 308
Arthur Godfrey and His Friends, 73
Arthur Godfrey's Talent Scouts, 73
Ashbrook, Dana, 447
Asner, Ed, 227, 315, 373, *373,* 374, 501, 502
Associates, The, 310
As the World Turns, 130, 132
Astroboy, 50
A Team, The, 160
Atkinson, Rowan, 524
Attanasio, Paul, 255, 460
Attell, Dave, 362
Autry, Gene, 422
Avengers, The, 61, 431, 432, 434, 435–36, *435,* 441
Aykroyd, Dan, 88, 91, 524
Ayres, Lew, 242, 243
Azaria, Hank, 52, 54

Baa Baa Black Sheep, 486
Bachelor Father, 270

Backus, Jim, 39
Bain, Barbara, 436, 437
Baker, Dylan, 221, 222
Baker, Kathy, 230
Baldwin, Alec, 382
Baldwin, Howard, 228–29
Balint, Eszter, 335, 336–37, 370
Ball, Alan, 453, 473
Ball, Lucille, 9, 117, 264, 265, *265,* 266–67, 268, 328, 371, 467
Bancroft, Anne, 109, 357
Band of Brothers (miniseries), 478, 489–91, *490,* 492
Banks, Jonathan, 160, 173, 174
Banner, Bob, 83, 114, 115–16
Baranski, Christine, 222, 223
Barbarians at the Gate (TV movie), 483
Barbera, Joseph, *see* Hanna-Barbera
Baretta, 155, 156
Barney Miller, 274, 292, 360
Barr, Roseanne, 274, 280–82, *281*
Barrymore, Lionel, 242, 243
Baseball (documentary), 5, 512, 515, 519
Baskets, 359, 370
Batman, 133, 160, 419
Battlestar Galactica, 402, 408
Bavier, Frances, 324, *325*–26
BBC, 9, 87, 176, 235, 288, 291, 292, 293, 304, 305, 306, *306,* 308, 368, 400, 402, 495, 501, 505, 506, 521, 522, *523,* 524, 541, 544, 545
BBC America, 305, 408, 506
Beatles, 50, 70, *71,* 72–73, 82, 87, 153, 431, 433
Beatles, The (cartoon show), 50
Beaumont, Hugh, 270
Beavis and Butt-Head, 55
Bechdel, Alison, 375
Becker, 472, 473
Begley, Ed, Jr., 245, 247–48, *247*
Belkin, Lisa, 462
Bellamy, Ralph, 210, 220
Belushi, John, 88, 91
Benaderet, Bea, 46, 47
Ben Casey, 242, 243–44, 247
Bendix, William, 262
Benny, Jack, 5, 61, 92, 110, 120, 261, 288, 320, 345, 349, 350, 354–55
Benson, 279
Ben Stiller Show, The, 385, 390
Berg, Gertrude, 262, 339, 382
Bergen, Candice, 4, 90, 219, 377, 381
Bergen, Edgar, 20, 68
Bergman, Ingmar, 504
Berle, Milton, 69, 72, 73, 103, 178, 287, 290, 339–40, 346–47, 351, 397, 426
Bernie Mac Show, The, 282, 532, 535, 539–40
Bernsen, Corbin, 215, 216
Berry, Halle, 503
Best Time Ever with Neil Patrick Harris, 97
Better Call Saul, 175, 199, 205–7, 224–25, 388
Between the World and Me (Coates), 534
Betz, Carl, 213, 270

Beulah, 312
Beverly Hillbillies, 271
Beverly Hills, 90210, 141
Beverly Hills Buntz, 428
Beymer, Richard, 447, 449
Big Bang Theory, The, 283, 344, 349
Big Show, 93
Billingsley, Barbara, 270
Birth and Death of Abraham Lincoln, The
    (miniseries), 497
Black-ish, 285, 542
Blackman, Hugh, 435–36
Black Mirror, 399
Blackmore, Bobby, 121
Blake, Amanda, 413, 415
Blake, Robert, 155
Blatter, Sepp, 531
Bleak House (miniseries), 513
Blind Ambition (miniseries), 504
Block, Martin, 100
Blood & Oil, 145
Bloodworth-Thomason, Linda, 375
Bloom, Rachel, 384
Blue Knight (miniseries), 500
Blue's Clues, 32
Boardwalk Empire, 152
Bob, 344
Bob Newhart Show, The (TV sitcom), 79–80, 250,
    261, 274, 314, 323, 329–31, *330,* 347–49, 373,
    375, 389, 465, 469
Bob Newhart Show, The (variety show), 344, 347
Bob's Burgers, 59
Bochco, Steven, 4–5, 9, 155, 156, 157, 158, 160, 162,
    164, 178–85, 215, 217, 218, 220, 229–30, 236,
    250, 426–27, 428, 466, 484, 492, 508, 510
Boedeker, Hal, 429
Boing Boing Show, The, 41
BoJack Horseman, 59
Bold and the Beautiful, The, 131
Bold Ones, The, 178, 180, 186, 187, 213, 452
Bonanza, 23, 47, 80, 417, 418
Bonerz, Peter, 329, 330, 348
Bonneville, Hugh, 513, 514
Book Group, The, 65
Boomtown, 170
Boondocks, 58
Boone, Richard, 187, 242, 418
Boot, Das (miniseries), 487
Booth, Connie, 292, 293–94, *293*
Boothe, Powers, 422, 429
Boreanaz, David, 405, *406*
Borgia, 546
Borgnine, Ernest, 479
Bosley, Tom, 51, 523
Bosson, Barbara, 156, 181
Boston 24/7, 254
Boston Legal, 5, 208, 219–21, *219,* 224, 226, 233,
    234, 274, 343
Boston Med, 254
Boston Public, 5, 226, 232–33
Bowen, Julie, 219, 283

Bowes, Edward, 68
Bowman, Rob, 201
Boyd, William, 412–13
Boyle, Lara Flynn, 447, 450
Bozo's Circus, 18
Bracco, Lorraine, 166, 168
Bradbury, Ray, 504
Brady Bunch, The, 192, 212, 261, 271, 469
Braff, Zach, 254
BrainDead, 235, 239
Brand, Joshua, 189, 245, 246, 250
Brand, Russell, 388
Brando, Marlon, 341, 503
Brandt, Betsy, 173, 206
Brannum, Hugh, 24–25
Bratt, Benjamin, 217
Bravo, 487
Breaking Bad, 1, 2, 5, 10, 11, 148, 160, 168, 173–75,
    175, 177, 199, 201, 202–6, 225, 237, 290, 291,
    388, 404, 405, 441, 443, 444, 548
Brenner, 151–52
Brennerman, Amy, *163*
Brideshead Revisited (miniseries), 504
Britton, Barbara, 328
Broad City, 95, 127
Broderick, James, 151–52
Broderick, Matthew, 106
Brolin, James, 213, 245
Brooklyn Bridge (documentary), 511, 515, 518
Brooklyn Bridge (TV show), 246, 261, 262
Brooks, Albert, 90, 471
Brooks, James L., 4, 5, 6, 52, 53, 54, 63, 64, 65, 94,
    135, 274, 295–96, 310–17, 372, 373, 374, 386,
    387, 388–89, 390, 466, 468, 479
Brooks, Mel, 1–2, 5, 12, 68, 74, 75, 77, 98–109, 126,
    179, 316, 338, 340–41, 356–57, 386, 418, 434,
    466, 483, 536
Brooks, Richard, 217
Brown, Blair, 4, 375, *376*
Brown, Sterling K., 225
Browne, Daniel Gregory, 134
Bry, Ellen, 245, 246
Buck Rogers in the 25th Century, 402, 407
Buffalo Bill, 302, 375, 378
Buffy the Vampire Slayer, 145, 170, 395, 405–7,
    406, 410
Bullwinkle Show, The, 36, 40, 43–46, *44,* 48, 139,
    246, 374, 517, 536
Burgess, Bobby, 21, 22
Burghoff, Gary, 482, 485
Burke, Delta, 375
Burnett, Carol, 5, 79, 83–84, *85,* 86, 110–18, 193,
    303, 322
Burns, Allan, 311, 313, 314, 315, 372, 373, 374
Burns, Ed, 455, 460, 462, 492
Burns, George, 61, 92, 104, 261, 282, 320, 354, 536,
    539
Burns, Ken, 5, 12, 277–78, 478, 480, 511, *511,* 512,
    515–20, 534
Burns, Ric, 511, 516, 519

Burns, Robert Kyle, 516, 517–18
Burr, Raymond, 153, 210, 211, *211*, 241
Burrell, Ty, 283
Burrows, James, 296, 297, 299
Burrows, Saffron, 219, *219*
Burton, LeVar, 25, 32, 501, *502, 503*
Burton, Tim, 32, 33, 130
Buscemi, Steve, 166, 370, 420, 509
Buttons, Red, 178
Buzzi, Ruth, 85
Byrne, Rose, 221, 222
Byrnes, Edd, 151

Caesar, Sid, 1, 5, 74, 75, *75, 76, 77, 78,* 92, 99, 101,
    102, 103, 104, 111, 115, 116, 178–79, 187, 328,
    340, 341, 351, 386, 482–83
Caesar's Hour, 77–78, 98, 103, 111–12, 115, 338, 341,
    342, 351, 466
Cagney & Lacey, 159
Call to Glory, 487
Campanella, Joseph, 213
Campbell, Flora, 131
Campbell, Glen, 123
Candid Camera, 536
Candy, John, 93
Cannell, Stephen J., 155, 159–60, 188, 194–95
Cannon, 153
Captain and Tennille, The, 92, 501
Captain Kangaroo, 15, 16, 24–26, *25,* 32, 33, 34, 41
Captain Midnight, 18, 120
Captains and the Kings (miniseries), 500
Captain Video and His Video Rangers, 18
Car 54, Where Are You?, 61, 292
Cardellini, Linda, 251, 391, 457
Carell, Steve, 304, 306, *306,* 307, 363, 527, 541, 542
Carey, Josie, 15, 24, *27,* 34
Carlin, George, 90, 123, 318, 360, 361
Carlock, Robert, 384
Carmichael, Jerrod, 278
Carmichael Show, The, 278, 285
Carne, Judy, 85
Carney, Art, 46, 263, 264, 311, 397
Carol Burnett Show, The, 67, 83–84, *85,* 86, 107,
    110, 113, 114–17, 126, 134, 136, 179, 193, 274, 314,
    375, 465, 469
Caroline's Comedy Hour, 359, 362
Caron, Glenn Gordon, 159, 296
Carradine, Keith, 422, 424
Carrey, Jim, 94, 303, 304, 322, 391, 538, 539
Carroll, Bob, Jr., 264, 266
Carroll, Diahann, 312
Carson, Johnny, 25, 54, 79, 95, 97, 193, 281, 302,
    319, 321, 322, 339, 521, 522, 547
Carter, Chris, 200, 202, 402, 403–4
Carter, Jim, 505, 513, 514
Cartoon Circus, 60
Cartoon Network, 58
Cartwright, Nancy, 52, 54, 316
Caruso, David, 162, 163, *163,* 164
Carver, Randall, *295*

Carvey, Dana, 88, 363
Castellaneta, Dan, 52, 54, 316
Cattrall, Kim, 380, *381*
Cavalcade of Stars, 73, 76, 263
CBC, 26
CBS, 3, 4, 5, 7, 15, 18, 19, 20, 24, 25–26, 32, 33, 36,
    39, 40, 41, 46, 48, 49, 50, 51, 67, 70, *71,* 73, 77,
    79, 80, 81, 82, 83, 86, 87, 92, 95, 96, 99, 103,
    105, 106, 107, 110, 114, 116, 119, 120, 121, 122,
    123, 129, 130, 131, 134, 135, 137, 139, 140, 143,
    144, 151, 153, 154, 156, 157, 158, 159, 160, 164,
    169, 170, 178, 179, 181, 186, 189, 191, 195, 199,
    208, 209, 210, 211, 212, 213, 214, 217, 218, 220,
    222, 226, 227, 230, 231, 235, 238, 239, 241, 242,
    244, 245, 246, 250, 251, 252, 258, 260, 261, 262,
    263–64, 266, 267, 269, 270, 271–72, 273, 274,
    275, 282, 283, 287, 290, 292, 296, 298, 300,
    303, 308, 309, 310, 313, 314, 319, 323, 324, 325,
    326, 327, 328, 329, 331, 334, 338, 339, 340, 342,
    344, 347, 348, 371, 372, 373, 375, 376, 377, 378,
    379, 395, 396, 398, 399, 407, 412, 413, 415, 417,
    418, 419, 420, 426, 431, 433, 434, 436, 438, 446,
    447, 449, 452, 465, 469, 472, 478, 479, 480,
    481, 482, 485, 487, 495, 497, 498, 499, 500,
    503, 504, 508, 509, 510, 521, 525, 530, 531, 532,
    546, 547
CBS Radio, 130, 266, 268, 414
Central Park Five, The (documentary), 515, 519
Chamberlain, Richard, 243, *243,* 244, 504
Channing, Stockard, 222, 450, 452
Chapman, Terry, 87
Chappelle's Show, 94, 126
Charles, Glen and Les, 296, 297, 299
Charles, Josh, 222, 223, 237
Charles, Larry, 353, 355
Charlie Brown Christmas, A (holiday special),
    36, 48, 49–50, *49*
Charlie's Angels, 154, 501
Chase, Chevy, 87, 88, 90, 91, 524
Chase, David, 5, 9, 166, 168, 169, 186–90, 302, 356,
    402, 472, 473, 474, 476
Chayefsky, Paddy, 2, 103–4, 239, 240, 310, 468
Cheers, 168, 248, 261, 275, 276, 291, 296, 297–300,
    298, 309, 331, 334, 355, 466, 472
Cherry, Marc, 142, 144
Chicago Hope, 226, 231, 251
Chicagoland Mystery Players, The, 149
Chicago Med, 258
Chiklis, Michael, 160, 170, 171, *171*
Children's Corner, The, 15–16, 24, *27,* 34
Children's Television Workshop, 29–30
China Beach, 250, 478, 487, 488–89, *488,* 491
Chris Rock Show, The, 94, 359, 364
Christopher, William, 482, 485
Cinemax, 93
City Hospital, 242
Civil War, The (documentary), 5, 478, 495, 510,
    511–12, *511,* 515, 519, 520
Clark, Marcia, 218, 225
Claster, Bert, 19
Claster, Nancy "Miss Nancy," 19, 24

Clausen, Alf, 54
Clavell, James, 504
Cleese, John, 87, 292–94, *293*, 295, 309, 522
Climax!, 433
Clooney, George, 56, 192, 251, 252, *252*, 253, 254, 280, 282
Close, Glenn, 170, 172, 221–22, *221*, 223, 545
Clutch Cargo, 42, 48
CNN, 218
Coates, Ta-Nehisi, 534
Cobb, Lee J., 213
Coca, Imogene, 74, 75, *75*, 76, 99, 102, 115, 179, 340, 341
Code Black, 258
Coe, Fred, 496
Cohen, David X., 52, 58, 64
Colasanto, Nicholas, 297, *298*, 300
Colbert, Stephen, 81, 343, 363, 387, 525, 527, 528–30, *529*, 531, 532, *533*, 547
Colbert Report, The, 521, 528–29, *529*, *533*
Cole, Gary, 222, 450
Cole, Michael, 154
Coleman, Dabney, 134, 302, 378
Colgate Comedy Hour, The, 77, 287, 288, 482
Collins, Joan, 141
Colonna, Jerry, 17
Columbia Pictures, 341
Columbo, 149, 151, 155, 156, 157, 178, 179, 180–81, 185, 193, 199, 244, 255, 257, 309
Combat!, 459, 478, 481–82, *481*, 487, 490, 491
Comedians in Cars Getting Coffee, 96
Comedy Central, 5, 36, 55, 56, 58, 60, 65, 70, 94, 95, 109, 125, 126, 127, 274, 306, 389, 521, 525, 528, 530, 531, 532, 535, 542
Comic Strip Live, 385, 389
Commander in Chief, 452
Commish, The, 160, 171
Conaway, Jeff, 295, *295*, 296
Connelly, Christopher, 131
Connery, Sean, 105, 432, 435
Connors, Chuck, 153, 501
Conrad, Robert, 192, 193, 419, 486
Conrad, William, 43, 44–45, 414
Conried, Hans, 43, 45
Conroy, Frances, 453, 454, *454*
Converse-Roberts, William, 375, 376
Conway, Tim, 83, 84, 113, 116–17, 179, 479
Cooke, Alistair, 499–500
Cooney, Joan Ganz, 29, 30
Cooper, Bradley, 440, 441
Cop Rock, 160, 178, 184, 508
COPS, 160
Corden, James, 96, 343, 547
Corner, The (miniseries), 459, 462, 493
Coronation Street, 132
Cosby, Bill, 51, 105, 274, 276–78, *277*, 279, 280, 312, 434, 543
Cosby Show, The, 260, 261, 276–80, *277*, 281, 282, 299, 470
Cosell, Howard, 88
Court TV, 217, 218

Cowboy Bebop, 58
Cox, Wally, 2, 50, 291
Crane, Bob, 479
Cranston, Bryan, 2, 173, 174, *175*, 201–2, 203, 332, 404
Crawford, Broderick, 150–51
Crazy Ex-girlfriend, 384
Crazy Ones, The, 226, 234
Crime Story, 159, 164, 194, 195
Critic, The (animated short), 98, 99, 105, 385, 390–91
Crook, Mackenzie, 304, 305
Crosby, Bing, 86, 93, 390
Crosby, Mary, 137, 138
Cross, Marcia, 142–43, *143*
Cruise, Tom, 56, 437–38, 466
Crusader Rabbit, 40, 44, 45, 60
Crystal, Billy, 32, 88, 137
CSI: Crime Scene Investigation, 143, 154, 169
Culp, Robert, 105, 434
Cumberbatch, Benedict, 176
Cumming, Alan, 222, *223*, 224, 237
Cummings, Robert, 209, 309
Curb Your Enthusiasm, 98, 108–9, 126, 294, 320, 351, 352, 353, 355–57, 358, 368, 471
Curtin, Jane, 88, 524
CW, 384, 439, 546

Daily Show with Jon Stewart, 274, 306, 363, 521, 526, 529, 530–31, *530*, 532, *533*, 535, 542
Daily Show with Trevor Noah, 531
Dallas (1978), 117, 129, 137–40, *138*, 141, 145, 146, 156, 168, 280, 282, 449, 503
Dallas (2016), 144–45
Daly, Tyne, 159
Damages, 172, 208, 221–22, *221*, 223, 224
Dana, Bill, 78
Dana Carvey Show, The, 359, 363–64
Dancing with the Stars, 538
Danes, Claire, 441, *442*
Danger Man, 434, 435, 438
Danger UXB, 487, 491, 504
Daniels, Greg, 52, 304, 306, 307, 363, 541–42
Daniels, Stan, 295, 315
Daniels, William, 245, 247–48, *247*
Daniel Tiger's Neighborhood, 34–35
Danny Kaye Show, The, 115
Danny Thomas Show, The, 269, 270, 325–26
Danson, Ted, 177, 221, 222, 297, *298*, 472
Danza, Tony, 295, *295*, 296
Darden, Christopher, 218, 225
Daria, 55
Dark Shadows, 130, 402
David, Larry, 5, 7, 94, 96, 108–9, 126, 294, 320, 332, 333, 351–58, 368, 471, 479, 546
David Letterman Show, 93
David L. Wolper Productions, 311
David Steinberg Show, The, 92–93
Davis, David, 295–96, 315, 329
Davis, Kristin, 380, *381*

Davis, Lucy, 304, 305
Davis, Sammy, Jr., 17, 72, 84, 274
Davis, Viola, 144, 146–47
Davy Crockett (miniseries), 20, 22, 413, 497–98
Dawson's Creek, 142
Day After, The (TV movie), 28, 444–45
Days and Nights of Molly Dodd, The, 4, 262, 371, 375–77, *376*
Days of Our Lives, 131, 132
Deadwood, 5, 158, 246, 412, 415, 422–24, *423,* 425, 426, 428–29, 430
Dean Martin Show, 79, 84
"Defender, The" (teleplay), 210, 212, 220–21
Defenders, The, 210, 212, 213, 215
DeGeneres, Ellen, 283
Delany, Dana, 488, *488*
Delirious (stand-up special), 361
Dempsey, Patrick, 257, *258*
Denver, Bob, 51
Depp, Johnny, 130, 159
Designing Women, 375, 380
Desilu Studios, 264–65, 266, 267–68, 328
Desperate Housewives, 129, 142–43, *143,* 144, 344
Devine, Andy, 17
Devious Maids, 144
DeVito, Danny, 295, *295,* 315
Dey, Susan, 215, 216
Diagnosis Murder, 250, 255
Diamond, Reed, 170, 171
Dickens, Kim, 422, 424, 429
Dickinson, Angie, 154
Dick Van Dyke Show, The, 5, 7, 193, 261, 268, 271, 303, 313, 320, 323, 327–29, *327,* 333, 338, 342, 373, *373,* 374, 382
Different World, A, 279, 280
Dillahunt, Garret, 422, 424, 429
Ding Dong School, 18–19, 24, 26
DirecTV, 208, 221
Disney, Walt, 19–22, 23–24, 38, 40, 413, 498
Disney Channel, 23, 24, 32
Divorce His/Divorce Hers (miniseries), 500
Doctors, The, 242
Doctors at Large, 292
Doctor Who, 400, 499
Dodd, Jimmie, 21, *21,* 22–23
Dollhouse, 406, 408
Donna Reed Show, The, 269, 270, 372
Donny & Marie, 92, 501
D'Onofrio, Vincent, 161
Doogie Howser, M.D., 178, 183–84, 226, 230, 250
Dora the Explorer, 32
Douglas, Michael, 154, 513
Dourif, Brad, 422, 424, 429
Downey, Robert, Jr., 88, 232
Downton Abbey (miniseries), 1, 495, 499, 500, 513–14, *514*
Dragnet, 133, 149–50, 151, 152, 153, 172, 241–42
Dragnet '67, 151, 153
Drake, Larry, 215, 217
Driver, Adam, 382, 383, 393
Dr. Katz, Professional Therapist, 55

Dr. Kildare, 241, 242–44, *243,* 245, 247, 258
Dr. Quinn, Medicine Woman, 250
Duchovny, David, 201, 403, *403,* 404, 447, 450
Duel (TV movie), 181, 361
Duffy, Patrick, 137, 138, 140, 145
Duffy's Tavern, 291, 297
DuMont network, 18, 39, 68, 69, 73, 74, 76, 98, 99, 101, 131, 149, 209, 261, 263, 340
Duncan, Sandy, 501, 502
Dunham, Lena, 4, 126, 382–83, *383,* 392, 393–94
Dust Bowl, The (documentary), 515
Duvall, Robert, 420–21, *421,* 509, *509*
Dynasty, 117, 140, 141, 146
Dysart, Richard, 215, 216, 217

Early Frost, An (TV movie), 247
East Side/West Side, 179, 446, 455–56
Eastwood, Clint, 417, 418, *419,* 422
Ebersol, Dick, 90
Edelstein, Lisa, 255, 257, 450
Edge of Darkness (miniseries), 505
Edge of the Night, The, 210–11
Ed Sullivan Show, The, 67, 70, 71–73, *71,* 78, 79, 81, 82, 88, 104, 120, 153, 324
Edward and Mrs. Simpson (miniseries), 504
Edwards, Anthony, 251, 253
E! Entertainment Television, 218
Efron, Marshall, 61, 87
Eglee, Charles H., 170, 185
Eikenberry, Jill, 215, 216
Einstein, Bob, 80, 86
Elba, Idris, 455, 456
Eleanor and Franklin (miniseries), 500
Electric Company, The, 32, 98
Elephant Parts (anthology special), 320
Elizabeth R (miniseries), 500
Ellen, 282–83
Elliott, Chris, 88, 389
Elliott, David James, 217
Emergency, 245
Emmerich, Noah, 443, 444
Empire, 129, 145–47, *146*
English, Diane, 377, 379
Entertainment Tonight, 95
Episodes, 308
Epps, Omar, 255, 256
Equalizer, The, 191, 194, 195
ER, 144, 223, 231, 241, 251–54, *252,* 282, 344
ESPN, 218, 466
Esposito, Giancarlo, 173, 174, 206
Essman, Susie, 355, 362
Evans, Dale, 413
Evans, Linda, 137, 141
Evening with Carol Burnett, An (TV special), 110
Everybody Hates Chris, 282
Everybody Loves Raymond, 282
Execution of Private Slovik, The (TV movie), 180
Extras, 308
EZ Streets, 151, 164

Fabares, Shelley, 270
Fabray, Nanette, 111
Facts of Life, The, 532, 535
Fairchild, Morgan, 140
Falco, Edie, 165, 166, *167,* 258, 370
Falcon Crest, 140
Falk, Peter, 155, 179, 199, 213, 309
Fallon, Jimmy, 67, 88, 95–96, 339, 343, 387, 489, 491, 524, 547
Falsey, John, 189, 245, 246, 250
Fame, 297
Family, 446
Family Guy, 48, 52, 58, 539
Family Ties, 275, 299
Faraway Hill, 131
Fargo, 9, 11, 177, 495, 497
Farr, Jamie, 482, 486
Farrell, Mike, 482, *483*
Farrow, Mia, 131, 132, *133*
Farscape, 407
Fashion Story, 340
Fassbender, Michael, 489, 491
Fat Albert and the Cosby Kids, 51
Father Knows Best, 269–70, 278, 372
Fawlty Towers, 291, 292–94, *293,* 295, 297, 302, 305, 308, 309
FBI, The, 150, 153, 160
Fear the Walking Dead, 410
Feig, Paul, 391–92
Felicity, 142, 440, 441, 444
Fellowes, Julian, 513
Fenn, Sherilyn, 447, 450
Ferguson, Craig, 95, 96
Ferguson, Jesse Tyler, 283, 284
Fernwood 2Night, 136, 287, 288–89, 302, 528
Ferrell, Will, 88, 91
Ferrer, Miguel, 447, 450
Ferrera, America, 144
Fey, Tina, 88, 91, 126, 128, 382, 384, 468, 524
Field, Sally, 128, 500
Fifty-Fourth Street Revue, 340
Fight Against Slavery, The (miniseries), 501
Fincher, David, 196, 197
Firefly, 406, 407–8
Fischer, Jenna, 304, 306
Fishburne, Laurence, 32, 34
Fisher, Terry Louise, 183, 215, 217
Flamingo Road, 140
Flanders, Ed, 245, 247, 248, 249
Fleming, Eric, 417, *419*
Flintstones, The, 36, 37, 46–48, *47,* 55, 236, 360, 536
Flip Wilson Show, 86, 193, 536
Flockhart, Calista, 218, 231, 232, 379
Florentine Films, 518
Flynn, Joe, 347
Flynn, Neil, 282
Fonda, Henry, 210, 288, 309, 523
Fontana, Tom, 5, 7, 161, 164–65, 166, 169, 245, 246, 248, 249, 250, 453, 460, 461, 546
Foote, Shelby, *511,* 512

Ford Star Revue, 287, 288
Forsyte Saga (miniseries), 499, 513
Fox, 5, 36, 37, 52, 53, 55, 56, 58, 59, 60, 63, 64–65, 94, 108, 110, 126, 129, 139, 141, 143, 145, 150, 158, 160, 166, 170, 189, 199, 200, 202, 218, 225, 226, 231, 241, 255, 279, 280, 282, 283, 296, 306, 310, 316, 318, 343, 364, 379, 385, 389, 390, 392, 395, 403, 407–8, 467, 469, 471, 472, 473, 496, 510, 532, 535, 538, 539, 541
Fox, Michael J., 222, 223, 275
Foxx, Jamie, 538
Frances, Miss, 18–19, 24, 26
Franciscus, James, 151
Frankenstein: The True Story (miniseries), 500
Franklin, Bonnie, 275, 288
Franz, Dennis, 156, 162, 163–64, *163,* 424, 427, 428
Frasier, 261, 275, 285, 300, 324, 331–32, 343
Freaks and Geeks, 5, 385, 391–93
Freeman, Martin, 176, 177, 304, 305, 495
Frees, Paul, 43, 45, 50
French, Leigh, 80, 82
Fresh Air with Terry Gross (radio show), 12, 109, 126, 198, 405, 406, 407, 409, 449
Fresh off the Boat, 285–86
Fresh Prince of Bel-Air, 282
Fresno (miniseries), 110, 117
Frid, Jonathan, 130
Friday Night Lights, 5, 233, 446
Fridays, 93–94, 351, 353, 358, 546
Friendly Fire (TV movie), 110, 117
Friends, 282
Fringe, 408
Fritz, Ken, 80, 121–22
From Here to Eternity (miniseries), 487, 504
From the Earth to the Moon (miniseries), 202
Frost, David, 522, 523, 524
Frost, Mark, 156, 158, 402, 447, 448, *448,* 499
Fuchs, Michael, 321–22
Fugitive, The (1963), 44–45, 73, 149, 152–53, 154, 187, 248, 334, 426, 441, 442, 449
Fugitive, The (2000), 170
Funicello, Annette, 21, *21,* 22, 23
Futurama, 58, 60, 64–65
FX, 7, 8, 9, 11, 58, 148, 152, 170, 171, 172, 176–77, 178, 185, 198, 208, 221, 225, 246, 254, 323, 334, 356, 359, 362, 367, 368–69, 370, 385, 408, 410, 428, 431, 443, 484, 492, 495, 497, 545

Gallant Man, The, 480, 481, 491, 515–16
Gambon, Michael, 505, *505,* 507, 513
Game Change (TV movie), 145
Game of Thrones, 410–11, 431, 463
Gandolfini, James, 166, 167, *167,* 189
Gangbusters, 150, 160
Garber, Victor, 375, 440, 441
Garner, James, 155, 188, 344, 416, *416,* 417
Garner, Jennifer, 440, *440,* 441
Garofalo, Janeane, 88, 301, 303, 322, 390, 450
Garrison's Gorillas, 480
Garry Moore Show, 79, 80, 84, 110, 112–14, 115, 116

Gazzara, Ben, 153, 500
Gelbart, Larry, 6, 78, 99, 341, 387, 466–67, 482–83, 484, 485
Gellar, Sarah Michelle, 234, 405, *406*, 407
Geller, Bruce, 244, 436
General Hospital, 130–31, 133, 244
Generation Kill (miniseries), 459, 462, 463, 478, 492–94, *493*
George, Lynda Day, 436, 437, 501
George & Leo, 344
George Burns and Gracie Allen Show, The, 320, 536
George Gobel Show, The, 288, 346–47
George of the Jungle, 50, 236
Gerolmo, Chris, 185, 492
Gervais, Ricky, 59, 304, 305, *306*, 307, 308, 368, 541
Get a Life, 389
Get Smart, 61, 98, 99, 105–6, 117, 126, 236, 374, 386, 434, 536
Giamatti, Paul, 127, 497
Gibson, Channing, 185, 249
Gibson, Henry, 85
Gillespie, Darlene, 21, 22
Gilligan, Vince, 5, 7, 11, 173, 174, 175, 199–207, 225, 388, 403, 404, 548
Gilligan's Island, 227, 261
Gilpin, Peri, 331–32
Girl from U.N.C.L.E., The, 433–34
Girls, 4, 5, 126, 127, 371, 376, 382–84, *383*, 385, 392–94
Gleason, Jackie, 46, 53, 73, 76, 77, 78, 187, 263–64, 292, 365, 426, 499
Glee, 110, 146
Glen Campbell Goodtime Hour, 86
Gless, Sharon, 159
Goaz, Harry, 447, 450
Gobel, George, 5, 120, 346–47
Godard, Jean-Luc, 536, 540
Godfrey, Arthur, 73
Goggins, Walton, 170, 172–73, 176
Goldberg, Gary David, 262, 275
Goldbergs, The (1949), 261, 262, 339, 371, 382
Goldbergs, The (2013), 261, 286
Goldblum, Jeff, 32, 127
Golden Girls, The, 142, 143
Goliath, 226, 234
Gomer Pyle, U.S.M.C., 326, 479
Goodman, John, 221, 222, 280, 281–82, *281*
Goodman, Tim, 366, 369
Good Times, 273, 287, 288, 360
Good Wife, The, 1, 7, 208, 222–25, *223*, 235, 236, 237–39, *252*, 376
Goodyear TV Playhouse, 103
Goranson, Alicia "Lecy," 280, *281*
Gordon, Howard, 403, 441
Gordon, Ruth, 342
Gorshin, Frank, 401
Gosselaar, Mark-Paul, 162, 492
Gossett, Louis, Jr., 501, 502, 503
Gould, Peter, 173, 205, 206
Grace Under Fire, 282

Graham, Heather, 447, 450
Grammer, Kelsey, 297, 300, 324, 331
Graves, Peter, 436, *437*, 438
Gray, Linda, 137, 138, 145
Great American Dream Machine, The, 61, 87
Great War (documentary), 478
Green Acres, 61
Grey's Anatomy, 144, 241, 254, 257–58, *258*
Grier, David Alan, 94, 278, 538
Griffith, Andy, 213, 270, 324–25, *325*, 326
Grinder, The, 225
Grizzard, George, 497
Groening, Matt, 6, 37, 44, 52–53, 54, 55, 58, 60–66, 94, 316, 317, 479, 548
Gross, Terry, 109
Guiding Light, The, 130, 132
Guillaume, Robert, 136–37, 279, 280
Gulliver's Travels (cartoon), 38, 39
Gunn, Anna, 173, 174, 205, 422
Gunsmoke, 399, 412, 413–15, *414*, 417, 418, 420, 422, 426

Hagen, Earle, 326, 328
Hagman, Larry, 129–30, 137, *138*, 139, 145
Hale, Barbara, 210, 211
Haley, Alex, 289–90, 470, 501, 502, *502*, 503
Hall, Arsenio, 94
Hall, Michael C., 453–54, *454*
Hamel, Veronica, 156, *157*
Hamilton, Joe, 83, 114, 115
Hamlin, Harry, 215, 216, 457
Hamm, Jon, 457, *457*, *458*, 475
Hanks, Colin, 489, 491
Hanks, Tom, 128, 489, 491
Hanna-Barbera, 41–42, 46, 48, 51
Hannah Montana, 32
Happy Days, 51, 261, 268, 275, 360
Hardy, Tom, 489, 491
Harmon, Mark, 245, 247, 251
Harper, Valerie, 314, 315, 373, 374
Harrelson, Woody, 176, 297, 300
Harrington, Pat, Jr., 78
Harris, Julie, 511, 518
Harris, Neil Patrick, 97, 183, 184, 230, 250
Harrison, George, 50, 54, *81*
Harry O, 154–55
Harry's Law, 226, 233
Hartman, Phil, 32, 88
Hart to Hart, 156
Harvest of Shame (documentary), 518, 527
Hatcher, Teri, 142–43, *143*, 332
Have Gun, Will Travel, 187, 242, 399, 415, 418
Hawaii Five-O, 154
Hawkes, John, 422, 429
Hawley, Noah, 11, 177
Hawn, Goldie, 85
Haynes, Lloyd, 312
HBO, 3, 4, 5, 7, 8–9, 15, 29, 31, 32, 59, 65, 94, 98, 99, 108, 110, 117, 123, 136, 145, 148, 152, 158, 161, 162, 165, 166, 169, 170, 171, 176, 186, 189, 198,

204, 214, 246, 251, 258, 285, 291, 301, 302, 303, 308, 318, 321–22, 343, 351, 352, 355, 356, 357, 359, 361, 362, 364, 365, 367, 368, 369, 371, 376, 378, 380, 382, 385, 390, 392, 393, 399, 402, 408, 410, 412, 415, 422, 423, 425, 426, 428, 429–30, 446, 450, 452, 453, 455, 459, 462–63, 465, 466, 467, 468, 469, 472, 473, 474, 478, 483, 489, 491, 492, 494, 495, 496, 497, 521, 524–25, 528, 530, *530*, 531, 545, 546
He & She, 374
Heartbeat, 248, 258
Hee Haw, 86
Helter Skelter (miniseries), 500
Hemsley, Sherman, 273
Hendricks, Christina, 457, 458, 475
Henner, Marilu, 295, *295*, 296
Hennessy, Jill, 217
Henry, Buck, 98, 99, 105, 434, 522, 523, 536
Henson, Jim, 29, 30, 31
Henson, Taraji P., 145–46, *146*, 219
Hercules: The Legendary Journeys, 405
Herman, Pee-Wee (Paul Reubens), 32–34, *33*
Heroes, 408
Herrmann, Edward, 486, 500
Hickman, Dwayne, 51
Highway Patrol, 150–51
Hiken, Nat, 310, 311, 478, 479
Hill, Steven, 217, 436
Hill Street Blues, 3, 4, 7, 8, 125, 133, 139–40, 148, 155, 156–59, *157*, 161, 163, 164, 172, 178, 179, 182–83, 184, 185, 188, 215, *216*, 218, 227–28, 229, 236, 244, 246, 250, 254, 257, 275, 298, 299, 373, 374–75, 402, 407, 425, 426–28, 456, 460, 466, 510, 544, 545
Hines, Cheryl, 355, 356
Hirsch, Judd, 221, 295, *295*, 296, 315
History Channel, 496, *502*, 503
Hitchcock, Alfred, 108, 187, 398, 498
Hitchhiker's Guide to the Galaxy, The (miniseries), 402
Hoffman, Dustin, 51, 54, 151, 214, 429
Hoffman, Philip Seymour, 440
Hogan's Heroes, 459, 479, 485
Holbrook, Hal, 452, 500
Hollywood Palace, 79
Holocaust (miniseries), 486–87
Homeboys in Outer Space, 260
Homefront, 489, 491
Home Improvement, 280, 282, 323, 363
Homeland, 431, 441–43, *442*, 444, 491
Homicide: Life on the Street, 5, 7, 161–62, 165, 171, 246, 255, 456, 459, 460, 461, 462, 546
Honeymooners, The, 46, 47, 53, 73, 77, 187, 199, 260, 261, 263–64, 273, 292, 310, 365, 426, 459–60, 548
Hooks, Jan, 88, 525
Hootenanny, 517
Hopalong Cassidy, 412–13, 422
Hope, Bob, 17, 93, 102, 390, 521
Hopkins 24/7, 254
Hopper, William, 210, 211, *211*, 224

Horace and Pete (Internet miniseries), 359, 362, 370
Horton, Edward Everett, 43, 45
Hoskins, Bob, 506
Hour Glass, 68
House, M.D., 224, 241, 255–57, *256*, 259
House of Cards (British version), 193, 196, 197, 513
House of Cards (Netflix), 7, 191, 196–98, 452, 513
Howard, Ken, 181
Howard, Ron, 270, 275, 324, 325, *325*, 335
Howard, Terence, 145, 146, *146*
Howdy Doody, 16, 18, 24, 25, 60, 186–87, 351, 425–26, 429
How the Grinch Stole Christmas (holiday special), 48
How the West Was Won (miniseries), 504
How to Get Away with Murder, 144, 146, 225, 257
H. R. Pufnstuf, 37, 469
Huckleberry Hound, 42
Huffman, Cady, 357
Huffman, Felicity, 142–43, *143*, 176
Huggins, Roy, 155, 187, 188, 416, 417
Hullabaloo, 67
Hulu, 7, 196
Humans, 408
Hurt, William, 221, 222
Huston, Anjelica, 420, 421, 509
Hutton, Timothy, 176

I, Claudius (miniseries), 504
Idle, Eric, 87, 107
I Dream of Jeannie, 236
IFC, 95
I Killed the Count (miniseries), 498
Iler, Robert, 166, *167*
I'll Fly Away, 186, 189, 246, 446, 457
I Love Lucy, 8, 73, 125, 149, 178, 260, 264–68, *265*, 271, 285, 320, 323, 326, 371, 467, 548
Imaginary Friends (TV movie), 235
Inherit the Wind, 209
In Justice, 235, 236, 237
In Living Color, 94, 126, 532, 535, 538–39, 543
Inner Sanctum, 398
Inside Amy Schumer, 5, 95, 109, 125, 126, 127–28
Into the Night Starring Rick Dees, 535, 537–38
In Treatment, 65
Ironside, 153
I Spy, 105, 276, 278, 279, 312, 434
It's Garry Shandling's Show, 318, 320–21
It's the Great Pumpkin, Charlie Brown (holiday special), 50
It Takes a Thief, 438, 439
ITV, 431, 433, 435, 478, 487, 495, 499, 513

Jack Benny Program, The, 20, 269, 324, 332, 354–55
Jackie Gleason Show, The, 77, 84, 263–64, 499
Jackson, Michael, *53*, 54

Jacksons, The, 92
Jacobi, Derek, 504
Jacobson, Peter, 255, 257
JAG, 217
James at 15, 141
Jane the Virgin, 546
Janney, Allison, 450, 452
Janssen, David, 152, 154
Jason, Rick, 481, 482
Jazz (documentary), 512, 515, 519
Jeffersons, The, 273, 287, 288, 289, 314, 360
Jeopardy!, 518
Jerry Lewis Show, 79
Jesus of Nazareth (miniseries), 504
Jetsons, The, 48, 58, 64
Jimmy Kimmel Live!, 95
John Adams (miniseries), 497
John from Cincinnati, 425, 429
Johnnie Walker National Comedy Search, 389
Johnson, Don, 145, 159, 170
Johnson, Mark, 200, 205
Jones, Chuck, 39, 48, 517
Jones, James Earl, 158, 182, 503
Jones, Tommy Lee, 420–21, 421, 509
Jon Stewart Show, 525
Jordan, Michael B., 455, 456
Josie's Corner, 26
Judd, for the Defense, 213
Judge, Mike, 55, 306
Judge Judy, 214
Judy Garland Show, 79–80
Julia, 270, 312
Julie and Carol at Carnegie Hall (TV special),
    84, 110, 114
Julie and Carol at Lincoln Center (TV special),
    110
Junior Frolics, 15
Justified, 1, 170, 176, 428
Juvenile Jury, 18

Kahn, Madeline, 68, 107
Kaling, Mindy, 304, 307, 541
Kallen, Lucille, 74, 75, 99, 340
Kartheiser, Vincent, 457, 476
Kate & Allie, 275
Katims, Jason, 5, 232–33
Kaufman, Andy, 90, 93, 295, 295, 296, 315
Kaufman, Charlie, 363
Kavner, Julie, 52, 54, 316
Keeshan, Bob, 16, 24, 25
Kelley, David E., 5, 141, 160, 183, 215, 217, 218–19,
    219, 220, 226–34, 251, 274, 343, 379, 447, 466,
    467, 484
Kelly, DeForest, 399, 415
Kelton, Pert, 263, 264
Kemper, Ellie, 304, 307, 384
Kennedy, John F., 139, 209, 458
Kennedy, Robert F., 28
Kercheval, Ken, 137, 138
Kessler, Todd A., 166, 221

Key & Peele, 94
Kimmel, Jimmy, 343
King, Michelle, 7, 222, 224, 235–40
King, Robert, 7, 222, 224, 235–40
King, Stephen, 235, 504
King Features, 50
King of the Hill, 55, 58, 306, 541
Kinoy, Ernest, 212, 244
Kirby, Durwood, 113
Kirke, Jemima, 382, 383
Klein, Dennis, 301, 302
Klugman, Jack, 154, 212, 396
Knight, Ted, 315, 373
Knight Rider, 260
Knots Landing, 137–38, 140–41
Knotts, Don, 78, 82, 324, 326
Knox, Terence, 245, 246, 487
Koestner, Paul, 337
Kojak, 154
Kolchak: The Night Stalker, 186, 187–88, 388, 402,
    403, 404
Konner, Jenni, 392, 393
Koppel, Ted, 28
Korman, Harvey, 83, 84, 107, 113, 115, 116, 308
Kovacs, Ernie, 6–7, 9, 11, 61, 76–77, 78, 84, 87,
    104, 340
Kozoll, Michael, 156, 157–58, 182, 188, 215, 402
Kraft Television Theatre, 179, 396, 496
Krakowski, Jane, 382, 384
Krasinski, John, 304, 306
Krause, Peter, 453, 454
Kukla, Fran, and Ollie, 15, 16, 17, 27–28, 523
Kung Fu, 420

L.A. Law, 5, 158, 178, 183, 208, 215–17, 216, 218, 220,
    224, 226, 229–30, 232, 234, 236, 237, 238, 246,
    254, 379, 425, 466
Landau, Martin, 436, 437
Landau, Michael, 419–20
Landgraf, John, 7–10, 11, 14, 172, 368–69, 385–86,
    545
Lane, Nathan, 106, 222, 225
Lange, Jessica, 370, 495, 545
Larroquette, John, 214, 219, 308
Larry Sanders Show, The, 5, 110, 117–18, 136, 171,
    285, 291, 301–4, 301, 308, 318, 321–22, 343, 368,
    378, 385, 390–91, 528
La Salle, Eriq, 251, 252
Lasser, Louise, 134, 135, 135, 288
Last Week Tonight with John Oliver, 521, 528, 530,
    530, 531
Late Late Show, The, 303
Late Late Show with Craig Ferguson, The, 95
Late Late Show with James Corden, The, 96, 547
Late Night with Conan O'Brien, 42, 359, 363
Late Night with David Letterman, 95
Late Night with Jimmy Fallon, 95, 96
Late Show with David Letterman, 95, 363
Late Show with Stephen Colbert, The, 193, 530
Laurie, Hugh, 255, 256, 257

Laverne & Shirley, 275, 360
Law & Order, 151, 153, 158, 160, 217, 223
Law & Order: Special Victims Unit, 217
Lawless, Lucy, 405
Lawrence, Vicki, 83, 84, 113, 116
Lawyers, The, 186, 187, 213
Leachman, Cloris, 313–14, 315, 373
Lear, Norman, 5, 9, 134, 135, *135,* 136, 227, 271, 273, 275, 278, 338, 340, 360, 365, 366–67, 387, 482, 528
Leary, Denis, 302, 362
Leave It to Beaver, 6, 61, 62, 269, 270, 372
LeBlanc, Matt, 308
Lee, Pinky, 17–18, 33
Lee, Sheryl, 447, 449, 450
Leeson, Michael, 276, 279
Leeves, Jane, 331, 332
Lehrer, Tom, 522, 523, 524
Leigh, Janet, 424
Lemmon, Jack, 191, 193–94, 195, 209
Leno, Jay, 95, 300, 302, 339
Leonard, Robert Sean, 255, 256, 257
Leonard, Sheldon, 324, 326, 328
Leoni, Téa, 472
Letterman, David, 78, 92, 95, 303, 322, 360, 362, 363, 525, 529, 532
Levinson, Barry, 83, 161, 460, 461
Levinson, Richard, 155, 180, 244
Levy, Eugene, 93
Lewis, Damian, 441, 442, 489, 490–91, *490*
Lewis, Jeffrey, 156, 426, 427, 428
Lewis, Jerry, 72, 77, 79, 160, 178, 288
Lewis, R. W. B., 426
Liebling, Jerome, 515
Liebman, Max, 74, 75, 99, 101, 112, 340, 341
Life and Legend of Wyatt Earp, 415
Life Goes On, 446
Life of Leonardo da Vinci, The (miniseries), 500
Life of Riley, The, 262–63, 269
Lifetime, 144, 371, 375, 376, 377
Lights Out, 398
Lincoln, Abraham, 346, 497, 500, 519
Lincoln, Andrew, 409, *409,* 410
Link, William, 155, 180, 244
Lionsgate, 477
Lipton, Peggy, 154, 447, 450
Liquid Television, 55
Little, Rich, 90
Live at Gotham, 125, 126
Lives of Benjamin Franklin, The (miniseries), 500
Living in Captivity, 472
Lloyd, Christopher, 283, 295, 296, 315, 388
Lloyd, Norman, 245, 247, 248, 249, 497
Locklear, Heather, 141–42
Lone Gunmen, The, 199, 202
Lone Ranger, The, 18, 413, 421, 422
Lonesome Dove (miniseries), 412, 420–22, *421,* 495, 508, 509–10, *509*
Long, Shelley, 297, 299, 300
Longoria, Eva, 142–43, *143*
Longstreet, 153

Lord, Jack, 154
Lord, Marjorie, 325
Lorre, Chuck, 283, 349
Lost, 204, 395, 408, 440, 447
Lost Prince, The (miniseries), 513
Lou Grant, 53, 157, 181, 310, 314–15, 374, 387–88, 447
Louie, 66, 126, 323, 334–37, *335,* 356, 359, 362, 367–69, 370, 484
Louis C.K., 5, 37, 66, 126, 302, 334, 335–37, *335,* 356, 359–70, 484, 526–27, 546
Louis C.K.: Shameless (stand-up special), 359, 362, 367
Louis-Dreyfus, Julia, 88, 128, 285, 332, 333, *333,* 353–54, 356
Love Is a Many Splendored Thing, 134
Lowe, Rob, 225, 450
Luck, 425, 429
Lucky Louie, 364–67, 369, 370
Lunch with Soupy Sales, 17
Lupus, Peter, 436, 437
Lynch, David, 99, 107, 402, 447, 448, *448,* 449, 450, 470, 471, 499

Mac, Bernie, 282, 539, 540
McAvoy, James, 489, 491
McCallum, David, 433
McCarthy, Charlie, 20
McCartney, Paul, 12, 50, 54
McCloud, 154
McConaughey, Matthew, 176, 495
McCormack, Eric, 283
McCullough, David, 511, 518
McDaniel, James, 162, *163*
McDermott, Dylan, 218, 231
Macdonald, Norm, 88, 524
McDonough, Neal, 489, 491
MacFarlane, Seth, 58
McGavin, Darren, 188, 402
McGinley, John C., 254
McGoohan, Patrick, 61, 105, 155, 434, 438, 498, 499
McHale's Navy, 347, 459, 479, 485
Mach GoGoGo, 50
Mack, Ted, 68–69
McKenna, Aline Brosh, 384
McKern, Leo, 504
Mackie, Bob, 84, *85,* 86, 116
McKinnon, Ray, 422, 429
MacLachlan, Kyle, 236, 447, 448, *448,* 450
MacLaine, Shirley, 315, *514*
McLerie, Allyn Ann, 375, 376
MacMurray, Fred, 270
McMurtry, Larry, 315, 420, 508, 509–10
Macnee, Patrick, 61, 435, *435*
McQueen, Steve, 210
McRaney, Gerald, 422, 429
McShane, Ian, 422, *423,* 424, 426, 428–29
Mad About You, 84, 98, 99, 108, 110, 117, 282, 338, 342, 343

Mad Men, 5, 37, 173, 190, 198, 202–3, 237, 274, 380, 441, 446, 457–58, *457,* 469, 472, 473–77
MADtv, 94
Maggi McNellis Crystal Room, 338, 340
Magnum, P.I., 156
Maher, Bill, 81, 525
Mahoney, Jerry, 112, 324
Mahoney, John, 331
Major Bowes' Original Amateur Hour, 68
Majors, Lee, 213
Make Room for Daddy, 269; *see also Danny Thomas Show, The*
Malcolm in the Middle, 202, 203
Malek, Rami, 491
Mama, 261, 262, 371
Mamet, Zosia, 382, 383
Mandel, Howie, 245, 247, 248
Man from U.N.C.L.E., The, 105, 433, 434, 515
Man in the High Castle, The, 7, 11, 404, 408
Mann, Leslie, 388, 391
Mann, Michael, 159, 429
Mannix, 153
Many Loves of Dobie Gillis, The, 51
March, Frederic, 209
Marchand, Nancy, 166, 167
March of Time, 311
Marcus, Ann, 134
Marcus Welby, M.D., 213, 244–45, 246, 247–48, 251
Margulies, Julianna, 222, 223, *223,* 239, 251, 252, *252*
Married . . . with Children, 134, 280, 284, 316
Marshall, E. G., 212
Marshall, Garry, 275
Marshall, Penny, 90
Martha Raye Show, The, 288
Martian Chronicles (miniseries), 504
Martin, Andrea, 93
Martin, Dean, 17, 72, 77, 79, 178, 288
Martin, Mary, 111
Martin, Millicent, 522
Martin, Quinn, 152–53
Martin, Ross, 191–92, 419, 437
Martin, Steve, 80, 82, 83, 86, 342, 360, 506
Martindale, Margo, 222, 223
Marty, 2, 131, 468
Marx, Groucho, 484, 536, 539
Mary, 92
Mary Hartman, Mary Hartman, 129, 134–36, *135,* 142, 287, 288, 289, 302
Mary Kay and Johnny, 261
Mary's Incredible Dream (special), 92
Mary Tyler Moore Show, The, 3, 4, 5, 8, 53, 135, 181, 227, 232, 248, 250, 268, 274, 296, 300, 303, 310, 313–14, 315, 329, 347, 371, 372, 373–75, *373,* 377, 379, 382, 387, 465, 466, 469, 479, 484
Masada (miniseries), 504
*M*A*S*H,* 6, 8, 78, 81, 139, 168, 227, 245, 250, 274, 291, 300, 312, 314, 319, 334, 341, 355, 360, 389, 465, 466–67, 469, 478, 480, 481, 482–86, *483,* 488, 489, 503

Masius, John, 245, 246
Massey, Raymond, 243, *243*
Masterpiece Theatre, 487, 499–500, 506
Mathers, Jerry, 270
Matheson, Tim, 91, 450
Matlock, 213
Maude, 134, 273, 287, 288, 290, 314
Maverick, 155, 412, 415, 416–17, *416,* 426
Max Headroom, 402
May, Elaine, 122, 364
Maya & Marty, 97
Mayor of Casterbridge, The (miniseries), 506
Meadows, Audrey, 264
Medic, 187, 242
Medical Center, 244
Medical Story, 245
Mel Brooks: Live at the Geffen (comedy special), 98, 108
Melendez, Bill, 49
Melrose Place, 141–42, 143
Menasha the Magnificent, 291
Men in Crisis, 310, 311
Merchant, Stephen, 304, 308
Meredith, Burgess, 129, 396, *397*
Merman, Ethel, 100, 111
Metalious, Grace, 131, 132
Metcalf, Laurie, 280, 281, *281*
Metcalfe, Jesse, 142, 144
MeTV, 199
Meyers, Seth, 88, 524, 547
MGM, 41
Miami Vice, 158, 159, 427
Michaels, Lorne, 85, 88, 89, 90, 91, 97, 353, 358
Mickey Mouse Club, The, 15, 20, 21–23, *21,* 24, 30, 34, 40–41
Middle, The, 282
Mighty Mouse Playhouse, 41, 387
Milch, David, 5, 7, 156, 158, 162, 164, 184, 415, 422–24, *423,* 425–30, 460, 466, 484
Miles, Sylvia, 328
Miller, Arthur, 466, 511, 518
Mills, David, 455, 460, 462
Mills, Donna, 140–41
Mirren, Helen, 161, 513
Mission: Impossible (1966), 244, 329, 419–20, 431, 436–38, *437,* 515
Mission: Impossible (1988), 437
Mister Rogers' Neighborhood, 15, 16, 26–28, *27,* 29, 31, 33, 34
Mitchell, Warren, 272, 288
Modern Family, 260, 283–85, *284*
Mod Squad, The, 154, 158, 450
Monash, Paul, 131–32
Monday Night Football, 88
Monk, 169–70
Monkees, The, 269
Monty Python, 87, 107, 294, 349, 360, 364, 386, 536
Monty Python's Flying Circus, 87, 93, 107, 292, 294, 522
Moonlighting, 159, 296

Moore, Garry, 112, 113, 115, 116
Moore, Mary Tyler, 4, 92, 118, 227, 266, 271, 313, 315, 327, *327*, 328, 373, 374
Moore, Roger, 416, 417, 433, 438
Moranis, Rick, 93
Morgan, Darin, 403, 404
Morgan, Harry, 153, 482
Morgan, Tracy, 88, 382
Moriarty, Michael, 217
Mork & Mindy, 275
Morris, Greg, 329, 436, 437
Morris, Howard, 74, 75, 103, 111, 179, 340, 341
Morrow, Vic, 481, *481,* 482, 501
Morse, David, 245, 246, 247, 248
Moss, Elisabeth, 450, 457, 458, 475
Mother Love (miniseries), 432
Movie Loft, 361
Moyers, Bill, 14
Mr. Magoo's Christmas Carol (special), 48
Mr. Peepers, 2, 291
Mr. Robot, 408, 491
Mr. Wizard, 18
MTM Enterprises, 264, 296, 313, 347
MTM Productions, 3, 157, 158, 181, 182, 183, 214, 246, 250, 266, 267–68, 314, 315, 329, 331, 372, 373, 374–75, 387, 545
MTV, 55, 70, 126, 159, 218, 320, 525, 540
Muldaur, Diana, 215, 217, 230, 237
Mull, Martin, 134, 136, 280, 288, 289, 528
Mullavey, Greg, 134, 135, *135*
Mulligan, Richard, 136
Munsters, The, 271
Muppets, 19, *30,* 31, 37, 92
Muppets, The, 305
Muppet Show, The, 31, 37, 92, 125
Murder, She Wrote, 158, 180
Murder in the First, 178, 185
Murder of Mary Phagan, The (miniseries), 191, 194
Murder One, 164, 178, 185, 218, 425, 510
Murphy, Eddie, 88, *89,* 90, 91, 360–61, 362, 539
Murphy, Ryan, 254
Murphy Brown, 371, 377–79, *378,* 484
Murray, Bill, 87–88, 90, 91, 524
Murrow, Edward R., 485, 518, 527
Myers, Mike, 88, 91
Myers, Phyllis, 405
My Little Margie, 371–72
My Mother the Car, 260, 311–12, 313
Mystery!, 160, 213, 432, 506
My Three Sons, 270, 312

Nabors, Jim, 324, 326, 479
Naked City, 149, 151
Naked Truth, The, 472
Name of the Game, 180
Nash Bridges, 170
Nashville, 146
NBC, 2, 3, 4, 5, 7, 8, 12, 16, 18, 19, 20, 23, 24, 36, 39, 40, 41, 42, 43, 46, 48, 50, 67, 68, 69, 70, 73, 74, 75, 76, 77, 78, 79, 80, 81, 84, 86, 88, 89, 90, 92, 93, 94, 95, 97, 98, 99, 101, 102, 103, 104, 105, 108, 110, 117, 121, 123, 130, 131, 133, 139, 140, 141, 142, 144, 148, 149, 150, 151, 153, 154, 155, 156, 158, 159, 160, 161, 166, 169, 170, 178, 179, 180, 181, 182, 183, 186, 187, 189, 193, 194, 202, 208, 209, 213, 214, 215, 217, 218, 226, 229, 231, 233, 234, 236, 241, 242, 244, 245, 246, 247, 248, 250, 253, 254, 255, 257, 258, 260, 261, 262, 263, 268, 269, 275, 276, 278, 279, 280, 282, 283, 285, 287–88, 291, 292, 295, 296, 297–98, 299, 300, 302, 303, 304, 306, *306,* 308, 310, 311, 312, 318, 319, 320, 321, 323, 324, 331, 332, 333, 334, 338, 339, 340, 341, 342, 343, 347, 351, 353, 354, 355, 356, 357, 359, 363, 371, 375, 376, 378, 379, 382, 385, 391, 395, 398, 399, *400,* 402, 408, 413, 415, 417, 418, 425, 426, 433, 434, 438, 446, 450, 451, 452, 456, 459, 460, 465, 466, 467, 468, 469, 482, 483, 486, 487, 496, 497, 500, 504, 510, 521, 522, 523, *523,* 525, 526, 531, 532, 535, 536, 541, 545, 546
NBC Entertainment, 182
NBC Mystery Movie, 154
NBC Radio, 130, 149, 209, 269–70
NBC Television Theater, 496
NCIS, 217
Nelson, Barry, 433
Nelson, Craig T., 487
Nelson, David, 268–69
Nelson, Harriet, 268
Nelson, Ozzie, 268, 269
Nelson, Ricky, 268–69
Nesmith, Michael, 319–20
NET (National Educational Television), 15, 26
Netflix, 7, 10, 13, 34, 59, 191, 196–98, 283, 384, 385, 399, 452, 453, 513, 546
Nevins, David, 8
Newell, David, 26, 27
Newhart, 105, 140, 296, 331, 344, 347, 348–49
Newhart, Bob, 5, 274, 318, 329–31, *330,* 344–50
Newman, Edwin, 544
Newman, Phyllis, 522, 523
Newman, Randy, 90, 184
Newsroom, The, 9, 465, 466, 467
New Steve Allen Show, The, 104
Nicholas, Denise, 312
Nichols, Mike, 114
Nichols, Nichelle, 399, 401
Nicholson, Jack, 315, 466
Nick at Nite, 125
Nickelodeon, 55
Night Court, 214, 280, 299
Night Gallery, 399
Nightline, 28–29, 55
Nightly Show with Larry Wilmore, The, 274, 521, 528, 531, 532–34, *533,* 535, 542–43
Night Stalker (2007 reboot), 199, 404
Night Stalker (TV movie), 402
Nilsson, Harry, 51
Nimoy, Leonard, 399, *400,* 401, 436, 437
1900 House, The, 540

Nip/Tuck, 254–55
Nixon, Cynthia, 380, *381*
Nixon, Richard, 84, 209
Noah, Trevor, 527
Noah's Ark, 242
Nolte, Nick, 429, 500
Norris, Dean, 173, 174, 205–6
Northern Exposure, 186, 189, 246, 250
Noth, Chris, 217, 222, 223, *223*, 380, 381
No Time for Sergeants (teleplay), 324–26
Not Necessarily the News, 524–25
Not the Nine O'Clock News, 524
Novak, B. J., 541
NPR, 12, 109, 126, 198, 405, 449
Nurse Jackie, 258–59
Nye, Louis, 78
NY Med, 254
NYPD Blue, 5, 148, 158, 162–64, *163,* 172, 173, 178,
    184–85, 246, 363, 424, 425, 427, 428, 460,
    466, 492

Obama, Barack, *526,* 532, 535, 543
O'Brien, Conan, 42, 52, 126–27, 339, 363, 364
O'Brien, Cubby, 21, 22
O'Connor, Carroll, 227, 271, 272–73, *272,* 365
Odenkirk, Bob, 173, 205, 206, 225, 301, 303, 322,
    363, 390
Office, The (BBC), 65, 291, 304–6, *306,* 307, 368,
    541
Office, The (NBC), 291, 304, 305, 306–7, 323, 384,
    535, 541–42
O'Hara, Catherine, 93
O. J. Simpson Story, The (TV movie), 218, 225
Olin, Ken, 164, 470
Oliver, John, 81, 96, 527, 530–31, *530, 533*
Olyphant, Timothy, 176, 422, 424, 428
Omnibus, 497, 500
O'Neal, Ryan, 131, 132
One Day at a Time, 270, 275, 282, 287, 288, 290
One Hour in Wonderland (holiday special), 20
O'Neill, Ed, 283, 284, *284*
O'Neill, Eugene, 193, 370
Ontkean, Michael, 447, *448*
On Trial, 209
Operating Room, 181–82
Oppenheimer, Jess, 264, 266
Orange Is the New Black, 10, 453
Orbach, Jerry, 217
Original Amateur Hour, 68–69, 73
Orphan Black, 408
Our Miss Brooks, 3, 267, 372, 379
Outer Limits, 399
Over There, 178, 185, 492
Owen Marshall, Counselor at Law, 213
Owens, Gary, 85
Oz, 5, 7, 164–65, 166, 171, 246, 453, 546

Paar, Jack, 12, 78–79, 112, 121, 339, 521, 547
Pacific, The (miniseries), 491–92

Paley, William S., 500
Palicki, Adrianne, 234
Palmerstown, U.S.A., 289–90
Paltrow, Bruce, 181, 245, 246, 248, 249
Paltrow, Gwyneth, 181, 248
Panjabi, Archie, 222, 224, 239
Pantoliano, Joe, 164, 166, 487
Paper Chase, The, 213–14
Paramount, 472
Parent, Gail, 83, 134, 136
Parenthood, 5, 233, 446
Paris, 158, 178, 182
Parker, Fess, 497
Parker, Molly, 422, 424, 429
Parker, Sarah Jessica, 4, 380, *381,* 383
Parker, Trey, 55–56, 57, 58
Parker, Ursula, 334, 335, 336–37, 370
Parks and Recreation, 292, 307–8, 359
Partridge Family, 469
Party Girl, 469, 471–72
Pastore, John, 28, 51
Patinkin, Mandy, 231, 251, 441, *442*
Pat Paulsen for President, 119
Patterns (teleplay), 2, 396, 496
Patty Duke Show, The, 449
Paul, Aaron, 173, 174, *175,* 203, 205
Paulsen, Pat, 80, 82, 123, 528–29
Paulson, Sarah, 225, 422
Paul Winchell and Jerry Mahoney Show, The,
    110, 112
Payne, 308
PBS (Public Broadcasting Service), 5, 11, 14, 15,
    25, 26, 29, 31, 32, 34, 61, 87, 125, 159, 160, 176,
    193, 213, 214, 432, 478, 486, 487, 495, 497,
    499–500, 504, 506, 507, 510, 511, 512, 513, 515,
    518, 519, 540, 544
Peele, Jordan, 94
Peer Gynt (miniseries), 497
Pee Wee's Playhouse, 15, 32–34, *33*
Penn, Kal, 255, 257
Pennies from Heaven (miniseries), 504, 506, 508,
    523
Penny Dreadful, 408, 410
People's Court, The, 214
People v. O. J. Simpson, The (miniseries), 177,
    218, 225
Perez, Rosie, 538
Perlman, Rhea, 248, 297
Perry Mason, 133, 208, 210–12, *211,* 213, 215, 224,
    226, 231, 241
Peter Gunn, 151, 159
Petrocelli, 213
Petticoat Junction, 47
Peyton Place, 129, 131–33, *133,* 134, 137, 139, 141
Phillips, Irna, 130, 132, 134
Phil Silvers Show, The, 291, 459, 478–79; *see also*
    You'll Never Get Rich
Phyllis, 314
Picardo, Robert, 488, *488*
Picket Fences, 160, 220, 226, 230–31, 232, 379,
    447

Pierce, David Hyde, 222, 223, 324, 331
Pierce, Wendell, 455, *455*, 456
Pig Goat Banana Cricket, 65
Pink Lady, 92
Pinky Lee Show, The, 18, 33, 291
Piscopo, Joe, 88, 90
Piven, Jeremy, 301, 303
Pixar, 19
Pizzolatto, Nic, 176
PJs, The, 535, 539, 541
Place, Mary Kay, 134, 136
Playboy's Penthouse, 344
Playhouse 90, 8, 103, 132, 310, 311, 396, 397, 459
Plemons, Jesse, 173, 177
Pleshette, Suzanne, 329, 330, *330,* 331, 347, 348–49
Poehler, Amy, 88, 308, 524
Point, The (animated musical), 51
Poirot series, 159, 512–13
Police Tapes, The (documentary), 157, 182
Police Woman, 154
Politically Incorrect, 525
Politics on Trial, 209
Pompeo, Ellen, 144, 257, 258, *258*
Popeye Theater, 15
Portlandia, 95
Posey, Parker, 471
Post, Markie, 214
Potter, Dennis, 12, 184, 292, 504, 505, *505,* 506, 507–8, 522–23, 544
Potts, Annie, 375
Pounder, CCH, 170, 251
Powell, William, 105
Powers, Stefanie, 434
Practice, The, 218–19, *219,* 226, 231–32, 233, 234, 467
Presley, Elvis, 16, 19, 70, 72, 78
Preston, Billy, 90
Prime Suspect, 160–61, 513
Principal, Victoria, 137, 140
Prisoner, The (miniseries), 61, 190, 438–39, 449, 499
Prisoners of War, 441
Private History of a Campaign That Failed, The (TV movie), 486
Private Practice, 258
Prohibition (documentary), 512, 515
Pryor, Richard, 90, 107, 360, 361
Public Defender, The, 209
Pugh, Madelyn, 264, 266
Puppet Playhouse, 16, 425; *see also Howdy Doody*
Pushing Daisies, 395

QB VII (miniseries), 500
Quatermass Experiment (miniseries), 499
Quayle, Dan, 4, 377, 378–79
Queen (miniseries), 503
Quick Draw McGraw, 42
Quincy, M.E., 154, 158
Quinn, Colin, 88, 362
Quiz Kids, 18

Rachins, Alan, 215, 216
Radner, Gilda, 88, 125–26
Randall, Tony, 214
Randolph, Joyce, 263, 264
Rashad, Phylicia, 276
Rat Patrol, The, 480
Ratzenberger, John, 248, 297
Rawhide, 412, 417–18, *419,* 422
Rayburn, Gene, 78
Raye, Martha, 112–13
RCA, 16, 23
Reading Rainbow, 25, 32
Real Time with Bill Maher, 123, 525, 531
Real World, The, 540
Rebel, 418
Recount (TV movie), 145, 191
Red Shoe Diaries, 213
Red Skelton Show, The, 47, 77, 84
Reed, Donna, 370
Reed, Robert, 212
Reedus, Norman, 409, *409*
Reid, Elliott, 522, 523
Reiner, Carl, 1, 5, 32, 74, 75, 77, 98, 99, 102, 103, 104, 106, 111, 115, 179, 271, 273, 288, 313, 327, 328, 329, 338–43, 373, 382, 466, 483
Reiner, Rob, 80, 82, 86, 90, 271, 273
Remington Steele, 158
Ren and Stimpy Show, 55
Reno 911, 66
Requiem for a Heavyweight (teleplay), 131, 396, 468
Reynolds, Gene, 312, 314, 315
RFD 6, 37
Rhimes, Shonda, 144, 225, 257–58
Rhoda, 310, 314, 316, 387
Rhys, Matthew, 443, *443,* 444
Rice, Jeff, 187–88
Richards, Michael, 94, 332, 333, *333,* 353, 354, 356
Richardson, Ian, 193, 513
Rich Man, Poor Man (miniseries), 137, 500
Rick & Morty, 65
Ricky Gervais Show, 59
Rifleman, 415, 418
Rigg, Diana, 61, 431–32, 434, 435, *435,* 436
Ritter, John, 275
Ritter, Krysten, 173, 174, 203–4
Rivers, Joan, 118
Road Runner Show, The, 50–51
Robards, Jason, 209, 511
Robot Chicken, 58
Rock, Chris, 88, 282, 360, 364
Rocket to Stardom, 119, 120
Rockford Files, The, 155, 156, 160, 186, 188–89, 194, 417
"Rocky and Bullwinkle" cartoons, 36, 40, 42–46, *44,* 54, 61, 139, 414
Rocky and His Friends, 36, 40, 42–46, *44,* 517
Roddenberry, Gene, 244, 399, 401, 415
Rodriguez, Freddy, 453, *454*
Roebling, Paul, 511, 518, 520

Rogen, Seth, 391, 392
Rogers, Fred McFeely, 11, 12, 15–16, 24, 26–29, 27, 34, 35
Rogers, Roy, 413
Rolle, Esther, 273
Romano, Ray, 274, 282
Romper Room, 19, 31
Rookies, 154
Room 222, 232, 310, 312–13, 372, 374, 388
Rooney, Andy, 87
Rooney, Mickey, 82, 397
Roosevelts, The: An Intimate History (documentary), 512, 515, 519
Roots (1977; miniseries), 137, 244, 289, 470, 495, 496, 497, 501–3, 502, 504, 509
Roots (2016; miniseries), 496, 502, 503
Roots: The Gift (miniseries), 503
Roots: The Next Generation (miniseries), 503, 504
Rose, Reginald, 103, 127, 209, 210, 212, 220, 309
Roseanne, 134, 260, 263, 280–82, 281, 284, 323, 470
Rose Marie, 327, 328
Rosenberg, Meta, 188
Rosenthal, Phil, 282
Route 66, 426
Rowan & Martin's Laugh-In, 61, 77, 81, 84–86, 123, 517, 521–22
Royle Family, The, 65
Roy Rogers Show, 413
Rubicon, 441
Rubin, Ellis, 214–15
Rudd, Paul, 388
Rudolph, Maya, 88, 97
Rudolph the Red-Nosed Reindeer (holiday special), 48
Ruff and Reddy Show, 41, 60
Rugrats, 55
Rumpole of the Bailey (miniseries), 213, 504
Run for Your Life, 426
Russell, David O., 370
Russell, Keri, 23, 142, 440, 443, 443, 444
Ruttan, Susan, 215, 217
Ryan, Shawn, 37, 170, 172, 173

Sachs, Andrew, 292, 293, 293
Saint, The, 433, 438
St. Elsewhere, 5, 7, 8, 140, 169, 182, 190, 220, 227, 241, 244, 245–50, 247, 252, 254, 255, 331, 373, 438, 460, 545, 546
Salem's Lot (miniseries), 504
Sales, Soupy, 17
Sandburg's Lincoln (miniseries), 500
Sanders, Bernie, 239, 351, 358
Sanderson, William, 422, 424, 429
Sandler, Adam, 88, 91, 389
Sands, Stark, 492, 493
Sanford and Son, 134, 193, 260, 287, 318, 319
Sargent, Herb, 522, 523
Saturday Night Live (ABC), 87–88
Saturday Night Live (NBC), 12, 67, 71, 74, 81, 87, 88–91, 89, 92, 97, 102, 125–26, 263, 306, 351,
353–54, 357, 358, 359, 360, 362, 363, 370, 382, 522, 523, 524, 525, 531
Saturday Night Live: 40th Anniversary Special, 357–58
Savage, Fred, 225
Saved by the Bell, 32, 125
Scales, Prunella, 292–93, 293
Scandal, 144, 257, 452
Scenes from a Marriage (miniseries), 504
Schiff, Richard, 450, 452
Schifrin, Lalo, 436
Schlamme, Thomas, 9, 253–54, 545
Schnauz, Tom, 202, 205
Schoolhouse Rock, 37
Schroder, Rick, 162, 420, 509, 509
Schulz, Charles M., 48, 49, 49, 50
Schumer, Amy, 5, 37, 95, 109, 125–28
Schur, Michael, 307
Schwimmer, David, 225, 357, 489, 491
Sci-Fi Channel, 407, 408
Scooby-Doo, Where Are You?, 51
Scooby-Doo cartoons, 37
Scott, Bill, 43, 45
Scott, George C., 179, 209, 446
Scrubs, 254, 255
SCTV, 93, 97, 386, 390
Seacrest, Ryan, 67
Secret Agent, 105, 434, 438
Seeger, Pete, 82, 120, 123
See It Now, 485
Segal, Alex, 324
Segal, George, 342
Seinfeld, 94, 96, 168, 202, 251, 262, 282, 323, 324, 326, 329, 331, 332–34, 333, 345, 351, 353, 354–55, 356, 358, 466
Seinfeld, Jerry, 96, 332, 333, 333, 334, 352–53, 354, 356, 358
Selleck, Tom, 156
Senator, The, 452, 453
Sepinwall, Alan, 169
Serling, Rod, 2, 11, 104, 113–14, 117, 311, 396–97, 397, 468, 480, 496, 498
Sesame Street, 15, 29–31, 30, 37, 125, 360
Sesame Street Workshop, 29–30
77 Sunset Strip, 151
Sex and the City, 4, 371, 376, 380–81, 381, 382, 383, 384, 393
Sgt. Bilko, 75
Shalhoub, Tony, 170, 200
Shandling, Garry, 5, 7, 96, 117–18, 301, 301, 302, 303–4, 318–22, 368, 378, 390, 391, 528, 547
Shapiro, Jonathan, 234
Shapiro, Robert, 218, 225
Sharkey, Ray, 160, 194
Shatner, William, 210, 219, 219, 220–21, 233, 396, 399, 400, 401
Shea, Christopher, 49, 50
Shearer, Harry, 52, 54
Sheen, Martin, 450, 451, 452
Sheindlin, Judy, 214
Shelley Duvall's Faerie Tale Theatre, 32, 34, 343

Shepherd, Cybill, 159
Sheridan, Nicollette, 142, *143*
Sherlock, 495
Shevelove, Burt, 483
Shield, The, 5, 37, 148, 152, 170–73, *171*, 177, 198, 204, 221
Shindig!, 67
Shogun (miniseries), 244, 504
Shore, David, 255
Short, Martin, 88, 92–93, 97, 221, *222*
Show Me a Hero (miniseries), 459, 462, 463–64
Showtime, 8, 32, 162, 191, 194, 209, 213, 214, 258, 308, 318, 321, 343, 408, 410, 431, 441, 447, 448, 491
Sid Caesar, Imogene Coca, Carl Reiner, Howard Morris Special, The (TV special), 98, 99, 106, 338
Sikking, James B., 133, 156
Silva, Frank, 447, 450
Silverman, Fred, 92, 134, 157, 182, 314, 501
Silverman, Sarah, 88, 95, 109, 126
Silvers, Phil, 48, 61, 310, 352, 459, 479
Simmons, Ed, 83, 287, 288
Simon, Danny, 74, 75, 99
Simon, David, 5, 10–11, 161, 170, 455, *455*, 456, 459–64, 492–93, 494
Simon, Neil, 74, 75, 99, 112, 113, 340
Simon, Sam, 52, 53, 296, 317
Simon & Simon, 298
Simpson, O. J., 164, 185, 218, 225, 501
Simpsons, The, 6, 36, 37, 44, 48, 52–55, *53*, 56, 57–58, 60–61, 62, 63–64, 94, 98, 139, 280, 296, 306, 310, 316–17, 385, 389–90, 479, 548
Sinatra, Frank, 17, 68, 79, 84, 132
Singing Detective, The (miniseries), 184, 292, 495, 505–8, *505*, 513, 523, 544
Six Feet Under, 446, 453–54, *454*, 456, 473
$64,000 Question, The, 18, 268
60 Minutes, 87, 275, 518
Six Wives of Henry VIII, The (miniseries), 500
Skarsgård, Alexander, 492, 494
Skelton, Red, 77, 179
Skokie (TV movie), 342–43
Sky King, 318
Slattery, John, 380, 457
Slings & Arrows, 10
Small Fry Club, 39
Smart, Jean, 375
Smigel, Robert, 42, 88, 363
Smiley's People (miniseries), 439
Smilin' Ed McConnell and His Buster Brown Gang, 17
Smith, "Buffalo" Bob, 16, 24
Smith, Kate, 82
Smith, Maggie, 513, *514*
Smith, Will, 192, 282
Smith, Yeardley, 52, 54, 316
Smits, Jimmy, 162, 164, 215, 216, 217, 428, 450, 453
Smothers, Dick, 80–81, *81*, 82–83, 84, 119, 120, 121, 122, 123
Smothers, Sherry, 120

Smothers, Thomas Bolyn, Jr., 119–20
Smothers, Tom, 5, 80–81, *81*, 82–83, 84, 119–24
Smothers Brothers, 54, 80–81, 82, 83, 84, 120, 121–24, 271, 318, 522
Smothers Brothers Comedy Hour, The, 7, 12, 61, 67, 80–83, *81*, 84, 86, 92, 94, 119, 122–24, 226, 271–72, 273, 515, 517, 521–22, 528–29
Smothers Brothers Show, The, 80, 121, 122
Smurfs, The, 32, 51
Snavely, 308
Snyder, Tom, 95, 303
Soap, 136–37, 279
Sobol, Ed, 496
Sohn, Sonja, 455, *455*
Somers, Suzanne, 275
Something About Amelia (TV movie), 222
Sonny and Cher Comedy Hour, The, 86
Sony, 96
Sopranos, The, 3, 5, 8–9, 10, 65, 148, 152, 165, 166–69, *167*, 171, 173, 176, 177, 186, 189–90, 198, 204, 237, 250, 258, 302, 356, 366, 402, 405, 438, 442–43, 450, 452, 463, 467, 469, 472–74, 475–76, 496, 545
Sorbo, Kevin, 405
Sorkin, Aaron, 5, 6, 7, 8, 9, 196, 253, 274, 302, 322, 450, *451*, 452, 453, 465–68, 484, 545
Soupy Sales Show, The, 17, 45
Soupy's On, 17
Soupy's Soda Shop, 17
South Park, 36, 52, 55–58, *57*
Spacey, Kevin, 5, 6, 7, 160, 191–98, 420, 513
Spader, James, 219, *219*, 220, 233
Speed Racer, 50
Spelling, Aaron, 121, 141, 154, 156
Spencer, John, 215, 450, 452
Spielberg, Steven, 51–52, 90, 155, 180–81, 252, 361, 399, 489, 490, 491
Spike TV, 96
SpongeBob SquarePants, 32, 55, 56, 58
SportsCenter, 466
Sports Night, 9, 465, 466, 467
Spotnitz, Frank, 7, 11, 403, 404, 408
Spunky and Tadpole, 60
Stack, Robert, 152
Stand, The (miniseries), 235
Stanley, 112
Stapleton, Jean, 227, 271, 272–73, *272*
Star, Darren, 141, 380, 384
Starland Vocal Band Show, The, 92
Starr, Ringo, 50, 54
Starsky & Hutch, 156, 501
Star Trek, 94, 220, 244, 268, 395, 398, 399–402, *400*, 404, 410, 415, 470, 538
Star Trek: Deep Space Nine, 401
Star Trek: Enterprise, 401
Star Trek: The Next Generation, 401, 402
Star Trek: Voyager, 401
State, 126
Stein, Joe, 74, 75
Steinberg, David, 83, 92–93, 123, 355
Steinem, Gloria, 379, 522, 523

Stephens, Alexander H., 532–33
Stephenson, Pamela, 88, 524
Stern, Howard, 303, 392
Steve Allen Show, The, 78
Stevens, Connie, *416*
Stevenson, McLean, 482, 485
Stewart, Jon, 79, 81, 322, 362, 387, 525–28, *526,* 529, 530–31, *530,* 532, 542–43
Stewart, Lynne Marie, 32, 34
Stewart, Patrick, 308, 401
Stiller, Ben, 88, 390, 391
Stone, Matt, 56, 57, 58
Stone, Milburn, 413, 415
Stone, Sharon, 303, 321, 322
Stonestreet, Eric, 283, 284
Storm, Gale, 371–72
Strain, 408, 410
Strathairn, David, 375, 377
Strauss, Peter, 500
Strauss Family, The (miniseries), 500
Streep, Meryl, 172, 486
Streets of San Francisco, 154
Stritch, Elaine, 263
Strong, Danny, 145, 405
Struthers, Sally, 271, 273
Studio 60 on the Sunset Strip, 465, 466, 467
Studio One, 103, 209, 210, 212, 220–21, 309
Suchet, David, 512–13
Sullivan, Ed, 20, 67, 70, 71–72, 73, 77, 339–40
Super Circus, 17
Survivor, 540
Susskind, David, 105
Sutherland, Donald, 484
Swartzwelder, John, 52, 55, 60
S.W.A.T., 156
Sybil (miniseries), 500

Talent Associates, 105
Tales from the Crypt, 399, 402
Tales of Wells Fargo, 415
Talman, William, 210, 211
Tamblyn, Amber, 255, 257
Tamblyn, Russ, 447, 449
Tambor, Jeffrey, 156, 285, 301, *301,* 303–4, 318, 322, 391
Tarses, Jay, 375
Tartikoff, Brandon, 234, 299
Taxi, 53, 199, 260, 274–75, 291, 295–98, *295,* 299, 309, 310, 315, 317, 360, 388, 389
Taylor, Elizabeth, 54, 130, 500
Taylor, Regina, 189, 457
TBS, 11
Teenage Mutant Ninja Turtles, 32
Tele-comics, 39
Television (documentary), 544
Television Parts, 320
Tergesen, Lee, 165, 492, *493,* 494
Texaco Star Theater, 69, 70, 73, 103, 287, 339, 340, 347, 351
That '70s Show, 261

That Girl, 3–4, 312, 372, 374, 379
That Was the Week That Was (BBC), 521, 522–23, 523
That Was the Week That Was (NBC), 80, 521, 522, 523–24, *523*
These Are My Children, 130
30 Rock, 126, 292, 323, 382, 384
thirtysomething, 446, 470–71
This Is Your Life, 74, 102
Thomas, Danny, 269, 287, 325
Thomas, Marlo, 4, 372, 379
Thorn Birds, The (miniseries), 244, 504
Thornton, Billy Bob, 177, 234
Thorson, Linda, 435, 436
Three's Company, 275
Three to Get Ready, 76
Thriller, 399
Till Death Us Do Part, 272, 288, 308
Tillstrom, Burr, 16, 523
Time for Beany, 45
Tinker, Grant, 3, 53, 181, 246, 250, 266, 299, 313, 315, 373, 374, 545
Tinker, Mark, 162, 245, 246, 249, 299
Tinker, Tailor, Soldier, Spy (miniseries), 439, 504
Tiny Toon Adventures, 52
TNT, 129, 144, 178, 185
Toast of the Town, 20, 67, 70, 71, 72, 73, 77, 339, 340; *see also Ed Sullivan Show, The*
Today, 74, 76
Tolkin, Mel, 74, 75, 99, 101, 340
Tom Arnold: The Naked Truth (special), 389
Tomlin, Lily, 85, 90, 221, 222, 450
Tomorrow, 303
Tom Terrific, 60
Tonight!, 74, 76, 78, 104, 343
Tonight Show, The, 25, 76, 78–79, 89, 95, 96, 112, 121, 193, 280–81, 300, 302, 318, 319, 321, 339, 521, 522, 547
Tony Orlando and Dawn, 86
Tony Randall Show, 214
Top Cat, 48
Torn, Rip, 301, *301,* 302–3, 318, 322
Tour of Duty, 487
Tracey Ullman Show, The, 52–53, 54, 60, 63, 94, 108, 310, 316, 317
Traffik (miniseries), 513
Trailer Park Boys, 66
Transparent, 10, 285
Travanti, Daniel J., 133, 156, *157,* 158
Travolta, John, 225
Treme, 459, 462, 463
Trials of O'Brien, 179, 213
Trillin, Calvin, 522, 523
True Blood, 408, 494
True Detective, 9, 176, 495
Truffaut, François, 536, 540
Truth or Consequences, 267
TruTV, 217
Tucker, Michael, 215, 216
Turnabout, 182
Turner Classic Movies, 432

Turturro, Nicholas, 162, *163*
TV Land, 384
"Twelve Angry Men," 127, 209, 309
Twelve O'Clock High, 480
20th Century–Fox, 313, 485
24, 510
24: Live Another Day, 496
Twenty-One, 40
21 Jump Street, 158–59
Twilight Zone, The, 6, 7, 43, 104, 113, 117, 127, 168, 187, 199, 310, 395, 396, 397–99, *397,* 402, 403, *403,* 404, 410, 470, 480, 498, 548
Twin Peaks (1990), 107, 158, 168, 190, 236–37, 395, 402, 407, 408, 446, 447–50, *448,* 471, 499
Two and a Half Men, 283
Tyson, Cicely, 179

Uggams, Leslie, 501, 502
Ugly Betty, 144
Ullman, Tracey, 94, 108, 316
Unbreakable Kimmy Schmidt, 384
Undeclared, 385, 392
Underdog, 50, 236
United States, 483
United States Steel Hour, 324
Universal, 179–81, 361
Untouchables, 131, 149, 152, 159, 166, 187, 268, 420
UPN, 395, 401, 405
Upstairs, Downstairs (miniseries), 500, 513, *514*
USA Network, 55, 169, 408, 439, 491

V (miniseries), 504
Vampire (TV movie), 182
Vance, Vivian, 264, 268
Van Dyke, Dick, 250, 271, 327, *327,* 328
Van Dyke, Jerry, 311–12
Vaughn, Robert, 433
Veep, 285, 452
Velvet Alley, The (*Playhouse 90* episode), 397, 398–99
Vereen, Ben, 501, 502
Vergara, Sofia, 283, 284, *284*
Victory at Sea (documentary), 478
Vietnam: A Television History (documentary), 478
Vince Gilligan's Island of MeTV (TV special), 199
Vonnegut, Kurt, 12, 300, 511, 518

Waggoner, Lyle, 83, 84
Wagner, Robert, 438, 439
Wagon Train, 415, 417
Wait Till Your Father Gets Home, 51
Walking Dead, The, 395, 404, 405, 408, 409–10, *409,* 463
Wallace, Marcia, 329, 330
Wallace, Mike, 377
Walston, Ray, 230

Walt Disney Christmas Show, The (holiday special), 20
Walt Disney Company, 24, 364
Walt Disney Studios, 20, 22, 38–39, 40, 41, 62
Walt Disney's Wonderful World of Color, 23
Walters, Barbara, 377
Waltons, The, 446, 457
Wanted: Dead or Alive, 418
War, The (documentary), 478, 512, 515, 516, 519
War and Remembrance (miniseries), 422, 487, 508
Ward, Geoffrey C., 511, 519
Ward, Jay, 40, 42, 43, 45, 50, 517
Ward, Ramona, 43
Warner, Malcolm-Jamal, 276, *277,* 279
Warner Bros., 38, 42, 52, 192, 210, 346
War Prayer, The (TV movie), 486
Warren, Charles Marquis, 413, 417
Warren, Lesley Ann, 436, 437
Washington, Denzel, 245, 247
Washington, Kerry, 144, 219
Waterston, Sam, 189, 217, 457, 511
Wayans, Damon, 88, 94, 538
Wayans, Keenen Ivory, 94, 538
WB, 142, 170, 395, 405, 407, 539
Weapons of Mass Distraction (TV movie), 483
Weaver, Dennis, 154, 361, 413, *414,* 415
Weaver, Sylvester "Pat," 74, 76, 78, 102
Webb, Jack, 149–50, 151, 152, 153, 155, 241, 242, 245
Webster, Tony, 74, 75
Weinberger, Ed, 276, 279, 295, 315
Weiner, Matthew, 5, 37, 166, 173, 190, 274, 457, 469–77
Weitz, Bruce, 156, 218
Welch, Ken, 112, 114
Welch, Raquel, 84
Welcome Back, Kotter, 319, 360
Weld, Tuesday, 51
Wells, John, 251, 252, 253
Wendt, George, 248, 297
West, Dominic, 455, *455,* 456
Westerner, 418
West Wing, The, 3, 5, 8, 9, 166, 237, 253, 274, 446, 450–53, *451,* 456, 465, 466, 467, 545
Westworld, 408
WGN, 130, 208, 209
Whedon, Joss, 170, 405, 406–7, *406,* 408
When Things Were Rotten, 107
Where In the World Is Carmen Sandiego?, 32
Whitaker, Forest, 170, 172
White, Betty, 219, 308, 344, 373
White Shadow, The, 157, 178, 181, 246
Whitford, Bradley, 450, 452
Wilde, Olivia, 255, 257
Wilder, Gene, 99, 106, 107
Wild Wild West, The, 6, 191–92, 419–20, 434, 437
Wild Wild West Revisited (TV movie), 192
Will & Grace, 282–83
Willard, Fred, 136, 288, 289
Williams, Allison, 382, 383
Williams, Andy, 288

Williams, Clarence, III, 154, 447, 450
Williams, Mason, 80, 82, 123
Williams, Matt, 279, 280
Williams, Michael Kenneth, 455, 456
Williams, Michelle, 142
Williams, Robin, 161, 234, 275, 460
Williams, Roy, 21, 22
Willis, Bruce, 159
Will Vinton Studios, 539
Wilmore, Larry, 5, 274, 387, 527, 530, 532–34, 533, 535–43, 546
Wilson, Flip, 86
Wilson, Patrick, 177
Wilson, Rainn, 304, 306
Wincer, Simon, 420, 422, 509
Winds of War, The (miniseries), 487, 504, 508
Winky Dink and You, 19, 40
Winningham, Mare, 192
Wire, The, 5, 10, 161, 170, 405, 446, 455–56, 455, 459, 462, 493, 494
Wise, Ray, 447, 450, 457
Wiseguy, 151, 159–60, 164, 194–96, 407, 510
Wishbone, 32
WKRP in Cincinnati, 261, 292
Wolf, Dick, 158, 160, 217
Wolf, Fred, 51
Wonderful World of Disney, The, 24, 469
Wonder Years, The, 261, 262, 544
Woodward, Joanne, 497, 500
Woody Woodpecker Show, 41
Wooley, Sheb, 417, 419
World at War (documentary), 478

World World, 32
Worley, Jo Anne, 85
Wright, Evan, 462, 492–93, 493, 494
Wrong, Terry, 254
Wu, Constance, 286
Wyle, Noah, 251, 253
Wyman, Jane, 140

Xena, Warrior Princess, 405
X-Files, The, 188, 199, 200–202, 203, 388, 395, 402, 403–5, 403, 408, 410

Yerkovich, Anthony, 156, 158, 159, 427
Yogi Bear, 42
Yorkin, Bud, 273, 288
Yoshimura, James, 461–62
Yo soy Betty, la fea, 144
Yost, Graham, 170, 176, 491
You Are There, 209
You'll Never Get Rich, 48, 291, 310–11, 352, 459, 478–79; see also Phil Silvers Show, The
Young, Robert, 213, 244, 269–70
Young and the Restless, The, 131
Younger, 384
Young Lawyers, The, 213
Your Show of Shows, 1, 5, 67, 74–76, 77, 92, 93, 98, 99, 101–3, 104, 106, 107, 112, 115, 126, 179, 288, 310, 316, 328, 338, 339, 340, 341–42, 351, 357, 382, 386, 521
YouTube, 95, 96, 97, 547